Under the Editorship of

John E. Horrocks
The Ohio State University

ABILITIES:
Their Structure,
Growth,
and Action

Raymond B. Cattell
University of Illinois

HOUGHTON MIFFLIN COMPANY   BOSTON
New York   Atlanta   Geneva, Illinois   Dallas   Palo Alto

Printed in the U.S.A.

Library of Congress Catalog Card Number:
77–143324

ISBN: 0–395–04275–5

To
John L. Horn,
indomitable
and insightful
fellow prospector
in the higher strata

EDITOR'S FOREWORD

The nature and measurement of man's abilities as a central preoccupation of psychology had its day in the closing years of the last century and in the early decades of the present one. Unfortunately, the enterprise faltered, and interest declined as other aspects of psychology became more fashionable. Perhaps it is not entirely fair to say that interest in abilities went out of style but rather that the field stagnated, suffering from a paucity of new ideas and characterized by the persistence of out-moded concepts. Such a state feeds upon itself, for able psychologists are attracted elsewhere, leaving the arena to those willing to accept and live within parameters set by the past.

However, times as well as fashions change. The events of the 1960's have radically modified the nature and direction of society, and with these changes have come corresponding alterations in the interests of behavioral scientists. One such change has been a recognition that a civilization has a duty to consider its human resources and to make the most of them, not only for the sake of the civilization itself but also for the benefit of the individuals and groups that comprise it. Modern society, taking its text from the Bible, is becoming increasingly "mindful of man" and looking for answers helpful in implementing its new programs. One resulting interest is in human abilities, as the reactions catalyzed by Arthur Jensen's article in the *Harvard Educational Review* attest. The 1969 meeting at the University of Illinois considering the revision of contemporary intelligence concepts is reminiscent of a similar meeting held nearly fifty years earlier at Indiana University. The circle appears to be closing. The last quarter of the twentieth century may well see the study of human abilities regain both the prominence and the quality that characterized it in the first quarter of the century. And Raymond Cattell's present volume is a giant step in that direction.

A new book by Professor Cattell is a major publishing event because his works are invariably stimulating, unorthodox, and controversial; one always senses a thrust into the future. *Abilities: Their Structure, Growth, and*

Action is no exception. Cattell brings impeccable credentials of training, experience, and personal research to the task of writing a definitive book on human abilities. Actually the volume deals almost entirely with intelligence, allotting relatively little space to motor and perceptual abilities or to occupational ability patterns. Professor Cattell ignores side issues that would distract the reader from a plan to give coherence and unity to the overall field of abilities.

Many readers who know the Cattell of recent years as a psychologist concerned primarily with personality and motivation may wonder why he has selected the present topic. Yet Cattell's pioneering work was in the field of intelligence, and it was he who developed and introduced culture-fair intelligence tests. Numerous research articles on intelligence and related topics, various intelligence scales, and such provocative concepts as fluid and crystallized intelligence attest to his eminent qualifications and interest in the field. As Professor Cattell notes in his own preface, he might have called this volume "Intelligence Revisited." One might truthfully add, "Defined, Extended, and Projected."

As a behavioral scientist Cattell contends that an understanding of the structure of intelligence must come mainly through the study and analysis of behavior, accomplished with cross reference to evidence from other cognate disciplines bearing upon the nature of man and his activities. His approach is holistic in that he demands the destruction of the artificial barriers erected by such restrictive categorizations as motivation, personality, and intelligence. The fourteen chapters of the book take the reader from psychometric beginnings through discussion on the nature of abilities and their exemplifications. Chapters dealing with heredity and environment and with intelligence and society speak directly to those concerned with the worlds of today and tomorrow. Of special theoretical interest is the discussion of the triadic theory of abilities, particularly in terms of developmental relationships. Throughout the book, his references to his own work, stretching over forty highly productive years, illuminate the points he makes from direct personal experience. Few scholars can draw upon such a prodigious personal backdrop of research and writing—a backdrop consisting of some thirty books and over three hundred articles.

Abilities is a book to be read with profit by the untrained psychologist as well as by specialists in other fields relating to the nature of man and to programs designed to further his welfare. Research workers interested in intelligence and its social implications will find it of particular interest. This volume will not answer all possible questions about human abilities and their potential role in social planning. Not everyone will agree with the author's formulations and conclusions. Yet *Abilities* is unmistakably a milestone in a chaotic field, and, despite the highly technical nature of much of the subject matter, an imaginative contribution which will stimulate both antagonist and supporter to pursue the crucial task at hand.

John E. Horrocks

PREFACE

          A preface to a scientific book has the purpose, in my opinion, of being more frank and personal than is appropriate in the scientific treatment itself. It can expose the backstage construction, knit up historical connections, and, by a freer use of the first person singular, permit the expression of values and reactions properly excluded in a textbook. Some critic, I venture to prophesy, will say that it would be hard to be more frank or singular than I have been in the text, and that my chapter on intelligence and society is already full of "Beyondist" values. That may be true, but there are still some things to say that may help the student.

As far as my own forty years of published research is concerned, this book might be called "intelligence revisited," for I may seem to have been absent on other frontiers for thirty years. Between 1928 and 1942, stimulated by personal research with three giants in the field—Spearman, Burt, and Thurstone—I published about a dozen contributions to the field of ability research. After that, as I set out on my own Odyssey into personality and motivation research, I can claim only sporadic contributions. What then justifies this return? I could reply, at a superficial level, that the best vacation is a change of work, or that the invitation of a good publisher is not to be spurned. But there are more solid reasons.

First, the traveler returning to his native land can see it with more understanding than can either the stay-at-home or the stranger. Second, I am convinced that the topic of abilities has such roots in the growing science of the total dynamics of personality that it should no longer be handled by an educational psychometrist. Third, in terms of the continental development of concepts about this area, I think I might paradoxically say that I never really left it.

Nevertheless, there is a sense in which I left my intellectual offspring— the research articles and books and the three intelligence scales of the thirties, the concept of fluid and crystallized intelligence born in 1940, and the introduction of culture-fair intelligence tests—to starvation. I had not learned—as older researchers know from the history of science—that more original and vital ideas than mine have collected dust on bookshelves for lack of exegesis by their parent or some scholarly leader.

Not that these contributions stagnated; the whole field seemed to stand still after the tremendous pioneer work of Binet, Burt, Piaget, Spearman, and Thurstone in the first quarter of the 20th century. The field of psychology that had been first to achieve a precision yielding a real technology, and which, in Spearman's development of factor analysis, opened up that major half of method we now call multivariate experimental psychology, seemed to stand still. A certain ant-like industry went on in psychometric details, but, judging by the kinds of tests which established themselves as standard educational instruments, the drifts in these stagnant waters were retrogressive—into pre-Spearmanian chaos.

Since I have described my absence as an Odyssey into personality research, I may continue the allegory and say that on returning I found myself at odds with the crowd of suitors who were unsuccessfully besieging my first love. With equal feeling they seemed to resent, and with conspicuous inadvertence to omit from their writing and teaching, both the theory of fluid and crystallized intelligence, and the argument that the new culture-fair tests should be given at least as large a role in applied psychology as traditional tests.

Fortunately, the citadel of the tired establishment was also simultaneously attacked at this juncture from the opposite side by Guilford and his colleagues researching on creativity. The sounds of our independent marchings began to awaken the whole countryside. Alas, in this book I am compelled to ask whether those stirringly active researchers in the area of creativity are marching in the right direction, in a basic research sense. Even if they were, I would not be very happy with the vulgar misunderstanding by the camp followers, who have tried to make creativity a popular cult. The thoughtful, subtle work of Galton, Lombroso, Spearman, Havelock Ellis, and Kretschmer is lost in monotonous drumbeats which assert that the individual has only to lose his inhibitions to become a da Vinci, a Newton, a Beethoven, or an Einstein.

However, the important fact is that ability study is on the move again, as shown by the appearance of half a dozen books by distinguished writers in these two or three years. My personal belief is that it is moving toward a new and more subtle view of structure, incorporating the concepts of fluid and crystallized intelligence in what I have called *the triadic theory,* and that it will now develop its relations far more richly with personality and motivation theory than ever before.

The concepts of ability structure, like those of any other psychological structure, must be derived from analysis of *behavior*. The concepts from actual behavior can then, if the time is ripe, be integrated with evidence from physiology and neurology, comparative animal behavior, machine simulation, developmental analysis, and the domains of personality and motivation. Thus, while my aim has been to meet a major need for integration across these fields, and while I feel that ability study must be rescued from the narrow confines of psychometry, I actually *begin* this book with technical psychometric presentations. I foresee difficulties here, both for the student and with the critic. The former has my sympathy, for, in view of his having been led along primrose paths by teachers who never taught the disciplines of factor analysis and other necessary multivariate concepts, he may find the first three chapters difficult. I can only suggest that he use this concrete problem as a stimulus for doing some reading in factor analysis indicated as a desirable supplement (in particular, the chapter in the *Handbook of Multivariate Experimental Psychology,* 1966) and the recent simplified presentation by Guertin and Bailey (1970).

On the other hand, from the critic, I anticipate possible dissatisfaction expressed in the accusation that I have handled the psychometric evidence with insufficient elaboration and rigor to give full support to my triadic theory. Throughout this book, however, I have attempted a judicious compromise among several utilities. Primarily it is intended to be a comprehensive and integrating statement of where this field of knowledge stands today. As such it is a textbook for the graduate student and the undergraduate major in psychology. Secondarily, it is intended to suggest leads to the researcher, and in this interest it asks awkward technical questions, and comments on more theoretical issues than would arise in an undergraduate text. These bits of crucial reasoning, I trust, will be treated as didactic opportunities by the good teacher who wants the flavor of exploration and research in his teaching from the beginning. The triadic theory is itself the most provocative of these issues, for it points to several areas where evidence is missing and where ideas for research can be found.

There is a third aim with which I have sought a successful compromise, that of communicating with the intelligent reader in other specialties who wants an up-to-date, research-oriented birds-eye view of the psychology of abilities. It is for this reader that I have extended discussion of current issues of debate in education and the social sciences further than I might otherwise have done. Nevertheless, I feel no need to apologize to the teacher of academic courses on tests, measurements, and abilities for the rather extensive treatment given to social aspects of expression, recruitment, and fostering of abilities (in the last chapter). Any student worth his salt will want to pursue these "activist" issues.

I am greatly indebted in the preparation of this book to two persons: my longtime secretary Mrs. Deborah Skehen, and my former student and present research colleague, Professor John L. Horn. It is through the continuing pioneer research work of the latter that the two of us hope, in the next few years, to produce a more extensive, and largely technical, reference book in the ability area, of which this may be regarded as the brief precursor. I wish also to express thanks to my colleagues Professors James Schuerger and Ted Dielman for comments on the manuscript, to Professor John Horrocks for his editorial eye on the main form of the book, and to M. J. Connors and K. Toivanen for painstaking editing in the Houghton

Mifflin office. Finally, as more than the usual required formality, I want to thank the committees of NIH, inasmuch as my personality researches, supported in part by Public Health Research Grants Nos. MH1733–8 through MH1733–12 from the National Institute of Mental Health, have helped toward this integration.

Raymond B. Cattell

CONTENTS

CHAPTER
THIRTEEN

GENIUS AND THE PROCESSES OF CREATIVE THOUGHT

CHAPTER
FOURTEEN

INTELLIGENCE AND SOCIETY

TABLES
AND FIGURES

ABILITIES:
Their Structure,
Growth,
and Action

CHAPTER ONE

THE SCIENTIFIC GOALS OF ABILITY STUDY

1. ON THE IMPORTANCE OF INTELLIGENCE

An opening remark familiar to a reader is that he is about to study the most important thing in the world. Further, it may be hinted that prior to the work in question the topic has been neglected. Neither of these claims can be made for the subject of intelligence. Students, it is true, place cleverness on a pedestal of importance, but a more experienced psychologist or an older man begins to perceive that other personality qualities can be more valuable than intelligence—even in school achievement. Indeed, with experience one may reach the conclusion that "the most important ability is dependability." Surveying human history, as Lowell did, we may agree with such individual judgments as "If Napoleon's heart had borne any proportion to his brain, he would have been one of the greatest men in all history," or with Terman's (1947) observation that the order of contribution of geniuses to human culture is by no means the same as that of their I.Q.'s. In all the writing in the New Testament, and since, about Christ, eulogies of sheer intelligence are not prominent.

Nevertheless, intelligence is a fascinating and important topic. The disciplined application of high intelligence by a few thousand leading scientists of genius between the Renaissance and today is almost solely responsible for the unprecedented health and wealth of the present vast population of the globe, for we are not conspicuously better than our ancestors in political sense or other things to which our fortune might alternatively be credited. Moreover, to the individual possessed of intelligence, the doors of universities and the ranks of the respected professions are freely

1

opened. And, apart from considerations of either competition or service, greater intelligence increases for its possessor perception of the esthetic grandeur and deeper significance of our universe. As by a great lens, or by those capacities to see color which distinguish man's view of scenery from the drab black and white world of the dog or the rat, the gift of intelligence creates an ever-enlarging spectacle.

Therefore let us concede our topic some importance. But certainly we cannot proceed further to say that it is also neglected! Many scientists in the field might wish heartily that it were—or at least that it could be freed from the misinterpretations heaped upon it by the hosts of amateur authorities in school, home, and industry. As the expenditure of time and money on education has increased, so has the volume of paper in magazines, books, and newspapers devoted to more or less superficial, or politically tainted, or grossly wishful views of the nature of human ability. The central interest of the topic is further witnessed by the birth in this generation of an international society, Mensa, entrance into which is based simply on being intelligent—beyond a certain, prescribed, high test hurdle. Great societies have begun to spend enormous amounts to raise the ability levels of their persistently less competent members. Thus, it is becoming socially important to find out what scientific knowledge about abilities and their development may lie hidden under the clouds of dust raised by recent disputations about the nature and distribution of human capacities.

2. A BRIEF HISTORY OF IDEAS ABOUT INTELLIGENCE

The history of ideas about intelligence is so long that whole books have been written about it. Plato compared the intellect to a charioteer guiding the powerful horses of the passions, i.e., he gave it both the power of perception and the power of control. He introduced the term "nous" for this reasoning power, which, via the classics, became in England an upper class slang term for almost the same subtle quality as was covered by the common word "gumption." It implies some sheer insight—some insusceptibility to being fooled—which is not to be identified either with a trained, polished intellect, or with the more emotional reasonableness of "common sense." But Plato and Aristotle saw things a little more simply than our modern sophisticate. Indeed, if the academic philosophers will excuse the blasphemy, they appear a little "stuffy" in wishing to make intelligence and reason practically synonymous. (As philosophers of that time they were naive physiologically too, in considering the brain a sort of sponge radiator for cooling the blood rather than the seat of intelligence, which they placed elsewhere.) During the Middle Ages, the "darkness" of which we love to overdo, the Scholastics divided this classical "intellect" into intellect as it remains today and a distinct, new entity to which Thomas Aquinas gave the new word "intelligence" or understanding, i.e., a "gumption" bereft of academic "culture."

The medieval age, one must admit, showed good observation in practical matters too, and Edward I of England enacted what now we should call a welfare law, distinguishing in advanced fashion between the "born fool" or imbecile and the psychotic who "hath had understanding, but by disease, grief, or other accident hath lost the use of his reason." Thus, the early distinction between lack of intelligence and an emotionally rooted lack of reasonableness—the division, as it were, between an engine too small or weak to take a load and one powerful enough but deranged and mistimed —was drawn very much as in psychiatric language today. Medical psychology retained and developed conceptions of the two types of failure, ultimately, into mental defect and psychosis. But even by the mid-nineteenth century there had been little advance in fundamental concepts about the nature of that intelligence which had failed so mysteriously in the mental defective. However, by the turn of the century, taxonomy and diagnosis had proceeded to a classification stabilized in the terms *idiot* for the most severely lacking, *imbecile* for an intermediate grade, and *moron* for a level little below what we are pleased to consider a "normal range of intelligence." Much medical knowledge which had accumulated showed a positive relation of brain damage or failure of brain development to failure of powers of insight, reasoning, and learning.

This is essentially where matters stood when the brilliant contributions of Spearman, Binet, Burt, Terman, and others broke upon the psychological scene in the opening decade of our century. As the most basic contributions to science often do, these contributions began with measurement. However, since few laymen (and not all scientists) realize how much the advance of science *has* hinged upon the discovery of *accurate ways to measure and describe,* a brief digression on scientific method is necessary at this point.

Today, in retrospect, one sees at many stages in scientific history a fog of elaborate, vague, and wildly erroneous theories in possession of some particular field. In due course these numerous theories are dispelled, to give way to a clear, acceptable, effective single theory. The layman seldom has enough acquaintance with the hard operational experiments that accomplished this conjuring trick, and still less often does he realize that the ability to effect the necessary, decisive, crucial experiment *at all* depended mainly upon the advent of measurement where there was no measurement before. He knows of the world-displacing theory of Copernicus and the harmony of mathematical explanation produced by Newton's law of gravity, but he seldom hears of Kepler's toilsome amassing of descriptive astronomical observations or Tycho Brahe's lifetime devotion to the development of accurate instruments. Similarly, turning from the remote to the more recent, how many realize that the defeat of poliomyelitis by production of vaccines was possible only because ways of *measuring* degrees of immunity achieved were discovered by following alternative theories of vaccine preparation?

The basis of effective description and measurement that duly appears in any science, sometimes designated as its "taxonomy," was slow to come to the science of psychology. Until recent times psychology has been the happy hunting ground of the literary and clinical theorists. Among the more mature sciences it has been derided, not unjustly sometimes, as a mere popular carnival of pasteboard concepts. But the area of ability study actually has had the honor of being one of the first in psychology (along with perception and memory research) to move onto firmer ground. Its steady advance is a tribute to the resolving power of measurement. In fact, ability study has been the real father of *psychometrics,* the branch of psychology concerned with technical developments of measurement. And from this area of firm order, psychometrics took over areas of personality and motivation previously left to psychoanalytic and other speculation. But those developments are another story (Cattell, 1965a).

Usually the first and most elementary step in taxonomy has been the recognition not of measures but of types. Medical psychology made a qualitative beginning with such distinct types of intelligence defect as microcephaly, mongolian imbecility (now renamed Down's syndrome), hydrocephaly, phenylketonuria, and galactosemia. But ultimately taxonomy requires measurement, and the introduction of intelligence testing was the prelude to the measurement of many aspects of cognitive behavior. Ultimately, in additional areas of psychology, accurate descriptions of behavior as it takes place at a given moment in time must be obtained if we are to get any laws worthy of the name. The theorist who wants to proceed to developmental laws about abilities—who wants to be "dynamic" in his explanations of the origin, growth, and nature of intelligence—must be patient to make and record observations first. He can no more focus meaningful movement without this "description of a given moment" than a movie director can get intelligible movement in a film without the individual "static" frames themselves presenting each a clearly focused "still."

3. THE TESTING AGE BEGINS

These truths became espoused and implemented in research around 1900 by two leading psychologists of very different backgrounds and goals. One was Charles Spearman (1904a) of London, about whom more will be said. The other, Alfred Binet (1905), was the son of a French physician. Prior to his work on intelligence, Binet had been a kind of knight-errant of science, treading several diverse paths of scientific investigation before psychology. He had investigated animal magnetism, the behavior of microbes, and finally the study of mental diseases. It was this last interest which led him, with the psychiatrist Simon, to the investigation of intelligence.

Their emphasis was on the pathology presented by subnormal intelligence. French psychology always has had a practical, medical bent, like much of the psychology in the Mediterranean countries. In fact, Binet was following in the footsteps of a predecessor, Séguin, who, with Itard, had succeeded in taming and teaching the famous "Wild Boy of Aveyron," who apparently had grown up without contact with human culture. Séguin, the inventor of a training device which later became a "formboard test of intelligence," thereby earned for himself the affectionate title "the apostle of the idiots." Binet himself, however, also had a lively theoretical interest in psychology, and, as early as 1889, he had founded the first psychological laboratory in his country (a few years after that founded by J. McKeen Cattell at Johns Hopkins University). In the end the actual provocation for the construction of the first intelligence tests came from the Parisian school authorities, who pointedly asked Binet and Simon to clarify the diagnosis of irremediable forms of backwardness in school children.

To get ideas Binet began an intensive study of the mental capacities of his own two children. His explicit objective was to devise a means of measuring the level of general intelligence possessed by any particular child as by "a metric scale of intelligence." Thus, he conceived that there was a mental capacity, different from school achievement, which could be measured "as with a ruler." The rationale of his procedure ultimately turned out to be one of sampling a person's ability in all directions by means of ingenious and carefully graded tests of comprehension, memory, judgment, ability to detect absurdities, capacity to resist foolish suggestion, cleverness, and penetration.

These tests, in various translations and developments, such as the Stanford-Binet, are too well known to psychologists to need illustration. But one might consider briefly the instance of a seven-year-old being asked, "Do you see this book? Put it on the chair by the door. Then open the door. Then come back here." To pass he has to execute all three commissions without error. Or, again, five numbers are read deliberately, e.g., 7, 5, 1, 9, 8, and the child is asked to repeat them. Then he is given five little cubes, which look very much the same to the eye but vary in weight, and he is asked to put them in order from the lightest to the heaviest. Then simple designs on paper are exposed to his view for a certain number of seconds, and he is asked to draw them from memory. Or again, a picture is placed before him, and he is asked to say what it is all about. Then he is asked to state what is wrong or ridiculous in such items as: "Yesterday the police found the body of a girl cut into eighteen pieces. They believe that she killed herself." (This somewhat ghoulish item was omitted from the American translation!)

Although this is the first, known, systematic realization of a standardized test of intelligence, the *idea* of intelligence tests was not new. In fact, such devices have been proposed a number of times over the course of centuries, for selection for special positions; indeed, Plato, by implication, proposed such selection in his *Republic*. However, as happens so often in human thought (witness Democritus' propounding of an atomic theory in the fifth century B.C., or H. G. Wells' description of a working time machine), there is all the difference in the world between a general verbal notion and its precise, imaginative, working out in practical steps.

Many teachers at the time saw the great virtue of the Binet-Simon test to lie in the practical realm—in fact in the greater certainty of distinguishing between true mental defect and mere lack of school progress. Psychological researchers saw also the gains in experimental design through being able to make concise measurement statements and proceed to exact comparison. But perhaps the greatest gain from this attempt at measurement was that it forced concentration on a definition of the concept of intelligence. For the problem always is thrust brutally upon any person proposing any measurement to *define* precisely the thing that he is measuring.

As we shall see, an armchair, philosophical definition of intelligence is not enough. Nature may have other ideas about how abilities actually are organized. Indeed, before the question, "How do you define intelligence?" we must ask, "Does there even *exist* a *single* power or focus of ability, or are there *several* distinct foci?" It is clear from the operations he followed as well as from what he wrote initially that Binet held a multifocal concept of intelligence. Actually he proceeded like a mining engineer wishing to get an estimate of the richness of some widespread deposit of ore; he took the equivalent of a series of borings at a number of points and averaged the assays. However, in various writings he *implied* also the unifocal view, that intelligence is some one thing, and he debated the relative appropriateness of the concepts in such terms as "cleverness" and "judgment."

Regardless of the soundness of his somewhat mercurial definitions, a very real contribution made by Binet was that of measuring by units of "mental age." This measuring unit has weathered the storms of decades of debate, though with minor modifications. Essentially, after arranging his tests in order of difficulty, he gave them to a large number of normal children to see which and how many tests the normal, average child at each age would pass. If a particular child passed all the questions normally passed by children of, say, eleven years, he was given that mental age level, whatever his actual age might be. From this, with the help of an idea by the German psychologist Stern, Binet proceeded to the concept of "intelligence quotient," a value obtained by dividing the mental age by the actual age and multiplying the result by 100. It was observed within a few years that the intelligence quotient tends to stay fairly constant for a particular child, but the issue of *how* constant it stays has been debated ever since, and will be taken up here later in technical detail.

Charles Spearman was a man of a very different stamp. Coming from an eminent family with military traditions, he was an officer in the Army in India, who very properly might have been occupying himself with polo but who rather eccentrically carried an extensive library of books around with him. Thus, he devoted a rather generous leisure to the satisfaction of a deeply inquiring mind. Even so, he came to regret the early years he had "wasted" in this amateur scientific status, saying: "I had made the mistake of my life. I had given myself up to the youthful illusion that life is long."

Comparatively late in life he came to be a professor at the University of London, where he built up a world-famous research center in psychology. Spearman took up the fundamental question of the definition of intelligence much more seriously than did Binet. He asked himself whether we should think of intelligence as a single power or as a bundle of very unrelated abilities—"a crowd of faculties," as seemed to be implied by Binet's multifocal view. In other words, he asked, "Could a person be quite a genius at mathematical problems, a perfect fool at expressing himself in writing, and an average man in handling sensitive social situations?" In fact, would the profile of abilities of a person pass through a series of ups and downs as one goes over a long list of possible performances? The value and uniqueness of Spearman's contribution was not only that he asked very clearly the fundamental questions first, but also that he developed a highly original and effective method for *answering* them.

4. THE BASIC ISSUE OF THE STRUCTURE AND DEFINITION OF ABILITIES

What was developed by the genius of Spearman as the scientific, technical means of answering these questions is a somewhat complex methodology of correlational statistics known as *factor analysis,* which must be approached in the next chapter. Here, at the outset, it is enough to recognize clearly that the approach of making up subjective, armchair definitions of intelligence is foredoomed, logically and methodologically.[1] In a short time definitions of intelligence could become as numerous as psychologists—more so, in fact, since any one psychologist can be inconsistent! As in any other area of science, our hope is to operate with a certain limited number of operationally precise concepts, derived as far as possible from nature. And the issue, before definition, is how *many* unitary abilities exist in behavior covering what can be designated semantically "intelligence." Thorndike, one of the most eminent of American workers in this area in the first two decades of this century, also asked this question very clearly (1931) and answered it to his own satisfaction by saying that there were three or four main groupings of ability—four "intelligences," if one likes. Thus, it transpired, fortunately, that every logically possible view found its sponsor. These were: (1) the unifocal or monarchic view in Spearman, (2) the oligarchic idea of a "few big abilities" in Thorndike, (3) the multifocal, "host of unrelated abilities" view appearing intermittently in Binet but most uncompromisingly in Watson (1914), and others of the "reflexological" school of learning theorists who considered intelligence a vast collection of specific acquired competences. Also, (4) there were various combinations of these three.

In spite of the differences among Binet, Spearman, Thorndike, and, eventually, Watson, Terman, Köhler, and others who joined the fray, this

---

[1] One is reminded of Haldane's pithy comment: "[In science] we are compelled to investigate before we know what we are investigating, and as our knowledge increases we must continually restate our questions." *The Causes of Evolution* (New York: Harper, 1932) p. 63.

group of early twentieth-century psychologists at least agreed—in contrast with their predecessors and many philosophical psychologists belatedly active as contemporaries—that one of the first goals of ability research is to discover the *structure* of abilities. That is to say, as good research strategists, they recognized that before science could attack the exciting questions of how intelligence develops, what part heredity plays in it, which parts of the brain are involved, and the like, the researcher must study *behavior itself* and find out the unitary patterns in which abilities are arranged. Further, in spite of contemporaries who created a further smoke screen by claiming that the human mind is beyond understanding, they had to proceed on the courage of their convictions that all psychology must begin with actual behavior *measurement*. They took the position that human nature, like any other object of scientific analysis, is susceptible to quantification. Here they were heartened by a dictum of Thorndike (which some say comes from the English eugenist, Karl Pearson) that "whatever exists, exists in some quantity, and can therefore be measured." Such a statement was not to be made without protests from many who represented the literary and clinical approach to psychology, who readily invoked such terms as the "soul," and whose writings were sprinkled with synonyms for "the ineffable and the unmeasurable."

While following positivist explorations, however, let us admit that when we advance toward the boundaries of psychology we shall find strange un-predictables, which such modern physicists as Heisenberg believe we find at the boundaries of physics also. Nevertheless, to make clear our general psychological position, let us assert that, like the physicists, we have to march on with staunch scientific faith in order and explicability, aiming to reduce the inexplicable until, if such be the case, something inscrutable finally stops us.

Beginning with actual behavioral measurement, therefore, the experimental psychologists whom we shall follow here proceeded to attack the structure of abilities. They rightly anticipated that beyond this understanding of structure, a further understanding of the development of abilities and their interactions with physiology and with the rest of personality would be reached. Historically, the first important step along this path was taken in 1904, when Binet's intelligence test was given to the world and Spearman's paper "General Intelligence, Objectively Determined and Measured" appeared in the American and the British *Journal of Psychology*. (In the former it appeared, as if to remind us of the times, alongside an article entitled "A Preliminary Study of the Psychology of the English Sparrow"!) These two sources of scientific endeavor, the practical contribution by Binet and the deeply theoretical and mathematical contribution by Spearman, later fused in a common, harmonious stream of research. But that came only after almost a generation of debate, some misunderstanding of the structural issues, and many traffic jams along the path of progress from premature attempts to answer questions of popular interest before the tougher, basic, scientific, and structural questions were tackled.

CHAPTER TWO

PRINCIPLES AND METHODS IN INVESTIGATING GENERAL MENTAL CAPACITY

1. THE NATURE OF VERBAL DEFINITIONS OF INTELLIGENCE

If it is agreed that, as suggested in the last chapter, one of the first steps in investigating the "natural history" of human abilities has to be the construction of measuring instruments, but that *before* setting up a measuring instrument one has to define what is to be measured, the investigator may find himself in a paradoxical position. For the definition of intelligence may become possible only after the unitary structures have been discovered experimentally, but they can be discovered only from measurement research. Let us consider this apparent paradox.

It is part of the greater methodological sophistication required of the psychologist, compared to some other investigators, that he must recognize that the process of definition is very different for the scientist, on the one hand, and the philosopher, mathematician, or logician on the other. The latter are free to define subjectively as they wish, whether they be defining a unicorn or the ideal man or the square root of -1. The scientist, on the other hand, has to proceed empirically and iteratively. That is to say, he starts with a rough definition of what he is looking for and gradually reshapes it as he begins to see what is really there. For example, Lavoisier, as shown by his choice of the name "oxygen," thought that all acids would include oxygen in their composition. In the end the firm definition of acid hinged on a somewhat different feature, since only the majority but not *all* chemicals fitting the acid type contained oxygen. An acid could not logically be defined *a priori*, once and for all. The definition of acid therefore shifted, in a series of such "iterations," as many other scientific definitions have done.

9

Purely *a priori* attempts to define intelligence verbally could be infinitely numerous, as the last chapter indicates. But three major emphases corresponding to fields of psychological endeavor can be recognized among those which actually were produced. First came the educators, perceiving intelligence as "the capacity to learn." Since school learning might also include sheer rote memorizing capacity, or the motivation to study, both of which most people considered semantically outside the concept, various more elegant and more restricted forms of "learning capacity" were proposed, such as "the capacity to acquire capacity." Second came the notion derived from the philosopher, the poet, and the mathematician, converging on the phrase "the ability to think abstractly." This is a notion one might reach especially from noticing the capacity of more intelligent humans, in notable contrast to mental defectives, to abstract and generalize correctly.

A third definition came from the world of comparative animal psychology in the phrase "intelligence is adaptability to new situations." Any comparison of what commonly are regarded as more and less intelligent animal species points to the former being better able to achieve their instinctual goals in circumstances where unusual abstractions have been introduced, so that some new, roundabout adaptation has to be made. In this definition it is necessary, however, to add a footnote to make clear that one does not mean merely adaptation in the sense of being "able to tolerate" as in the more clinical sense of "adjustment"—which intelligent rebels always think is anything but intelligent! Nor is it physiological and anatomical adaptability in the wide Darwinian sense.

Facile theorists of the untutored kind often overlook the fact that their ideas—like the enquiry, "when did you stop beating your wife?"—beg the real question. In our present study they beg the question of whether intelligence is a single thing, as noted above. If we have a phrase like "the capacity to abstract," there is a tendency, as Francis Bacon warned us back in Elizabethan times, automatically to assume from a single term that there is a single thing. The more fundamental thinking of Spearman did not overlook this logically necessary question. What is far more remarkable, he showed a novel means by which it could be answered in this tenuous field of behavior. For in that same year, 1904, he published an article, "The Proof and Measurement of Association between Two Things," which became basic to all examination of structure in psychology.

To appreciate the importance of this, one must first acquire a deep suspicion of words. Incidentally, in no science is this so important as in psychology, and countless, sorry, wild goose chases would have been avoided if psychologists, beginning, for example, with William James, had learned this in their elementary classes. In physical life we do not often go wrong about and are seldom asked to prove our intuitive belief that the cat is one object and the dog another. But in the vast jungle of observation which is behavior—the substance of psychology—the taxonomist has to become a far more sophisticated methodologist than in almost any other science. What in fact *do* we mean, and how do we prove it, when we assert, say, that "musical aptitude" is a unitary gift?

The basic rule for proving the unity of an entity is the same (as John Stuart Mill explained) regardless of whether it is physical or behavioral unity. A thing is a unity when its parts move together, change together, and respond together to some treatment or stimulation. The cat and dog may be a single amicable heap by the fireside, but when you call the dog, four legs, two ears, a nose, and a tail cross the room to you at once while the other, cat-like elements stay put. Similarly, if I hypothesize that perceiving analogies, judging the lengths of lines, and seeing the points of subtle jokes are parts of a single thing called intelligence, then if I put one hundred students in the rank order of their performances on each of these, my hypothesis can be tested by seeing if this rank order is the same (or nearly the same) for all three performances. This method has been applied widely in psychology. For example, Scheier and the present writer (1961) investigated the hypothesis that anxiety is a psychophysiological unity by measuring a patient on each of a hundred occasions on blood pressure, tendency to see threatening objects in pictures, electrical skin resistance, and level of confidence in a new performance. The fact that the raised blood pressure, lowered confidence, and the other measures correlated positively and adequately together pointed to the existence of a unitary anxiety state appearing as a single response to various influences. The central principle of this method, in the developed form of *factor analysis,* was born in Spearman's concern about the nature of intelligence.

2. IS INTELLIGENCE UNITARY? SURFACE AND SOURCE TRAITS

Although factor analysis is a complex subject, a general logical (if not mathematical) understanding of its principles is vital to any real penetration of the issues about structures and traits. Factor analysis, as its name implies, is concerned with identifying the unitary factors or influences accounting for the patterns of behavior that we see. It has been used similarly in other branches of science—from medicine to meteorology—where a large number of variables is involved and where it is difficult to pick out the single underlying influences. Often in psychology we use the term *trait* for such an influence or the single pattern it produces, as when we say that Smith believes thus and so because he has acquired a strong superego or that Jones is able to solve these problems and learn rapidly because he has more intelligence. In the present section the reader is asked to bring his intelligence to bear to grasp the vital logic of factor analysis, before we proceed to apply it to some debated issues.

Historically, factor-analytic and correlational methods began with the work of a handful of geniuses, among whom Karl Pearson, Sir Francis Galton, and Charles Spearman were the leaders. In Spearman's work they began with the above-mentioned article on "proof of association." Out of this have grown concepts of surface traits and source traits, unitary response processes, dimensions of psychological states, homostats, and segregate types, and other operational concepts which are among the most complex but also the most useful in psychology.

A grasp of three of the most basic concepts is absolutely necessary, however, before the student or even the "lay reader" can come to grips in any meaningful way with the real nature of the ability problem. First, he should know the *correlation coefficient,* which is a device, originated by Sir Francis Galton, for measuring the degree of agreement—of "going-togetherness"—between two series of measurements—such as performances in the analogies and line judgment tests mentioned above. Typically, in figuring a correlation, we start with a list of people and two columns of scores, one for each performance involved. The correlation coefficient works out from such data, in the form given it by Karl Pearson and the French statistician Bravais, so that it equals $+1.0$ when two series go together perfectly, becomes 0.0 when they are utterly unrelated, and drops to -1.0 when they are exactly inversely related (e.g., the speed of trains and the time they take to go from A to B).

Even if two manifestations of behavior spring from the same source, we should not expect them to show a perfect r, that is, a correlation[1] of $+1.0$, because various other things may influence them also. For example, the correlation between the statures of fathers and sons may reach only $+0.5$, because, although they have some genes in common, the son also has the mother's genes. Furthermore, they may be affected by differences of environment or by sheer errors of observation which may be contained in the measures as written down.

Now let us suppose we have a theory that six performances, a, b, c, d, e, and f, are all expressions of some single ability. We could test, say, 200 people on all six of these and work out all possible (fifteen) correlations among the six as shown in the correlation matrix in Table 2–1.

The experimental result shows that our theory is wrong. Actually a, b, and e form one correlation cluster, being linked significantly a with b, b with e, and a with e, while c, d, and f do not belong and form another cluster. And the first cluster is independent of the second, for there are virtually zero correlations of a, b, and e with c, d, and f. Here one would have to infer that two different abilities are at work; these might be called α and β.

A correlation cluster such as α or β is called a *surface trait,* because it simply shows that manifestations in some way "go together" but tells us no

---

[1] Henceforth, for brevity, we may write just r for correlation coefficient. The calculation of the Bravais-Pearson "product moment," r, from two series of measures, X and Y, on the same persons, N, is done by the formula:

$$\frac{\sum xy}{\sqrt{\sum x^2 \sum y^2}} = r = \frac{\sum xy}{N\sigma_x \sigma_y},$$

where x and y are the deviations of each person's scores from the mean of each series, $\bar{x}$ and $\bar{y}$ respectively, and Σxy means adding up the products of the two deviations over all persons; σ_x is the standard deviation of the x scores, and σ_y the standard deviation of the y scores. If the reader is unfamiliar with simple correlation, he should read at this point some brief introductory text, such as Baggaley (1964), Guilford (1954), or Ferguson (1959).

TABLE 2–1

The Recognition of Unitary Surface Traits by a Correlation Matrix

Variables

		a	b	c	d	e	f
Variables	a	1.0					
	b	[.8]	1.0	These correlations would			
	c	.1	0	1.0	repeat values in		
	d	0	−.1	(.8)	1.0	lower left.	
	e	[.6]	[.7]	.1	−.2	1.0	
	f	−.1	.2	(.9)	(.8)	.1	1.0

Correlations of ±.2 or less are here considered negligible.

First surface trait relations marked by [ ]. Surface trait $\alpha = a + b + e$

Second surface trait relations marked by ( ). Surface trait $\beta = c + d + f$

more. By contrast with this, we may talk of a *source trait* as some *underlying* influence which *causes* things to go together. In statistical terms, the former is just a correlation cluster, as immediately observable in Table 2–1, whereas the latter is a "simple structure" *factor* or a factor given a unique position by "confactor rotation" (these qualities of a factor will be described below). The fact that manifestations to some degree "go together" in a surface trait (in ability, personality, or even nonpsychological data) is no proof that they spring from a single source. For example, it is a fact that one obtains a surface trait (correlation cluster) among measures on school children on such variables as size of vocabulary, familiarity with history, knowledge of literature, and ability to solve mathematical puzzles. And it is easy to see that a tendency to get a high score on these will contrast the "educated and intelligent" type of man with the "unintelligent and poorly educated." But we recognize at once on commonsense grounds that this surface trait of "the educated man" is a *combination* of exposure to a good school *and* a good natural intelligence. We recognize that underneath it lie two distinct influences—natural giftedness and years of schooling—and that both contribute to all four observed variables. One can reach the highest score only with the help of both factors, and the existence of the cluster is brought about by the two factors—source traits—being superimposed in their effects. But how do we locate such factors in a mathematical way, beginning with the observed, given correlation matrix in Table 2–1?

3. BEHAVIOR STRUCTURE INVESTIGATION: FROM CORRELATION TO FACTOR ANALYSIS

Factor analysis, which began in psychology with Spearman and Pearson and has been carried forward since by Burt, Thurstone, Kelley, Hotelling, and more recent contributors, is a method of getting out the underlying factors when we are given, by experiment, only the matrix of correlation coefficients, as in Tables 2–1 and 2–2(b).

TABLE 2–2
Factor Structure Derived from Experimentally Given Correlations

(A) UNROTATED FACTOR MATRIX, V_o, SHOWING TEN VARIABLES POSSESSING
TWO BROAD FACTOR INFLUENCES UNDERLYING THEM.

	(i) Unrotated, V_o.		(ii) Rotated, V_{fp}.	
Variable	Loading on Factor 1	Loading on Factor 2	Loading on F_1	Loading on F_2
a	.75	−.13	.75	.02
b	.69	.25	.50	.40
c	.38	.56	.05	.66
d	.50	.69	.09	.82
e	.38	.69	−.02	.79
f	−.69	.13	−.70	−.00
g	−.93	.19	−.95	.01
h	−.31	−.50	−.02	.58
i	−.25	−.56	.07	.63
j	.25	−.06	.26	.01

(B) CORRELATION MATRIX, R, FROM WHICH V_o WAS DERIVED.

	a	b	c	d	e	f	g	h	i	j
a	100									
b	49	100								
c	21	40	100							
d	29	52	58	100						
e	20	43	53	67	100					
f	−53	−44	−19	−26	−17	100				
g	−72	−59	−25	−33	−22	67	100			
h	−17	−34	−40	−50	−46	15	19	100		
i	−11	−31	−41	−51	−48	10	13	36	100	
j	20	16	06	08	05	18	−24	−05	03	100

The process by which one calculates from the correlation matrix to what is called the factor matrix, such as that shown in Table 2–2(a), will not be explained here—it would require too much space—but the student should understand the meaning if not the arithmetic of this calculation and transformation. If we consider the slightly enlarged example with nine variables in Table 2–2(b), we are taking a case where the covariation (correlation) of the nine ability tests can be accounted for by only two sources of variance, as shown by Factors 1 and 2 in the *factor matrix* V_o in Table 2–2(a). For the moment let us not pause to ask just how the computer got this factor matrix V_o from the correlation matrix R, which we fed in. (It is a routine process well known to mathematicians.) The figures in any column in this factor matrix are called *loadings*, and they tell how much the given factor contributes to the variance of the given test. If the sign is positive, an increase in a person's endowment in the factor increases his performance in that variable; if the sign is negative, an increase in endowment in the factor decreases it.

The rows of the factor matrix V_o can be written as an algebraic equation, in this context commonly called the *behavior specification equation*—for example,

$$p_a = .75F_1 - .13F_2 + U_a$$

where p_a is anyone's performance in the test a, and F_1 and F_2 are that person's endowments in the factors. U_a represents an unknown, unique influence in p_a, i.e., something "special" affecting it beyond the two factors we know are definitely *common* to most of the variables a, b, c, d, e, f, g, h, and i.

The same statement of resolution into factor loadings can also be expressed geometrically, for those who enjoy geometry more than algebra, by plotting the ten tests a, b, c, etc., as points in a coordinate system given by the two factors, with projections arranged to be equal to the loadings in V_o, as shown in Figure 2–1(a). (Let the reader check the positions of a few points from Table 2–2 to satisfy himself.) In the geometrical system two tests are drawn so that the angle between them shows how big the correlation between them has been found to be (in R) from the experiment. The angle is drawn conventionally so that the *cosine* of the angle (multiplied by the length of the two test vectors[2]) equals the given *r*.

FIGURE 2–1
Plots Showing How the Variance on Variables Can Be Assigned a Factor Composition, by Source Trait Coordinates

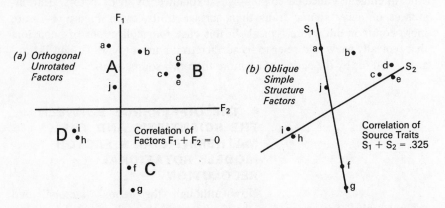

(a) Orthogonal Unrotated Factors — Correlation of Factors $F_1 + F_2 = 0$

(b) Oblique Simple Structure Factors — Correlation of Source Traits $S_1 + S_2 = .325$

---

[2] The term vector will be familiar from high school math. The lengths of these vectors are fixed by what are called the communalities—the amount of all common factors in the test, obtained by squaring and adding the loadings in the row of the V_o for that test. The communality is written h^2 (for test a it is .58), and the length of the test vector is h. The factors are in standard scores and are given unit length (i.e., 1). Usually no test vector reaches unit length, for that would mean that its variance was *totally* accounted for by these two common factors alone.

If the test vectors are drawn in with the angles between them fitting the obtained correlations, then by this convention, the "correlation clusters" can be seen literally as clusters, like sheaves of arrows, and it is at once evident that we have four such correlation clusters or surface traits here, A, B, C, and D, though A is less "tight" and clearly defined than the others.

In the geometrical system one can see now from the matrix in Table 2–2 what the computer's calculation of factors must amount to. It is the equivalent of drawing the tests with the proper angles to one another—as given by the experimental results (r's) directly—and then drawing in two coordinates. The factors are simply the coordinates F_1 and F_2 in Figure 2–1. Some angles among tests, incidentally, if tests were represented by billiard balls on sticks thrust into a potato, would force one to go into three-dimensional space. Beyond that one might be given by the experiment certain cosines that will mutually fit only if one goes into four- and five-dimensional "hyperspace"! That is to say, the correlation matrix, given by the experiments, *itself* decides (within certain experimental limits) *how many* factors are going to have to be called in to explain, i.e., to fit, the correlations. Let us note once and for all this fact that the number of major influences required to explain the behavior is not left to the whim (more often, the rooted theoretical prejudice) of the experimenter but is given by the experiment. However, as the alert reader may have noted, the *position* at which we draw in the coordinates is arbitrary (by habit we drew them vertically and at right angles in Figure 2–1) and on the solution of this more will be said.

In the above psychological example (Table 2–2) one surface trait— "the intelligent educated man"—was explained by two factors. But instances of *fewer* source traits than surface traits, as in Figure 2–1, are more common and more typical. In this case *four* collections of behaviors that typically we would refer to by surface trait names (A, B, C, and D) are accounted for by the action of no more than *two* source traits.

4. THE DIFFERENCE BETWEEN THE SCIENTIST'S AND THE MATHEMATICIAN'S FACTOR MODEL: ROTATIONAL RESOLUTION

Now although the terms "factors" and "source traits" (as opposed to "surface traits") have been used here initially as two almost interchangeable concepts, it may have become evident that some slight differences in definition exists which now can be stated. If factors are coordinates in a two- (or more) dimensional space—a space which in fact is marked out initially only by the given test vectors, which are placed at the angles given by the results of the experiment—then the number of coordinates is fixed, but they can be drawn in later at whatever angles we please. To the mathematician one set of orthogonal coordinates is representationally as good as another—one can spin them like a roulette wheel and still get equivalent (but different) sets of loadings, fixing the test points at whatever rotation one chooses. Indeed, as the results come out of the computer, by various programs, the position of the axes *is* arbitrary, and we can shift them later into any one of an infinite series of "rotated positions" without changing anything that the mathematician values in the results.

The scientist, however, wants something that has meaning not only in this particular calculation but also in those *from all his experiments*. He is not so nonchalant as the mathematician as to where the axis shall be spun, for actually a source trait proves to mean more to him than just a factor. He knows that, granted certain special restricting conditions on rotation, the coordinates he settles upon can have the additional properties of being real and particular influences or causes. In physical measurement correlations, for example, a coordinate axis can be placed in one position where it means temperature, another where it means mass, and another where it means volume. (Sullivan and the present writer (1962) factored fifteen measures on one hundred cups of hot coffee to show this.) However, these meaningful positions are reached only after rotation, for as the (vertical) coordinates were placed immediately as in the V_o matrix coming directly from the computer, their positions represented only obscure mixtures of mass, temperature, volume, etc.

The story about how the uniquely meaningful position—the perfect roulette spin of fortune—can be found is too recondite for brief description here. One way is by finding what is called "simple structure." This supposes that in any widely sampled set of variables *any one natural cause is unlikely to affect more than a minority of all variables*. Consequently, if we shift to a position where there are as many *zero loadings* as possible for the factor—a position realized by comparing the columns in V_{fp} with those in the original V_o from which it is spun in Table 2–2—this should correspond to the true position of the influences. A more complex—but in principle more positive—method than simple structure is called "confactor rotation." In either method, what the psychologist has achieved is the discovery of uniquely defined source traits underlying the observed manifestations (variables) of behavior—source traits to the meaning of which he can direct his next enquiries.

To recapitulate, the experimentally given correlation matrix is factored, and the plot expressing variables as vectors fixed by their projections has the coordinates shifted, until the position, as in Figure 2–1(b), corresponds to a simple structure. It will be seen that in Figure 2–1 the plots (a) and (b) are the drawings from the unrotated (V_o) and rotated (V_{fp}) matrices, respectively, in Table 2–2. (The expression V_{fp} means the variable-dimension matrix fixed at a *factor pattern* position.) Accordingly, an investigator would assume at this point that he has brought his factors to the unique source trait (S_1 and S_2 in Figure 2–1) positions at which they are likely to correspond to real underlying influences, accounting for the variations seen in his variables. It is good practice to check this unique position at once by a new experiment, mixing these variables in with others, to see if the simple structure rotational resolution in the different context gives the same source traits again.

Now, if the cosine of an angle, in this geometrical representation, represents a correlation, it is obvious that the source trait positions reached for the factors in Figure 2–1(b) must make S_1 and S_2 positively correlated. (Since Cos $90° = 0$, only *orthogonal* axes are uncorrelated.) Mathematicians are not fond of the complexity of calculations which come with oblique coordinates; but to the scientist it would be incredible that the various influences found in nature and interacting in a common universe should be *exactly* uncorrelated! The causes and forces we know in our universe do not "proceed on parallel lines to infinity" without interaction. Being in one universe, they interact.

Air pressure and air temperature are distinct factor *concepts,* corresponding to the distinct source trait factors we would get if we factored a lot of variables affected by air pressure and temperature—e.g., plant growth, sinus infection incidence, water consumption, and wind velocity—recorded at one hundred city observatories. But when we plotted them they would be oblique, as in Figure 2–1(b), not orthogonal as in 2–1(a), because with changing latitudes and altitudes the factors of pressure and temperature will become correlated. Similarly in psychological variables, if, say, intelligence and emotional stability come out as distinct factors (as we know they do), we scarcely should expect them to be uncorrelated. Among students who passed difficult scholarship exams, for example, we might expect intelligence and emotional stability even to be negatively correlated, because those who lack stability and persistence will get through only if they are very bright, whereas those who are not bright may hope to succeed only if they are particularly steady workers. Thus, the source traits we locate in psychological experiments quite typically turn out to be drawn obliquely as in Figure 2–1(b) and have some moderate degree of mutual correlation.

5. EARLY FACTOR FINDINGS: THE TWO-FACTOR (g AND s) HIERARCHICAL THEORY

It is to be hoped that the reader's patience has withstood this excursion into the abstractions of correlation coefficients, factors, rotations, and the surface trait and source trait concepts. At one time psychology courses were the recognized refuge of those who wished to take a "science" without facing the rigors of mathematics—as encountered, for example, in chemistry and physics. Nowadays the psychologist, and even the biologist need to be as good at mathematics as the engineering student. Indeed, in proportion as the human mind is more complex than the most complicated machine invented by man, the psychologist's mathematics needs to be *more* refined and subtle than that of the physical scientist or the engineer. No psychologist today can hope to understand the complexities of ability structure and learning without a grasp of at least the general principles of correlation and factor analysis. He needs insight also into such concepts as are met in the various probability propositions in learning theory, in multiple regression, and in variance analysis approaches required in all behavioral analyses. Nevertheless, the above sketch of the fundamentals in multivariate experimental methods and concepts can carry the reader most of the way, though some additional methodological reading may be suggested as we reach the heart of certain theoretical issues, for those who wish to look independently at our statement as to what the factor-analytic evidence implies.

Meanwhile, let us note that Spearman really did not get as far as these *multifactor analysis methods,* as they are called now. They grew in due course out of the further development of his ideas by others. What he actually stopped at has been called the *two-factor theory* of intelligence, which we should grasp before proceeding. In pursuing the question "What is intelligence?" he measured good-sized samples of children on a varied set of cognitive performances which other psychologists of his day claimed to be measures of intelligence. On examining the correlation matrices which he first obtained, he made the interesting discovery that by rearranging the order of the tests along the edge of the matrix he always could get what he called a "hierarchy." That is to say, as shown in Table 2–3, the correlation coefficients would decrease in size uniformly from above downwards and from left to right.

He showed that the existence of a hierarchy (later checked by something better than scanning the columns, namely, the statistical test known as the "tetrad differences" criterion) is compatible with the theory that every ability can be divided into two contributions: (1) a *general* mental ability which it shares with all other abilities and (2) an ability absolutely *specific* to that performance. The *two-factor theory* of a g and an s in every cognitive performance has had to face later modifications, but for twenty-five years it was a tower of strength in the form of a clean-cut, methodological, testable reference theory among the ragtag and bobtail of superficial speculation which sought to justify the rather feverish intelligence testing activities of those times.

TABLE 2–3
Correlations Among Diverse Abilities Arranged in a Hierarchy

Performance	1	2	3	4	5	6
1. Vocabulary Size	(1.0)					
2. Solving Math Problems	.7	(1.0)				
3. Spatial Thinking	.6	.5	(1.0)			
4. Following Complex Directions	.5	.4	.3	(1.0)		
5. Judging Musical Pitch	.4	.3	.2	.1	(1.0)	
6. Matching Colors	.3	.2	.1	.1	0	(1.0)

The experiments which the g and s theory provoked brought out interesting facts: (1) that almost all correlations in such matrices are positive; (2) that the ratio of the g to the s (necessarily higher in performances at the top of the hierarchy in such rearranged lists as in Table 2–3) is highest in complex mathematical and abstract verbal abilities and lowest in motor skills and repetitive tasks; and (3) that speed of intelligence item solution and final intelligence level in *intelligence-demanding* tasks are not so different. The fact that correlations among all abilities tend to be positive supports the idea of a really wide "general" mental capacity factor, and suggests that "negative transfer"—i.e., one ability getting in the way of and detracting from another—must be quite uncommon.

The determination of the ratio of g to s has both general interest and specific application to intelligence test construction. By the calculations available in the early twentieth century it was shown that success in mathematics is nine times as dependent upon g as upon s, and about the same for classics and understanding of grammar and syntax at an explicit level; that success in music (by grades) is about three times as dependent upon g as upon s, and that ability to draw (from nature) is about one-quarter times as dependent upon g as upon some special gift peculiar to drawing (Spearman, 1927).

Regarding speed, it was found that there is very little difference in the rank order of one hundred people (of similar age) on an intelligence test score when they are made to do it to a demanding time limit and when, alternatively, they are given all the time in the world. Naturally, there are more complaints from people under the first condition to the effect that they are not doing themselves justice; but the correlation of the two conditions is so high that it does not seem to matter much under which condition they are tested. Thorndike, with more mixed groups, evaluated the magnitude of the difference as more significant, and talked of "speed" and "power" (untimed) measures of intelligence as sufficiently different to justify separate measurement. As we shall see later, there *is* indeed a "general speed of mental work" factor *distinct* from general ability, but it shows itself more strongly in routine ideomotor performances like reading or cancellation of numbers and letters, whereas speed of solving complex problems (among coevals) is much more a matter of intelligence itself (Spearman, 1927).

6. A FIRST GLIMPSE OF THE PROPERTIES OF "GENERAL MENTAL CAPACITY"

Through the above approaches and much experimental work by Spearman, Thorndike, Holzinger, Terman, and their students, and particularly through the large-scale analysis of educational performances by Burt in London school children, the nature and properties of the general mental capacity factor were clarified greatly in the opening quarter of our century. That clarification gave firm ground, on the practical side, to the construction of intelligence tests (where formerly the only definition in practice had been the somewhat cynical "intelligence is what intelligence tests measure," sadly subject to "whose intelligence test?"), and on the theoretical side, it suggested a new framework for research.

If Spearman's theory were correct, the essential germ was now caught on the microscope slide, and it remained only to describe it and its natural history. The entity "g" was operationally defined as "that which enters 9:1 in mathematics, 3:1 in music, etc., and into *all* abilities in a pervasive fashion." Whether the predilections of a particular psychologist, or a whole school of psychologists, favored application of the popular word "intelligence" to this entity is almost a matter of fashion and actually of small importance. If they did not, to what else would they attach it? There could be little doubt that this most massive influence, demonstrated to be enshrined centrally in the field of human abilities, best merited the term intelligence. But, as elsewhere in science, the best designation of a precise entity requires one to get out of the morass of semantics and set up a new symbol, freed of the subjectivities and confusing associations of popular, loosely used terms. This Spearman proposed to designate "g." One then has an operational referent, and it is merely a secondary, semantic issue whether or not one uses "intelligence" to refer to "g." (The same argument supports the application of universal index numbers to personality dimensions discussed in Chapter 12, such as U.I. 24 for anxiety or U.I. 32, exvia, for the true core of extraversion.)

Actually, an examination of the properties of "g" showed that the best and most representative verbal definitions previously used for intelligence were not far off. The performances which load "g" most highly as a factor, *do* involve "the ability to think abstractly" to a far greater degree than do low-loading performances. The definition of intelligence as "capacity to acquire capacity" was supported by the correlations of 0.5 to 0.7 between g and measures of rate of learning of scholastic material. And it was shown in Laycock's experiments on resourceful adaptation in problem solving that "g" is indeed "adaptability (of means to ends) in new situations."

Questions still might be raised about "how general is general?", for it could be objected still that the concept of "the total field of cognitive performances," about which, as a basis for "fixing" the general factor, most theorists fortunately were in rough agreement, has remained subjectively defined. The difficulty exists, but is not acute, and "personality sphere" sampling of variables does offer some objectivity. However, nowadays it is recognized that there is no such thing as a truly "general" factor across all behavior. (General is a mathematical notion—general to a matrix—rather than a psychologically meaningful concept). *Broad* is a better term than general or common, and will be so contrasted with narrow or *specific* in our further discussions.

It is probably correct to say that most leading psychologists today accept the general or broad factor position which Spearman reached. With minor modifications this is the position of Burt, Humphreys, McNemar, Vernon, and other experienced reviewers of the field, while Guilford's position is in agreement at least to the extent of keeping an orthogonal system. Most of the work of test instructors, and those investigating the age trends, physiology, and general "natural history" of intelligence, operate on a single broad factor definition. However, in the present book, a development different from all of these is taken, which, while consistent with the spirit and technical methods of Spearman's basic approach, leads to the conclusion that in fact we have to deal with *two* broad or "general" ability factors, *fluid* and *crystallized*.

Naturally, this radically different view of two equally important but different "sister" factors has come in for some fierce debate; which makes it all the more important that the student should master methodological questions thoroughly. The attack on these technical issues is made—after the present preliminary introduction—in Chapter 5 below. But before entering that fray, we need to build up, in Chapters 3 and 4, an adequate body of substantive knowledge concerning the ability field generally.

CHAPTER THREE

THE NATURE OF PRIMARY ABILITIES

1. FROM THE GENERAL ABILITY FACTOR TO MULTIPLE FACTOR ANALYSIS

Our attention so far has been given to hunting the main quarry—g, or general ability—allowing the numerous small s's, or narrow special abilities, to escape, so to speak, in all directions. Quite early in the research of the London group, however, Spearman himself began to ask what these latter really might be. In explaining them he borrowed a model from engineering and said g was the size of the main power house, while the s's represented the magnitude of special engines in particular localities which employed the power. This is more of a colorful metaphor than a theory, though in physiological terms one *could* express it as level of total cortical electrical activity in relation to goodness of various local neuron structures.

Regardless of the particular interpretation of the individual s's, they began to give theoretical trouble. Quite early it was noticed that experiments kept cropping up in which Spearman's hierarchy failed—as for example by the occurrence of a correlation of 0.7 instead of the actual value of 0.4 in the "cell" of the correlation matrix where tests 2 and 4 intercorrelate (see Table 2–3 in Chapter 2). Spearman brushed these aside, saying that when this happened the experimenter had chosen two tests, as in 2 and 4 cited, which *were far more alike than they should be,* so that the intercorrelation was more than that due simply to the amount of g in them. A formula was known:

$$r_{ab} = r_{ag} \times r_{bg} \qquad \text{3.1}$$

which gave the correlation to be expected between two tests, a and b, through their having a given amount of g in common. Here r_{ag} and r_{bg} are

23

the correlations of a and b, respectively, with the common general factor, g. Anything greater than that r_{ab} value must be due to a and b sharing also the same s—or, at any rate, something perhaps a little broader than an s, that is *not* intelligence. Spearman's explanation of a break in the hierarchy was correct, but it left one wondering on what inspectional grounds one excludes a test as being "too much like" another.

Thorndike, who was not yet convinced of g, inclined to the view that such breaks in the hierarchy were considerable, in any actual experimental data, and were due to what he called "group factors." He believed that if one took a random set of tests one would find several massive group factors, e.g., verbal, mathematical, and dexterity abilities, which are so broad that they might reasonably be called distinct g's or varieties of intelligence. Spearman began to be accused of grooming his hierarchies by simply throwing out any test that upset them (and him!), and he was urged by critics to pursue the study of group factors instead of ignoring them. (As often happens in scientific research, the onlookers urgently ask the busiest man to do still more!) But he continued to concentrate on uncovering the nature of g, and like the able ex-officer that he was, his scientific maneuvers continued to follow the strategic aim of first annihilating the main body of the enemy.

In the end the so-called "group factors" came into their own from a very different analytical approach. Thurstone, a talented and inventive engineer-turned-psychologist, produced an elegant and powerful generalization of the factor-analytic model and method. Spearman originally had introduced factor analysis in a fit of absent-mindedness, as it were, as a necessary instrument to support his main theory of intelligence. He had kept close to the correlation matrix, showing a proof—by the "tetrad differences" criterion—of one general factor and of a specific factor for each test, when all the tests were of a similar general nature (cognitive). Thurstone transcended these first limitations and developed the general principles for taking off from *any* correlation matrix, no matter how mixed the variables, and arriving at the set of factors needed to "explain," or at least reproduce, the experimental correlations. Whether the factors thus found would be judged finally to be general, group, or specific rested on other criteria. The new factor model thus produced broad or "common" factors which further analysis could show to be either of universal monarchic influence, as in Spearman's g, or of only oligarchic influence among peers, as in Thorndike's group factors.

2. THURSTONE DEMONSTRATES THE EXISTENCE OF PRIMARY ABILITIES

The new mathematico-statistical tool of *multiple factor analysis*[1] thus brought into psychology has influenced theory in countless areas, but initially it affected ability theory most of all. For a moment it threatened to replace general intelligence and the I.Q. by a quite different structural picture, in which about a dozen "primary abilities" were salient concepts. To comprehend the next arguments we must recognize that though multi-factor analysis initially permits all kinds of factors to emerge, the question of whether they are recognized as common or group, broad or narrow, is decided eventually by the process of *rotation* described in the last chapter.

Thurstone, in short, no longer stuck close to the correlation matrix, as if the psychologist would know beforehand pretty well how each correlation should be interpreted. Instead, his method vaulted far from the correlation matrix, forthwith into hyperspace, i.e., typically into more than three factors, and settled the question of meaning by applying perfectly general principles (not tied to any particular substantive psychological theory) of factor resolution (rotation) in that hyperspace. (The difference of temperament and imagination between relatively earthbound psychometrists who, for example, in so-called facet analysis—as proposed by Guttman in 1955—resemble the first aeronauts, who believed in "flying slowly and keeping near the ground," and those more imaginative, open-minded souls who fly high and navigate freely in the new medium of hyperspace still divides the psychological field.)

When Thurstone applied his multiple factor analysis (published in 1931) to the realm of ability data (1938), he came out with a result which at first appeared to bring the whole Spearman position tumbling to the ground. Instead of one general ability he found seven or eight quite distinct *primary abilities*. It was treated as a psychological earthquake by many, and a considerable number of educational psychologists—especially those who had for various reasons been unhappy with the I.Q.—began burning their intelligence tests, convinced that with the overthrow of the single, monarchic general intelligence factor, the I.Q. was no longer a useful concept. Two years later, in a paper at the annual meeting of the American Psychological Association (Cattell, 1941), the present writer pointed out, and Thurstone fully concurred, that since a "g" factor could be obtained as a *second-order* factor among his primaries, the concept of g was still firm. The Spearman and Thurstone findings were reconcilable; and with mutual illumination.

---

[1] The historical origin of multiple factor analysis constitutes a complex and interesting scientific story in itself. The fact is that while it was being developed *by* psychologists *for* psychologists the mathematicians were developing independently what is called principal components analysis and the extraction of "latent roots"—in mathematical terms which no psychologist would recognize. Only later did the two streams merge. Truman Kelley at Harvard was developing multiple component analysis in the same decade as Thurstone. And also in that same decade Hotelling developed with mathematical finesse the full principal axes method. But there is also a "lost article" by J. C. M. Garnett in the *Proceedings of the Royal Society, 1919,* which discovers the principle, and recently Sir Cyril Burt has pointed out that Karl Pearson, still earlier, clearly set out the idea but did not follow it up. In short, as often happens in science, a new conception can have independent, practically simultaneous, and sometimes forgotten roots, each with the special flavor of the personality of the genius concerned.

The technical meaning of *second-order factors* will be introduced as we proceed further. It must suffice for the moment that Thurstone not only proved the existence of several distinct primary abilities—verbal, numerical, spatial, perceptual, etc.—but also showed that a single general ability could be considered to lie further back, in some sense as a source of these specialized developments. Thus, he was under no illusion that he had succeeded in abolishing g. Indeed, he pointed out an extremely important though subtle sense in which his approach to "g" through primaries actually defined "g" in a more scientifically satisfactory way (see page 74) than it had been defined by Spearman, Burt, and others of the London group.

Among practicing psychologists, the creation of this alternative of "primary or secondary" has led to swings of opinion on the relative practical importance of measuring children on the primaries and on the second-order general ability behind them. First the fashion ran to abolishing "g" and measuring primaries only, but recently Vernon (1964) and McNemar (1958) have urged independently that "g" is the more important predictive entity after all (somewhat as the present writer argued in 1940). By now, however, through those developments we shall describe (and as the next chapter will show) which are concerned with g having split into *two* general factors, g_c and g_f, these older disputes are irrelevant. To those tied to the pendulum of fashionable theoretical emphasis in schools and education departments, however, the standing record must be insisted upon— that Spearman was actually broad and comprehensive in his perspective. Despite his concentration on locating g, he never underestimated the practical importance of his s's (some few of which nowadays would be called primaries). At a meeting of the British Association in 1928 (on the brink of the economic depression and its discouraging unemployment), he delivered a lecture pointing out the likelihood that every individual is a genius at something. For since the s's are extremely numerous and unconnected with general intelligence, the high probability is that there is at least one of them on which any given individual, no matter what his intelligence, is very highly gifted.[2]

Thurstone's primary abilities give substance and precision to the element of truth in Thorndike's more vaguely perceived "group" factors. Thurstone had begun by both (a) looking more widely than had the London school at unusual and distinctive kinds of ability and (b) permitting more than one apparent representative of each kind of ability. The tests for the number of factors from a given correlation matrix were at that time admittedly crude, but Thurstone had no difficulty in showing that a single broad fac-

---

[2] An anecdote of that meeting may be of interest as illustrating the absent-mindedness of a great theorist. Before a large audience Spearman reeled off, without writing on the chalk board, the various complex formulae supporting his main theoretical position. Perceiving the expressions of the audience, the present writer, as research assistant to Spearman, ventured to put a piece of chalk in his hand. He held it faithfully to the end of the hour and then, saying, "And this is what I call the theory of 'g'," he wrote one small and very solitary "g" in the middle of the large board!

tor no longer sufficed, and that more likely there were six to a dozen factors in such behavior. The simple structure, however, showed that the primary abilities (as they have always been called since) were all somewhat *positively* intercorrelated, and that in consequence a single general ability might underlie them all at the second order. A reasonably assiduous but still not adequate search for further group factors has been made by various psychologists since that time (including the later work by Thurstone himself on factors in perception). Horn (1965) has attacked the problem comprehensively and French (1951) has published a list of what he considers reasonably well-established primaries, covering, initially some twenty such abilities (see Table 3–1).

3. A ROLL CALL OF PRESENTLY RECOGNIZED PRIMARY ABILITIES

The further pursuit of primary abilities, following Thurstone's methods has gone on not so much in a desultory as in an uncoordinated fashion, which renders a final map rather difficult to draw. The studies of Adkins (1952), Alexander (1935), Bechtoldt (1947), Broadbent (1965), Brown and Stephenson (1933), Carroll (1941), Cox (1928, 1934), El Koussy (1935), Fleishman (1954), Halstead (1947), Kelley (1954), Rimoldi (1951b), Swineford (1949), Woodrow (1938), and others have often produced new suspected primaries, sometimes as a byproduct. Even so, these and the more direct studies and summaries of Horn (1965), French (1963), and others cannot yet claim to have covered the whole domain.

Late in the day, largely in the last ten years, the picture of primaries has been enriched, but, by Thurstone standards, not clarified, through the industrious test construction of Guilford and his coworkers—Christenson (Guilford, Christenson, et al., 1954), Cox (1928), Frick (Guilford, Christenson, Frick, and Merrifield, 1961), Green (Guilford, Christenson, et al., 1954), Herzka (1954), Hoepfner (1964), Kettner (1959), Merrifield (Guilford, Christenson, Frick, and Merrifield, 1961), Peterson (1963), Zimmerman (Guilford and Zimmerman, 1948), and others. Some questionable features in Guilford's theoretical framework will be discussed in Chapter 11, and at this stage we have to note only that his factors (a) are kept orthogonal and (b) derive from tests constructed to fit an *a priori* scheme (see the box on page 54) which would yield about 130 different abilities. The first of these, in the present writer's opinion, is an entirely wrong principle. The second (see page 54) is only one of several possible arbitrary classification principles no one of which can guarantee covering the total field of human ability performance.

A better principle for the second purpose—covering the field—is one akin to the *personality sphere* concept (Cattell, 1946a, 1965a) used in personality research. This takes the total realm of behavior in our culture, essentially by sampling the twenty-four hours of our daily behavior, and reaches a stratified sample of the total population of human behaviors. The conversion of this to an ability modality subsection is made according to the principle on page 55 below. Such a concept of *a total realm of ability performances* is vital to a reliable map of primary abilities. For without some guide as to how performances are "spaced," i.e., whether one performance is very different from another or so close as to be considered a virtual duplicate, there can be no objectivity to our primary ability concepts. For example, a psychologist could (as Humphreys and others have accused Guilford of doing) "blow up" a specific factor into a group factor (a primary) by multiplying the number of separate tests in quite a small specialized area. Only moderate ingenuity is required to invent ten different measures of efficiency in putting on and lacing one's shoes, and thus (since they are likely mutually to correlate highly) produce a broad "primary ability" (covering ten variables) for "putting on shoes." Explicit attention to this *personality sphere* principle has been, at worst, simply lacking in the primary ability surveys of, say, French or Vernon. But it has been used deliberately, yet in a perverse and deluding sense, in the work of Guilford. For he deliberately makes the initial choice of tests fit a subjective academic framework rather than a naturalistic sampling of existing behaviors.

The maintenance in Guilford's work of orthogonal factors, where the natural structure requires oblique factors, necessarily means, as the examples of Cattell and Dickman (1962) show, that the supposed independent abilities extracted actually are mixtures of more fundamental primaries. However, the first factors in a study which is *not* rotated do come fairly near, as a rule, to the first two or three rotated ones. In factors later than the opening ones, however, chaos ensues. It is as if a man had ten cases of whiskey, each of a different brand, and then began switching the bottles from case to case in random fashion, doing so most thoroughly in the later cases. Now if he were to drop the first and second cases, and strain off the whiskey from the broken bottles, the first case might give him predominantly the flavor of scotch, the second of bourbon, but after that the flavors would be increasingly obscure. Just so, we may take Guilford's first, larger factors as reasonable approximations to the first couple of factors that a simple structure rotation would yield. However, it is time for someone carefully to rotate to maximum simple structure the rest of the excellent data of Guilford and his coworkers if we are to understand, with confidence, how the further factors from these researches confirm and extend the work done by Thurstone (and his successors using uniquely determined rotations) on primary abilities.

It is for these reasons that the attempt to present, in Table 3–1, a list of presently recognized primary abilities has its difficulties and limitations. The list of simple structure primaries lacks the firm cross-checking which the recent extensive work of Guilford, when rerotated, *could* give. Also, one must recognize that it has not extended itself exhaustively into the far spaces in the way that a systematic application of the personality sphere principle eventually may bring about. The question of how such a list

TABLE 3–1

A Tentative List of Empirically Based[1] Primary Ability Concepts

Proposed Universal Index Numbers[2] and Letter Index[3]	
U.I.(1)	*Verbal Ability*
a_v	Researches (40 or more): Burt (1940), Thurstone (1938),
or	Garrett (1946), Guilford (1967), Woodrow (1938).
(V)	Tests: Vocabulary comprehension, reading comprehension, grammar and syntax matching proverbs, etc.
U.I.(2)	*Numerical Ability (Basic Manipulation Facility;* not *Mathematics)*
a_n	Researches (30 or more): Garrett (1946), Guilford (1967),
or	Thurstone (1938), Woodrow (1938).
(N)	Tests: Addition, subtraction, multiplication, division.
U.I.(3)	*Spatial Ability*[4]
a_s	Researches (12 or more): Fruchter (1948), El Koussy (1935),
or	Thurstone (1938), Macfarlane (I. M.) Smith (1964).
(S)	Tests: "Hands," flags, cubes.

[1] This includes those of Guilford's orthogonal factors which (a) appear, as far as one can judge, likely to remain valid, with little reconstitution, under maximum simple structure (oblique) rotation, (b) are not so narrow as still to require demonstration of acceptable breadth, and (c) have some existence apart from variables specially created to fit the box schema.

[2] It has been proposed (Cattell, 1957; Pawlik, 1966) that seven U.I. numbers U.I.T. I, II, etc.) be given to *higher*-order personality T-data factors (the ability second orders beginning at U.I.T. VIII), and Arabic numerals to the present *primaries*. An order suggested earlier followed historical sequence entirely. The present order, superseding it, is made at a date at which it is possible to see which factors are of larger variance and stability. Accordingly, the larger are placed first, i.e., it is an order of diminishing "importance." After the gap due to the personality and motivation factors U.I. 16 through U.I. 69 (which are kept there because they are objective test factors and not distinguishable to the satisfaction of all psychologists from ability factors) the remaining ability factors are mainly in order of historical appearance as confirmed factors, and the list can be added to continually on that basis.

[3] Here, as in some other fields (e.g., chemistry), there is a practical mnemonic appeal in using letter symbols which remind one of the first letters of the name. Naturally, repetitions break this down as one gets beyond a couple dozen, and one has to go to two and even three letters, which is more cumbersome than the numerical system. In this case psychologists began with capitals, e.g., for V, N, and S, which are shown here. But in the larger context of higher-order abilities, and special kinds of abilities which we shall encounter in ensuing chapters, it is advantageous to distinguish the primaries, abilities, or agencies by the consistent use of "a." So we have set as a preferred alternative here the use of a's with subscripts appropriate to the original capitals. Thus, a_v, a_n, a_s, etc.

[4] Horn (1965) and Pawlik (1966) recognize the possibility of a second spatial ability factor, as the researchers below claim, but they point out that no single study has found *both* in the same matrix, and they suggest wisely that it may be the same factor in some new tests.

U_{so}	*Spatial Orientation*
or	Researches: Roff (1950), Comrey (1949), Michael (1957), Guilford & Lacey
(So)	(1947).
	Tests: Spatial problems, e.g., apparatus tasks in an airplane, in which the bodily orientation of the observer is involved, too.

U.I.(4) a_{ps} or (P)	*Perceptual Speed (Figural Identification)* Researches (more than 30): Guilford (1967), Thurstone (1938, 1950). Tests: Comparing similarity in visual material and configurations, mirror reading, dial recognition.
U.I.(5) a_{sc} or (C_s)	*Speed of Closure (Visual Cognition, Gestalt Perception)* Researches: Botzum (1951), Guilford (1967), Roff (1950), Thurstone (1958, 1950), Pemberton (1952), Meili (1949). Tests: Street Gestalt, Speed of dark adaptation.
U.I.(6) a_{ir} or (I & R)	*Inductive Reasoning (General Reasoning[5])* Regarding reasoning factor Pawlik (1966) concludes "Deductive is certainly distinct, whereas Inductive and General Reasoning may or may not represent separate factors." We assume here they do not. Researches (about 15): Thurstone (1938), Meili (1949), Guilford (1967). Tests: Thurstone's "mark test," discovering rule or principle, series, secret writing, pedigrees.
U.I.(7) a_{dr} or (D)	*Deductive Reasoning (Logical Evaluation)* Researches (Only half a dozen show it clearly): Thurstone (1938), Guilford (1967), Botzum (1951). Tests: Proceeding from general to specific, syllogisms (selective), assumptions made.
U.I.(5) a_{mr} or g_m or (M)	*Rote Memory[6] (Associative Memory)* Researches (about 25): Anastasi (1958b), Carlson (1937), Carroll (1941), Garrett (1946), Thurstone (1938), Guilford (1967). Tests: Word-word pairs, figure-word pairs, number-figure, etc.
U.I.(8) a_{mk} or (Mk)	*Mechanical Knowledge and Skill* Researches: Cox (1928, 1934), Guilford (1967), Bennett (1952). Tests: Knowledge of tools and machinery. Perception of mode of working of machines.
U.I.(9) a_w or (W)	*Word Fluency* Researches (about 30): Bernstein (1924), Cattell (1933b, 1936a), Guilford (1967), Hargreaves (1927), Studman (1935), Thurstone (1938). Tests: Words beginning or ending with ——, anagrams.

[5] Regarding the attempt to separate General Reasoning from Inductive Reasoning, our conclusion is that General Reasoning is nothing more than a partial perception of fluid general intelligence, g_f, in the first order. Such tests as Guilford's ship destination and arithmetic problems are obviously good g_f measures. See Marron (1953).

[6] Despite the very clear demonstration (see text, page 42) of a distinct Meaningful Memory factor by Kelley (1954), Roff (1950), and others, and also of some narrow factors like Memory Span (see Pawlik, 1966) we have not listed the former here, on the strong argument that it represents only a projection of intelligence, g, into memorizing performance. Our assumption is that Rote Memory represents a basic capacity to commit to memory and retain, which operates regardless of meaningfulness and complexity of the material. Later research should separate the general effectiveness of committing to memory from the general retentivity, but at present they are probably confounded here. This factor or factors should appear eventually as a "general capacity factor" and as such would not be listed eventually among the primaries. Consequently we have listed it here as U.I. (T)5 not (8), since the figures in parentheses are retained for primaries (see page 33).

U.I.(10) a_{if} or (If)	*Ideational Fluency* Researches: Cattell and Tiner (1949), Carroll (1941), Bechtoldt (1947), Guilford (1967), Taylor (1947), Meili (1949). Tests: Topics, Riddles, Plot titles, Uses.
U.I.(11) a_{rc} or (Cf)	*Restructuring Closure (Flexibility of Closure)* Researches: Thurstone (1938), Roff (1950), Guilford (1967), Meili (1949), Pemberton (1952), Schaedeli (1961). Tests: Gottschalk, Hidden figures, Hidden letters. A large part of the variance often included in this factor belongs to personality factors U.I. 19 and U.I. 21.
U.I.(6) g_x or (O)	*Flexibility-vs.-Firmness*[7] *(Originality)* Researches: Cattell and Tiner (1949). Possibly same factor in Guilford. Tests: Riddles, unusual uses, remote consequences of hypotheses.
U.I.(12) a_{mc} or (Mc)	*General Motor Coordination (Psychomotor coordination)* Researches (about 12): Cox (1928, 1934), Dudek (1948), Guilford (1967). Tests: Two hand coordination, pursuit meter, hand and foot adjustments.
U.I.(13) a_{md} or (A)	*Manual Dexterity (Also Aiming)* Researches: Cox (1928, 1934), Guilford (1967), Hempel and Fleishman (1955). Tests: Minnesota rate of manipulation, aiming small arm-hand movements. (Possibly also Kinaesthetic sense of Bass and of Fleishman [1954]; but note contrast with Finger Dexterity.)
U.I.(14) a_{mu}	*Musical Pitch and Tonal Sensitivity* Researches: Karlin (1941). Tests: Seashore Musical Aptitude.
U.I.(15) a_d	*Representational Drawing Skill* Researches: Spearman (1927), Burt (1940). Tests: Draw a man, Draw a house. The factorial boundaries of this test have not been well defined, nor has its relation been worked out to esthetic taste (as in the Meier Seashore Art Judgment test).

LESSER, NARROWER, LESS SUBSTANTIATED PRIMARIES

U.I.(70) a_{ef} or (Fe)	*Expressional Fluency* Researches: Carroll (1941), Taylor (1947), Guilford (1967). Tests: Not production of ideas but verbal expression for assigned ideas.

[7] Theoretically this is a very important factor (see pages 41 and 412) which needs closer investigation. It is classified here as a higher-order "capacity," on the assumption that it covers not only Cattell's "flexibility" phenomena, but also Guilford's "originality" and some of Guilford's adaptive "flexibility." This flexibility is posited to a general—and not always advantageous—quality of the nervous system. To avoid confusion, what used to be called flexibility of closure (U.I. 11 above) has been named Restructuring Closure, which is actually more apt. For the person who sees the figure he is looking for in Gottschalk figures is actually not being flexible; he is holding in mind tenaciously the figure he is to see.

U.I.(71)	*Motor Speed*
a$_{ms}$	Researches: Guilford (1967), Cattell & Kulhavy (1971).
U.I.(72)	*Speed of Symbol Discrimination*
a$_{sd}$	Researches: Guilford (1967)
U.I.(73)	*Musical Rhythm and Timing*
	Research: Karlin (1941)
	Test: Reproduction of musical rhythms.
U.I.(74)	*Judgment* (*Possibly Binet's "coup d'oeil"*)
a$_j$	Researches: Corter (1952), Guilford (1967).
or	Tests: Described by French (1963) as solutions to "practical
(J)	problems where some estimation or guesswork" is involved
	(see Pawlik [1966], p. 551).

And several smaller factors in Guilford's (1967) list.

It will be noted that two major factors commonly listed among primaries have been omitted above. Unlike U.I. 5 and U.I. 6 which might, with further research, prove to have a primary as well as a general component and therefore are listed above, visualization (U.I. 7) and speed (U.I. 4) are almost certainly higher-order factors and, as such, are listed in the powers below.

---

should be organized *taxonomically* has also been set aside for the present (see Chapters 4 and 11, however). For discussion would be necessary on such alternatives as grouping them by higher-order structure (an impossibility in the Guilford scheme), or by Guilford's scheme itself, or by some scheme hinging on cultural importance, or by some further, independent basis.

Meanwhile, as indicated in the footnote to Table 3–1, it has seemed best to begin with the factors of larger variances and strongest confirmation and pass to smaller ones, though after that (after U.I. 75) the order of historical discovery and confirmation must decide the indexing in the future. It should be noted that although present evidence on magnitude and certainty permits the first fifteen "major" primaries to be indexed somewhat differently from the earlier indexing by Cattell (1957a, 1957b) and French (1963), the main principles of that earlier indexing are maintained:

(a) Since ability and temperament factors cannot be segregated to everyone's satisfaction, all objective test (nonquestionnaire) personality and ability factors are run together in a single series.

(b) Since French had indexed up to U.I. (16) when the personality indexing (Hundleby, Pawlik, and Cattell, 1965) was begun (see also the present author's article in *Psychologia,* Cattell, 1957b), the primary personality and motivation factors run from U.I. (16) through U.I. (69), leaving the primary ability factors to run from U.I. (1) to (15) and again from U.I. (70) until the point where a further batch of personality factors are once more ready to be indexed.

(c) First-order factors have numbers in parentheses, as above. Second-order factors from these, which are at the same level as general intelligence and most objective-test general personality factors, are Arabic numbers without parentheses. The strata above these, as here and in the work of Pawlik on higher-order personality factors, proceed to Roman numerals and Greek letters.[3]

4. DESCRIPTION OF SOME REPRESENTATIVE PRIMARY ABILITY PATTERNS

In the perspective appropriate for the present book there is no need to discuss in detail the nature of all primary abilities and the concrete tests which measure them. French's test kit (1963), Thurstone's PMA test (1948), Pawlik's (1966) fine chapter on research sources, as well as the IPAT Primary Ability Tests will give detailed information, as will the exhaustive treatment by Guilford (1967). Actually, not enough is yet known, in any case, about the "natural history," e.g., age course, nature-nurture ratios, physiological and learning processes, of these primaries to justify extensive treatment, so illustration must be our aim.

Verbal ability (V or U.I.(T)13 or a_v) was characterized as a "hierarchy-breaker" by Spearman, and has figured (along with "education") as almost a "general" factor in the writings of Burt and Vernon. Thurstone's analysis showed verbal ability as an emphatic primary, and his and later works have revealed that it includes mainly size of vocabulary and command of syntactical (grammatical) and stylistic sense but also many other relatively minor aspects of verbal skill. (Spelling is a different ability, located partly in visual memory.)

The boundaries of numerical ability (N or U.I.(T)10 or a_n) are quite different from those one would expect from any subjective notion of "mathematical ability." In both school children and the average adult, N involves skills (accuracy and speed) in the basic processes of addition, multiplication, subtraction, and division, and the somewhat more complex procedures commonly superimposed on them. It is quite different from arithmetical reasoning or mathematical ability, which has much "g."

A very different factor pattern that one might hypothesize to arise similarly to a_v and a_n from cultural learning but which falls outside the scholastic area, is that of mechanical aptitude, a_{mk}. But something often popularly suspected to be the same, namely spatial ability, s or a_s, is

---

[3] This elaboration is unavoidable if confusion is not to ensue, since, in the personality realm, we have no less than four stratum levels now known: personality questionnaire primaries: U.I. (1), etc.; questionnaire secondaries and objective-test primaries, U.I. 1, etc.; second-stratum objectives U.I. I, etc.; and, finally, third-stratum factors on objective tests, U.I. α, etc.

We must also anticipate later conclusions about three taxonomic classes of ability factors if present indexing, e.g., that symbolizing visualization as p_v, is to be understood. That classification calls for higher-order "powers" which are either (1) *general capacities,* like intelligence and speed, which are indexed by g's, e.g., g_c, crystallized intelligence, or (2) *provincial organizations,* like visualization (p_v), or auditory organization (p_a), and finally, (3) *agencies* (mainly our present primary abilities) which are indexed as a's, e.g., a_v, a_n, for verbal and numerical primary abilities.

actually very different indeed, showing no apparent impress from any cultural institution.

Spatial thinking involves especially keeping "orientations" in mind, as shown by examples in the upper part of Figure 3–1 below. Thurstone brought some evidence to show that thinking in three dimensions might involve different skills from thinking in two dimensions. A simple verbally presentable example is to ask the subject to imagine a three-inch cube painted red and sawn into one-inch cubes. One then asks: "How many of the latter will have paint on one, two, three, four sides?" The emergence of a spatial reasoning factor and the discovery that visualization is also some-thing distinct—quite distinct in this case—from spatial thinking well illus-trates a point which cannot be emphasized too much to the beginner in psychology. It is that introspection and common sense are very unreliable bases for forming hypotheses about ability structure.

Visualization, p_v, as indicated in the footnote to Table 3–1, though commonly listed with primaries, has not been included because the evi-dence by Horn (1965) powerfully supports the concept that it is a broad, higher-order, "provincial" factor, i.e., broader than a primary. Visualiza-tion extends to a broad array of performances, such as "seeing" what will happen to a piece of paper when cuts are made in a folded state (W. Harrell, 1940), imagining the change of view when an object is rotated (see Figure 3–1(b), envisaging the direction of movement in one part of a machine when another part moves (this is also determined partly by a_{mk}; see Cox, 1928). What is involved is aptly described by Pawlik (1966, p. 543) as "the ability to imagine properly the movement of spatial displace-ment of a configuration or some of its parts." For reasons given later this is considered connected with a "province" in brain localization (hence, the p_v symbol) in the visual cortex.

Assuming that Table 3–1 will suffice to give the reader as much idea of the typical nature and variety of the chief fifteen (and possibly twenty) primary abilities as he needs, it might be more appropriate here to turn to the main controversies. As pointed out below, the whole area is rent and made difficult to integrate at the present time by the differences of methods and results between those who follow Thurstone, on the one hand, empiri-cally converging on (oblique) simple structure, dealing with perhaps twenty primaries, and recognizing a higher-order structure, and on the other hand, Guilford's followers, dealing only with orthogonal factors, creating tests according to a theory, and ending with well over a hundred primaries with no higher-order structure.

In a few regions in the ability domain, the difference can be reduced to speaking as if one Thurstone factor splits into four or so Guilford factors. Thus, Thurstone's "Perceptual Speed" is cut up into "figural perceptual speed," "symbolic perceptual speed," "symbolic discrimination perceptual speed," etc., by Guilford. But in other areas the differences in the two kinds of resolution will not permit even this degree of translation.

FIGURE 3–1

Operations in Spatial and Visualization Abilities

(*a*) *Spatial Abilities*

    In this test you are to try to imagine or visualize how a piece of paper can be folded to form some kind of object. Look at the two drawings below. The drawing on the left is of a piece of paper which can be folded on the dotted lines to form the object drawn at the right. You are to imagine the folding and are to figure out which of the lettered edges on the object are the same as the numbered edges on the piece of paper at the left. Write the letters of the answers in the numbered spaces at the far right.

    Now try the practice problem below. Numbers 1 and 4 are already correctly marked for you.

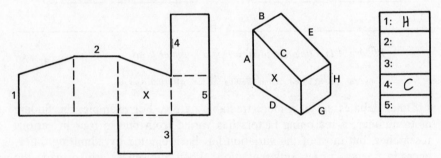

    NOTE: The side of the flat piece marked with the X will always be the same as the side of the object marked with the X. Therefore, the paper must always be folded so that the X will be on the outside of the object.

    In the above problem, if the side with edge 1 is folded around to form the back of the object, then edge 1 will be the same as edge H. If the side with edge 5 is folded back, then the side with edge 4 may be folded down so that edge 4 is the same as edge C. The other answers are as follows: 2 is B; 3 is G; and 5 is H. Notice that two of the answers can be the same.

Adapted from *Surface Development* by L. Thurstone. Copyright © 1962 by Educational Testing Service. Used with permission of Educational Testing Service.

(*b*) *Visualization Examples*

    This is a test of your ability to perceive a whole picture even though it is not completely drawn. You are to use your imagination to fill in the missing parts.

    Look at each incomplete picture and try to see what it is.

*Write on the line beneath it a word or a few words telling what
the picture is. You need not describe it in detail; just name
the picture or its important parts.*
   Try the sample pictures below.

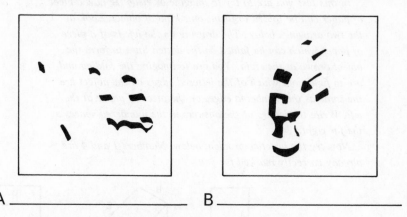

A _____   B _____

Picture A is a flag and picture B is a hammer head.

Other debates are of a more tractable nature. For example, the finding
as to number of reasoning factors has varied from one to four in various
researches, but most of the variation has been created by admitting differences in fineness of test differentiation. When allowances are so made the
issues have been reduced to a question of whether there are two reasoning
factors—inductive, a_{iv} (I), and deductive, a_{dv} (D)—or three, through
admitting a general reasoning factor (R). Three can be agreed to exist only
if all three are found *in the same research,* and our conclusion here must
be that there are only two (I and R becoming a_{iv}). Spearman, through the
work of his student Hargreaves (1927), recognized that reasoning is
something over and above intelligence (and many men, for example, are
willing to concede women equality on the latter but not the former!). Insofar as any factors other than fluid intelligence enter into the Culture-Fair
Intelligence Test (Cattell, 1940; Cattell, Feingold, and Sarason, 1941), it
would seem that the series subtest has some dependence on this power, as
illustrated at the top of Figure 5–2. (Men and women, however, do *not*
seem to differ in level on the Culture-Fair Test, so whatever sex difference
caused the above comment, it cannot be *ability* to reason.) Meanwhile, Figure 3–2 shows examples of such reasoning (inductive in the form of
classification problems.

Another general class of emerging primaries covers those in which the
knowledge and skill clearly belong to an area of cultural concentration. An
obvious and well-checked primary here is that of mechanical aptitude (Cox,
1928), in which there is, incidentally, a large sex difference. Another is
musical aptitude, and yet another is artistic aptitude, as shown in Burt's

FIGURE 3–2
Operations for Inductive Reasoning and Word Fluency
Primaries

(a) Inductive Reasoning

   This is a test of your ability to discover rules that explain
things. In each problem on this test there are either two or three
groups, each consisting of three figures. You are to look for
something that is the same about the three figures in any
one group and for things that make the groups different from
one another.
   Now look at the sample problem below. In the first line, the
figures are divided into Group 1 and Group 2. The squares
in Group 1 are shaded and the squares in Group 2 are not
shaded. In the second line a 1 has been written under each
figure that has a shaded square as in Group 1. A 2 has been
written under each figure with an unshaded square as in
group 2.

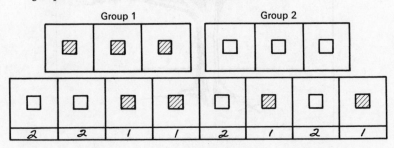

   Now try this more difficult example, which has three groups:

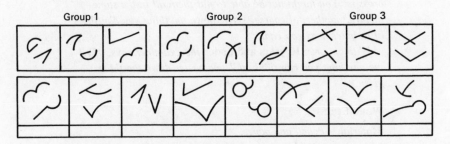

   The figures in Group 1 consist of both straight and curved
lines. The figures in Group 2 consist of curved lines only. The
figures of Group 3 consist of straight lines only. As you can
see, there are other details that have nothing to do with the
rule. The answers are 1, 1, 3, 1, 2, 1, 2, 2.

(b) Word Fluency Primaries

I want you to think of as many different *things as you can
that might be drawn under the tree somewhere about where the
cross is. You might not be able to put them all in the same
picture together, of course. Write down anything you can think
of as quickly as you can.*

With children 10 years and under *the examiner says, "Tell
me anything you can think of," and writes down the things
given.*

WORD SERIES

Material.—Pencil and paper.
Instructions to subject.

(a) *I am going to give you a minute, and I want you to
write down (or tell me) as many things as you can think
of that are 'round' or could be round. A penny would do.
Give me as many as you can. Ready? Go.*

(b) *Now write a list of things we can 'eat.'*

(1917) or Cattell's (*Guide to Mental Testing,* 1936c) drawing ability scale (different from intelligence, spatial ability, or manual dexterity). How close, again, is artistic executive skill to esthetic sensitivity, of the kind one might get at through the Meier-Seashore test of esthetic judgment? Although, as Spearman pointed out very early, these "artistic abilities" are little correlated with intelligence and require explanation in terms of what we should now call independent primaries, their structure is far from understood. For example, the careful work of Karlin (1941) on tests in the Seashore musical aptitude test shows several quite distinct factors, some having to do with apparently more innate gifts, such as judgment of absolute pitch, and others with acquired musical motor skills. Similarly in art, there is no clear evidence yet as to how motor drawing skill is related to the esthetic judgmental skills.

A serious problem which presents itself as one proceeds to the artistic, musical, poetic, literary, and similar areas is the absence of an objective criterion. This is actually a double problem: first, that society itself may be in doubt as to what *is* excellent performance, and second, that the nature of the performance is such that *conspective*[4] scoring is difficult or impossible for the psychologist.

5. FLUENCY, MEMORY, AND PERCEPTION PRIMARIES POSSIBLY TIED TO PERSONALITY

A class of alleged ability primaries about which there is much confusion are those variously called fluency, ideational fluency, associational fluency, flexibility, rigidity, dispositional rigidity, etc. Although these are mentioned in some recent writings as though they had begun as concepts in Guilford's divergent ability schema, the basic work on structuring them is much older, and they can be seen in proper perspective only by respecting the substantial and strategically planned original work done on them by Spearman (1927), Bernstein (1924), Hargreaves, (1927), Studman (1935), Cattell (1950a), Pinard (1932), Stephenson (1953), and many others.

Spearman and his coworkers demonstrated that fluency, speed, and perseveration must be considered general factors (not narrow primaries) outside the area of general intelligence and possibly of abilites.

---

[4] *Conspective* means scored in such a way that two psychometrists giving the same test are bound to get the same answer for a given individual's performance. In educational circles these are often called objective as opposed to essay type tests. But *objective,* in psychology proper, means much more than *conspective.* For example, in personality testing, a questionnaire requiring self-evaluation is not objective, but a behavioral test *is* objective, as in the O-A (Objective-Analytic) Batteries (Cattell, 1955b). *Multiple-choice* is not an adequate synonym for *conspective,* because the latter is a broader term covering *both* multiple-choice, *selective* answer tests and *open-ended, inventive* tests. For when the examiner has a key that will cover all eventualities, the latter can also be fully conspective.

Fluency was recognized, when intelligence was partialled out, as extending across such measures as speed of supplying words beginning with a given letter, volume of material per minute in completing stories or topics, and fertility of ideas in completing drawings. It appears as an oversight that Thurstone conceived it as "word association," W, when the earlier work of Cattell (1933b, 1936a) and Studman (1935) had shown it to be much broader, indeed a general fertility or facility of memory retrieval in regard to any kind of material.

Furthermore, the introduction of objective performance devices in measuring temperament factors by Cattell (1933a) in 1933, revealing a substantial role of the surgent personality factor in fluency, made it certain that fluency would have to be pursued with both ability and personality connotations, and that test performance in fluency must be assigned recognizably distinct ability and personality factor components. The recent work of Hundleby and Pawlik (1965), Riley Gardner (1958), and others fully confirms this tracing of a substantial part of fluency to a temperament source trait (U.I. 21, Exuberance). The picture was further clarified by Bernstein's (1924) demonstration of the distinctness of fluency and speed,[5] and by the present writer's and Studman's (1935) demonstrations that fluency extends as a single factor across both verbal fluency (later located by Thurstone, 1938) and high productivity in completing drawings by a stroke of the pencil. Although Thurstone gave the symbol W to his verbal fluency factor, his experiments were not designed so as to show that other fluencies were excluded and that what he found was not the previously isolated general fluency factor, then labeled F, which runs across all kinds of high fluency or retrieval capacity.

While studying fluency—which we shall later bring evidence to show is a higher-order, general capacity factor, g and not a primary—it is appropriate to show its relation to ideational fluency, a_{if}, in Table 3–1, and to flexibility, g_x, since in recent popular discussion they have been thrown into a ragbag of so-called "divergent thinking" abilities. To get valuable historical depth on the concept of flexibility, we must start with the concept of "perseveration"—of a momentum or inertia to be overcome in mental processes—which has reappeared again and again in psychology. Spearman, picking up the ball in 1920 from the Dutch psychologists Heymans and Wiersma and from the philosopher-psychologist Gross, viewed it essentially in terms of individual differences in speed and in degree of "impedance" from interference in switching from one mental process to another. However, further experiments by the present writer (1935a, 1935b) called for a transformation of the concept from one of perseveration to one of "disposition rigidity." For the evidence that de-

---

[5] Speed, which is a higher-order factor, will not be discussed further among the primary abilities, nor will the factors of body tempo, which Rimoldi so clearly demonstrated (1951a) and which have since been confirmed and extended as aspects of true temperament factors, notably U.I. 22, Cortertia, U.I. 26, Narcissistic Ego, and U.I. 29, Superego.

cidedly higher saturations on this factor are found for performances requiring *a switch-over from some old, accustomed, overlearned activity to a
new way of effecting the same end* rather than any mere perseverative
momentum as such, points to the need for a rigidity concept. This disposition rigidity, as an actual test performance, has since been shown to involve primarily the personality factor U.I. 23 (in the negative direction of
"Inability to mobilize"), or "Regression" (Hundleby, Pawlik, and Cattell,
1965), but it also has variance contributions, in the form of attempted
willed control of rigidity, from three other personality factors.

In 1945, in connection with personality research, it seemed to the writer
that fluency and disposition rigidity were not enough to account for certain
flexibilities and rigidities observed in the higher mental processes. Could
it be that although fluency and rigidity are, so to speak, very basic properties of *all* mental activity (as indeed Spearman had theorized, at least on
fluency and "perseveration"), yet we are dealing in the higher cognitive
processes with some more specialized "ideational fluency" and "ideational
flexibility versus ideational rigidity" which come into play only there? The
answer could be given only by a research design in which both the *old*
(fluency, disposition rigidity) and the *new* concepts (the latter represented
by new tests) were simultaneously measured and factored.

This the writer and Tiner proceeded to do, and a clear answer was published (1949) showing that in the general realm of fluency, *ideational
general fluency* appeared as a pattern in higher mental processes. It manifested itself by loadings on, for example, invention of many nonsense
syllables, retrieval of many words with some simple restriction, and also
flicker fusion and perspective oscillation. In the rigidity–flexibility area, on
the other hand, the usual broad disposition rigidity factor appeared in
perceptual–motor manifestations (backward writing, restructuring habitual
visual perception, etc.). But now there also appeared a second factor, loading the ability to answer riddles, to reconstruct hidden words (anagrams),
etc. This latter, called *Ideational Flexibility-versus-Firmness,* is set out and
discussed more fully in Chapter 13 on creativity. Suffice it to say that this
ideational flexibility, in the sense of being able to get out of a rut of inveterate habit, almost certainly has dynamic, personality roots, which can
be associated tentatively with personality factors U.I. 19 and U.I. 26.

About a decade later, the ideational general fluency and ideational flexibility factors were confirmed (and given slightly different names) by
Guilford and his coworkers, who made possible a more accurate assessment of the factors by adding some new tests, notably the match problem
(Luchins, 1959) the water jar problem, etc. Also in this area of ideational
flexibility measurement are the tests called unusual uses, figure grouping
("figure concepts") and number associations. Such work—extending the
known expressions of previously located factors—is very valuable. In this
context of orthogonal factors, however, the loading patterns must be
watched for the warpings due to incomplete rotation, while the fitting of
results into the Procrustean bed of Guilford's threefold schema leads to

labeling inconsistent with that which would be given on a Thurstonian basis of direct formation of concepts from empirical patterns.

Along with fluency, it is appropriate to study memory phenomena, since we shall develop the theory later that fluency is really a special aspect of memory—the facility and speed of the process of retrieval from a memory store. As mentioned, two memory (besides immediate and long distance) factors have been found, one rote, one intelligent, but we have listed only the rote—as a_{mr} or g_m—since we hypothesize that intelligent memorizing is finally to be resolved into intelligence and rote memory. Throughout the discussion here we have been unable, on present evidence, to reach a conclusion as to whether memory should be considered narrow enough to be a "primary," a_m, as Thurstone and other factorists have found it, or whether it has the status of a general power, perhaps to be indexed g_m (since g's are retained for general capacities).

The unfortunate fact is that not nearly enough steps and aspects of the learning and recall process—such as immediate committing to memory, rate of fading, mode of retrieval, and other manifestations important to the memorizing processes—have been used by psychometrists, who have tended instead to confine themselves to some total learning effect, either in meaningless material or in some one content area. As Pawlik well says (1966, p. 546), "Tests of memory functions have been somewhat underrepresented in factorial research on abilities." Thus, existing results cannot be taken as representative of the structure likely to emerge ultimately in factor analysis, and until the fuller factor picture is at hand, the rest of the evidence is hard to integrate. If we assume that the g_m factor is essentially a factor of goodness of *retention*—which, as Underwood (1957), Broadbent (1965), Melton (1963) (in the "decay hypothesis"), and others have shown, tends to be the same for meaningful and rote material, as if in a continuum—then any special factors found beyond this are likely to be largely in the *committing* to memory. Thus, Kelley's "meaningful memory" factor would have to be explained as a peculiarity of operation (intelligent ordering) in committing to memory. The present writer is inclined to favor this and to suggest that a number of primary powers might be expected to segregate out according to content, e.g., school achievement areas, because the individual's possession of reservoirs of content in an area would favor, up to a point, improved committing to memory of new content in that area.

Several researches indicate differences in power of committing to memory according to the nature of the material (Schwartz and Lippman, 1962; Hunt 1962). Gabriel (1963) and Kintsch (1963) have also made an argument for differences of fundaments and relations being associated with different "committing to memory" processes. This use of relations and fundaments we might connect with the general factor of fluid intelligence, as "perception of relations," on the one hand, and with "rote memory," on the other. In short, this finding in the realm of "process" observations fits Kelley's individual difference finding, if we grant that intelligence is necessary for the processing and storing of relations but that rote memory suffices for proper names and nonsense syllables. Thus Kelley's "intelligent memory" would be a derived composite of g_f and rote memory. Furthermore, the nature and development of the existing apperceptive masses (which give "meaning" to some stimuli) as well as of the dynamic interest systems (which tend to match apperceptive masses), will add further special memory factors likely to appear as narrower primary abilities.

One special influence in committing to memory comes to light from brain physiology—namely the special reduction of the power of committing to memory which comes with injury to the lower brain around the corpus callosum as well as with delirium tremens and senility. This *could* be an interference with whatever strength of motivation does to memorizing recognized here in physiological terms. The question is taken up again in a later chapter.

With this brief statement of some observations on fluency and memory, an hypothesis will be suggested about their relationship, namely, that what are called localized, special fluencies (except ideational fluency) are the increases in fluency which come in a particular area through a high *reservoir of material* already committed to memory in those areas. This is taken up in more detail in the next chapter, where it is argued that a general fluency factor, g_r, is essentially a general power of retrieval which is, however, a composite outcome of present physiological retrieval efficiency and past memorizing power, plus past exposure to what needs to be stored.

The multiplication of perception factors, which has occurred alike in Thurstone's and in Guilford's work, though for different reasons, and the variety of specific proposed perceptual abilities (except for a_{ps} and a_{sc} listed here), also present a rather confused picture at the present moment. Instances of perceptual ability factor tests are given in Figure 3–3. In this case, however, the solution to the apparent multiplication of factors may lie *outside* the field of abilities altogether, in the field of personality (as it did for fluency, to the extent that U.I. 21, Exuberance of Temperament, enters). By including markers for four or five of Thurstone's perceptual "ability" factors in objective test personality researches pursued from 1947 to 1957, the present writer and his colleagues were able to show that three of these Thurstonian perceptual abilities appeared to express the projection of personality factors into the cognitive perception realm. That is to say, if a reasonable number of personality and temperament variables were included in such experiments, the factoring showed that the cognitive, perceptual expressions were only part of a broader temperamental tendency. Thus, it seems that the factor (variously called ideational flexibility, intellectual flexibility, etc.) involving particularly Gottschalk figures—and which is also the heart of Witkin's cluster (1962) of "field independent" behaviors—is largely an expression of the personality factor in objective tests originally called Independence (or Promethean Will) and indexed as U.I. 19.

Indeed, it is true in all primary ability research that work on ability structure can approach clarity and precision of conclusion only if the

FIGURE 3–3
Tests Used as Markers for Perceptual Ability and Personality Factors

(a) Perceptual Ability

> This is a test of your ability to compare lengths of lines by eye. Shown below is a box containing 5 pairs of lines of differing lengths marked A, B, C, D, and E. Each pair consists of a vertical and a horizontal line of the same length. The lines marked A are the shortest and those marked E are the longest. (Both vertical and horizontal lines are shown in the box because some people think that 2 lines of the same length look different lengths when one is vertical and the other is horizontal.)
>
> Below the box of lines are two rows of test lines numbered from 1 to 10. The lines in the first row are the <u>same length</u> as the ones in the box. The lines in the second row are <u>twice as long</u> as the ones in the box. Beneath the number for each test line write the <u>letter</u> of the line which is the <u>same length</u> or <u>half as long</u> as the test line. Measure the lines with your eyes. Do not use your fingers or your pencil.
>
> Now try the practice items. The correct letter has been written beneath the number of the first item in each row.

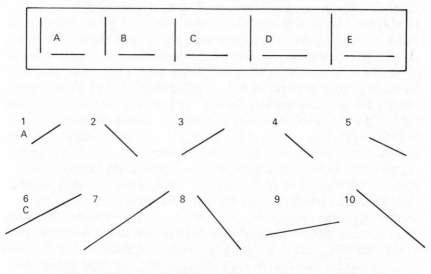

> The answers to the other practice items are as follows:
> 2—D; 3—E; 4—B; 5—C;
> 7—E; 8—A; 9—B; 10—D.

(b) Perceptual Tests in Personality Factors

Find out in which square of five both signs in left single square occur again. There may be more lines than necessary. The shapes may be moved but not directly turned and they retain their size. In the last example you would check "e" in the answer sheet. Don't lose time.

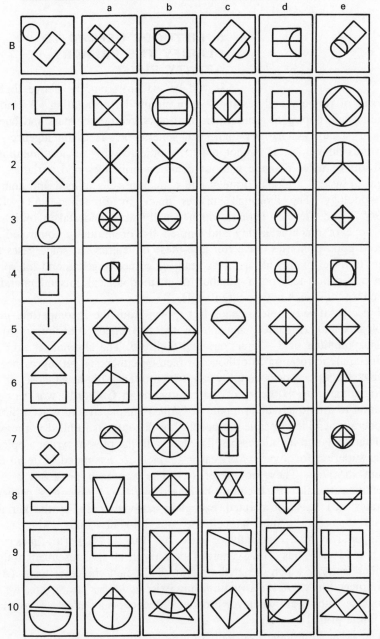

By kind permission of The Institute of Personality and Ability Testing, 1602 Coronado Drive, Champaign, Illinois.

variances due to personality factors are first "partialled out," by including personality factor markers and locating these factors along with what have been supposed to be special ability factors. The resolution of influences in perception largely into well-known personality factors has been well set out recently by Schneewind (see Cattell, 1971).

6. METHODS NEEDED TO CLARIFY THE PRIMARY ABILITY FIELD

It will be evident from the above that the pursuit of primary abilities that began simply by correlating all kinds of abilities and hoping to group them, first as correlation clusters and later as primary factors—narrower than such general factors as intelligence—has run into difficulties. It cannot reach its objective by an accumulation of individual studies planned without common principles and variables, but requires instead a global strategy and a far more disciplined and complex methodology. The thorough surveys made by French (1963), Horn (1965), and Pawlik (1966), which usually were undertaken initially in the hope of reaching a tidy and limited list of mutually confirmed and agreed upon primaries, have run into these difficulties. In some cases they seem to have foundered, as far as really good convergence and interpretation are concerned, on a number of methodological misunderstandings which we must seek now to disentangle.

First, as already noted, chaos has grown from the incompatible methodologies and associated concepts of the two major contributors to the primary abilities field—Thurstone and Guilford. The alternatives are: (a) factor-analytic rotation to orthogonal factors, either (i) getting as near to simple structure as *orthogonality* can, which often is not at all close, or (ii) fitting some *a priori* theory of the rotator, as in Guilford's work; or (b) rotation to a uniquely determinate (*oblique*) simple structure according to a general scientific principle not peculiar to the data, as fulfilled in the work of Thurstone and his successors. The latter, in the present writer's opinion, is far superior, for a variety of reasons, which are examined in detail elsewhere (1957a). They are these: (a) The approach possesses a basic scientific rationale. (b) It cannot be biased by the experimenters' particular theories. (c) It is not affected, except in a trivial sense, by the variables which the experimenter happens to put into his study, whereas the orthogonal system, especially as used by Burt (1940) (at times) and Vernon (1964), has a first general factor (with all its subsequent train of smaller factors) which lies at the mercy of the first choice of tests. (d) It can proceed to whatever structure may exist at *higher* strata; i.e., we can recognize with its aid whatever broader influences may affect and organize the initial primaries.

The issue of whether we gain or lose at this stage in applying some *a priori* schema in choosing the tests that we will factor is distinct from the above technical question of a meaningful resolution in factor analysis per se. But inasmuch as Guilford uses such a scheme, it is an additional difference causing divergence of findings from those of the Thurstonian approach. As will be seen in the next chapter, the Guilford ability schema, or *any* schema, is only *one of many* that could be applied. Unfortunately it is possible for any schema to connive, with weaknesses created in defective uses of the factor-analytic method, to give an apparent proof to almost any theory present in such a schema.

A taxonomy of abilities is a desirable aim, but, like the taxonomy of the biologist, the psychologist's scheme should derive from a *naturalistic* observation of discovered primary abilities. The only real necessity in a schema for choosing tests—and it *is* a real necessity—is the practice of sampling a population of ability performances *from life* (not the laboratory), in starting any correlational, factor-analytic study. As pointed out above, this has worked well in personality research, through the employment of the personality sphere concept, and similarly one could sample the cultural dictionary, or take a time sampling across time and people, in the ability domain.

When this is done—and it may be considered half-done in current results —the definition of a primary ability is "that which one obtains as a uniquely simple structure rotated, replicated, factor pattern. Secondly, it is one which holds across a set of performances far less broad than all behavior or, indeed, than all behaviors of a cognitive modality." At the same time, if primaries are to have scientific predictive value and utility in applied psychology, they must not be so narrow, i.e., so "manufactured" out of tests artificially multiplied in the laboratory, that the primary factor is really a mere blown-up "bloated specific" (Cattell and Tsujioka, 1964). Thus, one aim of sampling is to avoid the Scylla of confusing a primary with a general factor, while the other is to steer free of the Charybdis of innumerable overblown specifics. Instances of what may be errors of the first kind are given in Table 3–1 in U.I. 5 and U.I. 6, and of the latter in the last few factors allowed in Table 3–1 above and several of Guilford's going beyond that list.

Among primaries meeting these basic conditions there will be some natural correlation, of course. For example, verbal (a_v) and numerical (a_n) primaries will be appreciably correlated, for the good reason that (see Chapter 6) intelligence enters into the production of both of these structures. Consequently, higher-order factor analyses of firmly located true primaries typically will yield secondary and tertiary strata structures. These will be recognized as broader influences (as studied here in Chapter 7) of considerable theoretical importance. This higher-strata domain, bringing out the "wheels within wheels" in psychological determination, akin to the intriguing complexities with which other sciences are plentifully endowed, is completely locked away from the psychologist who insists on dealing with *orthogonal* primaries. To the latter approach this whole domain is as meaningless as the paintings of Manet to a color-blind man.

Although the reader may not yet have the facility in multivariate analysis to follow the detailed argument, he may well appreciate the intent of a technical point which should be made at this point. It concerns the decision regarding several instances above where the existence of a distinct primary has been doubted. In many of these instances—such as word fluency, figural perception speed, symbol perception speed, or meaningful memory —one perceives psychologically that the principle of Occam's razor (parsimony of explanation) could be better served by considering these to be *areas of overlap* between two already known general factors, rather than *ad hoc* primaries. For example, word fluency might be determined by the general fluency (speed of retrieval of memories in general) factor and the amount of word storage in the a_v, verbal ability factor. And, as we have surmised above, the meaningful memory factor (Kelley) might be an overlap of rote memory and intelligence, "g." The figural, symbolic, and other speed of perception clusters might be the overlap of a general speed factor with local neural organizations concerned with figural and symbolic processing. Only more careful factor extraction and rotation can settle these issues.

It is not asserted that present evidence favors *all* these alternatives to the currently popular explanation by primaries, but only that a mistake in structuring *could* have occurred along these lines. This may be dismaying to the psychologist who has learned to expect that factor analysis will be an objective analytic procedure, but, just as when we learn that the family physician errs in, say, twenty percent of his diagnoses, it behooves us to understand why.

Two ways in which an "extra" primary could be "created," where broader factors, by higher-order analyses, can actually be shown to exist, are illustrated in Figure 3–4. They concern inadequate choice of variables and use of a faulty number of factors. In the first the experimenter has made a mistake in not representing a well-known general factor, intelligence, by good markers, and has confined his study of memory to memory tests only, forgetting the principle of putting in "hyperplane stuff" (Cattell, 1952, 1966). The six-variable study (Figure 3–4 (a) (1): see plot and corresponding rotated matrix) yields two nonoverlapping factors, meaningful memory being one. The ten-variable study (Figure 3–4(a) (ii)), also yields two factors, rote memory and intelligence, but now with intelligence located by a sufficiency of variables, the primary of "meaningful memory" is shown to be superfluous, and one perceives it was falsely occasioned by an overlap of two broader capacities.

In the second research, Figure 3–4(b), if we suppose (i) to represent the true state of affairs, (ii) has taken out one factor too many—a mistake easily made. Here there are really two rather broad factors 1, 4, 5, 6, 7, 10 and 1, 4, 7, 10. The same correlations are restored from the factor analysis in (ii) as in (i), provided either that the relatively general perceptual speed factor has slightly higher loadings on 1, 4, 7, and 10 or that Symbolic and Figural are somewhat correlated. But in the second case separate primary abilities are assigned to the latter. An actual instance of this kind is the

FIGURE 3–4
Possible Systematic Causes of Recording Primaries
Where They Do Not Exist

Research (a). Failure of Marker Representativeness, Necessary for Hyperplane Delineation

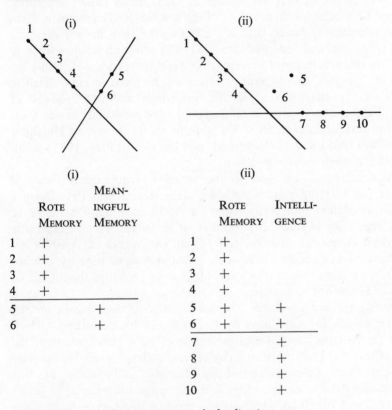

	(i)	
		Mean-
	Rote	ingful
	Memory	Memory
1	+	
2	+	
3	+	
4	+	
5		+
6		+

	(ii)	
	Rote	Intelli-
	Memory	gence
1	+	
2	+	
3	+	
4	+	
5	+	+
6	+	+
7		+
8		+
9		+
10		+

Note: Where no plus sign appears, the loading is zero.

Research (b). Dubious Estimate of the Number of Factors

(i)	Perceptual Speed	Crystallized Intelligence	(ii)	Perceptual Speed	Symbolic Perc. Speed	Figural Perc. Crystallized
1	+	+	1	+	+	
2			2			
3			3			
4	+	+	4	+	+	
5	+		5	+		
6	+		6	+		
7	+	+	7	+		+
8			8			
9			9			
10	+	+	10	+		+

alternative often presented in Burt's and Vernon's analyses. There, instead of V and N appearing as separate primaries, they come together with common loadings on a "V:ed factor" of general school achievement.

A major problem still to be faced in the mapping of primary abilities is the separation or partialling out[6] of temperament and motivation factor effects beforehand, so that the abilities as such can be clearly separated. Instances have been mentioned e.g., of the low inhibition present in Exuberance (Personality factor U.I. 21) affecting the total fluency measure, and of temperamental Independence (U.I. 19) affecting independence of perception (Restructuring of Perception or Field Independence). Other examples of "trespass" or cooperative action will be given in more detail in Chapter 12. To effect this separation insightfully and well requires, of course, that there be progress in mapping objective personality source traits parallel to that made in abilities, but with the recent surveys of Hundleby and Pawlik (1965) and of Nesselroade and Cattell (In Press 1971) available, this is a much reduced problem.

Granted increased attention to the technical requirements indicated above of (a) carrying marker variables across researches, (b) objective rotational resolution statistically tested for significance and congruence of pattern from study to study, (c) inclusion of personality factors, especially those which counterfeit abilities, and (d) an enrichment of variables beyond those conventionally included in pencil-and-paper tests by psychometrists; there is no reason why a reliable map of primaries should not be completed in one or two decades.

Regarding the last condition, one must recognize that, except for the deliberate search for new ideas by Guilford and his coworkers (which escapes the past only to fall into the prison of an *a priori* scheme), the choice of tests has been banal to a degree, rarely stepping outside the pencil-and-paper ruts of the educational psychometrist. Ability testing has had its boundaries fixed to an unconfessed degree by the convenience of pencil and paper, and of group administrable material—and even by the exigencies of a limited time for retests set by Ph.D. thesis timetables! The larger ability world to be sampled from laboratory learning experiments, animal ethology, cultural anthropology, and the "criterion performances" of everyday life, has been sadly neglected.

When a reasonably comprehensive list of primaries—clearly separated from broader factors, from personality dimensions, and from blown-up specifics, etc.—is reached, a taxonomic study must then be prepared to recognize that "primary abilities" will by no means turn out to be all of one species. They come as a single class only as empirical factor patterns,

---

[6] What the applied psychologist is often accustomed to thinking of as "partialling out" by a partial correlation coefficient, amounts in essentials to the same thing as setting aside a factor in factor analysis. However, in order to set aside personality factors in ability researches it is vital to have several test markers for the personality source trait *other* than the variables which express its effects in the ability field—and this is rarely planned in ability research designs.

but factors can spring from very diverse causes. Later in this book we reach a taxonomy of abilities as "agencies" or acquired instrumentalities (a's), as provincial neural organizations (p's), and as general capacities (g's). What we have taken here empirically as "primary abilities" will not be entirely identical with the class we designate later, by further propensities, as agencies, though mostly "a" (agency) symbols occur in Table 3–1. Some primaries are fairly obviously special aggregates of knowledge and skill reflecting, in their unity, the unity of a social institution. Verbal, numerical, mechanical abilities, etc., may thus arise from cultural molds. Other primaries such as body coordination and spatial ability, may be more constitutional, representing neurological endowments (p's) that are still relatively local in effect. Others, again, as suggested above, may really be broader, higher-order "g" factors, for the moment "caught by one corner," and therefore appearing only as primaries, and so on.

Any attempt to map primary abilities as of 1970 must be likened to an attempt to map the physical globe in 1470. The existing map is both limited by ignorance and distorted, and it leaves one only dimly aware of vast spaces outside it. Beyond its boundaries lie, for example, gourmet taste and hunter olfactory skills; many social interaction skills, e.g., facial expression skills; child management skills of nursery governess and teacher; all that the first-class housewife does in her kitchen (balancing the male's mechanical aptitude); sailing a boat; the proficiencies of military combat; and the spectrum of abilities in courtship and lovemaking; to name but a few of the absentees.

CHAPTER FOUR

PRINCIPLES IN DRAWING THE MAP OF ABILITIES

1. WHAT GOOD IS A TAXONOMY?

Our conceptions of the earth come to us from bold explorers and assiduous map-makers—from the Columbuses and the study rooms of Prince Henry the Navigator. Though Eric the Red was the first known European to find America, Amerigo Vespucci was the first to communicate clearly the idea that this land was a new continent, and, as a result, a German professor making maps in Nuremberg called the new land America. As with the earth, so with the world of human abilities: the concrete discoveries will take on their due richness of meaning only when they are sifted and placed in perspective by classification, indeed by a taxonomy based on due study of their properties.

A taxonomy of abilities, like a taxonomy anywhere else in science, is apt to strike a certain type of impatient student as a gratuitous orgy of pedantry. Doubtless, compulsions to intellectual tidiness express themselves prematurely at times, and excessively at others, but a good descriptive taxonomy, as Darwin found in developing his theory, and as Newton found in the work of Kepler, is the mother of laws and theories. On the other hand, a too subjective model or map, like some Graeco-Roman maps which showed nothing beyond the great river circling the Mediterranean empire, can be as much of a curiosity-stultifying curse as a factually inspired map can be a blessing.

Classifications of abilities as misleading as some of these ancient world maps were to geographical explorers can be found aplenty in the charts of phrenologists and in various pre-experimental writings such as those of faculty psychologists. Incidentally, since some psychologists actually reacted to factor analysis as if it were a rebirth of faculty psychology we should pause to underline the difference. The faculty psychologist of a hundred years ago found a word in the dictionary (or floating in his mind) and then described at length the manifestations of a unitary mental capacity which conformed to it. The factor analyst, or correlation analyst, does something very different when he finds the unitary pattern first, and then describes and names it according to its form. Furthermore, though we have not discussed this yet, he is not content to state that several behaviors are bound by some underlying unity. He proceeds as soon as possible to ask why they are bound, what mental processes are shared in their expression, and how they come to develop in that way.

However, as we have just seen, there is "many a slip twixt the cup and the lip" in cruder factor-analytic usages, so that debates still exist as to what the factor unities are. And we do *not* yet know what the properties and *natural history of growth* of most of the empirically discovered primary abilities in Table 3–1 are. A third natural objection to developing any sort of final taxonomy at this stage is that we are, so to speak, describing the solar system without the sun. As to the latter, the reader naturally will be wondering where general intelligence takes its place among these more localized primaries. However, he will have noted that we refer repeatedly to "higher strata," broader or more general capacities, and realize that the evidence for intelligence is yet to be marshalled (actually in Chapters 5 and 6 below).

Regarding the last we might for the moment be permitted to proceed on the assumption that something like Spearman's g is accepted by virtually all psychologists. By implication we have begun above to put alongside it, and on the same footing of generality, certain other concepts of *properties general to cognitive behavior,* such as rote retentivity, g_m, fluency, g_r, and general speed, g_s. Regarding the incomplete identification and description of the primary abilities themselves in Table 3–1, we may point out that since our aim is not to "place" particular primaries exactly in a framework but only to get ideas about how the framework might be constructed, the presently known "suggestive" properties are enough. It would, for example, probably be a mistake to undertake premature attempts to use *explanatory* principles, as in a division of abilities into those shaped by heredity and environment or by their neurological and biochemical sources or into derivatives of higher order general abilities, and so on.

However, for better or worse, psychologists wish to have something more than the simple list of assumed, discovered, empirical primaries in Table 3–1. They need to have some schema in mind for thinking about abilities, despite the fact that at present it cannot be a truly objectively based taxonomy and must include subjective elements. Such schemata, as mentioned, existed earlier in faculty psychology and phrenology at a speculative level and appeared again in Spearman's classification of general, group, and specific factors at a theoretical construct level. Although the two main newer schemes that we shall discuss—Guilford's form-content analysis and the present writer's triadic theory—are incomplete and are forced to skate over thin ice at times, they offer frameworks based on substantial observation and are useful for the ordering of data and further experiment.

2. A CRITIQUE AND FURTHER EXPLORATION OF SOME PROPOSED CLASSIFICATORY PRINCIPLES

Regardless of the particular descriptive categories one tends to favor, there are here, as elsewhere in science, two general ways in which one can proceed: (1) by waiting until more precise scientific knowledge has accumulated around most properties of the primaries—a course which we rejected as not possible at this juncture and (2) by creating a framework of subjective, philosophical-logical categories —on present data indications—according to one's own favored logic. This latter procedure of not waiting too much upon the correlations and organic relations experimentally emerging and instead analyzing the subjective "logical" categories which appeal to one always has been tempting to that philosopher who hides in every scientist. In the last two decades this procedure has been pursued extensively by Guilford, and a classification has been proposed by him according to operations, content, and "product," as shown in Figure 4–1.

FIGURE 4–1
Guilford's Three-Dimensional Box for an *A Priori*
Classification of Abilities

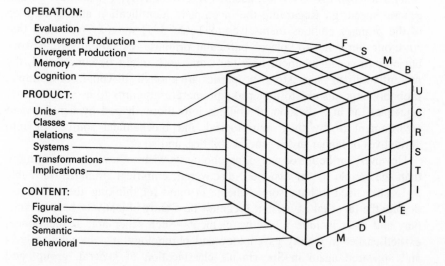

Guilford's "box" of three dimensions has been a valuable first step in stimulating interest in a taxonomy of abilities. Some may think nevertheless that its principal value lies in having raised the issue and presented one of several possible systems, for to various critics it has seemed, on the one hand, somewhat inadequate and, on the other, to have developed too many arbitrary features. For example, the product classes could readily be replaced by several others with equally good claims. And the content categories are by no means exhaustive or mutually independent. Finally, the operations—as witness the Cattell and Warburton (1967) and Fiske (1970) analyses of operations possible in psychological tests—omit several possibilities. In particular the terms convergent and divergent, though easy to remember, seem to express a less essential and central aspect of the differences here commonly intended. A convergent production is one where a correct answer exists, a divergent is one where several responses are acceptable and are given a score. However, in virtually all fluency and flexibility tests that have been good markers for the factors concerned in them, quite definite restrictions are in fact given in the instructions and accepted in scoring the answers.

A different and somewhat more extensive basis has been proposed by the present writer (see Figure 4–2, p. 56), the rationale for which will be given in a relatively condensed discussion. First, any systematic discussion of the possible classification of abilities must be preceded logically by a definition which segregates abilities themselves as a class, in fact as one of *three trait modalities,* namely: *abilities, temperament traits, and dynamic traits.* (This modality analysis is made in Chapters 11 and 12, where relations of ability with temperament and motivation are discussed). Second, a classification is likely to be merely philosophical and too artificial if it disregards the biological and physiological bases of behavior. The psychologist deals with behavior, but he should not deny himself clues from the nature of the physical organism. Principally this means that the ability taxonomist should keep an eye on the seven sensory and motor area brain bases in the central nervous system, especially as illuminated by study of comparative animal psychology. The large nose of the dog and the totally different proportion of olfactory to visual brain areas which goes therewith relative to humans suggests that comparative psychology can give leads to possible sensory and motor behavioral substrates or factors, even though they are not yet adequately brought out in human individual difference factorings.

The schema proposed in the Ability Dimension Analysis Chart (Table 4–1, p. 67) is centered on the same basic stimulus-organism-response model as in the personality structure realm (Cattell and Warburton, 1967). An approach to the final schema is best made by discussing some illustrative dimensions. First, a line can be drawn between perceptual abilities and performance abilities on the operational ground that the response to the former can in the last resort, in motor terms, be nothing but "a this or a that," or, indeed, "a this or a nothing." It involves such a response as pressing a button or not when a painting is judged better than a criterion

FIGURE 4–2
Some Ability Combinations Represented in Three-Dimensional Subspaces from the ADAC

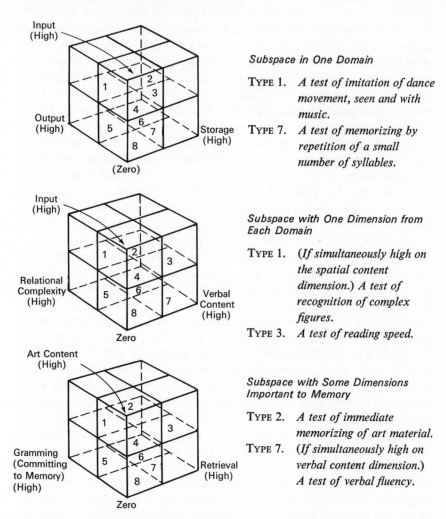

Subspace in One Domain

TYPE 1. *A test of imitation of dance movement, seen and with music.*

TYPE 7. *A test of memorizing by repetition of a small number of syllables.*

Subspace with One Dimension from Each Domain

TYPE 1. *(If simultaneously high on the spatial content dimension.) A test of recognition of complex figures.*

TYPE 3. *A test of reading speed.*

Subspace with Some Dimensions Important to Memory

TYPE 2. *A test of immediate memorizing of art material.*

TYPE 7. *(If simultaneously high on verbal content dimension.) A test of verbal fluency.*

or when an intelligence test alternative bears the right relations to a stimulus series. In what we may call "executive" ability (business meanings aside!), on the other hand, a fairly prolonged motor performance may be involved, e.g., as in a pursuit meter or in completing a story or in producing a series of navigation steps for a ship or plane. However, let us note that although motor abilities do not enter into the perception, perceptual abilities often enter into the executive performance. Executing a decision in car driving after the main situation is perceived still involves coordination of visual, kinesthetic, and other perceptions in the performance of the motor actions.

Second, there is an important dimension of distinction among abilities which combines what may be (for this purpose) the essence of both Spearman's noegenetic and anoegenetic and Guilford's convergent and divergent dimensions. In his *Principles of Cognition* (1923), Spearman defined noegenetic action as that leading to new mental content and anoegenetic as thinking which deals only with reproduction or recognition. Thus if a child recognizes that the solution to "a visitor at the door" is to call mother or if in solving for the square roots of 16, 9, and 4 he reaches figures 4, 3, and 2, he is utilizing concepts already in his mind. But if, proceeding with square roots, he reaches the idea of $\sqrt{-1}$, he has created (assuming he had not met it before) a new concept. To sketch a little more background for this, (which will be developed more fully in Chapter 13, p. 431) in considering the eduction of relations, let us note that Spearman recognized the eduction of relations and of fundaments as *the* central processes in thinking. Thus if one takes the following analogies:

4 is to 12 as 1 is to [1, 2, *3*, 4]

rabbit is to bird as auto: [dog, fish, engine, *airplane*]

the presented items and alternatives 4, 12, 2, rabbit, auto, engine, etc., are *fundaments*. One perceives a *relation* between 4 and 12 and applies it to 1 to get the new fundament 3, and correspondingly in the second analogy.

A person may create—if he is intelligent enough—a relation he never realized before, e.g., seeing time as a fourth dimension, or a fundament he never knew before, e.g., when someone who had never known an airplane got the idea (but not the word or the manner of making one) from considering the second analogy. If he responds with the word "airplane" (or checks it), he is completing a relation-correlate eduction process by dipping into memory for something that fits the relation.

While it may be incorrect to say that memory is needed in all kinds of ability performance, there is a continuum of increasing need for it across any ability spectrum. And although pure noegenetic action in Spearman's sense is perhaps rare in everyday life (a culture-fair, perceptual intelligence test comes near to it, and in the spatial realm we use it every moment, as when we decide where a tennis ball will be when we hit it), it enters similarly in varying amounts into all cognitive behavior. Since some performances obviously involve more reproductive memory (anoegenesis) and others more noegenesis, all abilities (perceptual or executive) can be placed on dimensional continua in these respects. Regardless of what further categories our taxonomic scheme must possess eventually, it therefore seems essential that we start with the two orthogonal coordinates—perceptual versus executive and high versus low memory action.

The categorization of convergent and divergent, by Guilford, stresses success in the former as due to a precise right or wrong answer and in the latter as due to a large output (ultimately perhaps assessed per minute) which, in the case of fluency and flexibility, would be due largely to high reproductive activity. However, it does not seem correct to label the concept we are approaching here as one more instance of high reproductive activity. Consider that successful learning or problem solution is either by insight or by trial-and-error. The former means correct relation eduction, but by no means does it imply noegenesis, since when the relation is applied, success still depends on reproduction. It does not solve the problem if, when bargaining in a Parisian shop, one can see that the required word is something the opposite of "more expensive," but cannot reproduce the cogent expression "à bon marché."

There are, indeed, really three dimensions in this area: one is the high-low memory demand just listed as dimension No. 2; another is the complexity of relation-eduction demanded for an insight type of solution, which we will call dimension No. 3; and the last is the extent of variability of response, which can contribute to bringing about a trial-and-error solution. Variability of response generally implies good memory resources, for even in the motor field the various movements tried actually may have to be stored. There are obviously other influences, however, such as *quickness of retrieval* of available stored memories and readiness to get away from responding in an old rut, which we have called flexibility and which, at the lower level, may also be low disposition rigidity.

Thus the distinction often made in abilities between insightful types of problem-solving and trial-and-error problem-solving would seem to depend, in defining the latter, on recognizing more than one conceptual dimension of abilities, namely, on (1) richness of storage of available responses, (2) flexibility or readiness to change some habitual, inveterate mode of response, and (3) speed of retrieval from storage.

In working toward a classification, certain systematic problems appear, notably that which often appears in factor conceptualization itself (and elsewhere) between a bi-polar dimension and two separate dimensions. For example, we can have a dimension from perceptual to executive (possibly even dichotomous) as above or one dimension indicating the extent to which the given ability requires perceptual skills and another the extent of executive skills. When they are not mutually exclusive (completely negatively correlated), as is true in this case, the schema of two distinct dimensions is better. Indeed, many mistakes and confusions have occurred in the factor field alone through oversimplification and the failure to recognize two dimensions each from zero to high on a given component, and thus permitting a performance to be simultaneously high on both.

A special case of this problem is encountered when we come to *areas* of memory storage, such as numerical, semantic, pictorial, etc. (Similar categories in Guilford's "content" dimension, Figure 4–1, are considered alternative categories along one side of his cube.) It would seem best, (if we are to operate with continua, as seems desirable) to make each of these a separate dimension. Thus we part company, at this point, with Guilford's system of mutually exclusive alternatives. For example, with jointly operative dimensions it would be possible to have an ability combining high evaluation with high memory, or with high symbolic or behavioral content, all having the possibility of being present in high degree. In some cases, notably in interest and motivation where a twenty-four hour day precludes being simultaneously high in all, we face a problem occasioned by the usual, slight, negative correlation among such *ipsatively scored* variables (Horn and Cattell, 1965). But such restrictions still do not preclude use of (correlated) coordinates.

Another general problem resides in the question of whether we are out to classify abilities according to certain conceived properties which may not be operationally measurable or to classify them according to certain instruction and measurement operations. For example, we shall introduce below a category of "amount of memory *processing* required," the operational definition of which may not be immediately evident. On the other hand, we deal also with the question of whether speed is a different ability from sheer (untimed) level of performance in a given content, and in this case there is a simple operational difference in instruction and scoring which constitutes the essence of our dimension. However, this dimension is applied separately to, say, perception, memory retrieval, and execution, with the implication that speed in each of these is different. Certainly, any good eventual scheme must admit "subspaces" in which a certain set of dimensions, m, n, o, is applicable only to another subset, t, u, v, though *apart* from this all dimensions cut across all other dimensions.

A pioneer attack on classification in terms of actual operations in tests has broken trail for us in the area of personality tests through the precise schema proposed by Cattell and Warburton (1967). In the objective personality test area six dimensions were finally considered comprehensive as follows: (1) differentiation between two responses versus between responding and not responding; (2) restricted (channelized, convergent) versus unrestricted (open-ended, divergent) requested response; (3) inventive versus selective response; (4) single response versus patterned and ordered sequence constituting a total response; (5) operating at natural speed of evaluation versus coerced or required speed of evaluation; (6) responding to immediate meaning or to symbolic referent meaning (e.g., judging length of lines versus judging tastiness of food described in words, and so on through less important aspects of test behavior). It will be seen that the current notions of divergent and convergent confuse dimensions (2) and (3) here. Whether the individual operates under a restriction to give a single, unique response fitting certain conditions or indicates a variety of responses acceptable to him is quite distinct from whether he reaches this by choosing among selective, multiple-choice answers, already given to him, or reproduces answers from his own fluency and memory. The categories just listed for personality tests, however, are given here only as a suggestive stimulus for the ability area, not a final proposition.

The fact that memory enters so universally into ability performances makes it certain that one dimension for classifying abilities should be *content.* However, in the next section we will argue that content must be dualistically conceived, namely, as *sensory-motor organization* content and as *experience (including cultural)* content. The *experience content* dimension in Figure 4–2 is a much more comprehensive concept than that in Figure 4–1, which applies largely to artificial test situations. Life experience content is implied here, and the encyclopedia is the basis for its divisions. For example, the curriculum categories of the educator—geography, mathematics, music, etc.—are involved here (so that we come completely in line over a limited tract with the educational test constructor) but so also are swimming, the family album, and campfire songs. The reconciliation of Guilford's four subdivisions with these is simply achieved when it is considered that the pie of content can be cut in all sorts of arbitrary directions. Musical content, for example, will include Guilford's symbolic, figural, and semantic subcategories. The question becomes simply one of the nature of cross-classifications with the latent issue: "Which cutting of content has the wider utility?"

Many other classifications of ability will suggest themselves, but some depend upon knowing more about the natural history of the primaries. This is true for example of the counsellor's preference for a division into aptitudes, considered to be more constitutional, and abilities, the patent result of learning experience. The degree of nature-nurture division is of interest but is less fundamental than the divisions proposed in the next section and which finally crystallize the discussions begun in this section into a constructive schema. Equally secondary, if we are really dealing with abilities, is any classification according to the dynamic life goals—ergs and sentiments—which abilities *serve.*

3. WHAT CATEGORIES ARE REALLY NEEDED IN A THEORETICAL CLASSIFICATION OF ABILITIES?

The above section, as its title indicated, aimed at a preliminary exploration of and skirmish with a variety of possible classificatory principles. Although discussion so far has been restricted to primary abilities, their characteristics are similar to and encompass those of the higher-order abilities abstracted from them. So the scheme now to be considered is one for *all* abilities.

Accepting the general stimulus-organism-response model stated above, we shall take as a basic framework for describing ability a schema which looks first at:

(a) a stimulus perception component, including a test instruction,
(b) a component describing the internal operation, i.e., the types of storage, sorting, etc., that must occur within the organism, and
(c) a motor response component.

These might more aptly be called "phase activities" because they are necessary phases in any ability performance and any given ability can in quantitative "dimensional" terms be assigned so much of each. In what is called a perceptual ability most of the activity, and therefore the chief limiting parameters, will lie in the perceptual activity regarding the stimulus, while the executive performance will be trivial. Conversely, in what is an executive performance, e.g., a motor dexterity skill, a fluency test, or a construction task, far more of the descriptive parameters will lie in the motor and verbal response organization tasks. The middle phase activity—internal storage and processing of data—has to have its characteristics inferred from the nature of the stimulus and the nature of the response, but it is certainly a distinct abstraction worthy of consideration on its own.

Now, at a commonsense level and without immediate resort to defining operations, one can see that abilities can be classified according to *amount* of activity at each of these three phases. That is to say, in a first reference to operations the level of success of different individuals in total performance in one ability will depend more on their relative standing in the perceptual phase or in another on their motor differences, and so on. These may be considered the first three dimensions along which any ability can be classified, and one would decide the classification according to the amount of activity of each dimension which characterizes the ability. For example, the a_{ps} primary of perceptual speed, is high on the first, moderate on storage, negligible on execution. Deductive reasoning, a_{dr}, is high on the first and the second and low on the third. In Table 4–1, the Ability Description Chart, the above three dimensions are set down accordingly as Domain or Panel A.

If we are to begin with the next most obvious set of dimensions which cut across and describe all these three activities, we should begin with *content*. The same *content* categories, with possible slight exceptions, will apply to perceptual input, manipulation-storage, and executive output dimensions. For this reason, Domain or Panel C, in Table 4–1 is set down in terms of two dimensions which cut across and interact with all others. However, it is equally important to notice that content in input for a given ability may be different from that for output. For example, in playing a piano the input content is visual, the output spatial-kinesthetic. Or again, one can see that the input in reading an engine assembly booklet may be fixed by verbal skills and the output in manipulating the engine by mechanical ability content.

Therefore, a very different schema of content from Guilford's "figural, symbolic, semantic, and behavioral" is proposed here, namely, first a duality of independent sets according to (a) the way in which *content* is grouped *experientially,* i.e., *in personal learning experience and in historical cultural institutions* and (b) the way in which the *biological, neural* structure of the organism groups content. The former yields such categories as verbal, numerical, spatial, mechanical, and social content. The latter yields visual, auditory, and kinesthetic motor sensation and control, and other organic function content categories. Some subdivision in the motor control category may also be necessary as suggested by the separate appearance of a general bodily dexterity and a hand dexterity factor. (It is possible that usefulness in some researches would appear also from other "general content property" dimensions cutting again across these cultural and organic categories such as breadth or variety of content in any one area. However, we shall not pursue these further.)

After content we turn to an entirely different facet. Indeed, the next most obvious dimension is that of the degree of demand upon the *ability to handle complex relations.* Although complexity of relation perception is virtually identical with Spearman's measure of general intelligence, it is not yet appropriate to commit ourselves here to the conclusion that this will be true also of complexity as it affects storage and output. All we assert is that the quality of an ability will be strongly affected by the degree of relational complexity existing in the content, no matter in what area of processing. Again, as the dimensional system reminds us, this complexity could be at quite different levels in the stimulus situation input and in the output, two extremes in this respect being an intelligence test, where a crude pencil stroke suffices for output, and walking a tight rope, where extremely complex relations must be built into the muscular output. Very little is known about the effect of relational complexity upon storage, though, as we have seen earlier in referring to the work of Kintsch and others, and, as will be seen later in the work of Lashley (Chapter 8), there is reason to believe that retention may operate differently upon *relations* abstracted from sensory fundaments and upon the *fundaments,* i.e., the literal, concrete experience itself.

It would be possible to confuse this dimension of complexity with what is surely different, namely, what we have called above the *amount of processing* which input, storage, and output may require. The two are different because the exercise of a particular ability could require a greater or smaller amount of processing—in terms of *the number of successive operations* required—at any one of several complexity levels in terms of abstractness of relations involved. Differences in amount of processing in input can be illustrated by checking whether one figure is larger than another compared with, say, recognizing which of four names is that of a foreigner who lived in the nineteenth century and wrote music. Differences in amount of processing on both input and output can be illustrated by comparing pressing a key when a light appears with responding to a piece of music by writing down the poem it seems to call to mind. That this dimension of "amount of processing" necessarily applies also to retention and internal manipulative processes is not so obvious. However, the phenomena of reminiscence, of retroactive inhibition, and of brain injury effects discussed in Chapter 8 suggest that for storage it is a fully relevant dimension. For there is ample evidence that the course of retention is affected by the degree of various consolidation and ordering "processings" that go on after perception and before retrieval.

Regarding the amount of processing required in the perceptual, internal processing, and executive aspects of an ability, two questions are likely to occur to the reader. Each concerns the conceptual boundaries of "process-ing." By processing is meant any kind of manipulation of the material given in the stimulus situation, or made available in the initial memory deposit, or in the storage offered as material for retrieval operations in the executive action that is necessary for performing what is needed in the response. Eduction of relations is obviously one such manipulation, as when the stimulus is an analogies test or when the response is to draw lines which represent a box in perspective. This being the case, we have already taken as a dimension a property—the level of complexity of relations utilized—which is a dimension of the processing activity. Why have we not taken other dimensions of the processing than its sheer amount, as first sug-gested, and the level of complexity of the relations used in it, as here?

The answer would seem to be that other dimensions of the processing activity can indeed be taken, such as speed or content, but that they are included already in dimensions of all abilities. There is, however, one remaining characteristic of processing which has not been defined, and that is what initially might be called "restrictiveness of mental set." For exam-ple, in a perceptual test the individual might be told "Find all instances where the figure on the left is the same shape as the figure on the right but of different size," or "Look for all people in the crowd whom you have known before and who are close to your own age." Or, in a test primarily in the executive region, he might be given a cancellation test with the in-structions "Cancel all e's except when they occur before t's, or "Bowl to knock down the second red pin from the left." In neither of these cases are the relations at all complex. The restrictions are not such as place the processing far out on the "complexity of relations" dimension or demand a high intelligence, but they are what might be called "compound or con-junctive restrictions."

Such restrictions operate psychologically in the form of a mental set which is "compound" because it has several parts operating simultane-ously or in immediate succession. The degree of complexity of the relations involved in the sets is quite an independent matter, yet it is tempting to use "complexity of restriction" for this dimension. However, to avoid con-fusion perhaps it had better be called *multiplexity of set*. Thus, giving *any* association word would be a task of low multiplexity whereas giving four-letter words beginning with w that have to do with daily tasks would be of high multiplexity. This multiplexity dimension applies to all three regions.

The question now arises whether we need retain under "demand" a sepa-rate facet of "amount of processing" or whether it is described and ac-counted for adequately by complexity of relations and multiplexity of sets. If we include in the latter the number of sequential steps in processing, e.g., collecting, comparing, selecting, enlarging, and so on, then it would seem that we do not need a separate category for amount of processing. Thus, for maximum simplicity until some more complicated treatment is demanded by the facts, it seems best to stop at two dimensions that together define "amount of processing."

Insufficient attention has perhaps been given to the middle process in the organism of referring, storing, sorting, etc. It has been suggested that these processes can be assigned levels on other parameters, such as relational level, multiplexity, amount of activity, and so on, but do we need to refer these to several distinct phases in the internal processing? Apparently we do. At the least there is experimental evidence that committing to memory, retention, and retrieval (or referral of input to existing storage in matching, etc.) are independent powers. Thus in Table 4–1 we shall insert in the present Domain P (process parameters) section, three parameters, one for amount of committing to storage that is involved, one for the extent to which goodness of persisting retention from earlier experience aids the performance, and one for dependence on efficiency of retrieval or comparison in connection with what is in storage. These continue, as 3, 4, and 5, the two (complexity and multiplexity) process parameters already set down.

Turning to other possible general process parameters we encounter flexibility. As brought out in the last chapter, there is still some uncertainty about the nature, i.e., the tests loaded in, a factor designated flexibility versus firmness of structure. At least we have evidence that it is distinct from the well-demarcated, broad factor of *disposition rigidity* (perseveration, motor-perceptual rigidity) which we have already set aside from the abilities as essentially a temperament factor (or factors). As tentatively defined, flexibility in the cognitive, ideational area is a freedom to restructure ideas due to a lack of firmness in the previously learned structures. This *ideational flexibility* (Cattell and Tiner, 1949) shows itself in riddles, i.e., getting meanings at variance with practical realistic meanings, in thinking of unusual uses for objects normally used in other ways, e.g., using a swimming pool to hold hot soup for a large dinner party, and probably in various kinds of absence of mind and failure of effective habits through some kind of oscillation (excessive flexibility?) in accessibility. *A priori* there is no reason why this should not be a general property operating through all three regions—perception, internal processing, and execution— and we shall posit it as another general dimension (with empirical evidence locating it as g_x).

Finally there is the vexed question of speed. As stated in Chapter 3, correlational evidence points to a number of different speeds rather than a single general speed. The issue is tied up with the very question of ability test scoring as such. In some areas of experiment, e.g., animal experiment, research has hinged explicitly on only two kinds of score—for speed and for freedom from errors—and in principle, if error is broadly interpreted, these constitute most of our means of measuring performance on *any* ability. They generally correlate positively, and in some areas, notably the intelligence test realm, amount done in a fixed time and amount correct in an unlimited time correlate very highly. The better a man is in any realm of ability—dexterity, esthetic judgment, intelligence, etc.—the quicker he does a given amount of a task correctly. However, there are two conditions necessary for this correlation to be high—that the subject be asked to work quickly, and that the subjects all be of much the same age.

Granted these conditions, there are as many speeds as there are distinct abilities, as located by measurements of goodness and correctness of response. But in a wide set of measures under speeded conditions when we partial out these primary abilities (and intelligence too), two or three *generalized* speed measures remain. Indeed the *tempo* measures remain even when subjects do not aspire to high speed of task performance, i.e., are not asked to work at top speed. Setting aside the tempo factors, which have been identified by Rimoldi (1951a) and Cattell (1957a) as due to a natural temperamental tempo component most clearly represented by personality factor U.I. 30 and the depression-elation factor U.I. 33, one finds two further sources of speed difference. First there are temperamental sources, notably a general arousal-activation factor, U.I. 22, which persists as a characteristic level of cortical alertness at which an individual operates. Second, there are various motivation factors (Cattell, Radcliffe and Sweney, 1963), most important of which is the broad factor U.I. 16, called Assertive Ego (and which can be ambition in the test situation).

The available evidence therefore can be interpreted most simply by saying that anything that is *general* in cognitive speed, namely, the general cognitive speed factor first found by Bernstein (1924), is actually temperamental (U.I. 22) or motivational (U.I. 16) in origin. Nevertheless, the U.I. 22 temperament component, being independent of motivation, depression-elation, and tempo, and favoring high speed in reaction time (simple and complex), in cancellation, in reversible perspective, etc., actually extends in a confusing fashion along the frontier between ability and temperament traits. It is said that in the present high speed age there are only the quick and the dead, and, by most people's judgment, surviving and getting things done quickly is being useful and "able." Thus there is even a semantic problem. However, careful evaluations suggest that the contribution of the basic neural speed in U.I. 22 to the variance in *high level* abilities is quite small, though it would appear to be appreciable in performances like driving a car or qualifying as an air pilot (Cattell, 1955a). Contingently it would seem more convenient, when discussing the ability domain, to include this general speed dimension in the *ability* schema, strictly in the U.I. 22 sense. In doing so we make the assumption (as yet insufficiently checked) that it operates across perception, internal processing (committing to and retrieving from storage), and executive performance (but scarcely in storage *retention*). It is understood that speed differences through temperamental tempo, mood, and motivation level are excluded from this conception of purely temperamental-cognitive speed. Even so, this is an anomalous component compared to the others, for it appears only when ability scores are made under "speed" instructions and in scoring a timed performance.

4. THE ADAC OR THEORETICAL "ABILITY DIMENSION ANALYSIS CHART"

Let us now put together in a total perspective the results of the analyses in the last section. There are one or two general questions to ask before the Ability Dimension Analysis Chart (ADAC) can be put together. First, are we describing tests or people? The answer is "both." For although our purpose began as that of gathering tests in a taxonomy, when we have said that any test can have more of this or that, we have also said that people can have more or less of what it takes to do this or that. (This is recognizable as a special illustration of the equivalence in factor analysis of the P × Q technique transposes.)

An analogous logical question arises in the vocational guidance expert's attempt at a taxonomy of occupations. But though it is partly answered there in the same way as we have answered it here, the fact still remains that the actual structuring of the taxonomy of demands and the taxonomy of people's abilities, though occupying the same "space," may be different. The recruit who was asked whether he thought he would do better with a machine gun or a rocket launcher replied that he knew only that he played better on the French horn than the violin and requested transfer to the band. A taxonomy of military and musical proficiencies would be very different, but the same intelligence, speed, spatial, etc., abilities would operate in most of both realms, and would offer yet a third taxonomy of unitary traits. Correspondingly, "amount of dependence on input activities" is a unitary category in the description of various abilities; but input activities depend on qualities in the individual, e.g., sensory powers, his level of stored content in the given area, and so on. Nevertheless, as pointed out at the beginning, in this case and notably in the content and process domains, we would expect alignment of test and individual descriptive characteristics.

If next the question is asked whether the taxonomy is descriptive or interpretive, the answer is that it seeks *ultimately* to be interpretive. A classification of primary and higher-strata abilities on some sort of simply descriptive basis can be pursued when empirical research proceeds further; but the ADAC chart is definitely in terms of processes, contents, and so on which are inferred to be underlying components of the observed variety of abilities.

It will be observed that the schema (Table 4–1, p. 67) has three *domains* of dimensions (facets, phases, parameters), that are not coordinate in nature. This is shown further by the fact that though the dimensions in any one permit all mutual combinations, occasionally a dimension, e.g., retrieval, will not apply across all divisions of some other domain.

The first domain is concerned with the predominance of one or another of the *phases of action* in any ability. Starting with the stimulus, organism, and response characteristics discussed in most psychological analysis (but developed here further in the computer model), the classification ends with

TABLE 4–1
The Ability Dimension Analysis Chart (ADAC):
A Theoretical Schema

DOMAIN OR PANEL A: ACTION PHASES (IN ABILITY ACTION)
1. *Involvement of Input* (largest in perceptual abilities). The value on this is the extent to which the ability score rests upon sensory input activity relative to the stimulus.
2. *Involvement of Internal Processing and Storage*[1] (largest in memory measures). The value on this is the extent to which processing of resources of storage (committing, retention, retrieving, comparing) determine the score.
3. *Involvement of Output* (largest in executive performances). The value on this is the extent to which qualities of output determine the score.

DOMAIN OR PANEL C: CONTENT
1. *Involvement of Experiential-Cultural Dimensions.* This includes such separate subdimensions as verbal (semantic), numerical, social, spatial, mechanical knowledge, art, music, science.
2. *Involvement of Neural-Organizational Dimensions.* This includes subdimensions of visual, auditory, kinesthetic, tactile, motor, cerebellar, etc.

DOMAIN OR PANEL P: PROCESS PARAMETERS
1. *Demand in Terms of Complexity Level of Relation Eduction.* This concerns the complexity of relations handled *as* relations, as well as the complexity implied in the eduction of correlates (fundaments) required in any process. This parameter defines level in a standard hierarchy[2] of relations.
2. *Demand in Terms of Multiplexity of Sets.* This concerns the amount of complication in processing, independent of relational complexity in any one operation. It could be analyzed into subsets covering (a) number of items handled, (b) number of simultaneously applied sets, e.g., belonging to class X, larger than a, beginning with letter B, etc., (c) number of sets in successive steps. A model for such an "amount of processing" evaluation exists in logic and in the computer. It may be thought of insofar as it applies to the output phase, as degree of restruction and control of output. In human and animal behavior they are expressed by the operation of mental sets, in multiplex systems of various rank levels, from the simplicity of a reaction time response, to the response of a diplomat at a UN committee.

---

[1] It is necessary at the outset to make a clear distinction between the rating of an ability on involvement of *storage* and of involvement of *particular contents*, in Domain C. The statement about a particular ability in terms of the content it demands in, say, the mechanical knowledge field, is a statement about the mechanical knowledge level presented in the particular test or job. What storage the individual has achieved in that area is quite another question. Furthermore, the content defines more than is concerned with storage. The input (perceptual) and output (executive) activities would deal also with Content X in an ability for which Content X is given a high value.

[2] The project of developing a hierarchy of relations according to inherent complexity, especially to test more precisely the general relation-eduction theory of intelligence has been mooted, to logicians and philosophers, several times by the present writer (1965c). Apparently it offers formidable demands on following through from theory to practice which so far have daunted the logicians. However, in principle, as discussed on page 310 below, one could start with relations at the lowest, sensory level, and build up a hierarchy of relations among relations, culminating in the highest conceptual abstractions. It is the level on such a hierarchy which is referred to here, as complexity of relations used in processing of material.

3. *Amount of Committing to Memory* ("Gramming"). This may seem to apply as a dimension only of the storage phase, and so it does in an *immediate* sense. But inasmuch as perceptual and executive abilities are dependent on level of storage, and level of storage is dependent on effectiveness of committing to memory, a person's score on gramming (as we may call, for brevity, "committing to memory") will affect *all* abilities. Conceivably, even when level of interest-motivation is set aside (as it is from all this cognitive analysis) a person's effectiveness in committing to memory (gramming) is dependent on more than one factor, e.g., a neural structure and a physiological efficiency factor. But for initial simplicity committing to memory is considered one dimension.

4. *Amount of Retentive Activity Involved.* Again this is a dimension obviously concerned with the storage phase but affecting all performances. In most memory abilities—other than immediate memory—level of success would depend substantially upon individual differences in whatever capacities enter into efficiency or retention. Again, as with gramming, the retaining of impressions may be found in the end to depend on more than one factor. As pointed out in Chapter 8, on physiology, this subject is at present in a highly speculative state.

5. *Amount of Retrieval Activity.* There is good reason to consider retrieval as an entirely distinct activity from retention. It may be affected in its *result*, of course, by the amount in storage, the nature of the content, the complexity of the relations, and the multiplexity of conditions requested in the retrieval. But by hypothesis there are individual differences in some general retrieval efficiency when all the above are held constant. In this case we have a dimension restricted, however, to a subspace, since the differences among abilities in the extent to which retrieval is involved can apply only to the executive panel, unless we assume that retrieval at a nondeliberate level applies also to perceptual recognition. Retrieval plays a major part in such abilities as fluency.

6. *Flexibility versus Firmness.* Every dimension or function so far discussed could vary on a dimension of flexibility versus firmness. Presumably flexibility would give advantages especially in trial and error learning but also in relational insight learning. Lack of firmness and freedom from fluctuation of response would also bring impairment of performances in other situations.

7. *Speed Demand.* Speed is an anomalous and extra dimension[3] in the sense that, as pointed out above, it arises only for that form of measuring abilities in which a time limit is set. However, the latter is at least a widespread requirement both in tests and life performances. Consequently it is an important dimension in the classification of abilities to state to what extent they involve speed. The extent to which the individual is able to score well on a speeded test is, however, decided by a whole subset of cognitive and temperamental speed factors, as indicated in the text above. Speed is a dimension obviously responsible for distinguishing between an ability as a "level" and as a "power" ability, as discussed below in connection, for example, with intelligence tests (see page 79).

---

[3] An extra dimension suggested by some psychologists, which we have rejected as truly superfluous, is that of selective versus inventive (closed versus open-ended). This is a characteristic differentiating tests which, in terms of abilities involved, would appear to be taken care of already by the dimension of Retrieval, P5, which is high on inventive and low on selective tests. Whether a special dimension should be given to recognition as a process is debatable, and we have assumed here that it is taken care of by the judgment of a relation of similarity (P1), and a special recognition set, P2.

---

categories of input, internal processing, and output. Although we have used the terms perceptual, memory, and executive abilities as approximately synonymous with these, the fact is strictly that no perceptual ability is entirely restricted to input action, and no executive ability is confined to output activity only. The former consists of perception made meaningful by instant comparison of sensory input with storage, while the latter requires some supply from storage and some constant guidance from input as perception.

The second panel or domain—that of *content*—intrinsically requires no explanation beyond what has been given above. But it should be understood that each of two "systems" or "spaces"—experiential and sensory motor—consists of a whole set of dimensions which, as pointed out above, may be considered virtually orthogonal coordinates within each. No need exists at present to attempt a complete listing of these subdimensions; but we can illustrate the first by verbal, numerical, mechanical, social, etc., and the second by auditory, visual, olfactory, motor, etc. Any given ability can be designated, *separately in its input, storage, and output,* as high or low on each of these, i.e., the *phase* and the *content* dimensions are independent coordinates.

The third panel or domain, as shown in Table 4–1, is that of the *dimensions of process.* Here seven parameters are apparently sufficient to cover all taxonomic differences in type of ability. They define the parameters along which processes may differ regardless (with slight exception) of which of the three phases in an ability is involved or what kind of content is used.

Since there are twelve dimensions in the ADAC, is is obviously impossible to represent the scheme in simple graphical fashion as a three-dimensional box, as in the Guilford schema in Figure 4–1. If one considers only above average or high and below average or low on each of these dimensions, there would in fact be $2^{12} = 4096$ types of ability. (Actually about 500 if we omit nonviable combinations.) This is even larger than the 120 of Guilford's schema but as will be seen from the ensuing discussion, we do *not* suppose here, as Guilford does there, that there should be as many factors as there are types.

Although the whole hyperspace cannot be represented visually in 3-space, subspaces can be so represented and some are given for illustration in Figure 4–2. It will be recognized that in abandoning the bi-polar (input versus output; verbal versus numerical, relational complexity versus speed) use of ability dimensionality as a false mode of analysis, we stay with dimensions each of which simply runs from high to low on the given parameter. Thus Type 7 in the first drawing in Figure 4–2 must be some test of low input, low output, and high storage. This could be, as suggested, a concentration on memorizing a comparatively small number of words or figures.

The three-dimensional chart alone cannot, of course, fully define the ability. Thus in Type 7 just described we are not told whether the memorizing is of verbal, mechanical, spatial, or other coordinates of content, or whether it is of relationally complex or simple material, or involves high or low multiplexity of sets in processing for memorization, and so on.

The question of how important primaries and other empirically established factors would fit into it is discussed below.

5. CONSTRUCTING TESTS TO FIT A SCHEMA VERSUS CREATING A TAXONOMY TO FIT DISCOVERED ABILITIES

The opening of this chapter has dealt in general terms with the use to which (a) an empirical, factor taxonomy and (b) an *a priori* "theoretical" (in the popular sense) classificatory scheme can be put, and some incidental comments on possible alignments have been made along the way. Our argument has been that for reaching a good natural taxonomy it is preferable to start with a representative sampling of variables from the natural personality sphere of human stimulus-response behavior.

However, the alternative—an *a priori, abstractive* (Cattell, 1966) design —should not be ruled out from factor-analytic search for unitary structures provided we recognize that some bias may be introduced in the form of (1) missing certain areas, areas not conceived initially by the theorist and (2) boosting what should be narrow specifics or near specifics into broad, important-looking abilities through the theorist manufacturing a host of tests in an area with which he happens personally to be preoccupied. Criticisms of both type 1 and type 2 have been leveled against Guilford's chart of abilities and could be applied also to the present writer's ADAC scheme *if it were employed in the same way.*

The creation of a subjective theoretical schema will not in itself prevent the ultimate verdict of experimental, correlational studies from stating fairly what the correlations actually are among the various abilities used. Consequently, a true final picture can emerge, *provided no powerful systematic selection of variables has been taken to favor a certain outcome.* This can be illustrated by the well-known, basic comparison of correlation experiment design and analysis of variance experiment design in Figure 4–3. Here an investigation has set out to test the significance of the relation of body weight and height to intelligence and has taken eight persons in each cell as shown at (a). Whatever relation he finds with intelligence, it is such as may be perceived after he has eliminated correlation of height with weight in his sample. However, a better view of the true state of affairs is shown in (b), by the correlogram, and it can be noted that, with thirty-six points in all, the analysis of variance experiment has included *all* cases from the NW and SE quadrants, but only half the cases from the NE and SW quadrants. If one *knows* that this has been done it affects one's interpretation of the analysis of variance result.

The artificial manipulation of the distribution of tests, to which we have objected in the Guilford schema, is precisely analogous to, though in detail different from, this manipulation of the distribution of people in Figure 4–3. The location of simple structure depends on tests being natu-

FIGURE 4–3
Obliteration of Natural Correlation in an Analysis of
Variance Experimental Design

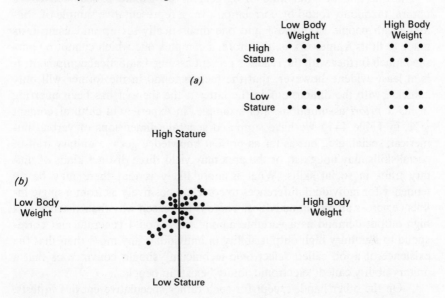

rally more densely distributed at some zones in the factor space than at others. This distribution is likely to be clear and decisive if we take a representative sample of human performances; but it can be lost if we deliberately set out with a schema such as that in Figure 4–1, and fill the empty spaces with artificially created combinations. At any rate, if the dimensions are assumed to be factors, the quadrants that should be empty will become homogeneously filled. The psychologist has as much right to resist this confusing influence as a biologist has to reject the artificial monsters called centaurs and dragons when he is seeking a natural biological taxonomic scheme.

Nevertheless, the issues are subtle for an early, introductory chapter. Another subtle issue, needing a glance at this point, concerns the difference between the loading of a test and the mean level of a test with regard to any factor. The parameters hypothesized in Table 4–1 are dimensions of tests, but we are most likely to *isolate* them as dimensions of people. For example, when we hypothesize a dimension such as A.1. of *degree of involvement of input activities,* our hope of checking this as a unitary factor depends on people being at different levels of efficiency or endowment on this capacity. If they are, then correlating tests over people will yield such a factor, and every test will have a loading on it. But when we classify tests in a taxonomy, we are going to ask whether a test is high or low in the level of input activities it demands, and this is not exactly the same as having a high or low loading. The logical statistical issue (which Burt and Ross have clarified) cannot be further pursued here, and it must suffice to notice the difference and to note that after factor analysis we shall have to go to further estimations to get this information as to where a test stands in regard to the level necessary on a certain process before the test performance can appear at all.

The question of what kind of agreement we should expect between a natural taxonomy found by correlation over a representative sample of abilities (with people as entries) and one theoretically set up and using tests made to fit its framework is, therefore, a complex one which cannot be pursued much further with the reader's present assumed statistical equipment. It is at least evident, however, that the factors found in the former will only coincide with the dimensions in the latter if the theorist has been unerring in his *a priori* assumptions. For example, in experiential-cultural content (C1, in Table 4–1) we have supposed separate dimensions of verbal, numerical, social, etc., but as far as present knowledge goes, a unitary trait of social skills may not exist, or the area may yield three distinct kinds of unitary traits in social skills. What is more likely is that there may be no tendency for individual differences to correlate positively as from a single influence across all output activities. There is no reason why the existence of a high output demand as a variable among tests should generate and correspond to a unitary high output ability in individuals any more than that the existence of a job called "electronic technician" should convince us that a unitary ability called "electronic ability" exists in people.

On the other hand, except for such rather speculative entities in tests, which could require several factor traits to cover them, we *are* hypothesizing in the ADAC that most dimensions will correspond to individual differences on unitary traits. Thus we are hypothesizing, corresponding to unitary test demand dimensions in the ADAC, a general ability to handle complex relations (which we already identify with Spearman's g), a general speed factor (U.I. 22 or g_s), a general retention factor (Kelley's rote memory), and a general retrieval factor (which we would identify with the main component in fluency). We would wish the definition of the verbal, numerical, spatial, social, etc. dimensions of content also to be considered so defined that they fit the primary abilities discovered and to be discovered. Also the neural-organizational content categories should be considered defined by the presently known visualization factor and such auditory, kinesthetic, and other factors as are discovered. Thus the position of the ADAC is that, though theoretically conceived, it is generated substantially on a basis of findings from presently existing research so that its categories would be expected to fit factor-analytic evidence. At the same time it aims to suggest tests to be tried in *new* factor-analytic researches, to discover in what way such categories as input and output, multiplexity of set, or flexibility versus firmness need to be modified or extended.

An important difference between the ADAC dimensions and the Guilford categories, over and above those discussed, is that Guilford hypothesizes that a factor will be found corresponding to each *cell* in his box, whereas the ADAC supposes a factor will correspond only with each of the twelve *dimensions* (plus perhaps further subdimensions), *not* with the combination (cells). The latter, in ADAC, may easily lead to as many as 4000 types of tests. However, by dimensions ADAC suggests only twelve (up, to say, thirty) factors; whereas the Guilford schema already leads to about 120 factors.

As in facet analysis, (Guttman, 1965) the Guilford scheme proposes to make enough tests in each cell, according to a prescription, to generate a factor from what, on a firm sampling basis, would almost certainly be only a specific factor. Whereas Alice in *Through the Looking Glass* says, "Words mean what I want them to mean," certain modern psychometrists are dangerously near saying, "Correlations can be made to have the values I want to give them." A long chain of mutually orthogonal (uncorrelated) tests undoubtedly can be built up from a sufficiency of items granted sufficient test design skill, patience, and research resources. However, upon using some different subjective theoretical schema, it would certainly be found that a considerable number (geometrically, an infinite number) of quite different series of ability concepts could also be built up—even in the same factor space, as through an orthogonal rotation.

In contrast to this scientific Tower of Babel, this nightmare of noncommunicating private worlds (ultimately one for each psychometrician), the approach presented here by stratified behavior sampling and simple structure unique rotations promises convergence on a common structure. It will be a structure which, as we pass from primary abilities in the next chapter, reveals second and higher-order simplifications. As we come to consider the fewer and broader powers then revealed—in contrast to the numerous primaries we have so far considered as the empirical harvest—the available results in the next chapter point to a fairly close agreement between experimental findings and the theoretical expectations of the ADAC taxonomic scheme.

CHAPTER FIVE

THE DISCOVERY OF FLUID AND CRYSTALLIZED GENERAL INTELLIGENCE

1. THE BIRTH OF THE "TWO INTELLIGENCES" CONCEPT

Looking back over the last fifty years to the immense amount of work devoted to surveying primary abilities, what we see concretely is a dozen or so (Table 3–1) firm peaks, such as Thurstone's primaries, rising out of a cloud-enshrouded mass of more speculative entities. Only by such conceptual and methodological improvements as have just been discussed can we expect to see these mountain ranges more clearly. However, one peak which clearly towers above others, but which, in the interest of an orderly approach, we have not yet discussed, is that of the ability called general ability, g, or intelligence.

That a massive general factor existed among all primaries (actually as a second-order factor, as explained below) and, indeed, among virtually all cognitive tests, had been accepted since the monumentally thorough work of Spearman in the first twenty years of this century. The structure had been examined by such giants in the field as Burt (1940), Holzinger, (1934–1935), Kelley (1954), Thomson (1939), and Thurstone (1938), and, except for the modifications of interpretation by the two last, had been declared sound. It became the scientist's touchstone to which all debated practical issues in interpreting and using intelligence tests and the I.Q. were referred.

However, in the mid-thirties some half-dozen different lines of evidence converged in the present writer's thinking to suggest the disturbing idea that g might be two general factors instead of one! The notion was disturbing to the writer personally because of his association with, and his great regard for, Spearman and his work. Furthermore, a questioning of the theory of g at that juncture seemed unfortunate in terms of the hard-won public status of intelligence testing. For although the theory actually had taken intelligence testing out of the realm of guesswork and quackery twenty years before, it was only in the thirties that most users of intelligence tests had realized this. By then most had a satisfactory grasp of the monolithic simplicity and solidarity of conception emerging from the programmatic and strategic experiment pursued by Spearman, Burt, Holzinger, Thomson,[1] Thurstone and many others who had participated in the clarification.

The indications which point to the new synthesis converge from some six main directions, as follows:

(1) The work in Spearman's own laboratory on "content free" or "perceptual" intelligence tests (later to become culture-fair intelligence tests), by Line (1931), Fortes (1932), Gopalaswami (1924), and others (see Figure 5–1), with discussion of the implications of which the present writer had been closely concerned. Examination of certain correlations here suggested that these "perceptual" forms of classification and analogies tests were probably measuring the central core of "g" with unusually high validity. They suggested also that many relatively "scholastic" tests, as accepted by most test constructors, were bringing a thick veneer of something besides g into the test score. Binet and Simon, whatever their verbal gymnastics regarding the definition of intelligence, were clear that the intelligence they were measuring was something constitutional. At least they indicated that they were aiming at something inherent in the individual apart from his education. Any alert psychologist in the twenties and thirties was bound to notice that alleged intelligence tests were being shaped by the educator increasingly in his own image. By contrast, the various tests of "gumption" in Binet and the new "perceptual" (non-pictorial, non-verbal) tests in the Spearman laboratory were yielding, when applied to children at least, unusually high correlations among themselves which suggested they might be different from the "g" of the more educationally oriented tests. Native wit and education were beginning to show their separate colors.

(2) From widespread try-outs of the perceptual tests (Figures 5–1 and 5–2) there were already indications, since confirmed, that the age increase in performance on such perceptual tests flattened out as a plateau distinctly earlier than did the synonyms, vocabulary, numerical ability, etc., of the school intelligence tests. In fact, the curve flattened around thirteen years instead of at about sixteen and seventeen years (see Figure 7–7 for detail).

(3) Examination of Thurstone's epoch-making, second-order analysis of the primary abilities (1938) indicated *more* than one general factor. As explained above, a second-order factor analysis begins by taking the primary

---

[1] As we shall see, Thomson did not concur in the whole interpretation, but agreed on the new ideas of method and statistical proof.

FIGURE 5–1
Early Development of Perceptual Tests

> *The principle suggested in the early monograph by Line*
> *(1931: from which these notes are taken) was to employ the*
> *relations used in intelligence tests, notably classification*
> *and analogies, upon simple sensory data, e.g. shades, colors,*
> *sizes, and shapes. Right and wrong alternatives are to be*
> *presented and irrelevant features deliberately introduced. Thus,*
> a priori *concepts of relational complexity could be compared*
> *with difficulty according to psychometric evidence.*

PRINCIPLES

Test in which illustrated	*Solution: Right*	*Solution: Wrong*	*'Order' of critical relation*	*Main irrelevant elements*
		Brightness		
II	Two objects, different grey, same shape	Two objects, same grey, same shape	2	Shape, size, absolute grey, absolute difference
III	Three objects, same or different shapes. The shapes are arranged so that the difference between the first and second is greater than that between the second and third	Three objects, same or different shapes. But the shades do not obey the rule; i.e. the difference between the first and second is equal to or less than that between the second and third	3	Shape, size, absolute shade, absolute differences
		Color		
IV	One object, blue	One object, any color but blue	1	Shape, size
V	One object, any shade of blue	One object, any color but blue	1	Shape, size shade of blue
VI	Two objects, one of which is green	Two objects, neither of which is green	1	Shape, size, color of second object
XX	Four lines, the ratio between the ratios of the second and third, and the third and fourth, is greater than that between the first and second, and the second and third	Four lines, not so constituted	4	Lengths of lines

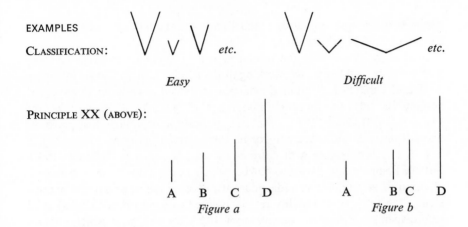

EXAMPLES

CLASSIFICATION: *etc.*   *etc.*

Easy   *Difficult*

PRINCIPLE XX (ABOVE):

A   B   C   D   A   B C   D
Figure a   *Figure b*

From Line, W., "The growth of visual perception in children," *British Journal of Psychology Monograph Supplement*, #15, 1931. Reproduced by permission of the *British Journal of Psychology*.

factors obtained from factoring actual *variables*. It then works out the correlations among these primary factors, puts them in a square correlation matrix, and factors them again. Unfortunately, good statistical tests fixing the number of factors to extract were at that time not available, and the decision as to whether there was really one factor or more was somewhat subjective. Nevertheless, this evidence pointing to two (or more) carried more weight than the uncertain conclusion gained from merely looking at the unevenness of the hierarch when the two kinds of tests—more and less educational—were correlated as described in (1) immediately above. It was also much more firm than the early finding of Burt (1909) when arbitrarily he took out three general factors (the second and third obscure) from sets of variables where Spearman had stopped at one. (In this case, however, there was no suggestion in his analysis of what have now become the concepts of fluid and crystallized intelligence.) For the unsatisfactory rotational method—or lack of rotation—which he used (see Figure 5–8 and explanation following) caused his second (and third) "general factors" to consist partly of mixtures of Thurstone's *primaries*.

Indeed, many writers, e.g., Vernon (1964), regarded the bi-polar factors[2] (the meaning will become clearer in Figure 5–8) of the Burtian kind of analysis as producing what were interpreted as "equivalents" of the primary abilities so unequivocally defined by Thurstone. From this point, indeed, a translation between the London and Chicago dialects began to be accepted rather popularly, in which the second factor by the London rotation was

---

[2] A bi-polar factor is one whose meaning is recognizable by its having approximately the same number of equal and opposite (positive and negative) loadings, the positive on one sort of content, the negative on another. For example, in the present ability context such a factor has appeared (as second or third factor) loading verbal performance positively and numerical performances negatively. It would be called "Verbal versus Numerical Ability." An alternative rotation, however, reveal separate "uni-polar" verbal and numerical abilities, as in Thurstone's analyses.

considered a rough equivalent (verbal and educational) of a compound of Chicago V and N primaries.

In the few years after the announcement (1941) of the *two general-factor theory,* and before its checking in the precise fashion shown in Figure 5–3b and Table 5–1, additional evidence continued to come in. It appeared notably in the very thorough researches of Rimoldi (1951b), Adkins (1952), and Botzum (1951), that one general factor in cognitive perform-ances is not enough to account for all the common variance.

(4) The first results with *culture-fair intelligence tests* (Cattell, 1940; Cattell, Feingold and Sarason, 1941), which (sometimes under the rubrics of culture-free and culture-reduced) have become the practical test expres-sion of the fluid general ability factor, pointed to a very different degree of I.Q. dispersion (standard deviation of I.Q.) for this new general factor compared with the old. Indeed, it seemed that fluid ability measures gave

TABLE 5–1
Two Researches Sampling the School Age Range Showing the Distinction of Fluid and Crystallized General Intelligences

277 7th and 8th Grade boys and girls[1]
(14–15 year old)

Primaries	Fluid Intelligence g_f	Crystallized Intelligence g_c
Thurstone primaries:		
Verbal ability	.15	.46
Spatial ability	.32	.14
Reasoning ability	.08	.50
Numerical ability	.05	.59
Fluency	.07	.19
IPAT Culture-Fair:		
Series	.35	.43
Classification	.63	−.02
Matrices	.50	.10
Topology	.51	.09
Personality, HSPQ:		
A Cyclothymia	−.04	.52
C Ego Strength	.21	−.07
D Excitability	−.04	−.44
E Dominance	−.15	−.01
F Surgency	−.05	.09
I Premsia	−.09	−.29
Q_4 Ergic Tension	−.04	.37

[1] Cattell, 1963a, page 14.

306 4th and 5th Grade boys and girls[2]
(*10–11 year old*)

Primaries	Fluid Intelligence g_f	Crystallized Intelligence g_c
Culture-Fair Intelligence:		
(IPAT)	.78	.09
Verbal Ability	.22	.63
Numerical Ability	.47	.35
Spatial Ability	.73	.03
Personality Factors:		
Extraversion	.01	.29
Anxiety	.05	.00
Pathemia	.04	.04
Independence	−.04	−.60
Neuroticism	−.09	.06

Note that in the school period the extravert qualities tend to associate with more rapid acquiring of crystallized intelligence (but not later). Temperamental independence is related somewhat negatively.

Regarding g_f, culture-fair, relation-perceiving tests are most loaded, but there is some loading on verbal, spatial, and numerical ability. The weights alter somewhat with age, but crystallized intelligence, by contrast, appears conspicuously in verbal ability, trained reasoning, and numerical and other scholastic abilities.

[2] Cattell, 1967b, page 148.

a standard deviation of I.Q. around 24 instead of the older value of 16 (or 15) which had become accepted for traditional intelligence tests.

(5) Approximately the same two types of intelligence test performance —those of the "perceptual," "culture-fair" type and those of the traditional verbal and other "intelligence" tests—as separated out in factor analysis also differentiated themselves in a variety of ways in their physiological associations. First there is evidence, summarized below, that brain injury may affect performance on the traditional tests most noticeably in a person's performance in some one kind of subtest or performance, while leaving others little affected if at all. For example, an injury in the Broca area of the brain may produce aphasia—loss of verbal command—but no discernible loss in spatial or numerical ability. On the other hand, such cortical damage almost anywhere seems to produce *some* loss in the fluid ability performances (Reitan, 1955; Lashley, 1963). Furthermore, as shown in the evidence finally organized by Hebb some years later (1942), considerable recovery typically occurs in the crystallized abilities if the damage occurs after maturity, whereas damage in the same areas before maturity brings more lasting impairment. This fits the theory (page 98) that crystallized ability is a product over time of earlier fluid ability action.

(6) The age curves of change of general ability level *after* initial maturity —in the period beginning at 20 and running to 65—are quite different for

the two classes of test. The perceptual, culture-fair type shows a steady decline from about 20–25 years, whereas the verbal, numerical, mechanical curve continues after 20–25 at the same level and may even rise slightly throughout life.

There are thus many indications converging from at least six directions that there are *two* general relation-perceiving, intelligence-like abilities that are quite distinct in their properties. However, the basic identification of each, upon which all the other differences of property hinge, has to begin in the behavioral (not the physiological, age shift, or psychometric I.Q. property) structure. Accordingly, we shall now give close attention to the techniques which permit recognition of unitary structures in more complex behavioral fields.

2. THE MEANING OF FACTOR STRATA

At the time when the present writer ventured the fluid and crystallized intelligence theory (1941) at an APA Annual Meeting, each of the above threads of evidence was available for picking up, though sometimes in obscure work and relatively unconfirmed. Indeed, at the very same meeting, physiological evidence was reviewed by Hebb for two kinds of brain power which he called "A" and "B" intelligences. His arrangement of the physiological evidence in ways which other brain physiologists had not recognized was masterly. But the ultimate foundation of the fluid and crystallized intelligence concepts rested on the way in which *all* of the above six diverse sources "clicked into place" when put together, and without all of them the full properties of the concepts could not be realized. However, so long as psychology deals with behavior it must be the delicate evidence of covariation of behaviors presented in factor analysis that alone will provide the justification for distinct structural concepts and for their psychological natures. With the structures located and reliably measurable, all other properties, e.g., age change, learning effects, physiological influences, etc., can be investigated confidently and fruitfully in relation to such foci.

Parenthically, let it be said that the meaning of the expressions "fluid" and "crystallized" which the present experimenter began to adopt at this time for the two intelligences cannot be explained fully until the nature of all the collated evidence has been discussed. But contingently it is evident that one of these powers—that unconnected with cultural skills, which rises at its own rate and falls despite cultural stimulus and which is affected in no specific behavioral area by brain injury—has the "fluid" quality of being directable to almost any problem. By contrast, the other is invested in particular areas of crystallized skills which can be upset individually without affecting the others. These two g's, as we shall call them,—since there is much to be said for retaining continuity with Spearman—we shall henceforth symbolize respectively as g_f and g_c, the subscripts indicating "fluid" and "crystallized."

FIGURE 5–2
Examples of Five Culture-Fair Perceptual, Relation-Eduction Subtests of Proven Validity for Fluid Intelligence

Choose one to fill dotted square.

Series

Choose odd one.

Classification

Choose one wherein dot could be placed as in item on left.

Topology

Choose one to complete analogy.

Analogies

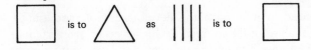

Choose one to fill empty square at left.

Matrices

From Form B, Scales II and III, IPAT Culture-Fair Test. By kind permission of the Institute of Personality and Ability Testing, 1602 Coronado Drive, Champaign, Illinois

Analogies section from Cattell Scale II, Harrap & Co.

In this chapter we shall concentrate on the evidence for the distinct characteristics of g_f and g_c. In order that the reader may get some concrete sense of g_f, let us pause to look at the material in culture-fair intelligence tests. For from the moment when g_f was recognized as a distinct factor, the present writer and his colleagues began to search for more "saturated" measures to define it; and these turned out, almost as a byproduct, to have promising properties as culture-fair tests. The culture-fairness (culture-reduced quality) of such tests, however, is relegated for later discussion in a social psychological context (Chapter 10). Our main discovery in working on these "culture-fair subtests" (Cattell, Feingold and Sarason, 1941) in the early forties was consistent with the parallel work of Line (1931), Fortes (1930), and Raven (1947), namely, that just as such devices as analogies, classifications, and the matrix type of relation-educing tests had proved, most g saturated in cultural materials so they continued to be among the best in perceptual stimulus material.

If a concept is best first tied down in behavior, then the prime need in pursuing the fluid and crystallized ability concepts was to clarify the structure of the correlational evidence on actual performances. To form the foundation for such structural experiment it seemed necessary to the present writer first to get more "saturated" measures of the fluid ability factor, and for that reason work was done in the early 1940s on developing effective, perceptual, culture-fair subtests. The question of relative freedom from cultural influences and the design of tests for cultural comparisons is best considered later in its social context, but as will be seen in Figure 5–2, for culture-fair tests one needed only to translate relation-educing performances, such as series, classifications, topology, matrices,[3] and analogies into alternative nonverbal nonnumerical, noncultural fundaments such as novel shapes, scents, or sounds (or incidentally, into words so simple that all subjects know them equally well).

Partly due to the need to wait upon the development of more subtle techniques in factor analysis itself as regards higher-order factorization, really adequate proof of two distinct factors was not given until twenty years after this original work. ("Partly" is used because in fact there were more mundane reasons well known to researchers, namely, that the laboratory most interested in these developments took off on a long expedition into personality structure factoring!) This was not entirely wasted as far

---

[3] The particular design of subtest called matrices, derived from the work of Line and Fortes, and used in the present writers Culture-Fair Scales, has been put out by Raven as an "intelligence test" in and of itself. However, by psychometric standards this is a faulty design since no *single* subtest in the culture-fair realm, *any more than in any other realm,* is fully loaded with the required general factor. There is always appreciable contribution in one type of performance from something specific to it. It has proved a sound and necessary principle in all psychometric construction of tests for a given factor, in abilities as in personality, never to "put all one's eggs in one basket." For this reason a well-designed Culture-Fair Scale balances the specifics by using as many as four to six different types of subtests, thus eliminating the greater part of any one bias.

as ability research was concerned because the trial of the methods in new areas, such as personality, where the "positive manifold"[4] of abilities no longer held, contributed to a flexibility needed in the new approach to abilities. During this period, however, the greater part of ability research continued, as in the Wechsler-Bellevue, WAIS, Miller, and similar tests, without "turning the corner." The ability research area became regarded by enterprising investigators as a conservative and relatively worked-out area, where research concentrated on practical minutiae, e.g., effects of practice, repeated factorings of existing tests, finer determinations of the stability of the I.Q., etc.

With such a predominance of tradition in the theoretical background of ability study and so great an investment of skills of applied psychologists in existing published tests, it is not surprising that, as Newland has pointed out, it took psychologists around 1945 five to ten years to realize that ideas had started off on a new track. Since so sudden a swerve jolts comfortable convictions, there is bound to be much debate over the necessity for substituting g_f and g_c for g. Consequently, despite their complexity, the technical issues in factor analyses on which the change initially turns, require some concentration here by the student.

What indeed, is a second or higher-order factor, and how is it located? Let us go back to look at Thurstone's and others' discovered primaries, as set out in Table 3–1. The steps in going to higher-order structure are: (1) to obtain the scores of, say, 300 people, on perhaps twenty primaries; (2) to work out the correlations among the primaries[5] (typically positive and in some cases, e.g., between a_v and a_n, quite large); and (3) to factor-analyze and obtain the factors necessary to explain the correlations. The factors now obtained are "factors among factors." They account for much of the variance in the primaries but leave over something specific to each primary. The second-order factors, as they are now called, also show simple structure positions just as primaries do, and turn out at these positions to be somewhat mutually correlated. Of course, as far as ultimate influence on variables is concerned (acting through the primaries), higher-order factors tend to be broader in their influence than are primaries.

For reasons which will become apparent, it is more accurate to speak of a factor being at a certain *stratum* rather than a certain *order*. (Among

---

[4] A positive manifold means that no matter what dimensionality we are dealing with, the actual test vectors appear only in the positive quadrants. That is to say, a test turns out to be positively loaded on *any* pair of ability dimensions we care to take. It carries further Spearman's observation that most cognitive measures tend to be positively intercorrelated.

[5] The primary scores are estimated from the actual tests. However, an alternative approach for obtaining the correlations among the primaries has been used in some of our studies and explained in the research articles. In this the factor analysis which gives the primaries is rotated to maximum simple structure with great care, and the angles obtained are used to obtain the correlations among the true factors (not *estimates* of primaries as in the other method). The two approaches agree quite closely.

other things the "order" is relative to the position from which one takes off, whereas stratum refers to a constant, absolute level and position of operation.) If we accept the position—which seems scientifically most justifiable—that a factor is an influence, then a first-stratum factor operates on variables and a second-stratum factor has an influence on first-stratum factors. That is to say, it contributes to the variance of first-stratum factors, though some of their variance remains their own. To illustrate from something that is always with us—the weather—one can imagine that if measures on variables influenced by weather, e.g., rate of grass growth, frequency of repainting a house, rate of denudation of a hilltop, number of days of fog, were taken at 200 stations over the earth, a factoring might give primaries such as inches of rainfall, hours of sunshine, mean strength of winds, etc. A factoring of these might yield still more pervasive second-stratum factors such as temperature, air pressure, average humidity. If these in turn are correlated over the 200 stations, possibly one would get altitude and relation to the Van Allen belt as partial determiners of temperature, pressure, and humidity. (Closer examination shows that in some cases we do not have a simple one-way strata effect, but a complex network of mutual influences, in what has been called "the reticular model" (Cattell, 1965c); but here the strata model appears to suffice.)

However, for the moment let us keep to first-strata factors and ask what factor theory means in terms of equations. It means that we approximate to what may be more complex relations (if something more complex than linearity actually should hold in the data) by a linear, additive equation. What in general may be called the *behavioral equation* then states that a test performance on test j, scored for an individaul i, as t_{ji}, can be written:

$$t_{ji} = b_{jv}\, a_{vi} + b_{jn} a_{ni} + \cdots + b_j a_{ji} \tag{5.1}$$

where the a's are primary abilities (a_v = verbal ability, a_n = numerical ability, etc.), the last, a_j, being an ability specific to the test j. The b's ("behavioral indices") in this formula are *factor loadings* telling how much the given primary is involved in the performance j. The i's indicate that the scores on the abilities are those of a particular individual, i.

If it should be that the next jump from primaries lands us in the general intelligence and general speed, etc., stratum level, then from the second-order factoring we would write for any one primary, a_n—say, numerical ability:

$$a_{ni} = b_{ngf} g_{fi} + b_{ngc} g_{ci} + b_{ngs} g_{si} + \cdots + b_n \bar{a}_{ni} \tag{5.2}$$

where g_f, g_c, and g_s are the general fluid intelligence, crystallized intelligence and general speed factors, and $\bar{a}_n$ is what is specific to numerical ability when the effect upon it of general intelligence has been allowed for.

A number of very useful things, in terms of psychological theory, can be done with these equations. For example, knowing a person's factor scores, one obviously can *estimate* his performance on a test; one can find out (by squaring the correlations) *how much* of the variance of any performance score is accounted for singly or collectively by the various conceived abilities; and one can note the resemblance of *one* performance situation to another by comparing their profiles on the behavioral indices (b's). In terms of getting structural information, however, one needs to know principally which one of the actual performances—the t's—is affected by each first-stratum ability, and what the lines of influence are from higher to lower-stratum abilities. Such a picture of influence, from a concrete example in which the connections were known before the factor analysis, is drawn from the factor loadings (Cattell and Jaspars, 1967) in Figure 5–3.

FIGURE 5–3
Diagrammatic Representation of Factor Influences in
Successive Strata, from a Concrete Prescribed Example:
A Plasmode

(A) The Planned, Known Influence Structure

> *The figures in circles on each arrow show the amount of*
> *influence, positive or negative, assigned to each factor (as*
> *weights; square for variance) on the factor at the next stratum.*
> *The values for first-stratum (primary) factors as they affect*
> *variables are not inserted because of the limited space but may*
> *be read off on page 12, Table 1 of Cattell (1967a).*

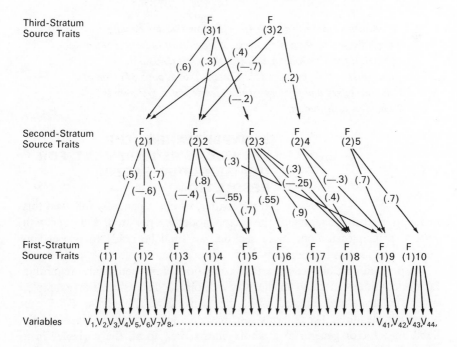

*(B) Actual Correlation Matrices Obtained From
Factoring Variables Concretely Built Up
According to the Above Influence Pattern*

SECOND STRATUM SOURCE
TRAITS (AS VARIABLES)   THIRD STRATUM FACTORS

	$F_{(3)1}$	$F_{(3)2}$[1]
$F_{(2)1}$	.33	.19
$F_{(2)2}$	.46	−.34
$F_{(2)3}$	−.21	—
$F_{(2)4}$	—	.57
$F_{(2)5}$	—	—

[1] (Values below .19 and third "error" factor omitted.)

FIRST STRATUM SOURCE
TRAITS (AS VARIABLES)   SECOND STRATUM FACTORS

	$F_{(2)1}$	$F_{(2)2}$	$F_{(2)3}$	$F_{(2)4}$	$F_{(2)5}$[2]
$F_{(1)1}$	.39				
$F_{(1)2}$	−.56				
$F_{(1)3}$	.70	−.56			
$F_{(1)4}$		.72			
$F_{(1)5}$		−.45	.68		
$F_{(1)6}$			−.52		
$F_{(1)7}$			.89		
$F_{(1)8}$		.46	−.26	.40	
$F_{(1)9}$			.38	−.24	.67
$F_{(1)10}$					.63

[2] (All values below .19 and the sixth "error" factor plotted.)

> *A comparison of (a) with (b) will show that the actual
> analysis gets back to the pattern of significant influences intro-
> duced in the plasmode model, (a), though it does so more
> accurately at the primary (see Cattell, 1967a, page 34) than at
> the secondary and tertiary stratum levels which typically is
> found in such studies.*

3. HYPERPLANES: THE TECHNICAL REQUIREMENT FOR UNAMBIGUOUS FACTOR RESOLUTION

If the reader, who has patiently followed this
description of the meaning of the factor model for research, will bear with
general principles for one more section, we shall be ready to proceed to
definite conclusions in the ability field.

As pointed out above, a certain confusion of nomenclature regarding
factors continues to stand in the way of pointed discussion. For example,
order and strata are confused, while the terms "general" and "specific" can
be very misleading. These terms suit mathematicians who can speak justifiably of a factor general to a whole matrix, i.e., to all the variables in a

correlation of factor matrix, and contrast it with one specific to a single test. However, in life, i.e., over all the behaviors which men show, it is safe to assert that *there can be no such thing as a categorical general factor;*[6] there are only more or less broad factors. What is general to a particular experiment of a couple of dozen variables is more or less an accident of the variables chosen. We are much more interested in knowing how *broad* a factor is in regard to life, and if, for continuity we continue to talk about general factors, we mean thereby only the broadest class among broad factors. Strictly, we should speak only of *broad* factors,[7] *narrow* factors, and *specific* factors. Except for the last all is relative, and the relativity has meaning only in regard to what we have discussed above as a stratified sample from a population of behaviors and situations in our physico-cultural world.

Recognition that the "general" i.e., *broad* traits reported in the matrices of Spearman, Burt, Rimoldi, Vernon, Adkins, McNemar and others are *not* general but only broad saves much time previously spent debating spurious issues. It also reminds us that the distinction between what is called a very broad (formerly "general") and not so broad (formerly "group") factor has been largely an artifact of the experimenter's choice of variables. (And about that choice many an experimenter has been inexplicit, to say the least!) With this understood, we can proceed both to defend one particular factor resolution rather than another and also to substantiate the statement made earlier, in passing, that Thurstone's obtaining of a "general" factor at the second order had the advantage of fixing that factor uniquely as to meaning. For, as Thurstone claimed, a unique fixing of the general factor had not been possible with the Spearman-Burt-Vernon approach with hierarchies and "tetrad differences."

To grasp the argument here it is necessary to develop a little further the conception of simple structure introduced in Chapter 2. If factors are influences or determiners, and no influence can be entirely general to all variables in the universe it follows that any factor—even a broad one—will leave a rather large fraction of the variables that are used with only a zero loading showing upon them. For example, intelligence affects a child's solving algebra problems and winning chess games, but not necessarily his sociability, quickness of temper, blood type, the time taken to get to school, or the number of maiden aunts he possesses. These latter are said to "lie in

---

[6] Even if someone should assert that all behavior begins and ends with breathing, so that breathing should appear as a general factor, we should have to point out that many behavior measures are ratios, e.g., amount in the first minute relative to the second, which cancel absolute level—even if absolute level is affected by breathing efficiency, which is very doubtful over normal ranges.

[7] The reason for using *broad* instead of reverting to "common" for this concept is that much confusion would then result (again, among psychologists rather than in the smaller world of statistics) because *common,* as opposed to *unique* (in the sense of Allport (1961) and Cattell (1946a)), is used to describe a pattern *common to all people,* whereas a unique trait is one obtained by P-technique describing a trait form which no one else possesses.

the hyperplane" to the factor or strictly to what is called the "reference vector."[8] That is to say, these tests fan out from the origin orthogonally to the reference vector, forming, in three dimensions, a plane. The typical outcome is that if we plotted the position of tests, as described above, by their loadings (or the angles showing their correlations with other tests), we should expect a lot of tests to have a projection of zero on the factor concerned, as points in the first nebula (hyperplane mass) do on factor T_1 in Figure 5–4(a)(2). In three-space this would form a nebula of points like a disc or plane, but with more factors than three it lies in hyperspace and thus in general is called a hyperplane.

The coordinates in Figure 5–4(a)(1) are drawn vertically and horizontally, since the "factors" as they come out of the computer are orthogonal. On the plot of points obtained from the projections of tests on these orthogonal factors the hyperplanes then become visible, as seen in this same

FIGURE 5–4
Simple Structure Illustrated Abstractly and by Substantive Instance of Anxiety and Intelligence

(*A*) *Abstract Ideal Illustration of Simple Structure*

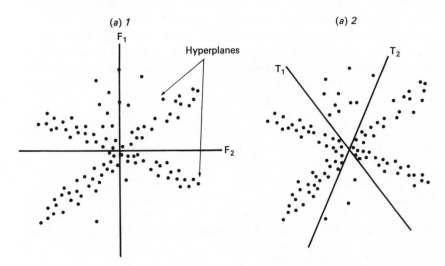

(a) 1

F_1 and F_2 are the factor coordinates from the computer analysis.

(a) 2

T_1 and T_2 are the source traits (reference vectors) placed at the simple structure position, perpendicular to the hyperplanes, here seen like spiral nebulae perceived edgewise.

---

[8] Apart from technicalities which the general psychologist can bypass at this time, we can continue to call this reference vector the *factor*.

(B) Concrete Instance: Intelligence and Anxiety

> *This is a plot from an experiment with 500 airmen measured on some eighty behavioral variables. Two well known factors, out of several located, have been plotted against each other. The anxiety factor is marked partly by such objective tests as annoyability and suggestibility and partly by questionnaire (16 P.F.) responses. The hyperplanes to the two factors are unmistakable and the intelligence source trait is fixed along the thick (near horizontal) axis. It loads most highly the test of series and of classification and negatively, low accuracy in estimating time. The identity of the unlabeled points can be found in the research indicated (Cattell, 1955a, 1956) since the main purpose of this figure is to give a concrete view of hyperplanes in intelligence definition.*

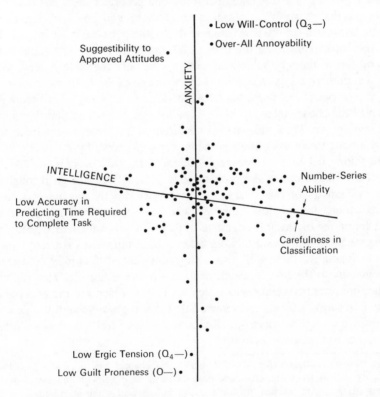

Figure 5–4(a)(1). One then perceives that the reference vectors (a first form of the factor) drawn as perpendiculars to these nebulae (since simple structure means just this) as in Figure 5–4(a)(2), are in fact mutually oblique (somewhat correlated), as is usual in nature.

In Figure 5–4(b) two concrete illustrations of simple structure are presented. As Plato realized, the actual is usually a somewhat battered replica of the ideal! So the hyperplanes in (b) are not quite the perfect discs seen on edge that are approximated in (a). However, they show what typically is obtained, and it is clear that there are no other positions in either drawing at which the factors could be placed. These examples, incidentally, are deliberately taken from noncognitive fields—personality and motivation—in order to permit a comparison with the research data on fluid ability soon to be presented, in which the standards of simple structure are very similar.

Now the essential impotence of the Spearman general factor position, which seems to have been realized only very slowly, is that no provision was made in rotation for providing material for hyperplanes—for the "ground" to be of a different color, so to speak, so that the "design" would stand out against it. Spearman's "tetrad difference criterion"[9] (Spearman, 1927) ensured that his matrices contained only one general factor, but it did not guarantee that it would constitute a uniquely rotated position. The matter can be illustrated briefly if we assume that some personality or interest factor, say, interest in doing the tests at all, enters roughly orthogonally to a general factor, though the general factor is the only cognitive general factor and accounts for the greater part of the variance of the tests, as follows.

Let us suppose that some ten tests—marked as a through j in Figure 5–5 —have been chosen by a psychologist on his ripe conviction that they represent intelligence. They will—unless his intuition is hopeless—correlate positively among themselves in all possible ways, as shown by no cosine in the figure falling below zero (no angle among them 90° or more). The first component taken out in the process of factor analysis will go through the center of gravity of this swarm of tests, as shown by the axis g_1. Along comes another investigator, however, who believes that k, l, and m are also good measures of general cognitive ability. These—added in dotted lines in Figure 5–5—will swing this big first factor component extracted over to g_2. (Incidentally, they will also swing the second factor P_1, extracted orthogonally to the first as usual, over to a new position P_2. This shift has further important consequences which we shall follow up at the appropriate point.) In short, a factor so extracted that it just goes through the centroid of all the tests has no more stability than a surface trait: it chases clusters, having no hyperplane to hold it.[10]

---

[9] As with several other technical points which this chapter has to respect in defining its theory, the undergraduate student probably will need help on this one from his teacher. At any rate, he has 'little alternative but to accept the statement at a first reading and pass on, or to enquire with the help of his professor into the background of scientific literature which enlarges on the theme.

[10] Spearman's tetrad difference criterion, as just mentioned, was really a device that groomed the matrix free of group factors and produced a unifactor (or "univocal") matrix, but it did not guarantee that the axis of this factor would always be in the same position. Furthermore, in the case where a second broad factor entered every variable *with exact proportionality to the first factor* it would not even recognize that two (not one) factors would be at work. The distinction between *uni*factorial and

FIGURE 5–5
Dependence of Definition of Intelligence (in Burt-Vernon
Sense) on Choice of Variables

> *Shift of meaning of intelligence—from g_1 to g_2—when it is defined only as a cluster. The addition of such tests as k, l, and m pulls the center of gravity over and at the same time shifts the meaning of P, a trait made to be independent of intelligence.*

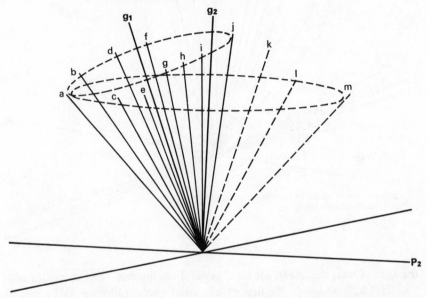

By contrast to the situation in Figure 5–5, the experimental designs which we have used in pursuing the concepts of fluid and crystallized general intelligence have deliberately included in the research variables of a kind—shown as n, o, p, q, r, s, t, u, v, w, x, y, z in Figure 5–6—that would be expected to be *unrelated* to intelligence. They could be personality questionnaire factors, motivation strength measures, and even physical strength variables. These yield for the investigator the guiding hyperplanes shown in Figure 5–6, in which all the cognitive variables of Figure 5–5 are repeated (and therefore appear with the same correlations) but in this more illuminating context of hyperplanes. *Now* the factor for general ability has its reference vector fixed at g (the old g_1 is shown for comparison, as well as the old P_1) while the present *true* position for the personality factor is fixed at P. (Note n and o did not turn out to fall as expected, but the rest sufficed to define the hyperplane.)

From Figure 5–6 it will be realized that if a second psychologist enters the Figure 5–5 experiment with different subjective convictions concerning

---

pure factorial structure in a test should be read elsewhere (Cattell and Warburton, 1967, Chapter 8). The same kind of objection holds, incidentally, to Guttman scaling: it may show that all items possess only one dimension in common, but that dimension can be factorially complex in terms of known psychological factors.

FIGURE 5–6
**Resolution of Indeterminacy of Intelligence, by New
Context to Figure 5–5 in Form of Hyperplane Variables**

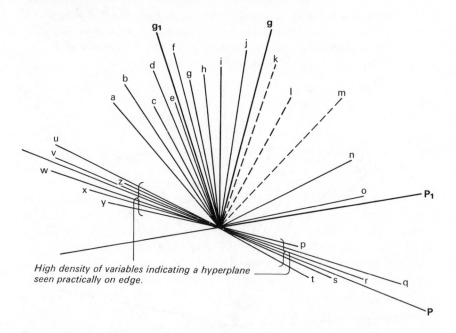

High density of variables indicating a hyperplane
seen practically on edge.

the kind of tests that mean for him "general intelligence" and therefore adds variables k, l, and m to the first psychologist's set (a through j) he will no longer produce the change of result which this addition formerly produced. For the rotation is anchored by the hyperplanes at the position g, and is no longer pulled about as g_1 was to a new center of gravity. Neither the enthusiast for the tests a through j, nor he who believes in k through m, with their subjective drifts to the surface traits g_1 and g_2—nor any number of other inspired positions—can claim to be right. In the end the simple structure position, g, may stabilize away from all of them. The first *unrotated* component, as it comes out of the computer admittedly still will shift over to the right, as before, when the new tests are added, relative to the first component with the old set. But actually we are no longer at the mercy of unrotated components. *Whatever* those first components might have been we should have rotated away from them by the new method to the position defined by the hyperplanes. The hyperplanes are part of the *configuration* of correlations yielded directly by the experiment, and as such are not subject to the form of factor extraction used.[11] Thus the disagreement of the

---

[11] It might be objected that, if extra variables can alter the cluster which gives the centroid or first component, they can also alter the positions of hyperplanes. This false impression would not arise if we could draw in many dimensions, instead of only two, as here. The hyperplane is affected by more or fewer variables only in the sense of sampling, not by a systematic bias. They remain in place just as the lines of

two first investigators would be solved in experiment 5–6 by taking up a third position independent of either of their starting points.

4. THE EMERGENCE OF THE SECOND-STRATUM FLUID AND CRYSTALLIZED ABILITY PATTERNS

The technical issues of the last section perhaps have presented a steep climb for those first entering the domain of multivariate experimental designs. But if the main ideas have been mastered, the reader is now safely over the rarefied air of the pass and may swing along more easily for the rest of the book. The issues may seem specialized, but one must remember that it is in the nature of science that theories of great moment often turn on an intensive examination of some quite specific technical method. The three most important conditions of meaningful factor analysis, less often met than missed in studies published to date, are, in summary: (1) a check by two or three independent methods (the Scree, the Kaiser-Guttman, or the Lawley criteria) on the actual *number* of factors to take; (2) a *simple structure* or *confactor* rotation to a demonstrably *unique* resolution; as well as (3) certain broader, experimental design principles beyond statistics, e.g., ensuring a wide choice of behaviors, of types of people, etc., in relation to theory.

Despite the half-hidden Achilles heel just discussed, which actually left the whole theory vulnerable, Spearman's theory of *g* had prevailed among thoughtful psychologists for thirty to forty years when the fluid and crystallized ability theory appeared. Actually the tranquil assurance of intelligence test technology, like that of the Pax Romana which prevailed over the classical world, lived by inexplicit compromises between the local predilections of specific test constructors, as in the Wechsler, the Stanford-Binet, the Otis, the Cattell Scales (in Britain), the CPE, the Miller, etc., and the central, official theory of "g" which nominally received general tribute. For virtually every one of the intelligence tests which dominated practice and publication in America had not been cleanly founded on thorough and basic prior research centered on the theory of g, though one or two in Britain had a more scientifically felicitous relation to this theory (notably Spearman's own little-known test (1929), Sir Godfrey Thomson's Northumberland (1935) and Moray House Tests, Ballard's (1927), and some others.) In America, as in the factor analysis of the Stanford-Binet, and of the Wechsler, by Cohen (1952, 1957, 1959) and by Saunders (1960), the

---

force drawn in iron filings around a magnet will not really alter their direction by shaking in more or fewer iron filings. Working with only a thin sprinkling of variables may result in a hyperplane being relatively tenuous, and most studies would in fact do better to carry more "hyperplane stuff," i.e., by including, say thirty "irrelevant" variables with every twenty that cover the factor area in which the experimenter is interested, for this enlarged sample of variables will produce a more emphatic hyperplane.

analysis was an attempt to understand afterwards what had been constructed on "commonsense" principles, and the factorially mixed-up state of the Wechsler-Bellevue and WAIS, for example, or the grotesque overloading with verbal ability of the Miller Analogies, were an inevitable consequence. In Britain, around 1930 (Cattell and Bristol, 1933) Bristol had found the g factor saturations of various Binet tests to be quite low, but had taken the dozen most highly saturated and developed them further into what is now the IPAT Scale 1 Intelligence Test. What will be a curious story for the historian of this 1910–1960 half-century to unravel is, on the one hand, the lip service paid almost unquestioningly by the competent to Spearman's theory, and, on the other, the essential ignoring of such principles by many popular test constructors. The goodness of an intelligence test in that period seemed to be evaluated more by its reliability coefficient, the social prestige of its author, and the use of astronomical numbers of subjects in its standardization, than by its validity in the light of any rational theory.

If the basic theory received any overt criticism from the test users and constructors, it was on trivial misunderstandings rather than with respect to truly promising improvements therein that remained in the womb of time. The theory of fluid and crystallized intelligence, the researches of Line, Fortes, and others, and the initial papers on culture-fair intelligence tests in the early 1940s thus waited nearly twenty years for the attention of substantial and crucial experiment. The first and relatively slender experiment begun in 1960 was, nevertheless, startlingly clear in its verdict. It showed (Cattell, 1963a) that if enough material for hyperplane identification is included—which had never been done before for second-order analysis—there are indeed *two* general intelligence factors, as the theory had stated, and that their properties come very close to being those expected. It also showed that two further general factors appeared—the speed and retrieval factors suggested above—which lacked any properties that could be called intelligence factors. All four of these patterns will be examined below, but meanwhile we may note that the second stratum had been opened up with a vengeance! For, whereas it had been customary to end the tentative penetration into the second-order domain neatly with a single "g" like the lonely summit of a pyramid, it became evident with improved techniques that at least four massive factors had to be explained at this upper stratum and that two of them were, so to speak, twin forms of Spearman's g.

There followed immediately a second and far more extensive research by John Horn of the University of Denver, on 297 men and women, and this was followed by another on 277 boys and girls of twelve and thirteen years, and another on 62 children of six and one-half years. The results for two of these researches only are set out in Table 5–1 in order not to "clutter'" the view on a first occasion. (See Table 6–1, page 106, below for more complete presentation.) They strikingly support the view that there are two general ability factors in the cognitive area concerned with solving difficult cognitive problems, and they show that this difference exists over the whole age range for which intelligence tests have hitherto proved effective. In seeking, in the opening three researches, to span the age from 6 to 60, we risked not seeming to get such good agreement among factor patterns as might exist if the researchers had restricted to a uniform type in regard to the range and nature of the groups, for it is well known that all known factors, in ability or personality, change their pattern of expression with age.

Not all the variables that were used as "hyperplane stuff" are set out. In fact only the last seven rows in the first research and the last five in the second, which are primary personality factors measured by questionnaire, illustrate the variables which perform the precious function of having essentially zero loading on one or another of the ability factors. Their presence permits not only a second but also a third-stratum ability factor to be rotated despite its extending as a "general factor" across *all* these (cognitive) tests that have hitherto typically been investigated only in isolated groups and without personality variables. For clarity the table omits the extra columns for the third and fourth (and sometimes fifth) broad second-stratum factors generally found, and which correspond to speed, fluency, and visualization as discussed later.

It will be seen that the crystallized intelligence factor, g_c, corresponding in content to many traditional tests of I.Q., loads typically verbal ability (.46 to .74), reasoning (.30 to .72), the number primary (.29 to .59), and, to a lesser degree, word fluency (.10 to .25). The fluid general ability factor, g_f, has some loading on some of these same primaries, e.g., .05 to .47 on number, .30 to .73 on spatial, and .08 to .23 on reasoning; but its main loadings are on the perceptual, culture-fair tests. In these latter tests of relation eduction, undertaken without help from prior schooling, the loadings are .35 on series, .50 on matrices, .51 on topology, and .48 to .78 on classification.

Although differences in pattern of expression with age will interest us later (Chapter 7) it is what is common and central to the different experiments that interests us most at this point. One of the most interesting features is that although crystallized ability in general does not enter into the culture-fair subtest performances, fluid ability *does* enter, though to a lesser extent than the crystallized general ability, into those primaries such as verbal, numerical, and reasoning abilities which have been used in traditional intelligence tests. In other words *purely learned* judgmental skills are not enough, even in the *traditional* intelligence test, to enable such problems to be solved. Some fluidity of relation eduction is needed and some adaptability to new situations is demanded, even when using acquired judgments.

Incidentally, it is a demonstration of the effectiveness and sensitivity of the factor-analytic design, when entered with due precautions and adequate equipment, that this partial overlap can be detected. The tendency of the usual distribution of variables chosen in research in the ability field would be to favor a drift toward a complete split of fluid and crystallized loadings; but the hyperplanes are so firmly anchored by the *personality* variables that the rotation cannot be disturbed in this direction and it seems that psychologists henceforth must accept the fact that the primary abilities *are* complex, factorially. Figure 5–7 shows the crucial plots from two of these researches, so that the reader now familiar with the simple structure concept may judge for himself just how compelling these resolutions are relative to any alternative. The two researches agree not only in the patterns of the fluid and crystallized general abilities (i.e., in the fluid having *some* projection into V and R) but also in leaving the majority of the personality factors in the hyperplane. One can notice here already, however, a tendency which we shall find supported in later studies, for the *crystallized* (but seldom the fluid) ability to get somewhat involved with personality. This would be expected if the fuller development of the theory below is correct; namely that crystallized ability arises not only from better educational opportunity but also from a history of persistence and good motivation in applying fluid intelligence to approved areas of learning.

FIGURE 5–7
Plots of Two Age Levels Showing the Hyperplanes
Determining Distinct Fluid and Crystallized Intelligence
Factors and Their Salient Expression

(A) High School Age Showing the Typical Substantial Positive
Correlation (r = .47; 277 Thirteen to Fourteen Year Olds)

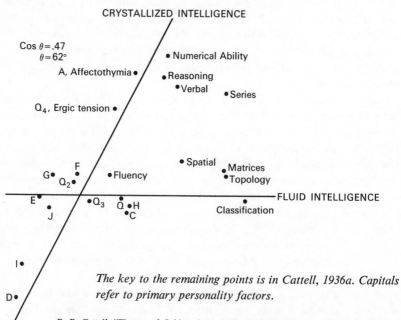

The key to the remaining points is in Cattell, 1936a. Capitals refer to primary personality factors.

*(B) Adults Showing the Much Smaller Positive Correlation
Usually Found After School Years (477 Lower Education Adults)*

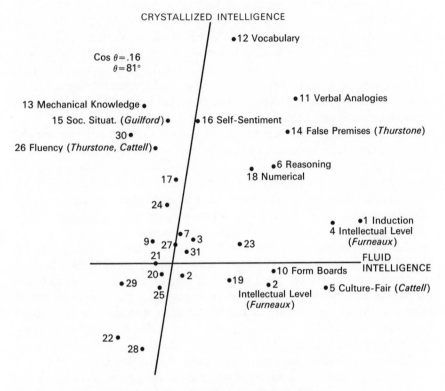

The key to the numbering of points is in Horn and Cattell, 1967.

J. Horn and Cattell, R. B., "Age differences in fluid and crystallized intelligence." *Acta Psychologica*, 26, 1967, 107–129. Reproduced by permission of North-Holland Publishing Company, Amsterdam.

5. g_f AND g_c: THEIR DIFFERENCES FROM EACH OTHER AND FROM PREVIOUS CONCEPTS

The theory of fluid and crystallized intelligence does not rest only on factor-analytic researches of structure itself, as shown above. It draws further support from the five or six additional directions of evidence—developmental, physiological, etc.—mentioned above and soon to be followed up. But its *initial* sanction necessarily comes purely from the evidence of behavioral structure as such, and an understanding of the factor-analytic evidence for two factors presented in the last section is essential to appreciation of all later arguments.

Four independent researches are by any ordinary scientific standard sufficient to confirm a proposition; but larger researches are now in progress under Horn—especially to fix change of pattern with age—and should be available in journals at the time this book is published.

The main behavioral character of these two patterns of general ability is, meanwhile, clear enough. Crystallized general mental capacity shows itself heavily in such primary abilities as verbal factor, V; numerical ability, N; reasoning, R or I; mechanical information and skills, Mk; and experiential judgment (in social and other fields). Fluid ability appears in series, classifications, analogies, topology, and other well-known intelligence tests, when couched in shapes which are neither verbal nor pictorial, but such as would be equally accessible to a person of any background.

It is noteworthy that even verbal (synonym, analogies) tests can be made to load fluid intelligence very substantially (and crystallized relatively little) if the words are chosen to be easily within the vocabulary of the group tested, as Horn (1965) has shown. This is in accordance with the principle that fluid intelligence shows itself in successfully educing complex relations among simple fundaments whose properties are known to everyone, i.e., are overlearned, in the group being tested. In existing "verbal" intelligence tests this principle has been applied most carefully in the Cattell Intelligence Scales (1933c and Cattell and Cattell, 1959), Scale 3 of which, for "high-level intelligence" adults, is used as a criterion for the Mensa Society membership. The consequence is that, although verbal in content to all six subtests, it reaches as high a loading in fluid as in crystallized intelligence. This is to be contrasted with other "high-level intelligence" tests, such as the Miller Analogies, which achieve their high level of difficulty by invoking uncommon and even esoteric words.

A full discussion of the nature of the mental operations involved in the expression of fluid and crystallized general abilities is best taken up later (Chapter 13, page 428). But, immediately it can be seen that the crystallized ability (g_c) expressions, though of a judgmental, discriminatory, and reasoning nature, operate in areas where the judgments have been taught systematically or experienced before. The differences between the words, say "aplomb" and "savoir faire," or between "definite" and "definitive" in a synonyms test, or, in a mechanical knowledge primary test, between using an ordinary wrench or a box spanner on part of one's automobile, requires intelligence for the initial perception and learning of the discrimination (wherefore some never will learn it). But thereafter it becomes a crystallized skill, relatively automatically applied. The fact that the g_c also loads fluency (see Tables 5–1 and 6–2), and g_f does not, supports the conclusion that crystallized intelligence draws on the same reservoir of appropriate acquired ideas as that on which fluency of output draws. Perhaps judgments (relations), as well as fundaments, are actually in the memory reservoir on which fluency of retrieval draws, though the fluency factor, as we shall see later, seems to be largely a function of the sheer power of retrieval of fundaments.

Fluid ability, by contrast, appears to operate whenever the sheer perception of complex relations is involved. It thus shows up in tests where borrowing from stored, crystallized, judgmental skills brings no advantage. As far as logic is concerned, it seems to spread over all kinds of relationships: part-whole, classificatory similarity ("sets"), causal relations, spatial relations, inductive reasoning, new abstract relations in numbers, and inferential relations. In short, fluid intelligence, g_f, is an expression of the level of complexity of relationships which an individual can perceive and act upon when he does not have recourse to answers to such complex issues already stored in memory.

Although we have spoken of culture-fair tests as if they are synonymous with the means of measurement of fluid ability, an important distinction must now be drawn. As pointed out above, the Cattell Intelligence Tests, Scales 1, 2, and 3, were not designed (as were Cattell's IPAT Culture-Fair Scales 1, 2, and 3, later) to be measures of fluid intelligence (although they were the first tests (1933c) to include also "perceptual type" tests as a small, leavening fraction of the whole). They used apparent crystallized ability material such as synonyms, verbal analogies, arithmetical problems, etc. Nevertheless, they went a long way toward eliminating the effects of cultural differences, at least as social status and regional differences in our society, *by deliberately asking for difficult choices among highly familiar words.* Thus fluid-intelligence-measuring and perceptual, culture-fair designs are not synonymous for the former are not always free of culture.

Freedom from variance due to cultural and educational background can be achieved either by (a) presenting items that are new to everyone, or (b) presenting items that are equally old and familiar to everyone. The Cattell General Intelligence Tests (1933c) aimed at the latter, but, of course, could not succeed entirely. Consequently, as far as international comparisons are concerned, this test cannot compare for culture-fairness with the IPAT Culture-Fair. However, the point to bear in mind is that when a test does succeed in eliminating cultural difference effects within one country, by the device of arranging difficult word choices among words well within the vocabulary possessed by all, what is being measured still may have a very substantial component of crystallized intelligence in a different situation, as with an international group of subjects. Even in a group entirely in one culture, the skill in using common words today expresses the level of fluid intelligence as it operated in word learning perhaps two or three years previously. Such test designs, while desirable, are therefore not as good as those employing the full culture-fair (perceptual noegenetic) principle.

Among the structural results of the last section is a vital one (visible in Figure 5–7 but not yet discussed) namely, that the fluid and crystallized factors, g_f and g_c, are positively correlated very significantly at all ages. This correlation, which hovers around 0.4–0.5, could be interpreted according to a variety of theories, but the theory favored here, and made more explicit in the next chapter, is that the acquisition of the crystallized ability skills, e.g., learning how to calculate the area of a circle, as πr^2, or how to differentiate the way in which strong and weak verbs make their past tense, depends *partly* on the level of insightful "fluid" ability and *partly* on hours spent in school, etc. Consequently, a substantial but far from perfect positive correlation would be expected between the two.

One wonders if these two abilities, though overlapping and correlated, are so distinct that some intuitions of this duality by perceptive psychologists and others may have appeared previously. Surely the popular distinction of "gumption" or "nous" versus "trained intelligence" could be a foreshadowing of this g_f versus g_c distinction, and probably Thomas Aquinas's "intelligence" and "intellect" differentiation is getting near it. (Except that the dictionary use of "intellect"—at any rate in Oxford and a few American inbred institutions—would not include in intellect the fine judgments of a garage mechanic graduated in engineering, or the social skills of a good salesman—whereas g_c does.)

Three other currently popular dualities that are definitely *not* to be confused with that which we are now stating, are: (1) the distinction in some traditional American intelligence tests between the "verbal" and the "numerical-quantitative" ability scores, (2) Guilford's *convergent* versus *divergent* thinking abilities, and (3) Vernon's (and sometimes Burt's) distinction of *verbal-educational* (V:ed) versus *practical mechanical* (M:k factor) general abilities. The first is an obsolete conceptualization, confusing two Thurstone primaries, V and N, with broad secondaries. The second, we suggest, itself needs reorienting (see page 55), but there is no risk of any careful reader confusing it with the g_f and g_c distinction. The last, on the other hand, is sufficiently cast in the same framework of factor-analytic structural research to be in danger of real confusion. Nevertheless, the fact that the duality V:ed, as opposed to M:k, is not the same as g_f contrasted with g_c should be evident at once from two facts: (a) mechanical ability, as a primary, loads mainly g_c, i.e., it is a culturally acquired pattern, not part of g_f; (b) by the severe distortion from simple structure rotation in Vernon's resolution, on which we have commented above, V:ed and M:k are never in the same position as g_f and g_c even if taken out as second-order factors. Vernon himself (1964) agrees that the two pairs of concepts are distinct, and the present writer has shown V:ed and M:k to be complex confoundings of g_f and g_c. To see this latter more clearly, let us suppose that factors are taken out as principal components at the first order, without rotation (as in Burt's and Vernon's main analyses) from a set of tests that are chosen to represent "general cognitive mental capacities." A characteristic pattern of loadings among successive factors (called "genealogical" for fairly obvious reasons or, by Burt, "the Tree of Porphyry") follows, as shown in Figure 5–8. There only three successive matrix-general factors are taken out, but theoretically the pattern could run on to whatever number of "general" factors is indicated. The first factor is called general intelligence by analysts who use this scheme. The second is positively loaded on verbal and general scholastic education material and negatively on mechanical and what have been called "practical" abilities (Vernon, 1964). As stated above, this second factor may

FIGURE 5–8
The "Genealogical" Pattern (Tree of Porphyry) of Loadings
Required by the Original Hierarchical Theory of Abilities

FACTORS IN ORDER OF EXTRACTION

	1	2	3
Verbal Comprehension	+	+	+
Opposites	+	+	+
Reading	+	+	−
Verbal Problems	+	+	−
Mechanical Abilities	+	−	+
Form Boards	+	−	+
Spatial Ability	+	−	−
Geometrical Problems	+	−	−

POSSIBLE REORGANIZATION BY ROTATION

	1	2	3
Verbal Comprehension	+		+
Opposites	+		+
Reading	+		−
Verbal Problems	+		−
Mechanical Abilities		+	+
Form Boards		+	+
Spatial Ability		+	−
Geometrical Problems		+	−

be called a bi-polar factor—verbal versus mechanical—and so left. But by rotating the coordinates through 45° one can reinterpret the correlations in terms of two uni-polar factors, one designatable as verbal-educational—because these are its highest loadings—and the other as practical-mechanical—since mechanical ability, form boards, etc., will load this most highly. The reader should plot the eight test vectors in Figure 5–8, calling each + and −, say +.60 and −.60. To get the clearest effect the two uni-polar axes should go oblique and approach mutually to about sixty degrees. If the third factor is also included in rotations, separation may be still a little better.

There are three reasons why this scheme of verbal-educational versus mechanical cannot possibly be considered compatible with or an alternate approach to the theory of g_f and g_c. First, it has three factors (when positivized) instead of two. Second, it introduces conceptually a flavor of the Hindu caste system, which placed verbal skills as intellectually higher than mechanical and practical skills, and which does not exist in g_c and g_f. The latter contains *all* acquired cultural judgmental skills, and, as Humphreys (1962) has pointed out correctly (even when attempting to be critical!) crystallized intelligence loads mechanical knowledge and skills positively

(Table 6–2; Horn, 1965), not negatively as required and stated in the Burt-Vernon "V:ed" factor. Third, the Vernon V:ed versus M:k factor theory (or the two separate factors derived from it) lacks the experimental stability of the g_r and g_c resolution. For this V:ed versus k axis tilts here and there necessarily as the prior extracted "general ability" factor itself tilts. A glance back at Figure 5–5 and associated test (page 91) will make this clear. For this "practical" factor has to keep orthogonal to the "verbal, and right between them (at 45°) lies the Spearman "general intelligence" factor. By that approach the "g" factor depends on the choice of ability variables (even if the hierarchy had not been lost already by introducing the tests for the second, third, and later factors) and is unstable. Such factor analyses might seem almost to be undertaken merely to give the dignity and status of a uni-factor concept to what happens to be the investigator's subjective conception of what should go into an intelligence test battery. What seems to be overlooked repeatedly in these experimental designs is that as the first factor wobbles and wanders, all *subsequently* extracted factors swing their tails in sympathy. V:ed and M:k cannot be equated to g_f and g_c if only for the reason that what is factor-analytically subjective and indeterminate cannot be equated to what is precise—though the other, more specific reasons are also weighty. Yet a fourth concept that is sometimes mooted as a possible match to g_f and g_c is that of an innate intelligence as contrasted with the acquired "intellect" (but in a more modern sense than that of the Scholastics mentioned above). Burt's conception of intelligence as innate, all-round, mental ability in fact gets very close in meaning to g_f, but not through the same basis in actual factoring of tests. It is very probable that as nature-nurture research proceeds (see Chapter 10 below), g_f will be found much more innate than g_c. But g_f itself is subject to environment, particularly to brain damage or whatever effects neurological efficiency. So again, no simple equating can be done.

The reader who wishes to delve in more detail into the history of research in this area, including that of the primaries, but to keep to recent surveys, should see Butcher (1969), Horn (1968), and Pawlik's Chapter 18, in the *Handbook of Multivariate Experimental Psychology* (Cattell, 1966).

From this account of the emergence and essential foundation of what may be called the "investment theory" of fluid and crystallized ability (because crystallized ability becomes the trustee of gains from investment by fluid ability), let us pass in the next chapter to a more intensive study of the wider psychological implications.

CHAPTER SIX

HIGHER STRATUM ABILITY STRUCTURE AND THE INVESTMENT THEORY OF INTELLIGENCE

1. WHAT COMES AFTER THE PYRAMIDS?

So long as our attention focused mainly on the concepts of fluid and crystallized general intelligence as they emerged from the second-stratum factoring of primary abilities, we necessarily paid little heed to some other important shapes that began to loom in this higher domain. But, let us now satisfy our curiosity about this whole higher-stratum structure. Until a decade or so ago, lacking certain technical devices for factoring this higher realm, our chances of getting there would have been no better than Jack's chances of meeting the giant without his beanstalk. For one needs both the groundwork of a broad roster of well-established primaries, and the experimental designs to handle complex higher-order factor analyses. Without these one must stay at the first-story structures. As to the first of these needs, many diligent researchers, from Thurstone to Horn, as surveyed by French (1951) had, by 1965, established a reasonable collection of primary abilities at the first-stratum level. Consequently, the latest inquiries into the second stratum have been able to start off from a wider base of primaries than had been possible in previous attempts.

It is not surprising, therefore, that the second-stratum view obtained by Horn and the present writer in the researches mentioned—like that which opens up to those who leave the plain and reach the crests of the foothills —included ranges of second-stratum ability structures that had not been suspected previously. The two main factors, g_f and g_c, which had been the subject of so much theoretical discussion, now stood out clearly, but they were not alone. For there now appeared other broad factors never described before and which deserve immediate examination. Before attempting this it is necessary to warn the reader of a standard "conceptual illusion" in this technical area. By the nature of factor analysis—technically by the fact that no mathematically unique solution exists for the communalities if one takes out more factors than half the number of variables—the number of secondaries found from a dozen primaries rarely exceeds five and is more likely to err in the direction of taking out only three or four. When these secondaries, in turn, are factored, three or four of them can, by the nature of factor determination, yield only one or two tertiaries.

The result of this approximate halving of the number of entities dealt with at each successive analysis is thus always (in any sufficiently continued factor analysis) to produce a pyramid. Psychologists with the personal experience of having generated such a pyramid with great labor seem prone fondly to believe that this satisfying monument is the natural shape of the intellectual universe. Indeed, psychometrists have become accustomed to talk of hierarchies much as people who live in square rooms are apt to talk about the four corners of the earth. At any rate, the literature of the past fifty years is full of "hierarchical" models of cognitive ability structure. We have refrained from troubling the reader with most of these because no spontaneously convincing evidence for that pattern has yet really been encountered in the data commonly cited. Of course, evidence for this *may* yet be encountered, and there is a somewhat more subtle sense in which some kind of a hierarchy may be said to exist (page 310)—as a cap to some particular subset of tests. But the popularity of the idea in its crass form undoubtedly springs from (a) a misunderstanding of the empirical evidence through the "factorial pyramid illusion" explained above, and (b) some subjective intellectual compulsion, which perhaps the Pharaohs could best explain, to have a map of abilities beginning with the groundling variables and finishing neatly in a supreme point!

An unconscious weakness of the cognitive pyramid builder—the believer in the grand hierarchy—is that he takes for granted the unquestionable sanctity of the particular ground area of variables from which he starts. But what happens if pyramids are started all over the place from slightly but continuously different selections of cognitive ground performances? In principle there is no reason why one should not then finish up with simple parallel *strata* (as one sees in looking at the Grand Canyon of the Colorado), where a whole level stratum of pyramid peaks arises from slightly different bases, as shown in Figure 6–1. Geographically this kind of thing is common, as in the series of peaks at almost identical heights in the Great Divide of the Rockies. In psychology one has to collate many researches in order to become aware of it. And in collating these researches one becomes aware of a second possibility—that the peak of one set (if starting from a small base) actually may be a primary—a "groundling"—in another. Indeed, all sorts of chains and cross-connections are possible—as in

FIGURE 6–1
The Relativity of Hierarchies to the Base of Chosen
Variables: Pyramids Versus Strata

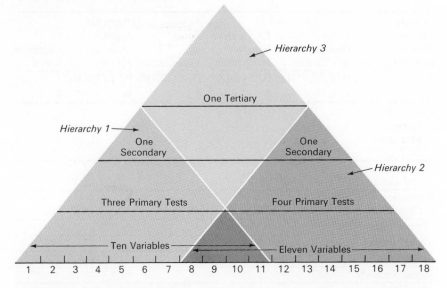

positive and negative feedback effects, for instance—among the influences which we call factors. The present writer has called this freer factor structure a *reticular* or *network* model and contrasted it with the *strata* model which, up to this point, has been accepted here implicitly.

In such a network we are likely to have an indefinitely extended set of interacting influences, so quite special factor-analytic experimental designs are necessary to explore a suspected reticular system. Fortunately, we can get a long way on the strata model alone, provided we recognize that any pyramids found therein in any one research may be artifacts of the above necessity for successive reductions of numbers of factors. In that case, several researches put together may show a whole stratum of, say, third-order factors where a single research might leave the impression that there is a single peak (see Figure 6–1). Certainly, in many reported researches one must recognize that, if variables had been more widely sampled in the first place, the researchers would be likely to finish with a plateau, at a certain order, whereas, with a more niggardly choice of the experimental coverage of data at the start, he had previously finished up with a pyramid.

In applying this to the ability area, we are pointing out that whereas the pioneer analysis of little more than half a dozen primary abilities by Thurstone had appeared to produce a single second-order factor (consistent with Spearman's hierarchy requiring a single "g"), the more ambitiously planned researches of Horn, for example, based on French's extension of primaries to more than twenty, revealed at least five, broad, second-order abilities as shown in Table 6–1 on p. 106.

TABLE 6–1
The Broad Second-Stratum ("Capacity") Factors in the Ability Realm

Primary Abilities Used in Correlation[1]	Fluid General Intelligence [U.I.(T)VIII][2] g_f	Crystallized General Intelligence [U.I.(T)IX][2] g_c	Power of Visualization [U.I.(T)X][2] g_v	Retrieval Capacity or General Fluency [U.I.(T)XII][2] g_r	Cognitive Speed g_s
Culture-Fair (Series, Matrices, etc.)	64				
Reasoning (Inference)	35	38			
Reasoning (Induction)	45	32			
Memory Span	72				
Verbal Ability		72			
Originality		82			
Assoc. Fluency		33		61	
Ideational Fluency				69	
Irrelevant Associations				85	
Flexibility of Closure	44		23		
Aiming			55		
Perceptual Speed			77		
Visualization			66		
Writing Speed					63
Cancellation Speed					46
Backward Writing					48

[1] This sets out a reduced (purely ability) set from the full 31 variables in Horn and Cattell, 1966, p. 262. For ease of scanning, all loadings below .19 have been omitted. The subjects are 480 male prison inmates of average age 28 years, sigma 10.6 years.

[2] These are the basic reference indices henceforth used for these factors in the proposed *universal index* (U.I.) of factors in objective tests (T). Roman numerals indicate second-order factors.

2. THE INTERPRETATION OF THE MAIN SECOND-STRATUM BROAD FACTORS

As usual, science must begin by forming conceptions of the nature of factors from the actual variables which prove to load them highly, both positively and negatively. (These are called the "salients".) They are to be contrasted with variables which are quite un-affected by the factor influences. (These are called the variables "standing in the hyperplane".) In this case (Table 6–1), "fluid general ability," g_f, appears to be the broadest factor and, in addition to the culture-fair, per-ceptual type of tests, it loads the Induction Primary, the Intellectual Speed and Level measures of the tests developed in England by Furneaux, the Inferential Reasoning Primary, such measures as Verbal Analogies, and the Associative Memory Speed Primary. What this implies regarding its nature will be discussed below. For the loadings on Intellectual Speed, (about .40), Associative Memory (about .42), and a wider array of other variables than in Table 6–1, the reader should see Horn and Cattell, 1966a, p. 282, remembering that the figures there have still to be transformed to the factor pattern matrix.

The crystallized general ability factor, g_c, of traditional intelligence tests has the next broadest span (seven primaries) covering the expected verbal, mechanical, numerical, and social skills primaries. After this comes a new broad factor not previously discussed, called g_v, visualization at its dis-covery, (but later to be called p_v). This factor evidently covers all kinds of performance—spatial orientation, form boards, gestalt closure—that are aided by good visualization resources. Previous to this perspective-giving work of Horn, a visualization factor of some kind had been reported fre-quently as a *primary* (see page 34). But this is often the fate of a secondary —that it is first spotted as an apparent primary—and it is now evident through the better design of Horn that this "visualization" spans several clear primaries, such as spatial ability (Thurstone, 1950), adaptive flexibility (Guilford, 1967), speed of closure (Thurstone, 1950) and flexibility of closure. It even has some loading on the Culture-Fair perceptual tests and on inductive reasoning and inferential reasoning. This indicates that visuali-zation may be used to solve what are thought of normally as intelligence-demanding problems, by resort to a visual representation.

The next broad secondary, g_s or U.I.(T)XI, is a speed of cognitive performance factor. This goes back a long way, to early and thorough demonstrations of its existence as a "group factor" in Spearman's labora-tory by Bernstein (1924). No really serious argument has ever been made that it is in fact just a primary, but nevertheless, it has floated around in a psychometrist's limbo awaiting placement. As mentioned above (page 40) there was a theory in the late twenties (Cattell, 1933a) that it reasonably could be considered a personality-temperament factor, and, in the present work of Horn (1967), the possibility is mooted that it represents a motiva-tional strength occurring in the actual test situation. Our conclusion above (page 65) is that the possibility that it is a temperamental or motivational influence must be considered seriously and carefully, but that the balance of evidence suggests that after large fractions of variance in general speed of behavior are allotted to such personality factors as U.I. 22, there will remain a general speed factor across the *abilities,* and for the present we shall so consider it. It affects speed in a broad spectrum of abilities, in-cluding such primaries as numerical performance, social skills, perceptual speed, and ideational fluency, but especially such mechanical speeds as writing (and, elsewhere than in Table 6–1, also reading). Its contribution is minor, however, to the speed of the more difficult, intelligence-demanding problems.

As pointed out earlier, the question of intelligence and speed was raised originally by Spearman (1904b). We have concluded that there is a sense in which a speed factor corresponds to each and every ability, primary or secondary. In intelligence itself it has been shown repeatedly that speed in complex, intelligence-demanding performances (power intelligence) is largely an expression of the same ability as is measured in fitness and error-freeness of response ("product intelligence"). Table 6–1 supports this in placing Furneaux's intellectual speed only trivially in the present cognitive speed factor and largely in fluid intelligence. By any reasonable perspective this simple speed factor is a distinctly broader factor even in the cognitive realm itself, than are the two intelligences. For example, it operates even more obviously in mechanical and perceptual performances than in intelligence. Speed measured in successful, intelligence problem-solving is local to intelligence (being zero if a person cannot solve the problems!). If intelligence is considered speed at all, it is speed in more complex performances than those that are typically strongly loaded by g_s.

Finally, the fifth, broad, ability source trait in the second stratum is g_r, which we are calling the "retrieval from memory storage" factor. Some times called general fluency, this source trait should not be confused with the primary abilities called word fluency and ideational fluency. The indications that some quite broad power operates in these areas also began early in this century, in three, strategically planned, factor analyses by Hargreaves (1927), by Bernstein (1924), and by the present writer in Spearman's laboratory, all of which show that such fluency performances over a wide range of test performances of various kinds are independent both of intelligence and speed, as discussed above.

It has been suggested by the present writer above and elsewhere (Cattell, 1936a, 1957a) that one would theoretically expect fluency to appear as two factors, only one of which strictly corresponds to the facility of the *retrieval* activity, while the other represents the actual *reserves* of memory storage in the given performance area. A somewhat similar theory was suggested on the basis of experimental results by D. M. Johnson and his coworkers (Johnson, Johnson and Mark, 1951), and by Guilford (1967) as well as by some learning theorists. If cumulative output in a fluency test is recorded every minute or two minutes, a curve is obtained which fits the equation:

$$f = s(1 - e^{-rt})$$

where f is the fluency score, s is a supposed total size of storage (number of available items in the category), e is the natural logarithm base, t is time, and r is a constant having to do with rate at which the supply is being exhausted. From measures at different points in time, yielding different f values, simultaneous equations of the form:

$$e^{rt} = \frac{s}{s - f}$$

can be developed which are theoretically capable of solution for r and s. A formulation of this kind would be substantiated if we could eventually show two factors in the fluency area, one for r—rate of retrieval—and one for volume of content stored in the areas, s. The question is whether the g_r we at present find empirically corresponds to r or some joint function of r and s.

It has been suggested above that the "word fluency" is actually two factors—the general "F" of Spearman (g_r here) plus a specific primary of word content and interest—but this remains to be checked. However, in some test situations the variance from g_r could so predominate that one might not notice the other factor. Actually, as the Bernstein study (1924) shows, any actual performance in fluency will also have a loading from the general speed factor, g_s, insofar as that is involved in the writing down of the words thought of. Thus any attempt at scoring pure g_r is likely to require careful test design, paying heed to a balance of various storage content areas, to speed (g_s), and to certain personality factors of an inhibitory nature, notably U.I. 17 and U.I. 21 ($-$) which also affect output in certain situations. But the analysis by Horn (1967) gives us clear indications that a *general* retrieval or fluency factor exists.

3. WHAT CAN FUTURE RESEARCH ADD TO STRUCTURAL CONCEPTS AT THE SECOND STRATUM?

Psychologists evidently have to alter their conceptions considerably from the monarchic view of a single broad cognitive ability factor, which has dominated thinking in the first half of this century. To return to our metaphor, there is not one vast mountain range, or even two (g_f and g_c), but several great ranges in the domain of cognitive effectiveness. That is to say, even when the wide range of test performances of various kinds has been grouped neatly in a few score primary abilities, each of some appreciable extent, several second-stratum influences that each make some contributions over a wide area of primaries.

Some will assert that psychologists should accept this revolutionary view with caution, since we ourselves have admitted that one factor-analytic experiment in itself, even using so widely and carefully chosen a set of primaries as Horn employed (as represented in Table 6–1), and on so substantial a sample and age range of adults, is not conclusive proof. Any one study of this kind could be inconclusive because of a faulty decision on the number of factors or because of inadequate rotation. However, we have accepted in the four or five researches here only those in which, as the reader may see in the research monographs, sophisticated technical standards and adequate sample sizes have been attained.

The possibility must also be considered that one particular kind of people or age group could give odd results, and for this reason there is almost no end to the number of researches one would like to see done. However, the five here—two major researches by Horn, and three of lesser, average scope by the present writer and coworkers—already cover the main age ranges, and, fortunately for clarity of conclusion, agree very well on the higher-stratum structures.

An introductory statement on the higher-stratum outcome has been given in the previous chapter, but we aim now to examine the more extensively marshaled data in Table 6–2, in order to proceed to more detailed conclusions. The main conclusions are that: (1) Except for a few slight loadings, the *personality* primary factors lie in the hyperplanes of the general ability factors, i.e., their loadings do not depart significantly from zero. (2) The *general* form of the g_f and g_c broad factors is the same for all three ages and types of group. Possibly it is significant that Table 6–2 shows numerical ability to involve fluid ability in five to six-year-olds but negligibly in thirteen to fourteen-year-olds, for at the former age addition and substraction are feats of understanding rather than computing habits. Other, lesser differences of loading could be due simply to different construction of particular tests at different age levels. (3) Where *more* primaries are taken into a study (see Table 6–1), as in Horn's second research, the visualization, g_v, and memory retrieval, g_r, secondaries appear again—having disappeared where there are too few tests to represent them —in the same form as we saw before.

In regard to the last point, the nature of the other, broad, second-stratum factors, such as g_v, g_s, g_r, etc., must be left for later consideration. Our aim here is to focus on the nature and relations of the two main intelligence factors. A cramping situation faces us, however, either in conceptualizing these other broad ("general") powers, such as g_s and g_r, or in attempting to sharpen the concepts of g_c and g_f, namely, that the ground stratum of primaries on which they all rest is still grievously limited in number. It is not only that after fifty years of ability investigation we might expect more coverage and definition, but also that all we have obviously has been systematically biased by a passive drift to the educational and academic domains. Indeed, this whole study of areas of ability has been sadly uninformed by any imaginative safaris into new areas, guided by something akin to the personality sphere concept which gave so vital a sense of perspective to personality research.

It is true that Guilford's search for types of cognitive performance that might be called "creative" has resulted in a whole new addition. For the list of a hundred or more primaries that might be there considered the reader is referred to his book (1967). However, many critics want to call some of them only artificially enlarged specifics, i.e., very narrow abilities made to appear broad factors in matrices by repetition of closely similar tests. In any case, the pursuit of the "ability space" by an *a priori* framework of operation, product and content is a very different one from using

TABLE 6–2
A More Extensive Research View of Loading Patterns of
Fluid and Crystallized Intelligence

(A) *5–6 Year Olds (114)*
   (*Cattell, 1967a*)

	g_f	g_c
Culture-Fair		
(Fluidity Markers)	58	−11
Reasoning	10	72
Verbal	−17	74
Numerical	43	49
Personality 2	04	−05
Personality 3	07	−08
Personality C	−07	−09
Personality H	15	17
Personality Q2	01	02

(B) *9–12 Year Olds (306)*
   (*Cattell, 1967b*)

	g_f	g_c
Culture-Fair (All)	78	09
Reasoning[1]	30	40
Verbal	22	63
Numerical	47	35
Spatial	73	03
Exvia	01	29
Anxiety	05	00
Pathemia	04	04
Neuroticism	−09	06

(C) *13–14 Year Olds (277)*
   (*Cattell, 1963a*)

	g_f	g_c
Culture-Fair		
(Classification)	63	−02
Reasoning	08	50
Verbal	15	46
Numerical	05	59
Spatial	32	14
Personality F	−05	09
Personality C	21	−07
Personality H	21	−04
Personality Q2	−06	05
Personality Q3	05	−02

(D) *Adults (477)*
   (*Horn, 1965*)

	g_f	g_c
Culture-Fair (All)	48	−08
Reasoning	26	30
Verbal	08	69
Numerical	20	29
Spatial	04	−04
Mechanical Knowledge	−15	48
Speed of Perceptual		
Closure	18	−05
Ideational Fluency	−03	25
Inductive Reasoning	55	12
Personality, U.I. 16	−04	18
Personality, U.I. 19	05	07
Personality, U.I. 21	−03	−08
Personality, U.I. 36	01	43
Personality,		
Anxiety, U.I. 24	−05	−26

For ease of comparison the variables have been arranged here in the same order, not in g_f and g_c blocks. Where personality factors are lettered they are the same as designations in the 16 Personality Factor Questionnaire.

[1] In this case since reasoning was not a separate primary, an estimate (rounded) was made from tests known to load it.

a personality sphere naturalistically sampling all human behavior. One step in the right direction in Guilford's work, however, is his encompassing of a number of social behaviors—grievously neglected in the prevailing scholastic framework.

Nevertheless, the fact remains that the exploration of "ability space," which has been left largely in the hands of educational psychologists, has been parochial to a degree. General psychology should see that all its domains of research are represented. Guilford's inclusion of social behavior is still only behavior on paper. There remains the whole area of *in situ* (not pencil and paper) social management and adeptness in word and act. Where are all the tasting skills and smelling skills of a good cook or a gourmet? What has happened to the skills of the carpenter, the plumber, the gardener, and the ploughman? Who has investigated and correlated the know-how of the sailor who infers a specific change of weather from the different movement of his bunk and the sound of the wind? How many studies exist of performances with crayon, paint brush, and sculptor's chisel? What is known about prediction of performance in poker, chess, boxing, car-driving, and skiing? How many measures have been taken of performance on committees, on market bargaining, on judging implications from the tone of a voice? How many psychometrists have pursued the naturalistic ability sphere sampling so far as to give scores in courtship and love-making?

In terms of any sort of personality sphere concept, it is indeed easy to see that the convenience of pencil and paper and measurement by groups has virtually ruled out the discovery also of whatever ability structures may be based on sensory input other than by the visual (pencil-and-paper) channel. Auditory skills (recognizing melodies, performing analogies on pitch, classifying forms of noise) require elaborate apparatus, as also does scoring of vocalization, picking up accents in a foreign language, etc. Olfactory skills are neglected almost completely, though they are quite significant, for a good judgment in analyzing a strange odor has saved many a life. Tactile skills—except in connection with studies of Braille, or the point discrimination test of fatigue—have practically never been correlated. Rupert Brooke speaks for more than poets when he recalls the significance of having "touched flowers, and furs, and cheeks." Within the realm of touch and kinesthetic experience there is probably a substantial array of perceptual, reproductive, and motor primary abilities still untouched—as perhaps the blind know best. Incidentally, Newland's test (1962) of relation eduction (intelligence) for the blind is one of the few sustained researches that has thrown a little light into the tactile-kinesthetic area, showing, as our theory of g_f would require, that complex relation perception in this area expresses the same fluid ability factor as in the visual area.

As we penetrate here further into the evidence on the nature of primary, secondary, and even third-order structure as revealed by strategic, factor-analytic experiment, it becomes necessary to point out that the ultimate classification of abilities will be made by no means on stratum-order alone. It will include reference to the various content, process, action phase, etc., parameters in Table 4–1, discussed in Chapter 4. Consequently, the conceptual categories will not be simply those of stratum—even if we could rely—which we cannot—on strata assignments made at this early stage of research. It may help to illustrate this by instancing the capacities associated with local sensory and motor neural endowments, and which we shall define later as "provincial powers" or p's, to distinguish them from central, general, brain capacities, or g's. To complete the series we shall symbolize the typical unitary abilities (but not all) found at the primary factor level as a's.

The point to be made is that with certain choices of primary variables, and with certain deficiencies of present factor analysis, some g's may appear initially as second-order factors and some p's may show themselves in first or third rather than second-stratum factors. The p's or "provincial" neural organization endowments can be illustrated by visualization, which has been written sometimes as g_v, a general capacity. (Actually, up to now, some writers have been inclined to write it as a g_v and some as a_v). Visualization represents a type of ability which applies only over one sensory or one motor domain. These areas typically are first suggested to us by the biological structure and motor perceptual activity of the particular organism, and later (Chapter 8) by physiological evidence of a certain neural localization and unity of action in the brain. Beyond the instances presented by p_v and p_m—visualization activity and general motor coordination—these factors have not yet been clearly, individually revealed by factor analysis, but researchers have noted that they tend to hover between first and second-order positions.

The question of whether they are to be expected consistently to make an appearance at first or second order, operationally, can be set aside for the moment. But from other evidence it is likely that eventually we might expect six or seven p factors, of which visualization and general motor coordination are two. That is to say, this provincial capacity of visualization, brought out most clearly by Horn, has properties that we may expect in some five or six large new "continents" in the world of abilities. When relation-perceiving capacities are measured simultaneously in different sensory areas and brought into a single correlation matrix, there should be an emergence, probably mostly at the second stratum, of factors also for p_a, auditory skills; p_t, tactile judgments; and so on.

These would apply over both storage and simple relation perception in the given sensory area, whereas the more complex relation eduction which we see in g_f and g_c will integrate all these local areas. These powers which affect all "p's" and "a's" we have indexed as "g's", affecting cognitive performance with complete generality. It may happen that p's and g's in present day experiments will emerge at the second stratum, together, but this does not mean that the p's are coordinate with the g's in any "peer" sense. Speed, retrieval, and some others yet dimly seen, may constitute the first emerging members of a whole set of g's, by no means restricted to fluid and crystallized intelligence. Their general character consists in running across all primaries and all p areas of sensory and motor content. As the theory developed in Chapter 4 and 5 suggests, the g's correspond to the dimensions in Table 4–1 governing such general process qualities as speed, output breadth, and so on. Well-planned experiment, breaking into the second and third strata, is necessary to check the nature and relation of these factors.

4. THE NEW PERSPECTIVE
FROM THE THIRD STRATUM

A view from a height is generally rewarding. Would it not be worthwhile to climb to the third stratum in the factor analysis of abilities? Curiosity alone might motivate one to do this, for it never has been done. Moreover, in this case, psychologists nostalgic for the good old days of a single, simple general intelligence factor may urge that if we go one stratum higher we shall find the missing peak of the pyramid—a single general factor subtending both g_f and g_c.

A few years ago any serious exploration at a third-order level would have seemed about as practicable as stratospheric flight in the Wright brothers' biplane. Even today it is an expedition which has to be undertaken with considerable foresight in design. Among the problems needing proper handling are: (1) If one is not to come to a single factor spuriously, merely because of an insufficiently broad foundation to support more, it is certainly necessary to take off from a basis of more than two second-stratum factors, which means, in turn, decidedly more primaries than are generally taken into researches of this kind. (2) As we have seen, if the reference vector is to be rotated reliably to a unique position at this higher level, there must still persist into the second stratum enough hyperplane stuff— enough variables (in this case, second-order factors)—*likely to be uninfluenced by anything common to the whole cognitive field.* In other words, there must be personality or other non-cognitive factors among the second-order factors. This is a long way to "haul," since to get, say, three or more non-cognitive factors at the second stratum requires quite a lot of primaries to start with. Fortunately, the personality area has been explored so well that one can enter with relatively few variables, each reliably hitting on one primary. (3) As one goes to higher orders, the correlations among factors have to be determined increasingly by the simple structure rotation itself, whereas in variables and in primaries (where a good primary battery exists) the correlations can be obtained simply between test scores. It has been shown (Cattell, 1965c) that by the third order these correlations are only rough. The only present means of overcoming this difficulty is to average results of several experiments, which requires extensive and coordinated research.

These principles have been followed attentively if not always completely in the four or five researches yet achieved, the consensus of which however, comes close to adequacy for most conclusions drawn. One principle is to have enough "hyperplane stuff," and this is illustrated in Tables 5–1 and 6–1 where one perceives a string of personality variables at the end which, like a kite tail, performs a different function from that performed by the variables of central interest. Also, as the original research articles will show, extreme care has been given to polishing the simple structure determination by almost unprecedented numbers of fine rotations.

Before actually factoring the correlations among those second-order "general factors," with which we are now familiar in these researches, we

TABLE 6–3
Typical Correlations Found Among Broad Ability Secondaries

(A) *5–6 Year Olds*
   (Cattell, 1967a)

	g_f	g_c	Person. Trait 1	Person. Trait 2
g_f		.32	−.21	−.21
g_c			−.28	−.10
Person. Trait 1				−.15
Person. Trait 2				

(B) *9–12 Year Olds*
   (Cattell, 1967b)

	g_f	g_c	Anxiety
g_f		.42	−.08
g_c			.01
Anxiety			

(C) *277 13–14 Year Olds (Cattell, 1963a)*

	g_f	g_c	Exvia	Anxiety
g_f		.47	.29	.35
g_c			.17	.15
Exvia				.17
Anxiety				

(D) *477 Adults (Horn, 1965)*

	g_f	g_c	g_r	g_s	p_v	Person. Trait (U.I. 19)
g_f		.16	.21	.39	.34	.06
g_c			−.12	.10	.36	.33
g_r				.22	.09	.22
g_s					.37	−.26
p_v						−.02
Person. Trait (U.I. 19)						

The correlation of fluid and crystallized intelligence seems to be highest (.42, .47) in the school years, and lowest (.16) among adults.

can see by a glance at the correlations in Table 6–3, that, except where personality factors are concerned, the correlations are (with one exception) uniformly positive, and particularly large between g_f and g_c.

Nevertheless, the vital question of whether a single general factor at the third order will suffice—as would satisfy a return to a Spearman position —was answered unequivocally in the negative as soon as the results of factorization appeared. In the first place, even where (as in Table 6–3(c) (d)) the personality factors also correlate positively, the verdict is (Table 6–4) that personality tertiaries form distinct factors and do not fit a hierarchy. But—and this is the central point here—the ability factors in two of the four researches also do not come together at the third order, and require a fourth-stratum analysis before they show up on one factor. Moreover, whether they come together at the third or the fourth order this cognitive

TABLE 6–4
Exploring Ability Structure at the Third Stratum

(A) 5–6 Year Olds (114) (Cattell, 1967a)

	$g_{f(h)}$	Educational Effectiveness Factor	Possible Maturity Factor
g_f	.94	-.06	.13
g_c	.41	.38	-.12
Personality Factor X	.10	.89	.03
Personality Factor Y	.01	-.01	.93

(B) 9–12 Year Olds (306) (Cattell, 1967b)

	$g_{f(h)}$	Educational Effectiveness Factor	Possible Maturity Factor
g_f	.70	-.02	.25
g_c	.59	.48	-.06
Anxiety	-.09	.07	-.32
Personality Factor 1	-.41	.00	.05
Personality Factor 2	-.02	.62	.04

(C) 13–14 Year Olds (277) (Cattell, 1963a)

	$g_{f(h)}$	Educational Effectiveness Factor	General Personality Factor — Alpha	— Beta
g_f	.69	.00	.02	-.07
g_c	.63	.32	-.04	.07
Anxiety U.I. 24	-.01	.79	-.51	-.07
Exvia U.I. 32	.18	.23	.01	.00
Cortertia U.I. 22	.09	.32	-.51	-.07
Personality Factor A	.01	-.05	.99	-.03
Personality Factor B	.00	.04	.03	-.74
Personality Factor C	.02	.06	-.69	.08

(D) Adult Criminals (477) (Horn, 1965)

	$g_{f(h)}$	Educational Effectiveness Factor	General Personality Factor — Alpha	— Gamma
g_f	.53	.02	-.08	-.10
g_c	-.04	.73	.20	-.08
g_r	.42	-.21	-.08	-.40
g_s	.60	-.01	.33	.10
p_v	.57	.38	-.13	.18
Person. U.I.	.00	.11	-.32	-.66
Anxiety U.I. 24	-.03	-.41	-.31	.02
Personality Factor A	.00	-.01	.45	-.00
Personality Factor D	.34	.00	.11	.21

The subscript (h) in $g_{f(h)}$ indicates that this is understood as an "historical" g_f, years before this experiment. At these levels we know virtually nothing about the meaning of the personality factors, brought mainly as "hyperplane stuff," and except for U.I. numbers, they are represented by A's, B's, X's, Y's, etc., specific to these matrices. Our concern is with the g_f and g_c and the steadily recurrent $g_{f(h)}$—hypothesized as the "historical" fluid ability, and a somewhat vaguer "education and experience" second factor. The Horn study is of special interest in showing that g_r, g_s, and p_v—two of which are general powers in the cognitive field—seem positively related. It is anomalous, however, in showing no significant loading of g_c on the "historical" g_f. The fact that (d) deals with a criminal, convict group may account for this, suggesting that in this type of population the "historical" (childhood) fluid ability was *not* invested in gaining school knowledge and skills.

Note that with one or two exceptions the personality factors are not given general identifications but are at present kept local to matrices.

factor which covers the two ability factors does *not* give a loading approaching unity on g_c, which would be required if what is central in traditional intelligence tests—Spearman's g and the second-order pattern among Thurstone's primaries—is to be identified with our third or fourth-order factor general to the cognitive field. In fact, in all four researches it loads fluid intelligence, g_f, *more* than g_c—and in general appreciably more so. How is one to explain this tendency of the "historical" g_f (i.e., $g_{f(h)}$) to load g_f more than it does g_c?

5. CAUSAL SEQUENCES AND FACTOR ANALYSIS: THE INVESTMENT THEORY

Naturally there are a variety of theories—some more probable than others—that might explain the particular balance of approximately .80 and .60 of the uppermost stratum, $(g_{f(h)})$ general, cognitive factor upon the second-stratum, fluid and crystallized, general ability factors. But to achieve the most probable we have to reach further into physiological, developmental, and social evidence than the psychometrist usually does. Since this evidence is largely in later chapters, here we shall state the theory—the *investment* theory—which fits the present facts, and leave it to later chapters to show why it fits better than some others. Parenthetically, we shall spend no time here on the finding that sometimes the unification occurs at the third order and sometimes at the fourth. This is relatively unimportant, having to do with the initial breadth of choice of variables, and though it has interesting sidelights, they must be left until later.

The investment theory supposes that in the development of the individual there is initially (perhaps after two or three years of maturational shaping from birth) a single, general, relation-perceiving ability connected with the total, associational, neuron development of the cortex. This general power is applicable to any sensory or motor area and any process of selective retrieval from storage. Because it is not tied to any specific habits or sensory, motor, or memory area, we have called it *fluid* ability, g_f.

In the course of gaining experience, a large number of perceptual discriminatory skills and executive skills are added to the individual's repertoire. His rate of learning in matters requiring little grasp of complex relations will depend on motivation, rote memory, frequency of reward, etc. On the other hand his rate of learning in fields demanding insight into complex relations—and these fields include especially the problems of reading, arithmetic, and abstract reasoning with which he struggles in school—will depend appreciably on his level of fluid intelligence (though motivation, goodness of teaching, etc., will still play their part, as with the acquisitions of low relational complexity). These complex, acquired abilities, in the form of high-level judgmental skills in particular perceptual and motor areas, we are calling "crystallized intelligence," because their expression is tied to a series of particular areas. For example, there is no reason why a nice judgment acquired in perceiving the relationships of some high-level vocabulary items should be able to come into play and help one solve an algebra problem, or why fluid ability crystallized in social diplomacy should help one decide whether the distributor or the plugs are the probable source of some trouble in an automobile. Parenthetically, the old illusion of transfer of training, which kept Latin long in the grammar school, is probably due to the correct observation that a person good at Latin is likely to be good at mathematics, but accompanied by a failure to realize that this is an effect of high fluid ability, not of learning transfer operating in high crystallized ability acquired by training.

Now in all kinds of relation-eduction in new material requiring fluid ability, the child high in one manifestation will be high in another, and from correlations rooted in such observations eventually we obtain the fluid ability factor. But as a result of the fluid ability being *invested* in all kinds of complex learning situations, correlations among these acquired, crystallized abilities will also be large and positive, and tend to yield a general factor. However, the g_f factor will not account for *all* of the correlation in this case, as it does in the non-cultural, overlearned, or new problem-solving, because years at school, interest in school work, and other influences will also determine, perhaps substantially, the level of crystallized abilities.

Measures of the two factors would be expected to correlate positively and appreciably, as we see in Table 6–3 (about 0.3 to 0.4 on an average). For this year's crystallized ability level is a function of last year's fluid ability level—and last year's interest in school work and abstract problems generally. To be exact, it is a cumulative function of several years' operation levels of g_f, but the last year will be most important—in the case of growing children, but not adults—because the fluid ability a year earlier will not have been at a high enough level to account for the summit level of this year's crystallized intelligence.

It will be noted that so far we have tended to take for granted the experimental finding that crystallized intelligence *is* a single power. Yet, what the suggested explanation above offers is primarily an account of how a well-motivated attempt to learn in some complex new area will depend on the individual's level of fluid ability and will result in depositing judgmental skills. This investment of fluid ability in the experimentally-gained, crystallized skills may, as far as we yet know, result in their having a life and durability of their own, in independence of the fluid ability which begot them. The term "crystallized" is meant to imply this freezing in a specific shape of what was once fluid ability. But we have implied another property in this crystallized ability, namely, that the various manifestations of it— the various areas in which it is produced—show a positive correlation of their levels. A person high in one crystallized ability tends to be high in any other, and the person low is also low all-round. For we have asserted that, like fluid ability, it is a broad, *general* factor, and this is the meaning of a general factor.

The seasoned multivariate experimentalist and factor analyst will point out that the unity of the fluid ability factor could account for the common variance in the crystallized ability factor manifestations, but that, unless time or circumstance dislocated the two, they would not clearly result in two distinct factors. Further, through the intrusion of intermediate influences in the specific learnings, the loadings on the crystallized ability, g_c, would not be as high as those found on g_f, if g_f were the only cause. Since they do seem to run *about* equally high in the two factors (if anything, those of g_c are higher), one is inclined to look for some *second, common* influence operating on those manifestations of crystallized ability over and above the common influence of the historically active g_f. Such a common influence is found in the combined result of the form of the school curriculum, and of the social, familial, and personal influences which create interest and time for learning simultaneously in any and all forms of intellectual learning. If we consider first what is probably the most potent of these common influences, the content of the school curriculum, we see that if schools teach mathematics, English essay writing, and social science, and if some people remain in school longer than others, these three disciplines will, when tested over a single adult population, show positive intercorrelations —common variance.

Thus, it is evident that the "insightful, discriminatory," and "adaptive skills" measured in fluid ability and that part of crystallized ability not due to fluid ability show intercorrelations due to different principles in the two cases. In other words, crystallized ability as a whole has additional causes of correlation over the first. This would be expected to make the loadings for g_c higher than for g_f, and since this actually happens—at least at certain ages—it is perhaps not surprising that Spearman's g and the traditional intelligence test have found g_c first and adopted it as their guide to tests, and to conceptions of a general ability factor.

A second question that some factor analysts will ask concerns the interpretation of the third-stratum version of g_f, as an historical $g_{f(h)}$—that which operated in the few years before the experiment. How can a factor be something not here at the present moment, but present back in the individual's history? The question is highly relevant because we are going to argue that the fluid ability factor typically found at the second stratum, and which can be estimated from the individual's present scores on the primary abilities, *is* his *present* fluid intelligence level, but that the single ability appearing at the third (or fourth) stratum and loading both second-stratum g_f and g_c is the fluid ability of yesteryear, which fathered the present fluid ability directly and begot the present crystallized ability out of past experiences. Some special experimental conditions, e.g., factoring a sample containing a fair proportion of persons with recent brain injury, or samples with certain age selections discussed below will be necessary to check on this. Meanwhile, the case for this interpretation can be discussed in terms of the basic meaning of factor analysis.

The notion that factor analysis can be a means of detecting unitary influences not at present operative, but which have operated in the past is apparently revolutionary to some psychologists. But, in fact, it has always been implicit, and sometimes explicit, in the concept of a trait (Cattell, 1946c). A unitary structure may represent some single living influence at the present moment, or it may be a still-operating set of powers representing the creative act of an earlier living entity. Even the pattern of an explosion can be perceived either while the explosion is occurring or from evidence long afterward. Similarly, a doctor can recognize the specific pattern in a living patient of the scarlet or rheumatic fever germ which did its fell work many years before. Or again, the geologist infers from the pattern of the great circular amphitheater which stands out unique and unitary in the Arizona desert the action of a single meteor long ago.

In psychology the personality and ability structures, which we recognize by correlation patterns existing among features of behavior, can represent either a presently existing influence, e.g., a high state of anxiety, or, alternatively, a set of habits which mutually correlate because they were imposed together years ago. For example, if we take a hundred middle-aged adults, some of whom have never skied since they were fifteen, and others never, there assuredly will be a substantial correlation between ability to do a stem turn and to herring-bone up a hill now, low though the abilities and the correlations may now be.

The nature of the present fluid ability factor is relatively straightforward. We may designate it temporarily as a general, relation-perceiving span based on the magnitude of a neurologically efficient cell mass, and appearing as an existing energy in any current behavior. The nature of the factor found as crystallized ability is as yet less specified, and we still have before us the task of explaining how a pattern apparently composite in its origins appears as a single factor. Empirically, we have to recognize that this unitary pattern, long the target of traditional intelligence tests, expresses itself in the school years and for some indefinite time afterwards as a set of high correlations among numerical ability, grammatical sense, size of vocabulary, and other relationally complex and abstract skills trained in the typical school curriculum.

One must not forget that nine-tenths of generalizations and theorizing about intelligence and intelligence tests are based on observations in school, and that beyond the school age there exists a penumbra much filled in by guesswork until recently. The suspicion must be entertained that the role of purely scholastic experience has been overstressed in explaining its origin and in understanding its adult form. As to the latter we must note that after school, as investments of intelligence in different occupational and other skills are added to scholastic skills (e.g., skills in selling, in engineering, in driving buses, in making pies, and in managing small children) the older pattern common to all people who attend school should begin to disperse—or, at least, abrade—and give way to the rise of new kingdoms.

Empirically, this means that the correlations constituting the earlier crystallized ability pattern should begin to be less dependable. Probably the main correlational disturbance arises not so much from the fact that scholastic skills deteriorate (at different rates in different people) as from new investment patterns arising. As to the compositeness of crystallized general intelligence, one must recognize that the positive correlations arise not only from the widespread uniformity of the school curriculum—at least in the three R's—and the fact that different individuals are exposed to it for different numbers of years, but they arise also from dynamic causes, in the form of some children being more strongly interested in all that may be called intellectual matters and school achievement. Examined closely, these influences that are not g_f, and not length of learning in school, are themselves complex. The personality researcher will pry them apart into such demonstrated contributors as affectothymia (A factor), superego strength (G), strength of self-sentiment (Q_3), and so on. Nevertheless, despite these composite origins, it can be shown that in a broad, higher-stratum, factor analysis, it is not unreasonable to expect (as will be discussed in more detail below) that the joint effect (in the middle and late school period) would be a single, broad, crystallized ability factor.

However, these composite origins must be kept in mind when we begin to ask what happens to crystallized general intelligence, and the traditional intelligence tests that measure it, *after* school. The crystallized intelligence factor then goes awry both conceptually and in regard to the practical predictions to be made from traditional intelligence tests. In the twenty years following school, the judgmental skills that one should properly be measuring as the expression of learning by fluid ability must become different for different people. If these are sufficiently varied and lack any common core, the very concept of general intelligence begins to disappear. One can no longer hope to predict from one ability level to that of another or from a test to a criterion. If the coronet of commonly learned abilities falls to pieces, the monarchic intelligence concept vanishes. To be more experimentally exact, it dies hard rather than vanishes, for early imprinting is more powerful than the experience in middle life which generates new general factors for the engineers, the doctors, and the housewives.

But with the decline of the concept, the raison d'être of the traditional intelligence test also declines. The practicing psychologist must recognize, as just seen, that crystallized ability begins after school to extend into Protean forms and that no single investment such as playing bridge or skill in dentistry can be used as a manifestation by which to test all people. His alternatives are then: (a) to sample behavior still more widely than in the traditional test, using a formula expressing the role of fluid intelligence in learning in each of many different fields (an approach which, in practice, might amount to producing as many different tests as there are occupations, etc.); (b) to change completely to fluid intelligence measures, soon to be discussed; or (c) to continue to measure by the "school version" of crystallized ability essentially leaning on what the individual's intelligence was at the time of leaving school. Admittedly, this relic has considerable persistence and one would be seriously misled in such adult-testing by traditional tests only in the case of the child whose schooling was defective, or the adult who has suffered brain injury.

Thus, in the case where traditional intelligence tests are applied to middle-aged adults, the inferences go awry theoretically and practically to the moderate extent that the existing crystallized scholastic intelligence is only a *tolerably* exact relic. For (a) it has been variously eroded by time, and (b) it deputizes for a fluid ability that was in existence thirty years before, not for the present fluid ability. Two projections are involved, in both of which we do not know enough about the projection formula to be accurate: the first from the present crystallized ability score backwards to that of thirty years ago, and the second from the inferred fluid ability forward to the fluid ability today through mischances of life as they concern brain damage.

A very different problem in defining crystallized ability exactly is that of its basic compositeness, which the sophisticated factor analyst will soon pose. If the unity of crystallized ability—in the late school period when the correlations of verbal, mathematical, spatial, etc., judgments are most adequate and satisfactory—is really due to (at least) two sources, namely, common fluid ability level and common degrees of learning experience in a common curriculum, why should this appear as a *single* factor? Surely it is strictly only a surface trait or correlation cluster produced by the combined action of an inherent individual ability pattern, g_f, and a pattern of education, which we will call S_e (to indicate it is a mold in the *situation,* not originally in the person).

Figure 6–2 says in geometrical terms that the present g_c projects initially on two axes ($g_{f(h)}$ and S_e), much of its variance being accounted for by variance on these. It is saying just the same thing as the numerical data in A–D in Table 6–4, namely, that the "historical" $g_{f(h)}$, (the subscript (h) indicating the individual's level of fluid ability in the preceding years), operates, along with educational experience in school and home and some third influence from personality (in Table 6–4, (a) and (b) called immaturity), in combination to produce the present level of g_c. If we take the second rows in (a), (b), and (c) in Table 6–4 and average them, we get, in fact, $+.55$, $+.37$, and $-.07$ as the loading contributions respectively of fluid intelligence, education, and some personality influence in the production of crystallized intelligence. Incidentally, for the moment we are "splitting no hairs" over the meaning of these other factors and simply accepting them for the time being as some broad influences of education and personality. On intensive examination the former may prove to split into contributions from time at school, interest, and motivation, and even general goodness of rote memory (outside intelligence), but at a broad analysis we shall simply call it "exposure to education".

FIGURE 6–2
The Interaction of Fluid Ability, Time, Curriculum Pressure,
and Rote Learning Ability

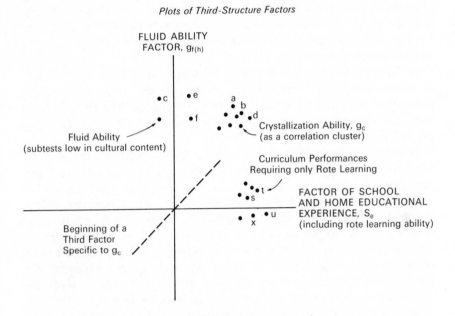

Plots of Third-Structure Factors

The same interactive relationship is set out more completely in different form in Figure 6–3 which appears on page 129 and also in Figure 11–1, on page 309, in connection with another aspect of ability structure discussed in Chapter 11.

The fact that the loadings, and therefore presumably the causal influences, act in this manner will be discussed further as we proceed. But to anyone familiar with the concepts of *surface* and *source* traits, an initial potential contradiction has to be clarified in Figure 6–2. It is that g_c appears here as a surface trait—a correlation cluster of variables brought close together by having simultaneously substantial loadings on $g_{f(h)}$ and S_e. Yet in most contexts it has itself been regarded as an independent factor —a source trait on its own. This we have attempted to indicate in Figure 6–2 by introducing a third axis as an interrupted line, suggesting that some new dimensions specific to g_c arise. It might be that simple addition of $g_{f(h)}$ and S_e are not enough to account for the variance in g_c, but that some interaction occurs, indicating need of a specific dimension. On the other hand, if g_c were represented here as a single variable, not a cluster, the situation would be in accord with what we usually recognize in factor-order (strata) relations, namely, that what is a *factor* at a lower order is a dependent variable at a higher order. The issue is a subtle one and must be discussed further in the next section.

6. PROBLEMS OF AUTONOMY AND PROTEAN INCONSTANCY OF g_c

By now the reader hopefully will see more insightfully the appropriateness of calling this theory, which recognizes the fact of a g_c and g_f duality, the investment theory. It says that g_c arises and has its particular form as a result of investing a general capacity, $g_{f(h)}$, in suitable learning experience.

In the growing-up period at school, an added coherence and unitariness of pattern are given to the learning product by the form of the school curriculum itself and by what the culture (operating through the family and other institutions outside the school) considers it desirable for young people to learn.

However, in connecting the pattern of loaded performances that we have obtained empirically with that which might be expected from this theory, the discerning reader will object that "the things which society believes a properly socialized person should learn," will include many things besides those which are aided conspicuously by g_f. It will include good manners, moral inhibitions, athletic proficiency, and much rote learning. Thus, whereas performances a, b, c, d, e, and f might be the complex kinds of things that are learned more easily with high g_f, the somewhat different set of variables a, b, d, s, t, u, and x might be those which the school and society actually concentrate on teaching. And, if this is the case, would not the factor of crystallized ability include many "routines" in the school molding process that are due merely to rote learning and imitation?

Figure 6–2, which portrays the essential nature of this conjunction of two very different kinds of influence, certainly demonstrates that this could happen. Many rote-learned skills such as variable t could be far out on factor S_e and have no projection much above zero on g_f. However, the probability of the truth of the subsidiary theory of coincidence of high loadings, necessary to the investment theory, is increased by the saving consideration that teachers or "pedagogues" sometimes also are called "pedants". That is to say, they are strongly prejudiced in favor of "intellectual" education. In spite of the pressure of "progressives" to stay with finger paintings, eurythmics, languages, learning without grammatical analysis, and subjects attractively free of hard demands for mental discipline, enough schools continue to follow a scholastic intuition that education should be concerned with subjects that severely exercise intelligence. That intuition leads to putting much emphasis on the abstract subjects—mathematics, expression in language—which lie at the heart of many areas of application. Even in rural areas schools do not teach plowing, though they may teach the physics and chemistry which make comprehensible the motor plow or the use of fertilizers.

In short, it is really no accident that institutions of learning concentrate on intelligence-demanding subjects significantly more than do the extra-scholastic sources of various more desultory kinds of learning in our lives.

Therefore, although we should expect in Figure 6–2 that some things, e.g., card games, skill in courtship, might load on fluid ability but not schooling, as at c and e, and that various rote learnings would load schooling but not intelligence, as at t and u, a definite concentration would be expected high up in the north-east quadrant through the many performances, e.g., a, b, and d in the figure—familiar to us in the performances affected by crystallized intelligence—which conspicuously load both.

With this background let us turn again to the paradox encountered above that g_c looks at one level like a surface trait, yet operates at the next lower level as a factor in its own right. A surface trait is normally a bunch of strongly intercorrelating variables produced by overlap of the substantial effects (of the same sign) of two or more factors on those variables. What we have here, however, is a *surface trait* (or possibly just the measures, as in a traditional intelligence test of the factor g_c) *at a higher stratum*. Such a variable has the compositeness of a surface trait at the upper stratum, but by definition and mode of appearing there it must be a factor at the lower level, i.e., at the second stratum.

Now we have taken the scientific (not just statistical) model that a factor is an influence. How can this composite thing have the status of an influence itself?[1] Does it, indeed, have the status of an influence? The answer to the latter is "Yes," because at the second order it leaves a hyperplane, as clearly as a powerful tide leaves a fringe of seaweed at high-water mark, or as the movement of a ship is proven to the air pilot by the visible V of its bow and stern waves.

What the nature of the emphatic autonomy is that arises in this offspring of fluid intelligence and learning experience is a question to which more space needs to be given—and fuller further discussion is given in Chapters 11 and 12. The student will note that a somewhat related idea in the personality field was stated by Allport's "functional autonomy," though this was only a name without an explanation. Nevertheless, observations of similar action elsewhere help support the invocation here of the notion that this created cluster or surface trait in some manner begins to operate psychologically as an independent influence. The statistical evidence of (a) development of an extra dimension, and (b) the appearance of a hyperplane, clearly indicate that it has gained powers of self-perpetuation as a single entity, and that it enters with other influences into various primary ability growths and a wide range of problem-solving performances. Some kind of dynamic interest qualities perhaps suffice to give it a life of its own. At any rate, in the history of the individual it will be seen later that fluid intelligence and this new investment product pull apart and follow different curves of growth and decline.

---

[1] One is reminded of the poetess's would-be disdain of the lover who has captivated her:

> "What is this thing, that built of salt and lime
> And such dry motes as in the sunbeam shine
> Has power upon me. . . ?"

In spite of this autonomy, and the characteristically high intercorrelation of the kind of abstract and largely scholastic performances which go into the traditional intelligence test and which make this factor g_c hard to miss in even the crudest factor analysis, the factor really has a precarious existence. Cultural change, shift of mixture of areas intellectually fashionable, or a change in the school curriculum can weaken its identity and unity as a discernible factor, even in the teenage school period when it is most prominent. This decline in a clear-cut, self-conscious, cognitive unity might also upset its dynamic unity and autonomy. Indeed, in correlational studies after the school period, in middle life, it would be hard to find if we took the various occupational skills developed since school days as the basis of correlations. As far as we yet know the only safe way—in the crystallized ability test realm—to compare intelligences of forty-year-olds is to go back, like a nostalgic alumnus, to the experiences of school days. And these will deceive us to the extent that they have undergone different degrees of fading and rehabilitation in different lives. Finally, when we step out and design tests across cultures, to the extent that we give verbal analogies in English, classification in Urdu, and synonyms in Swahili, to a hundred school children from different cultures, we are bound to find that the crystallized intelligence factor has vanished into thin air.

The most important thing to remember about the g_c factor on which the traditional intelligence test leans for its validity is that despite a brief uniformity in the school period of any culture, it really has a Protean character. Its shape is forever changing with the social class, age level, subculture, occupational group, nation, and historical era. It happens that in a stable, well-organized, well-knit culture with a powerful school system the pattern is common enough in form and sufficiently varied in strength of impress to generate a broad factor having impressive predictive power from one ability to another, e.g., from a set of six subtests to a criterion ability. But it is a treacherous thing for any one but a sophisticated psychometrist to handle.

A third and last issue of primary importance in understanding the investment theory is provoked by looking at the third-order analysis (or the fourth in some studies) shown in Table 6–4. Our theory is that the highest, broad, cognitive factor in problem-solving and relation-perception (not the highest in other cognitive areas, e.g., speed, retrieval), standing alone at the third order, is the individual's "historical", $g_{f(h)}$, level of fluid ability at the time when it was invested in learning to produce his present level of crystallized ability. We have given reasons above, e.g., from geology and other sciences, for believing that a factor can in general represent either a present entity or an historical entity. In this case, at the third order, it appears as the father of the second-order crystallized ability, out of Learning, and also the father of the present, second order, g_f, out of Time.

If $g_{f(h)}$ is separated from g_f by time only, it may be objected that we should expect it to correlate with (to load, actually) g_f decidedly more than g_c. For into the variance of the latter enters also a contribution from a quite variable learning experience. However, it can be argued (1) that the life course of fluid ability need not run smoothly, for physiological events intervene, and (2) that we have been unspecific, almost to the point of prevarication, about how far back $g_{f(h)}$ in our third stratum is supposed to go. The only logical definition of it is that it represents the g_f level over the crucial formative years of the g_c actually measured in the experiment. The crucial years in the growing child will be the most recent. This hypothesis brings mathematical subtleties. For example, if our subjects are fifteen-year-old children, $g_{f(h)}$ will have been at a different (though steadily increasing) level for all the preceding years, and the g_c level would be expected to be an integral of fluid intelligence and learning over the curve of growth.

This is set out in formula (6.1) which simply says that during each year of age $g_{f(h)}$, the acting fluid ability level at the time, and S_e, the form of the educational influence at the time, interact to deposit so much g_c, crystallized ability. The g_c level at any given year is the summation of these products up to that time, thus:

$$g_{c_a} = \int_o^a (g_{f(h)} \cdot S_e) \, dt \ \text{ or } \ \int_o^a (g_{f(h)} + S_e) \, dt \qquad \textbf{(6.1)}$$

where a is the t value—the age—at the time. This could be carried further by including expressions for the individual growth or change curves of $g_{f(h)}$ and S_e, and by specifying more precisely their mode of interaction. The curve for $g_{f(h)}$ over the growth years might be roughly parabolic ($g = t^{1/2}$) or have the form $g = x(1 - e^{rt})$ while S_e would be irregular or perhaps a gently rising, straight line. The mode of interaction one might be inclined, psychologically, to set down as a product, but at least in the factor-analytic framework, and, therefore, in regard to the loadings of $g_{f(h)}$ and S_e as now obtained (Table 6–4), we would treat it as a sum. If further analysis shows interaction to exist (in the statistical sense) some formula may need to be adopted, having both summation and product terms, but the further working out of (6.1) derivatives obviously will be much easier if we accept summation as a sufficiently close appproximation.

From anticipations of the growth curves, and from factor-analytic considerations, one can see that the loadings of $g_{f(h)}$ on g_f and g_c, respectively, should be very different for factorings of a group of ten-year-olds and of a group of fifty-year-olds. In the former, fluid intelligence is rising so rapidly that it treads closely on the heels of g_c. That is to say, a child has no sooner acquired judgmental, discriminatory skills, e.g., in mathematics, representing the limit of action of his g_f, at, say, nine years, than they are submerged beneath more sophisticated skills, the learning of which has been made possible by his rising g_f in the next year. In these circumstances of a rising g_f level and a steady, appropriately adjusted sequence of learning we should expect a very high correlation of $g_{f(h)}$ with g_c, of $g_{f(h)}$ with g_f, and of g_f with g_c. (A practical consequence is that culture-fair and traditional intelligence tests would give pretty similar results, just so long as we keep to school children in the same culture.)

On the other hand, with fifty-year-olds, the g_c, if measured by the usual intelligence test, which harks back to what most of the subjects knew when they left school, will have its highest correlation with g_f of thirty years ago, and the $g_{f(h)}$ which comes from factoring such data to the third stratum would be the $g_{f(h)}$ of the high-school period. The *present* g_f could well be something very different indeed, and the correlations of $g_{f(h)}$ with the present g_f at the second stratum would be expected to be positive but low. The investment theory thus warns that even when we recognize distinct g_f and g_c factors, their nature and value, and meaning in prediction need to be watched constantly. The matters to be watched and the allowances to be made will become more fully evident in the next chapters dealing with natural history, age changes, and physiological and social influences.

The issues in this section are subtle ones, as we were forewarned by the term "inconstancy of g_c" in its title. Perhaps "elusiveness" would have been better than "inconstancy". For it is not that a single thing is inconstant in its level. Rather the situation is that it changes its very nature with culture and age, and, like a much-modified, old house, may straggle even into essentially separate sub-dwellings. A basic issue in g_c which, despite its fundamental nature, we have thought best to leave to the extensive discussion possible in the nature-nurture analysis of Chapter 10, concerns the question of whether the investment theory implies that investment of g_f in one g_c area means less investment in another. If a child is pushed to invest in scholastic areas is he likely to be poorer in the social skill areas of g_c; and, if the modern farm boy learns more about calculus will his discriminations be poorer regarding the weather and the song of birds? Granted we accept the undoubted limitation of total interest and hours in a day, the conclusion must be drawn that growth of g_c in one dimension to some degree (yet to be worked out) means lack of development in another. The ignoring of observations of this kind is back of most claims to have "raised the I.Q." by measuring g_c in the area of training only.

With the aid of Figure 6–3 let us now summarize and separate the important final conclusions from the somewhat complex facts and inferences of second and third-order factorizations on which they depended. The investment theory of g_f and g_c is that fluid intelligence in the growing period invests itself in the learning of judgmental skills, particularly in the more abstract features of the school curriculum. The level reached in school achievement is a function both of g_f and a bunch of opportunity, motivation, and memory factors, which, at first, tend to appear as a single S_e factor. However, the crystallized intelligence skills in which g_f is especially invested pull apart from the rest of the school and life-acquired skills which depend more on rote memory largely because they have *use as tools in solving a wide array of problems.* By self-conscious awareness of this kind of ability, and its constant use in the school type of performance, later it may itself acquire unity as an influence and show itself in factor analysis very soon as an independent factor in abilities. These factorial and causal relations are finally summarized in Figure 6–3.

FIGURE 6–3
Hypothesized Causal Action in the Investment Theory

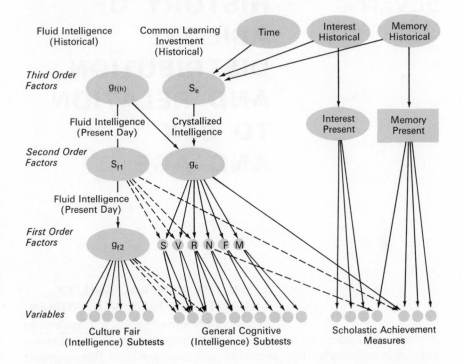

Culture Fair
(Intelligence) Subtests

General Cognitive
(Intelligence) Subtests

Scholastic Achievement
Measures

Nevertheless, although g_c is a very useful entity in prediction of school performances and tends throughout the school years to be highly correlated with g_f, it is not an entirely satisfactory psychological measurement concept. For the pattern of unity will tend to be somewhat different in different schools and curricula (and certaintly in different cultures). And, according to the investment theory, we would expect that the relation of g_c to g_f would be better to the g_f a year or more earlier (that is, to $g_{f(h)}$) than to the present g_f. Indeed, beyond the school years the correlation of present g_f and present g_c may become relatively poor.

CHAPTER SEVEN

THE NATURAL HISTORY OF ABILITY: DISTRIBUTION AND RELATION TO SEX AND AGE

1. ON THE GENERAL ABILITY EQUALITY OF MEN AND WOMEN

Progress in behavioral science is made most elegantly when the researcher begins with establishing definite structures—and the accompanying recognition of new concepts—and then proceeds strategically to ask:

(a) What are the age curves and population distributions with respect to these structures?

(b) How can the structures have developed through genetic and environmental influences? and

(c) What are the physiological associations (when the genetic determination is high)? and what are the learning and molding social institution associations (when environment has been shown to predominate)?

Our purpose in this chapter is to sketch in (a), above,—"the natural history"—though it must remain a picture with several obscure patches in it. Such incompleteness exists for the simple reason that the triadic theory is too new for answers to have appeared to the questions which it provokes. Obtaining samples of sufficient size to define age and cultural trends is in any case a massive undertaking which, together with subsequent analysis, could take a task force of psychologists the better part of twenty years. Thus it is inevitable that this generation's knowledge of distribution should be restricted in some degree to last generation's conceptions of structure. Nevertheless some strenuous and well-directed research by Horn (1967), Knapp (1963), McArthur and Elley (1963), Marquart and Bailey (1955), Rodd (1958) and others has given us glimpses of distributions, etc., in more modern terms. For example, it has filled in (in a preliminary way) the most needed knowledge about the population distribution and age changes of fluid ability and the relations to crystallized intelligence.

But about the other generalized "powers" as we may call them, such as speed, g_s, retrieval, g_r, memorizing, g_m, visualization, p_v, motor powers, p_m, etc., we know next to nothing. We also know precious little, indeed, about the primary abilities or *agencies* (as we shall later designate them), a_v, a_n, a_s, etc. Perhaps student readers may experience some compensation for this unsatisfactory incompleteness of the present chapter in finding that the natural history topic provides some relief—in the form of simple statements —from the technical complexities of the last two chapters!

Throughout history it has seldom been contested that the summit of mature intellectual judgment in almost all fields—literature, science, art, musical composition, and statemanship—is possessed mainly by the group of males old enough to be mature and experienced but not so antique as to risk the charge of senility. From this summit, however, the middle-aged man has seemingly been demoted recently by the discoveries which psychologists have made about abilities. On the one hand it is found that the peak of fluid ability indubitably comes much earlier than middle age, and on the other, it is now shown that there.is no apparent basis for men rather than women claiming this mature intellectual leadership. (It has become indeed "a time to try men's souls"—in more senses than one.)

As to the equality of women, it is now demonstrated by countless and large sample researches that on the two main general cognitive capacities— fluid and crystallized intelligence—men and women, boys and girls show no significant differences—at any rate, none sustained over all ages and cultures. Refined analyses at particular age levels may show slight differences, e.g., the tendency of girls to mature a little earlier in crystallized intelligence, and of women in some cultural groups not to grow in crystallized intelligence during middle age to the same extent as men. But the finding which most squarely meets our eye is the *equality*—when race and culture are equated.

How is this to be reconciled with literary insights about the special qualities of the feminine mind, or the stubborn conviction of the man- (and woman) in-the-street that men are, say, more able mechanically and women more competent verbally and perhaps in perception of emotional relationships? These folkloric observations are reconciled readily enough when we turn from the broad field of general intelligence to the primary abilities and special performances, as shown in Table 7–1.

In such primaries as spatial thinking, and still more in mechanical aptitude, there can be no question that men are substantially better—to a degree such that perhaps only a quarter of women exceed the male average or median. The writer recalls a difficult situation in World War II when women commissioned officers in the Air Force were to be measured on the same battery as men—in the name of equality of opportunity. Since the

TABLE 7–1

Age Trends and Sex Differences on Primary Mental Abilities

Clark, 1944:

Primary Mental Abilities Scale	Age 11 (N = 126)		Age 13 (N = 117)		Age 15 (N = 103)	
	$\overline{X}$	σ	$\overline{X}$	σ	$\overline{X}$	σ
Numbers	85.57	33.20	103.04	30.44	127.85	36.29
Verbal Meaning	51.66	22.57	69.94	24.20	87.83	23.55
Space	41.80	31.36	59.35	31.48	83.35	37.02
Word Fluency	41.68	14.65	58.73	16.29	69.24	20.04
Reasoning	31.48	14.66	45.65	17.38	54.99	17.71

Reprinted with permission of the author from M.P. Clark,"Changes in Primary Mental Abilities with Age," *Archives of Psychology*, 1944, 291.

Hobson, 1947:

Primary Mental Abilities Scale	9th Graders (Approx. 15 yrs.) Males (N = 222)		Females (N = 250)		Diff. $\overline{X}$	Diff. σ	C.R.
	$\overline{X}$	σ	$\overline{X}$	σ			
Numbers	126.71	34.38	129.32	31.57	−2.6	3.06	−0.85
Verbal Meaning	89.43	20.09	91.38	17.32	−1.95	1.77	−1.10
Space	83.38	30.62	68.97	30.34	14.41	2.79	5.16
Word Fluency	68.41	16.62	75.17	17.56	−6.76	1.56	−4.33
Reasoning	53.94	14.58	61.72	15.00	−7.78	1.36	−5.72

Reprinted with permission of the author and publisher from J.R. Hobson, "Sex Differences in Primary Mental Abilities," *Journal of Educational Research*, 1947, 41, 126-132.

Herzberg and Lepkin, 1954:

Primary Mental Abilities Scale	Age 16 $\overline{X}$ Males (N = 76)	$\overline{X}$ Females (N = 113)	t	Age 18 $\overline{X}$ Males (N = 101)	$\overline{X}$ Females (N = 54)	t
Numbers	23.91	24.34	—	23.95	22.83	0.72
Verbal Meaning	34.42	35.75	1.22	29.82	32.09	1.68
Space	28.09	23.85	2.83[1]	25.62	20.41	2.63[1]
Word Fluency	46.16	44.88	2.19[2]	43.40	48.22	2.56[2]
Reasoning	18.01	19.71	1.96	15.71	16.00	—

[1] Significant at 1% level of confidence.
[2] Significant at 5% level of confidence.

Reproduced with permission from F. Herzberg and M. Lepkin, "A Study of Sex Differences in the PMA Test, *Educational and Psychological Measurement*, 1954, 14, 687.

women candidates persistently fell almost a standard deviation below the men on mechanical aptitude, and policy dictated no discrimination, a solution of a kind was found by adding a constant to bring men and women to the same average before evaluating the individual case. (Similar suggestions have been made for other bio-social groups, e.g., racio-cultural groups.) Incidentally, not only is spatial ability at a higher level in boys, but, according to Werdelin (1959) two distinct space factor "primaries" appear in boys but only one in girls. This investigator found in Swedish samples that girls were superior in both verbal and numerical performances, and boys in reasoning as well as space.

Of course, as Table 7–1 shows, the balance is redressed in other areas. Girls at all ages tend to do better than boys in the verbal area and in fluency, as was noticed (not in terms of precise factors of course) long ago in Havelock Ellis's classical study of *Man and Woman* (1894). Girls start talking earlier than boys and are popularly believed to keep the lead all their lives. ("Never argue with your wife: it is only one word of yours against hundreds of hers.") In the field of school attainment girls tend to outclass boys in English, spelling, and the vocabulary and amount written in essays. Boys tend to lead in science, and to some degree in mathematics, though in the sheer numerical speed and accuracy of a_n, the numerical ability factor, girls usually lead.

In the next section we shall examine evidence in more detail, but, although voluminous, it is not always conclusive. Such conditions as whether the schools are coeducational or not, or what skills are tied to prospects of future occupations, or what the masculine and feminine images mean in different cultures, cannot be kept constant across all experiments. In Moscow one may see woman working as street laborers, raking tar gravel, and driving rollers. They are also skippers of ships and constitute more than half of all practicing doctors. Obviously, interest and experience do much, e.g., might account for the boys' greater performance in mathematics and girls' greater numerical skill. Separating whatever may be biological is, as usual, a second step, and for a beginning we must be simply descriptive.

2. ON THE MORE SPECIFIC ABILITY DIFFERENCES AND THEIR SUBTLE PERSONALITY ASSOCIATIONS

Some of the best work on ability differences in the sexes was done in the thirties and forties when the primary abilities were already beginning to be recognized reliably. Garrett, Bryan, and Perl (1935) found girls better in memory tests and speed tests at nine, twelve, and fifteen, and boys beginning to lead in mathematical ability by fifteen years. Schiller (1933–34) found girls better in reading, sentence completion, and arithmetic computation; boys in number series, performance tests, and arithmetic reasoning, but *not* reliably so in spatial ability. (This last is an aberrant result.) Concentrating on the mathematical ability question Blackwell (1940) brought out an extra factor of "care and exactness" in girls. One cannot view this and other evidence of better computing, cancellation, etc., in girls with better problem-solving mathematics in boys without suspecting that a personality factor—the greater dominance of boys and docility of girls—is here projecting its effects into the ability field.

Recent work (e.g., Very, 1967) confirms that there are not only significant differences of level, but also systematic differences of ability structure, in that most factors have some difference of loading pattern and some have large differences of variance. Until researches concentrate on factor-analytic technical thoroughness, especially in rotation, it is difficult to distinguish, however, between differences that are experimental error and genuine, significant differences.

Recent studies on primary abilities continue to verify, at a descriptive level, what is given above and in Table 7–1. Hobson (1947) found girls leading on W, R, and M (g_r, a_r, and g_m in our triadic indexing below), and boys decidedly on spatial ability, a_s. Meyer and Bendig (1961), at grades 8 and 11 found girls higher on V, R, N, and W (a_v, a_r, a_n, and g_r, in our later indexing) the R result being somewhat indefinite, but boys higher on spatial ability, a_s, though not at good significance. Some of the differing emphases in various researches appear due to the groups not being balanced on total ability, which tends to load verbal more than some other primaries. Thus Meyer and Bendig found girls leading in what would here be called total crystallized intelligence by seventeen years of age, which agrees with their usual and probably personality-based spurt in achievement at that age period, for we have shown evidence elsewhere that crystallized intelligence test measures are contaminated with achievement.

An extensive research by Herzberg and Lepkin (1954) (see Table 7–1) found that at sixteen to eighteen years girls led on word fluency, verbal comprehension, and reasoning, and boys on spatial ability, while numerical ability showed no difference. In other countries of the same cultural development as our own (see W. O. Horn, 1960; Vandenberg, 1962), approximately the same general differences are seen: girls score higher on verbal comprehension, a_v, fluency, g_r, and memory, g_m, and boys on spatial, a_s, and inductive reasoning, with general reasoning, numerical ability, and perceptual speed going to one side or the other with age and culture.

Turning from actually *measured* achievement one can see these childhood and adolescent primary ability profile differences persisting in cultural achievement. But there is something more, for the disproportions in areas of adult performance are far greater than the differences of means would suggest. Why is it that leading women scientists, engineers, and musical composers are uncommon, but leading women novelists and poetesses are widely recognized? Since cultural restrictions and traditional clichés about women's capacities have played a role in influencing final opportunity and performance, the historical cultural count of performance cannot be taken at its face value. Yet in the areas where one would expect *life* differences from the nature of the actual ability *test* results they certainly appear consistently. In this matter of indirect, personality influences on the final ability performance our discussion impinges on the question of creativity and is best postponed to the more thorough treatment of creativity in Chapter 13. But the personality qualities of greater conformity and docility in girls, which partly account for their noticeably better general school examination performance (and especially scores in montonous repetitive tasks) despite essentially equal intelligence, probably account also for their lower cultural creativity in later life, where the boys' independence favors originality.

A proper understanding of sex differences in ability needs to be interpretive as well as descriptive. And the interpretation must systematically consider (1) maturational differences, genetically determined in neurology and hormone balances, and (2) culturally produced differences through training for specified roles and ego ideals, and (3) systematic differences in opportunity. Since description should come first, let us summarize all the above at the data level by indicating that boys tend to excel in spatial and mechanical ability, in performance tests, in problem-solving creativity, and in achievement in science and mathematical fields. Girls excel in the verbal primary, in fluency, in numerical ability (distinguished from math as speed and accuracy in the basic operations), in memory and in speed, care, and exactness in most repetitive areas. They also excel in achievement in reading, and in a fairly wide array of school performances such as history and literature. As to reasoning ability, the results are conflicting and might be interpreted as a slight superiority of girls in the deductive and of boys in the inductive field. The majority of these differences hold across most ages and several national cultures. The mean differences are, however, rather small compared to individual differences. As pointed out in the last chapter, the area of primary abilities has so far by no means been mapped completely. One suspects that women might show superiority in certain socio-emotional skill areas and in esthetic sensitivities which have not yet been included in pencil-and-paper ability explorations. But the full story of the ability peculiarities of men and women is in any case more subtle than a simple primary profile difference: it requires attention also to interactions with personality and to changes over the age developmental period.

Regarding the maturational interpretation of the latter, there can be little doubt that girls are set by a different inner clock of maturation causing them, for example, to be ahead in mental—as in physical—development in early adolescence but relatively slower in later adolescence. And the cultural situation also intrudes. For example, being taught (in America) largely by women in the first two years, and by men and women later, with all the implicit projection of sex standards which this involves, does something (as Grams, Hafner, and Quast (1965) have attempted to show) to the early school adjustment of boys, and to girls in their experience of moving from a more to a less congenial atmosphere. (Bruner (1957) stresses the "importance" of boys receiving at an early age a continuing maternal warmth; but this is a matter of values.) In Western culture, as indicated above, there arises a twist, as it were, in the crystallized general ability, g_c, so that girls do better in verbal and probably social skills and men in mechanical. Incidentally, this has been shown on a large scale (nearly 4000 fourth and eighth graders) by Parsley (1964) who reports girls significantly better than boys of the same age on reading vocabulary and reading comprehension, but boys better on arithmetical reasoning. Brown and Bryan (1957) have reviewed the general evidence on sex differences in school intellectual performance and conclude that these are real enough in the particular areas we have discussed.

Butcher (1969) makes a beginning in analyzing the relative importance of environment and cultural role by pointing out that reading disability in boys is more common than in girls in America, where women teachers predominate at the earlier ages, but not in Japan, where half the primary teachers are male. The matter might also be examined by (1) comparing one-sex and coeducational schools, (2) relating ability differences to the "approved" role differences across cultures (though this *could* be two-way causation), and (3) relating the differences to differences in the degrees of inheritance found for the abilities. In co-educational schools it is hard to see any experiential difference sufficient to account for the superiority of girls in reading and vocabulary. As to the third approach above—that of examination of the nature-nurture evidence—Chapter 10 suggests a heavy genetic component to those abilities which are concerned in the sex differences. (And except in obviously sociological role-determined effects, most psychologists naturally incline to a genetic explanation of sex differences.) But on the crystallized abilities that evidence is relatively ambiguous, and at least the genetic determination is not so preponderant that we must assume the superiority of women in V and of men in Mk to be genetic. Incidentally, these differences create an awkward practical problem in the construction of crystallized general intelligence tests. As in different cultural groups, so here we ought to give somewhat different weights to the subtests in the two groups. This is increasingly important at middle age, when the search for a "Common denominator" or experiential areas for such disparate groups as businessmen and housewives becomes difficult.

One must also bear in mind the possibility that though the genetic difference may not be in the abilities themselves, it may lie in personality and temperament factors which in turn affect the development of abilities. For example, since the E factor of dominance (Cattell, 1957a) is substantially genetic, and has also a similar sex difference in most mammals, we may be reasonably sure that the greater submissiveness of females, which makes for an efficient docility in learning, is largely genetic. It is noticeable above that the acquired abilities significantly higher in girls—reading, verbal acquisition, numerical skill, and "crystallized ability" generally—are those concentrated upon in early schooling. They illustrate the way in which a temperamental difference develops, in a certain learning situation, into an ability difference. In this connection it is interesting to notice that

Boyne and Clark (1959), comparing boys' and girls' scores over twenty years on the Moray House Intelligence Tests, found that the scores of girls at 11+ increased more than boys. This again suggests, though it does not prove, an environmental effect connected with pupil role and motivation—if we assume that these are taken with greater seriousness and acceptance by girls than boys in the early adolescent period. Honzik (1963) even believes that a sex difference can be shown in the age at which both the level and the form of the child's intelligence (in the traditional crystallized intelligence test) begin to show higher correlation with those of the parents. Since in adults the years of schooling correlate with ability about 0.2 to 0.25, and with crystallized ability about 0.3 to 0.40, we are accustomed to a certain complexly determined correlation between intelligence of child and years of schooling of parent. Honzik found that this appears at three years in girls but not until five in boys. Several explanations are possible, but one is, again, that girls respond more quickly, in crystallized intelligence performances, to the cultural emphasis.

A priori, unless the natural selection of the hunting field and the domestic cave, respectively, over half a million years have been far more powerful than we imagine, one would expect the undoubtedly great biologically rooted differences between men and women to be likely to express themselves more in temperament and motivation endowments than in abilities. For the latter are the servants of *all* motivations. When the French cry, "Vive la différence," we must assume they are not thinking of intellectual abilities. Admittedly, culture could, a priori, be expected to be a powerful originator of differences in skills. But the question—of how malleable feminine abilities may be—which has received serious scientific attention since Havelock Ellis's *Man and Woman,* and has excited thoughtful comment by eminent writers such as Bertrand Russell, remains of great social importance. If equality of the sexes is to be aimed at in a progressive world, the question of the origins of the present differences deserves whatever small light we can throw on it now.

In the middle-age range there is data—admittedly not yet on sufficient samples—showing that, although the decline on g_f is no different for men and women, the latter tend to fall behind in the forties on measures of crystallized intelligence. Women who are not exposed to business and professional stimulation might well be expected to advance less in g_c. But, as the last chapter's reference to the Protean character of g_c makes clear, these results depend on the *investment area* in which we choose to measure crystallized ability. Certainly there must be areas of abstract skills in housework and managing children which can grow as a function of the amount of g_f invested, and to which the housewife's g_c can be referred more correctly for measurement, rather than to the defunct, standard, scholastic g_c area. On this basis the apparent lower scores of middle-aged women in traditional crystallized intelligence tests would mean nothing except that the psychologist has made a poor choice of test, or the woman a poor choice of area of intelligent self-expression.

But the most subtle and important differences of males and females on ability almost certainly lie, as suggested, more in the field of personality differences *projected* into ability expression than in the true abilities *per se.* An intriguing collection of evidence in this direction has been put forward recently by Broverman and his colleagues (1968) in connection with observations comparable to those in Table 7–1 (above) that females do better in speeded perceptual and motor tasks. What they show to a personality theorist is that perceptual and motor speediness, such as is regularly expressed in the personality factor U.I. 22 *Cortertia,* are regularly higher for women, whereas males do better in more inhibited, "second-thoughted," penetrating decisions typically instanced in U.I. 19, the *Independence* personality factor, which is significantly higher for men. These investigators proceed further to relate this behavioral difference to differences in the balance of *adrenergic,* activating hormones (which we recognize as active in the state dimensions P.U.I.1, Activation, and P.U.I.5, Adrenergic Response (Cattell, 1957a)), on the one hand, and *cholinergic* hormones with inhibitory actions, on the other hand. In support of this hormone explanation through U.I. 22, and U.I. 19 there stands the observation that the adrenergic and cholinergic patterns are physiologically responsive to estrogen and androgen concentrations.

Such relations of ability performances to personality and to physiological conditions undoubtedly occur, but have received little attention as yet from psychometrists in the ability field. They are discussed in a more systematic framework in Chapters 12 and 8, respectively. One must keep in mind that in the traditional ability-testing situation one deliberately sets out—and to an appreciable degree succeeds—to get separation of ability from personality factors. But in life performances they operate in intricate functional unity, and, as Chapter 11 brings out, new ability structures may appear from the expression of dynamic traits in crystallized skills. Sex differences in those areas remain largely unexplored.

3. INTELLIGENCE CHANGES IN THE GROWTH PERIOD AND THE PROBLEM OF INTELLIGENCE UNITS AND DISTRIBUTION

After an employer has asked, "Is the applicant a man or a woman?" the next question is apt to concern the applicant's age. Sex and age are nevertheless admittedly less important in giving an idea of intelligence than they are in serving as a guide to personality qualities and other necessary, e.g., social role, qualifications. Only in one period —infancy to adolescence—does age change account for much of the variation—and that period consequently will be the concern of this section. As it happens, the whole issue of defining the distribution of intelligence anywhere in the world is tied up with this growth curve, for it has hitherto provided the basis for units of intelligence increment. So both distribution and child growth rates become interwined issues at this point.

Two discoveries in relation to age marked the early work on intelligence in this century. First, increase on intelligence test performance ceased remarkably early—around fourteen to fifteen years. If middle-aged adults have a better intellectual performance than junior high school children it must be on some other type of performance for which the good old word "wisdom" may suffice temporarily. (The still more shocking discovery that the typical intelligence test performance may actually decline after about twenty had yet to be accepted.)

Secondly, a useful law about age and intelligence was found to hold over the growth years. Stern's proposal that individual differences be expressed in an intelligence quotient, derived from Binet and Simon's mental age concept,

$$\text{I.Q.} = \frac{\text{mental age}}{\text{actual age}} \times 100$$

proved eminently practical. Its practical use was significantly aided by the ensuing discovery that this particular value tended to remain constant over the individual's period of growth. Obviously, if development stops at fourteen years, this index as it stands ceases to be constant thereafter. The law holds only over the growth years. If so promising an index of individual intelligence differences is to be retained into adult life (i.e., if we are to talk of I.Q.'s for adults) we must obtain a translation—a rate of exchange—between I.Q. and some feature of the distribution curve, and then assume that this translation rate from percentile to I.Q. continues to hold among adults as it does among children.

For as yet there is no platinum bar for intelligence units, such as the measure for a meter of length originally preserved in Paris. The suggestion below (page 429) that all perceptual relations can theoretically be built into a hierarchy of complexity (as instanced in Line's work, Figure 5–1) may some day lead to such an objective, nonbiological basis for designating equal units of increment in complexity of problems solved. But at present the unit is bio-social, tied down with respect only to a particularly racial and cultural spread of scores. A mental age unit is the average increase in test performance in a particular year *in a certain racio-cultural group,* though later it may be averaged across many.

Another "given" bio-social measure is the spread of scores on an intelligence test for all people at one age. From this well-known "normal distribution curve," as shown in Figure 7–1, we can obtain standard score units defined in terms of so many raw score units in the test. Thus it is possible, beginning with the actual raw score, to express the scatter of a population all members of which stand at a given age in terms of mental age units (or I.Q.'s if we take the "growth-finishing" age of fourteen to fifteen years as our denominator).

FIGURE 7–1
Normal Distribution of Intelligence for Crystallized and
Fluid Intelligence

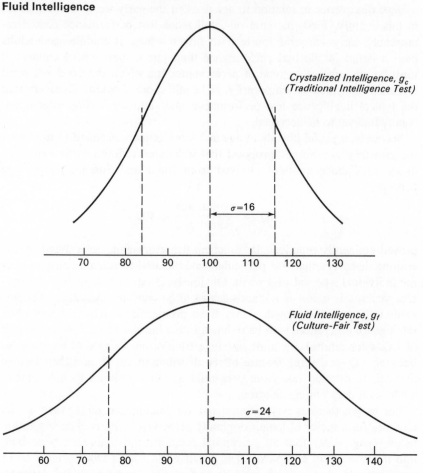

When this is done, a marked and interesting difference is found between traditional intelligence tests measuring g_c, and culture-fair intelligence tests measuring g_f. The latter have a standard deviation just about 50 percent greater, corresponding to an I.Q. sigma of twenty-four instead of one of sixteen previously accepted in, say, the Stanford, the British Intelligence Test, the Wechsler, and the WAIS tests. In either case, granted that (a) we know the age increase per year on the test for the average person from, say, six to fifteen years, and (b) we are willing to assume that the I.Q. *distribution* curve form found at, say nine and ten years of age continues to maintain itself into adult years, we can continue to translate from any adult's standard or percentile score into what Johnson (1948) has called a "standard score I.Q." It is as if we assumed, in the calculation of I.Q.'s after fifteen years, that the actual age stood still and the adult continued with the mental age he had at fifteen years.

It is useful, since we are accustomed to think in terms of the magnitude of the childhood I.Q. and its implications, to continue this convenient, though now abstract, I.Q. in dealing with adult intelligence levels. But the standard I.Q.—and indeed any I.Q.—is a value that needs to be watched critically. The meaning is not always what it seems to be, and even when more carefully formulated, the present formulations have weaknesses that should have been examined and eradicated years ago. Much of the alleged instability of individual I.Q. values may really lie in these weaknesses of formulation.

In the first place, if we are dealing with a largely genetic, maturational index, as we certainly are in fluid intelligence, g_f, then the real age in the denominator should surely be from conception rather than birth. By dividing by "chronological age plus nine months" the upward creep in average I.Q. sometimes reported in later childhood would tend to be corrected.

Secondly, there are distortions from uncertainties and differences in assumption about the age in adolescence at which the growth curve flattens. A reasonably stable estimate can be made for g_f, but, as will be increasingly apparent from the natural history of g_c, the age of cessation will vary with the culture and the area included in the high-loaded tests. For example, on verbal-numerical-reasoning primaries as subtests, it flattens in English semi-skilled worker apprentices at about sixteen but in American university undergraduates, little different in absolute mean level, it may be 18 to 20. The generalization has been made that high I.Q.'s reach the maximum later, but so far this has been indicated better in g_c than g_f, and may arise simply from the probability of brighter children being given longer education. But this is probably true only for tests in the "cultural investment area."

In the third place, there is the vast area of uncertainty about what to do with the I.Q. in adult life. The main solution, as indicated above, lies in the direction of determining actual ability-score distributions at each age and using the standard score I.Q. concept, i.e., translating from a centile rank or standard raw score at the given age to the same I.Q. as would match that centile in some agreed reference population. The reference population that is most practicable is that of nine or ten-year-olds, and, as far as present evidence goes, that retains its "centile to classical I.Q." relation on such parts of the distribution as can be checked on younger and older groups—up to sixteen and down as far as g_c and g_f can be located and measured as dependable factors. But if we carry this rate of exchange from centile to I.Q. into adult life, let us be alert to the fact that though we are likely to preserve the constancy of I.Q. for individuals better than by other methods, we are not preserving the constancy of the mental age yardstick. For in g_f the age curve, after a comparatively flat summit from about sixteen to twenty-two, drops steadily, while in g_c it may do anything, depending on the culture. (In our culture it stays flat or climbs very slightly indeed to about sixty-five.) As far as derivation from actual raw scores is concerned, the I.Q. is therefore a chronological age corrected derivative *after* twenty-two, just as it was *before* sixteen.

A fourth source of error or instability in I.Q.'s arises from considering the distribution of mental ages in a given year (as it affects the above calculation) to be that of the ideal normal curve. As Sir Cyril Burt has cogently argued from widely assembled data, it is highly probable that the I.Q. distribution curve—at least in Western European cultures—is not symmetric but is skewed slightly in some populations to the lower, and in others to the upper end, as in Figure 7–2 (continuous line, upper and lower). If the upper should prove to be more correct, a likely interpretation would be that mating is more assortive—intelligent tending to marry intelligent and vice versa—at the upper than at the lower part of the intelligence distribution. In addition we have to consider the probability that the curve is leptokurtic (7–2a) or platykurtic (7–2b), departing from the true normal curve, by constituting what Karl Pearson called a "Type 4" distribution. Such a curve could result from genetic mechanisms which allow a few relatively large genic effects to operate along with a predominance of small polygenic effects. It should be noted that the urban data in Fig. 7–2(a) is from an industrial city where the immigration of semi-skilled labor may account for the bulge immediately below an I.Q. of 100.

Finally we encounter the problem of different *genetic maturation rates,* to be discussed more fully in a later chapter. Its meaning is most readily seen if we consider different species, say humans and chimpanzees when it is evident that each has a pre-set rate of biological maturation, adjusted to—among other things—the period of parental care and the lifespan of the species. Thus, in the first year or two, the chimpanzee, with a faster rate of progress to adulthood, actually shows a better "mental age" than the child in such areas as motor control and speed. There are suggestions of such differences among the races of man and certainly we must assume that there are individual genetic differences in the prescribed rate of maturing. For example, they are well-documented as between girls and boys in such physical measures as stature and the lateness of reaching the final value. Incidentally one should distinguish between this real individuality of age of maximization and the euphemistic use of "late developer" for an individual of subaverage ability, about whom all that is really certain is that he is not an early developer.

If we knew what the differences in length of maturation period were for individuals, our predictions of adult mental age from childhood I.Q. could be more accurate; but so far the maturation-span concept is more discussed than investigated. As indicated above, a parallel phenomenon to this effect, expected primarily in g_f, occurs in the differences of subcultures which environmentally produce differences in maximization age for g_c. As more indicators of these "types" (of genetic breed and cultural matrix) become known, increased constancy of I.Q. may be achieved by suitably correcting the denominator. Regardless of these defects, the I.Q. remains probably the most useful index, and, properly calculated and used, conveys more information than most.

FIGURE 7–2
Some Actual Population Distributions Deviating from the Normal Model

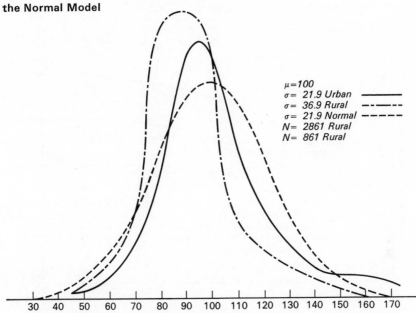

$\mu = 100$
$\sigma = 21.9$ Urban ——————
$\sigma = 36.9$ Rural —·—·—·
$\sigma = 21.9$ Normal ——————
$N = 2861$ Rural
$N = 861$ Rural

From C. Burt, "Is intelligence distributed normally?", *The British Journal of Statistical Psychology*, 26, 1963, 178.

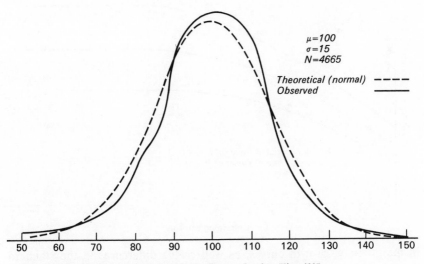

$\mu = 100$
$\sigma = 15$
$N = 4665$

Theoretical (normal) ————
Observed ——————

From R. B. Cattell, *The fight for our national intelligence.* London: King, 1937a.

From the above, somewhat involved issues we turn next to Figures 7–3 and 7–4, and discuss possible causes for the difference in flattening-out-age

FIGURE 7–3

Growth and Plateau Onset in Fluid and Crystallized General Intelligence

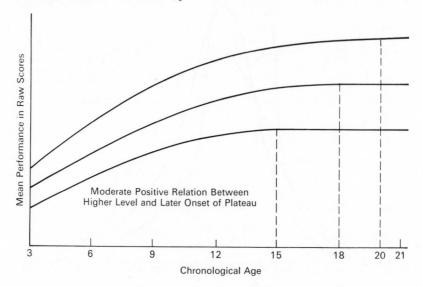

Crystallized General Intelligence, g_c

Mean Performance in Raw Scores

Moderate Positive Relation Between
Higher Level and Later Onset of Plateau

Chronological Age

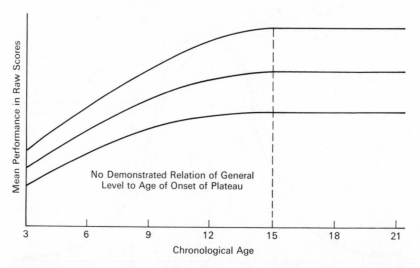

Fluid General Intelligence, g_f

Mean Performance in Raw Scores

No Demonstrated Relation of General
Level to Age of Onset of Plateau

Chronological Age

in the g_f and g_c growth curves, as well as the differences in the standard deviation of the classical I.Q.'s from these two measures. As the following additions to the discussion may show, the main reason for the earlier flattening of the g_f curve is that it is more fixed biologically, whereas g_c is more dependent on the age of leaving school. The latter shifted between 1830 and 1930 in English-speaking countries from about nine to about fifteen years, and if test results went back that far, perhaps some marked differences would be found, as have been found in lesser degree between 1915 and 1945. It is certainly noticeable, as the present writer showed in 1933, that as one takes groups experiencing a longer education, the supposed fourteen-to-fifteen cessation point extends to seventeen, eighteen, and beyond when using crystallized ability measures. Similarly, in regard to *decline* of g_c, the work of Burns (1966), Nisbet (1957), and Owens (1966) suggests, and Vernon (1969) has pointed out, that there is less decline in those of initially higher ability.

It is the "spread" of I.Q., however, that has occasioned most comment and speculation. The magnitude of the spread, i.e., the standard deviation, of adult mental ages, when it first became apparent, was a matter of astonishment to thinking people. Few other human characteristics (e.g., stature, blood pressure) show such a coefficient of variation. As Burt, Terman, and others were quick to realize, it meant that some members of the same adult community could be considered two or three times as "old," "mature," or "advanced" as others. Indeed, if we bring in a new scale—that of human evolution over a million years—and take an acceptable exchange rate from mental age to brain weight (inferred from fossils and corrected for body size), we have, living side by side in modern communities, people some hundreds of thousands of years apart in evolutionary level.

The problem for our immediate consideration, however, is why this scatter (see Figure 7–1) should be so conspicuously greater with culture-fair tests. (Indeed, it was this discovery of the wider scatter which constituted one of the early pieces of evidence provoking the theory of distinct fluid and crystallized intelligences.) One explanation of the lesser g_c scatter is that classroom education is dominated by the organizational necessity (and sometimes also a questionable egalitarian philosophy) of concentrating most on the backward while making the bright mark time. This does not allow the crystallized abilities to get so far apart as they would if the differences of fluid ability received their natural return on investment.

There is little doubt that our understanding of the age changes and the population ability distributions on intelligence will become much clearer as more data become available *separately* on fluid and crystallized intelligence measures. But technical issues of the kind discussed above now need to be worked out more explicitly. In regard to the effect of cultural conditions, especially in the school, upon the g_c distribution relative to that of g_f, experiment could easily be done. For example, one could contrast an ordinary single-stream school with one in which arrangements are made for, say, at least four different ability-level streams within each age, in regard to effects on culture-fair and traditional I.Q.'s. (Some approach to this was made by Borg (1965), but still with ambiguous results. Children would need to be in such distinct systems all their school lives for results to show clearly.)

Let us start with the basic assumption that in any system of school organization—indeed in life itself—*experience* accumulates as a function

FIGURE 7–4
Primary Abilities Age Changes Over the School Period

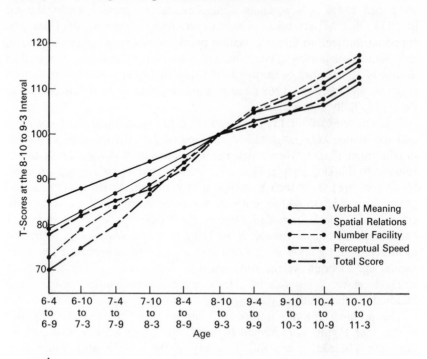

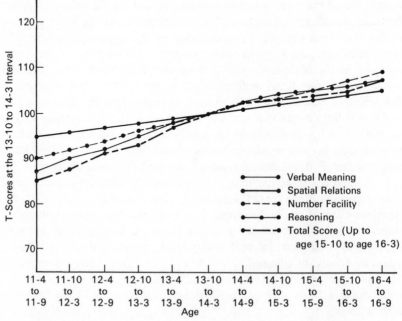

of chronological age. It is surely likely that persons in any one age group will be more uniform in amount of experience than they are in levels of endowment on g_f but in what follows we assume that coefficients of variation for g_f and e are equal. Let us work out what would happen to the g_c and g_f I.Q. sigmas in consequence. Essentially, as we have seen, the standard deviation of I.Q. is a function of the ratio of between-age-group and within-age-group variances. If (see Cattell, 1963a) $\sigma^2_{f(p)}$ defines the variance of fluid ability score *within* any one age group, i.e., across persons (hence the p subscript to sigma) and $\sigma^2_{f(a)}$ is the variance of fluid ability *across* the various age group means (across age $=$ a, say for the means on ten successive year-groups), then the sigma of $\sigma_{I.Q.(f)}$ will be a linear function, say k, of this, i.e.,

$$\sigma_{I.Q.(f)} = k \frac{\sigma_{f(p)}}{\sigma_{f(a)}}. \tag{7.1}$$

If we call $\sigma^2_{e(p)}$ the variance among individuals in experience, which is the new ingredient converting fluid to crystallized intelligence, and $\sigma^2_{e(a)}$ the corresponding variance across yearly experience means, the standard deviation of the *crystallized* intelligence I.Q. will be:

$$\sigma_{I.Q.(c)} = k \sqrt{\frac{\sigma^2_{f(p)} + \sigma^2_{e(p)} + 2r_{fe(p)}\sigma_{f(p)}\sigma_{e(p)}}{\sigma^2_{f(a)} + \sigma^2_{e(a)} + 2r_{fe(a)}\sigma_{f(a)}\sigma_{e(a)}}} \tag{7.2}$$

where $r_{fe(p)}$ is the correlation of intelligence and experience for individuals (people) and $r_{fe(a)}$ for means of age groups. The latter will be unity (for the group as a whole increases in experience as it increases in intelligence), the former perhaps slightly positive. With this reasonable assumption, $\sigma_{I.Q.(c)}$ is going to be less than $\sigma_{I.Q.(f)}$. Only if *both* $r_{fe(p)}$ and $r_{fe(a)}$ reached unity and $\sigma^2_{e(p)}/\sigma^2_{e(a)}$ were greater than the corresponding ratio for $\sigma^2_{f(p)}/\sigma^2_{e(a)}$ would this fail to be true.

It will be evident from the above that—so long as we talk of I.Q.'s, or, at least, go beyond meaningless raw scores in some other ways—statements about the distribution of intelligence cannot be separated from conclusions about age changes. The latter are so different for g_f and g_s that questions on this theme are best asked separately for fluid and crystallized abilities. A stable answer can be more definitely given for the former. Since the genetic make-up of a population changes relatively slowly, and fluid ability is more genetically based (see Chapter 10), values fixed for age change and I.Q. deviation in culture-fair tests may remain firm landmarks. But in regard to crystallized ability we may have to change our standardization and our thinking even with such sociological changes as occur in the brief space of one generation. If, for example, school efficiency increased in the sense of bringing more average gain from year to year in crystallized abilities (without affecting individual differences), the standard I.Q. deviation for crystallized ability would become still less. On the other hand; if school efficiency increased in the direction of producing a higher correlation between fluid ability and learning opportunity, e.g., by "streaming" of classes and by scholarships giving opportunity to ability, the traditional intelligence test standard deviation would increase, approaching that of fluid ability.

4. DISTRIBUTION PROBLEMS CONNECTED WITH DEFINING INTELLIGENCE, ESPECIALLY IN INFANCY

The attempts of psychologists to be precise about the natural history of intelligence—its growth rates and its distribution—require attention to still other problems than those of units and the age at which a plateau is commonly reached. Although we have been careful to define intelligence, as g_f and g_c, before asking about its age and population distribution, and although we have recognized that g_c will be protean and local to a culture, some difficulties still await us. First, even with g_f as a factor, it will change its mode of expression with age, as factors always do, and, second, we have spoken of *the* population, ignoring real biological differences in expression of intelligence and rate and duration of maturation that might be peculiar to certain strains.

Regarding the first, we are familiar with factor-analytic evidence that performances which are "saturated" (to 0.7 or 0.8) by the g_f factor at one mental age may be much less saturated at another. For example, ordinary small multiplication and division sums are loaded appreciably on intelligence at ten or eleven years of age, but scarcely at all among university students; and form boards, like the Séguin or Goddard, are good intelligence measures with six-year-olds or mentally defective adults, but scarcely with normal adults. With the latter they become measures partly of visualization but largely of the speed factor, for the relation eduction demanded is too simple.

Over most of the school-age range there is little doubt that our age plots are dealing with the same entity—g_c or g_f, according to which we are out to measure—provided we adjust the weights given to the subtests to what is appropriate at each age, as shown by the factor structure. The technical problems of bringing about this adjustment to age, on a continuous scale for intelligence level, have been clarified elsewhere (Cattell, 1969b, 1970a) in the isopodic and equipotent techniques. The real obstacle to continuing identity is encountered at the infancy age level. It does not concern how theoretically to handle the "changing weight" problem, but arises from the sheer absence of suitably gathered and analyzed data regarding the form of expression of intelligence.

In spite of the steadfast pursuit of researches by L. Stott and Rachel Ball (1965), Nancy Bayley (1949), Psyche Cattell (1940), McNemar (see Stott and Ball, 1965), Gesell and Ilg (1943), and others and the theoretical suggestions by Cattell and Kulhavy (In press), Piaget (1960), Hofstaetter (1954), Richards and Nelson (1939), Hurst (1935), and others, we are still, to some extent, groping for a firm conception of what happens structurally during the first five years. Bayley's work has the solid value of all programmatic research, and in this case the Berkeley growth study has explored the same subjects over forty years. Yet, for structural, factor-analytic purposes, a sample of twenty-five is practically useless. (Bayley rightly kept boy and girl samples separate, the total now being twenty-five on each.) Such variables were used as "eye movements in visual following" (used by Gesell and Ilg) at two to three months; "responsiveness to people" at three to seven months; "perceptual interest" at two to three months and again at fifteen to seventeen months; "manual dexterity", four to seven months; "vocalization", five to fourteen months; and "object relations", ten to seventeen months.

These variables obviously cover personality as well as cognitive function dimensions, which is perhaps desirable, and in any case, unavoidable at this age. (The researcher should, however, be alert to recognize personality factors in the outcome, which he has not always done.) At the same time, the choice of variables to cover cognitive function has generally lacked, in these preschool and infant level researches, several kinds of performance that regard for Spearman's g (or, more recently, g_f and g_c) would definitely suggest. (The tendency has been to make up measures from performances in children's play, rather than set up experimental measures that theory, e.g., in animal experiment, would suggest.) Furthermore, instead of attacking the problem of structure in what is ultimately the only satisfactory way —by a delicate and comprehensive factor-analytic research across many variables and carried through first and second orders—the child researchers have tended to take a second-best approach. This consists in measuring behavior in the infancy period of "unknown structure" and trying to find what it means by correlating with intelligence test scores from the same children when they reach intelligence testable age. In the Bayley data this has meant correlation with later performance (up to thirty-six years of age) on verbal comprehension, which we can consider a good measure (as far as any rather specific test goes) of g_c and a fair one for g_f. A striking feature of the results is the differences of males and females. "Response to persons" at 10–30 months, rated "happiness" 11–24 months in females, "shyness" 11–24 months in males, "positive behavior" in males 10–36 months, had apparently zero correlation with later intelligence scores. Intelligence through youth and adult life correlated negatively with "high activity" at 11–24 months but positively with "activity" at 21–32 months. Incidentally, this is one of the few pieces of evidence bearing on our theory (below page 155) that individual differences in intelligence are tied up with biological differences in maturation, and that early motor maturation is associated with lower final intelligence level.

The variables which showed some consistent positive correlation (though only over these same 25 cases) with later intelligence were "calmness" (about 0.3 in males), "positive behavior", about 0.3 in males, and "shyness", about 0.2 females. The last has bearing on the speculative hypothesis (page 370) that a large g_f endowment is a hazard as far as generating anxiety in early years is concerned. Bayley's data was also directly factored by Hofstaetter (1954) yielding three factors, which changed greatly in their contribution to the variance during the first three years. Both the scantiness of the data sample and the method of factoring used prohibit any firm integration of the analyses just discussed with other evidence.

More extensive psychometric research at the infancy level, using the somewhat defective factor analytic techniques of the thirties by Richards and Nelson (1939) (cross sectioning at six, twelve, and eighteen months) gave an *alertness* and a *motor* general factor at the lowest age, while at the highest the alertness factor showed itself as spreading into an alertness-language pattern. Above this age the work of Meyers, Dingman, and others, for example Schiller (1933–1934), hit upon what seemed to be primaries, in the Thurstone sense. At 36 to 42 months Hurst (1935) found six factors, which, however, still seem, like those of Richards and Nelson, to be at the second order. His "finding relations" and "motor coordination" could well be their "alertness-language" and "motor." In addition he has personality factors of "willingness to cooperate," and "persistence" which remind one of A, affectothymia, and C, ego strength, as well as a broad ability factor of perceptual speed and a smaller one of spatial reasoning.

In view of the inadequacies of factor analytic technique that have plagued these pre-school level analyses of ability structure, and led to inconsistent results (from which we have tried to salvage a consensus above), Kulhavy and the present writer undertook to start afresh from the "ground floor" in 1969–1970. Data was obtained from no fewer than 14 researches on samples extending from eighteen months to five years of age. These extensive and sound researches included the correlational studies at three, four, and five years on the Stanford-Binet (McNemar and others); the very thorough studies by Stott and Ball (1965, 1968), with the help of Merrifield, at 2, 3, 4, and 5 on the Merrill Palmer; and the studies by Cattell and Bristol (1933), Cattell (1967a), and Damarin and Cattell (1968). Unfortunately, except for the two last, even these lack inclusion of *non*ability variables to create hyperplanes for definitive rotation of any factor that might be found *general* to all ability performances.

The outcome for the three through five year range was surprisingly similar in essentials to what has been found at higher ages. The outcome even at one and a half and two years was not incompatible with a single fluid intelligence and the provincials (visualization, motor facility, etc.) but will not be discussed here because our results clearly indicated certain special hypotheses needing further experiment.

It is a widespread "philosophical" theory that "differentiation" accompanies all growth and that the ability and personality structure of a six year old should be simpler than that of a twelve-year-old, and that a three-year-old should show still simpler structure. In *personality* this has not proved true: from 18 down to 4 the dimensions drop only from about 20 to 15, and this drop occurs in certain obviously "environmental mold" types of traits and not at all in the innate. After all, the child at birth is fully differ-entiated as to its physical organs, and though he changes in size therafter the maturations in form are comparatively minor.

The main finding in the ability area fits this principle and does not support the speculations about dramatic changes. What emerge as primary abilities at three years of age (and from two through five) are almost as numerous as those found by Thurstone (1938) and Horn (1965) at the adult level, and when these in turn are factored one obtains at the second order level about half a dozen broad ("general") factors as at the adult level, two of which justify the labels "fluid" and "crystallized" intelligence, while others are the general speed, and retrieval (fluency) factors found before with adults.

The techniques necessary for coordinating findings across as many as fourteen researches were complex, and must be read elsewhere (Cattell and Kulhavy, In press, 1971). Objective tests for numbers of factors and significance of primary rotations were uniformly applied across the fourteen researches. Then since the same variables had been used across subsets of these studies, the pattern matching indices showed the same primary factors repeating across them. Actually some fifteen primaries were located, but only the most "hardy" twelve were carried to a second order analysis as shown in Table 7–2.

TABLE 7–2
Pre-School Intelligence Structure: Second-Stratum
Factors Among Primary Abilities

	Second-Stratum Factors					
	g_f	a_g	g_s	p_m	p_v	g_r[1]
Primary Ability Factors	1	2	3	4	5	6
1. Motor Speed		−.2	.7	.5		
2. Memory for Instructions	.3	.3	−.4			.1
3. Verbal Facility	.1	.4			−.2	.1
4. Manipulative Spatial Skill				.3	−.3	.3
5. Perceiving Relationships	.7	.4				
6. Extracting Explicit Spatial Relations	.4	.5	.5			
7. Fast Cube Manipulation		−.2				.4
8. Visual Form Completion	−.2	.2			.6	.3
9. Pyramid Building	.2			.2		.5
10. Inductive, Constructive Reasoning	.7				−.5	−.5
11. Cultural Level in Visual Matters					.3	
12. Visual Perceptual Memory					.5	

Loadings are means, rounded to one decimal place, from 10 researches reanalyzed and integrated by Cattell and Kulhavy (1971).

[1] This has claim to being the g_r pattern, but actually, an argument could also be made for Factor 2 being g_r.

The natures of the primaries (illustrated in 1 through 12 in Table 7–2) can be studied as to their loadings on actual tests (Cattell and Kulhavy, In press 1971); but it will be noted that something akin to verbal, perceptual, and spatial (though not numerical) abilities appear. The labels of primaries in this research has deliberately been kept descriptive rather than interpretively formal, so that, for example, "Memory for Instructions" or "Alertness to Instructions and Maintenance of Sets" is used where some investigators might speak of a "Memory Factor." Certainly there are some primaries here, e.g., "Pyramid Building," which descriptively are quite narrow. With two or three of the primaries not listed in Table 7–2 showing narrowness to particular pairs of Merrill Palmer or Stanford-Binet tests one would have to be cautious in saying that as many as fifteen are definitely on the same level as the usual primaries. But the number is not significantly different from that at later ages.

At the second stratum level, the results again show, as just mentioned, a set of five or six general capacities (including, perhaps, a provincial power, visualization, as at the school level; see page 106 above). Here we see a fluid general intelligence source trait (No. 1) shown mostly in *perceiving relationships* and in *reasoning,* but also in following instructions and in extracting explicit spatial relations. Two others factors—2 and 6—have high generality, and we shall discuss in a moment their relative claims to being crystallized intelligence and general retrieval (fluency). Meanwhile, it is evident that there are two "provincials"—p's—as recognized before, one, No. 4, which appears to be motor and manipulative skill, as observed also by the investigators above, and one which is definitely visualization (No. 5). What is interpreted here as the general speed factor, g_s (No. 3), has unusually large investment in motor speed and admits of other interpretations. For example, it could be a spatial factor carried to the second order level, but if so why does it not load No. 4? It seems more reasonable to suppose that at this age speed can show itself largely only in motor action and in verbalizing spatial relations (not verbal vocabulary understanding as such, as in No. 3).

A curious feature is that despite oblique simple structure (which in the ability field generally eliminates bi-polar factors) there are several appreciable negative correlations in Table 7–2. Our conclusion is that at this age abilities will show more effects of motivation and personality relations than later. Thus the negative loading of g_s on "Memory for Instructions" (−0.4) may be due to impulsiveness in speed interfering with following instructions. Again, both motor skill (p_m) and what we take to be retrieval capacity (g_r) apparently interfere with inductive reasoning (loadings of −.5). Does this mean that there are more "either/or" rigidities in ways of problem solving at this age? The present writer's observations of four-year-olds in one of the studies included (Cattell and Bristol, 1933) suggests this may be the case. In the puzzle box problems pieces of chocolate were placed plainly visible in wire cage boxes (the designs were of the same nature as Köhler's experiments with chimpanzees), and some inductive reasoning would suggest ways of reaching the chocolate. It was noticable, however, that four-year-old boys who had shown strong manipulative skills would by habit try to lever the wires apart, and thus actually performed below average on the reasoning approach. Thus in periods of rapid growth of abilities it is conceivable that talents in one will for the time interfere with experience needed for the growth of another. In the fullness of time, the interaction of ability with experience will have a chance to fulfill itself for all abilities, and these negative correlations should disappear.

However, the main mystery at the two to five year level concerns the failure of earlier researches to come up with a clear answer either on the existence of a Spearman g or on the form of the "embryonic" division into g_f and g_c (crystallized intelligence). The present results across fourteen researches give a highly internally consistent answer which we must now discuss. The massive loading of Factor 1 on perceiving relationships and inductive reasoning are central to fluid intelligence and leave little doubt in so naming it. Two other factors—No. 2 and No. 6—are general enough to need consideration as a possible crystallized intelligence.

Now we must be alert to the fact that at this early age the form of crystallized intelligence might be substantially different from that to which we have been accustomed over the ages from seven to seventy. Crystallized intelligence is the set of judgmental skills from investing g_f in those cultural activities which need high g_f. From seven on they are the school curriculum —verbal, mechanical, social and numerical skills, for example. At three years of age the most complex activity encountered is language, so we should certainly expect it to load that. In lesser degree, however, it would enter into such activities as putting on one's clothes, learning the relations among relatives, and—much more than later—into mechanical skills with wood blocks, doors, taps, and so on. Except for its negative loading in inductive reasoning No. 6 would have appreciable claim to being crystallized intelligence, but No. 2 has the heaviest loading on verbal understanding, and memory for instructions, while still having loadings on those relation perceptions which are normal in any intelligence manifestations. Accordingly, No. 2 is labeled a_g—crystallized intelligence—while No. 6 is more speculatively put up for further testing as the otherwise missing general fluency, on the assumption that no tests other than manipulative ones have been introduced to catch this uninhibited flow of activity. (The reason for symbolizing crystallized intelligence alternatively as a_g, instead of g_c, will be explained shortly.)

The above analysis is thus offered as a firm basis of theoretical indications, to be tested especially by (a) a wider and more theoretically pertinent array of behaviorable variables than the limited span in the Stanford-Binet and Merrill-Palmer, (b) the inclusion of nonability variables to permit good rotation at the third order. The six second order factors in Table 7–2 *have* been carried to the third order, and deliver a picture of structure very similar to that in Table 6–4, i.e., the fluid general intelligence preceding the age of testing determines both the present fluid level and part of the present crystallized level. But without the "hyperplane stuff" the rotation does not justify reproduction here.

Actually, theory would expect that the form of crystallized intelligence would be more vague and of smaller *common* variance here and in middle age than in the school years and the following decade—say seven through twenty-seven years. For whereas the curriculum is reasonably uniform, but at the same time applied unevenly as to time length in our population, the pre-school home environment is less uniform and all are exposed to it for the same time. Mechanical toys, parental vocabulary, sibling stimulation, and visual acquaintance with pictures of objects not seen daily will vary enough, however, to begin the creation of a second "invested intelligence in culture" factor, and it would seem that the pre-school researches above point uniformly to such an a_g pattern—at least in the middle and lower middle class subjects taken.

In conclusion as far as these ten to twenty adequate researches go, the triadic theory checks out well. In reference to the developmental stages through two to five years, it would seem that the main structures, g's, p's and a's are already present, though the particular a's are somewhat different and a question mark remains among the general capacities as to whether g_c is present other than with smaller variance and at a higher order level.

Apart from certain challenging questions about the degree of early development in g_c (a_g), i.e., about structure, there remain here also some challenging questions about the curve of age development. We need, in fact, to discuss further the proposition debated above that different human biological strains are set to a *different* time clock even with regard to the *same* kind of intelligence. It has been pointed out that if a chimpanzee is brought up with a human child (Kellogg and Kellogg, 1933) the early progress of the former in manipulating the environment is faster and its later progress is slower and sooner ended. (Incidentally, it is not absolutely certain that the cognitive skills in the early performances of these two species which have been observed in this comparison *are* equally entitled to the term intelligence, because we are in doubt about what *is* intelligence even in man's infant years as well as in lower species [see Chapter 9].)

However, there is no reason whatever why two species, or two local varieties, e.g., breeds of men, should not have both different final intelligence levels and different rates of maturation, so that a comparison when the two are, say, one year old, would tell less than the I.Q. usually does about their differences at full flowering. And, while the human population does not span different species, it mixes what a biologist might call "local varieties" with different expectations of inherent longevity and different rates of maturation. Consequently, there could be slight differences between family strains such that child A cannot compete with B at an early age, but decidedly surpasses him in later life.

Especially could we get wrong predictions if we confounded the motor activity factor, p_m, with fluid intelligence, g_f measures, for it is evident that different human races differ in motor activity, and also that high early motor activity is inclined to correlate negatively with later intelligence. (No human infants are as active as a cageful of young monkeys!)

Since boys and girls are biologically, genetically different, they offer an easily available test-case for seeing how real these maturational differences may be. At a qualitative level educators have long been aware of such differences in "growth spurts" which affect the teaching of boys and girls together. One curriculum director asks, "Why do we not recognize that boys will be slower in elementary school, and avoid giving them a sense of comparative failure?" And another sees such substantial differences in pattern of abilities (see Table 7–1) that he argues that the European system and the American private school system of separate classes is desirable. There are social and other advantages of coeducation, but in the ability field these differences of the sexes at least provide an illustration that the same railway timetable cannot be applied to both.

If inter-familial longevity and maturation differences amount to anything, the constancy of the I.Q. may never be exact and its projection from childhood into adult life may require allowances for what we know about the individual in regard to his genetic class. Much of the alleged inconstancy of the I.Q.—expressible by saying that half the children measured may change by less, and half by more, than five points on a re-test—is due to sloppy measurement, and to the effect of environmental influences, notably on crystallized intelligence tests. But we now recognize that part of such inconstancy may be due to the effects now being discussed, namely, to differences in genetic maturation rate in different families. Nature has prolonged the period of early helplessness and flexibility precisely for the most intelligent species. It is probable that evolutionary forces are constantly in conflict in balancing the survival gains for the individual from an early start with those gains to the individual and society which acrue from the longer maturational trail, leading to Browning's "the last of life for which the first was made." In racially and culturally mixed groups we may be deceived if we cannot recognize and allow for these differences by tests, and proceed to arrange appropriate adjustments of education.

Another needed conception in improving predictions from the I.Q. is a recognition of the possibility (again apart from any individual instabilities as such) that the population standard deviation of the I.Q. may become greater in certain developmental periods. That is to say, I.Q.'s of 80 and 120 at eight years of age might become (when taken as an average of all children at these two levels, say, 75 and 125 at twelve years. No such major effect *has* been observed, but there are some experimental claims for minor trends of this kind. Since what we might call I.Q.$_{(c)}$, based on measurements of crystallized general intelligence, is decidedly more subject to environmental, cultural circumstances than is I.Q.$_{(f)}$, there are possibilities of quite a variety of local distortions of the I.Q. trends and distributions from those found more universally. A study at the London School of Economics, for example, shows that after about nine years of age the typical trend in children of the same I.Q. at nine is for those in better homes to increase a little and those in less cultured homes to drop a little. It could well be that traditional I.Q. tests at nine do not need to go beyond experience common to most homes to encompass intelligence-testing complexities, whereas, later, test designers, are forced to use more specifically cultural material (in contrast to the culture-fair, g_f test).

It has just been pointed out that, although it is an approximately correct and most universally appropriate statement to refer to the distribution of I.Q. (or mental age in children) as "a normal curve," Burt (1948) has shown that in Britain the largest and best samples available show some departure. A similar departure, showing a flattening of the curve, was found by the writer in putting together the first stratified adult sample from occupations, made in Britain on the Cattell Test in 1932 (Cattell, 1934). Now a normal distribution, mathematically defined, is something that results when a large number of small influences contribute in a random fashion. This would be expected in a freely intermarrying population in a richly varied environment, for either the genetic or the environmental component of intelligence. For, as will be seen in the discussion on heredity (Chapter 10), the consensus is that a large number of genes will be involved, just as in stature, and each gene could be present in one of two allelic forms. There is then far greater chance of an individual having 50 percent favorable and 50 percent unfavorable than getting say, 90 percent favorable and 10 percent unfavorable genes.

However, marriage is not random, but assortive, i.e., like tends to marry like, husbands and wives being found to be correlated in intelligence about +0.3 to +0.6 in various social classes. This would tend, genetically, to *extend and flatten* the curve, (technically, make it platykurtic). However, as found in the Burt and the Cattell studies mentioned above, and shown in Figure 7–2 the effect is as if assortiveness were operative only at the lowest and uppermost ranges, especially the latter. Burt brings in a genetic theory that there are a few large genes as well as many small ones. This may be, but there are other features of Figure 7–2a to be explained. Essentially it shows: (a) a higher prevalence of the "modal man" (I.Q. 100) than would be expected; (b) a tendency of the curve, as in surface tension in a fluid meeting a solid, to pull itself out and cling to the extremes; and (c) a tendency for (b) to be more marked at the upper than the lower end. As a resultant of these, the intermediate fairly bright and fairly dull are less frequent than a random normal distribution would require. The present writer is inclined to account for (a) by his principle (Cattell, 1957a) of "coercion to the bio-social mean (or mode)"—a general law that groups tend to cater to, preserve, and foster the average type more than any other. Resistance to this is effective only at the extremes—the mental defective and very low I.Q.'s who behave and reproduce with little awareness of the cultural pull, and the leaders who reject the average values for other reasons. And, as we have seen, in countries of good morale there has been an increasing tendency for the intelligentsia and general leaders to accept the responsibility of larger families as genetic education increasingly incorporates such ideals as part of the ethic of *"noblesse oblige."* At any rate, both this effect and a more careful assortative mating seem to have produced an extension of the curve at its uppermost levels. Additionally, in crystallized ability tests (Figure 7–2b is a better example of such data), this thin upper extension (ten to twenty times the expected values around I.Q. 130–140, according to Burt) could be due to a higher correlation of intelligence with education in this range than in the population generally.

However, there are numerous other influences, e.g., intermarrying within religious groups, inbreeding racial minorities, local concentrations of skilled or unskilled industries, migrations, coeducational universities and colleges (taking about one-fourth in the United States), sudden social changes in relative birth rates, etc., that could cause momentary or historically more prolonged bulges and attenuations in the distribution curve. These apply especially to the child I.Q. distribution and will be discussed more fully under social effects in Chapter 14. In regard to the adult I.Q., there are further complications due to age trends, discussed below, though the only really large adult samples available, from occupational studies (Cattell, 1934; Harrell, 1940; Fryer, 1922) and World War II drafts (Tuddenham, 1948) continue to show an essentially normal distribution. From time to time, various proposals are made for a substitute for the I.Q., but most have all the defects of the I.Q. plus others of their own. Considering that these anomalies of flattened and skewed distributions also tend to give some distortion to the basis for I.Q. calculations (including the standard score I.Q.), it is surprising that I.Q.'s work out to be as steady and apt as they do. Indeed, one may surmise that if the various distorting influences were allowed for, the real constancy would be better than is suggested by the present ±5 points of error on retest.

In drawing the curve of annual typical intelligence increase, in terms of the mean raw score for all children, we conclude by calling each year's raw score increment "one unit" of mental age. The fact that each successive year's increment (after ten years, at any rate) is significantly less (in terms of raw score) than the preceding may seem to imply an anomaly. Actually, we never assume in psychology that equal raw-score intervals are equal real intervals, and the practice of measuring annual increments (up to the plateau) as equal mental-age increases along the base line of our normal distribution curve is not yet proven to be definitely wrong. It will be observed, from Figure 7–4, that the growth of the primary abilities over the school period has the same general steadiness as in the g factors underlying them.

Application of the *simplex theory,* employable in psychology generally for obtaining equal interval scales (Cattell, 1962), and using Lingoes (1965) computer program now might be applied advantageously to this problem to see if at least over the middle period mental-age units *are* equal intervals. Meanwhile the use of I.Q.'s, or standard scores in mental ages, in any one-age cross-section of the population remains the favorite and probably the best unit for most purposes, including growth studies.

5. SOME PROBLEMS IN REACHING MEANINGFUL TRENDS AND DISTRIBUTIONS IN THE ADULT PERIOD

The age changes in g_f and g_c in the growth period discussed above are comparatively clear. As Figure 7–3 summarizes, the first results with culture-fair, fluid ability measures showed a definite difference in age trend from those found by most careful studies on crystallized ability scores, in that the curve reaches its plateau earlier—around fourteen instead of fifteen, sixteen, or seventeen. Indeed, the latter curve continues beyond fourteen to an uncertain age, usually fourteen to twenty, depending on whether it is a non-college or college group.

By contrast, a clear picture of what happens after adolescence is much harder to get. The most commonly represented curves in textbooks—those of Miles, Conrad, and Lorge (see Figure 7–5)—show a decline in intelligence test performance after about twenty-five years of age. Apparent contradictions arise, however, from such work as that of Bayley and Oden (1955) and Schaie and Strother (1968), showing that on at least some kinds of subtests (see also Horn and Cattell, 1967) improvement goes on up to fifty years and beyond (see Figures 7–6, 7–7, and 7–9).

Much of the confusion on age trends is a natural harvest of inattention, in the first place, to the structural realities. It arises not only through (1) using intelligence tests which are varying mixtures of g_f and g_c, and (2) failure to recognize g_s, g_r, and other general capacities and their effects on g_c estimates through the usual subtests, but also, (3) through lack of adequate confirmation of indicated decline still persisting with untimed tests.[1]

There are really four distinct main issues to be watched in age change: (1) the changing *relative loading pattern* of performances in the general factors (g_c, g_f, and also g_s and g_r), (2) the *mean magnitude* of the variance contribution of intelligence (g_c or g_f) at various age levels, (3) the extent

---

[1] Among writings in this field there has never been any clear conception of the role of speed, retrieval, and other *general* cognitive performance factors, as defined above, in the tests used. An alertness to the possible role of speed was shown earliest (except for Spearman's basic attack) by Thorndike who, arguing from the familiar fact that older people are slower, produced evidence for the view that, though the curve took the age drop in Figures 7–5 and 7–6 with *speeded* tests, it did not do so with unspeeded. The recently renewed attack on the problem by Furneaux, discussed below, although in new terminology, supports the basic position of Spearman, that speed in g-saturated tasks is part of intelligence itself, and is inversely related to the g-difficulty of the item. But this still leaves much variance in most intellectual tasks to be accounted for by the additional speed contribution from g_s, and if recall is involved, from g_r. In our language here, *power* (product per minute) does fall off with age, but in g_c performances, *goodness* of product *per se* does not. (Please note, however, that as already mentioned, Thorndike happened to use "power" in the opposite and inappropriate sense of *unspeeded* performance. But as far as the physicist (and our use here) is concerned, power is performance per minute (work divided by time). Present results with untimed culture-fair tests *do* still show a drop, as shown in Figure 7–5 (Cattell and Eber, unpublished results).

FIGURE 7–5
Life Range Curves on Traditional Intelligence Tests
(Various Mixtures of g_c and g_f)

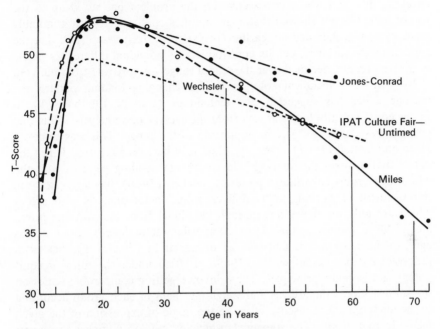

From R. B. Cattell, *Your mind and mine*, George C. Harrap Publishers.

to which the declining mean variance of one factor is compensated by increase in some other, and (4) the extent to which, even when intelligence, speed, retrieval, etc., are clearly, conceptually, factorially separated, the actual *estimate* of a person's score on one gets contaminated by overlap of loaded subtests with those of another.

That the loading pattern, and therefore the estimation pattern for g_f or g_c, will alter with age and level of the subjects has long been recognized and has been mentioned above. Evidence is available in such studies as those of: Asch (1936) at nine and twelve years, showing, incidentally, that intercorrelations and general factor variance are higher at nine than twelve years; Clark (1944), on eleven, thirteen, and fifteen-year-olds, showing increasing variance in fluency, reasoning, verbal, memory, space and number (in declining order) with age, together with decreasing covariance, i.e. decline in the general factor role; (3) Cohen (1957) similarly found the general factor (in WAIS) to decline in importance from between early adulthood and old age, and showed further that it is compensated for by an increasing role of a memory factor, possibly g_r or g_m; and (4) Balinsky (1941) similarly on the Wechsler-Bellevue cut the age range at six intervals between nine and sixty years and found changing factor structure. He added to the picture a strong suggestion that the decline of the general factor variance continues only to thirty years and then begins to increase again.

Much of this work was stimulated by the early hypothesis of Spearman, that g changes its loading pattern with age and level, and the comparatively early experimental work of Garrett (Garrett, Bryan, and Perl, 1935) checking this, and whose perspective on the problem has stood up to the test of time. Garrett showed that some abilities confounded with g, notably memory power, flattened out earlier (twelve to thirteen years) and that the general factor variance, i.e., its contribution to individual differences in the cognitive domain, declined over the school range—at any rate from nine on.

By way of a technical solution to the changing loading pattern the present writer has suggested two techniques (Cattell, 1969b): (1) to factor equal contributory samples from all ages in one analysis. Thus one gets the best "average" weight applicable to the range. This was done by Horn and Cattell (1967) in the age plots seen here on page 168. It has the defect that it mixes the inter-age, developmental loading patterns with the within-age group covariation patterns. Tucker (1966) has suggested the improvement of working in the full cross-age factor analysis with scores which are only the deviations of each individual from his own age group mean. More radical solutions for comparing factor scores either across ages, as here, or across cultures, as discussed in Chapter 14, has been proposed by the present writer (1969b, 1970a) under the titles of equipotent and isopodic principles. These involve getting comparable scales on the subtest scores themselves and weighting them in each group according to the loading pattern discovered to be the mode of expression of the given factor in that group. The statistical principles are too complex to discuss here, but they do offer a solution to the problem, sometimes considered hopeless, of providing a scientifically meaningful comparison of scores despite the changing pattern of factor expression with age and culture.

None of the existing published results has used the last, more refined method. The Horn results here used the cross-age factoring. The rest have used fixed weights—often those derived from only one end of the range and hazardously projected all through. The familiar curves in Figure 7–4, from Miles, Jones, Conrad, Lorge, and others are of this kind. Not only do they omit regard for weights but they in fact use unknown mixtures of g_f and g_c as most traditional intelligence tests were.

Closer scrutiny of such calculations shows, moreover, that they suffer from an additional and very different source of distortion. The curves as presented are actually a mixture of what we may call "the typical normal life course" with the "accidental" (but important) culture events of a particular life span era. For example, the typical life course in all cultures might be for a man to become more well-read as he gets older. But in some cultures the supply of good reading material might increase more than in another (in a particular generation), so the curve would rise more steeply for people repeatedly measured in that culture. In the last few years considerable progress has been made toward a more sophisticated conceptual handling of the analysis of age trends, through the independent but converging attacks by Schaie and Strother (1968), Baltes (1968), and the present writer (1968, 1969b). Several curves are conceptually separable, as shown in Table 7–3, and with suitable data gathering they can also be operationally separated.

Let us deal with the conceptual separation first. First we can divide the given curve into an abstracted "normative curve"—the typical age curve in the typical biological and cultural conditions, sampled across several epochs—and an *epogenic curve*—the special part due to the particular historical conditions in that epoch. Secondly, we can divide each of these into a biological or, better, *endogenous* part, and a cultural or *exogenous* part, as shown at the top of the lower half of Table 7–3. The other possible

TABLE 7–3
Data Matrices for Separating Endogenous, Ecogenic, and
Epogenic Components of the Life Span Curve

(A) POSSIBLE COMBINATIONS OF OBSERVATIONS

| | Same Age at Testing | | Different Age at Testing | |
	Same Birthday	Different Birthday	Same Birthday	Different Birthday
Same Year of Testing	No Series	Impossible	Impossible	SC
Different Year of Testing	Impossible	FCE	SL and CL	EE

Note: Only one category permits a further subdivision into same subjects or different subjects (from the same age group), namely, SL and CL.

(B) RESULTING SERIES

Calendar Year of Birth	Different Persons Tested Age at Testing						
	10	20	30	40	50	60	
1910	1920	1930	1940	1950	1960	1970	SL
1900	1910	1920	1930	1940	1950	1960	
1890	1900	1910	1920	1930	1940	1950	
1880	1890	1900	1910	1920	1930	1940	FE
1870	1880	1890	1900	1910	1920	1930	SC
1860	1870	1880	1890	1900	1910	1920	
1850	1860	1870	1880	1890	1900	1910	
	FCE						

Calendar Year of Birth	Same Persons Tested Age at Testing						
	10	20	30	40	50	60	
1910	1920	1930	1940	1950	1960	1970	CL$_1$
1900	1910	1920	1930	1940	1950	1960	
1890	1900	1910	1920	1930	1940	1950	CL$_2$

Suggested Designations of Six Major Experimental Series
SL = *Simple Longitudinal* series: same birth year, different subjects, different ages, different testing dates.

CL = *Cursive (or Cohort) Longitudinal* series: same birth year, same subjects, different ages, different testing dates. Two sub-series, $CL_{(1)}$ and $CL_{(2)}$ are put in here because one may test *all* of the cohort at every point, as proposed, designated $CL_{(1)}$; or test all at age 10, divide into five groups, and retest each at a different decade, to avoid retesting effects (practice), as in $CL_{(2)}$.

SC = *Simple (Fixed-date) Cross-Sectional* series: different birth years, different ages, same testing date.

FCE = *Fixed Age Changing Epoch Cross-Sectional* series: different birth years, same age, different testing data.

FE = *Fixed Epoch* series: different birth years, different age at testing, different testing date, but with life span centered on the same calendar year (epoch).

CCL = *Combined Cursive Longitudinal* series: same as CL above, except that for a planned collation of results for several different age groups in the same epoch.

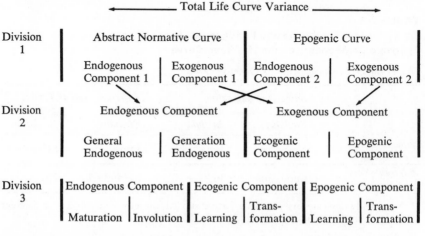

Main possible conceptual divisions in analyzing the total life course curve

divisions are self explanatory and need not be pursued here. The misleading effects of such curves as have been shown in Figure 7–1 is due to the failure of those interpreting them to separate the epogenic from the normative component. (The latter, as the lowest line on Table 7–3 shows can in turn be divided into an *endogenous* and an *ecogenic* component.)

The operational separation of these conceptual curves is carried out through gathering and analyzing data as shown in the upper part of Table 7–3. The nature of the six possibilities—simple longitudinal, SL; cursive longitudinal, CL; simple fixed date cross-section, SC, etc.—is set out below. The data so far available for intelligence comparison is that of Schaie and Strother (1968) and Horn and Cattell (1966b) and provides a comparison of two of the above data gathering curves—the SC (simple cross sectional) and the CCL (common, or cohort, cursive longitudinal) in which the same people (hence common) are followed up (hence cursive) for a short period and retested, starting at each of several ages (hence longitudinal).

No investigation has yet obtained the complete matrices in Table 7–3, and it is convenient to describe those which exist according to the facets of these matrices that they cover. As far as existing intelligence data over age is concerned, the kind of thing we have to watch is the cumulative effect of culture, in that for example, the crystallized intelligence score in 1970 of a 45-year-old in relation to that of a 25-year-old must primarily take into account that the "scholastic g_c" levels come from investments of g_f respectively in the schools of, say 1931–1943 and 1951–1963. Secondarily, one must recognize some lesser cumulative daily experience contribution to verbal, numerical, etc., components from the intervening years 1943–1970 compared to 1963–1970. Except for the valuable results of Schaie we have yet little to go on that is not restricted to the CS method. For the well planned *purely longitudinal* study of Jones (1959) and Bayley (1949) has suffered attrition to such small samples that the statistical limits of inference are gross. They used what we have called above the subdivision CL or the "running" method in which one heroically holds on to the same group throughout its life course. This reduces sampling error, but the regular SL can, as far as these kinds of results are concerned, beat it by taking far larger samples.

There are other problems mainly demographic in nature, to be solved once one leaves the safe corridor of research in children within the age range of the school system. No research on adults has yet obtained truly stratified samples, i.e., compounding classes, geographical areas, etc., nor has allowance been made for increasing selection effects from death, migration, etc. Thus, as Sealy has pointed out in Britain, although a_v factor goes on increasing in moderately well educated groups—as shown for typical groups in Figure 7–6 below—it actually drops in his data, after school leaving, *among those in less skilled occupations*. Most conclusions at present have to be tentative.

6. AGE CHANGES IN PRIMARY ABILITIES AND LOCAL ORGANIZATIONS BY SL, CL, AND CCL METHODS

In the triadic theory we have distinguished three classes of abilities (1) the primary abilities or agencies—the a's; (2) the provincial neural-experimental organizations, visual, auditory, etc.—the p's, and (3) the general capacities—the g's. It is convenient to examine the age trend evidence on these in two sections—the a's and p's here; the g's (except for the above rough introduction by the traditional intelligence test curves) in later analyses below. For there are some wider issues needing discussion with respect to the general capacities.

Significant age trends have been found on practically all the primary abilities, both on the rising tide of the youthful age span and in diverse upward and downwards courses in middle life.[2] Instead of taking space

---

[2] Although the problem of changing loading pattern does not arise so much to cause uncertainties in identifying younger and older measures of the same agency, as it does for crystallized intelligence (see below), yet, as Mukherjee (1902) shows, loading changes do occur. Verbal ability rises in g_c loading, for example, from Grade 8 to 10.

FIGURE 7–6
Primary Ability Age Changes in the Middle Life (Contrasting
MLC [Maintained Life Course] Measurement Results
with CAS)

> *In these diagrams the interrupted line represents the simple*
> *or cousive longitudinal data series put together from measures*
> *repeated at seven years, and the continuous line, the simple*
> *cross sectional data series, i.e., different ages at one testing.*

(1) Estimated Age Gradients: Verbal Meaning.

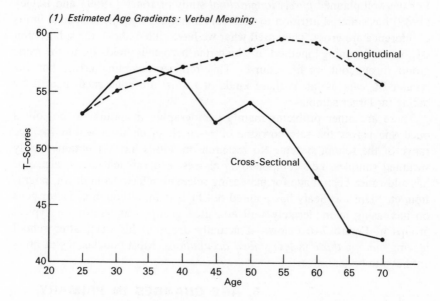

(2) Estimated Age Gradients: Number.

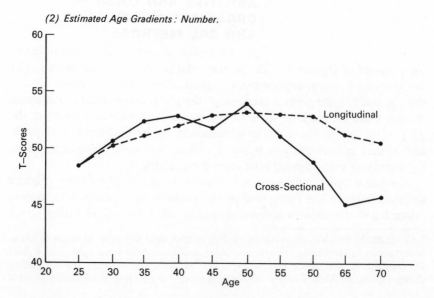

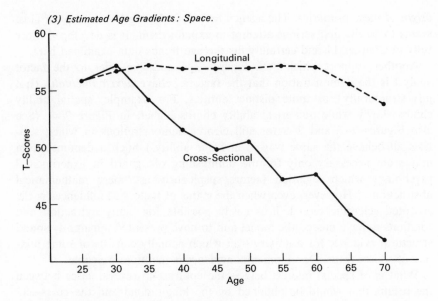

(3) Estimated Age Gradients: Space.

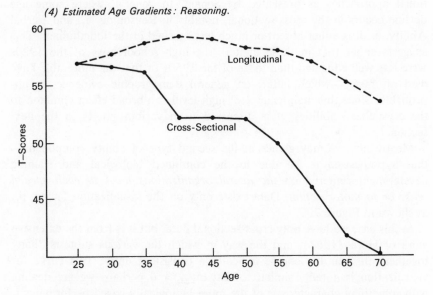

(4) Estimated Age Gradients: Reasoning.

K. Warner Schaie, "A cross-sequential study of age changes in cognitive behavior." *Psychological Bulletin*, 1968, 68.
Copyright 1968 by the American Psychological Association and reproduced by permission.

with verbal description, we have summarized the findings succinctly in Figures 7–5 and 7–6. These results, when confirmed and extended, will have considerable value for theories about the nature of the primaries. Incidentally, it is astonishing how little theory or even speculation has arisen among psychometrists (who have daily used the Thurstone PMA since the structural discoveries twenty years ago) about the *nature* and *origin* of these primaries. The agency theory, including the concept of aids, seems to be the first serious attempt to explain them. It is developed more fully in Chapter 11 and certainly fits the age trends data examined here.

Another support which both Figures 7–4 and 7–6 offer to the factor analyst is the demonstration that the factors behave *developmentally* (not just structurally) as quite distinct entities. For example, spatial ability climbs slowly while numerical ability climbs higher, in Figure 7–4. (See also Figures 7–7 and 7–8 for still clearer demonstrations in which subtests all behave the same way in any one ability.) Such a demonstration may seem necessary only for the diminishing old guard in experimental psychology which regarded factors suspiciously as "mere mathematical abstractions." However, even when the status of factors as influences is the accepted scientific model, it is easily possible for faulty extraction and rotations to have missed the model and to have presented apparently sound structural evidence for a unitary trait which actually consists of some mixture of source traits. Developmental evidence is therefore welcome.

What is of special interest here is the contrast in several cases between the results that would be obtained by the longitudinal and the cross-sectional approaches as presented by Schaie. In general, where some age decline occurs in the cross-sectional, notably in Reasoning, a_r, and Verbal Ability, a_v, it is either absent or much less marked in the longitudinal. This suggests either that in these matters the high school boys of the 1920s were less well educated than those of the 1950s or that the more able have died off faster—which latter, on general demographic evidence, is improbable. Since this maintenance of high level is a broad effect common to the crystallized abilities, it is discussed from various angles in the next section.

Meanwhile, we may glance at the second type of ability component—that hypothesized to be due to the combined biological and training development centered on *the neural organizations local to each special sense or to motor action*. Data exists only on the visualization factor, p_v, as shown in Figure 7–7.

In this case we have only cross-sectional data, but it is from the extensive work of Horn (1967), and the way in which the various subtests "hang together" in their life course indicates a consistent unity. This curve for visualization is notably similar to that of g_f, and perhaps we are dealing with something characteristic of the more biologically based performances.

One must not leave the data of this section without the cautionary comments which Schaie himself makes. First, as in all distribution and trend assessments, in any attempt at a stratified sample we are likely to go astray with such small numbers; second, there may be some slight test sophistication at the second testing. Finally, we must remember that even the longitudinal curve above is not the history-free, "average" *abstract normative* age trend abstracted from the epoch, but contains still a little peculiar to the era (to what happened during the seven years until retest in this case).

FIGURE 7–7
Age Changes in a Provincial "Power," or p: Visualization

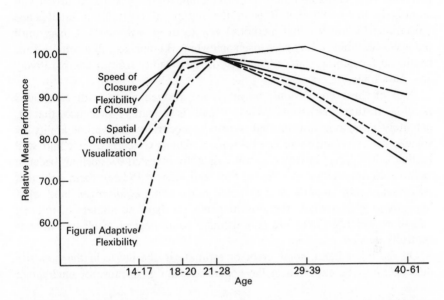

7. AGE CHANGES IN INTELLIGENCE AND THE GENERAL CAPACITIES

For many years the age change in intelligence, as general mental capacity, and as measured in such traditional tests as the Stanford, Wechsler, WAIS, Thorndike-Lorge, or the tests used by Miles, Jones, and Conrad and others, was believed to be as in Figure 7–4 above. It is only recently that Horn and the present writer were able to show that the curves are in fact very different for fluid and crystallized general intelligence and that the usually accepted curves so far discussed above are almost certainly mixtures of the two.

In Figure 7–8 the plots are shown for the separate tests which are highly loaded in these factors, and again, as in Figure 7–7, the unity of the source traits g_f and g_c is attested further by the consistency of the subtest trends. Figure 7–8(c) brings essentially congruent results from Schaie's longitudinal method, though the cross-sectional series dips in a way suggesting that Schaie's sample is showing some age decline not present in Horn's. The standard cross-sectional crystallized plus fluid ability plot from traditional intelligence tests, as shown in Figure 7–4, however, agrees with Schaie's result for cross-sectional results and is most typical of this type of series analysis.

By extrapolation to still purer measures of g_c, as well as by other results (such as those of Balinsky (1941), Bayley and Oden (1955), Christian and Paterson, Horn and Cattell (1967), and others), the conclusion can tentatively be drawn that it is in the nature of crystallized intelligence (examined by longitudinal methods) *not* to drop with age—at least until old age—and that it may even rise somewhat. By contrast, fluid intelligence results so far demonstrate a tendency to fall steadily from a comparatively early adult age.

Both of these conclusions, however, are hedged about with conditions needing further discussion. Where there is apparent evidence that g_c definitely rises, one notices that it usually occurs where verbal ability or some other *constantly and centrally used* skill is concerned. It could well be that other things in which g_f was originally invested *do* decline, because as life goes on, one has insufficient time and interest to keep them polished. *Any steady state in skills is a dynamic not a static equilibrium,* and what happens to g_c as a whole therefore depends on dynamic matters of interest and time, which, in later life may demand some neglect of all but what is centrally needed.

On the other hand, some error of estimate in the curve in the *opposite* direction may be expected in the conclusions on g_c because of inadequate

FIGURE 7–8
Age Changes in Fluid and Crystallized General Abilities and a Composite

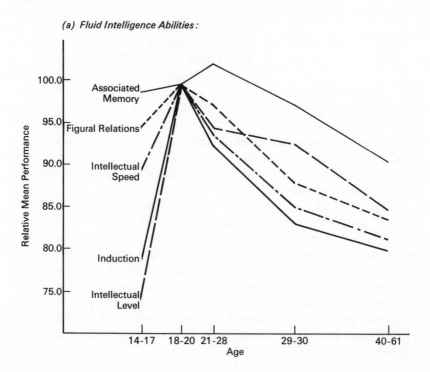

(a) Fluid Intelligence Abilities:

(b) Crystallized Intelligence Abilities:

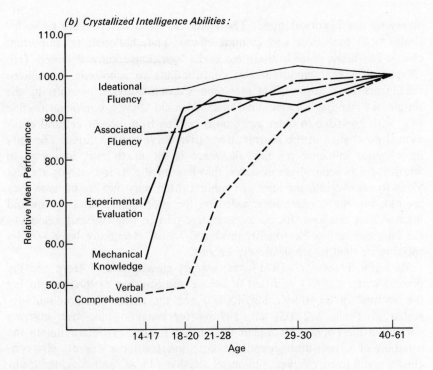

J. Horn and Cattell, R. B., "Age differences in primary mental ability factors." *Journal of Gerontology*, 1966, 21, 210–220.

(c) Estimated Age Gradients: Traditional Tests

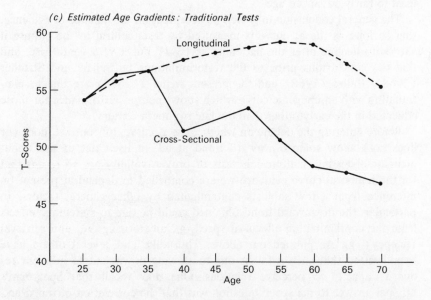

K. Warner Schaie, "A cross-sequential study of age changes in cognitive behavior." *Psychological Bulletin*, 1968, 68.
Copyright 1968 by the American Psychological Association and reproduced by permission.

allowance for historical trend. The historical trend or epogenic curve includes both biological and cultural effects, and, although no important change has taken place in that time in the former, we know definitely (see Chapter 10) that environmental contributions to scholastic crystallized intelligence have improved in that time. Consequently, any results by the simple or "standing" longitudinal method would show a significant decline in g_c with age (due to older age groups coming from poorer cultural eras) even if no change in the abstract normative curve really existed. The only other major influence needing allowance is the death rate, in regard to which there is some slight evidence that less intelligent individuals are less likely to survive into the later age cohorts. Men may be wise because they are old, but the correlation is aided by the probability that they are old because they are wise. Incidentally, a large part of what we call wisdom— the part that is not personality-produced—must essentially be g_c—in its social more than its scholastic expressions.

Recently, Wackwitz (1971) has re-analyzed age data of Horn and the present writer (1967) and that of Schaie and Strother (1968) employing the contrast of the simple longitudinal and the cursive longitudinal suggested in Table 7–2 (Cattell, 1970b) for obtaining the true abstract normative life course. He added the further feature of differentiating the equation of a best-fitting quadratic equation for these curves. His conclusions, still to be checked, of course, are that (1) as regards a_g, the traditional crystallized intelligence, the normative life course is slowly upward virtually all the way, and (2) as regards g_f the extraction of the epogenic curve trend *also* leaves the normative curve free of downward trend, at least to fairly advanced age.

The general conclusion may well be accepted, on the balance of evidence, that so long as the a_g curve is measured by tests central to the culture it shows no decline after the flattening at 16–17 but a very gentle rise, and that the conclusions prior to the re-formulations by Schaie and Strother (1968), Baltes (1968) and the present writer (1969b) are due to confounding with an epogenic curve which shows poorer performance for those educated in the early rather than the late twentieth century.

Before entering the debate on whether the g_f curve, by contrast, does (or does not) show some downward trend at all, in itself, let us ask about artifacts of testing. Culture-fair tests of proven validity are so recent that for the temporal curve evidence we are compelled to depend at present on inference from a few subtests contaminated by other general factors. In particular, the downward trend obtained could be due to systematic effects from the contaminating effects of speed, g_s, memorizing, g_m, and retrieval (fluency), g_r. As pointed out above, Thorndike and several others have hypothesized that such a fall is due to slowing down, not to inherent reduced capacity to perceive relations. One may recall that Spearman's original answer to the speed question was that the correlation of timed and untimed intelligence tests is so very high that speed *in intelligent judgments* is nothing but intelligence. Speed in simple cognitive processes, though, as in g_s, is something else. However, Spearman's subjects were generally at one age, and, as Bernstein's, Studman's and Horn's and others results show, one can find a distinct general speed capacity, g_s, and a distinct fluency (retrieval) capacity, g_r. These admittedly load simple performance much more than they do complex relation eduction. However, when a wide age range is factored, they do show *some* correlation with intelligence, and in any ordinary choice of g_f subtests *some* effect on curves, etc., from contamination with speed must be considered present in the former.

Thus although the theoretical situation is clearer since modern researchers have recognized the other general capacities—g_s, g_r, etc., *technical factor estimation* problems balk us notably in that a speed-free g_f measure has been difficult to accurately obtain. In other words, it still remains true, despite our ability to conceptualize and recognize speed and fluency as factors distinct from g_f, that in any actual g_f score estimate (measurement) by subtests we cannot easily find tests purely loaded in g_f and not also loaded in g_s and g_r. In looking at present curves we must not forget the possibility, therefore, that *these* capacities may decline steeply with age, and that, by their contamination of the g_f subtest measures, they give to the latter the appearance of declining too.

Figure 7–9 shows what is yet known about the age course of g_s and g_r. The latter does show a real age drop, but, at least if we give equal weight to Horn's research with Wackwitz and others, the drop in g_s—general cognitive speed—is not nearly as great as has been popularly supposed.[3] Perhaps the present conclusion is that general speed, g_s, shows a moderate decline with age, and fluency, g_r, a more steep one, especially in the later years. These are interesting findings in themselves, but as regards their implications for the interpretation of the g_f curve some doubt must remain. It would be wrong simply to subtract g_s and g_r out of g_f in the Horn data because, owing to the strong correlations of the former with age, one would be partialing out much age too. It would be better directly to free the estimates of g_f from tests loaded in these extraneous factors and observe the true correlation of g_f, as a pure factor, with age. Without exact data for this, a shrewd estimate would be that a pure g_f measure is *still* likely to show some age decline after about twenty years, though less than the current curves indicate.

---

[3] There is, of course, an appreciable margin of uncertainty here because of the scantiness and noncomparability of results. Thus Schaie's speed measure here is a single test and not a well-balanced measure of g_s, as in Horn's data. On the other hand, Horn's data is on a somewhat unusual (prison or delinquent) population. Similarly in the g_r curves, some are single tests, verbally biased, and one is a factor estimate. Again Schaie's results are somewhat anomalous on g_r in that the longitudinal actually declines less than the cross-sectional. Possibly as generations rise in g_c they decline in g_r, substituting learning for spontaneity! Some confidence can be added to the acceptance of a normal steep decline in g_r, however, from the fact that personality factors associated with high fluency, namely surgency (F in the questionnaire series), and U.I. 21, Exuberance (in objective batteries), both show a very decided age decline (Cattell, 1957a).

FIGURE 7–9
Age Changes in the Speed and Fluency-Retrieval General Capacities

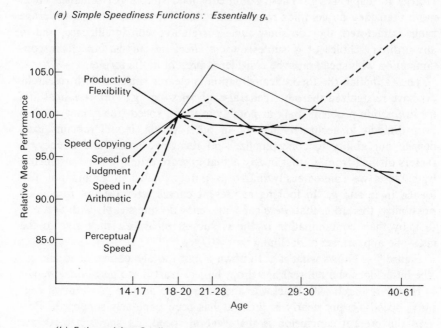

(a) Simple Speediness Functions : Essentially g_s

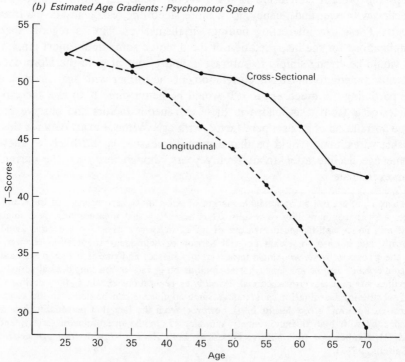

(b) Estimated Age Gradients : Psychomotor Speed

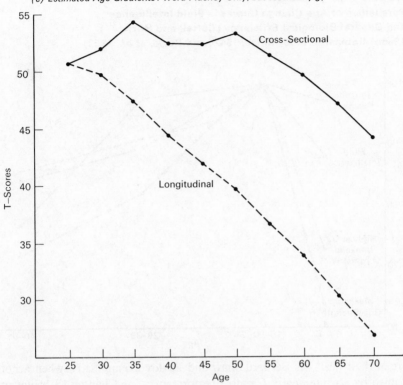

(c) *Estimated Age Gradients : Word Fluency Only, but essentially* g_f

(a) from J. Horn and Cattell, R. B., "Age differences in primary mental ability factors," *Journal of Gerontology*, 1966, 21, 210–220.

(b) and (c) from K. Warner Schaie, "A cross-sequential study of age changes in cognitive behavior." *Psychological Bulletin*, 1968, 68.
Copyright 1968 by the American Psychological Association and reproduced by permission.

Why should this be? Later evidence will tie g_f considerably to biological, neural efficient, and the fact is that almost every known biological index shows some decline from about twenty years of age. (Hearing begins to decline even from about eighteen years.) Certainly, as the dotted line in Figure 7–10 shows, there is a remarkable parallelism of g_f and general biological efficiency measures, especially oxygen metabolism.

Since these conclusions are likely to clash not only with one's fondest illusions but also with certain general human experience, let us look at the latter more closely. The peak in g_f is actually not so different from what we realistically recognize in athletic performances. Olympic champions are generally at peak performance in their teens or twenties, and a world-champion boxer is on the shelf (or at least on the floor!) by twenty-five or thirty. Sensory performances of vision and hearing are beginning to lose their range and elasticity from about twenty, and feats of memory are less common thereafter. Yet in cultured circles an obstinate conviction persists that some important qualities in the world of intellect ripen with age and

FIGURE 7–10

**Parallelism of Age Change Curves in Fluid Intelligence
and General Biological Efficiency (Cattell and Horn,
1966b; Robinson, 1938; Miles, 1942; and Burle, *et al.*, 1953)**

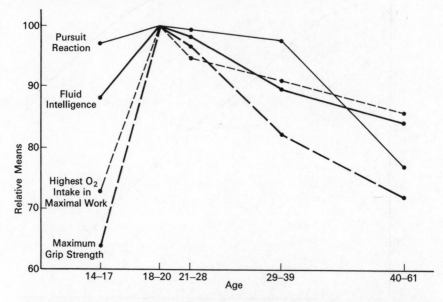

are at their best—as Bernard Shaw and Pavlov exemplified—when accompanied by a white beard. Creative performances, as Chapter 13 brings out, have their peak at different ages in different areas. But the pure "relational" performances, as in mathematics and nuclear physics (as in the works of Galois, Newton, Abel, Einstein and others), are the earliest to reach a peak of major contribution, which fits the g_f curve.

On the other hand, peak performances in cultural areas like history and politics, where a rich wisdom of experience is required, often come very late, as the performances of such men as Churchill, Darwin, Marx, Plutarch, Socrates and the writers of the Old Testament show.

Because of the way in which fluid intelligence is known to decline by reason of definitely known brain damage in individual cases, it has been almost assumed by some psychologists that the fall in *average* fluid ability in the whole population must represent some kind of widespread cumulative minor brain damage occurring in our population. It is an alarming challenge, and one that deserves to be met by thorough investigation (see page 79). But changes that amount to less than "damage" might be involved, such as a slowing down of metabolic rate in the nervous system, due to falling off in certain chemical pacemakers connected with hormones or oxygen transportation. If this latter is the true explanation fantastic possibilities arise of raising community mental capacity where it would most powerfully help society—in the experienced members—perhaps by some drug, as has been effected by tranquilizers in other directions.

It is a common oversight—needing to be watched in Chapter 10 where the relative variances due to heredity and environment are studied—to assume that environmental variance means educational variance. Teachers naturally fall into this trap, but the good guess today would be that nearly half of the environmental effect on intelligence is physiological: chemical and nutritional deficiencies in the womb, birth injuries, head injuries in childhood, atherosclerosis and gland deficiencies in middle age, and so on. Now the possibility must be seriously considered that the normative curve for g_f—whether it be the declining one of Figure 7–9 or the almost horizontal or very slightly declining one which Wackwitz's calculation (1971) suggests—is still not fully known to us because of our ignorance of the current epogenic curve which has to be subtracted to yield the normative curve.

As Windle (1969) concludes from his extensive studies, some degree of birth injury (in advanced societies which save the mother from pain) is more common than has been supposed, particularly in terms of partial asphyxia. He points out that in data from 14 participating U.S. medical institutions, "21 percent of the infants in the study had low apgar scores at birth" (op. cit., p. 83). These patent neurological defects tend to disappear in weeks or a few years, but his experimental studies with asphyxiation in new born monkeys show that the neural damage persists, the behavioral control presumably being transferred to undamaged areas. There is no need to be alarmed over this state of affairs (only 1½ % of all infants show neurological defects persisting to the end of the first year); but it is obvious that different obstetric and pre-natal care customs in particular could influence the population distribution of the neural substrate for g_f.

In short, g_f could also have its epogenic curve effects, altering from generation to generation, and what we get in this generation from the scanty data available for comparison of the SL and CCL curves (Figure 7–2) is not yet telling us what the true normative curve is. The best estimate is that with persons free of any of the physical diseases which affect brain function the g_f curve should stay relatively steady from 16 to 60, perhaps with a slight decline in the later years.

It is perhaps a puzzling question why g_c does not also show some similar decline to g_f, since, although it consists of learnt judgmental habits, they have to operate through a biological neural substrate. The answer would seem to be partly (a) that what declines in g_f is some global neural efficiency, not a local one, as in a reflex or specific skill (and the evidence of Chapter 8 is that the neural storage of g_c is much more localized); and (b) that the dynamic equilibrium of which we spoke is compatible with some loss in the original collection of g_c habits, but that learning and relearning more than make up for these losses.

The latter statement brings us back to the problem of the protean, polymorphic, and unstable character of g_c. We have recognized above that it is as protean as the forms of culture, and that the factor-loading pattern continues to metamorphize with age. (Notably, in early childhood it may

show in play with building blocks, following simple directions, code substitution, or putting a wooden manikin together; later in Koh's block,
verbal synonyms, and sentence completion, and so on; and later still in
bright persons by abstract performance such as complex number series—
which forever remain over the horizon of difficulty for the average intelligence.)

Particulars of the changing loading pattern of ordinary intelligence tests
with age have already been discussed above. But here we are considering
changes both from age and differing cultures and subcultures. These differences are far greater than the ordinary intelligence test user or the amateur
in cross-cultural research likes to contemplate. To take an extreme example
across both age and culture: how are we to compare the intelligence of an
American high school boy, measured on English vocabulary and number
series, say, with that of a middle-aged Tartar nomad of the time of Genghis
Khan, whose judgmental skills are in the world of desert climate, the construction of tent cities, and the tactics of bow and arrow battles from
horseback? At a common-sense level, people are content to speak of the
intelligences of such remote persons as being practically equal, as if indeed
the word could have a common meaning. As we may show in Chapter 10,
cross-cultural and, therefore, cross-age measures *are* theoretically possible
with due attention to technical points (Cattell, 1970a). There is really no
philosophical problem that cannot be resolved into a scientific and technical
one. However, the technical problems are so complex and so neglected
that many comparisons currently made with traditional, crystallized intelligence tests are not of a kind to permit *firm* conclusions about differences
over age or culture.

Finally, a word is necessary on what our present conclusions about g_f
and g_c age change mean for our conceptions of the real intelligence distribution in adults. Any measurements on a group of adults ranging from
twenty to sixty-five will give an altogether inflated idea of the range of I.Q.
For the standard deviation obtained will *compound* common age differences with individual differences. The present writer's pioneer study
(1933a) of intelligence in a more truly representative adult population
sample than had been previously available (only students had been surveyed previously) evoked surprise and scepticism by reason of the large
sigma (about 24 points of I.Q.) of I.Q.'s obtained. Yet later researches
with the full resources of government agencies supported the finding, and,
as we now see, the most likely theory *required* it. To "place" the intelligence of an adult, whether with g_c or g_f concepts, we need separate distributions for each interval (five years?) of adult age, and the I.Q. and
mental age concepts must take their meaning from those separate distributions. If we throw all ages together, and calculate from the raw score-to-
I.Q. transformation found at, say, sixteen years, the I.Q. sigma will be as
high as 24, even on g_c measures, as the present writer's 1933 study showed,
for the interindividual and interage group variances are added.

The present chapter has been fully occupied with stating our knowledge about the natural history of intelligence in quantitative analysis of distribution, sex differences, age curves, structural changes, etc., and must leave certain qualitative interpretations of these changes, e.g., of the age measurement changes in terms of conceptual reconstructions, to later chapters, notably Chapter 13 on the processes of creative thinking. It is important to have the perspectives of data relations firmly in mind before embarking on theory construction.

CHAPTER EIGHT

THE PHYSIOLOGICAL AND NEUROLOGICAL BASES OF INTELLIGENCE

1. ABILITY AND GROSS BRAIN FEATURES

"That man has brains!" is the somewhat elliptical metonym by which people often refer to outstanding intelligence. The conviction that for all practical purposes brain and intelligence are one is widespread—and in a basic sense not unreasonably so. For it is obvious that increasing brain size goes with increasingly intelligent adaptation in the animal world, and that damage to the brain in man can produce idiocy. Nevertheless, one of the first things that psychologists did in this century was to cast doubt on any simplicity of connection between brain and ability.

Some of this was the sheer hubris of the specialist out to debunk any popular idea. Students were taught that there is no correlation of head size with intelligence; that some of the largest heads are those of hydrocephalic imbeciles (the head being enlarged by the disease process); and that men of genius have been known to have subaverage brain weight, e.g., the case of Anatole France. (He died at eighty with a somewhat subaverage brain weight, conceivably due to the usual shrinkage of weight which occurs with age.[1] See Table 8–1.) On the other hand there is a class of imbecile

[1] As Cobb (1965) remarks, "Anatole France . . . might well have lost 100 grams from atrophy." The position of Whitman surely should not surprise readers not brainwashed by certain professors of literature.

In this neglected field the last extensive survey, by Hamilton (1936) thirty years ago, showed positive correlations prevailing but at values of only .05 to .10. These r's could be significant on large samples, but there is every reason to believe that they

TABLE 8–1
Weights of Certain Normal Human Brains in Grams

Australian bushwoman	794
Anatole France	1,017
Japanese woman (average)	1,250
Walt Whitman	1,282
European woman (average)	1,300
European man (average)	1,400
Thackeray	1,658
Bismarck	1,807
Cuvier	1,820

Reprinted with permission of the publisher from S. Cobb, "Brain Size," *Archives of Neurology*, 1965, 12, 555–561.

more "normal" and more numerous than hydrocephalics, called micro-cephalics, whose low intelligence is definitely associated with decidedly small size of a healthily functioning brain. More careful studies of brain weight show that persons of high intelligence tend to have significantly higher brain capacity. And one also discovers that the meagre correlations of +0.1 only between head size and intelligence, such as Pearson found, are often based on poor intelligence tests and poor measurement of cranial capacity. Recent studies (though still without culture-fair tests) give a more significant relation, for as Tyler (1956, p. 622) summarizes "Eleven studies have been made of the relationship between intelligence . . . and cranial capacity. In all instances, the correlations have been positive, although small, ranging from .08 to .34."

Head size is, of course, partly proportional to size of body, and part of the brain is concerned with sheer bodily management; but if we know how to allow for that part (see Jerison, 1955) from outside measurements, we might well get a decidedly better correlation between the size of the rest of the cortex and intelligence. However, the correlation of brain size and head size is only slight, and there is no question of substituting measures of the latter for intelligence tests. Certainly head size is only an extremely rough guide, because of different skull thicknesses, differing proportions of white and gray matter in the brain, differing body size, etc. The correlation even of brain size (post mortem) with the *number* of effective cortical neurons which are most involved in intelligence is again imperfect, on account of differences in genetic texture, number of convolutions, etc. By texture we mean among other things, number of cells per cubic centimeter and, as Cobb points out (1965), brains can vary considerably in this respect. (In spite of these several intermediate sources of error, and the

would be raised by (a) more modern intelligence tests, (b) allowance for body size, (c) equating for age, and (d) better methods of estimating brain size from head size. In connection with the last, Radinsky (1967) has recently proposed better approaches. Similarly Jerison (1955) discusses functions for better estimating expected brain weight from given body weight.

resulting low correlation of mere head size with intelligence, if you look at a roomful of top executives or leaders in science you may see more large heads than you see on the street! Nevertheless, intellectuals are *not* necessarily egg-headed, as the popular phrase has it—and had it two thousand years ago, when the Athenians noted that Pericles had an egg-shaped head!) At any rate, it was these suggestions of correlation of brain size with intelligence, in men and animals, as well as observations of behavioral effects of brain injuries that helped stimulate early investigators to study the brain in the hope of understanding intelligence.

Among researchers in the psychology of intelligence there has been a certain manifest reluctance to depend on brain investigation to get at the laws of ability—a reluctance which springs from more subtle and justifiable reasons than those of discouraging students from expecting a correlation of 1.0 between intelligence and head size! Throughout the history of behavioral science there has been a tendency, wherever the going got rough, to retreat from the baffling complexities of *structuring behavior itself* (such as we have wrestled with in the first six chapters here) to the consoling concreteness of the physical brain. The popularity of phrenology, even in the ranks of the professions, was an expression of this symptom. Somehow there lingers a belief that by peeping inside the cranium one will catch consciousness at work. The relating of neural and physiological conceptions to the concepts derived from behavioral science is a most fruitful undertaking—if *both* sides, neurologists and psychologists, come with something in hand to trade. The reluctance of the more farsighted psychologists to "go physiological" too early is a wise recognition of this false lure of the concrete and the mirage of expecting something for nothing in trade.

However, only in the last fifteen to twenty years have psychologists known enough about ability structure from behavior, and about the fluctuation and growth of abilities from reasonably exact ways of measuring these, to seek firm relations of behavioral findings with physiology and neurology.

2. THE DEGREE OF LOCALIZATION OF BRAIN FUNCTION

Because of this lack of dependable knowledge about ability structure—until quite recently—any attempt to make inferences about brain structure and ability structure at present must rest largely upon inquiries made with relatively obsolete tests and performances. Since records are in terms of tests not ideally chosen, they can only lead to somewhat speculative conclusions. Nevertheless, much actually was accomplished by brain surgeons and others working even at a purely qualitative level of behavior description. Indeed, the chief debates at the turn of the century about brain localization were fought out, and the main outlines of a settlement reached, largely on gross observations that such and such performances were affected in a virtually all-or-nothing fashion.

A brief discussion on brain localization of psychological functions is necessary before proceeding to brain and ability relations. One of the earlier more dramatic localizations was that of the center for speech at the left rear of the frontal lobe by Pierre Broca, the French anthropologist and surgeon. But the further discoveries about the middle of the last century of other such genuine localizations as Broca's area were obscured by the theories of phrenology which set people looking for a different kind of localization from that which actually seems to exist. Whereas Darwin's father actually surveyed his son's head for a bump of "patience" or some protuberance indicating a well-developed "faculty" of logical analysis, the truly confirmable localizations turned out in the end to be those of simple sensory and motor activities.

As Figure 8–1 shows, the visual center proved to be at the occipital cortex, the auditory center at the upper part of the temporal lobe, and the muscular control areas laid out, as if by a map of the body upside-down, on the mid-parietal region. Touch followed in a tactile area back of the motor cortex, and taste and smell on the in- and undersides of the temporal region. There is ample evidence that the region surrounding the occipital cortex, where the form of the visual retina is itself projected, is concerned with visual memories and meanings. Similarly, images and memories specifically of a certain sensory modality appear most clearly in the area around the neurons concerned with another particular sensory perception area. A central loss, in the visual area, means blindness, despite the eye being intact; but brain damage more peripherally may bring only loss of visual meaning. For example, in a case tested by the writer, of carbon-monoxide damage around the visual area, the patient could draw a fork (when shown it) but could not give its name or say what it is for. However, the outlying association areas that affect a given sensory center can be fairly remote, and, in the last resort, almost any part of the cortex can have relevance in regard to some symbolic or other association of a particular sensory center. Thus Luria (1970) presents evidence on the effect of gunshot wounds in Russian soldiers, showing that the percentage of interference with recognizing sounds declines almost uniformly in all directions with distance of the lesion from the left hemisphere auditory center, but that some slight effect is noted even at the most distant areas from the auditory zone.

More of the evidence on these matters has come from observing loss of function when the brain is damaged, either accidentally and in necessary surgical removal in humans, or in carefully controlled experiments with animals. It also comes from electrical stimulation, without any brain damage, of the exposed brain. With humans the evidence has frequently seemed highly contradictory, and though we now realize the nature of certain misleading assumptions responsible for our confusion, there are still lessons in subtlety of thought that we evidently have yet to learn. One of the more simple sources of confusion has been our failure to realize,

FIGURE 8–1
Some Principal Localizations of Cognitive Functions in the Brain

The most definitely localized areas are those of the five senses and muscular movement. Other capacities are divided up among the sense and movement areas according to the extent to which these are involved. Thus there is no single center for words, but a center for seen words, in the visual association areas, a center for heard words, around the auditory center, and so on. Any one of these capacities may be lost without the others being affected.

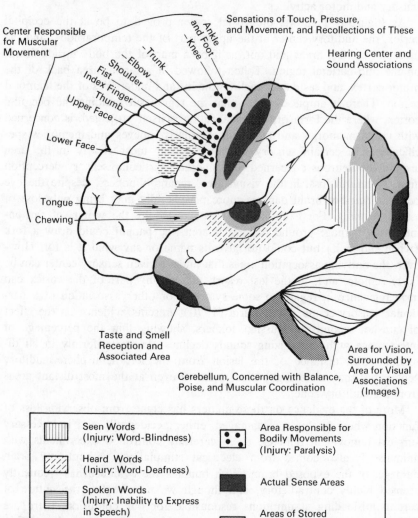

R. B. Cattell, *Your Mind and Mine*, George C. Harrap Publishers.

until certain experiments were done by Sperry and others, that a person can do practically everything (except bodily movements) with one hemisphere that he can do with two. It is as if the second hemisphere were not so much a means of augmenting the first, as a "spare" or an insurance against damage, operating in much the same role as the duplicate file that a foresighted man keeps for important copies of documents.

Very little loss of general learning ability and memory, for example, occurs in animals with one lobe removed—except for those few abilities—including motor control of the opposite side of the body, which lodge on one side only. Remarkable experiments have been done by cutting the connections between the two halves, producing independently learning and operating brains. But that is another and rather specialized story, and the important point from it for ordinary brain localization as discussed here is only that confusing inferences are drawn in animal experiments unless bilaterally symmetrical parts are removed, since one half otherwise can take over easily for the other. Puzzling contradictions also arise from two other sources: (1) that the effect of damage or ablation of the very same area will be different at one age from that found at another, and (2) that effects will be different according to the stage of learning of a particular skill. In addition to these special cautions the student of behavior and brain injury must be alert to the systematic principle that cessation of behavior X with a neurological injury Y does not prove that X is "located" there. The absence of Mr. X from a conference when there is fog at the airport Y does not prove that Mr. X lives at the airport. In more general terms, anything depending on a chain of events—as most neural action does—can be stopped by a break in any one of several links. A necessary is not a sufficient condition. These characteristics place neuro-psychology in especial need of being handled by multivariate experimental designs, but unfortunately, until recently few of its exponents have been qualified in such techniques as factor analysis, canonical correlation work, etc.

Prior to systematic experimental work it was at least clear, however, that localization held best for quite specific sensory and motor functions and that more complex mental functions are located more diffusely. It was also evident that, in the event of local loss, one part of the brain can take over to some extent the functions formerly belonging to another. This occurs much more readily at an early age with functions that do not have so inveterate a localization as the sensory experience itself.

Although functions corresponding to more abstract psychological concepts, e.g., linguistic ability (which has visual, auditory, and motor elements), seem less localizable and clearly involve a variety of interconnecting tracts among the sensory and motor zones, yet certain relatively general functions, especially those dealing with personality and emotion, show some localization. A notable instance is the locating of controlling, associative, and inhibiting functions in the frontal lobes. This is shown in animal experiment by the inability of frontal-lobectomized monkeys, for example, to learn to make *delayed* discriminatory responses. Thus, if they can learn to choose food from under a square rather than a triangle, but then have to learn to wait ten seconds before taking the food, they become confused if frontal lobe tissue has been removed. Similarly, in human beings, frontal injuries typically cause no specific sensory or motor loss as such, but a loss of ability to concentrate, to control impulses and emotions, and to recall and respect the social inhibitions one has been taught. Another instance of a decided localization of a general ability is revealed by the inability to commit recent events of any kind to memory which follows certain bilateral injuries to the hippocampus (and amydala) on the lower, mid-inner sides of the two hemispheres.

As to intelligence, if the neurologist acquainted primarily with the qualitative findings up to, say, 1920, had been asked to locate it anywhere, he would probably have designated the frontal lobes. It must be admitted, however, that this would be partly because (a) no specific sensori-motor functions were found there, and by exclusion one had to find *something* that the region was doing; (b) the verbal control area (Broca's area) was at the beginning of the frontal area, suggesting that some "abstract skills" are projected further forward; and (c) the accessory powers of attention, concentration, and "reasoning," which are so necessary to much intelligent problem-solving, seemed to be located there. Apart from this, all that could be said was that gross brain injury *anywhere* generally brought some apparent reduction of intelligence.

3. EVIDENCE FOR INTELLIGENCE AS GENERALIZED COORDINATED CORTICAL ACTION

One of the first extensive experimental explorations of brain function was due to Karl Lashley who operated on the brains of rats in the 1920s. As a small boy Lashley had accompanied his father on the Klondike gold rush, and something of that exploratory fever remained with him, though in his new conception of Eldorado, the lure of gold had become transmuted into that of scientific truth. Certain scholars today are apt to point to some errors in his work, as the armchair pundits will doubtless continue to do till doomsday in their characteristic, effeminate envy of the trail-breaker with ice in his hair and his eye sweeping previously unseen expanses. Some mistakes always will be made on the rugged trail where decisions have to be made relentlessly—one, two, three. Lashley drew maps of the rat brain and systematically ablated different parts in different sets of rats until all areas were covered. As this was done, he investigated the effects both upon the learning of new habits and on the use of maze and problem-solutions which the rats already had learned.

He found the anticipated losses of, for example, visual learning and memory from injuries to the visual area, and the usual sensory-motor losses from the motor areas, but also something new. He found that a wider brain area was necessary in effectively *learning* a new habit than in *retaining* it. It had long been realized that certain processes—loosely called "consolidation"—go on in the storage of things in memory for an appreciable time *after* the actual experience. This is shown, for example, by the existence of retroactive inhibition—the impairment of memory for learning process A, if instead of the brain lying fallow, a new learning task, B, follows immediately afterwards. It is evidenced also by losses of memory that people suffer for an incident if the brain receives some kind of shock immediately after the incident. So here, in later work, it was found that removal of tissue before or immediately after learning did more damage to the habit than it did after the habit was well ingrained. One likely explanation of this would be that when *most* of consciousness and attention are involved in the learning, *much* of the brain is also involved. Further, appreciable areas evidently continue to be involved in the consolidation, but as the behavior settles to an almost unconscious habit it is relegated neurologically to less diffuse paths, indeed to narrow channels lower in the cortex, and in some cases ultimately even to a lower brain or spinal level.

Finding that, with *complex* learning, removal of brain tissue almost anywhere impaired learning, Lashley proposed a *principle of equipotentiality* of neural resources. Spearman perceived in this an excellent possible agreement with his notion of "g" as a general "energy," and, as the present writer recalls from being present at a discussion in the London laboratory between Spearman and Lashley in the mid-twenties, Lashley felt reasonably satisfied with this explanation at the time. Later he encountered evidence in his work which seemed to make this too simple, and he veered toward Thurstone's emphasis on primary abilities. Evidence of human brain damage also seems in some cases to place emphasis on "mass action" and in others on "special area" explanations, thus paralleling the swings of emphasis between second-order general factors and first-order primaries which we have seen to occur in the ability structure realms with each new piece of evidence (see Chapters 3 and 4 above).

The kind of evidence which favors the notion of certain, special-area abilities is the occurrence of amnesic aphasia from left pre-frontal lobe injury. The physician's definition of aphasia, incidentally, Thurstone equates in quantitative measurement terms to a drop in the W or V primaries (page 79). Again, lobectomy for temporal-lobe damage (near the hearing center) has been shown to reduce performance on the Seashore test of musical ability, notably in tonal quality and tonal pattern discrimination. And although such injury does not upset the ordinary, overlearned ability to recognize spoken words, it does reduce capacity to recognize words unusually pronounced, or embedded in noise, and the power to repeat stories orally presented.

In later chapters (notably 11 and 13) the notion is developed that the most abstract logical relations and concepts stand at the head of a hierarchy of relations which, on the "ground floor" consist of relations at a simple sensory level and in one sense. For example, spot A is bigger than spot B; note X is higher in pitch than note Y. Abstraction (necessarily followed by adopting symbols for the manipulation and reference storage of such abstractions) is intrinsically a building up of relations among relations. Usually, such a development of higher order abstractions carries one almost from the beginning far outside any single sensory or motor area. Consequently, in brain structure, we should expect that relations lower in the logical hierarchy would have some intermediate degree of localization, whereas the higher abstractions would transcend any one "provincial" sensory or motor domain. Thus, initially, there might, for example, be an association area for lower order abstractions linking only visual and auditory experiences, which, while not as large as the whole cortex—concerned with the most general relations of all—still requires an appreciable extent of brain mass for its action (compared to recognition within a single sense channel). Luria (1970) notes that a lesion in the lower part of the left parietal lobe affects perception of spatial orientation, e.g., on a map, ability to compute and sense of grammatical form, and asks what these can have in common. He concludes that appreciation of relations of sequence are necessary for success in all of these, and that an abstraction of sequence occurs both in spatial and temporal perceptions, which tend to be carried symbolically more by spatial thinking which has been partly located in the lower left parietal area. Indeed, the parietal area, which lacks any extensive specific sensory lobalization, must be considered an appreciable part of that association mass required for the ultimate abstractions.

In summary, it can now be generalized with some confidence that ablation or injury to the "projection area" of any one of the sensory—sound, vision, taste, somesthesia, etc.—or motor centers, i.e., the surrounding area of projection fibers, upsets an ability. That ability is the capacity to perceive any complexity of pattern, spatial or temporal (i.e., involving sense of duration) in connection with the given sense. When injuries occur at greater radial distances from the sensory center the loss of finer patterns and discriminations *as such* is often more evident than when the central sensory area alone is damaged. For example, the early work of Rejlander found injury distally placed around the speech area might not affect the apparent size of vocabulary, but did affect the nice use of abstract word meaning. Such discrimination is definitely of the nature of what we measure in primary abilities and moves in the general direction of what is commonly meant by intelligence as the capacity to perceive relationships.

However, it is also true, as far as can be inferred from results with tests not previously oriented to modern ability structure concepts, that injury almost anywhere in the cortex produces a reduction in intelligence—for the moment in a sense common to g_f and g_c. Russian investigators, who have concentrated a good deal on brain physiology, claim that no less than three-quarters of the cortex has nothing to do *directly* and specifically with either any one of the sensory input centers or the motor output activities. This mass we shall call the "association mass." But it may be added that even sensory area X may act as a source of integrating associations for sensory center Y. There is no contradiction between specificity and generality: there *is* specific brain localization, and there *is* a general mass action of the total cortex. Thus, by recent findings Lashley's mass action is by no means abolished, but only qualified. Indeed, granted that we speak of cortical tissue (not basal ganglia, cerebellum, etc.) there remains a fundamental truth in the simple statement that "intelligence can be weighed by the pound." The recent careful work of Ross (1958) for example, shows slight but significant loss of I.Q. after quite varied forms of brain injury. (This does not deny, however, that as McFie (1960) shows, the special primary abilities are also selectively impaired, according to brain area.) Another research showing how more sensitive measures give clearer evidence is that of Lansdell (1968) showing that amount of injury and brain removal in the temporal lobe, which one might at first expect to affect verbal ability, and by left more than right side injuries, actually shows the most consistent relation not to verbal but to general reasoning ability (among the primary abilities tested). The correlation of injury and loss was 0.51 (P < .05), and it was equipotential on right or left sides.

The more sensitive the intelligence measurement devices, the more clearly is it demonstrable that in addition to the particular primary or sensory area ability loss first noticed, there is also some loss in general ability. Aphasics, for example, also show some deterioration in nonverbal tasks, i.e., not only in such subtests as sentence completion, analogies, opposites and synonyms, but also in the "spatial" matrices, complex and speeded form boards, mazes, and the detection of absurdities.

4. QUALIFICATIONS AND COMPLICATIONS OF MASS ACTION THEORY

It is perhaps almost unnecessary to say, at this point, that the field of brain neurology, in relation to ability, would require highly complex and qualified statements as well as many new terms—even if we knew all. Thus, for example, frontal-lobe operations on humans for therapeutic purposes often do *not* produce the I.Q. loss that the above statement would suggest. But operations in their particular cases probably brought improvement by remedying unusual emotional blocks to the use of ability. The ensuing increase in power of concentration then more than compensated for loss of relation-perceiving capacity due to the neurological loss. However, one of the most systematic sources of necessary qualification of the above generalizations concerns the effect of age of the subjects. It had long been observed in the work of Beach, Lashley, Tsang, Vygotsky, and others in this area that damage of the same relative magnitude in the brain of a young child or animal did not seem to result in the same loss as in an adult. Neurologists are indebted particularly to D. O. Hebb (1959a) for perceiving the order in what was, before his article, a rather bewildering and seemingly contradictory array of evidence.

The capacity for memories and skills to relocate themselves in the child brain is apparently much greater than in the adult, and where the latter may suffer losses which are, in part, permanent, the former may recover completely. Considering this in conjunction with the different degrees to which other performances are affected—namely, a loss of a more specific and local kind of ability in the older person—Hebb developed the neurological basis of a concept of two kinds of general ability, which he called "A and B abilities" (page 80). The theory of fluid and crystallized ability, put forward by the present writer while these neurological findings were emerging, integrated into a single theory this neurological evidence for two kinds of ability with (1) the basic factor-analytic evidence, (2) the evidence of standard deviation differences in the g_c and g_f I.Q.'s, (3) the findings on the very distinct age curves throughout life, and (4) the evidence for changing cultural forms of the g_c patterns.

Russian neuropsychologists have put forward related theories and observations, which are partly re-interpretable in the simple mass action principle used by Hebb to explain the g_f and g_c difference, and partly in the further investment theory and the dual hierarchy set theory discussed below. Vygotsky (1934 in 1965) pointed out that classical localization theory could not explain certain observations. In particular he instanced that a change occurs in a behavioral function "located" in brain area A, when relatively remote brain areas B, C, etc., connected with other functions are destroyed. For example an apraxia (motor disturbance) may be determined partly by damage causing a verbal aphasia. Also he insisted that the nature of the disturbance at A depended partly upon whether B or C areas were involved. None of the semi-mystical concepts of Vygotsky are necessary, however, to account for these observations. First, the mass referral law (a suitably modified statement of the mass action principle in which the primary emphasis is that all the cortex enters into *any* relation eduction) will account for the effect of B and C upon A's functions. Secondly, the specific nature of the effects respectively of B and C can be traced to the "provincial powers" or p factors in the triadic theory (Chapter 11), which are differently sensorially localized. Thirdly, the dual hierarchy set theory (Section 7, below) reminds us that both the localization and the mass referral principles require, to complete the explanation, a dynamic theory of "sets." That is to say, the outcome of whatever potentialities are local or massive and general depends on the way these potentialities are put together by the dynamic sets of the moment. The aspect of these lawful observations that has to do with differential effects from developmental age will be considered with the *investment theory* in Section 7 below.

Meanwhile a word is necessary on some apparently conflicting experimental results with regard to the *mass referral* (or mass action, or equipotentiality, to use slightly different conceptualizations) principle. In the first place, because of the marked crudity at present of measures aimed to test the equivalent of g_f in animals, the present writer doubts the precision of certain experimential conclusions that animals brain-injured early in life not only recover the particular abilities but reach a *general* intelligence level no different from that of uninjured animals. Even in experiments on the corresponding theme in humans, the intelligence testing has not been sensitive enough in terms of sufficiently factorially clear test-concepts to prove this. The basic fact must not be overlooked that neural tissue does not regenerate itself. One must distinguish, moreover, between the notion of mass referral (equipotentiality or mass action), which is apparently sound enough, and that of *unlimited* substitutability, or boundless capacity to relocate. The young animal can relocate, and return to a high level of performance, but it cannot escape the law of mass action and almost certainly suffers some general learning-ability loss. Indeed, it may be hypothesized that there is a sense in which the young animal's loss from early brain injury is greater. *For he loses not only the capital but the gains from the years of interest at which that capital would have been invested in producing crystallized abilities*—whereas, the adult injured in adult life has already collected these gains.

Some further discussions of special kinds of evidence must follow before justifying our particular theoretical resolution, but briefly to anticipate that conclusion, we may say that fluid ability is conceived as a power which is a function of the total, effective, associative, cortical cell mass and of certain parameters of efficiency in those cells. The efficiencies are concerned with metabolic rate, biochemical qualities discussed in the next section, and freedom from too high a burden of memory storage. But at any rate, they are parameters which seem to be at an optimum level in early maturity. This power of a given neurological mass at a given physiological efficiency goes to work with learning experience, as described in Chapter 11 below, to build up a wide spectrum of acquired judgmental skills. The majority of these are concerned with complex relationships and constitute what are called "crystallized general intelligence," the parts of which can be quite locally "stored."

To fit the neurological findings with respect to age we must bring to the theory the additional hypothesis that in the young animal the operation of a particular skill is not so rigidly and narrowly neurologically channelled as later. By this hypothesis a localized injury would not produce such a localized behavioral deficit in a younger as in an older animal, but would produce the same loss in fluid ability. This same-sized loss in fluid ability would, however, show up, as usual, in other areas than the local one, and probably more so in early injury, because all areas are more sustained in their action by fluid ability in the young, while more judgment-behavior has been shifted to crystallized ability in the old. Young and old would show this loss equally in learning something entirely new, but the loss might be more important for the post-mature adult who (see the age curves of page 168) has less capital left even before the traumatic loss. On the other hand, if certain complex, say, mathematical notions require a certain g_f level, the individual who sustains injury in adult life, after he has mastered and stored these, is better off, as pointed out in the paragraph above, than if he had sustained the g_f less early, and never mastered these discriminations as g_c investments.

This much integration of observations can be attempted with reasonable safety at the present time, resulting in a theory which possesses appreciable simplicity along with a rather wide efficiency of prediction. But at the present moment, in the path of further advance stands a virtually insurmountable obstacle left by the failure of learning theory to come to terms with neurology over the nature of *memory*. Attempting a reconnaissance of the road block, we may see in the following section that there are at least three equally entertainable and highly divergent theories of what happens in memorizing. And since we cannot properly handle the relation of g_f to g_c without some knowledge of the neurology and physiology of memory, our further steps in theory development have to remain tentative.

5. EVIDENCE FROM ELECTRICAL ACTION OF THE BRAIN

Before returning in Section 7 to a final attempt at integration, despite some difficult issues there, let us take stock of findings in areas beyond neural anatomy, namely, in neural function, in electroencephalography, and physiology. The expectation that the brain would "work by electricity" is as old as Galvani's early experiments with frog's nerves and the electric current. Demonstration of the existence of electrical potential waves during brain action was given first for animal brains by the English physiologist Caton in 1875. A German psychiatrist, Berger, developed in 1924–1929 the technique of taking what we now call encephalograms, or EEG records, from the human skull and showed their value in exploring brain damage and epilepsy. Since then an extremely widespread use of EEG records, along with computers, has given a fairly substantial, but still somewhat obscure foundation, along with the chemical findings of such great contributors as Adrian (1947) and Eccles (1966) for inferences on neural functioning in brain action.

From two or more leads lightly gummed to the skull (or in some cases, electrodes placed on the brain itself) currents based on fifty to one-hundred millionths of a volt are picked up, amplified, and printed on a record as shown in Figure 8–2. The average amplitude seems to be about fifty microvolts. The problem of how to read this odd handwriting of the brain was answered first by the recognition of the presence of some four or five different wave frequencies: an alpha rhythm of 8–13 per second, a beta much quicker, and delta and theta rhythms which are slower and less regular. Most work has been done on the alpha waves which vary in frequency, in amplitude, and in the extent of their interruption. (A high "alpha index" means that alpha frequency is steadily present much of the time.) However, amplitude, frequency, phase relationship, and other aspects equally deserve attention.

Visual stimuli, mental computation, and other evidences of concentration momentarily blot out the occipital alpha rhythm. Incidentally, the findings regarding alpha interruption agree with the brain localization concepts from the other methods above, in that a visual stimulus produces most

FIGURE 8–2
Wave Forms Visible in an Electroencephalogram

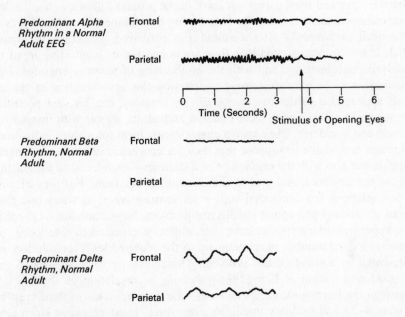

Predominant Alpha Rhythm in a Normal Adult EEG — Frontal — Parietal

Time (Seconds) — Stimulus of Opening Eyes

Predominant Beta Rhythm, Normal Adult — Frontal — Parietal

Predominant Delta Rhythm, Normal Adult — Frontal — Parietal

interruption in the occipital lobe, and abnormality of the left prefrontal region alpha coincides with verbal ability loss, and so on. The first impact of any stimulus produces wave changes largely at one amplitude, but, as Gernstein at MIT demonstrates, the disturbance then spreads over a wider range of amplitudes. A stone dropped into a barrel of water at first sets up regular waves, which then are reduced and augmented by reflections, and we may conjecture that "processing" by other brain regions similarly sends back more varied sets of reverberations.

Three ways of extracting some order that would permit more intelligible reading of the complex handwriting suggest themselves. One is a Fourier analysis, mechanically breaking down the observed wave form into components (such as the five or so above). Another is the simple notion of repeating a stimulation or other process dozens of times and averaging say, the first ten seconds of brain potential changes following the stimulus. Thus one gets a single essential process curve, cleared of "noise," as in what have recently been called "evoked potentials." The third possibility is to take as variables many measurable features of the electroencephalographic outputs of a large number of people and to factor analyze them. This would assume that the varying amplitudes of the various frequencies can be traced to a small number of underlying influences, each with its particular spectrum of influence across the frequencies. (See discussion of process analysis, i.e., resolution into basic process curves; Cattell, 1966.)

The second has been performed very extensively, and an elaborate computer—the "average response computer" (ARC)—has shown that indeed there are marked regularities—at least, in the process following stimulation. For example, there is a regular long-lasting but dampening series of waves ("evoked potentials") after a stimulus is perceived, as shown in Figure 8–3. It has been suggested that they are connected with referring input to analyzing mechanisms, and with the establishing of memory engrams. For circumstances (e.g., anaesthesia) which stop this reverberation of potentials appear also to destroy committing to memory, etc. Evoked potential waves become faster with older children and adults, slower with thyroid removal and in old age. They keep a characteristic form for a given individual. It seems reasonable to suppose that they are concerned not only with memorizing but also with the *evaluation* of a stimulus—its referral to the sorting in the sensory area, and also to the eduction of relations. For they appear when relations are demanded with other sensory areas, as when one presents a standard perceptual intelligence problem. Now a smaller total cortical apparatus, like a smaller computer, might be expected to take longer to process a fixed number of relations up to the required level for solution, as presented by a standard test problem. This is exactly what appears in the original observation of Ertl (1966) showing a correlation of about -0.7 between the latency measure (taken as time from stimulus to third crest in Figure 8–3) and ordinary intelligence measures. Incidentally, as Horn also shows, the reliability of the latency measure as a "trait" is high (.7 to .9) so that, with a reliable intelligence test, such a correlation is not intrinsically impossible. A careful followup by Horn (1969) confirms the rather surprising significances of Ertl and his associates, though the magnitude of the correlations in an adequate sample and a well-chosen array of ability factors proves to be nearer to -0.3. The special virtue of Horn's analysis is his testing the latency against a whole array of measures, in which he finds the largest r's with g_f and g_c, but also, in certain phases of the curve, with g_r—retrieval effectiveness or fluency. Thus a shorter latency is a result not only of the larger cortical mass for relation eduction, underlying g_f, but also of the effectiveness of assembling relevant information and judgmental skills. Horn also brought out the important fact that the correlation is better if subjects receive stimuli when at a low level of arousal. It would be interesting next to see if the correlations for g_f and g_r are better respectively when the stimulus is a culture-fair intelligence problem and a problem requiring much referral to memory resources.

Turning next to relations of ability to the "resting state" EEG, we encounter such contradictory results as to justify the comment that if investigators in this field had first structured (factor-analytically) the EEG specttrum (Cattell and Elmgren, In press), the findings would have been more consistent. Naturally, one speaks here of both individual difference factor analysis and also what has been called differential factor analysis or process factor analysis. It is a sad illustration of the slowness of techniques to cross academic boundaries that among thousands of EEG researches it is impos-

FIGURE 8-3
Evoked Potentials as a Measure of Intelligence

>   *Dr. Ertl's method picks out the critical (typically the third)*
>   *wave crest, as indicated by the dots on these specimens from*
>   *seven of his subjects. The time in milliseconds from the*
>   *moment of stimulus is then found to be simply inversely related*
>   *to the I.Q.*

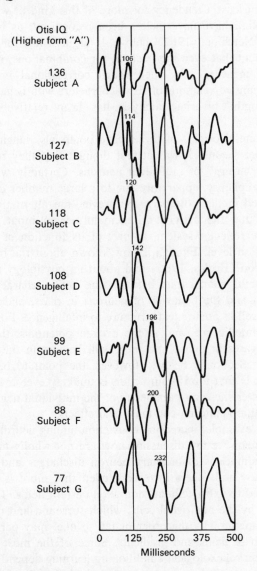

Otis IQ
(Higher form "A")

136
Subject A

127
Subject B

118
Subject C

108
Subject D

99
Subject E

88
Subject F

77
Subject G

0   125   250   375   500
Milliseconds

● Indicates Third Event

J. P. Ertl, "Evoked potentials and intelligence," *Revue de l'Université d'Ottawa*, 1966, 36(4), 599–607.

sible to find more than half a dozen experiments (and those, alas, inadequate) that have attacked EEG wave analysis factor-analytically. Indeed, the first crude method—simply examining associations with individual wave frequencies—has prevailed. What one would expect to get from the other technique is the discovery of a number of focal origins corresponding to distinguishable spectra extracted by the factor analysis, as the astronomer and chemist recognize in a single broad spectrum the presence of several distinct elements by the different *spectra* characteristic of each. Correlations showing at least a tendency for more of this kind of wave to go with more of that kind have nevertheless been recognized, as in the work of Netchine and Netchine (1962) below. It argues well for a full factor-analytic treatment that even their search for combinations of scores (from separate wave measures) by such rough correlational impression have brought significant correlations of EEG characters with behavior which the "one wave length" bivariate analysis has been relatively impotent to show.

As to the general origins of these wave potentials, ranging from six to eighty cycles per second, it was at first thought that they represented the summation of "firings" of individual neurons. Certainly wave forms are known, e.g., in epilepsy, apparently due to a large number of cells becoming synchronized in their discharge. However, the alternative also has to be considered that the activity arises mainly from input, notably from pulses from the reticular system, as part of its function of maintaining a suitable activation level. Enough is now known about the behavior of the individual neuron (Eccles, 1966) and about its physiology for us soon to make some useful connections between the action characteristic of the isolated neuron and the behavior of neurons in mass, and thus to relate physiology as well as anatomical structure to intelligence. For example, the known fall in intelligence, and in the evoked potentials, through thyroid deficiency are cases in point, and more will be met in the discussion on biochemistry in Section 6 below. However, the point to be made in the present context is that total brain action is unlikely ever to be predictable from the characteristics and parameters of the individual neuron alone, but only from position (pattern) and mass field effects.

There is, for example, increasing conviction among neurologists that the general phenomena we are discussing now are not wholly to be explained in terms of summations of ordinary neuron discharges and synapse phenomena. Rusinov and others have concluded that more is due than was formerly realized to extra-cellular, non-axon current fields. The white matter constituted by the neuroglial cells, which surround and outnumber the neurons (grey matter) by the order of ten to one, may participate in the formation of these fields and gradients. Some of the most successful attempts to explain reflexological conditioning learning depend on the notion that centers of excitation set up general field "sets" within which the synapse behavior of particular, individual neurons is altered. It is specifically theorized, in fact, that fields of frequency-modulated signals create the conditions for synapse connections to function. Thus the macroscopic and the microscopic approaches ultimately may be brought into convergence in more than a speculative, theoretical sense.

To return to the EEG phenomena *per se,* it is evident that whatever the full nature of these regular wave forms picked up by the electrodes may be, the alpha wave is some kind of homeostatic energy system. Like a flywheel it betokens energy "resting," ready to be used. Brazier suggests it may be a rhythmic excitement level in the dendritic layers of the cortex. When a person perceives, concentrates, or thinks, the simple oscillation is wiped out as by some kind of discharge. Furthermore, it has been noted that its very existence depends on the existence of a sufficiently large volume of associational cortex, i.e., cortex not directly concerned to cope with sensorimotor immediate experience as such. For example, it is quite hard to find alpha in animals, or in children before a certain stage of brain development, and, as we shall now see, it is apt to be of slower frequency in mental defectives.

The general finding in experiments exploring the relation of alpha waves to intelligence was initially thought to be a significant positive relation between higher alpha frequency and higher mental age. However, it is now realized that this relation is far more consistent and large among those with subnormal intelligence, and brain size or with age-sclerosis or brain-damaged deteriorations than in the normal adult range, in which it scarcely exists. Vogel and Broverman (1966), who note this, suggest that the poor and often insignificant relations in the adult range may be due to the adult areas of intelligence expression—what we would designate the crystallized intelligence manifestations—being very different in different people. This amounts to saying that adult intelligence in the experiments concerned has not been properly measured by traditional intelligence tests; to which we can only say 'amen.' If the protean non-comparability of adult intelligence tests is the problem, the correlations should become as significant as those with children when culture-fair (fluid ability) intelligence tests are used in these experiments instead.

The initial hopes for a simple relation of ability measures to alpha rhythm are thus clearly ruled out by the careful surveys of Lindsley (1961), Ostow (1954) and Ellingson, indicating there is no relation in normal adults but only in the early years—where slower gamma and delta waves give way to faster and more prevalent alpha—and in brain-injured persons, where the whole EEG is, in any case, upset. On such bases two hypotheses about the EEG that need to be considered are as follows: First, as we have seen, there is the suggestion that a "critical mass"—analogous to the critical mass necessary for selfsupporting nuclear fission—of "free associational" brain tissue, i.e., neurons not absorbed in specific, sensory, local organizations, may be necessary to produce these rhythms. That mass is somewhere in the intelligence range between the higher mammals and man. Among younger children and mental defectives or deteriorated adults of about a six to ten-year mental age, the correlation of more rapid, developed alpha rhythm with mental age is appreciable—about $+ 0.3$ to $+ 0.6$. However, as others have noted, the relation is more significant with mental age than with I.Q., i.e., there are developmental as well as sheer magnitude associations. Thus the evidence is, in any case, that the relation is curvilinear, and as we get to cortical masses in the adult and superior adult ranges, further increase in intelligence-growth become irrelevant to increase in alpha characteristics.

The second hypothesis is that the alpha rhythm frequency, though *related* to some cortical feature highly responsible for intelligence, is not a direct and unmediated expression of it. Alpha frequency may, for example, be an index of latent resources. If this is so, good research strategy would suggest that, instead of taking "resting" measures on the EEG, we should take measures of how these wave features change, especially when complex stimuli and intelligence-demanding problems are presented, as in the pioneer work of Ertl and Horn, with its finding that latency of the third wave phase in the evoked potential does correlate with intelligence and that the subject's level of prior arousal is important. Along the same line of strategy is the above-mentioned claim of Netchine in Paris that the correlations with mental age are much better if one takes, instead of alpha frequency, a compound index of this value with amplitude and certain patterns in the EEG. One would be inclined to hypothesize that it would be better still if beta rhythm (positively) and presence of delta and theta rhythm (negatively) were included in the regression weights for the index, since they also correlate with intelligence as indicated by certain exploratory researches.[2]

In summary, even at the present stage of research, if one is prepared to discount certain failures to demonstrate connections as probably due to poor choice of type of intelligence tests, and low correlations as due to using single variables (with much specific in them) instead of weighted estimates of EEG factors, one would conclude that very suggestive relations have been found. At least over lower intelligence ranges there is evidence from the field of electrical observations, which converges with that from anatomical observations discussed previously to the important conclusion that intelligence is closely related to the magnitude of the physiologically active cortical mass of "associational" interconnective neurons. Recent more direct approaches to evaluating this neuronal mass as in pneumoencephalographic (X-ray examination) studies (Kiev, Chapman, Guthrie, and Wolf, 1962) generalize that "the degree of impairment of the highest integrative functions

---

[2] We return with this reflection to the argument above, that if a technically good factor analysis of individual difference variables of the EEG were carried out, there is every prospect that a factor would be found (i.e., a weighting of various manifestations more meaningfully devised than the already promising rough index of the Parisian researchers) that would correlate very highly with intelligence. Furthermore, from the demonstrations of Landantytkina, A. Glass, and others, that the desynchronization of waves (as in alpha index interruption) seems proportional in individuals to the effort of concentration they are required to make to a problem, correlations surely should appear between the magnitude of such evoked disturbances when different people are presented with problems of standard difficulty.

is directly related to total number of inadequately functioning cortical neurons."

In time, this cortical associational neuron mass must be anatomically and histologically more precisely defined for the more exact testing of the theory that it corresponds to g_f. One gets hints, for example, from both the electrical (e.g., Netchine correlations) and the anatomical evidence, that this associational mass is less concentrated in the occipital and frontal lobes than in the more central cortex. For instance, correlations of brain injury with intelligence, as Weinstein and Teuber and others show, are somewhat lower when the mass lost is measured in these frontal and occipital areas than when in parietal, rolandic, and temporal areas. There are even suggestions (DeRenzi and Faglione, 1965; Smith, 1964) that the left hemisphere is slightly more important not only in verbal ability (Broca area) but in general intelligence.

An intriguing problem for the psychologist looking for the neural basis of abilities resides in the peculiar status of the frontal lobes, which we have barely discussed. From the early days of neurology it was realized that these lobes had no immediate sensory or motor function, and there was a distinct inclination, at the "phrenology" stage of investigation, to associate a high forehead with high intelligence. Observations of brain injuries quickly showed that emotional control, foresight, and prudence were the chief loss from such injury, and intelligence tests seemed to show no more reduction than would follow from comparable injury anywhere else in the brain.

Much valuable controlled experimental work on animals by Pribram (1960), Bianki (1962), Franz (1902), and Konorski (1948), as well as the special studies of Harlow (1949), support this general conclusion, and show the area to be concerned with planning, maintaining sequential sets, and handling the motivation impulses and general arousal signals that arise from the brain stem and the reticular system. Harlow, Pribram, and others have shown that animals with frontal lobe injuries lose delayed-action but not discriminatory powers. The studies of electrical brain action by Grey Walter (see Section 5 below), also confirm the role of frontal lobes in handling excitatory input. Evidently the assignment of many frontal lobe association traits to projections from the hypothalamic area, and therefore to the important tasks of *emotional* analysis and conduct control (which it has not been our business yet to discuss in this book on abilities) accounts for the less than expected role of the frontal lobes in intelligence as such. However, that composite derivative of intelligence and personality control which we call "problem solving capacity," and which tends in animal research to be erroneously equated with intelligence as "relation perceiving capacity" (see Chapter 13) *does* have more definite association with the frontal lobes. In Section 7 this issue is taken up again in connection with the concept of "plans" by Miller, Galanter, and Pribram (1960). Meanwhile, let us see what contribution to the problem resides additionally in the biochemical evidence.

6. EVIDENCE FROM CHEMICAL RESPONSE PROPERTIES OF THE BRAIN

It is obvious that some reduction of correlations and some uncertainty of conclusions in regard to functional connection of anatomical brain structure with various behavioral functions could be due to that fact that existing structures may not always be fully functioning, because of biochemical conditions. A clear but extreme illustration of such factors is the development of mental defect from phenylketonuria, where initially normal brain structure is powerless to function because of a critical lack of a metabolite (5-hydroxytryptamine) in early infancy. Incidentally, animals also perform poorly on mazes if fed a high phenylalanine diet which is equivalent to the biochemical upset seen in these children.

Such simple relations to biochemical action are at present not widely demonstrable despite the appearance of some comparatively straightforward correlations like the above, and the relation of thyroxin or oxygen or glucose level to general behavioral response efficiency. The more general rule is that biochemistry and anatomical structure interact more complexly. Thus a particular chemical (at least, when we go beyond simple oxygen metabolism) is effective in one anatomical organization and not in another, as is clearly brought out by Berger (1960). For this reason, understanding chemical action often depends also on understanding the "wiring diagram," i.e., the structure of neuroanatomy discussed above. Nevertheless, it is good to begin study here with the basic chemistry of the ordinary neuron, as it operates practically everywhere, and turn to local specialization later.

Necessarily, a brief survey, such as this book attempts, cannot consider neuro-chemistry systematically, but we may note that the sodium-potassium ion ratio is a basic determiner in the process of transmission of impulses along the nerve axon. Similarly, grasping the action of acetylcholine (and the substance which keeps it in equilibrium—cholinesterase) is vital to understanding transmission at the synapses, where one neuron links onto another. The application of potassium chloride solution to the cortex, for example, can so upset the sodium-potassium ion balance that a whole region goes out of action, as shown by inertness of electrical signs and the temporary disappearance of ability to learn, equivalent to that found more permanently when such a region is excised. Since synapses are everywhere in all brain regions, changes in acetylcholine, an excitant of conduction at the synapses, and cholinesterase, which inhibits it by increasing conductance of membranes to potassium and chlorine ions, can similarly produce widespread effects. These effects of general overexcitation are about such as would be expected from the summation over large masses of the known effects on individual neurons and the surrounding glia. As far as brief summary is possible, it would be correct to say that the known chemistry of the sodium-potassium balance of cholinesterase, serotonin, noradrenaline, etc., as they act on the neuron is helpful in understanding upsets of excitation and inhibitory balances. For we can see how these natural biochemical regulators lead to regional overexcitation, on the one hand, as in severe anxiety or epilepsy, and, on the other, to sleep or sluggishness with impaired functioning. However, the more striking effects of drugs upon intelligence and learning arise from chemicals the action of which at the cell and synapse level is probably not so simple and certainly not so well understood.

By considering first what is known about the gross action of chemicals —"drugs"— foreign to the body, or, at least, "abnormal" in condition, we are aided in our understanding of the more subtle natural regulators. From the time when the first prehistoric man brewed alcohol, to the latest, post-LSD, psycho-active drug, man has become accustomed to expecting fairly definite behavioral effects from ingesting certain chemicals. The effect of alcohol is marked in slowing reaction time, upsetting cerebellar control, reducing the emotional control associated with normal action of the frontal lobes, and in decreasing intelligence. The present writer (1930) was able to show that although ten grams of absolute alcohol produced intelligence loss of a few points of I.Q. for most people, a quite small dose of five grams, though lowering intelligence in some, showed a distinctly variable action. That this variability of effect was not experimental error was shown by the pattern being strikingly consistent for members of the same family. Caffeine, as in coffee, on the other hand, produced some gain in memory recall and slight but insignificant increases in what we should now call crystallized intelligence-test performance. Had fluid (culture-fair) tests been available then, it seems likely that no change in g_f would have been recorded, since the crystallized increase is sufficiently explicable by caffeine's familiar action in improving memory access and retrieval. A more recent study directly investigating effects on general ability, specifically on g_c and g_f, is that of P. S. Hundal (Punjab University) who found that, although the direction of effects of benzedrine (upward) and phenobarbitol (downward) are the same on fluid and crystallized intelligence measures, the only significant ($P < .01$) effect was that of phenobarbitol on the former. This agrees with some general conclusions below that (1) fluid intelligence is more affected by generalized cortical influence, (2) most effects are downward from a natural efficiency level, and (3) retrieval and crystallized intelligence may instead be more affected by drugs producing facilitation of recall.

Among the "tranquilizers" and sedatives such as meprobamate and phenobarbitol, Townsend and Mirsky (1960) show that digit symbol-substitution (which, with appropriate groups, is a moderately good intelligence test), is susceptible to more impairment than tasks involving only mechanical attention and alertness. Most results, however, show negligible impairment by meprobamate of judgment and intelligence function, except possibly slightly in memory; but appreciable impairment of such test performance occurs by phenobarbitol. On the other hand, large meprobamate doses in monkeys (Weiskrantz, Gross and Baltzer, 1965) do reduce discrimination performance, but may slightly improve delayed responses in monkeys with frontal lobe injuries. The experimenters suggest that it reduces an excessive and inappropriately ordered intake of sensory information due to the impaired frontal lobes. Frankenhaeuser and Myrsten (1968), with large doses of this tranquilizer, found more impairment with increased task difficulty and less as the prior amount of learning increased. Miller (1960) gives a clue to some inconsistent results by arguing that meprobamate actually increases speed of learning in performances with which anxiety interferes. Injection of procaine into frontal lobes (Paolino and Friedman, 1959) apparently produces no intellectual impairment (again adding a mite of evidence that the frontal lobes are involved more in control than intelligence, though still one must conclude *some* intelligence involvement). The effects of LSD seem generally deteriorative, especially in regard to memory functions.

A major difficulty in giving the main outlines of conclusions here comes from the lack of agreement among physiologists on the dimensions of drug classification by effects. Terms like "stimulant" and "depressive" are pointless when the same drug stimulates a dozen things and simultaneously depresses half a dozen others. An empirical demonstration of nine main independent dimensions-of-state change (Cattell, 1960) suggests that a meaningful vector or profile characterization is possible, however, for any particular drug action. Berger (1960) has brought some order into the pharmacological side by designating five main types of psychoactive drugs —phenothiazines, Rauwolfia derivatives, diphenylmethanes, propanediols, and substituted amines—and two main types of action—cerebral depression and autonomic suppression. He shows that the third and fifth of the chemical types act depressively on the cortex and the first three on the hypothalamus. However, the more sensitive measures of total cortical efficiency are made, the more they tend to show slight impairment with most sedating drugs. And with stimulants like caffeine and strychnine the improvements are slight and mainly in recall.

The above conclusions mainly concern normal subjects. When persons suffering from psychosis or some temporary impairment are concerned, more significant improvements in intellectual performance may result. Such improvements, under diseased or pathological conditions, include the finding that amphetamine (benzedrine, etc.), as shown by Blackburn with the present writer's culture-fair tests, will improve the intelligence performance of hospitalized depressives. But, as Brubaker and Pierson (1962) show, dexadrine (benzedrine) gives no significant difference for normals on intelligence or the primary mental abilities. In the case of depressives it would seem the improvement is through change in motivation, since persons in normal emotional states do not improve. Again Gilgash (1957) finds significant improvement on the Wechsler test with psychotics from chlorpromazine (an anxiety reducer), but Porteus, using the maze test of intelligence, closer to g_f, finds a consistent and significant loss of I.Q. from this drug over a series of careful experiments.

Even in depressed or mentally ill persons, the clearest conclusion seems to be that alleged I.Q. improvements are probably due to being able to gain the patient's attention and motivation, not to increased relation-perceiving capacity as such. As Uhr (Uhr and Miller, 1960, p. 620) well summarizes, "Improvements in effective intelligence reflect a lessening of disruption rather than any direct affect of the drug upon performance." An exception to this is the improvement in senile persons or those suffering from brain circulatory disorders, where drugs which remedy the condition—as in the findings of improvement through small doses of a convulsant (metrazol) drug, of an anti-coagulant (Dicumarol), and of sodium glutamate (a protein nutrient), (Caldwell, 1958)—produce real, cortical, efficiency increases.

To cut an intrinsically long (though inherently fascinating) story short, one must conclude that, *except for people in diseased or subnormal conditions,* no artificial drug has appeared that is capable of significantly increasing fluid general intelligence or bringing more than momentary improvements in crystallized intelligence (which may be mediated by changes produced in g_r and g_s). To anticipate outcomes of our next discussion—on nature's own chemicals—the same generalization essentially holds there too: a nerve network, as presently genetically given, has the best biochemicals for its most efficient functioning. However, although this is true in the long run, in relation to all the mental and emotional adjustments and recuperations we have to make, there is no intrinsic reason why temporary improvements should not be made, as everyone experiences (or thinks he experiences) if he sustains performance on cups of strong coffee, though he suffers jitters and jadedness afterwards. Certainly everyone has introspections of variation of his intelligence and insight, and, if Horn's results (page 491) are confirmed and extended, we are likely to conclude that the main capacities—g_f, g_c, g_r, g_s, etc.—fluctuate from hour to hour, each with its characteristic pattern. Presumably this is partly external stimulation, leading to higher activation level or increased fatigue, and partly internal biochemical change.

The chief, natural, physiological determiners of neural action that might be investigated as affecting the intelligence performance from given neural masses are the nutrients—oxygen, glucose, etc.—the general bodily hormones—adrenalin, noradrenalin, thyroxin, the ketosteroids, etc.—and certain chemical pacemakers in conduction at synapses—acetylcholine, serotonin, cholinesterase, etc. Let us briefly consider them in this sequence.

There are ample studies showing both intelligence and memory reduction from shortage of the primary fuels, oxygen and sugar (though incidentally it is realized now that brain cells metabolize proteins and lipids in lesser degree also). High altitudes, or oxygen chamber pressure drops corresponding to 10,000 feet or over, begin to reduce intelligence, memory, and control. Sugar level reductions do the same and impair learning. Reductions in the sheer quantity of blood circulation in the brain, below certain limits, can account for the same effects. Brozek, the present writer, and others (1946) showed on World War II volunteers for experiment that vitamin B (thiamin) deficiency produces anxiety depression, sensitivity to noise, and lack of ability to concentrate. Other experiments have confirmed that with this degree of severity of deprivation there is also intelligence test loss. The effects of vitamin deficiency in mothers have been set out in Chapter 7 on heredity.

About the effect of degrees of malnutrition within reversible limits there is much debate. Studies of German children with relatively severe malnutrition in World War I were unable to conclude any I.Q. loss. Recently the issue has taken on political overtones in relation to the real degree of intelligence improvement to be expected from welfare programs, with resulting extreme claims in both directions and the production of more emotion than knowledge. Like almost every other influence, nutritional differences seem to have their larger and more permanent effects in very early life. As typical of the more environmental emphasis one may take the conclusions of Cravioto (1966) that raising both protein and calorie consumption in children with marked malnutrition slightly but significantly increases intelligence test performance. He concludes also that malnutrition prior to six months is especially liable to cause loss of I.Q. and that, whereas losses in later life may be recovered, these are not. These inferences from reconnoitering research are necessarily shaky and not yet to be taken too seriously because no dependable intelligence test is known for six-months-old—or even two-year-old—children. The evidence with culture-fair tests (page 463) is that the increase in bodily size in this generation from richer nutrition has *not* been accompanied by any general fluid intelligence increase. The increase in crystallized intelligence seems due to better schooling. If there were any fluid intelligence increase one would need to prove, before considering it part of the larger physical growth, that it is not due to reduction, by better hygiene, of the size of the minority suffering from brain damage through disease. The general medical evidence is that in severe malnutrition, as in famine, the body sacrifices all kinds of other tissue before nervous tissue. In the range of nutrition in Western cultures it seems unlikely that much intelligence variance is associated with calorie intake, though it might be with unwise eating habits, e.g., those giving vitamin B deficiencies or excessive cholesterol from overfeeding.

Turning from fuel and protein, to the regulating hormones and brain pacemakers, let us dismiss most hormone effects as already widely known to readers. The only one having major effect on intelligence is thyroxin, which, when reduced, produces retarded thought (myxoedema) and imbecility (cretinism). Early reduction of brain metabolism may also mean a reduction of neural growth. Speculatively, there has been suspicion of other hormone deficiency effects, including the sex hormones. Since some performances, notably, fluid intelligence, but also fluency (retrieval) show a maximum in late adolescence, it is easy to argue that sex hormones play some indirect part. The German psychiatrist Möbius once remarked, in noting the lively minds of most adolescents and the dullness of most adult conversation, that "some degree of mental defect supervenes in all people after adolescence," and it is an easy step from this comment to the notion that the highest production of sex hormone produces, rather than merely coincides with, this intellectual stimulation. But no tangible evidence on such connections exist, and eunuchs have not been noted for stupidity.

Understanding of the action of acetylcholine, serotonin, noradrenaline and other "neurohormones" and their balances (hydrolysers, esterases) such as cholinesterase, monoamine oxidase is rendered difficult partly by the fact that the action of most is primarily on the mid-brain and old brain (limbic system) rather than the cortex. (Serotonin, for example, is most concentrated in the hypothalamus (Himwich, 1960) as also in noradrenaline and adrenaline.) Also the strong emphasis in research has been on understanding schizophrenic impairment, which happens to show in the cognitive area more as disordered motivation than lack of intelligence. The possibility exists (from evidence mainly on learning in animals, by Rosenzweig, Krech, and Bennett (1961) and others, that raised acetylcholine in the cortex is associated with increased anxiety, alertness, and problem-solving activity. They analyzed the ratio of cholinesterase in the cortex to that in the subcortical levels of the brain. This c/s ratio becomes higher in rats and mice whose environment presents more stimulation or disturbing features. The increase of the ratio of cortical weight to cholinesterase in the more stimulated rats could be a function of cortical enlargement or of greater demands for cholinesterase at the subcortical, hypothalamic level, occasioned by greater arousal. However, Tapp and Markowitz (1963) found that stimulation increased ventral cortex and subcortical weights and thus *decreased* subcortical cholinesterase. With marked increases in life stimulation the cortex is thicker and more developed, and as indicated, it remains a possibility that the lower cholinesterase proportions could be a consequence of this greater cell development. (Since *number* of cells cannot be increased by environment, one must infer that the average cell size is increased.) Brighter genetic strains of rats in maze-running (from Tryon's experiments) also show a higher ratio. These results need to be related to the P-technique (state) findings by Williams and the present writer (1953) that in human beings low cholinesterase in the blood serum is found in anxiety ($r = .78$) and high cholinesterase in stress. This suggests that animals said to be living in a more "stimulating" environment actually may be living at a more anxiety-creating level, and that it is this which stimulates cortical growth. A generalized overactivity with acetylcholine rise, associated with increase in brain volume growth, may be shown also to bring some increase of intelligence test performance with it, but this has to be checked.

Biochemical research in behavioral science is only in its infancy, but a very promising infancy. As far as abilities are concerned it is particularly relevant to effects across the age range. As Levine and Mullins (1966) point out, the correct operation of hormones (sex, thyroid, or adrenal) at critical periods of development exerts necessary efforts on the early development of the central nervous system and on subsequent behavior. It has already been pointed out, in connection with Hebb's generalizations, that deprivation of stimulation in early life, e.g., as in Nissen's (Nissen, Chow, and Semmes, 1951) experiments depriving chimpanzees of visual stimuli and other experiments on auditory stimuli, will cause lack of development of normal discriminatory skills in that sense area. Apparently the structural development of cells is normal, but their biochemical preparedness and reactivity is virtually permanently lost. Some of the age changes discussed in Chapter 7 can be correlated with such physiological changes. For example, between the age of thirty and ninety the mass of the brain typically declines about ten percent. The concentration of RNA (Ribonucleic acid) in nerve cells first increases with maturation and then decreases from about fifty-five to sixty years of age. Probably RNA is more important to memory (and therefore g_c and g_r) than to g_f, but it also coincides with curves of loss of the latter.

Probably the most important biochemical conclusion for ability psychology, however, is that the brain cells are normally at a high pitch of efficiency. They have the highest metabolic rate of any body cells and when the brain is active there are, according to Hyden, of the order of three billion impulses operating per second (two billion in the visual system alone). It is not surprising therefore that most "foreign" chemicals, e.g., alcohol, LSD, merely reduce effective abilities. There is no magic "elixir" for intelligence, but only the natural biochemicals (thyroxin, acetylcholine, adrenaline, and its simulator amphetamine, etc.) the addition of which, *if the brain is subnormal through their absence,* can raise intelligence and learning capacity back to their proper level as expected from the structural limits.

7. THE PHYSIOLOGICAL INTERPRETATION OF FLUID AND CRYSTALLIZED INTELLIGENCE, QUALIFIED BY SOME UNSOLVED RIDDLES OF MEMORY

In the above sections presenting evidence from neuroanatomy, chemical action, and electrical phenomena we have largely refrained from syntheses attempting interpretations beyond the zone of each sectional area. For in the present inchoate state of the subject the cautious reader may want to separate fact from interpretation in whatever necessarily condensed general propositions are here offered. Even our factual survey, by reason of its having to dissect out from the enormous area of neurophysiology what is most vital only to the subject of abilities, has had to neglect those aspects of neurology which have to do with the dynamic and emotional life—notably the roles of hypothalamus, mid-brain, medulla, limbic system, and autonomic system—and with the reticular system and spinal cord.

The major theoretical difficulty in reaching a more exact neurological meaning for intelligence and other abilities is that the bulk of the experimental evidence has to do with observations on learning, especially in animal studies. And learning in most cases involves not only intelligence, but also drive, memory, and other lesser factors. In allowing for effects due to effectiveness of memory we are hampered at the present juncture in research by the fact that the neurological basis of memory is extremely speculative. Theories vary from (1) "reverberating circuits" (to which there are serious objections), to (2) qualities of "facilitation" or "readiness" induced in synapses (anatomical or chemical), (3) preferred neural pathways and networks determined by electrical "fields," and (4) molecular changes in universally neurally distributed RNA and other proteins. Since at present some of these are equally attractive attempts to integrate intelligence theory with the memory aspects of learning, theory has all the complications of intellectual polygamy.

Whatever alternatives or combinations are accepted they have to square with the generally accepted conclusion, from both behavioral and physiological evidence, that memory has three major aspects:

(1) A short-distance memory, from seconds or minutes to an hour or so which is a maintained activity and involves interaction with present storage leading to further storage. The "reverberating circuits" concept, which has had to be almost abandoned as an explanation of long-term memory, is quite apt here. At least some persisting neural electrical activity is involved.

(2) A long-term storage, in principle not unlike a library or a computer storage, but which now seems likely to depend on specific protein molecule formation, as genetic storage depends on nucleic acid molecules. McGaugh's experiments with strychnine, picrotoxin, and pentyline tetrazol show some stimulation of learning possibly in connection with this process, but others with pemoline and ribanol, which show significant memory improvement in aged patients and in the learning of rats, suggest a protein synthesis in memory. W. B. Essman has similarly shown that "engramming" of memories is improved by uric acid ingestion. Studies of S. H. Barandes, showing that drugs upsetting protein synthesis upset memory, and G. Ungar's work, showing that transfer of brain extracts may transfer such learning as avoidance of certain stimuli, point to memory as chemical storage, and probably related to protein molecules.

Within this storage procedure, however, we can recognize a continuum between storage of the immediate, "photographic" event and the abstractions that can be made from that and many other events, by intelligent relation eduction. The latter are probably the work of the short-term memory sorting and referral activity in (1) above, and are stored under symbols and abstractions. This difference probably corresponds to the factor-analytically substantiated difference between "intelligent" or "meaningful" and "rote" memory factors revealed by Kelley (1954). However, this difference arises in the committing to memory ((1) above), where the more intelligent person proceeds much further in processing the data. For, as Underwood (1957) convincingly argues, the rate of decay of a memory is very similar indeed for rote memory on the one hand, and intelligent learning on the other. The chemical storage properties may therefore be identical, while the more intelligent, preliminary, committing to memory in the one case has to do with reverberations in the cortical association mass before being "stored away." As we have seen, final sensory storage tends to need only some relatively narrow and economical neural areas to which memories are ultimately relegated. This also fits the finding that simple learning, of the classical conditioning kind, can occur in the absence of practically the whole cortex. Or, if learning is performed with an intact cortex, it is not lost when the cortex is removed. On the other hand, as Lashley showed, a more complex sensory, e.g., visual habit is impaired when the visual association area is ablated, though it can be relearned.

Whatever else may be found about memory, we thus conclude that learning of *complex* adaptive behavior requires the "intelligence" contribution which, by our hypothesis, derives from what we have been calling contingently the "total cortical" or "associative" mass. Learning utilizes this in the act of relational perception and additionally, but perhaps diminishingly, in the ensuing consolidation processes.

Yet a third aspect of the storage procedure—the dynamic aspect—needs to be introduced. On the psychological, behavioral side it is evident that not only the committing to memory but also the efficiency of storage hinges partly on strength of interest, and the relevance of the material to dynamic motivational systems. As far as their role in committing to memory is concerned, it seems that we can implicate already in the neurological expression of dynamic interest, the hippocampus and the amygdala, which have to be intact for committing to memory. That they have to do with the role of motivation sets is indicated also by their activity in retrieval, since there also the direction of search is a matter of motivation sets.

(3) Thus we come to the third major aspect of the memory process—that of retrieval or recall. Here, apart from intactness of the hippocampus and amydala zones, and the physiological indications that such drugs as caffeine, benzedrine (and hyperbaric oxygen, in the senile) help the process, the picture is scanty. In the psychological realm, dynamic sets are the chief determiners of what and how much is retrieved from storage, but what a dynamic interest set means physiologically is still beyond us.

Before attempting to integrate conclusions on abilities and brain action a brief return is required to the question of localization, with the addition of more sophisticated interpretation made possible from matters discussed recently. For the question of localization includes that of recognizing the "association mass" which increasingly has to be recognized as the seat of fluid intelligence. The main doubts and qualifications of Lashley's mass action theory of intelligent learning have been two; first, that every ablation removes some particular sensory capacity and presumably damages one of the factors which in the triadic theory we have called a "power." Since *most* complex learning involves *several* senses at once, this sensory damage, i.e., damage to the powers, could itself account for the loss without any resort to the notion of a damaged "association mass." Arguing against this is Lashley's own demonstration that a rat taught to run a maze blind nevertheless suffers loss of adaptation by removal of purely visual area nerve mass. Secondly, the human intelligence data shows some departure from "equipotentiality" in that the occipital and frontal cortex seem rather less important than the rest of the cortex. Incidentally, we have learned from numerous experiments that the question of localization is greatly complicated by developmental events. In the main, initial localization can be flexible, whereas later the location of particular skills is more definite, narrow, and harder to find substitutes for. Furthermore, as Luria (1965) points out, "If in the early stages of mental development destruction of specific zones of the cortex leads to undevelopment of *higher* parts constructed on their basis, then destruction of these same zones at a mature age evokes a failure of *lower* systems depending on them." In other words, a zone may have a necessary constructive function during the early stages which it loses later. Possibly the decline of fluid intelligence with age is to be explained partly as a loss of duality of function—the cessation in some local zone of action as part of the association mass, over and above the local, specific action.

The notion that the associational mass to be identified with fluid intelligence is in any case not the total cortical mass, but something less, involved particularly in the frontal and occipital and sensory power zones, fits the fact that we readily find other behavioral factors—powers and controlling mechanisms—corresponding to the specialization of these zones. The p_v (page 34) or local "visualization ability" factor can be ascribed with some confidence to the degree of development of the occipital lobes; the ego strength[3] factor to the degree of frontal lobe development; the general motor ability factor to the motor area, and so on.

At this point, as we scrutinize the "associational mass" conception more closely, it seems desirable for the sake of more precise definition, to name it finally the "combinatorial (or combining) mass." For the theory is that its functions are (1) to associate or interconnect the various local sensory and motor organizations, and (2) to extract new relations and emergents. These functions are perhaps better expressed by the term "combining." The question naturally arises as to where the local zone action leaves off and the combining mass action begins. At this point in discussion a fruitful integration of concepts may be made between the combining mass, as the physiological basis for general relation eduction, and the notion of Miller, Galanter, and Pribram (1960) that the forebrain, limbic system, and frontal association area of the cortex are the basis for operations which they call "plans." Plans are essentially an action scheme for testing congruities, such as one would expect to see connected with forebrain action.

---

[3] That the frontal lobes are concerned with emotional control and the initiating and direction of activity has long been known. The more precise theory here put forward is that frontal lobe development corresponds to the higher-stratum personality factor TII found by Pawlik and the present writer and called "ego assertiveness and problem-solving strength" (1964). In this factor, indexed as (T),U.I. 16 (ego strength, in objective test primaries and measured also by C in the questionnaire realm) control is prominent. It has been shown (Pawlik and Cattell, 1965) the frontal EGG phenomena are significantly correlated with measures of action of this factor.

These action plans and testings operate in conjunction with what these writers call "images," constituted by the available stored information about the world and the acting subject. The former associated with the forebrain and limbic system, has to do with devising and controlling a suitable action sequence, or hierarchical fitting of subactions into a total course of action. The latter ("images") correspond roughly to what we would designate more precisely here as the g_c system—the system of reality-tested information and judgmental skills, developed through g_f and experience, and stored neurologically in the more specialized zones where g_c skills are ultimately stored. Distinct from both of these—the plan control in the limbic system and forebrain, and the g_c resources around the sensory motor areas—is the combining mass offering powers of relation eduction necessary to the further development of both plans and images (g_c).

A question which naturally arises at this point concerns where the relation eduction within a particular sensory power zone ends and the *general* relation eduction begins. This is paralleled by the question of where, anatomically, a sensory or motor zone ends and the combining mass begins. In the factor analysis of behavior we see a fair degree of relational hierarchy development to be present in the local organizations themselves, e.g., in the visualization capacity to develop purely visual patterns. At some point the relational analysis is carried to higher hierarchies in the combining mass as the pattern is understood in broader sensory contexts, e.g., a visual music score as an auditory sound pattern. It might seem sufficient to say that the combining mass takes over the moment that interaction begins between two or more senses, or a relation passes beyond the meaning of a particular sensory domain. But more likely the higher relations, even within one sensory domain, already involve the combining mass. The notion that two and two make four can be learned purely in the visual field, but it does not have its full sanction and meaning until it has been compared and integrated with a similar finding in, say, the auditory and tactile fields. The "logic" of one sense could be and is sometimes peculiar, as conjurors realize. The experience from other areas may thus feedback through the combining mass to the higher level relation eductions in any one local organization. This is perhaps why it is possible, as in culture-fair intelligence tests, to measure g_f by complex relations presented purely in one (visual) sensory channel.

At present little is known about the anatomical boundaries of the neurological combining mass, partly for the obvious reason that it grades without sharp boundaries into the sensory and motor power association area. Present conclusions would be that it is central in the cortical mass, that it does not involve the outlying quite specialized cortical areas, and that it is no more projected into the frontal lobes (with their plan-controlling specialization) than into other local power zones. For, as we have seen, there is much evidence that the frontal lobes and forebrain are concerned with impulse control, anticipation of future consequences, and the arranging of action plans in proper sequences and hierarchies determined by external realities.

The relation of intelligence to perception and control in socio-emotional action situations—paralleling the anatomical relation of frontal lobes to combining mass—is an intriguing one to the investigator, which we shall approach more systematically in Chapter 12, on personality-ability inter-actions. But in the present context of the neurological bases of ability one can only point to the expectation—by analogy to what is found from the other provincial power localizations—that a p (power) factor would be found in behavior corresponding to the frontal lobe. This should be con-cerned with good relation eduction ("intelligent perception") in the field of emotional relations and actions, and of cultural values. It should appear as a rather broad beginning of "politico-ethical" ability, before that be-comes incorporated in crystallized intelligence. Because of that poverty of imagination in the devising of a sufficiently broad spectrum of psychometric tests which we have had to deplore in Chapters 2–6, no factor—either as a primary or as a provincial power secondary—has yet been established in this general area.

In default of research by ability investigators, it is personality research, as documented in Chapter 12, that has picked up what is probably also the ability structure of this area. The basis for this assertion lies in the ego strength (C) and superego strength (G or U.I. 29) factors. What one would like to see is a factor definition more strictly of their ability expres-sions in terms of the novelist's sensitive perception of emotional relation-ships and behavioral consequences. And inasmuch as conduct obeys the same quality of lawfulness as the physical world, the same logic of summa-tion, substitution, etc., one would expect the special relations educed in this power to be successfully handled in proportion to the individual's endowment in fluid intelligence, and to be deposited as a part of crystallized intelligence. Unfortunately for the neurological investigation of this area, animal experiment is useless, since the socio-cultural-ethical world of animals is miniscule compared to that of humans, and the corresponding neuro-anatomy is almost certainly equally rudimentary. Indeed, the sociol-ogists, and the dialectic materialists among neurologists, such as Vygotsky, are tempted, by the importance of this brain area in human life, to reverse the causal perspective. For them the flow of culture, not the brain, is the determiner, and the frontal lobes might be better thought of as so many individual radio receivers dipping into a vast sea of electromagnetic wave transmissions which constitute the culture. But two-way action still holds, and the neurological determiners of individual brain action are also de-terminers of the total culture.

Although we can begin to give, in Shakespeare's phrase "a local habita-tion and a name" to some functions, such as the motor areas, and the spe-cial senses (with their association areas), to impulse (the midbrain) and impulse control (the forebrain), to memory storage input and output (the hippocampus), and to fluid intelligence (the central cortical combining mass), a habitation for the primaries and crystallized intelligence has been left indefinite. That indefiniteness is an offspring of our uncertainty about memory storage, and the common feature of these abilities is that they involve storage of memories that are abstract, symbolic, and transcending any one sensory or motor power. All that is certain is that they finish up as narrowly localized and requiring little space—like Broca's area for speech symbols. The behavioral nature of the factorially unitary powers, such as vizualization and auditory skill (see Holmes and Singer, 1966, for indications of an auditory provincial power) is that they deal with relations strictly within the sense, and at a lower order, closer to sensory perception, than g_f performances. For that reason, because sensory experience is common to all people except the uncommon deaf and blind, the p factors may be weakly defined within a species, though they would obviously be powerful between species (as between eagle and bloodhound). Somewhere on the neuroanatomical crossroads between these areas is the most likely place for the primaries and crystallized abilities, as verbal ability lies in part between the auditory zone and the motor area for the tongue. Because of the uneven mixture of sensory-motor powers involved, and the dependence of all of them on the combining mass of g_f, one would expect these locations of the various aspects of g_c to be relatively variant and unstable.

In spite of some remaining puzzles, the alignment of behavioral factorial findings and neurological anatomical and functional findings is encouraging. Any attempt at such a total picture, it is true, has to depend at present on some shrewd guesswork. For example, there are practically no instances where drug action or electrical brain function records correspond neatly to one factorial category, and we have had to guess, above, that, for example, the slight improvement of intelligence with caffeine may really be due to better speed and recall in the storage on which g_c judgments depend. Methodologically the whole field would be clearer if factor analysis were applied in experiments on *change* measures under manipulation, as it has been to absolute behavior measures. Then we might hope to discover, for example, how much the various performance changes under drugs can be allocated to particular sources, and we might demonstrate, for example, that caffeine leaves g_f entirely untouched and produces its effects through g_r or g_s.

The briefly summarizable anatomical picture seems to be that both the "provincial organizations" (sensory and motor association areas) and general fluid intelligence are expressions of the effective functional mass of sensorimotor and general association (combining network) zones. As such one would expect these p's and g_f to have considerable genetic determination,[4] whereas the primary agencies, a's, and g_c would depend also on the effectiveness of the storage and committing-retrieving areas in the hippocampal area and physiological efficiencies at learning and recall. All correlations with anatomical features are, of course, subject to modifica-

---

[4] A testable inference from this theory is that the genetic-environmental variance ratios determined for various a's, e.g., verbal, numerical agencies, should coincide with the degrees to which they are affected by chemical conditions known primarily to affect g_f.

tion by transient physiological efficiencies, e.g., oxygen availability. In this connection we might expect, as Horn has found, that diurnal cognitive performance swings, when factored, show that g_f as a unit has its own swings. Also physiological and behavioral data will show two-way effects, so that, as Rosenzweig, Krech, and Bennett have demonstrated (1961), behavioral overstimulation will have detectable neurological effects. In the neurology-to-behavior direction many testable deductions can now be made from the above structural theory. For example, any drug affecting the total combining mass should influence the rate of insightful learning, but not of conditioning, whereas influences, e.g., anxiety, affecting the autonomic system, should (and do) alter autonomic conditioning learning but not g_f-determined, intelligent learning.

Neither space nor available research data permits pointed and profitable discussion of the neurological correlates of the other general capacities—g_s, g_r, etc. Their lability with age, their susceptibility to drug action, etc., indicates that they depend on general neural efficiency, and we know in addition that g_r depends on functionality of hippocampal areas near the corpus callosum. But, whereas g_f obviously depends primarily on sheer magnitude of neural fibre mass, it would seem that general speed, g_s, depends more on physiological efficiency conditions. The fact that g_f and g_r seem to unite, in part, in a still higher-order factor (Table 6–4) does suggest, however, that some common condition of cortical efficiency affects them both. These are riddles worthy of combined research by psychologists and physiologists starting, however, from a truly broad conceptualization and using multivariate experimental designs.

CHAPTER NINE

ULTRA-HUMAN INTELLIGENCE: ILLUMINATION FROM EVOLUTION OF ANIMALS AND MACHINES

1. THE DISTINCTION OF INTELLIGENCE AS A SUBCATEGORY WITHIN PURPOSE—ADAPTIVE BEHAVIOR

While not forgetting that our central topic is human ability, we may yet find virtue in seeking perspective on it from broader domains. For it is an axiom of scientific method that no area is fully illuminated until we step out into comparative views, utilizing perspectives which transcend the internal approach. The biological dictum that to know a species we must also know the wider genus to which it belongs, applies to all knowledge.

If we ask where else intelligence is found, some, like Newton and Copernicus, will point to the heavens; others will refer us to the living world, especially the higher mammals and certain insects, while the modernist, intoxicated with cybernetics, will suggest that we look at the remarkable behavior of a computer or logic machine. As to the first, the vast and cloudy purposes of the cosmos still elude our comprehension, but in animals and machines we see organizations which cope with problems similar to those handled by our own intelligence, and from which we can surely enlarge our concepts. Admittedly, the behavior of apes, bees, birds, and porpoises is more like our own than is that of an ancient Egyptian water mill, a Roman catapult, a Norman turnspit, a Polynesian fish hook, a Victorian alarm clock or a modern American computer. Animal and machine constitute two species rather than one; but they share the behavior of a genus which "responds adaptively to external stimuli." Let us begin, however, with the more familiar domain of animal intelligence.

Viewing animal behavior, it is obvious that man has been more concerned over most of his history—at least prior to Darwin—to emphasize the differences rather than the similarities. The dearth of intelligence in a school-mate is considered fully indicated when he is called a stupid ape. The theologians denied the animal a soul, and the early naturalists denied him intelligence—permitting him "instinct" instead. Indeed it is soon evident that adaptive behavior of the latter kind is not a sufficiently restricted characteristic for locating what we call intelligence. If intelligence is to have the particular, usefully restricted meaning we have given it in the general factor g_f, then we must distinguish in animal behavior between that which is intelligently adaptive—in the general sense of aiding the animal's survival—and that subvariety of such behavior which continues to be adaptive even *when the normal conditions are changed,* and which alone can strictly be called intelligent. We have to distinguish indeed between what is *purposive* and what *purposeful.* The instinctual behavior of animals, e.g., of the squirrel burying the nut he will need next winter, is very *purposively adapted,* but need have no intelligent insight. As Cannon brought out in *The Wisdom of the Body,* not only much of our outward behavior, e.g., walking, but all kinds of inner physiological processes, are far more "intelligent," in this "adaptive" sense than the possessor of them usually understands.

Our position here will be that in fact *two* kinds of *purposive* adaptation must be distinguished from *purposeful* intelligence. They are, first, the instinctual processes—achieved by the genetic trial-and-error learning of phylogenetic evolution—and secondly, the skilled and well-adapted, *intuitive* judgments we make, without knowing why. The latter may be as blindly acquired by individual, ontogenetic trial and error experience as the former are by racial, phylogenetic, natural selection of trial and error behavior. The former type of purposiveness is seen at work in the beautifully adapted instinctive behavior of animals and especially insects; the latter is demonstrated in the intelligence with which a skilled cyclist handles a bicycle—while being utterly unable to say why he does what he does.

What we shall distinguish as the subclass of consciously *purposefully* intelligent behavior, often developing within purposively effectively-adapted behavior, is marked by (1) conscious *insight* into the connections that are operating, and (2) the fact that, as seen by the observer, it obviously represents the achievement of a desired goal despite *re-arrangements of the stimulus situation* from the accustomed pattern associated with instinctual behavior. Proof of the existence of insight is somewhat unsatisfactory so long as it rests purely on introspection, and we shall later give it a more behavioristic touchstone[1] than a remark by the subject: "Ah, I see!"

---

[1] Pointing to insight as the touchstone of intelligence definition may seem inconsistent with the position taken in the last chapter that g_f is involved in learning even where no insight is demonstrable, but only *improvement,* in learning and adaptation in a complex situation. In the last resort, the suddenness of behavior change from a quite poor to a completely correct solution, by which we recognize insight, may be only

Although shrewder common sense observation, and the theology of the Scholastic philosophers, have kept animal intelligence to an evaluation decidedly below that accorded to our own, popular sentimentality over animal pets never ceases to supply gratifyingly impressive, if questionable, anecdotal evidence for virtually human levels of performance. One of the classical early works on animal intelligence—that of Romanes—mixed such domestic anecdotal evidence with scarcely more reliable observations by hunters and others. At the present juncture, however, the field can call upon reasonably systematic knowledge and disciplined methodology from (1) ethologists, whose skilled and systematic observation of animals in natural surroundings has grown from that of McDougall on propensities to that of Carpenter (1934), Lorenz (1958), Von Holst, Tinbergen (1951), Eibl-Ebesfeldt (1967) and many others patiently pursuing this new branch of psycho-biology; and (2) manipulated experiment in the laboratory, as pioneered by Köhler (1925) and McDougall (1932) and now illustrated by such work as that of Maier and Schneirla (1964), Bitterman (1965), Hess (1959), Beach (1948), Harlow (1949), Scott (1959) and many others. Let us glance next at evidence from both of these sources.

2. INSTINCT IN RELATION TO TRACTABILITY AND INTELLIGENCE

To speak of animal intelligence it is helpful first to glance briefly at the more rigid purposive instinctual behavior with which it is contrasted. Instinctual behavior is seen in such activities as nest-building, courting ceremonies, hunting for food, methods of attack and escape—all showing exquisite purposive adaptation. It has been argued by some sociologists and even some ethologists that much instinctual behavior is actually learned. (No one disputes that it gets modified and is variously intermixed with intelligent acts.) Eibl-Ebesfeldt, Lorenz, Tinbergen, and others who question that all is learned, have repeated experiments by Kies, Lehrman, and others (who claim that most is acquired) by more ingenious

---

the most obvious and easy criterion. There may be other behavioral criteria characterizing an insightful solution, notably, that the animal does not return from it to other less effective solutions. Although we can assume that insight and a high degree of conscious awareness of a relation nearly always go together, the "consciousness" cannot be taken as the criterion by a behaviorist, either with humans or animals. Instances could probably be documented in human behavior, for that matter, where an individual's g_f has permitted him to use a new, complex relationship, *as* a relationship, without full conscious awareness of it. Many complex correct applications of syntax in speech are probably of that kind. The best behavioral criteria of the application of intelligence, resulting in problem-solving use of a newly perceived relation, are probably (1) the sudden change in the learning curve, (2) the absence of further *regressive* varied trial and error, (3) the ability to transfer the learned relation to new and different sets of concrete situations, and (4) changes of behavior in the situation itself that the observer can demonstrate to be direct "inferences" from the "theory" constituted by acceptance of a new relation.

experiments of their own. Rats make nests out of bits of paper and straw and retrieve their wandering young despite having been prevented from seeing their own parents and others do this. It is true that certain appropriate conditions for the species are necessary—cool temperatures, low enough to suggest nest-building, a shady corner, babies (real or artificial) that squeak, and so on. Without these suitable stimulus and background conditions, rats may carry bits of paper around rather aimlessly, cut up bits of straw and leave them around, and drop "babies" if they show unusual properties, such as being (despite correct coloring, etc.) as inert as bits of wood. Furthermore, some experience of the right situations with objects at the right maturational time apparently does much to put the pieces of the innately given behavior elements together in a harmonious and effective whole.

Similar appropriate conditions for innate response development have been found in other instincts that have been studied, e.g., hunting in the polecat. At first, when an animal of this species is brought up away from other polecats, it does not attack a rat when immediately presented. Only when it is provoked by the added stimulus of the rat running away does the pattern emerge. If brought up from earliest infancy with rats, so that a pre-established conflicting gregarious satisfaction arises, it will be even slower to attack, and require a raised level of hunger to discover its own hunting propensities. The typical consummatory behavior in hunting—shaking the rat, rolling it on its back, biting it fatally in the back of the head—also matures with certainty only with respect to the separate necessary elements in the chain, e.g., taking the rat and shaking it. The smooth coordination of the whole chain comes only with time and experience. Whether this delay in appearance of the full pattern is dependent on learning or on maturation is a question to be answered only by subtly designed experiment. Certainly, many complex behaviors, e.g., the flight of swallows, have been shown unquestionably to occur without any possibility of imitation or practice. Where, in the natural situation, *possibilities* of imitation occur, it may still be questioned whether it is *actually* imitation of adults or simply the possibilities of playful exercise, which improve the coordination. The playful fighting of lion cubs gives scope for coordination of many innately given "springs" and "grasps," and indeed, play has long been recognized (at least since Herbert Spencer) as the schooling of animals.

The argument seems reasonable that the coordination and sequential run of part behaviors, when the part behaviors are themselves unquestionably inherited, is also itself partly inherited. Then—as in "imprinting"—a timely experience in play assists the maturation, without that experience having to be rewarding (except as play)—as in ordinary learning. The crucial test for this theory could be designed by manipulating the environment so that the appearance of the instinctual sequence process gives experience but not reward, so that no learning in the ordinary sense could be assumed. (Usually the experience *is* rewarding, assuming the instinctual goal is a reward, and *could* therefore reinforce the appearance of the best order of coordinating the parts.) But the Galapagos dove continues after centuries to show "injury feigning" behavior to draw visitors away from its nest, though there are no predatory carnivores in all the Galapagos islands. The best explanation is surely that the pattern was reached without learning, and that this is a phylogenetic carry-over from ancestral areas where the behavior was actually rewarding to the maternal instinct.

Other instances of indubitable maturation of complex behavior are increasingly being turned up by careful ethological observation. Birds which catch insects on the wing have been noted, when hungry, to go through all swooping and snapping behavior in the complete absence of stimuli, namely, flies (though in this case there has been no proof that they have not been rewarded by insects before). Then there are situations where instinctual patterns are not only useless but positively punishing. There is an instinctive ritual of combat between turkey cocks wherein they lock beaks, interwine necks, and wrestle. When one lies down in a particular way it is a signal that he accepts defeat, and he is allowed to withdraw unharmed. Many other species of large birds, however, have developed a different instinctual combat pattern, including vicious striking at face and stomach with claws and spurs when the opponent lies down. A combat between a turkey and, say, a peacock, is likely to be fatal to the former, both because the peacock does not observe "the Marquis of Queensbury Rules" and also because the instinctual behavior of surrender, effectively life-saving in turkey society, merely encourages further attack in other species.

Instances of maladaptation of instinct in a strange or rapidly changing environment are fairly numerous in the animal world. Their prevalence suggests that a certain looseness in organization would be advantageous. Nature has to take care that something in "instinct" can be left to learning. Evolution has to aim, therefore, at a purely actuarial balance between the life-saving gains from a modicum of flexibility and those from having a firm tendency to behave in ways that are usually rewarding. Obviously, man is an extreme instance of high permissiveness and flexibility, though, as the associates of the present writer have shown by factor-analytic methods (Cattell and Miller, 1952; Cattell and Horn, 1963; Cattell, Horn, Sweney, and Radcliffe, 1964), there *are* still detectable distinct and unitary "instincts" in man. Because of their extreme difference from lower animal instincts on this plasticity continuum they have been called *ergs,* i.e., sources of energy in the form of "stimulus reactivity operating toward a particular kind of final consummatory satisfaction." The reader may study these eight or nine human ergs in texts on dynamics elsewhere (Cattell, 1965a) and will see that there is seemingly little left in man but a prescribed consummatory activity and a special quality of reward for whatever (learned) behavior leads toward that specific goal. In man intelligence evidently has reached a level relative to the complexity of his environment where it can be depended upon to find a way to the biological goal in the absence of specific instinctive intuitions.

An important conceptual issue now presents itself in the question: "How much of the plasticity—the lack of complete hereditary prescription—of instinctual behavior should be assigned to some quality of 'openness to new responses as effects of reward learning,' i.e., to a quality of passive plasticity, and how much positively to intelligence, i.e., to a helpful capacity to perceive new relations?" Calling the former, for future discussion, "tractability," (or, as a factor in humans, "flexibility versus tensity," see Chapter 13) we are bound to recognize that though it may tend to correlate positively, across species, with intelligence, it is by no means identical with it. And at the nervous system level, as discussed in the preceding chapter, we can see that intelligence as relation-perception demands substantial representation in the brain by a coordinating "combining mass," whereas tractability could be in part a purely biochemically or physiologically determined mutability in the nerve paths which normally fix the instinctual chain of responses.

Evolutionary adjustment indeed has a difficult problem here, for to increase tractability without increasing intelligence is to court disaster, while the converse—intelligence with rigidity—is useless. A permissiveness to rearrange the instinctive coordinated sequences and satisfactions invites biological perversion just as much as it does improved adaptation. The dangers of tractability or flexibility can be seen in the perversions of the human sex drive, or the devices by which men trap animals and (recently) eliminate insects. The rigidity of the instinct sequences in insects, in the last resort, must be ascribed to Nature's inability to give them—because of the size-weight limit imposed by the skeletal and breathing system—any appreciable mass of purely coordinative, brain tissue, i.e., tissue not committed to a specific use. Individual adaptability demands a somewhat reckless expenditure on brain tissue in the form of association tracts. But if flexibility is introduced without this prerequisite for insightful adaptability, to knit together some new complex behaviors by learning, the animal world departs from the path of exactly prescribed instinctual behavior only at its extreme peril.

Presumably, however, the capacity to vary from a genetically prescribed path, is a weakening, not an abolition, of an exact genetic maturation prescription. Such tractability or flexibility is surely, nevertheless, in part, a trait or condition of the nervous system independent from that of possessing a large endowment in intelligence. For example, tractability is a necessary precondition also for advance in blind trial and error learning, which is not itself intelligence. The "reversal learning" design which Holmes and Bitterman (1966), Skinner (1953), and others (see below) have used to explore animal learning would seem conceptually to be more a measure of tractability than of intelligence. But since these two capacities must be appreciably correlated (according to our theory above), at least *across species,* one would expect reversal learning to improve, in general, as one goes up the evolutionary scale, just like intelligence.

With this brief definition of the properties of the instinctual mechanisms with which intelligence has to interact, and the necessary conceptual separation of intelligence from tractability, we are in a position to concentrate on intelligence as such in the animal world.

3. THE CONDITIONS AND RANGES OF UNREFLECTIVE AND INSIGHTFUL LEARNING IN ANIMALS

By "purpose" above we have referred to the framework of biological goals or consummatory behaviors—eating, escape, gregarious gathering in a herd, courtship and copulation, destruction of an enemy in combat—for what, in man, have been demonstrated to be at least nine distinct ergic structures. As a classificatory philosopher may later comment, these seem designed by evolution to contribute *either* to the survival of the individual *or* that of the species, though that *purposive* classification has little relevance to their *physiological and psychological properties* and classificatory characteristics as such.

Psychologically let us now recognize more specifically what may be called purposive or purpose-adapted behavior. In all of these cases we can assume that the ergic goals define the purposes. Purpose-adapted behavior is likely, however, to show itself in elements at various subsidiation steps (goal distances) from the final goal, not only at the consummatory stages. All purpose-adapting behavior is innately rewarded by reaching the biological goal. But beyond these general characteristics one must distinguish two and probably three forms of purpose-adapted behavior: (1) that which has by evolution become innately and unconsciously adaptive to reaching the goal; (2) that which is learned but not consciously connected with its goal; and (3) that which is learned *and* consciously connected with the idea of reaching the goal. Instinct is *genetically* purpose-adapted, but with this we can contrast *acquired* purpose-adapted behavior. As just suggested, the latter can be subdivided—if we may momentarily use the word "conscious"—into blind trial-and-error learning without awareness of how the new behavior secures the desired goal, and intelligent, insightful learning in which the organism is conscious of how the new behavior succeeds in reaching the goal, or, at least, relates means to ends. We have already pointed out (Underwood, 1957) that as far as memory trace characteristics are concerned, the two forms of learning behave, after the initial short-term memory consolidation phase, in the same way, e.g., as regards rate of fading.

As we have seen, one behavioral criterion for differentiating insight—without the illegitimate and undependable peep into human consciousness or anthropocentric projection into animals—is the occurrence of a sudden change in the typical form of the trial-and-error learning curve. The time or errors curve takes an immediate vertical drop as the individual sees "how it works"—or, at least, learns an abstract relation—as shown in Figure 9–1 (b) compared with (a). Other associated phenomena are a period of pondering before, a complete change of strategy, etc., around the moment of insight, absence of further trial and error, and the appearance of "inferences." Below, we shall ask how such insights appear in various animal species; but it is obvious that in man the fumbling of trial-and-error learning is fairly often superseded by sudden insights. After several attempts to get

FIGURE 9–1
Learning Curves With and Without Insight

(a) Without Relation
  Perception:

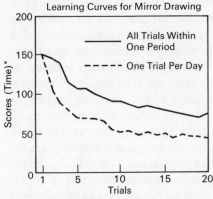

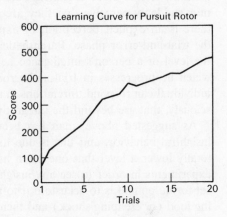

*Note: This inverts direction of learning gain.

The scores that constitute the curves are related to the amount of time required to trace a figure in the mirror, and hence decrease as skill goes up. The top curve is for continuous practice, all trials within one period. The bottom curve is for trials spaced one trial per day. (After Lorge, 1930)

The scores that make up the curve are for successive trials and represent the time on the target per 1-minute trial and 1-minute rest with a maximum possible score of 600; i.e., a possible score of 10 per second if the stylus remains on the target. (After Ball, 1950)

(b) With Relation Response,
  or "Insight":

Learning curve depicting the course of learning with insight. Whereas gradual learning is the rule in the trial-and-error situation, sudden solution is the rule in insight learning. Once a solution occurs with insight, it can be repeated promptly.

(b) With Relation Response, or "Insight":

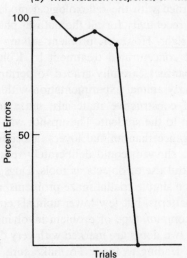

E. R. Hilgard and Atkinson, R. C., *Introduction to Psychology.* New York: Harcourt Brace Jovanovich Inc., 1967.

a key into a lock a man may "perceive" from the shape of the keyhole that he was holding the key upside down; or, in a more abstract example, after some unsuccessful attempts to solve three simultaneous equations he may suddenly recognize that one is simply dependent on another; or after some attempts to smooth an argument between a man and a woman at a party he may suddenly perceive that they are husband and wife. In all these cases there is an explicit perception of expressible relationships not realized in the trial-and-error phase. Parenthetically, however, we must reiterate that the level of a person's intelligence helps also to determine the speed with which he progresses in trial-and-error learning, since in such learning no individual can respond to relations in the situation, even blindly and unconsciously, that are beyond the integrative scope of his combining masses.

As suggested above, man has been slow to credit animals with much insightful behavior, and this is due to its being, except in primates, on so totally lower a level that one often has to set up special, carefully graded experiments in order to see any insightful steps at all. The typical problem set for an animal is to accustom it to a certain, natural, easy way of reaching food (or escaping shock) and then to block the direct path and see how far it is capable of finding a way around the barrier (the "detour" design). If the animal reacts correctly to each such detour problem—such as starting off, in a glass hedged maze, in the opposite direction to the food in order to reach it—we may assume insight. Actually, most successful animal detour learning usually occurs after much wandering around and proceeds by small increments of certainty, like any human trial-and-error learning.

Some initial, relatively unsystematic, "experimental" studies of animal intelligence were begun by Lloyd Morgan in 1890, but animal experimentation received its real impetus from E. L. Thorndike (1932) and Pavlov (1927) in work around the turn of the century. Pavlov's work was strictly concerned with the reflexological model of learning, but Thorndike had a wider receptivity for all the natural phenomena of animal learning, including insight. However, problem solving and intelligence in animals first received concentrated treatment by Köhler, who thought out problems for chimpanzees carefully graded to permit manifestations of insight. Most of this early animal experimentation with "labelled" doorways, sound signals, use of constructive materials, maze forms, etc., we must assume to be known to the student. The upshot was a much more sober view of animal intelligence than animal lovers' anecdotes had broadcast. Chimpanzees, as Köhler showed, could deliberately reason for a few seconds and make an insightful use of objects as tools. Dogs, cats, and some birds, could get insight on simple spatial maze problems, and learn to recognize differences in new patterns, but few lower animals could do either.

A common type of problem involving spatial and visual relations is that where two doors are marked with very different shapes—a cross and a circle —one leading to food. To make sure that the pattern form itself (rather than the position) is explicitly recognized and that one is not dealing with a global trial-and-error learning, the symbol can be shifted from the right to the left, altered in size and color, etc. Under these "pure pattern perception" conditions only apes indubitably solve it. Harlow has called this the "learning set" criterion performance, when the animal recognizes that only one solution is correct, and, having hit on it, it never returns (as it would sporadically in trial-and-error learning) to the wrong choice. Almost any of the standard, relation-perception, intelligence subtests used with humans—classification, analogies, opposites, topology—could be adapted to this reward-with-correct-choice design of experiment employable with animals. Incidentally, it is a sad reflection on the parochialism of divisions of psychology that animal research has so far availed itself very little of the resources of human individual difference research. Even the names used show this, the *classification* problem being named in animal research an "oddities" test, and the *eduction of a relation* a "learning set." The latter specialized use is perhaps reasonable in that a set seemingly is developed, in the classical sense of a mental set, to apply one particular relationship (if it will fit) to the repeated stimulus presentations, just as a child is set by the intelligence test example to apply analogy reasoning to each successive test item. But in a wider sense animal intelligence investigation has not made an informed use of the types of situation which the investigation of human ability structure has shown to represent important categories.

In groping for what distinguishes intelligent from unintelligent behavior in animals, animal psychologists have used such expressions as "recognizing a general principle," "combining elements effectively," "abstracting an essential quality," "reasoning," "reacting to symbolic stimuli" and so on. As we shall point out in Chapter 11, probably the important common feature in all of these descriptions is the ability *to perceive relationships* and to react to relations as such. With this conception it would seem desirable to test animal intelligence by the same designs of subtest as have been most g_f-saturated in humans, namely, classification, series, analogies, etc., though, of course, greatly simplified. Also one would look for the distinct general capacities of speed, retrieval (fluency), etc., and the local organization of visual, auditory, and motor powers.

A simple classification test is one in which two things are alike and a third different. In what animal researchers have called "oddity-principle learning" a monkey is allowed one "reach" through the bars of his cage at three "dish covers." After some trial-and-error reward—the equivalent of "instructions" in tests for humans—rhesus monkeys will "get the general idea" as Stone (1961) has shown, and henceforth choose the non-class dish cover (regardless of the particular class symbol) in each new presentation. From there on this can be developed into a graded intelligence test.

A series test can also be translated into animal testing, as in the well-known "double alternation" test, where the animal has to learn a sequence of "left correct; right correct; right correct" etc., in presentations of identical right and left objects. As commonly presented it could be, it is true, nothing but a memory test, no different in essence from the performance of a person repeating a long telephone number. Even so, it spreads out the animal kingdom, cats managing a sequence of four, raccoons of six, and primates eight (LL RR LL RR). The well-known triple-plate problem, in which the rat has to cross three plates in a particular sequence is another series test and here rats can do up to three, cats to seven, and rhesus monkeys to sixteen or more. However, to correspond correctly to relation eduction in series perception, the animal would have to (a) show transfer from one location and type of stimulus to another, and (b) extrapolate from the given series to new terms. In general, that common laboratory mammal, the rat, can barely be said to start at all on true series or classification behavior; cats, dogs, birds, raccoons show traces, and primates really begin to catch on. These facts we shall consider in the next section in asking if a general ability factor arises in animals.

Other experiments with animals bear only in a less direct fashion on the nature of insights. Bitterman (1965; Holmes and Bitterman, 1966; Lowes and Bitterman, 1967; Schade and Bitterman, 1965) experimented on fish, turtles, rats, and pigeons on reversal learning and maximization learning. In the former, as mentioned, an animal learns by trial and error that stimulus A, not B, is rewarded, and when he has learned this, the reward is switched and he is made to learn the reverse. (It is noteworthy that this has been used as a temperament (tractability) test on humans! See Cattell and Warburton, 1967, pages 464, 485.) The animal might seem to have the equivalent of "one is always right, but what is right may change at intervals." In maximization learning one choice, A, is rewarded, say seventy percent of the time and the other, B, thirty percent. The informed thing to do, if you are a professor of mathematical statistics, is not to choose A seventy percent of the time and B thirty percent, but to choose A always. What kinds, i.e., structures, of abilities would theoretically be expected to operate in a lower animal in these two kinds of experience is by no means clear. However, rats, monkeys, and pigeons succeed at both this and reversal learning; fish do not, and turtles oscillate between success and failure.

In delayed action learning, in which the animal has to hold a simple decision in mind for some seconds or minutes (as described in the last chapter) cats, rats, and dogs tend to point their noses and can solve it as long as they are allowed to do this, but raccoons and especially monkeys hold longer and without "pointing" aid. It is sometimes said that this behavior and alternation learning imply that a "symbol" is being used, but this is debatable, and the performances would seem to be composites of intelligence (relation eduction), tractability, and a temperament trait of inhibition of more immediate action (frontal lobe action) among others.

The clearest examples of behavior strictly corresponding to intelligent insight in man are probably still those of the classical experiments of Köhler carried out on chimpanzees. (Classical also as a good use of spare time, for they were done while World War I and the British Navy kept him marooned on the island of Teneriffe.) When bananas were hung high up out of arm's reach, many chimps gave up, but some eventually carried over some boxes and piled them up under the bananas. In another experiment where bananas were placed too far outside the cage to reach, but short sticks were left about, they tried to scrape them in with the sticks. The sticks were too short, but Köhler had made them so that one stick could be fitted into the hollow end of the other. At length Sultan, a genius among ages, put the two sticks together and with an evident glorious insight, proceeded to push one firmly into the "tube" in the other, and scraped in the bananas with his "synthetic" stick.

Roughly equivalent adaptation demand, and difficulties in arranging means to ends were presented by Bristol and the present writer for solution by human three-year-olds when candy was placed in open-work (visible connection) puzzle boxes in intelligence testing (Cattell and Bristol, 1933). Two- and three-year-old human behavior was about the same level as the adult primate behavior. Of course, as before, a distinction must be made between the insightful and purposeful *perception* of relations involved here and in *some* animal experiment, and that mere *utilization* of the relations which intelligence permits without conscious insight in other designs of animal experiment above. In the latter, e.g., by conditioning in trial-and-error experience, the behavior ends up by being "intelligently adaptive" (purposive, but not purposeful) just as in the former. For example, an odd-even series can be mastered either with or without insight, but differences have still to be recognized between the two. Two areas of difference are (1) the sudden "curve of learning acquisition" history (the abruptness of the intelligent, insightful perception) and (2) the capacity to transfer the learning, in case of insight, immediately to different concrete stimuli.

Just as we have divided *purpose-adapted* behavior into *instinctual* and *learned,* so we must divide the latter—learning by problem solving—into *unreflective* (blindly conditioned, trial-and-error) learning and *insightful* (conscious, or relation-perceiving, purposeful) learning. The *instinctual* and the *unreflective*—although one applies to the life of the *species* and to *genetics,* while the other applies to the *individual and experience*—have an important similarity of form. In terms of a mathematical model, they lead to making the response which (a) has a higher probability of being presently correct because (b) it has been rewarded more frequently, but which may not yet be completely apt to the individual situation. Despite the insightless, trial-and-error origin, the *rate* at which unreflective learning takes place and the *level* which it reaches in the individual may demand and be dependent upon an amount of combining brain mass—of intelligence substrate—not required in the *species* inheritance of the same complexity of behavior. This is emphatically evident when one considers the complexity of insect behavior, and connects with our neurological rule that it requires more brain mass to learn than to store.

Turning to the relation of *unreflective* to *insightful* learning, we see at once an intriguing parallel to the concepts of crystallized and fluid intelligence. As the above notion that intelligence resources (neural combining mass) are necessary even in insightless learning of complex relations would suggest, the evidence of Harlow, Stone, Bitterman, Wells, and others here discussed shows that even in unreflective learning the various species fall in much the same rank order as we find for insightful learning. (However, systematic experiments admittedly have not yet been carried very far down the evolutionary scale.)

The conclusion would seem inevitable that the capacity to learn to employ in *any* way, consciously or unconsciously, a given complexity of relation depends on some brain capacity (the "combining mass" of fibers). This is the basis for insightful, explicit perception of such relations and also for their utilization in learning. The animal which is able to learn to respond in, say, a complex required series, may be said to have "operative concepts" approaching what becomes explicit in insight or the capacity to transfer relations. However, "approaching" is an important qualification. For, physiologically, although a certain level of brain development is necessary in those who learn such operative concepts, one may hypothesize from as yet unorganized experimental results that the combining mass for learning correctly to respond to a certain "cue complexity" is not quite as large as that needed to handle with insight the explicit concept, per se. This latter is shown by ability to transfer, and to use a symbol for the relation. Without this we find the learning restricted to one sensory or motor locality. The clown walking the tightrope, or the hummingbird hovering over a flower, may have cerebellar development and "operative concepts" in the area of physical dynamics and air flow better than those which the aeronautics professor puts in the mathematical concepts in his textbook. But even when their adaptive responses imply equations as complex as any which he sets out in his book, they actually cannot express them in formulae or use them elsewhere.

4. PHYLOGENETIC EVIDENCE ON ANIMAL ABILITY STRUCTURE

To get the most out of the comparative study of animal intelligence it is necessary to combine it with observations of that physiological and neurological substrate—the brain—which we studied more specifically in man in the preceding chapter. Even at a superficial glance, the well-known generalization is supported that the higher we climb in the evolutionary tree, in terms of behavioral adaptation, the more physically developed does the brain become. But "level of evolution" is apt to be an anthropocentric concept. There are *many* directions of evolution from the most primitive animal life, and before any reduction to a single dimension can be contemplated, one does well to explore the many interesting varieties of behavioral adjustment and neurological form.

Upon doing so, one becomes impressed by the special emphases given to neurological development by habitat, by the physical structure of the animal, and especially by the greater dependence in different species on this or that sense organ. It has frequently been said, for example, that much of the brain development of man has arisen from (a) his use of tools or weapons (Ardrey, 1961), and (b) his need to communicate in a gregarious species.

The former became possible through his having hands, which, in turn, was a product of his starting to walk upright—and so on.

Another point of interest is that beyond the various basic neurological differences of various branches of the tree of evolution, one begins to encounter repeated occurrence of independent, parallel inventions, both in sensory organs and in brain structure. For example, the octopus, which has the largest brain of all invertebrates, has vision and eye structure more like that of man than some intermediate genuses. It can be conditioned to decline a dish of crab when presented with a white card (after being shocked simultaneously with the latter). But even this genius among the invertebrates is very rigid. It fails on simple detour tests or even in learning some new patterns of muscular coordination.

A *nervous system* capable of rapid transmission of a message (as distinct from slow transmissions by ordinary cells, responding contiguously by normal cell sensitivity) first appears in those lowly aquatic creatures, the hydras. It is the merest development of a connection between a touch sense organ and a motor response cell—the simplest typical reflex. In the coelenterata— including the common jellyfish—a circular nerve network appears, along with some new sensitivities (a vague reaction to change of light and gravitational position). Considering that it has no brain, and only a poor muscular coordination achieved through this nerve ring, it is amazing to see how successful the creature can be, biologically. In a sense, it can even claim to "hunt" its prey by rising to the surface of the water (by coordinated contractions of the bell-shaped body) and then, by floating down some distance with extended tentacles like a trawling net, picking up what food it can. Its sting kills the prey, and it can convey the food to the central mouth. All this is sheer "instinctual wisdom"—purposive adaptation maintained in this uniform and simple environment on the most meager nervous mechanism. Incidentally, physiologists (Prosser, 1939), have shown that there is also much *spontaneous* nervous discharge even at such lowly levels (crayfish, jellyfish, starfish), indicating that the nervous system is not merely a passive responder to stimuli, but a generator of action and electric potentials within itself.

Higher non-vertebrate levels already begin to show more *interconnecting* neurons—the beginning of that "combining mass" which eventually comes fully into its own in the mammals. For example, the starfish with a nervous system still radial, and therefore not centralized, has quite a repertoire of different and coordinated behaviors. The organism achieves this pool of alternative behavior patterns without a brain, but by a "democratic" interaction of several plexuses, each responsible for local control. And whereas a decapitated flatworm does just nothing, the spontaneous, endogenous, nervous activity just referred to increases as we go up the scale of neurological mass: a restless inner "purpose" appears. With this one begins to observe also other important adaptive structures, such as the primitive neurosecretory cells in worms—the predecessors of the ductless glands which continue to develop a role in the inner nervous activity.

Not only suitable, innately prescribed, adaptive behavior, but even simple learning is demonstrable already in various of the invertebrate phyla.
For example, a rewarded snail will learn to take the correct turn in a T-maze
after about sixty trials. Insects make a special development in the sensory
area. Their effectiveness in vision (despite the compound eye) is considerable, and they have developed an extreme olfactory sensitivity. Their capacity in two areas: social organization and spatial command of terrain is especially high in bees and ants, and by any standard of final behavioral
effectiveness, they rival the mammals.

Nevertheless, it is only with the appearance of the vertebrate, bilaterally
symmetrical, nervous system that the key to a substantial neural expansion
seems to have been found in the animal kingdom. The forward end of an
elongated body—the shape that occurs in most mobile animals and insects
—is the natural place for developing the sensitivities—the effectively integrated sensorium—necessary for a constant encountering of new environment. Once vision, taste, smell, and hearing become closely mutually located and bound with association tracts, the basis for growth of a single
brain area, with an effector (and tactile receptor) spinal cord, is created.
Certainly it is the vertebrates that eventually outshine all other phyla in
developing the kind of behavior that fits our definition of intelligence as perceiving relationships. And in the phylum the order of mammals outclasses
all others.

Figure 9–2 gives a slightly simplified, schematic picture of the development of brain areas as we go to increasingly adaptive, non-stereotyped behavior in the vertebrate (Stettner and Matzniak, 1968). In the fish a
slightly protuberant cerebrum is already evident. But more clearly evident,
and as yet not bound in a single cortex, are the separate sensory area lobes
—the optic lobes, the olfactory lobes, etc.—and, of course, for motor coordination, the separate cerebellum—the gyroscope of the physical body. In
the amphibia (frog) the cerebellum has already begun to spread over the olfactory and to overhang the optic lobes. Some relative increase in the cerebellum enables the bird to handle the extra bodily balance and coordination
of flight. In the dog the special sensory and motor areas are already bound
in a single large cortical organization, beneath which the old brain, brain
stem, and cerebellum are beginning to disappear as under an umbrella.

The changes in absolute size of the cortex are considerable. From two
or three grams in a fish two feet in length, or in rat or dove, it reaches 100
to 150 in the dog, 400 in the gorilla, and 1500 in man (see Table 9–1).
Below the vertebrates, some increase in brain size is simply due to intake
—to the creature taking greater advantage of the information the world has
to offer, in color, sound, range of taste, and smell. Since the sensory field
and physical adjustments required are much the same for all (except for
the differential emphasis of land, air, and ocean) we should expect that all
kinds of species would show approximately parallel discoveries of five or six
sense organs and development of corresponding analysis areas in the brain.
The main difference one notes at this sensory analysis level is for the more

FIGURE 9–2
Stages of Evolution of the Brain

*The relatively great growth of the forward end of the brain
in higher forms, seen by comparing sagittal sections of the brain.*

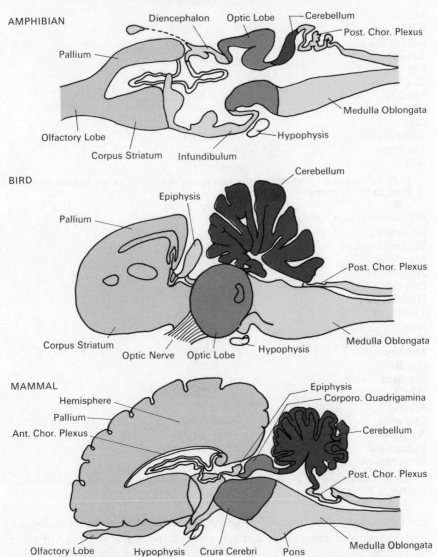

S. Ochs, *Elements of Neurophysiology*, New York: John Wiley & Sons, Inc., 1965, p. 273.

broadly adapted, "intelligent" animals to develop more in the "remote" senses (vision and hearing) relative to touch and taste, for these developments handle a wider, more anticipatory contact with environmental problems. But the most obvious increase accompanying the increases in what we

TABLE 9–1

Brain Weights of Twelve Species or Genuses of Mammals (Adult)

(a) Absolute

	Gram Weight
Mouse	0.4
Rat	1.6
Guinea Pig	4.8
Rabbit	9.5
Cat	31.0
Dog[1]	65.0
Monkey	88.0
Chimpanzee	350.0
Man	1450.0
Dolphin	1700.0
Elephant	5000.0
Whale	7000.0

[1]Note, in the usual variability of dog breeds as Cobb (1965) notes, weights may vary from 20 to 120 grams.

(b) Relative to Body Weight

Mammals

Squirrel Monkey	1:12
Marmoset	1:19
Japanese Mouse	1:22
Porpoise	1:38
House mouse	1:40
Tree Shrew	1:40
Man	1:45
Ground Shrew	1:50
Monkey	1:170
Gorilla	1:200
Elephant	1:600
Whale	1:10,000

Reptiles

Crocodile	1:5,000
Anatosaurus	1:20,000
Stegosaurus	1:30,000
Brontosaurus	1:100,000

Part (b) reprinted with permission of the publisher from S. Cobb, "Brain Size," *Archives of Neurology,* 1965, 12, 555–561.

have classified as intelligence in the last section is that in the neurological, associative, *combining mass* and *sensory-analytic,* cortical areas. In other words, the specific sense experience and perceptual meaning areas increase in size, but not so rapidly as the associational areas which, in mammals, constitute the most rapidly increasing mass of the cortex.

An interesting light on essential versus nonessential cerebral relations to intelligence is gained by comparing birds with mammals. Both spring from the common reptile pattern, but the morphology of their brains has developed very differently. Quite apart from the greater relative cerebellar development demanded in birds by the greater motor and gravitational sensitivity needed to ride the unstable winds and move in three dimensions, the whole cortical proportion is different. Whereas in mammals the cortex is all-enveloping, as shown at the bottom of Figure 9–2, in birds it has receded almost

FIGURE 9–3
The Main Paths of Brain Development in the Vertebrate Phyllum

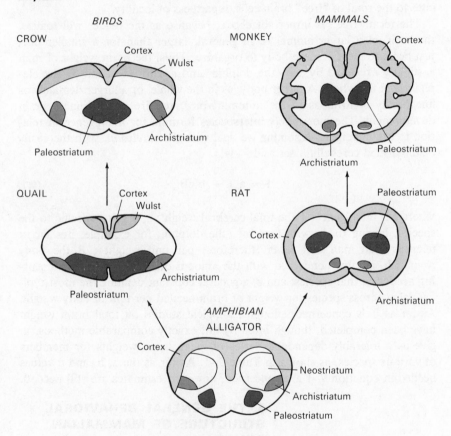

The wulst is a structural, histological zone peculiar to birds, apparently with functions similar to those of the cortex. However, the whole development of zones is distinctly different. The increasing development of "intelligence" in birds is associated more with enlargement of the wulst and upper striatum (next to it), whereas in mammals it parallels growing volume and area of the cortex. (The above are simplified, schematized drawings from actual transverse sections of the brain, as in various anatomical texts.)

From "The brain of birds," by L. J. Stettner and K. A. Matzniak. Copyright © by Scientific American, Inc. All rights reserved.

to a vestige, and the various subdivisions of the striatum (hyperstriatum, etc.) now make up the bulk of the cerebrum. Nevertheless, as the ablation studies of Ziegler and comparative studies of Krushinsky, show, learning of the kind indicative of intelligence, in birds as elsewhere, seems to depend on the total functioning cerebral mass as elsewhere, but mainly striatal, with the cortex playing no special part. This is a useful warning not to take local phylogenetic morphology and histology too seriously when we are dealing with this most general of capacities—intelligence—which consistently relates to the total of "free" brain cells, regardless of locality.

The term "free" is important above, because as the reader will realize, the brain of a larger animal is, in general, larger than for a smaller one, just because there is more body to organize. Thus, the brain weight of man is slightly exceeded by, say, the dolphin, and greatly exceeded by the elephant and the whale. A larger body, as in the whale, or a larger demand for fine bodily control, as in the humming-bird, require proportionate brain development. The most likely interspecies formula for intelligence in relation to brain weight—assuming we deal with the *cerebrum,* with the easily distinguished cerebellum set aside—is:

$$I = a_s T - b_s cB \tag{9.1}$$

where I is intelligence, T the total cerebral weight; a_s a value specific to the species, having to do with texture[2] (the dolphin, for example, has larger neurons than man and fewer, therefore, per unit weight); B the body weight; b_s a value concerned with the amount of bodily control and sensing needed in that species; and c, a general constant defining the most typical value across species for weight of brain needed per unit of body weight. As far as T is concerned, enough zoological studies on total brain weight have been completed, though often by not exactly comparable methods, to give us a tolerably dependable series of mean brain weights for members of various species, as shown in Table 9–1. As far as the a, b, and c values needed in equation 9–1 are concerned, however, estimates are still needed.

5. THE GENERAL BEHAVIORAL STRUCTURE OF MAMMALIAN ABILITY

At this point let us push forward our taxonomic "zoom lens" and focus henceforth only on comparisons within the mammalian order, with some reference occasionally to bird behavior. At the same time we shall shift the emphasis from general, ethological "behavior in situ" and largely anatomical comparison to actual, laboratory, behavioral test measures, and the "structure" of such behavior itself. Unfortunately, it must be confessed from the outset that we do not possess in the realm of

---

[2] Neurons per cubic millimeter vary from about 140,000 in the mouse, through about 21,000 in man, to 6,000 to 7,000 in elephant or whale.

animal experiment anything approaching the systematic, correlational, structural analyses studied in Chapters 3, 4, and 5 above for man. Nevertheless, in principle, two kinds of individual-difference ("R-technique") correlational analysis are possible (besides the factoring of change scores) that could yield evidence of animal ability structure. They are (a) the ordinary one of experimenting simultaneously with many "ability" performances on a sufficient sample of animals within a species, and (b) what we may call *trans-species factorization* in which correlations are made between the *mean* performances of each of a sufficient variety of species.

Studies of type (a), though unfortunately not yet covering a sufficiently representative set of ability performances, have become available in the work of Anastasi et al. (1955), Cattell, Korth, and Brace (1971), Royce (1966), Scott et al. (1959), Vaughn (1937) and Wherry (1941.) However, factor structure determinations made on comparative psychological data in the way suggested in (b) has *not* yet been thoroughly carried out. In a rough sense, however, it is already evident from Section 4 above that one would be likely to arrive, across species, at a unitary general ability factor. That is to say, the rank order of different species in one type of performance, e.g., detour learning, or classification ("oddity learning"), seems to be much the same as in any other complex learning, e.g., reversal learning, series, etc. However, by the criteria accepted as standards in ordinary psychometric work, the results are not at the precision level needed for factor analysis. Livesay, in a recent study (1966) with rats, rabbits, and cats, indicates technical difficulties with the Hebb-Williams closed field comparisons of different species and changes of reliability with method of scoring. Das and Broadhurst (1959) show a reliability of only .48 for such tests, and in fact finish up with a difference in species rank order from that independently obtained by others.

Experimentally we are thus at a lower level of precision, as yet, than in the work with humans. But such surveys as those of Krech (1966) on animal problem solving, and especially the fine correlational analyses by Royce (1966) leave little doubt that problem-solving capacities of diverse kinds tend to increase together. Similarly the connection of this general ability with increasing size of the neural combining mass is supported by brain operation results on animals, such as those seen in Section 4 above. It is supported also by Bagshaw and Pribram's (1965) and Dabrowska's (1964) demonstration of reduced learning, discrimination, and generalization through damage in almost any cortical area. A general survey by Wechsler (1958) in fact concludes that general intellectual deficit is not linked to damage in any *particular* center. Furthermore, there are fairly strong indications that in lower animals localization of special sense transactions are less rigid than in humans, and that mass action, appearing as "substitutability," is more prevalent.

Because the bulk of the structural analyses in Chapters 2 to 5 above are made on relatively homogeneous human groups, the greatest interest in possibilities of close comparisons with the animal field centers on the first of the two correlational approaches just indicated: that in which animals in one species are measured on a good variety of experimental performances, which are intercorrelated to show how they cohere. A classical instance of this is Wherry's (1941) factor analysis of Tryon's maze-running data on bright and dull rats. Another is that of Anastasi et al. (1955) on the performances of seventy-three dogs, and of Vaughn on eighty-three rats. Typically four or five factors have been found in such studies, but there have been great difficulties in checking the findings through dependable matches across replicative researches. For, as Royce (1950) points out, the rotation of factors in some studies has been quite poor, and the choice of variables has not provided enough markers to plan any use of precise matching indices.

The best attempt to align and interpret such work is that of Royce (1950), who rightly recognizes that *both* temperament and ability factors are likely to emerge from the kinds of performance used in much animal learning research. In rats he concludes that there is stability for a factor of (a) docility versus readiness to venture, (b) of visual responsiveness, (c) of speed or motility, and (d) of insight or complex learning capacity. The first and third might be written off as temperamental and motivational, and we are perhaps left with two ability structures: a factor akin to p_v visualization (page 34) in humans, and if Royce is correct, one corresponding to fluid general intelligence, g_f. Other sensory or motor "local organization" factors might conceivably have appeared if there had been variables to mark them. The actual performances in which the hypothetical g_f shows itself in rats are: freedom from errors on the elevated maze; fewness of trials needed in the simple maze; freedom from errors on the simple maze; success in latch box solution; multiple platform learning; and the Maier reasoning test by multiple light signals.

In temporarily calling this "fluid intelligence," general factor "insight," Royce states that he does not imply that all behavior involved is insightful, and in fact the concept comes nearer to what is general in success in purpose-adaptive learning, even when it is trial-and-error in nature. We have already suggested that this must be a function of the same general relation-utilization capacity (based on the neural combining mass) as appears, with added qualities of conscious recognition and generalizability, in insight. Now that the notion is further supported by Royce's conclusions, it might be clearer to refer to this operative "conscious and unconscious insight" explicitly as *relation-handling* potential. Research is needed to see whether the complexity level of relations that can be absorbed and fixed in habits by trial-and-error learning is in fact exactly proportional to that shown by the same animals or persons in insightful performances, but Royce's findings point that way for animals, and there are several studies that do so for humans.

Considerable advances in precision of conclusion from animal researches could be made if the performances were conceived and created in relation to wider theories of the nature of abilities, rather than only in the tradition created by the prevalence of certain pieces of apparatus. Royce, whose own work like that of Howarth (1966) has imaginatively opened up new realms, comments (1966) on the contrast between over four hundred varieties of performance test explicitly invented (Cattell and Warburton, 1967) and brought to standard form in the human area, and the extreme paucity of comparable measures in the classical animal experimental area. The former measures have been developed in relation to a variety of theories about human ability and personality structure; but until recently no such breadth of theory about animal individual differences and the variety of common cognitive processes has directed "comparative psychology." And, as Royce points out, the attempts to unravel animal ability structure have "not prevailed against the practical difficulties of conceiving diverse situations."

Meanwhile, there is tolerably convincing evidence in the above animal behavior analyses of some general ability running across sensory areas and operating in general relation perception, and of a factor governing specifically visual discriminations. Further, there are hints that with a broadening of the experimental performances tested, corresponding discrimination factors might be found, like the regional "power" factors found in man, for olfactory, auditory, and motor performances. The range of these sensory area factors, judging by the relative separatedness of visual, olfactory, and other lobes in animals compared to man, might be more influential across performances than in man, where the general ability, g_f and g_c, factors predominate. So far, however, nothing has been found equivalent to the V, N, S, etc., primary abilities (cultural "agencies") in humans, though recent, unpublished work on "sentiments" in rats by Dielman, Schneewind, and the present writer, point to such "culturally acquired" ability complexes as intrinsically possible. As in humans, what are primarily ability performances substantially involve, also, temperamental and motivational factors with which we are not here concerned. Indeed, much of the "delayed action" and "attention preserving" actions of the frontal lobes in animals seem similar to those which also express human intelligence in controlled reasoning, and additionally involve ego strength (Hundleby, Pawlik, and Cattell, 1965).

Basic advances in this field await not only that wider choice of relation-educing behaviors which Royce has urged upon the animal experimenter as so necessary for interpreting concepts by multivariate analysis, but also a conceptual clarification of what to do when behaviors across species are qualitatively so different. In the latter connection, some intriguing issues have been raised by Lilly's (1961) experiments pointing to the porpoise as the unrecognized genius of the animal world. As Table 9–1 shows, if we were to do a rough calculation of formula 9.1 above, i.e., allowing for body weight, the dolphin would finish up with an effective brain weight not so very different from that of man. And Lilly believes "It is probable that their intelligence is comparable to ours, though in a very strange fashion" (Lilly, 1961, p. 39). Generalizing that in man a brain must reach about 1000 grams in order to learn the abstract symbolism which we call a language, he claims an appreciable language communication exists in schools of porpoises. He urges that, in higher mammals, intelligence levels cannot be fully appreciated unless we realize that many important and relevant measures have been entirely absent from laboratory research on animal ability. It would seem that either the laboratory researchers must become ethologists in outlook or the natural ethologists must master quantitative, multivariate experiment.

The fact that the life of the dolphin does not permit the use of tools or the carrying of possessions, means that intelligence must express itself in fields of experience having a very different emphasis from the environment-manipulating preoccupation of man. Possibly the limited manipulating capacity of birds explains why (except for the Egyptian vulture, the seagull, and the crow), they show no intelligent use of "tools." But if our theory of (a) g_f, (b) the "combining neural mass," and (c) the existence of an abstract hierarchy of relationships applicable to the real world independent, at its apex of abstraction, of the particular nature of its sensory bases, is true as a whole, then certain consequences follow for the comparison of intelligence across species. The performances which covary in the g_f factor will cover in part different sensory and behavior areas in various species, but will have a common loading pattern where they overlap, when they are at the same general level of ability. In any case, a general ability factor common to them all can be extracted by going across species, i.e., entering each species as a single individual case in the correlations, thus making objective comparisons of intelligence conceptually possible.

6. THE COMPARATIVE STRUCTURE OF THE ABILITIES OF MACHINES AND COMPUTERS

Animal abilities, though differing enough from human intelligence to yield fresh prespectives, yet belong in a generic sense to the same kingdom, and, in most cases to the same family. Only from a wider comparison with the behavior of machines can one get a radical, searching—and sometimes eerie—light on the more basic meaning of intelligence. At the moment we live rather intoxicatingly in the lusty youth of computers—in what Wiener called the "cybernetic revolution" appearing as the first, main, social-scientific change since the industrial revolution. The access of cheap power which made the industrial revolution is followed by one of new horizons through automatic calculation, reasoning, and control; but many of the features of digital and analogue computers were present in essence in simpler machines, e.g., in the Chinese abacus, the negative feedback of the turnspit in the Elizabethan kitchen, and the response to the condenser in the first steam engine. The term cybernetics, incidentally, was coined by Ampère in 1834, and a little digging in the work and writings of Babbage, in 1888, will show that good thinking along these lines is not as recent as the newspapers would suggest.

The behavior of a machine has its primary resemblance to animal intelligence because it is a problem-solving, environment-manipulating device. But even the layman will object at once that the parallel breaks down because (a) the machine is a passive slave of man with no motivation and goal of its own, responding only when man sets it to respond, as in, say, a mouse trap, and (b) it does not continuously learn from experience. The first objection holds in a complete sense only for a simple machine like a bow and arrow. From the beginning of powered machines, like a steam engine, we have something akin to motivation "built in." And the unfortunate military pilot pursued by, say, a heat-homing rocket missile, would nowadays admit that a machine can strive, with constant readjustment to situations, toward a consummatory goal!

Regarding the possibility of learning, which is closer to our issue of machine intelligence, judgment about machine learning is best withheld until we have studied computers more closely. However, it has been the sport of ingenious minds for generations to make mechanical devices that seem to think and learn. Recent instances are Grey Walter's mechanical tortoise (1960), Shannon's maze runner, and Ashby's homeostatic "design for a brain" (1960). If we include examples only on paper, we must include McCulloch and Uttley and go back to Babbage (who, Sir Cyril Burt reminds us, had "working models in hardware" more than a century ago). (If literary speculation is included, one can go back to Mary Shelley's "Frankenstein" and Well's "Island of Dr. Moreau.")

While recognizing that some degree of "intelligence" has to be admitted in machines from their beginning, let us consider the most modern claimant, the advanced electronic computer. It has essentially five parts: (1) a device for *input,* where information is read in from cards or discs; (2) a *control* or self-regulating plan of operations, as typically seen in "a program"; (3) a *storage* for data needed in the transactions, e.g., a memory drum; (4) a *processing* or calculation unit; (5) an *output,* e.g., a teletype or card-punching addition.

We have already used this model in a schematic way as an aid to developing a classification of abilities in Chapter 5, but we admitted certain important differences from the human mind which made any literal and exact translation unwise, the reasons for which must now be discussed further. To begin with, the input, though it is the analogue of the animal sensorium, is quite a poor relative of the latter. It does not have a roving eye, nor does it search out the environment. It selects only in a simple way, usually taking what is given on the card—and this is material that has been predigested from the physical world by a human. Later we shall point to the machine's enormous discrepancy in the reasoning area between inductive and deductive reasoning compared to humans. If presented with, say, five shapes in the typical classification test, and asked to pick out a sixth that "goes" with them from, say, four others, the machine is far behind the human, largely due to this perceptual weakness. On the other hand, in deductive reasoning, presented with a set of premises and a set of logical rules, it reaches all possible conclusions better than most philosophers, as has been recently demonstrated in regard to inferences from postulates in particular geometrical systems. The syllogism "All luminous stars also radiate gamma rays" and

236 Ultra-Human Intelligence

"Our sun is a luminous star" etc., is presented to the machine, however, only as two or three symbols to which it mechanically applies the logical rules. It knows nothing about the scintillation of stars at night or the warmth of the midday sun. The human being has predigested the greater part of the input that *he* would experience as global input, before the machine receives *its* bare input, upon which to apply exhaustively its mechanical logic.

Although the capacity of the machine to respond to the totality of its environment, by its "input mechanisms" is thus very limited compared to an animal brain, its performance in the second phase—that of processing, including reasoning—is more nearly equal, if two very different qualities can be called equal. Its quality is obviously more mechanical, but also—in the area of computing in which it is mainly asked to perform—altogether more rapid and accurate. Since logical inference can also be automatized—and ordinary algebra, Boolean algebra, and general mathematical logic are examples of this—a machine can definitely be programmed to reason, especially in deductive reasoning (inductive reasoning, as indicated above and explained below, is somewhat different). Another field of reasoning in which machines can do well—in fact, far better than the human brain, is that associated with probabilities. Much of our everyday reasoning is concerned with combining probabilities or contingencies of this or that event affecting our purposes, and here the computer does a superb job.

Turning to the third kind of operation—memory or storage—one becomes aware of decidedly greater differences of man and machine. In man memory is a living thing; in machines it is static. In animal memory operation two phases are widely recognized—the short distance memory in which experiences are not stored but kept in some active reverberation, while their associations that determine storage are worked out; and the long distance memory in which recollections and ideas are stored and retrieved in ways more closely resembling storage on the machine's magnetic drum. The machine, it is true, also has a duality—the storage of the program and the main storage of what the program has to work upon; but there is no obvious or helpful parallelism here. The greatest difference of all in this respect is that the computer is characteristically completely cleared of its particular storages after each piece of work, whereas the human mind goes on accumulating and being affected by its memories till its dying day. When we discuss later Turing's idea that a computer should be "sent to school" to learn, this issue of its memory organization becomes important. Meanwhile we note that, in the present-day computer, nothing quite corresponds to the extensive use of the "combining (and sorting) mass" of neurons in the first phase of animal memorizing, leading gradually to the placing of a memory in a comparatively restricted storage area. The data in the computer goes directly to its storage space.

Finally we come to the output, which the typical user of a typical computer knows as a "print out," but which in, say, an automatic pilot or a homing rocket, issues as a physical control, more akin to the executive muscular action finishing the deliberations of the animal mind. Here no radical difference exists; the computer of a space ship and the human cerebellum have much in common.

In seeking by such comparisons to throw light on human intelligence, one has to distinguish between differences that are essential and revealing and differences that are merely due to the special way in which computers happen to have been developed as handmaidens serving the purposes of the human mind. Obviously, the computer has not been designed in the first place to give the maximum resemblance possible to human perception and decision. Computers, after all, began in the abacus and Pascal's early machine, primarily for adding and subtracting and removing the stressful chore of accurate detail from the human conscience. They proceeded in the still-mechanical, pre-electric stage of Briggs's slide rule and Babbage's mechanical monster, to processes of multiplying, dividing, and working out general equations. Today they calculate, compare, and evaluate systems presented to them, search for particular patterns in sets fed into them; recognize objects; translate languages; and choose the best purchases on the stock exchange. They have also been taught to play games of checkers and chess; and (in the Illiac, product of the University of Illinois), to compose music and make drawings.

As to the sensory apparata, in which above we noted so major a defect in comparison with animals, it would apparently be quite possible to build in vision by selenium cell additions and auditory skills through the telephone. Already the former is at a point where scanning machines score test answer sheets and respond to shapes cast by an "eye" lens on an electric retina. The Bell Telephone Company's "Audrey" also reacts to sound coded from a microphone, and can thus respond to spoken instructions. There seems little doubt that it can be made to move in a direction better to parallel human perception, but in this respect the computer still has a long way to go.

And in spite of these impressive analogies of machine to brain, the pattern of performances, even apart from present limitations of development, is in important ways very different. An obvious difference appears when we compare the empirically discovered primary abilities or agencies of humans with a corresponding profile of the machine. In numerical ability, defined just as in Thurstone's N, the computer fantastically exceeds human performance. (The writer has known one or two prima donnas of lightning calculation who can keep up with a simple desk computer on certain operations, perhaps for five minutes; but they soon make errors and in a few minutes collapse from fatigue while the machine serenely proceeds.) In the area represented by the human deductive reasoning primary ability, since logic can be programmed for the machine as a series of calculations (expressed in Boolean algebra) etc., the computer also far exceeds human powers, at any rate in terms of speed and comprehensiveness. As stated above, it has also succeeded in detecting, in a rather large number of logical propositions, inconsistencies not previously noticed by logicians. The computer is reported actually to have supplied some more elegant proofs for propositions by Russell and Whitehead than those previously known. Inductive logic receives special consideration below. In spatial ability—Thurstone's S—it can do wonders with an oscillograph. In memory—Thurstone's M—it is infallible in storing and retrieving; but its range of "material" is small relative to what goes into human memory—when one considers the diverse sensory modalities of human memory.

But what of the "higher-order" factors, of fluid intelligence, g_f, general retrieval, g_r, and general speed, g_s? The last needs little discussion: the machine is enormously faster, and the nature of the processes that enable it to be faster may well be on the same continuum—a continuum of time for a single neural process—as differentiates human beings. How far the retrieval process in man and machine can be referred to the same principles can only become clear as the machine process "hypotheses" are tried out in brain investigation. What is clear is that both the accuracy and the scope of machine retrieval already decidedly exceed those of the human brain.

This needs a little further discussion because it underlies comments below on machine "learning" in relation to the meaning of intelligence. The memory space of a machine is as large as one cares to make it, whereas that of a brain is sadly limited. In what we commonly think of as "sound reasoning," memory is as important as relation-perceiving capacity, as it is also in the functioning of crystallized intelligence. For example, a doctor, or a clinical psychologist, in making a diagnosis, draws on various generalizations, each perhaps simple in itself, but requiring to be put together, often in no more complex an interrelationship than that of simple "weighting" of probabilities. It has been shown in actual clinical data by Meehl (1954) that as more pieces of information are supplied to a clinician he tends to make better judgments up to some five, six, or seven pieces, but after that he makes little improvement and may even get confused. The machine, on the other hand, not only weights the first half dozen bits of knowledge more accurately (in a probability or regression sense), but continues to use further information so long as it adds to certainty. In range of retrievable information, and efficiency of using it, at least in a mathematical sense, the machine far surpasses man.

However, the vital point is that the machine has to be programmed by someone, and that it does not normally continue to learn and revise its programs as does the human being. Nevertheless, as pointed out above, the totality of "ability to learn" includes both plasticity and relation-perceiving capacity and, among animal research psychologists, at least, the ability to learn has been accepted too uncritically as a basis for ranking intelligence, as if all of it were intelligence. Learning and intelligence are two very different things, and not enough has been done to devise animal learning experiments which clearly separate them. Sometimes it is blind, trial-and-error learning—explainable in reflexological terms and requiring

only plasticity—and sometimes it is insightful[3] learning (both usually requiring reward). Parenthetically, we have recognized that some non-
insightful trial-and-error learning may also involve intelligence, according
to the complexity of the perceptual and motor relations required in the
discriminations, regardless of whether they are consciously and insightfully
recognized as relations.

The "learning" of machines as they are now constituted separates trial-
and-error from insightful learning still more clearly than we may have
separated them before, because the machine, with a sufficiently vast memory storage, can perform fantastically well by trial-and-error learning; it
can beat a good chess player by recalling more successful moves from
previous games (beginning at the given point in the game) than he can—
but it does very poorly at learning by insightful perception, i.e., eduction
of relations. Indeed, most of the game-playing successes of machines are
the behavior of an "assiduous ass" which stores up in its memory all past
games and when a situation arises chooses the play which in the past
has most frequently led to a winning game from that point on.

As so programmed, it works on general probabilities rewarded in past
games. It can also advance to more specific probabilities through recording the probabilities of moves by the given type of opponent—his style—
as it comes to be recognized—as a human player tries to do. But even
programmed in the simpler way it beats all but the very best human
players. Present day weather forecasting is partly based on the same
procedure: find a pattern of humidity, pressure, etc., in the past records
that most closely resembles today and see what came next. This is a
measure of our present lack of insight into the laws of meteorology! The
work on the strategy of games followed by Von Neumann and Morgen-
stern's pioneer analysis has advanced enormously; but in some higher
unusual constellation (demanding g_f rather than g_c) one suspects that the
insight of an Alexander or a Napoleon would beat the computer. Parenthetically, the "stored wisdom" of the computer cannot strictly be equated
to the human g_c, because the latter is a deposit of wise decision capacities
resulting from an initial application of g_f, i.e., insight. The "machine wisdom" is rather that part of human learning by trial and error which is not
g_c, but appears in the more rote-learned school subjects. The comparison
does bring out, however, that in humans such rote learning must lead to a
number of decisions which simulate, and are mistaken for, the action of
fluid intelligence, and that the boundaries of such learning would be expected to be determined appreciably by the span of memory.

However, in all the machine problem solving discussed up to this point,
the "experience" has been collected by humans and stored in the machine.

[3] Incidentally, we are continuing to use the term insight in the strict behavioral sense
we gave above, i.e., not depending on evidence of conscious report of the experience.
For who knows whether an organization such as a modern computer, with a million,
highly complex, electronic circuits, has consciousness?

The latter shows that end result of trial-and-error or insightful learning in coping with a problem, rather than the learning itself. A decade or so ago, this was the only way a computer was known to behave—as a passive executor of human instructions. It did what the program told it, and so precisely that its response resembled those of the rigid but effective instincts of an insect. However, a computer can be programmed to learn tactical tricks within the strategy of its program as well as to handle digital facts. Already, as in, for example, the factor rotation program known as Maxplane (Cattell and Muerle, 1960), it can be programmed to respond adaptively to a quite complex variety of situations, without depending on having met the exact situation before; but this is still not self-learning. One perceives that the absence of learning in a machine is really synonymous with the other obvious lack in any comparison with a human being —the absence of motivation and "pleasure" at getting a successful end result. Once some awareness of success, relative to a goal, can be made perceptible to the machine, some rewarding of the responses that have led up to the given result can be installed. At that point it can be programmed to alter its own program as a result of the "success" of a particular response. That means that that response is "weighted" to be made more readily, frequently, or early in the series in future. As Minsky (1966) points out, this means that the machine must have some "knowledge" of how to operate upon its own program; but this use of a program within a program should offer no insuperable difficulty. Thus, learning, both as a "response preference" (as in conditioning) and as "inhibition" (as delaying a response longer) can be set up in a computer. Even by the time these words are printed, there may be advances so striking as to make this analysis seem crude. Nevertheless, enormously potent though such learning devices might become, they would still, as described up to this point, remain on the level of insightless, trial-and-error learning. Parenthetically, the extent to which machines can nevertheless acquire what humanly we would call "judgment" from such experiences may be appreciated from Kleinmuntz's recent book (1968). An interesting variant is Enslein's (1967) training of a computer to distinguish representatives, as by perception, of two classes of objects. This is done by varying internal connections in a systematic way, much as in human reward learning, to increase and retain those which favor more correct responses, though this varying of connections is done by the human experimenter.

The last and the hardest nut to crack in conceiving the machine simulation of intelligence concerns the manner in which relations can be educed by anything resembling a digital computer. For this capacity to perceive relations is the central definition which has been given to fluid intelligence. However, before we tackle the computer's perception of patterns, it is informative (especially since many readers will be test-oriented psychologists) to digress for the space of one page into the ways in which actual perceptual test responses are typically evaluated in human beings. For the varieties of perceptual performance and of response performance can be

TABLE 9-2
A Classification of Test Performance Parameters

Operational Character of Response

1. Known by subject to be *objectively* evaluated	vs.	Produced explicitly as a Self-Evaluation
2. Evaluated on External Behavior	vs.	Evaluated by Physiological, Internal Changes
3. Evaluated on a Single Variety and Dimension of Response	vs.	Evaluated on Each of Several Possible Responses
4. Evaluated on Total Number of Responses (Retrieval Fluency)	vs.	Evaluated on Subsection of Responses that Meet Conditions
5. Evaluated on a Single Score	vs.	Evaluated on a Total *Pattern* of Element Responses
6. Evaluated on *Producing* the Response (Inventive)	vs.	Evaluated on *Selecting* the Response (Selective)

closely interconnected. Certainly the ways, in general, in which computer and human abilities can be brought into a common conceptual scheme are likely to be more soundly appreciated through a basic analysis of what behavior we measure in tests. Table 9-2 is an attempt at such a basic analysis of the forms of behavior that are put into measurable form in tests. It is explained in more detail elsewhere (Cattell and Warburton, 1967), but the essentials of the taxonomy are here evident. One must be careful, incidentally, to distinguish between the classification of abilities by their inherent parameters, as in the Ability Dimension Analysis Chart (ADAC) in Table 4-1, which pursues a higher-level abstraction than the present *operational* categorization.

A rather constantly recurring dichotomy brought out in the above taxonomy, and one applicable to both human and machine performances, is one which Burt (1949) called "inventive" versus "applicative," and which Guilford later revised as "divergent" versus "convergent." Though popular, these terms invite confusion, the former with "inventive" versus "selective," which, as a truly operational concept, is covered by No. 6 in Table 9-2, and the latter with No. 4 in Table 9-2, namely, degree of fluency. The confusion in the "divergent-vs.-convergent" jargon is one of a mode of *production* of response with a mode of *scoring* it. The individual can produce on a mental set simply to give a *lot* of responses (like a manic psychotic), or on a set which respects the relation-eductive and complexity-of-sequence conditions, designated in Table 4-1, as ability properties. The examiner or experimenter, according to Table 9-2, can set conditions which are inventive or selective (parameter 6) and, in either case, score on sheer number of responses (parameter 4) or on their correctness according to some key. Similarly a machine output can be evaluated by its total volume versus correctness as fitness to some condition or by its having to invent or to select. This ambiguity of the phrase "convergent-versus-divergent" is discussed in other connections elsewhere (pages 55 and 57).

With this glance at a classification of test performances, we may return with a little more precision to considering the uniqueness of relation perception. For it is here that the greatest difference exists between computer and brain, and here that we have greatest difficulty in getting assistance from the well-understood computer toward finding out what happens in the little-understood brain. And here we see the sharp difference between deductive and inductive reasoning. For a computer can readily be programmed for the former—each relation, such as "greater than," "part of" or "like" being represented by a digital term. On the other hand if it is asked to look at a triangle, a square, and a circle, with its selenium eye and say which is the odd one out, it is likely to perform more poorly than a five-year-old child. In fact, it does very poorly at recognized *patterns* in any sense modality. Whereas to a child a box is a box, or a puppy a puppy, no matter what the perspective or lighting, so that he can recognize a shape in a different context or a tune with a change of key, the machine is apt to be literal. A chimpanzee, or even a rat, can be taught to recognize a triangle, despite differences of size (distance) or angle of vision, but the computer, despite its facility with other problems, initially reacts to a triangle only when all in the presentation is preserved exactly constant.

It is true that recently the computer has been programmed so that it will (by following the edge) say to itself: "This has three corners," or "This has four straight edges." And from this step some ingenious work by Selfridge and Neisser (1960) has made it actually able to solve some analogies and classification problems (as in examples in Figure 5–2 above or Figure 9–4 below) which have hitherto been considered the essence of a fluid intelligence problem. In pushing into this field, computer specialists have become increasingly aware that the very precision of the computer is its downfall when it faces problems of this type. Like the insect with its rigid instinct, or the behavior of a too meticulous human, it fails to see the wood for the trees. The problem is partly the main one we are bringing out: that it reacts to "facts" rather than "relations"; but it is also that it lacks plasticity and does not know how to accept approximate presentations, in which the t's have not been crossed nor the i's dotted.

Another way of saying this is that the machine is mathematical rather than statistical. It takes the literal, precise value of each individual presentation, instead of recognizing what it is in terms of a central tendency which the individual presentations resemble to a certain statistical probability. What is common to all kinds of cats has first to be found statistically. The machine can handle very well, as we have seen, logical deductive classifications. If "All cats have long tails" and it is told "This is a cat" it will tell you "It has a long tail." The inductive and statistical problem is "What exactly *is* the shape of a tail and *when* does it begin to be long?" and "When does a set of qualities begin to look like a cat?"

Before we can make a computer do this, we have to discover more about the logic and the process by which we ourselves begin to recognize distinct types of objects, despite differences in size, in absolute brightness, in per-

FIGURE 9–4
Pattern Discrimination Beginning To Be Possible by the Computer

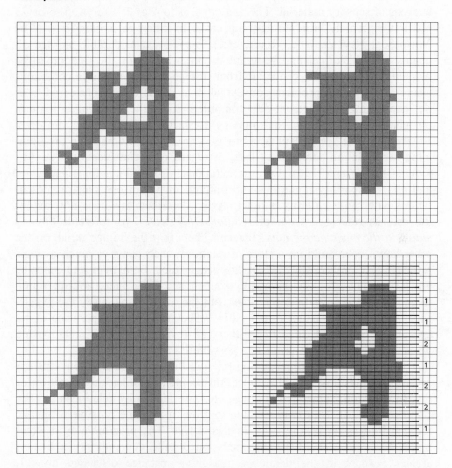

spective, etc. Some interesting answers to "the formal representation of human judgment" have been given by Kleinmuntz (1968). One practically successful attempt to get the computer to sort its world into distinct classes of objects, and to recognize any one individual as belonging to a class, is the Taxonome program of Coulter and the present writer, reported by Kleinmuntz. Just as a child may be a little puzzled at first by the behavior of a Siamese cat, wondering whether it is a cat or a dog, but eventually settles for a cat, so the computer will recognize that the "distance" of a case from several type models gives it varying resemblances, which it can appreciate. On this basis, which implicitly involves determining the relationship, in quantitative terms, between two patterns, the computer can begin to "perceive relationships," giving it the beginning of insight.

The recognition of patterns by computers is perhaps a beginning, and it certainly suggests that the eduction of relationships from the real world, rather than from humanly pre-digested, encoded data, implies vast prior analysis of sensory material. The analogy 2 is to 4 as 3 is to (4, 5, 6 or 7) requires extremely little storage; but cat is to kitten as Britain is to (The North Sea, New Zealand, Rome, etc.) implies a considerable storage of, in this case, historical and geographical knowledge for the relation to be worked out. However, even apart from storage problems, and in conditions where a perceptual problem conveys all that needs to be considered, it is not convincing that present-day computers solve the problem of pattern recognition, classification, and analogy use in the *way* that the brain does. Butcher's (1968) excellent account of some current computer programming for "relation-perception" lists, in regard to a classification test, (1) looking for *differences* of two presentations, (2) looking for *similarities,* and (3) comparing similarities and differences within one pair of presentations with those entering another. As so described this does not involve the use, as reference data, of *relations themselves,* as referents *already stored in the machine memory*. It seems likely that the human mind, on the other hand, does build up a store of relations, each being as much a single retrievable reference object as is any single fact. Both man and machine are programmed to, say, compare six men and three men, and do something if one is greater than the other, but the mind stores away the experience of the relation as a "2 to 1 ratio." The subsequent experience of six eggs in one nest and three in another can revive the "twice" relationship *per se,* with its attendant predictive possibilities as a relationship.

The next step beyond perceiving relationships is perceiving relationships among relationships, e.g., that twice, thrice, etc., are all forms of ratios, or that mother-son, father-grandfather, etc., are all family relationships. For such hierarchical relation-perception to grow, it must be possible to invoke relationships as retrievable units in themselves. The programming of computers for most current use has occasioned little demand for such hierarchies (except in the deductive reasoning instance discussed above), whereas it is the everyday business of the human brain.

A distinction was drawn above between man and machine in respect to their facility in handling inductive and deductive reasoning. This puzzles the philosopher logician, because he recognizes that in every inductive reasoning act, e.g., that drawings a, b, and c belong to one class and d to another, there are deductive steps. Their tendency to show up as two distinct primary factors, and for men to be better than machines on induction, is presumably due to the special processes involved in the initial "eduction of relations" between given fundaments. Once these relationships are educed, i.e., abstracted, they can be manipulated, as relationships just as in deductive reasoning. Indeed, as we have seen, the manipulation of these deductive relationships can be relatively mechanical, so that in respect to comprehensiveness of conclusions and infallibility of inference from the premises, a machine can do better than a philosopher. (Similarly a child taught the rules of algebra can apply them to reach conclusions more quickly and accurately than a wise adult unschooled in algebra.)

One sees here the rise of what is behaviorally a pseudointelligence, and anatomically a capacity to handle complex relations with very little neural storage mass. What is its relation to fluid and crystallized intelligence concepts? Evidently it comes under crystallized intelligence, as a capacity for the generation of which fluid intelligence—the capacity to educe relations—is first necessary. For this reason, we would predict that inductive reasoning should load g_f more than g_c, relative to deductive reasoning. However, the results of deductive reasoning, including those of mathematics, though mechanically reached, are in fact never accepted at face value without checking them in other ways. The mathematician, as distinct from the idiot savant of rapid calculation, is never far in his formulae from his degree of direct insight. Indeed, as Poincaré (1914) pointed out, he often reaches a conclusion first by "intuitive" insights and then builds up the mechanics of formal derivation afterward. Consequently, we should not expect the crystallized intelligence of man, by any mechanical manipulation of its stored relational abstractions, far to exceed its fluid intelligence capacity for direct relation-perception. At least this would be rare enough not to upset the usual correlation picture in the general population. With the machine, on the other hand, which has no reluctance to exceed its insight, crystallized intelligence could acquire more of a life of its own, and mechanically proliferate relations among relations. Since the laws of the manipulation are only known for lower levels, much of the product might be nonsense.

There remains, when all is said, a certain mystery about the initial relation eduction, largely in the experiential world and by inductive methods, performed by the central, associative, brain mass and closely tied with what we measure as fluid intelligence. When I conclude there are two windows on Smith's house and only one on Jones's, a great deal of rapid comparison of similarities and differences has gone on to permit the use of "house" and "window" (regardless of whether I yet have words for them). There is evidence that even in culture-fair intelligence tests, with "nameless" objects, the speed and accuracy of performance is increased by importing verbal or other symbols for the relationship; but if speed is not involved, the grasping and use of a more complex relationship seems to correlate best with other measures of fluid intelligence.

Possibly we have in the inductive relation eduction of fluid intelligence something not yet developed in the use of computers. If this relation eduction issues from basic experience[4] then the higher in the relational

---

[4] Although we take our main stand on the position that relations are so derived, the possibility must also be considered (corresponding to instinct in the dynamic realm) that the neural combining mass actually inherits a tendency to accept certain axioms and deductions, e.g., "that one and one make two," "that two objects cannot exist in

hierarchy the relations stand, the more complex and broad must the sensory basis be, and the larger would be the number of objects they derive from and apply to. Probably one reason (apart from little work having been done in this direction by persons needing computer service) why computers have not succeeded well in these insightful decision-processes is that an enormous amount of virtually simultaneous comparison and connection would be required to sustain this broad "meaning" of a complex relation. It could be that the secret of the brain's greater capacity to abstract a pattern from many particulars, and to handle, for example, complex analogies, lies essentially in its immensely greater number of units: ten billion cells in the brain against fifty to one hundred thousand transistors in a large computer. The storing of relations as such, which requires comparatively little space, is thus no substitute for the generation of relations on a broad base of relevant data. The computer, in short, is good at the "primary abilities" and it can learn, but, as constructed at present, it lacks: (a) the massive capacity to handle "real world" input (we should expect to find no factor, if we factored the comparative behavior of many computers, corresponding to the second-order visual and other capacities); (b) it cannot easily recognize approximate answers—statistically acceptable but not exact—and (c) it is relatively unable to handle patterns and to solve by "insightful" *relation eduction*—as distinct from reproductive, trial-and-error learned methods. And the fact that (d) it can handle deductive reasoning when supplied with formulae, should perhaps make us somewhat suspicious of deductive logic as a measure of intelligence, and even of mathematical "reasoning" that requires only manipulation of numbers of formulae according to pre-established rules.

Little has been said here about the obvious major difference of computers from the animal brain in its totality, namely the computer's lack of motivation, dynamic goals, and emotions—because that is less relevant to our examination of cognitive function. However, in the end this would become relevant, and, as we have seen, it *is* relevant to understanding the defects of machine learning, inasmuch as machines lack the built-in goals and satisfactions that give a basis for response preference and reward in learning.

Although we have encountered some puzzles which only more prolonged pursuit might clarify, it should be evident that the comparison of brains and computers is rewarding for the understanding of both. Similarly, the study of animal behavior, and of the phylogenetic perspective, has brought added confidence to our analysis of ability structure.

---

the same space," "that two negatives make a positive," or "that a straight line is the shortest distance between two points." This, to the dismay of the logician, implies that logic is relative to phylogenetic experience, and may be inapt for new domains, e.g., nuclear physics. At any rate, the theory that the combining mass inherits certain relation-perception tendencies is as worthy of investigation as that the hypothalamus inherits certain dynamic "instinctual" tendencies.

CHAPTER TEN

THE DEBATE ON HEREDITY AND ENVIRONMENT: ABILITIES IN RELATION TO RACE AND CULTURE

1. THE NEED FOR SCIENTIFIC OBJECTIVITY

Rarely in science has so much clearance of jungle growths of prejudice and false assumption to be made, in order that the clean lines of the laboratory can be seen, as when studying heredity. An inordinate proportion of extremists is ready to say either that heredity does not matter, or that environment can be forgotten. False assumptions and inferences regarding supposed necessary connections of this or that scientific position with various social, political, and religious beliefs are rife. Dogmatic and emotional epithets[1] are hurled across the heads of scientists between racists and ignoracists.

The one certainty with which we can begin is that any difference of behavior between two persons who are not identical twins is to be traced *partly to environmental and partly to hereditary differences.* The next thing that is certain is that quite complex scientific reasoning has to be followed if we wish to get at the truth regarding these interacting components. Scientists have developed some beautiful techniques for analyzing the contributions and interactions of genetic and environmental influences. In the discussions of scientists, the difference of opinion can be narrowed to much smaller margins than in the debates which breed more heat than light in political exchanges and in the press.

---

[1] To make clear that we are not using racist and ignoracists as meaningless words of opprobrium, let us define (1) an ignoracist as one who believes there can be no statistically significant differences on innate components in behavior between two physically distinguished groups of people, e.g., races, and (2) a racist as one who dogmatically asserts that his race is better than all others.

Obstacles to clear concepts in this area due to emotionalism[2] are rendered unusually formidable because prejudice can readily hide in intrinsic conceptual subtleties and evade disciplined statistical thinking. As an example of the former, not everything that is *innate* is *hereditary*, since mutations can produce in a person innate tendencies not present in the parents; furthermore, not everything that is congenital, i.e., something that is *born* with, is innate, since influences in gestation or the process of birth can produce marked effects, e.g., the sterility of the "free martin" at birth. In the same class as these conceptual confusions of *hereditary, innate,* and *congenital* are such semiphilosophical issues as the debate whether behavior, as distinct from a material structure, *can* be inherited. The latter is an empty dispute, so long as body and mind go together. We inherit, for example, a physical stomach, but also, if we are lucky, one that knows how to behave like a stomach. We inherit the chemistry of the cell—in brain or stomach—along with the cell structure.

Another conceptual hurdle that the student in this area must be able to take is the demand upon statistical thinking. Like the Victorian sceptic regarding the physicists conception of the atom ("Show me one"), the lay critic is apt to demand of the behavioral geneticist, "Show me the part of this behavior that is supposed to be inherited." In any actual behavior, genetic and learning contributions are as thoroughly mixed as tin and copper in a piece of bronze; but, like the metallurgical chemist, the psychologist has means of finding how much of each element is involved. The situation is no different for behavior than for physical structure, except (1) that we are relatively unaccustomed to seeing a virtually unchanged genetic component in behavior, and (2) that the environmental influence is, in general, probably greater in behavior. Mendel's dwarf peas were never so greatly affected by nutrition that he was in danger of confusing

---

[2] Probably another rather forbidding emotional block to progress in behavioral genetics has been the fact that most known instances of definite hereditary action, due to their having first been located by medical research, deal with *diseases* of various kinds. Many examples of clear genetic action stress the inexorable *limitations* of heredity rather than its *gifts*. Human nature is such that the average man is apt to think of the law of gravity as something which prevents his jumping over mountains rather than something which permits him to get traction in walking over the plain. Civilized man, looking at the brute, surely does better to recognize the gifts which heredity brings to modern races—such as unusual longevity, high intelligence, and resistance to diseases. If behavioral science is most illuminating when there is regard for *both* genetic and environmental influences, any obscurity, as Max Houtchens has recently pointed out, is rarely due to the geneticists, who constantly investigate interaction with environment, but it may be due to certain sociologists who recognize *nothing* beyond environment. For example, in a recent issue of *Contemporary Psychology,* a sociologist criticizes a psychologist as an emphasizer of heredity (and with an attempt at a Nazi smear by using the expression "Germanic," though the latter is English on all sides!). It turns out that the latter has done careful research for years to evaluate environmental and hereditary influences on behavior, whereas the critic has done none, presumably being satisfied with the conviction that all behavioral differences are environmentally determined.

them with the tall variety, and a lobeless ear is rarely so effected by environment, even in the pugilist, that one mistakes it for the lobed variety.

There are a few forms of behavior or ability, such as Huntington's chorea, color blindness, phenylketonuria, and special taste sensitivities, which are essentially "all-or-nothing" qualities and can therefore be studied at once, directly, in terms of a possible Mendelian mode of gene action, e.g., single or multiple gene, dominant, or recessive, and so on. But, since the hereditary component of most behavioral traits is evidently polygenic, i.e., due to multiple gene action, the psychologist has to content himself with statements such as: "Seventy percent of the variance in surgery is environmental, twenty percent is hereditary and ten percent is due to some interactive effect of heredity and environment." Public discussion, however, rarely pauses for statistical realities. It makes such subjective demands as "I want a clear answer as to whether intelligence is hereditary or not." Or, in an assertive mood, it reasons: "You say that mental defect is hereditary [or environmental], but I know an actual case where. . . ."

2. THE MENDELIAN AND THE NATURE-NURTURE VARIANCE RATIO APPROACHES

Since our topic here is intelligence, so that we have no space for long digressions into genetics as such, it must be assumed that the reader has a general knowledge of genetic terms and principles. He should also know that the "variability" on any trait within a group is commonly technically measured as *variance*—the square of the standard deviation on the trait measure concerned. He should also bear in mind the rule that if two influences are uncorrelated and not productive of nonlinear "interaction," the variance produced when they act together is simply the sum of those produced when they act separately. Thus the standard deviation of I.Q. on a crystallized ability (traditional) intelligence test is 16, and the variance, therefore, is 256. If heredity made a contribution of 206 to that total, then we should know (granted the conditions just stated) that environment made a contribution of 50. For although it is all very well to get rid of the idea, as Vandenberg (1962) suggests, that environment is "opposed" to heredity, we must not lose the important notion that they are undoubtedly complementary. That is to say there is no third term: what is not contributed by environment must be due to heredity. (True, one can have, as above, an "interaction" term, but this third term also finally resolves wholly into heredity and environment components, but with some additional law saying they are not *simply* additive in their effects.)[3]

---

[3] Another sense in which the term "opposed" is sometimes declared to be incorrect is contained in the statement that "because the effect of heredity is large, it does not mean that the effect of environment must be small: they could both be large (or small)." The weakness of this last would-be-correcting statement (by Hirsch) is that

One way of thinking about the variance contribution analysis concept is to recognize that each separate component represents how big the variance (in raw score units) would be if the other scource of variance were held at zero, i.e., if people did not vary at all on the other component. For example, the above instance taking $\frac{50}{206} \times 100\%$ of the existing variance on intelligence as environmental, means that if, instead of taking children at large, we took only a sample of children of *exactly the same heredity,* then the observed variance in I.Q. in that sample would fall from 256 (in the general population) to 50, and, therefore, the sigma of I.Q. from 16 to 7 units (approximately). Conversely, if we took children from their parents and brought them up in an *identical* environment we should expect from these figures that the usually observed variance (commonly symbolized as σ^2) would fall from 256 to 206, and the standard deviation of I.Q. (σ) from 16 to 14 (to the nearest unity) points. Incidentally, the values we have taken here for illustration are in fact fairly close to those which the investigations below show to be the best estimate.

A geneticist, as such, would like to know more than these statistical facts about *relative* importance. His science deals with the question of whether one, two, or more genes are responsible for the genetic differences, where they act with certain dominance, and other interactions, and so on. He would like to point to a particular individual and say he has such-and-such genes. Something close to this can be done with a few behavioral oddities, as illustrated above, but in the most important and universal traits, e.g., intelligence, stature, emotional stability, etc., we deal with polygenic effects not yet so analyzable. The issue of what we may say about *a given individual* is discussed below (page 255).

However, it makes a vast difference to what a teacher, a law court, or a clinician does about a particular case if we know for the behavior in question, what the *nature-nurture* ratio, *in general,* is. This N ratio is expressed:

$$\text{N ratio} = \frac{\text{variance due to heredity}}{\text{variance due to environment}} \tag{10.1}$$

---

we cannot compare the variance of one kind of measurement unit with that of another. Do men vary in stature more than they do in intelligence? If we can answer yes to this, then it would be possible to say that hereditary and environmental contributions are *both* greater in stature than in intelligence. But most psychological metrics are *not* ratio scales, i.e., do not have an absolute zero, so that a coefficient of variation, permitting one to say that stature varies more than intelligence, is not possible. (In this case, stature *does* have a zero, but few psychologists would be prepared to define what is zero intelligence.) In sum, we are commonly compelled to say that the total observed variance of any behavioral measure has a standard score value of *one*. In that case, the hereditary and environmental contributions *are* "opposed," or, to be exact, complementary, so that if the percentage due to one is high, that of the other must be low.

To illustrate in the above instance, this is:

$$N = \frac{206}{50} = 4.1$$

showing a decided predominance of "nature."

In many researches the value is expressed slightly differently in what has come to be called[4] the heritability ratio (or simply heritability) and represented by h. This is:

$$h = \frac{\text{variance due to heredity}}{\text{total variance}} = \frac{\sigma_g^2}{\sigma_g^2 + \sigma_e^2} \qquad \textbf{(10.2)}$$

The equivalent, reciprocal value for environment—$\dfrac{\sigma_e^2}{\sigma_g^2 + \sigma_e^2}$—might

be called the *modifiability ratio,* m. The h and m values[5] would be respectively 80% and 20% in the above instance, thus adding up to 100%, as logic requires. Note also that $N = \dfrac{h}{m} = \dfrac{h}{1-h}$.

However, the population variance ratio is not all that we can reach by the statistical approach. A very helpful further development for school and clinic—and for social reformers—is the more detailed analysis into ratios within and between families. It might be, for example, that for a certain ability the nature-nurture ratio *within* families, i.e., among children brought up in the same family is, say 3, whereas *between* families, i.e., considering the variance among the means (each from children in one family) of families with respect to the main population mean, the ratio is 1. This would tell us that environmental differences *between* families are relatively very important. In fact, discussion will finally turn to *four* variances; within family hereditary, σ_{wh}^2; within family environmental, σ_{we}^2; between family hereditary, σ_{bh}^2; and between family environmental σ_{be}^2. These four within and between family variances will add up to the observed variance of the population at large. Statistical approaches can also tell us how far environmental and genetic influences get *correlated,* as discussed below.

An alternative but statistically cruder approach to expressing the relative importance of heredity and environment—and one more frequently used in medical circles and when the Mendelian structure is known —uses the concept of *penetrance.* If among one hundred people known (from family records) to possess a certain gene, only seventy-three show the actual disease or behavior, the gene is said to have seventy-three

---

[4] Sometimes written h^2, which is unfortunate, for it is not itself a variance and h^2 has long been used for communality (a variance) in factor analysis.

[5] Strictly, h and m should never be presented without subscripts to show whether they refer to general population, as in h_p, to *between* family, as in h_b, or *within* family as in h_w. Most studies from twins are h_w values, not h_p, yet many textbooks fail to point this out. The final important value is h_p.

percent *penetrance*. Although this is more "obvious," it is statistically less useful than the variance ratio, and is usually based on less certain evidence and less clear concepts. For example, a fair amount of handling of the inheritance of schizophrenia has been based on the assumption that the presence of the gene in relatives can be accurately inferred, and that penetrance can consequently be calculated by the percentage located in mental hospitals.

Both variance analysis and penetrance are somewhat gross ways of making general statements about heredity that we would ideally like to make with more flexible assumptions, and in regard to the individual case. For example, the usual twin research method (unlike the MAVA method described below) assumes both that hereditary and environmental influences are uncorrelated, and that they combine in a simple additive way, without interaction. Animal experiments, in which manipulative control of both mating and environment is possible, clearly show, however, that the effect of an environmental influence depends upon the age at which it is applied, and upon the level of hereditary endowment. The same can be perceived, even if not evaluated, in humans. For example, the "headstart" type of special educational help would be quite pointless with a very bright child, and add nothing to his performance. This example of an environmental effect depending on the hereditary level can be matched by instances where the hereditary effect depends on the environmental level. For example, the difference in intelligence between a child of average, normal heredity and one with phenylketonuria is great if they are brought up on the normal range of diet. But if they are brought up on a special diet which does not permit the phenylketonuric chemical action to occur, the observed variance in intelligence will be reduced. Consequently, our statistical model should really accept "interaction," i.e., recognize that the hereditary and environmental contributions will not simply add, regardless of levels, but that at some levels of one, the effect of the other may be peculiarly powerful.

Of course, one can handle this with the simpler additive model by repeating the variance analysis at each of several levels and ranges of each variable, and then putting the whole together. In animal experiments we can do an equivalent job by using clones, i.e., highly inbred specimens, such that many animals can be taken to be identical in heredity. Then we can subject each member of a clone to a different environment and measure the ultimate effect. In this way, with several clones, the effect of each level of environment applied at each level of heredity can be determined, and interaction precisely evaluated. However, with humans, the only clones are identical twins, and two are not enough to try all levels of environment, even if ethical considerations permitted subjecting twins to manipulation on vital aspects of environment.

However, even when we know all about interaction effects through such simple animal experiment, or through the strategically planned analysis of variance with humans mentioned above (and described in more detail below), we still would not know, if presented with a creature at level x on trait A, how much of x *in that given case* was a contribution from environment, and how much from heredity. It is not necessarily a false conception that so much of, say, a given individual's stature is due to inner maturation (heredity) and so much to environment; but at present we have no operations that will permit us to answer such a question. We have only the statements of variance contributions operating over a whole *population.*

Geneticists have long recognized this with respect to physical genetics by saying that two (or more) different genotypes may result in the same phenotype. (The term "phenocopies" has been used for these equivalents.) This is best known, of course, with regard to the Dd genotype (in a single gene case) producing the same phenotype as the DD genotype, where D is the dominant and d the recessive allele, and the dominance of D hides the recessive d effect in the heterozygote. However, where a trait is determined by many genes, two or more different combinations may produce virtually the same result. On top of this, even when the average "potential" phenotype from two genotypes is *different,* especially powerful environmental action on one may bring it to the same final expression as the other. Thus there are usually several different "routes" possible—with combinations of genetic and environmental paths—to what looks like the same end result. An added complication is that some genetic structures may be more susceptible to environment (as in the well-known "imprinting" effect) at one stage of maturation and others at another.

In this connection, a certain confusion has resulted in behavioral genetics with continuous variables, through students of genetics mechanically carrying over the genetic terminology of "genotype" and "phenotype" suited to physical data and clearly distinct, discrete phenotypes, like tall and dwarf peas. There is no such thing as *the* phenotype in continuous variables far more strongly modified by environment, as behavioral variables generally are. In behavioral genetics we need a trinity, not a duality, of concepts, namely *genotype, standard phenotype,* and measured, *concrete phenotype.* The standard phenotype is not a literal, concrete, end result but an abstraction, an average, in a given, defined environment. Any single, concrete phenotype may be very different from this standard abstraction. (This has always been true, even in classical genetics, but the deviations have not been serious enough to demand recognition of the concepts in the terminology.)

Since, in human beings, we cannot control matings, or manipulate environments as can be done by dividing clones in animals into different experimental groups, our only potent approach is by analysis of variance. And here the MAVA method is about twice as effective as the twin method, since it can give the *correlations* between environmental and hereditary effects, and the *between families* hereditary and environmental variances. By quite complex, population, biometric, genetic methods (which we shall not study here), and by determining the variances in different age groups and cultures, it is theoretically possible to proceed from such data to all the types of findings, e.g., about heredity-environment imprinting relations, discussed above from manipulative animal research.

The nature-nurture ratio, N, is thus no fixed and eternal value, like, say, an atomic number, but, is like the value for acceleration due to gravity at the earth's surface, or the boiling point of water—something that depends on other circumstances. Like these latter, it is something very much needing to be determined, partly because of its practical utility, and partly because it is the necessary first step in reasoning to conclusions regarding more ultimate values. Any given nature-nurture ratio, e.g., that for intelligence, determined say for adults in America and ten-year-olds in Japan varies about some central value for a number of obvious reasons. For example, the range of genes determining the genetic component may be less in one race than another. Or the range of genetic contribution in a given organism from a given set of genes (and internal gene environment) may be definite and constant enough in terms of chromosome chemistry, but the environment alters continuously with historical, cultural, and climatic developments. For example, if a given culture began to treat its citizens more sensitively and differentially, e.g., by arranging longer, scholarship-supported education for the more highly intelligent, or more sheltered lives for those inherently more emotionally unstable, then the percentage of variance due to environment in N above might be expected to increase (with negative correlations in the latter case and positive in the former). Reciprocally, if racial selection occurred, e.g., by the brighter members of an impoverished country migrating abroad, so that the natural variance in ability in the particular racial mixture remaining in the given country became reduced, then the discovered percent variance due to heredity would fall. Thus the nature-nurture ratio must always have a subscript to indicate to what population, racial mixture, and cultural epoch it belongs. Although it is an important value in itself, e.g., for current clinical and social psychology, and for personality theory, it might therefore be said to be a still more important recorded value for understanding human historical and sociological trends.

As pointed out above, the behavioral scientist can go far with various refinements of the nature-nurture ratio, but the ultimate aim of the geneticist is always to find how many and what kind of genes (the genotype) are at work in determining the standard phenotype. But in traits much subject to environmental modification, his analytical inquiry into Mendelian effects and mechanisms can begin only after the statistical geneticist has finished setting aside, e.g., by MAVA, the variances in various groups that are purely genetic. The steps here of lawful transformation from gene structure to genotype variances are very complex, and generally are referred to as the science of "population genetics" analysis.

In behavior genetics our understanding of what happens in proceeding from genotype to standard phenotype and to concrete phenotype is still very incomplete. This is especially true of the first of these steps. Indeed the only certainties regarding specific genes and specific abilities and behaviors are restricted to the few exceptionally prominent oddities. In the ability field they are mainly forms of mental defect—phenylketonuria and what used to be called Mongolian imbecility but is now known as Down's syndrome. A gene determining faulty brain chemistry is responsible for the first, and a faulty replication of a certain chromosome for the second. But for the rest of the ability field, inference stops at variance analysis— short of describing genetic structure, Mendelian processes, and the steps between genes and neurological effects. So here our main aim—even yet still only partly achieved—must be to reach nature-nurture variance ratio statements.

3. DETERMINING NATURE-NURTURE RATIOS: THE MAVA METHOD

The adjective "environmentally-determined" is so clumsy that precise discussion is hampered, and the present writer (Cattell and Nesselroade, 1971) has suggested "threptic" as a brief technical term. Eugenics and euthreptics are thus terms to represent efforts to improve man respectively by genetic and environmental means. The Greek root of threptic was originally used by both Aristotle and Galen in this sense and it seems the most acceptable term available. Threptic and genetic are thus useful terms for exact reference respectively to abstracted contributions from environment and from genes. (Hereditary, as we have seen above, is not the same as genetic, since a child's genetic endowment is not exactly the same as an average or other mathematical function, of his parents overt genetic make-up. Mutations, crossing over, gene selection, epistacy, etc., may make the outcome different from a simple average of parental qualities. And Galton's law of ancestral contribution, which refers half an individual's peculiarity to his parents, a quarter to grandparents, and so on, is still only a global approximation.)

Setting aside for the moment the problem of relating the genetic make-up of the child to that of the parent, let us assume that a genetic endowment exists for him, and ask how we are to find what fraction of a child's phenotypic final appearance, in general, is due to this endowment and how much to his environmental fortune. In other words, and in regard to an ability, granted that we have for all children in the population a measure sigma (squared to give a variance) on intelligence test scores, and that we aim to break this down into hereditary and environmental ("genetic" and "threptic") components. How can we go about it? Most psychologists are familiar with the twin method of getting at these components; but nowadays we can do better than that with a few methods (notably the MAVA method) capable of giving more complete answers. If the reader will bear with a page or two of further methodological discussion, it will be possible to proceed thereafter to some definite answers on abilities.

The basic proposition on which all analysis hinges is best stated in the condensed form of an algebraic equation, splitting up the ability trait score, T, as follows:

$$T = c_g + c_t + (f)c_g c_t \qquad \textbf{(10.5)}$$

where c_g is the genetic contribution, c_t the threptic contribution, and $(f)c_g c_t$ is what the statistician calls *interaction,* i.e., some function (f) of c_g and c_t together, which is no simple addition of them, but some more complex function, e.g., a product of the values, each raised by some exponent. In accordance with the above usage of genetics and threptics, Nesselroade, Tsujioka, and Cattell have suggested in researches elsewhere (Cattell and Nesselroade, 1971; Cattel, Tsujioka and Ishikawa, In press) the term *genothreptics* for the special science of analyzing the *interplay* of genetic and threptic influences, at any rate in psychological material. Genothreptics concerns itself, of course, not only with the technical "interaction" term above, (f) $c_g c_t$, but with the whole equation and all aspects of its analysis into genetic and threptic components. A great deal of study today on, for example, imprinting (the more powerful effect of environment, produced when it strikes just at the right maturational stage) and on the changing hereditary contribution with age has made genothreptics already a broad, useful, and intricate branch of science.

Considering the interaction term alone—(f) $c_g c_t$ in equation (10.5)— we have to recognize that there is no doubt about its existence, and that presently available rough estimates assign to it anything from 1% to 20% contribution to the total variance. For example, an excellent university environment would be meaningless, and add practically nothing to the ability of a borderline mental defective, whereas it certainly adds greatly to the g_c of a really bright young person, and might even add to the g_f. Or again, turning to physical influences, the evidence suggests that differences of mutation have little effect on I.Q.'s from infancy onward, except perhaps with large brain growth, whereas in the womb and the infant years some observers have claimed to see reductions of I.Q. from relatively poor nutrition. The important issue here is that which we have referred to elsewhere in connection with "imprinting," namely, that the average addition from a given environmental influence can be interactively increased or decreased according to the phase in the developmental process at which it occurs. Effects of this kind have recently been shown in animal physiological development by Ginsberg (1965). There threptic influence, occurring at one phase in the chain of enzyme sequences which constitute the unfolding of a gene, has a more powerful influence on the end result than at another phase. It may, in fact, shift a "defective" genetic pattern on to a new curve of growth practically the same as that of a genetically more adequate endowment.

In this connection, geneticists often speak of a "norm of reaction" for a certain gene endowment, which would describe the normal possibilities of interaction with the environment at various stages and in various types of environment. An identical score on some dimension of the phenotype can obviously be reached by different individuals by several different temporal paths and through several different combinations of genetic and threptic contributions (equations 10.5 and 10.6). With advances in behavioral genetics, it may be possible in time to see what those paths and combinations were for a given individual, as a woodsman, looking at the rings of growth in a tree, can trace the individual history. But, at present, our progress lies in the direction of determining the *general* laws of contribution of heredity and environment for typical members of our culture and race.

By approaches too statistically complex to discuss here, it is becoming possible to estimate the general interaction magnitudes, through the MAVA method. But here we shall, for simplicity, pursue the model of simple additive relations, which permits us to drop the term $(f)c_g c_t$ from (10.5) and proceed with:

$$T = c_g + c_t \tag{10.6}$$

This simply says that a part score on a genetic part and another on a threptic learning contribution add up to the person's total observed trait score.[6]

Now, although we can doubt interaction, we cannot assume that c_g and c_t are at all likely to be uncorrelated. Especially in personality there is much circumstantial evidence that an hereditary tendency to certain behavior may get correlated with environmental features which affect the same trait. For example, if a father's intelligence favors his rising in the socioeconomic scale, his children may, because of his better financial resources, get better education, and since there is a probability that his children will inherit some of his intelligence, favorable intelligence and favorable education will tend to get correlated in that generation. (A similar effect would follow from scholarships.) To instance, on the other hand, a negative correlation, the child who is naturally more dominant is likely to get more reactions tending to "put him in his place," while the meek is more likely to be encouraged to assert himself and "inherit the earth." Thus a significant *negative* relation could arise both within families and between families in regard to the amount of environmental help toward dominance and the innate disposition toward dominance. The statistician recognizes that if such effects exist, the observed variance on a trait is *not* the simple sum of genetic and environmental variances as one might initially expect from (10.6) above, but rather:

$$\sigma_o{}^2 = \sigma_g{}^2 + \sigma_t{}^2 + 2_{gt}\sigma_g\sigma_t \tag{10.7}$$

---

[6] Psychologists who argue for the largest possible acceptable value for the environmental contribution, e.g., Hunt (1961) have criticized this simplified model, saying it does not give full scope to environment. If the interaction term is called an environmental effect, this is true; but it could just as logically be called a genetic effect. Although we have granted that ideally one should leave space for interaction, yet there is no proof that it generally exists, and in accordance with the good scientific principle of keeping to the simplest explanation unless forced to another, the present investigator and a majority of others have started with this formula.

Here σ_o^2 is the observed (experimentally measured) variance; the last term is called the covariance. (Note we have now shifted from scores to variance in scores.) If we consider both covariance and interaction and consider interaction to be simply a product, multiplied by a suitable constant, k, the basic model in (10.7) now becomes the rather more complicated looking:

$$\sigma_o^2 = \sigma_g^2 + \sigma_t^2 + k\sigma_{gt}^2 + 2r_{gt}\sigma_g\sigma_t \tag{10.8}$$

Because this complication may not in fact exist, and we claim the scientist's birthright (as stated above, and following Newton) to take the simplest hypothesis unless and until one is forced to the complex, we shall proceed here with the relationship or "model" stated in Equation (10.7).

Now one must go a step further and ask the reader to accept the general principle in analysis of variance (not specifically tied to genetics at all) that the variance one sees in the population at large, in, say, intelligence, can be considered the *sum* of a *within-family* variance and a *between-family* variance (i.e., the variance among sibs in the typical family and the variance among the means of families, considered over all families). Next each of these family variances can be broken down, just like the value for general population as a whole in Equation 10.7 above, into a genetic and a thenic part. Thus we arrive finally at four sources of intelligence variance, as follows:

(a) σ_{wg}^2 = The variability among sibs due to within-family genetic variance. No two children of the same parents (except identical twins) have identical genetic make-up, but are a different "throw of the dice" from the same genetic bank of the parents. So we let wg mean "within-genetic" variance.

(b) σ_{wt}^2 = The variance *within* the family due to threptic, environmental influences. Parents (and the school) treat sibs somewhat differently, partly due to differences of age, and sibs get different treatment from one another. So wt means "within-threptic."

(c) σ_{bg}^2 = That part of the variance *between* families, i.e., between the *average* level of one family and another, that is due to genetic influences, i.e., family heredity.

(d) σ_{bt}^2 = The variance between families traceable to their environmental differences, including family atmosphere and socioeconomic status.

Thus our basic equation can now be written (neglecting covariances) in extended,[7] more analytical form:

$$\sigma_o^2 = \sigma_{wg}^2 + \sigma_{wt}^2 + \sigma_{bg}^2 + \sigma_{bt}^2 \tag{10.9}$$

σ_o^2 (o for observed) is of course the value one would get from actually measuring people at large on the given trait, e.g., intelligence.

From these equations we can see that when obscurantists tell students that "heredity and environmental influences are *inextricably* mixed and no

---

[7] Note that it is still not fully extended. If, as in some actual researches, the more sophisticated model in Equation 10.8 above is used, 10.9 would also have terms for interaction and covariance.

meaning can be quantitatively given to each," they reckon without the ingenuity of the mathematician. (Before the days of chemistry, the sceptics were similarly confounded at Archimedes' being able to tell the percentage of gold in a crown, and at Eratosthenes' being able to calculate, from the shadow of two obelisks, the earth's circumference—which no man had traveled.) For it is easy to see that if concrete, numerical values can be found for the expressions on the left of equations (3) or (4), and if we can obtain several such equations, we can solve for the unknowns on the right, just as in any exercise with simultaneous equations. A key to the variances —σ_{bt}^2, σ_{wg}^2, etc.—that cannot be directly measured, is thus in our hands. However, there is the inexorable law that to solve for n unknowns one must have n independent equations. We have, in the first place, four unknowns (σ_{wg}^2, σ_{wt}^2, σ_{bg}^2, σ_{bt}^2). Where can four equations be found?

That for observed variance among family means will break up as follows:

$$\sigma^2_{BF.O} = \sigma_{bg}^2 + \sigma_{bt}^2 \tag{10.10}$$

It can be obtained by getting the mean of the sibs in each family, repeating this calculation for many families, and obtaining the variance of these means. This gives us $\sigma^2_{BF.O}$ (BF = between families, O = observed) in equation (10.10). Subtracting (10.10 from 10.9) (which has a subscript, GP.O for General Population, Observed), we have:

$$\sigma^2_{GP.O} - \sigma^2_{BF.O} = \sigma_{wg}^2 + \sigma_{wt}^2 \tag{10.11}$$

Let us next take pairs of identical twins and measure their differences from the family mean, leading to the within-family variance σ^2 (ITT for *i*dentical *t*wins raised *t*ogether). In this case, being genetically identical, they can have no genetic variance, but only within-family environmental variance, thus:

$$\sigma^2_{ITT.O} = \sigma_{wt}^2 \tag{10.12}$$

Subtracting this from (10.11) we have one of the unknowns we want, namely, $\sigma^2_{wg} = \sigma^2_{GP.O} - \sigma^2_{GF.O} - \sigma^2_{ITT.O}$. Let us next look for a fourth equation in:

$$\sigma^2_{SA.O} = \sigma_{wg}^2 + \sigma_{wt}^2 + \sigma_{bt}^2 \tag{10.13}$$

(SA = sibs raised apart). The σ_{bt}^2 must come in here because they experience the environmental difference of two distinct families. Subtracting this from (10.9) we solve for σ_{bg}^2. Thus, by extending this principle to other cases, and comparing all obtainable kinds of hereditary and environmental mixtures (sibs raised together, sibs raised apart, unrelated children raised together, fraternal twins together, identical twins apart, etc.) other unknowns can be determined. In fact, by using such equations we can solve not only for the four major unknown *variances* but also for the *correlations* between hereditary and environmental influences (and ultimately for interaction). However, for solutions of the slightly more complicated equations with correlation (covariance) terms, the reader must be referred elsewhere (Cattell, 1963a).

The method of analysis just described has been called the MAVA method, for *Multiple Abstract Variance Analysis*. The σ_{wg}^2, σ_{bt}^2, etc., are *abstract variances* because they are inferred from the *concrete variances* —BF.O, etc.—actually obtained in the experiments. They are "abstract" because no one has ever "seen" a pure hereditary component, i.e., obtained it as a direct measure, as one can calculate σ^2 from an actual sample. But σ_{bt}^2, σ_{wg}^2, etc., are best described as abstract, not "hypothetical" variances because they *undoubtedly exist* from the causes indicated.

The first use of the MAVA method on human subjects by Beloff, Blewett, Kristy, Stice, and the present writer in 1955 and 1957 (Cattell, Blewett, and Beloff, 1955; Cattell, Stice, and Kristy, 1957) yielded results for fluid and crystallized intelligence tests as shown in Table 10–1. For a variety of technical reasons[8] these results are put forward as both approximate and somewhat biased in the direction of giving excessive weight to environment. They should soon be replaced by results from the improved MAVA method now being applied by th epresent writer's research associates—Tsujioka, Ishikawa, Schmid and Schuerger—in this country and Japan. Even so, they are superior in size of sample (N = 647 and 1024) to the widely accepted studies reviewed in the next section, as we have seen, the MAVA method is superior in that it gives information on matters, e.g., between-family variance, correlations, which the twin method and other older methods are powerless to supply.

From this and many other studies, the general indications on nature-nurture ratios for intelligence are clear. Close to four-fifths of the total variance is hereditary, if we consider fluid intelligence, and distinctly less —about two-thirds to three-quarters—if we consider crystallized intelligence. Secondly, there is evidence of some appreciable correlation of the action of hereditary and environmental influences, slight in fluid intelligence, but probably reaching about 0.5 in crystallized intelligence. Both of these findings fit what previous theory about g_f and g_c would require.

---

[8] The equations assembled for the MAVA method at that time were not capable of solving simultaneously for the magnitude and sign of a correlation, and we have made a correlation value choice (as one does on extraneous scientific indications among roots given for a quadratic equation) on the basis of global considerations too numerous to mention here. Since the studies to be compared in the next section are on the basis of twins, we have also accepted the within-family environmental variance estimate associated with twins. Other consistent combinations of estimate could thus be made, but we have taken what seems best on the basis of these early MAVA studies. Probably another sign of the inadequacy of this pioneer study in 1955 is some apparent inflation of the within-family variance at the expense of the between-family variance. By these results, a bright child (+ 1 sigma) in an average family is likely to be brighter than an average child in a bright family (+ 1 sigma), a result we should not expect with a high degree of assortive mating.

TABLE 10–1
Nature and Nurture Variances, Ratios, and Correlations for Intelligence (Fluid and Crystallized) by First MAVA Experiment

Source of Each Component	Variance from Each Component: As Raw Score	As Percent of Total		Component As Percent of Total Observed Variance	Nature-Nurture Ratio	Estimated Correlation of Deviation (from mean) of the Genetic Influence with the Deviation (from mean) of the Environmental Influence
FLUID INTELLIGENCE						
Within-family genetic differences (among sibs)	122.5	46%	} Total Genetic Component	77%		0
Between-family genetic differences (among means of families)	83.3	31%			3.4	
Within-family environmental differences (among sibs)	52.9	20%	} Total Environmental Component	23%		.25
Between-family environmental differences (among means of families)	6.7	3%				
CRYSTALLIZED INTELLIGENCE						
Within-family genetic differences (among sibs)	2.27	66%	} Total Genetic Component	73%		.5
Between-family genetic differences (among means of families)	.23	7%			2.7	
Within-family environmental differences (among sibs)	.76	22%	} Total Environmental Component	27%		.5
Between-family environmental differences (among means of families)	.17	5%				

No. of Cases: 647 sibs together and apart, identical twins, fraternal twins and unrelateds reared together.

No. of Cases: 1024 sibs together and apart, identical twins, fraternal twins and unrelateds raised together.

As indicated in the text, these are preliminary results, since fluid intelligence measures are themselves recent. By comparison with a larger study not ready at the moment for publication the genetic component in fluid intelligence is here an underestimate. The unexpected feature in this first MAVA application is the large within-family compared to between-family variance. The results must be regarded more as an example of the *form* of results than as quantitatively dependable.

To anticipate discussion in Chapter 14 and Section 7 below, we may consider the possibility that the only appreciable effect of environment on fluid ability is through better nutrition and wiser general health care being given to their children by more intelligent parents. This would explain why there is apparently no correlation of heredity and environment within families (due to possible different "intellectual" stimulus) and only a slight positive correlation of these between families (the latter again presumably due to more intelligent parents tending to provide better physical environments). On the other hand, with crystallized intelligence the correlation appears larger—since intellectual opportunity also can influence growth here. It is perhaps a little surprising that it is as big within as between families. This points to an effect whereby the more gifted may either read more or become the object of more stimulus, e.g., from adult conversation, than the less intelligent.

One reason for suspecting that these results are biased toward environment—as so penetrating a critic as Loehlin (1962) has suggested they are—is that the culture-fair intelligence tests used were short (12½ minutes) and therefore distinctly less than perfectly reliable. Moreover, intelligence test scores fluctuate from time to time for the same person, not only on account of test unreliability but also because (see Chapter 8) one's capacity to function fluctuates somewhat from day to day. By the nature of the measurement in such an experiment this variance from momentary changes—the *function fluctuation* and *error of measurement*—becomes included in the environmental portion. But by any reasonable interpretation they do not conceptually belong there, and statistical improvements now available should exclude them. (The conceptual position is clear if we remember that higher resistance to certain diseases may be inherited, yet presumably it fluctuates with fatigue from day to day. Capacity to get hungry is inherited, but hunger fluctuates with mealtimes. Reversible daily and momentary fluctuation should therefore be averaged out when we assess an individual's level on a trait, *not* counted as environmental variance.) *Steady* trends may be due to learning or other real sources of environmental change, on the other hand. But since practically none of the researches on inheritance of intelligence has measured each person several times, *the current estimates of the percentage due to environment are inflated by including fluctuation*—and the genetic percentages are proportionately reduced. A rough but conservative correction along the lines indicated by Loehlin might raise the genetic percentage in fluid ability by about 5 to 10%—i.e., from 77% to about 82–87%.

4. ADDITIONAL EVIDENCE FROM TWIN AND FAMILY CORRELATION STUDIES

The MAVA method has been described first because it gives the most comprehensive theoretical overview of the essence of the problem and the most complete array of numerical solutions. But historically it was the last to be developed, and in the field of abilities most of our conclusions must rest, until the MAVA method is more widely used, upon more numerous researches based on some form of twin analysis. Before studying these findings, however, it would be well to summarize what more ideally we should be striving to get by the MAVA approach. In the first place, it does not have to confine itself to total environmental and total hereditary variance, but examines separately the effects within families and between families. The social class effects between families may be very different from the different ways in which parents treat children within families. Incidentally, egalitarian measures to remove environmental differences between families can do nothing to the latter. Secondly, MAVA informs us of the correlations of genic and threptic effects, and does so separately for within and between families. Incidentally, it suggests that between families the correlation is positive— the better stock tends to get the better education—but that within families it is zero or negative, i.e., more pressure is brought on the duller child to progress. With this reminder to be alert to gaps in the evidence, we can turn to the numerous twin studies since the pioneer investigations of Galton and Pearson, wherein psychologists have tackled the matter in more piecemeal ways.

Twin research is still much used in genetic researches, psychological and medical, and although when used alone it is best considered an introductory exploration, data from twins remains a constituent (but not indispensable) part of the MAVA design. Identical twins are always of the same sex, are physically virtually indistinguishable (except by such small signs as finger prints), and undergo gestation in the same chorion. Fraternal twins may be of different sex, do not develop from a single fertilized egg, and are no more alike than ordinary siblings. (The fact that they have the early environmental experince of sharing the womb can produce some negative as well as positive correlations.) Whereas identicals have identical heredity but different experience, fraternals are different in both respects, the variances of the differences of each kind being set out in formulae as follows:

(Same as 10.11 above)

$$\sigma^2_{\text{ITT.O}} = \sigma_{\text{wt}}^2 \tag{10.14}$$

$$\sigma^2_{\text{FTT.O}} = \sigma_{\text{wt}}^2 + \sigma_{\text{wg}}^2 + (2r\sigma_{\text{wt}}\sigma_{\text{wg}}) \tag{10.15}$$

(ITT.O = identical twins raised together, observed variance; and correspondingly for FTT.O).

A first weakness of twin research methods is that the figure in parentheses has to be assumed zero, and we know from MAVA findings that it is not. It has to be assumed zero, because there is no way of calculating it, for one must get the nature-nurture ratio from twin studies, as follows:

$$\frac{\sigma^2_{\text{nat.}}}{\sigma^2_{\text{nurt.}}} = \frac{\sigma^2_{\text{FTT.O}} - \sigma^2_{\text{ITT.O}}}{\sigma^2_{\text{ITT.O}}} \tag{10.16}$$

Another weakness is the assumption that the environmental difference between twins raised together is the same (a) for identicals and fraternals, (b) for twins as for ordinary sibs (in some inferences). The fact that two people are indistinguishable to most observers must do something to the similarity of the way they are treated. Most discussants assume that identical twin environments will be more similar than for fraternals and for the latter than for ordinary sibs. Less widely accepted but more subtle arguments, point out that twins strive more consciously than ordinary sibs to stake out and assert their individual identities, e.g., in dress and manner; that parents try to accentuate their differences, etc. Thus there are also reasons and ways in regard to which twins should be environmentally *more* different.

An important point to remember in any case, with sibs *or* twins—is that one is an appreciable part of the environment of the other, especially with identical twins. And one must remember that when two chestnuts are in the same pod, a convexity in one is apt to fit a concavity in the other (a point noted in the classical definition of a pessimist as a man who has grown up with an optimist). The MAVA method, incidentally, allows for a correlation of one child's environment with the other child's heredity. As yet, therefore, from twin studies alone, we do not know much about the nature of twin environmental similarity except that it is almost certainly peculiar.

Parenthetically, although what is commonly designated "the twin method" is strictly expressed in equation (11) above, twin investigation *may* include the very different tack from the above constituted by comparing identicals raised together with identicals raised apart, in different families. It is infrequently pursued, because it is difficult. Indeed, the discovery of a statistically big enough group of twins reared apart is the unfound El Dorado of the behavioral geneticist. So far it has not been reached in intelligence research despite the gallant search of Barbara Burks (1942) across the U.S.A. forty years ago and of Burt (1925, 1946), Burt and Howard (1956), and others since. Measuring such a set would permit an estimate of the size of *between-family* environmental variance, but in the sense of twin research as usually accomplished, one can still get only two of the four terms in the MAVA method; namely, *within-genetic* and *within-environmental* variance—and none of the correlations.

Some very fine researches on intelligence by the twin method were done forty years ago by Freeman, Holzinger, and Mitchell (1928), Burks (1942), Gardner and Newman (1940), and by others more recently (Vandenberg, 1965), all using traditional intelligence tests. They converge consistently on a nature-nurture ratio in the region of 4:1. This value, which is a within-family value in terms of MAVA (Table 10–1), is actually higher than the value we (Cattell, Blewett and Beloff, 1955; Cattell, Stice, and Kristy, 1957) obtained (3:1), but the exploratory MAVA was rough and the 4:1 agrees better with values from other sources. Further, although non-culture-fair tests were used, they were well chosen to get as far as possible in the direction of the fluid ability concept.

The remaining source of general evidence in intelligence heredity—and it is considerable even if somewhat uneven in quality—is in the form of correlations found among relatives of varying degrees of consanguinity. The result of more than fifty researches are set out in the two parts of Figure 10–1. Clearly there is a consensus and central tendency showing that as the degree of blood relation (kinship) of the relatives correlated gets closer, the correlation becomes higher. Thus cousins correlate less than sibs; sibs less than twins, and so on. Erlenmeyer-Kimling and Jarvik (1963) point out from their data that the "correlations closely approach the theoretical value predicted on the basis of genetic relationship *alone.*" However, as the MAVA design reminds one, a higher correlation of nearer relatives could happen also when there is marked parallelism between the closeness of genetic relation and of cultural family atmosphere, and it would be fallacious to assume that we can infer the genetic resemblance *directly* from these correlations.

FIGURE 10–1
Composite Result of Many Studies on Resemblance
(Evaluated by Correlation) of Groups of Varying
Consanguinity

Correlations of intelligence test results from fifty-six publications, 1911–1962. More than one study per category reported in several populations.

(a)

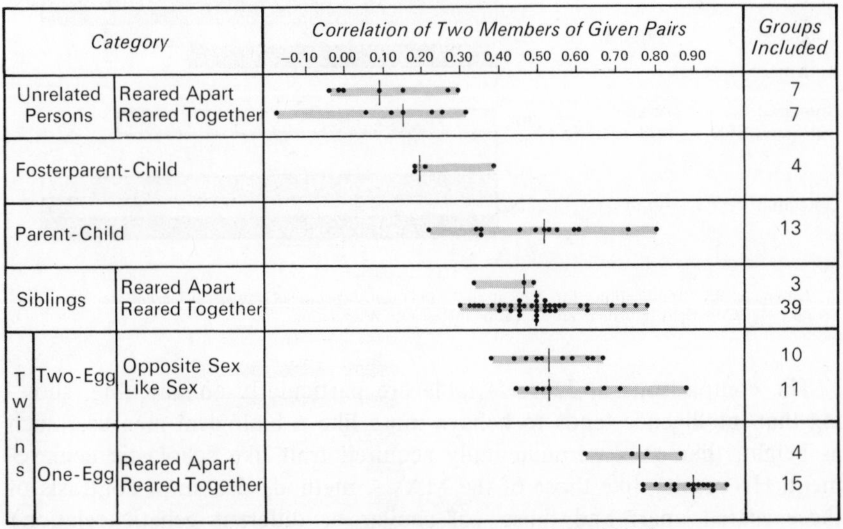

(Median Indicated by Vertical Line)

From "Genetics and intelligence: a review," by Erlenmeyer-Kimling and Jarvik, L. F., *Science,* 142, 1477–1479, 13 December 1963.

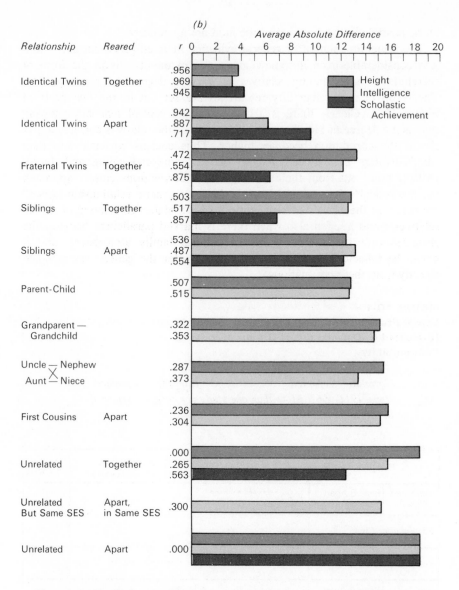

(b)

Relationship	Reared	r	Average Absolute Difference

Jensen, A. R., "Implications for Education," *American Educational Research Journal*, January, 1968, pp.1–42. Copyright by American Educational Research Association.

The comparisons in Jensen's table are particularly enlightening, showing that intelligence tends to behave more like a biological measure, such as height, than an environmentally acquired trait like scholastic achievement. His results, like those of the MAVA method, also show contrasts of those reared apart and those (of similar or different genetic relation) reared together. Identical twins reared apart, for example, show greater resemblance in intelligence than in scholastic achievement. In intelligence they show far greater similarity (r = .89, mean diff. = 6) than is found, for instance in siblings reared together (r = .52, mean diff. = 12.5 (approx.)). A very thorough analysis by Burt agrees with Jensen in concluding that physical measures, such as stature, for which there is considerable evidence of heredity, behave very similarly to intelligence. If space existed here to pursue also the genetic mechanisms as such, we should at this point ask more specifically how many genes are considered operative in intelligence, whether there are dominance (non-additive) effects, and so on. But at present one proceeds here on the simpler assumptions, and one finds that the obtained similarities of relatives in intelligence came close to those expected largely on genetic grounds alone, over the eight degrees of affinity that Burt studied from identical twins to second cousins. However, note that this still does not mean that interfamily differences are altogether the most important. If there were no assortive mating and no dominance, the variance among children within families would be just as great as that between families. A bright child in an average family would be as good or better than an average child in a bright family. However, we know that marriage *is* assortive: the bright marry the bright and the dull the dull, so that the divergence between families increases.

Before pursuing the genetic analysis *per se* to greater refinement, one should perhaps glance at some practical conclusion and practical cautions regarding such familial correlations. There need be no association of social conservatism with a full appreciation of heredity, because the above numerical values for inheritance do not give any high justification for select schools favoring (as far as ability prospects are concerned) the sons of their alumni; or for government by an hereditary aristocracy. The literal prediction of ability from father to son has the approximate form:

$$I_s = I_f \times .5 + C \qquad (10.17)$$

(where 0.5 is the average regression from Fig. 10–1, and C is an intergenerational constant that we will discuss on pages 276 and 278 below). This would mean (squaring the 0.5 correlation) that seventy-five percent of the variance of intelligence in sons has to be accounted for by something other than the genetic legacies of their fathers. A fairly intense concern for social stability and avoidance of civil war (a concern justified in the centuries before the ballot box) is necessary to accept hereditary kingship (despite competency considerations) in the light of such a chancy degree of inheritance!

However, it will be pointed out by the geneticist that, although prediction from the father is not so good, prediction from both parents is better —and a wise father is likely to choose an intelligent wife. (Further, a psychologist might point out that the greatness of kings or other public leaders does not rest on intelligence alone, but on personality and temperament qualities, themselves partly inheritable. The likelihood of the son approaching the father over the *average* of several such traits is better.) If the mother is also considered the equation (assuming an r of .4 between parents) becomes:

$$I_s = \frac{(I_f + I_m)}{2} \times 0.6 + C \qquad (10.18)$$

Where an appreciable correlation of intelligence of husband and wife exists—as in most civilized, freely mating, and socially stratified societies —the correlation of son's with father's intelligences is considerable. Nesselroade (Cattell and Nesselroade, 1967) found (in American society where a substantial co-educational college attendance facilitates intelligent boy meeting intelligent girl) a correlation of 0.4 to 0.5 between I.Q.'s of husband and wife. H. E. Jones found in another group a husband-wife correlation of 0.6, and the present writer, with Willson (1938), (N = 101) in a special sample with a distinctly wide social range in Britain, found the correlation rising to 0.8. The former yielded a mid-parent-mid-child correlation of 0.7 and a correlation among siblings of 0.5, while these rose in the latter to 0.9 and 0.8 (which are exceptional, due to a wide population span).

In a world where good habits and intellectual interests at the environmental level are handed on as much by the family as the school, these correlations telling about the combined effect of heredity and environment, are the practical values which the community has to employ when it hopes for more children per family from bright than dull homes. But the theoretically enquiring behavioral geneticist wishes to split up these effects and to understand from what influences the correlations come about. In this connection, the student should recognize (as a statistician could explain) that the findings on correlations are not in a different domain from those which have been set out in the simpler terms of additive variances in the MAVA method on page 255 above. There is a direct translation from the intra-class correlation to the variance ratio treatment, as follows:

(a) $\quad 1 - \dfrac{\sigma^2_{ITT.O}}{\sigma^2_{GP.O}} = r_{ITT.O} = 1 - \dfrac{\sigma^2_{wt}}{\sigma_{wt}^2 + \sigma_{wg}^2 + \sigma_{bg}^2 + \sigma_{bt}^2},$ $\quad$ (10.19)

(b) $\quad 1 - \dfrac{\sigma^2_{FTT.O}}{\sigma^2_{GP.O}} = r_{FTT.O} = 1 - \dfrac{\sigma_{wt}^2 + \sigma_{wg}^2}{\sigma_{wt}^2 + \sigma_{wg}^2 + \sigma_{bg}^2 + \sigma_{bt}^2}$

whereupon

(c) $\quad \dfrac{\sigma_{wg}^2}{\sigma_{wt}^2} = \dfrac{r_{ITT.O} - r_{FTT.O}}{1 - r_{ITT.O}} = N_w \cdot$ $\quad$ (10.20)

The last, (c) is the usual nature-nurture ratio (within-family) which can thus be derived from correlation coefficients. If we substitute in (c) the r's (.86 and .53) for identical and fraternal twins in Figure 10–1, we obtain for N_w a value 2.36, and for h, 0.70, which is about the same as what has been derived from other experiments.

In general, the results from the correlational studies with specific sub-groups agree very well with those yet available from the comprehensive MAVA approach—though they do not extend to all the unknowns discoverable by the latter. Thus Burks (1942) found 66% of intelligence variance due to environment (but settled on 80% from her best studies); Leaky (1935) found 78%; Newman, Freeman, and others (1937) found from 65 to 80%; Woodworth (1938) settled for 60%; while the more up-to-date studies surveyed by Jensen (1968) point centrally to about 80%. Burt (see below) bases his conclusions partly on his finding of a correlation of 0.87 on 53 identical twins *raised apart*. The case records indicate no selective placement, i.e., to highly similar families, that would bias such a result. For fraternals (dizygotics) reared apart, however, the value fell to 0.50. By contrast, ordinary scholastic achievement gave an r of 0.62 for the identicals reared apart and 0.83 for fraternals reared together. The important contribution from Burt's analysis is this clear demonstration of a far lower nature-nurture ratio for school work than for intelligence in the same sets of twins.

Evidence on the genetic-threptic ratio in intelligence has recently been given, within the twin method approach but by an interestingly different technique, through the work of Vandenberg (1962) and Loehlin (1962) who were concerned with the genetic structure of abilities generally. The experiment consists in taking the *differences* within pairs of identical and of fraternal twins on quite a number of primary abilities, and then *factoring these differences* (instead of the absolute scores, as is usual). If fluid ability is largely genetic, no factor pattern such as we have so far identified as fluid intelligence should appear between identicals, but only a crystallized factor, or, rather, the environmental part of g_c, corresponding with their difference in school application and other stimulation. But with fraternals, *two* factors should appear—one fluid, one crystallized. This, in essence is what these investigators found, and it simultaneously adds strength both to (a) the fundamental conception of a fluid and a crystallized component in intelligence and (b) the hypothesis that one is decidedly more genetically determined and the other relatively more environmentally determined.

As the brief survey of principles above indicates, the results of nature-nurture investigations are going to depend, in the first place, on whether the tests are oriented to crystallized or fluid intelligence. Good studies are in progress on the latter, but we remain in ignorance because they still have to report. Secondly, results will depend on the conceptual analysis in terms of allowance for test error, function fluctuation, and interaction. By far the most comprehensive and subtle analysis regarding the latter is in the series by Burt and Howard (1956) which the professional psychologist should peruse along with the MAVA method (see Thompson in Cattell, 1966). They make a distinction between "random" environmental effects and "systematic" environmental effects, the latter being equivalent to our MAVA terms where we note the environment that is correlated with, and perhaps a systematic reaction to, the individual's heredity. Their results are in Table 10–2.

TABLE 10–2
A Refined Assessment of Nature and Nurture Variance
Contributions to Intelligence

	Crude Test Marks	Adjusted Assessments
Heredity	77.06	87.56
Environment[1]	16.51	7.20
Unreliability of data	6.43	5.24
	100.00	100.00
[1] Divided into:		
(a) Random	5.91	5.77
(b) Systematically related	10.60	1.43

From Burt and Howard, 1956.

The adjusted values involve some assumptions which all psychologists will not wish to make, but Burt and Howard consider that they offer the best final figures today, though they are well above the 70–80% values central to most cruder data analyses. In fact, if we put error aside, as we should, the sophisticated analysis of Burt and Howard, based on ample data, gives a nature-nurture ratio of 82.5 to 17.5 or of 92.7 to 7.5, according to acceptance of alternative likely assumptions. An educated hunch from data and trends would be that, when culture-fair, fluid ability tests are used, we are going to find a 9:1 ratio of genetic to environmental influence. In crystallized ability, however, the value will typically be lower and more dependent on the accidents of the particular cultural regime. As the term "investment theory" indicates, g_f is liable, in its generation of g_c, to all the risks of an investment. Laziness may cause it scarcely to be invested at all; differences of individual interest may cause it to be invested in directions different from that in which "traditional" intelligence tests measure it—as Darwin's schoolboy interest went to discriminating butterflies and insects instead of the Latin participles by which his teachers judged his intelligence. Whole cultures may invest their g_f resources in what seem peculiar directions to others, as the superb skill in pictograms of the Chinese mandarin culture seemed to Europe, with the latter's concern with science and steam engines. The nature-nurture ratios for g_c are thus at least as much of sociological as of psychological interest, and are not fully described until content area as well as ratio becomes fixed. Nevertheless, there is a limit to which the G/T ratio can be pulled by culture, for g_c measures, because, wherever they are taken, g_f has had to play a substantial role in generating g_c. Obviously the g_c ratio will be highest where there is "perfect" education, i.e., where every individual's interest and opportunity are such that g_c is a perfect function of g_f.

5. THE INTERPLAY OF LEARNING AND SCHOOL EXPERIENCE WITH THE INTELLIGENCES AND PRIMARY ABILITIES

The whole of the twin, and for that matter the MAVA approach, hinges on correlation, and, as every student knows, correlation ignores means. If one obtained, say, a .55 correlation of intelligence scores of fathers and sons in a particular sample, and then added 4 points of I.Q. to every son, the correlation would remain just the same.[9] It reflects the agreement on the individual family rank order, but ignores the inter-generational shift. We know (see Chapter 14) that there is undoubtedly, in America (but less so in an older culture like Britain) a presently proceeding upward inter-generational shift on scores in crystallized intelligence, perhaps partly due to lesser childhood disease, but largely to increased educational investment. It has been suggested, e.g., by Hilgard, that the difference in emphasis between extreme environmentalists and hereditarians is due to their looking at different parts of the picture: the former to the average rise, the latter to the constancy of correlational rank.

In the present section we propose to give attention to effects of inter-generational educational effects; but, in so doing, it is necessary to draw a rather fine line between the experimental and the social implications. For the latter—with all the issues of differences of social groups, races, etc.—are considered in their collective aspects in Chapter 14. The reader who wishes to embrace both the scientific psychological and the broader social issues in a single reading should continue straight on from this section to Chapter 14. In this section we shall continue mainly with what is unquestionably generalizable within a given culture, and in so doing we propose to consider also physical and physiological influences, with speculations about what brain damage may be occurring, how neurone maturation occurs, and other possible intervening mechanisms. However, the important point to keep in mind is that however diligent we may be in uncovering environmental sources of variance, and however persuasive in stressing their potency, our conclusions must balance with the final account which tells us that 80% is ascribable to heredity and 20% to environment (in a mixed g_f-g_c measure).

Actually, two quite distinct lines of further investigation need to take off from the nature-nurture ratio findings: (1) an investigation of what Mendelian mechanisms are needed to account for the *genetic* part, and (2) an investigation, as proposed here, of the way in which environment

---

[9] Parenthetically, the father-son correlation as directly obtained is usually less than the true one. For in addition to the "I.Q. correction" to mental age for the actual age of the son, an age correction should be carried out on the fathers' scores. Thus, according to Figures 7–4 or 7–10, older fathers' scores should be raised relative to younger, before correlating with sons.

interacts to produce the noted changes. For this latter scientific specialty, which we shall pursue here—that of interaction effects—Nesselroade and the present writer have suggested the name genothreptics. Regarding the genetic structure and laws *per se,* what we can reasonably conjecture at the present time can be discussed in a couple of sentences. Despite some ingenious attempts to explain the distribution and inheritance of intelligence (see Fuller and Thompson, 1960; Hurst, 1935) in terms of six to ten genes, the evidence better fits a more polygenic structure. That is to say, intelligence genetically looks more like stature and other features which are known with tolerable certainty to involve many gene effects, in which different genes have different sizes of contribution. On the other hand, one has to recognize specific genes of rare occurrence which have a major effect, as seen in special forms of mental defect. Commonly, the defective gene allele takes away some general chemical necessity of the body, as in phenylketonuria or galactosemina, which ruins intelligence (along with much else) by denying development of normal neuron action. By contrast, the small decrements of intelligence, associated with absence of the presumed, small, cumulative, gene actions over the normal range, are associated with no other obvious abnormality of health.

Even with that freedom to experiment with special matings which animal experiment provides, the Mendelian action remains obscure, as the last chapter indicates, partly because of our defective delineation of intelligence in animal behavior. All that we get from that source is additional assurance that whatever seems to correspond to human intelligence in the animal world shows a pretty high degree of heritability *within* species. As *between* species—even within the mammalian order—the relative powerlessness of environment is obvious. No amount of training and experience can bring the most intelligent mouse within the range of the least intelligent monkey in *general* problem-solving capacity.

In the rest of this section our concern is with the second issue above— the manner of genothreptic interaction with environment. Therein we shall take the opportunity to satisfy the reader's curiosity also about nature-nurture with other abilities than intelligence, namely the primary abilities. However, this section can be only a first brush with intelligence-learning relations, which are treated more extensively in Chapters 11 and 12 below.

Regarding the general relation of genetic and cultural influences, it has already been pointed out above that the obtained nature-nurture ratio would be expected to vary somewhat from culture to culture (there is no positive evidence yet that it does) and from epoch to epoch, because the range of racial mixtures may differ in different countries, and the range of educational pressures may differ. If this is so, it may well be asked, perhaps some intensive education beyond anything now normally existing in the community *could* affect intelligence environmentally more than we realize at the present time? Some such nostrum has been the dream of teachers from time immemorial and of those attempting to eradicate unemployment and poverty in our present generation. Sundry psychologists, such as

Séguin, and the exponents of such commercial systems as Pelmanism, have claimed to increase "muscle" in brain power by suitable exercises. The view received support in educational circles for a time from the claims of Skeels and Stoddard for remarkably large I.Q. changes from environmental remedying of low intelligence in children of low intelligence mothers, but the critical statistical examinations by McNemar demolished this. Hunt (1961) and others have taken up the argument again recently. Certainly we can expect that everything that *can* be done will be done in the next few years by attention to diet, mental stimulation, etc., to raise lower I.Q.'s and, while preserving an open mind, one hopes that the large sums involved in research here will utilize meaningful concepts and exact statistical methods in order to avoid raising false hopes and evading real issues.

The most sympathetic presentation of the environmental arguments—gleaning the field of evidence for the most minute contributions—is that of Vernon (1969). It is nevertheless critical, to point out regarding the Skeels results (1940), for example, that "other investigators obtain inconsistent results" (with Skeels's). The fact is, as McNemar pointed out, the Skeels conclusions capitalize on that "regression to the mean" which we know occurs (through error of measurement, etc.) in any group initially chosen for extreme intelligence (high or low) when it is retested. Furthermore, cases were taken from an extreme environmental deficit to begin with. (Vernon and others quote judgments that the orphanage was about three standard deviations of environmental level below what would be considered normal environment.) Additionally there was no care about the design of experiment features which Campbell has since stressed—namely, the gain in this case through test sophistication effects in repeated testing. Finally, the tests used were substantially contaminated with attainment and reflect g_c gain with no clear evidence of g_f gain.

Investigations have been made, not only of early lack of stimulus in the environment, but also of poor nutrition and of poor motivational atmosphere, in terms of lack of parental affection. Only in quite extreme cases, such as amount of disease from malnutrition, have effects been noted on apparent intelligence. Thus in Africa, with respect to the "wasting disease," *kwashiokor,* which is due to lack of high energy protein diet and which produces subnormal body weight, it has been shown with tolerable certainty by such investigators as Churchill, Chow, and Cravioto, that young children of lesser weight learn more slowly. However, since Churchill found that even in twins (of identical genetic make-up and upbringing) the twin of lesser weight tends to learn more slowly, the simpler conclusion is that this slower learning is a nutritional lack of energy, rather than any proven discrepancy in intelligence as such.

As to affectional relations, it has been known for some time that children who receive less affection early in life tend to be less "extraverted," emotionally demonstrative, and less given to interacting with people. It is easy to assume that this impassivity is a lack of intelligence, and researches such as those of Spitz (1946), Bowlby (1953) and Schaeffer and Bayley (1963) have been quoted in support of this position. However, closer scrutiny necessitates discarding this conclusion. For example, though Schaeffer found lower developmental quotients (13 points) on the Cattell Pre-School Scale for Infants who were long hospitalized (and cut off from maternal contact) around twelve weeks of age, it was found that after return to their homes for even two weeks they completely caught up with the control group. In this connection we should consider also the "Rosenthal effect." If teachers are told (erroneously) that children A, B, and C are brighter on intelligence tests than D, E, and F, it appears in some cases that the former actually score better on intelligence tests when re-tested after a semester or so. The fact that teachers enjoy giving more attention to their bright children is well known, and this greater attention leads to greater advancement in the school subjects, e.g., verbal skills and vocabulary, used in crystallized intelligence tests.

Besides nutrition, richness of environment, and favorableness of emotional atmosphere, the possible environmental influences needing exploration are those of patterns of child rearing practices, parental occupation, freedom from physical diseases, family size, exposure to large vocabulary in the language of the culture (including effects of a second, minority language), income, books, T.V., social class, and race backgrounds. Correlations of some of these with intelligence are set out (p. 487) in Table 14–4. A phrase to avoid in exact work (though used above for reference) is the virtually meaningless term "enriched environment." As now used, it is either hopelessly vague or circular, i.e., improved intelligence is what comes from an enriched environment. Is a child, brought up in the din of a city center with hourly T.V. and constant innovative trivialities, enjoying an enriched environment relative to the life of an Indian on a reservation (as studied by Wayne Dennis for example), or the solitary farm on which Newton was raised? Krech's use of "enriched environment" for his animals meant the constant environmental interruptions of the first kind (presumably bad for thoughtful children), but like many others (e.g., Goldfarb, Spitz, and Dennis) he did not hesitate to draw conclusions that should properly apply only to some more precise definition. Actually, as we shall see in Chapter 14, Indians on reservations average notably better on traditional intelligence tests than Negroes in city centers, though what conclusions can be drawn from this are obscure, because of the looseness of definition and measurement that run through most environmental influence research.

The upshot of the recent comprehensive study by Vernon (1969) is that some modest upward shift—perhaps 3 to 5 points of I.Q.—may be brought about by intensive educational efforts, but that the least "doubtful" and inconsistent evidence to this effect occurs for influences in the first two or three years of life. Indeed, he summarizes Harrell, Woodyard, and Gates (1956) and Stoch to the effect that environment exercises most of its influence "from three months before to six months after birth."

Whatever value is found eventually for a mean shift, it will, of course, like the nature-nurture ratio, have meaning only relative to a particular culture.

As of 1970, no researches exist claiming to show a significant shift of a mean group I.Q. through intensive environmental influences (other than physical ones) that are free from disqualifying methodological weaknesses. The fact that the claims are largest for the infancy period is itself noteworthy, in view of the fact that this is where our tests of intelligence—and even our knowledge of what structures we are measuring (see Chapter 7)—are weakest. Indeed, the main issue remains, as before, whether the shifts are occurring in g_c or g_f. There is no doubt whatever that g_c can be raised by training, but such changes in g_c are misunderstood if conceived in terms of one "general intelligence." They bring no proof of any real change in fluid intelligence, g_f, and a change in g_c is only to a small degree one that will go on investing itself in further change (see Chapter 9) in the way an increase in g_f would.

Although there may be doubt as to whether an average shift on g_c of 3, 4, 5, or 6 points is obtainable in our particular culture at this point in particular social class groups by teaching machines, or redoubled educational effort and cost, there is no doubt about the general magnitude of the inter-generational shift for the bulk of the population. The inter-class issue we will set aside until Chapter 14 can define social class more precisely. A first indication of the inter-generation shift was given by Finch in 1946, followed quickly by the studies of Tuddenham (1948), the present writer (1950b), and latter by the Scottish Council for Research in Education (1949, 1961). In terms of theoretical possibilities and formulations, such a drift had been examined by the present writer in 1936(b) and 1938(c). Examining the achievement and intelligence scores in Mid-West high schools over the previous generation, Finch showed a steady, and surprisingly large increase per year in performance. Tuddenham (1948) concurred, for when he compared the Army Alpha Test performances of World War II and World War I draftees, his results showed an emphatic advance in the mean level of the latter. Sampling problems do not entirely obscure this conclusion. Later, in Britain, Sir Godfrey Thomson's very complete survey of the Scottish school population on the Binet and Moray House Tests showed a significant but small increase over a shorter period (magnitude depending on which test was used). Fortunately, in this same historical period under analysis, the present writer retested after a thirteen-year lapse (1936–1941) a complete 10-11-year-old cross section of the child population of a large city, Leicester, in England, with a culture-fair test *and found no statistically significant change* in average level. Tests on traditional intelligence tests available in city school records at the time suggested the usual slight upward creep of about 1 point per decade (though in the U.S. the shift would be about 2 to 5 per decade). The conclusion must be that the inter-generation changes found are exclusively in the crystallized ability component in intelligence tests, probably representing the unquestionably marked improvement in schooling and the reduced exposure to cerebral illnesses, to damaging fevers, etc., for the general population over this period.

Incidentally, this added constant (1 to 4 points, perhaps in different cultures during 1900–1960) is the C term in equations (10.16) and (10.17) above, used to estimate a child's from a parent's intelligence. In culture-fair tests, the evidence, just cited, is that it is zero; but in crystallized intelligence various results suggest that it might be 1–4 points (or even up to 8 in initially backward cultures) that we need to add in using that regression equation. It is important to remind the educator that not *all* of this inter-generation shift should be ascribed to schooling, but some could be due to improved health measures reducing brain damage, or even to improved early nutrition. This inter-generation shift probably has come to a plateau and virtually stopped in most Western cultures in this generation, and perhaps lasted little more than a hundred years. Incidentally, the common popular ascription of the rise both in stature and in intelligence over this period to improved nutrition is probably wrong. Stature has undoubtedly stepped up (notably through diet changes in countries such as Europe and Japan). But expert analysis shows natural and sexual selection[10] in a period of food plentifulness to have played a major role. As regards nutrition and intelligence, we must remember also that what is good for stature might be bad (through cholesterol deposition in early life) for intelligence.

On the hypothesis that a crystallized intelligence increase is due largely to schooling, one might expect—as one finds—that the upward trend would be larger in the rural schools, say of the American South, than in a long-established, scholarly, educational system, as in Scotland or Germany. Also one would expect that the increase would not go on indefinitely, but would represent a passing historical phase of adjustment. Of course, in the above calculations, both on nutrition and on education, one must recognize that the shift in average is due to bringing up the rearguard, and that the best educated one-tenth is probably no better educated today than, say, in Elizabethan England or ancient Athens.

Available evidence, supplementary to that of culture shift, analyzable for light on this hypothesis that g_c and not g_f is affected, is the comparison of two groups distinguished by a different amount of educational expenditure, socio-educational status, or length of schooling. Figure 10–2 from Spuhler and Lindzey (1967) shows somewhat old data from mean Army Alpha

[10] Parenthetically, we should not naively assume the stature increase to be "progress" until we see what this does to physiological efficiency, longevity, etc. In any case, as here indicated, at least one leading geneticist has rightly questioned whether this shift is all due to environment. It could be due (if Fisher's (1930) evidence on epistasis is correct) to the usual effect of hybridization (heterosis) consequent upon more travel and social mobility. Unless the causes of the stature and the crystallized intelligence shifts are different, however, a largely genetic selection and heterosis explanation for the former seems unlikely, for the evidence is that only g_c, crystallizd intelligence, and *not* g_f, has improved in the last generation (Cattell, 1950c).

FIGURE 10–2
**Army Alpha Intelligence Scores Among Draftees According
to Race and Mean Expenditures on Schooling Per Capita,
Plotted by States**

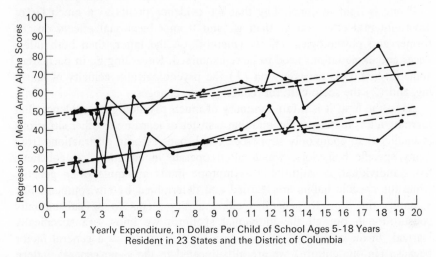

Yearly Expenditure, in Dollars Per Child of School Ages 5-18 Years
Resident in 23 States and the District of Columbia

From "Racial differences in behavior," by J. N. Spuhler and Lindzey, G. in J. Hirsh, *Behavior-genetic Analysis*. Copyright 1967 by McGraw-Hill. Used with permission of McGraw-Hill Book Company.

test scores of whites and Negroes in relation to per capita expenditure on education (different for states and for whites and Negroes).

What one sees here is an approximately linear relation of traditional intelligence test scores to amount of education—a relation replicated across the two groups. It may be unnecessary to point out to present readers that even the most steady, obvious, and significant linear relation of two variables, as here, should not be mistaken to mean that one *wholly* accounts for the other or that the causal action is one-way (though with time as one variable the latter is more clear). Only a minor fraction of the individual difference range in intelligence when two generations are thrown together is accounted for by the big change in educational effort between the generations.

Any apparent contradiction between the strong hereditary findings by MAVA or by the inter-familial correlation results on the one hand, and the evidence of a broad, upward shift on crystallized ability between generations or of changes with regional cultural differences, on the other, is illusory.[11] The results are entirely mutually consistent, provided one considers the role of causal directions different from those often assumed, and

---

[11] There has been some wishful concluding, without the least evidence, that a more "stimulating" environment raises g_f as well as g_c. Two kinds of evidence that might suggest this as a *possibility* are that on imprinting and that cited in Chapter 8 (Rosenzweig, Krech, and Bennett, 1961) showing larger brain weight appearing in much-stimulated mice or rats (page 203 above). The former actually shows that experience

provided the inability of the correlation to recognize mean shifts—as pointed out above—is recognized. If we keep the latter in mind, and realize that results point definitely to the inter-generational change being a change of crystallized, not fluid ability, any contradiction vanishes.

If one is right in concluding that the evidence points to a much larger environmental effect on g_c than g_f, and from educational effects on the former and physiological effects (mainly) on the latter, then both inferences and explanations need to be re-examined. Regarding g_c, in particular, some discussion is necessary on (1) the psychological specificity of learning, and (2) the socio-cultural relativity of g_c changes.

As to the first, it is a fair summary of much psychological evidence that learning tends to be specific, and that transfer of learning to other situations is smaller than commonly supposed. The broad factorial abstractions from many specific behaviors, which often operate in equations as constants fixing individual, constitutional asymptotic limits are quite often genetic, while the specific habits are learned and determined by environment. For example, the limit to general spelling ability seems to be substantially constitutional, but all the individual spellings we know are specifically learned. In the case of g_c we have seen that it appears as a general factor because (in one culture) we are all subjected to the same general pattern of "curriculum." Additionally, there is evidence that some of the intellectual habits learned, e.g., in mathematics, are of such generality that they *do* transfer and give generality of application. The growth in g_c from education, unlike much other learning, can thus be partly a genuine learning of a generalized capacity.

As to the socio-cultural perspective on this environmental gain, let us reflect on what has been said about the Protean possible forms of the crystallized intelligence pattern. First, this will give us a very different and more enlightened view of the nature of the inter-generational constant, C, which there is evidence to believe has recently been added to "the average I.Q." Any such elevation in crystallized intelligence has meaning primarily only in relation to a culture. It is an increment in discriminatory skills in the given culture's language, in numerical ability (which, indeed, is more universal), in mechanical ability (in Western culture), and so on, due to the investment of fluid ability in what school and society prescribe. In another culture the center of gravity (the centroid of a g_c factor) would be different—for Eskimos it might have its highest loadings in anticipating the behavior of a seal, or foretelling what a west wind will do to the ice pack. Note we are not talking here simply of "achievement" in a culture

---

is tied to improvement in particular pathways, not to general relation perception, and the latter is more easily interpreted as a biochemical effect on brain tissue (not intelligence) through stress and arousal—or even anxiety. A "culturally deprived" environment is, however, by no means lacking in stimulation and in demands on problem-solving ability, for, as Binet well recognized, the "gamin" of the Paris back streets may have a sharper education than the pampered middle class child.

which is broader and includes rote learning, but about those automatically used, high-level, judgmental skills requiring high g_f for their learning.

There are two distinct aspects to this potentially *Protean character* of g_c across countries and eras. First, it brings with it a still more necessary instability and incomparability of measures of intelligence (as g_c) at different times and places. In these (g_c) terms we cannot compare a Victorian with a modern, or a Maori farmer with a London solicitor. Secondly, as in all human performances that are partially products of time and motivational energy, the "ipsative" law holds that a gain in one direction of expression is necessarily at the cost of another. The old joke about the professor of zoology who forgot the name of a fish whenever he committed to memory the name of a new student is unfortunately not simply a joke. When a generation increases in performance on scholastic abilities, what has it forgotten?

It may have forgotten something—like skill in tracking animals (boys) or sewing shirts (girls)—which by most reasonable standards is less important than the newer g_f investments demanded by the culture. But at any acceptable level of scientific assurance, we do not know what has really happened. For, unfortunately, the number of experimentalists who can handle global, multivariate researches is still pitifully small and only multivariate research can answer the ipsative question. However, one may surmise with tolerable certainty that the Midwestern farm boy, like Huckleberry Finn, could make a lot of shrewd judgments about bird song, about growing plants and farm machinery, and about how to persuade a river boat skipper to give him a ride, at which the present generation A-student would fail. The former probably have less adaptive generality of use than the intelligence investments which a wise school and society set out to teach, i.e., the fine judgments yield a less wide gain in environmental control when taught in one domain than in another. But the decision as to what is a "gain" comes also into the field of values, and it might be that a broad investment in social skills, neglected by investigations on primary abilities, and arising from much lazy and casual interaction with people—even Mississippi people—*is* important and *has* declined in the generation in which scholastic skills have risen. There is also a constant danger in the "Mandarin" type of education that mechanical wisdom may be a casualty in hothouse curricula. The present writer (unpublished data) found that American schoolboys around 1940 were lower on verbal skill (V factor) than English boys of the same age, but higher on mechanical judgment, and one gets hints that upper-caste Hindu culture (whence we get the word pundit) would show a still bigger shift toward displacing mechanical intelligence (a lower-caste specialty) in favor of verbal philosophical skills.

Unless it is brought back to contact with cosmic reality (as by physicists, biologists, and astronomers), culture tends to drift into a narcissistic preoccupation with interactions within the human species—into purely verbal and legal skills. From Oxford to the Chinese literati cultures have explicitly or implicitly set up definitions of intelligence entirely in their own image. What is more, they probably create in the *actual* mental structure of a generation, a detectable, broad, factor pattern—g_c—in the image of their culture. In fact, when properly weighted according to the factor pattern found for these skills, the pattern can be used as the best expression for measurement (other than g_f) of intelligence in that culture. Here, incidentally, lies the central theoretical and practical problem of cross-culture comparisons of intelligence level—if we insist on trying to measure intelligence as g_c rather than as g_f. (The same problem arises in selecting for scholarships among university students, when it becomes necessary to compare individuals belonging to different branches of what C. P. Snow in Britain has called "the two cultures.")

At the present time, and in our culture (see discussion and tables in Chapter 6), most of the variance contributions which locate and define the crystallized general ability factor reside in such primaries as verbal, numerical, reasoning, mechanical, and other clearly definable areas of culture acquisition. Consequently, we can get at a more detailed view of the way the nurture component works in g_c by studying the primary ability nature-nurture ratios. In any case, the nature-nurture ratios for primary abilities constituted information desirable for its own sake, and which no survey of human abilities should omit. In this arena of research activity, however, there is as yet dependable evidence only on half a dozen out of the twenty or so mentioned in Chapter 3. As Table 10–3 shows, except for the discrepancy of Vandenberg and Blewett values (which is somewhat alarming, and for which the discrepant values are here ensconced in parentheses) there is a consensus that verbal and spatial ability have a high genetic component, fluency a lower one, and number skill a low value. The high environmental determination of number is easy enough to appreciate, but the low environmental value on V is a bit surprising, and serves to remind us of some of the subtleties of thinking needed here. Although an anthropologist would point out that language is the most environmentally, culturally determined form of behavior, yet, *within* a culture, the extent to which it is acquired could be considerably genetically determined. In fact, what the above figures imply is that everyone gets such a strong chance to become "overlearned" on language (relative to, say, numerical skills) that the ultimate determiner of an individual's level is less due to variance in exposure to language learning than to his inner capacities. Sheer vocabulary, it is true, might be expected to vary with home and social status, and the environmental role might be larger if the experimenters included wider ranges of social status. However, in the present ranges we seem to be dealing with skills which, through general conversation and reading, are relatively overlearned, so that more is left to hereditary constants. (Here we see another instance of the generalization made elsewhere that, as the general level of education is improved in society, hereditary differences will become increasingly important.)

TABLE 10–3
Researches on Heritability of Primary Abilities

Blewett	*h*	*Vandenberg*	*h*	*Strandskov*	*Rank Order of h*
Verbal (V)	.68	Verbal (V)	.62	Space (S)	1
Reasoning (Ir)[1]	.64	Reasoning (Ir)	(.28)	Verbal (V)	2
Fluency (W)	.64	Fluency (W)	.61	Fluency (W)	3
Space (S)	.51	Space (S)	.59	Memory (M)	4
Number (N)	.07	Number (N)	(.61)	Number (N)	5
		Memory (M)	(.20)		

[1] The somewhat disconcerting differences in certain values in the above researches—notably on N and Ir need comment. That in the latter case could be due to the form of the test of reason (whether conventional and learned or otherwise). That in the former could be due to differences of age and education in the subjects. Only when children are in a steep learning phase in arithmetic, or adults are pressed to limits of ultimate capacity (as in a nation of shopkeepers!) would one expect N to have much constitutional determination.

One would expect, as is roughly the case in Table 10–3, that a lower nature-nurture ratio would be found for those primary abilities which load high on g_c and a much higher one for those high on g_f. However, additionally, there could be different nature-nurture ratios to the *specific* factor parts of the primaries each in its own right. It is too early to draw conclusions, however, at this stage. It will be noted that we have considered fluency (not just verbal fluency) as a general factor, labelling it g_r, or general capacity for memory retrieval. The above results could possibly indicate that much of the total retrieval effectiveness is a function of the amount (or "internal pressure") of storage, i.e., of the cumulative effect of environment and learning. Probably this field of study will need to consider, in addition to volume of specific memory contents, a concept of "retrieval effectiveness regardless of content" (which declines a good deal in age and with certain drug conditions). In finer factor analyses, this may appear as a second factor to be split off from g_r, and later research may show that this, as distinct from content, does have more genetic determination. Parenthetically, the low N value does not imply, as one of the investigators listed in Table 10–3 has suggested, that mathematical ability is largely an environmental gift. After all, as pointed out above, N is facility with simple numerical calculation (which mathematicians tend to despise and often possess but poorly!), not mathematical ability. (As far as real mathematical ability is concerned, the instances of "mathematics in the family"—as in the Birkhoff's, Bernouilli's, Jacobi's, and others—could, of course, be explained *either* way.)

To fit the genetic eivdence with other evidence about the specific nature of primary abilities would be premature at this moment, because we know so little about them! If some of them represent entirely environmentally molded structures, one should expect that their "shapes" (as factor-loading patterns) would differ a good deal from one subculture to another. The only clear-cut, cross-cultural evidence available—that of Vandenberg on Chinese students and Horn on German school children—shows the same primaries to exist, in form and number, as in American subjects. This is compatible with the rather high heritabilities above, suggesting that at least the scores of such abilities as verbal, numerical, spatial, and reasoning propensities are somehow "given." Doubtless they built up environmentally, as what we have called "aids" (page 319), powerfully—and perhaps somewhat differently in very different cultures. Alternatively to their beginning around some hereditary facility, one may entertain the notion that there is sufficient in common to most cultures and to the character of the physical world to preserve these initial unities by environmental action.

6. THE EFFECTS OF SPECIFIC DIFFERENTIAL EXPERIENCES

The preceding section, going beyond the evidence from the twin and MAVA methods, has asked what evaluation of evidence on environmental action can be obtained from considering directly the relation of ability to forces in society. The present section pursues this line further, in the direction of a methodology of actually manipulating, experimentally, some influences that might be important.

Indeed, one can, in imagination, hear some readers asking at the beginning of this chapter why we chose to plunge into complex variance analysis procedures, when one might surely follow "classical" bivariate experiment by exposing people to different environments and asking what that does to the I.Q. One has to reply that the effects we are concerned with can *in principle* be simply analyzed by: (1) exposing persons of the same or fixed difference heredities to different environments, and (2) exposing persons of different heredity to the same, constant environment, and observing the resulting differences. Parenthetically, we may answer that the "constant environment; different heredity" and "constant heredity; different environment" designs *have* in fact been used in the above MAVA method. But they have been used without manipulation and often by combining both variations at once and employing complex analytical methods to separate them. The person desiring a simpler approach will reply that he would like to see something like a "controlled," i.e., *manipulative* experimental design, in which we deliberately apply experiences designed to improve intelligence to one group but not to another.

However, by reason of the practical difficulties and ethical objections which soon become obvious to experienced researchers, nothing very effective has ever become available in these terms. Indeed, it is for this reason that we have deferred consideration of such a forlorn hope until after the more solid evidence of MAVA and twin methods has been discussed. For example, no data exists in which one member of each of several hundred twin pairs has been subjected precisely to environment A and the others to environment B. Nor do we have situations where persons of known hereditary difference, e.g., sibs, have been exposed in sufficient numbers to exactly the same training environment. (Commonly, for example, the parents who can only afford to send one child to college send the conspicuously brighter one, often the only one who passes the entrance exams.) Where instances of uniform training exist, they exist only for small samples and with respect to relatively trivial differences of experience. (Cattell, Feingold, and Sarason, 1941, for example, trained children on the perceptual experience in culture-fair intelligence tests for short periods —without effect.)

It is possible to *find* naturally occurring differences of childhood-long exposure to stimulus, of course, as in the early British studies comparing canal-boat children (who got no schooling) or children of the chronically unemployed (Cattell, 1937b) with others, or in the present day repetitions of this type of study with "disadvantaged" social groups. The trouble with such approaches is that we have no guarantee that the genetic components in the disadvantaged are equal to those of the children under greater cultural pressure with whom we compare them. As we have seen (page 157), the investigator is forced by virtually unanswerable arguments to the view that some selection of intelligence goes on by social class (occupational level of parent). The evidence has been marshalled by Burt (1943) and others (page 384), and it appears in social class differences in culture-fair intelligence tests (pages 451 and 488) and in findings such as those of Findlay and McGuire (1957) where block-sorting and other tests scarcely related to schooling are done significantly better by children of parents in social classes corresponding to more complex occupations.

Nevertheless, some situations arise where the required conditions for comparison are tolerably met, and those with positive findings have been carefully gathered by J. McV. Hunt (1961). As pointed out above, the evidence, by Stoddard (1943), Wellman (1940), and Skeels (1940), of substantial changes of I.Q. in children of low intelligence, born of low intelligence mothers, when the children have been given special educational advantages is nowadays largely discounted. It has been shown by McNemar (1942) and others (see Vernon, 1969) not to stand up to searching psychological and statistical examination. On the other hand, Kirk (1958) studied eighty-one retarded children between three and six years of age, of whom more than half were given every advantage a modern nursery school could provide, while the rest stayed in their ordinary institutional environment. On the particular test used, seventy percent of those who got the special training showed gains, and the mean shift from that of the control group was significant, though only at the $P < .05$ level. Moss and Kagan (1958) correlated what they estimated to be "maternal concern with child's achievement" with Stanford-Binet scores at ages of three and six years. For boys they found correlations of .42 at three years, and .27 at six years, and −.07 and .01, correspondingly, for girls. In another small group they found .41 and .08 for boys and .16 and .09 for girls. More than half of these correlations are insignificant. Two considerations make unlikely the interpretation that "concern for achievement" raises the I.Q.: (1) The likelihood that the more intelligent mothers of naturally more intelligent children *would* show more interest and concern. It is a consequence—not a cause—of higher intelligence and its associations. And (2) The fact that tests of g_c rather than g_f were used, and increase in g_c has dubious meaning (see pages 124 and 483).

Under the impetus of hopeful welfare programs to eradicate backwardness and raise employability, there has been enormous expenditure in this decade on research carried out by "social work" oriented individuals who would not normally be doing research. Not surprisingly, a lot of the early reports of substantial gain in I.Q. by special training do not stand up to the scrutiny they are beginning to receive. Thus the review by Jensen (*Harvard Educational Review*, 1969) may be set out in his own informal précis.

An average of 29 intensive early intervention studies shows an average gain over control groups of between 5 and 10 I.Q. points on the Stanford-Binet and other conventional tests. The largest mean gain reported in any study I have been able to find is 23 I.Q. points on the Stanford-Binet, for a group of 11 disadvantaged children in a nursery program at the University of Illinois run by Merle Karnes. I find some interesting "correlations" in reviewing this literature: (a) reports of greatest gains are found in informal oral reports and personal letters, next greatest in papers read at conventions, and least when reported in journal articles and books—the same authors can lose 10 to 15 points on presumably the same study between informal and formal reporting of the results; (b) there is a negative correlation between the size of gain and the N of the group in which it is found.

Still more surprising revelations on recent research claiming (in newspapers) substantial I.Q. gains are given in Jean Glass's piquant "Educational Piltdown Man," 1968. A survey at the Hoover Institute, Stanford University by Freeman concludes: "Headstart results were encouraging *in some cases,* and suggested an average gain of 8 to 10 points on verbal tests. But it soon became apparent that the gain was only temporary and disappeared entirely within a few months."

A recently reported claim for large environmental influence is based on the finding in Israel that, whereas Jewish immigrants from different regions show initially substantial intelligence differences (those from Western Europe, for example, scoring significantly higher than those from the Yemen), yet their children brought up in a common kibbutz environment cease to show differences of this significance. This misses the essential features of a good experiment necessary to answer the present issues. It deals with ill-defined masses instead of families; it fails to measure the parents on culture-fair tests, despite their enormous differences of cultural background; it seems not to expect regression to the mean; and it tests the children themselves—in a kibbutz environment where vocabularies would necessarily become very similar—with verbal Terman-Binet types of test, obviously centered largely on crystallized intelligence.

In summary of the work in the last two decades aiming to investigate (or far more frequently to *prove*) the effect of specific improved environments on children's intelligence, one must regretfully conclude, with those who have set out their criticisms in more detail, that an incursion of tendentious but amateur Lysenkoism, aimed at the press, has ruined most of it. The evaluations of a group of eminent researchers, called to a three-day symposium at the University of Illinois to comment on the treatment of Jensen's paper in the Harvard Review (1969), are worthy of close study (Cancro, 1971). In particular, searching analyses have been made by Bereiter, Eckland, Ginsburg, Glass, Horn, Humphreys, Li, McNemar, Merrifield, Vandenberg, and Vernon. Most of the existing studies fail to yield reliable or consistent results through defects of design, such as: comparing effects of educational conditions without holding the parents' intelligence constant; failing to use well-defined measures of structural primaries; using samples altogether too small; taking cases so far deviant from average intelligence that the appreciable error of measurement favors considerable regression to the mean; drawing conclusions about intelligence in the infant range, where we do not yet have reliable tests or even knowledge of ability structure; failing to report selection (drop-out) effects between the test and retest; failing to allow for test sophistication; using tests which measure "intelligence" only in the very narrow range of performance in which specific training has been given; measuring only the results of improved environment without reciprocal evidence on effects of reduction of environmental stimulation; and, above all, of making no attempt on the measurements to distinguish between the effects on g_f and g_c. Admittedly, this is a difficult field in which to conduct experiment, even for experienced researchers. The influences that can ethically and practically be manipulated are small, hard to assign quantitative value to; apt to be correlated with genetic levels, and often swamped by uncontrolled and uncontrollable influences. For these reasons, the main conclusions must, at present, be based, as we have based them here, on the MAVA and twin approaches, which yield more meaningful, broadly based, and accurate answers.

The manipulative design of experiment which is thus so questionable with humans, can, however, be carried out effectively and accurately with animals, and at least two good studies exist. The design of holding environment constant and manipulating heredity was well exemplified in Tryon's (1940) familiar study with rats, selectively inbred for high and low-maze-running ability over ten generations from a common stock. The distribution curves of ability of the two strains pulled apart until there was very little overlap, despite identical treatment as to food, training, etc.

Experiments have also been carried out retaining the genetic stock constant while providing differences of environmental training. Such work, unfortunately, is at present invalidated by two deficiencies: (1) inability to define an "enriched" as distinct from a "disturbing" environment, and (2) lack of knowledge of what are tests for "general ability" in animals. As to the first, it was pointed out above that the term "enriched," which is fashionable at the moment, is for humans, both psychologically vague and operationally question-begging. If we are referring to a numerically high score of the environment for diversity of stimuli and curiosity-provoking objects, the environment of the poorest slum dweller today is greatly "enriched" compared with that of Archimedes, or Shakespeare, or Newton, or Rutherford on his remote New Zealand beach.

As for its use in animals from the physiological evidence of cholinesterase change in rats, the present writer might argue that the "enrichment" in these rat experiments was, instead, an exposure to a more anxiety and stress-creating environment. Hoagland and Burloe (1962) and others have shown that crowding rats, or even giving them too much exposure to strangers (which Bertrand Russell pointed out, before the physiologists, as a disadvantage of human urban life) brings glandular changes of the kind associated with anxiety and stress. The most quoted "enrichment" results —those of Krech—are suspect on these grounds.

Thus the advantage gained by experimentation with animals (but not feasible with humans) is more than negated by the several kinds of obscurities of interpretation which afflict the animal evidence. For example, it was immediately, and rightly, demanded of Tryon that he demonstrate that the maze-running ability he measured in rats had any relation to human intelligence. Obviously, differences of temperamental speed, sensitivity of motivation, etc., could be more strongly involved than a "general ability" factor. The factor-analytic study of animal behavior by Royce (1966; see Chapter 21), Scott, Fuller, and King (1959), Cattell, Korth, and Brace (1970), Vandenberg (1965), and others shows certainly that maze-learning behavior is not simply intelligence, and indeed leaves us still in part groping for good measures of the general abiilty factor or factors in animals.

As the readers consider the evaluation of the manipulative and social background influences in this and the previous section, in conjunction with the statistical analyses of the previous sections, he may well agree that the missing ingredient in many designs and conclusions has been a sense of perspective. For example, many claims for possibilities of raising I.Q. by exposures to particular environments overlook that there are only twenty-four hours in a day, and that time and interest spent on one direction of g_f investment, say the numerical facet of crystallized intelligence, to some extent means less learning in another direction.

A second dearth of perspective lies in considering our contemporary culture in country X as "culture" in the abstract. As pointed out earlier, the protean forms of g_c are theoretically endless, and though it may be socially rewarding to score higher on the g_c test accepted in our culture, we have no right to claim we are thereby increasing intelligence in a less parochial, more cosmic meaning.

Thirdly, there is a pedagogue's lack of perspective in assuming that the 15% to 20% which comprehensive calculations ultimately assign to environmental effects on intelligence in our culture is due to cognitive exercise. Much of it may well be the consequence of variations in interest and motivation, or to health and physiological accidents. For example, there is evidence (see Chapter 8) of thiamin and other vitamin deficiencies retarding intellectual performances. There is also the above suggestion that most environmental effect occurs in infancy or in the gestation conditions in the mother. (The recent, tragic epidemic of thalidomide babies reminds us what can happen to other aspects of development.) The Churchill (1965) research mentioned above, showing that, although the I.Q. differences of identical twins are small, the heavier twin at birth has more than chance probability of being the more intelligent, suggests some early physiological environmental influence. We have noted also that Harrell, Woodyard, and Gates (1956) found, in a group of 612 urban women (Norfolk, Virginia) whose diet was substandard, that feeding vitamin supplements in later pregnancy produced a slight but significant increase of I.Q. (measured at three to four years, where measurement is admittedly still uncertain in meaning, however) compared with the control group fed a placebo (inert pill). (Results disagreed, however, for Kentucky mountain women, of no higher social status than the Harrell group, where no difference was produced. Attempts to reconcile the two have taken the line that rural food was more nearly adequate.) However, this same wider perspective, now called for, would also dictate that we do not give all attention to the popular preoccupation with what are doubtful effects of existing ranges of nutrition in Western societies, but turn additionally to city carbon-monoxide exposure, possible permanent intelligence scars from certain drugs, arterial degenerations, accidents in medical anaesthesia, partial drownings, and just simple blows on the head.

Doubtless, in the near future, many more decisive studies will be done tracking down the sources of environmental variances in fluid general intelligence (probably 5%) and crystallized intelligence (probably 20% to 25%) to specific causes operating in our culture. Those studies will need to recognize that the nature-nurture percentages may alter for different ages, different cultures, different endemic disease patterns, and so on.

7. ABILITIES AS MOLDED BY RACE AND CULTURE

The notion that there could be significant racial differences in inherited behavioral potential excites panic in some minds. Others are distinctly allergic to it or dogmatically assertive about it, thus falling into two groups as defined above (page 247), namely, racists, on the one hand, who claim that a particular race is in some global sense better than all others, and ignoracists, who maintain that no significant intelligence or other temperamental behavioral difference *can* exist among races. Both, if the underlying value assumptions in their views are examined, share the conviction that any demonstrated difference should lead to hostility and mutual rejection, rather than an attitude of "How interesting and useful!" (For biological variation is so "useful," as Darwin has taught us once and for all, that there could be no evolution without it.) That this paragraph is, in fact, still in 1969, a necessary reminder, is shown by the reactions this year in the *Harvard Review* and elsewhere, to Professor Jensen's conscientiously scholarly statement[12] that there is evidence for slight but real racial differences in average intelligence level!

If there can be real differences of hereditary potential between one individual and another—which is unquestionable—then there *can* be significant hereditary behavioral differences between the mean of one group of, say, twenty people, and another group of twenty people. And, since national populations and races are simply collections of people, genetic differences are *possible* between two populations of any size. Incidentally, it might help if, in these connections, we forget the word racial, and speak of "a people." National populations mostly consist of racial mixtures, except for a few like China which is largely Mongolian, Spain largely Mediterranean, and Sweden largely Nordic. Even in subsections within a people, migration and other forms of selection *could* easily lead to statistically significant differences of average intelligence. For example, though the New Zealand population is virtually entirely British, it has been argued that results indicate a 1 or 2 I.Q. unit higher average than the parent population. (It could be that for certain classes it is an intelligent act to migrate from Britain to New Zealand, and there is in all such migrations a tendency for those of low initiative and high dependency to accumulate in the sample left behind.) Similarly the writer has seen unpublished results clearly suggesting that the intelligence of northern Italians averages better than southern Italians and Sicilians, and that south island Japanese (Honshu) may average better on culture-fair tests than those from the north (Hokkaido).

The detailed substantiation of area differences in fluid intelligence within the same nation would require more research funds than are now available, but, fortunately, the issue is basically a logical, not an empirical, one. If there are any forces at work to cause more intelligent people to move to one zone, and if, as is certain, some degree of inbreeding takes place within zones ("marrying the girl next door"), then genetic differences in average fluid intelligence will arise between the "subraces" thus formed. It is no less reasonable to assume that such differences can arise between sections of our present races, which have been separated and inbred for at least tens of thousands of years (Coon, 1962a, 1962b)—enough to produce easily recognizable physical differences. (As a leading geneticist has said recently (C. Stern, 1967), "It seems unreasonable to conclude that 'because there is [as yet] no evidence of inherent inequalities, the situation could not exist.' ") Every breeder of dogs is aware that the physical differences of dogs (which are, like the races of man, *all within one species*) are accompanied by noticeable differences in ability to learn certain skills. It has been recently shown (Cattell, Korth, and Brace, 1970) that quite

---

[12] The essence of his position was succinctly stated (1969): "If we have a multiple regression equation made up of a host of socio-economic and other environmental variables that predict educationally important criteria, and if the prediction is substantially improved by adding the variable called race to the prediction equation, I maintain that race is by definition a relevant and valid variable."

recent breeds (in terms of human race history) of dogs can be reliably statistically separated on their behavior measurements without the experimenter having seen the physical features of the animals. Incidentally, it is this equal segregation of behavioral and physical characteristics which underlies attempts to investigate mental heredity by relating behavior to particular physical features, and which has already been successful, for example, in relation to blood groups (Cattell, Young, and Hundleby, 1964).

Races were originally defined by anthropologists (Coon, 1962b) by: (1) patterns of physical appearance, (2) evidence of common historical descent, (3) the existence of inbreeding due to common cultural bonds, and (4) demonstrable special gene frequencies (Boyd, 1960; Spuhler and Lindzey, 1967). This "total" approach obviously combines evidence of present entity with explanation of origin. The present writer would be inclined to argue that we should not lean on history, but should recognize that an entity has to be first purely empirically defined by present correlations, like any species or breed in a Linnaean, zoological taxonomy. Nowadays there are objective ways of doing this by "numerical taxonomy" (Sokal and Sneath, 1964), which, in its most developed form, is embodied in a pattern-seeking computer program: "Taxonome" (Cattell and Coulter, 1966). Granted that we deal with races and subraces thus located by physical and physiological description—as complex patterns, not single genes —one can then ask if any behavioral associations are significant. Among those found is a marked difference of Caucasians and others in susceptibility to the Muller-Lyer illusion, auditory sensitivity to tone differences, taste discrimination (PCT nontasters occur much more frequently among Melanesians than Africans), partial color-blindness (much higher, for example, in some peoples of India than in Caucasians or American Indians), and other sensory capacities (Spuhler and Lindzey, 1967). Temperamental associations have also been found, as mentioned above, with blood groups, a particularly interesting one being that of higher premsia (I factor in the 16 P.F. and HSPQ—a form of emotional sensitivity) with the A group (Cattell, Young, and Hundleby, 1964). This finding has recently been supported by one other research and doubted by another, but it fits the definite findings of blood group associations with higher blood pressure and proneness to gastric ulcer (Nance et al.).

Thus, associations of innate behavioral tendencies with racial physical type are not only theoretically possible, but actually do exist. However, no truly absolutely indubitable proof of their existence in the area of intelligence exists as of 1970—there are only probabilities. Research with culture-fair intelligence tests has only just begun, and its first outcome is simply to show that racial groups as culturally diverse as Taiwanese Chinese and American Midwestern Caucasians can have means and sigmas (standard deviations) that approach identity, to a remarkable degree of precision (see pages 455 and 486 in Chapter 14). Incidentally, this offers strong pragmatic reassurance that the IPAT culture-fair intelligence tests are as culture-free as they claim to be, but it leaves a dearth of *positive* evidence on racial differences. Table 10–3, page 281, shows the kinds of difference that have typically been obtained with *traditional* (crystallized general ability) intelligence tests between American Negroes and whites, but although the results are highly consistent in hundreds of researches (Shuey, 1958), the utmost variety of opinion holds on their interpretation. The reader is referred to Spuhler and Lindzey (1967), Shuey (1958), McGurk (1961) and others for the detailed pros and cons. All that is certain is that neither the definite existence nor the non-existence of significant innate racial intelligence differences has been proved.[13]

Provided the question is properly stated, however, one can answer with stated degrees of probability (which is as much as one ever gets in social science), and the probability is that small but real differences of mean fluid general ability exist among various racial groups, subgroups, and peoples (racial mixtures). To get the question "properly stated" however, forces one to long digressions into technically complex methodological conceptions in cross-cultural comparisons. One problem in any evaluation of *crystallized* intelligence is illustrated by Einstein's remark (*Time,* September 29, 1967) that in the Australian Aborigine's society he would "rightly be regarded as an intellectual idiot who could neither track a wallaby nor throw a boomerang." From such problems, created by the changing form of crystallized intelligence, some writers (mainly social anthropologists, but inclusive of some psychologists) take refuge in the obscurantism that they "have abandoned the notion that intelligence can be accurately tested; it is difficult even to define the term." If, instead of creating these verbal quagmires we build our definition on the factorial structure of behavior, we can arrive broadly at two technical means by which cross-cultural or cross-racial comparisons can be made (see Cattell, 1957a):

(1) *The Generic Pattern Method.* Here one first locates the apparently corresponding factor in each culture and, then, by examining pattern similarity coefficients, among a wide collection of patterns comprising several from each culture, sorts them out into distinct types of pattern, each with one representative instance in every culture. If, in fact, the loading patterns by the taxonome program (Cattell and Coulter, 1966) shake down into a number of genera in that way, one is then standing on the same logic as the naturalist in bringing distinct local breeds into one species or the manu-

---

[13] The SPSSI, a political-action-oriented group of the APA, has recently issued a manifesto, in response to Jensen's publication of results on racial intelligence differences, as examined later scientifically at the Illinois Symposium (Cancro, 1971). It reads: "We find that observed racial differences in intelligence can be attributed to environmental differences" and "intervention can have a substantially positive influence" [by context, "on the intelligence scores of backward individuals"] and adds, "we believe that statements specifying the hereditary components of intelligence are unwarranted by the present state of scientific knowledge." Scientific knowledge is always in degrees of probability. The distortion of the best probability estimates by these dogmatic statements may best be judged by the reader himself, in the light of the opening comments to Section 6 above.

facturer who compares the horsepower of various cars despite differences in the curve "form" of the engine performances. Or, to take in man a physical analogy, one is in the position of measuring and comparing stature in different races of men, despite the fact that in some it is composed rather more of leg, in others of trunk, in others of neck length, and so on. So, in some races or cultures, as we shall show below, general intelligence may show a slightly greater weighting in verbal, in others in spatial components, and so on. By this generic identity approach, the answer to the comparison problem is first to discover the corresponding factors, and then to find a cross-cultural group permitting us to bring the scores to comparability on the actual performances that will be weighted differently in estimating the factor scores in each case. The technical issues have been discussed elsewhere (Cattell, 1970a).

(2) *The Cross-Cultural, Common Factor Method.* Here one factors the *mean* scores on each of *many* abilities gathered over each of *many* cultural groups and thus reaches a single "cross-cultural" factor. The problem here is that of finding a sufficient array of variables equally applicable to all cultures. For example, speed of reading in Urdu, judgment in descending Andean mountain paths, and ability to take an Opel car to pieces will not appear among them, but reasoning (solving syllogisms), remembering unknown symbols, and performing a classification on purely perceptual material (as in the IPAT Culture-Fair Test) may well appear.

In short, there *are* ways, technically complex though they may be, whereby intelligence levels can ultimately be compared across cultures. In the case of crystallized general intelligence, the comparison cannot be simple and exact, because the *form* of crystallized intelligence is never the same in two cultures, and problems of weighting arise (see proposed solution in Cattell, 1969b, 1970a). Actually, the same problem really exists, though we seldom face it, in comparing intelligence of any two groups, e.g., different age groups, *within* our own culture. Culture molds the form of its expression, and the two intelligence concepts—in culture 1 and culture 2—are not identical but only belong to the same *class*. So the psychologist comparing the mean scores of say, eleven-year-olds and twelve-year-olds is actually caught up, though he may be unwilling to recognize it, in the "generic" case described above. He is comparing the size of two chairs (of different) shape or the power of two cars (of different make). Some remnant of this weighting problem, to a far lesser degree, remains with respect to different races in the same culture even when fluid ability is measured by culture-fair tests (see Chapter 9 for discussion). Perhaps the primary of spatial thinking is stronger in one and that of verbal reasoning in the other, so that the loading patterns are somewhat different.

That the psychologist should be seriously concerned with facing and solving this methodological problem is brought home by the existence of highly characteristic subgroup differences in the manner of expression of intelligence as shown in the following data (Figure 10–3) from Lesser, Fifer, and Clark (1965).

FIGURE 10–3
Differing Racio-Cultural Primary Ability (Possibly Crystallized Intelligence) Patterns

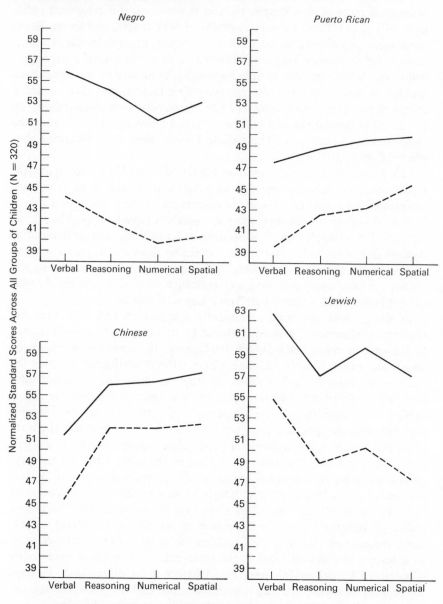

From "Mental abilities of children from different social class and cultural groups," by Lesser, G.S., Fifer, G. and Clark, D. H. Monographs of the Society for Research in Child Development, 1965, 30, #4 (series number 102). © 1965 by the Society for Research in Child Development, Inc.

The important point here is that the primary ability profile remains invariant in each racio-cultural group, despite those social differences we normally associate with class. (Within each class, the racio-cultural difference is significant but does not interact with class level.) Whether these differences are also differences in the loading pattern of the crystallized ability factor could be decided only by factoring across groups; but by almost any weighting system the crystallized general intelligence factor would be significantly higher in each group for upper status, and higher in Chinese and Jewish groups than the others. The U.S. majority profile (not shown) runs horizontally (being the standard) at about 54 for the upper and 46 for the lower class subgroups. Further discussion of these results can be found at their source (cited above) and in Jensen (1968).

So long as we depend on traditional tests of crystallized intelligence, present ignorance of the values needed for solving by the above "generic" method make any attempt to get dependable figures on differences in intelligence level between one people and another virtually impossible. But the path is open now to get meaningful results with culture-fair tests, providing certain precautions are taken in regard to cultural habits in actual test-taking and the correct weighting of subtests. This matter will be looked at again in the sociological context of Chapter 14, but, as Anastasi points out (1958b), any culture-fair test must find some common ground between two cultures. The Chinese, Indian, European, American, Australian, and Japanese use of the IPAT Culture-Fair tests shows that this common overlap ground has been found for many cultures, and the loadings for these subtests set out in Chapter 5 show that they indeed load highly on a common factor.

On the other hand, comparative measures on traditional, crystallized intelligence subtests are scarcely interpretable, because in every case a racial difference is mixed with a cultural difference. Of sheer test results *per se* with different groups (on traditional I.Q. tests) there is no dearth, and the actual scores, when real racial difference is involved, are *usually* significantly different. In the U.S.A. reasonably consistent differences have been obtained by traditional intelligence tests among peoples classified by parental origin and immigrant culture. For example, Jews, Scots, and Scandinavians characteristically hover high in rank. But these are also groups which have traditionally believed strongly in education. With individuals, as shown by the MAVA method, there are ways of teasing the hereditary and environmental components apart, because various combinations of heredity and cultural exposure can be found, but there are not enough combinations of different races with different cultures to get good answers at the group level. A few comparisons have been made of racial Japanese in Japanese and American cultures, of Italian racial mixtures in Florence and Boston, and so on; but the richness of combinations required for MAVA is missing.

As far as the present chapter is concerned, we are in any case not so much concerned with the racial and cultural differences *as such* (for which see Chapter 14) as we are interested in what light they throw on the general manner of interaction of heredity and environment in relation to intelligence. The approach suffices to remind us again that the nature-nurture ratio will vary for most crystallized ability measures appreciably with the culture, the age of the subjects, and the form which school education takes. That does not mean that N_c (the nature-nurture ratio for crystallized intelligence) is a worthless statistic; on the contrary, if we had enough N_c's for different people, ages, etc., a lot of valuable conclusions could be drawn from the comparisons. However, it is the N_f value (as derived from more culture-fair tests and other, high, g_f-saturated measures) that is probably of greater interest, because of the more central and stable concept involved in it. And to sum conclusions on these in a sentence, from the above surveys it seems likely that N_c could vary anywhere from 40% to 80%, whereas (accepting Burt's complex allowances) N_f is typically in the region of 80% to 90%.

Furthermore, the evidence suggests that much of the 10% to 20% of environmental effect in fluid intelligence should be sought in physiological variations not education or "mental training" as such. In particular, there are many deviations from the prescribed hereditary level in the downward direction due to malnutrition (more rare now in advanced countries), head injury, transient anoxia (shortage of oxygen), e.g., in childbirth, and possibly from faulty anesthesia or drugs taken by mothers during the gestation period. The universality of organized medicine in western cultures has done much to reduce the environmental variance due to inadequate physiological conditions and incidental diseases in the developmental period. Probably minor degrees of brain damage were very widespread in earlier historical epochs (even imperial Caesar suffered from epilepsy). One could expect that some average, slight, upward, intergeneration change, analogous to the increase in stature, could occur from such changing circumstances—especially the reduction in incidence of brain injury—between even this and the last generation. The only available results on a large sample with culture-fair tests—those of the present writer from Britain (1950c)—do not, however, show such a change, at least, at 10–11 years of age. Quite possibly, the inverse relation of intelligence to birth rate, which was also demonstrated to exist in that period (see Chapter 14), wiped out, genetically, the potential improvement from environment.

In accordance with the position advocated at the opening of this chapter, we have tried to be alert to the need to dissect prejudice out of scientific evidence on this socially vexed issue of heredity and environment. However, to interject an "action research" note, in clear separation now from the scientific analyses, we would point out that our present understanding of the role of heredity offers prospects of more hopeful social action than was conceivable so long as we thought intelligence depended largely on environment. If we wish to raise the mean I.Q. of our population by, say, 5 points above what it might otherwise be, the environmental path to doing so is individually stressful (through "cultural pressure") and in community terms costly (because all high-pressure, special education is expensive). But if, alternatively, the problem is attacked genetically, by reducing birth rates at lower relative to higher intelligence (and therefore, today, educational) levels of home, a 5-point increase of average I.Q. could conceivably be achieved in a generation. The important, and frequently overlooked, difference of the two approaches is that by the environmental approach the cost and labor are all to do again in every generation, like the labors of the legendary Tantalus, rolling his stone uphill. Whereas, if brought about genetically, the greater part of the uplift would "stay put" for future generations, and education could direct its resources to more positive goals.

CHAPTER ELEVEN

THE TRIADIC THEORY OF ABILITIES DEVELOP- MENTALLY RELATED TO STRUCTURAL LEARNING THEORY

1. GENERAL INTRODUCTION TO THEORY

With the evidence on ability structure, on genetic and developmental trends, on neurological substrate and animal comparisons before us, the time has come to set out more explicitly the integrating *triadic theory*. In so doing we plan also to begin considering the relations to dynamic and temperamental aspects of the total personality.

Although our main conclusions regarding structure rest on factor analysis, they do so with due regard for the properties of the correlational approach. In the first place, one must not forget that the (R-technique) results describe *common* and individual difference factors. In addition there will be purely individual developments of skills arising from idiosyncratic interests and conditionings, the delineation of which escapes anything but a developmental P-technique factoring of the single individual. Secondly, let us note what is well understood by the psychological user of factor analysis—if not by the mathematical statistician—namely, that because a set of patterns crop out as factors at the same order (stratum) it does not follow that they are the same kind of *psychological* entity.

The experienced analyst watches a variety of clues, e.g., the factor stratum level, the changing variances in different age groups, the changing test content, etc., which help check on his psychological hypotheses. In the ability realm of factoring, the reference to such cues—as given in the preceding chapters—must make it evident that we are heading toward a theory which makes *some* general factors the expression of limiting properties of the brain: fluid intelligence as the total associational or combining mass; speed as some physiological pacemaker; and general retrieval efficiency as yet another property of all cognitive action, while other general factors, and narrower primaries, may take shape from other causes.

Beyond the patterns which have their origin as limiting *capacities,* stretching across all kinds of cognitive measures of a certain type, we have recognized a whole class of more local *powers.* These are typically seen in the sensory area factors, some broader, some narrower, such as vizualization, auditory structuring ability, and the putative olfactory and gustatory judgmental factors, as well as general motor and kinesthetic aptitudes. So far, they have been assumed to be partly genetic and partly environmental in origin. That is to say, they are assumed to correspond to sensory and motor brain areas than can be cytogenetically recognized by the neurologist, but their functional power levels depend not only on the individual's endowment in that brain zone but also on his enriching experience in the given area. To contrast with the general capacities, which have been symbolized by g's, these *"provincial"* powers are symbolized by p's.

Finally, there is a third class of unitary structure, visible in correlations and other ways, corresponding largely to what have so far been called the primary abilities, but which, for reasons to be developed, we shall designate *agencies* or a's. They take their shape largely from cultural and general learning, and are the agencies through which fluid intelligence and the powers express themselves. To this total formulation of a model, whereby any actual instance of cognitive behavior is reduced (as far as abilities are concerned) to the joint action of *three* distinct types of ability, we shall give the name *triadic theory* (from the derivation "three in one"). The triadic theory is thus a statement both about the specific nature of each of three kinds of components, and about their tendency commonly to combine in joint action in any actually observed behavior.

The first two components might be said to have the common property of being "powers," in the sense that they fix limits to the developments that can go on through environmental experience or learning. As our expansion of the theory will indicate, they do not fix sudden and absolute limits, but appear as terms in a functional equation which fix an asymptote to what learning and motivation can do. Within these powers, however, we can make a basic distinction between the *general capacities* on the one hand, and the *local* organizations or *provincials* (as we shall call them for short), on the other.

The general *capacities* are limits to brain action as a whole, and appear as general factors across all cognitive performances. Apart from this character of being general parameters to the total neural performance, however, these capacities have little else in common. One—g_f, defining the action of the total neural combining mass—is, in its neural substrate, literally the size of an anatomical brain structure and might be viewed therefore as only a glorified "provincial" structure. Others, like the general speed factor, g_s, and the general retrieval (fluency) efficiency factor, might be chemical properties of the brain as a whole, i.e., not mainly describable as physical structure. Further, we must recognize that there can exist general parameters of brain action that are not cognitive but temperamental. As will become evident below, the line between these and cognitive parameters requires methodological sophistication for its drawing, but it can be drawn, and what we are dealing with in the triadic theory is the general factors strictly in the *cognitive* realm, leaving temperament and personality to other studies.

The term local organization (or provincial) is necessary for the second class of powers because "sensory organization" (which some might prefer) actually would not do. These powers include behavioral factors corresponding both to sensory organizations—visual, auditory, kinesthetic, etc. —and to motor areas. Although, as we have seen in our comparative studies, there are substantial differences between species in the development of these provincial powers, it would seem that among humans the differences are not marked, and, factor-analytically, since only two clear cases have been found (visual and motor), it *may* turn out that their variance contribution is, in general, less than the other two classes in the triadic theory. (However, as Chapter 14 indicates, there may be substantial racial differences in the pattern of levels on these provincials and the primaries.)

At a first level of statement, and as a basis for development, the triadic theory is summarized in Table 11–1. It states initially that any given ability performance is a function (*as far as cognitive roots only are concerned*) of representatives of three classes of factors: two classes of powers—capacities and provincial powers—and one class of acquired structures designated *agencies,* for reasons to be given shortly.

TABLE 11–1
The Basic Types of Ability Components in the Triadic Theory

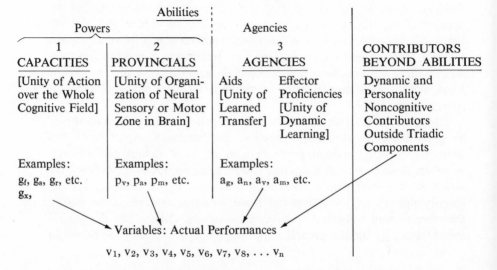

Abilities			
Powers		Agencies	
1	2	3	CONTRIBUTORS BEYOND ABILITIES
CAPACITIES	PROVINCIALS	AGENCIES	
[Unity of Action over the Whole Cognitive Field]	[Unity of Organization of Neural Sensory or Motor Zone in Brain]	Aids Effector [Unity of Proficiencies Learned [Unity of Transfer] Dynamic Learning]	Dynamic and Personality Noncognitive Contributors Outside Triadic Components
Examples:	Examples:	Examples:	
g_f, g_s, g_r, etc. g_x,	p_v, p_a, p_m, etc.	a_g, a_n, a_v, a_m, etc.	

Variables: Actual Performances

v_1, v_2, v_3, v_4, v_5, v_6, v_7, v_8, $\ldots$ v_n

2. CLARIFICATION OF POWER-AGENCY AND NATURE-NURTURE ASPECTS OF THE TRIADIC THEORY

The triadic theory—like any theory—is an abstraction, integrating a diversity of concrete findings. With such a new theory it is often important to guard against degenerative confusions with older, roughly similar abstractions, and this we shall do forthwith. In the first place, it is not simply and solely a statement about factor strata levels in a hierarchy. Most of the primary abilities, it is true, are agencies (class 3) and most of the statistically general higher-order factors are capacities, but this is not the primary and essential basis of distinction, and consequently there are exceptions. "General factor" is, in any case, only a mathematician's term, applicable to a particular matrix operation, not to scientific concepts, and we have seen that what we really have in psychology, *when domains of variables are properly sampled,* are factors of varying breadth. For historical continuity, the symbol g is retained for the *broadest* factors, but (a) no one of the "general factors" yet known—g_f, g_s, g_r, for instance—loads significantly *all* cognitive performances, and (b) some *equally* general factors found factor-analytically are not listed with the above cognitive capacities because they belong to temperament or motivation. Conversely, though crystallized general ability has, up to this point, for the sake of continuity with Spearman's work, been labelled g_c, it is becoming clear that its real character is that of an agency. Consequently, it should be symbolized correctly and logically by an "a," and from this point on we are going to ask the reader to refer to it by the symbol a_g—a notation stating that it is a *general* agency. It occupies in fact a unique position; that of an agency simulating the pattern of a general limiting capacity.

Secondly, the division is not one of hereditary versus environmental origins, though g_f is largely hereditary, while the particular patterns of the agencies are formed by learning and grow as segregated unities on that basis. In this respect the real distinction of powers and agencies is that the initial *growing-point*—the center which determines the nature of the organization—is, on the one hand, genetic and, on the other, the stimulus of a cultural mold. But the individual's level on any and all of these is in part a contribution from heredity and in part from environment. Probably, however, the environmental influence on the *capacities* is minimally through learning, and largely indirect, through physiological environment and events. A *provincial power,* such as visualization, presumably gets both its shape and its level initially from the genetic development specifically of the visual brain areas. But, as we know from the work of Lashley, Hebb, Klüver, Weaver, and others on visual deprivation in the early life of chimpanzees, lack of visual experience at a vital growth period can impair functioning seriously. Probably, in the *normal* human range, differences in sensory experience opportunities are trivial and rare, so that the differences we measure in p_v will turn out to be largely those in neural endowment, granted a normal quota of stimulation for all. But other kinds of environmental influence, e.g., such as produce local brain damage or inefficiency, might well enter into our measures of the "provincials." Similarly in fluid intelligence—a capacity—an atherosclerosis-producing environment might alter performance as a whole.

In this connection, we must distinguish the final *structural form* of an ability—as a unitary correlation cluster or surface trait—from the possible diverse origins of this covariance. For more than one source could produce the observed structures of covariance. Any lower-strata factor, such as a primary ability, might have its form, as a primary factor, entirely bestowed and determined by a type of learning experience. And, as far as one would know if he stopped at the first-order factor analysis, it might have no origin other than this. Only when one gets to a higher order of analysis is it revealed that part of the variance in these primaries is due to a general factor, g_f, which (as it turns out in this case) is largely genetic. Other research might show other parts of the primary factor variance to come from the provincials. The actual, observed variance—that in terms of which we determine an individual's level—is thus the end result of an interaction of *learning* influences with largely *genetic* powers; but the form of the primaries (not their intercorrelations) is probably—as will be argued in more detail later—fully an expression of the cultural environmental mold itself.[1] Incidentally, if any factor primaries should turn out *not* to be environmentally determined as to form, but to correspond to some as yet unlocated genetic-neural source, such abilities would have to be classified among the nongeneral *powers*, i.e., the p's or provincials.

The general implication of the term "agency" will perhaps have become familiar to the reader from the chapters leading up to the present theoretical integration. It is to the effect that the unity shown factorially to exist in any primary, such as verbal, numerical, mechanical, or deductive reasoning ability, arises from the repeated use of fluid ability in learning in a particular kind of cultural-environmental situation. The situation is a culturally rewarded one, e.g., the child's increasing grasp of verbal communication is socially rewarded to different degrees for different children, and the skill concerned is therefore an "agency" whereby the individual strives toward his ergic rewards. The essential conception includes (1) that the primary ability is an *instrument* or systematized *means-to-ends* in

---

[1] Parenthetically, the position here is that expressed in the concept of "genothreptics" in the recent book by Cattell and Nesselroade (1971). Genothreptics deals with the general *principles of interaction of heredity and environment*. In this connection we must beware of equating environmental with "cultural." Cultural anthropologists are prone to hypnotize students into the habit of doing this; but physical, climatic, and physiological experiences can be—in variance terms and factor structure patterns— almost as important as human culture itself. (Indeed, it would be helpful to think of such environmental-experiential categories as (1) physical, (2) physiological, (3) climatic, (4) socio-cultural—splitting the last into (a) institutional, e.g., formal education, and (b) idiosyncratic or biographical experience.)

civilized life; (a good grasp of number operations, for example, can become an agency for the attainment of a diverse variety of ergic life goals; the term thus helps to place these abilities in perspective in relation to the culture and the individual motivation system.) (2) that general fluid ability is utilized in constructing the instruments—and therefore comes out as a second-order factor among them; and (3) that the unitary character of the system of skilled judgments and habits arises from a unitariness in the learning experience which remains to be more fully investigated and explained here.

The triadic theory must, of course, at this stage of incompleteness of findings, leave certain gaps—such as that just pointed out with respect to possibly unknown p's lying back of some already structurally recognized primaries. Furthermore, it must be recognized that it is a *gross* classification, admitting finer subdivisions as more aspects of abilities become firmly established. For example, in the capacities, a further subdivision is evident (and might prove useful) between general brain parameters that arise from *neural structure,* such as g_f, and those arising from *physiological efficiencies,* which might perhaps include g_s and g_r. And an important subdivision will become evident also among agencies, as we discuss in Sections 5 and 6 below, their properties and origins.

3. CLOSER CONSIDERATION OF PROPERTIES OF THE SENSORY AND MOTOR ORGANIZATIONS —THE p'S

From this point we aim to look more closely at the special characters of the three main classes of abilities in the triadic theory. However, since the capacities have already received attention along these lines, they will occupy no single section here but will receive a review incidentally, as they come to be considered in the section on interaction of all three components (Section 4 below).

The abilities we are symbolizing now as p's, and which are defined theoretically as deriving from local neural organizations (and their associated banks of experience) rather than from general brain action parameters have been much neglected in ability research. Factor-analytically, for example, they have been thrown into anything from first to third-strata positions, as a result of distortions arising from inadequacies in behavior sampling and technical failures in higher-order factor analyses. Only recently (as Chapters 5 and 6 show) have the technical difficulties been resolved enough to lead to replication of three factor strata in each of the number of independent experiments. In these studies the abilities, now theorized to be p's here, cropped up with some ambiguousness of rank, at least as to their belonging to the primary or the secondary strata, but this ambiguity is not serious because first or second order is always dependent on choice of variables. With a sufficiently broad and well-chosen set of ability performances, as discussed in the next paragraph, one would expect the p's to appear at a higher order than the agencies—a's—because facility on any one of the provincials could contribute to the acquisition of many a's.

If we take as a typical "provincial" some sensory instance, such as vizualization, p_v, it must first be made clear that we are *not* concerned with any sensory acuity as such. It is the surrounding association area, rather than the small area concerned with sensory sensitivity as such, which by hypothesis, accounts for the unitary factor. However, in total sensory failure, as in the blind or deaf, one might anticipate some resulting association area impoverishment too, so that some correlation with sheer sensory effectiveness might exist. Nevertheless, the variables, which theory would expect to be loaded by a p factor of, say, visualization, would be perceptions of more complex relations, e.g., those involved in perceiving differences of shape and color (Pickford, 1965), the comparison of input with memorized visual forms, the manipulation and combination of visual forms as in art, capacity to judge areas, completion of a jigsaw puzzle, judgment of visual similarity, judging sizes and distances, handling maps, preference for geometrical rather than algebraic solutions, ability to manipulate cubes, etc., to obtain solutions to re-arrangements by visual imagination, ability to complete pictures, e.g., the gestalt completion test, and so on. In fact all that goes with handling complexities of relationship purely in the visual field, and presumably, also that part of memorizing and retrieval which is contributed from the visual field.

Similarly, in the auditory area we would theorize that the p_a factor will have some loading and contribution to recognizing auditory patterns, manipulating auditory patterns (but not the motor aspect), completing half-heard words, judging tones, learning to respond more quickly to auditory cues, and so on. Incidentally, there was a phase in education, around the turn of the century when, in connection at least with imagery, it was proposed to find out to which "type" each child belonged, and to teach him through that avenue. We now realize the impracticableness of this design; there are no true types, i.e., discrete, species types, as found by Taxonome (Cattell and Coulter, 1966). Besides, the two other triadic components, g's and a's, would be just as important. Nevertheless, the old observations of sensory capacities being factors that stand at different levels for different people is being substantiated and made more precise in meaning by the conception and measurement of the provincial powers, or p's.

Actually, the evidence for the existence and nature of the p's resides not only in the factor-analytic structuring of behavior as such, but also in the cytological evidence from neurology, and in the phylogenetic evidence. That enormous differences exist among species and general phylogenetically, e.g., the difference of man and dog in olfactory "intelligence," is widely recognized. Recently Roger Williams has called attention to relatively large individual differences among men in the size of areas of the brain cytologically recognizable as connected with particular sensory and motor organizations (see Sarkisov, 1966). It is true that at the moment we have clean cut and checked factor-analytic evidence mainly for visualization, p_v, plus some fragmentary sketches of an auditory factor, e.g., in Seashore's musical aptitude research, plus uneven support for a broad kinesthetic-motor factor (related to cerebellar efficiency?), and perhaps for a tactile-kinesthetic factor. But researches have now been designed by Horn and the present writer to explore the boundaries of olfactory, tactile, and even gustatory organizations.

In these perceptual instances of provincial organizations, the central feature is first the sheer ability to interpret sensory stimulation including, probably, even the simpler relations studied, for example, in psychophysical laws. Thus, in the visual organization, loadings of the factor will perhaps be found to include perception of changes in light intensity, resolution of color (when the retinal apparatus is adequate), distance evaluation and perspective recognition, etc. In the auditory field one should similarly investigate the possible inclusion of skills in appreciating, first, those psycho-physical relations of pitch, loudness, etc., which Stevens (1960), Karlin (1942), and others have investigated, and which are included in the components of musical aptitude as measured by Seashore (1947).

At some point in the development of such a "provincial organization," the operations which it performs in the given sensory area must begin to involve reference to data in other provincial (sensory and motor) areas, as a result of the mode of organization of the physical world itself. For example, the full meaning of perspective involves cross reference to the kinesthetic organization's (p_k) experiences begun as soon as the child starts to crawl.

One must consider also the relations of the p powers to the agencies—the a's. It has been suggested that the cultural learning which shapes an agency will be determined in rate of growth partly by the level of g_f, which determines rate of growth in any skills depending on perception of relations. However, a real but lesser loading on the agencies may be expected from the p's, inasmuch as resources of skill within a specific sensory or motor zone are involved in the cultural activity. Thus verbal learning, issuing in V factor (a_v in our symbols), requires both auditory and visual perception of words, and is presumably aided also by awareness of words in the motor experience of uttering them. Similarly, the spatial ability factor, a_s, is presumably the product of a synthesis of experience from the visual, tactile, and kinesthetic organizations. As second-stratum factor analyses are more broadly designed and accurately checked, the emerging loading patterns of visualization, p_v, tactual aptitude, p_t, kinesthetic and motor ability, p_k, etc., at different ages and in different cultures, will tell us more about the roles of the p's in relation to the a's generally.

As the level of complexity of the relations handled in any particular sensory or motor unitary organization increases, one would expect that the operations would begin to involve not only other sensory organizations, but also the fluid general ability. In fact, we know that the loadings of the latter begin to go up as, for example, the visualization tests in p_v measures get more complex. The subtle question now arises whether the higher level of abstraction indicating the intrusion of g_f is possible *without* this simultaneous broadening to other sensory organizations. In other words, can it occur within the provincial development itself, or is the invoking of g_f, for higher-level abstractions essentially the same as cross reference directly to a broader sensory basis, presented through other sensory areas? The idea of number as rank, or the question of whether the product of 3×4 is the same as that of 2×6 can be answered with seemingly quite adequate logic in a derivation either from visual dots alone or from auditory notes alone. Yet experientially it may be that the realization that the rule holds *both* in auditory and visual fields in some way enriches or, at the least, supports its use in either domain separately.

Logicians and philosophers sometimes verge on intellectual arrogance, or, at least, lack of imagination, when they insist dogmatically that the hard coinage of their symbolic logic represents universal, self-evident truth. The scientist and the naturalist can *conceive* that $3 \times 4 = 2 \times 6$ might be true in visual data but not hold in the phenomena of sound—at least in a world differently constructed from our own. What one seeks to illustrate by such conjecture is, of course, the notion that what the human mind chooses to call immutable laws of logic are, in the last resort, distillations of experience (including phylogenetic experience embedded in the genes). It insinuates the suspicion that deductive reasoning is, by one remove, just as dependent on world structure as is inductive reasoning.

An important thesis at this point is that a general bias is accidentally introduced into most discussions of deductive reasoning, and the handling of relations among relations (the g_f hierarchy), by the convenient habit (for illustration) of stripping relations down to mathematical form or to logical syllogisms into which no haze of statistical probability enters. By contrast, most of our deductive reasoning in everyday life deals with propositions which are at once intrinsically richer and beset with probability questions. If my girlfriend is passionately fond of Chopin and I have music only of Bach, would I be wise to play Bach when my rival is also present, who is very critical of Bach?

Here we encounter again the difference discussed on the last chapter between the computer and the human brain, when we wonder if the computer's facility with stripped logic and mathematical propositions can be called intelligence. The issue is important for the construction of intelligence tests, since, if the highest forms of relational complexity can in fact be found and set up in the domain of a single sense, e.g., if g_f enters into the highest visual complexities without bringing in any cross-sensory reference to the p's of hearing or touch, we can command the convenience of testing g_f through just one sensory domain.

In the discussions of the last chapter we argued that inductive reasoning, and the relations based on a broader base of experience, are in the last resort somehow more subtle and complex than the abstractions of, for example, number. Although the difference might be trivial, we should, on this basis, argue that $3 \times 4 = 2 \times 6$ has gained in the abstractness of the truth grasped and the behavioral efficiency of its application if it is based both on visual and auditory organizational experience. But one can imagine other instances where the abstract idea is rather threadbare, or even downright impossible without simultaneous use of experience across all sensory organizations. For example, when Shakespeare says to his beloved "Shall I compare thee to a summer's day? Thou art more lovely and more temperate," the whole gamut of sensory experience and the learning of common sequences in social and physical climates are necessary to grasp the relationship.

However, the verdict of experiment seems to be that, in all ranges of human ability yet tested, we can get the necessary degree of complexity for testing the highest levels of g_f within one sensory area alone (as in the Culture-Fair Intelligence Test's use of the visual field).[2] That the measure may be weighted and biased by the adding in of one particular p, or a, rather than a balanced assortment of them, is a different matter from any failure in measuring g_f itself.

The above problem, of the degree of inescapable interdependence among the provinces in the development of each toward perception and handling of relations higher in its hierarchy, has to be raised here, because it has implications for the position of g_f in the structure of abilities. But further pursuit of the idea must be deferred to Chapter 13, where, in the context of creativity, some last enrichments and refinements may need to be added to the intelligence concept and its definition. Yet the triadic theory poses new questions and is likely to stimulate much beyond the meager experimental work now available in precise exploration of the higher strata.

Meanwhile, the most likely conclusion is that, as perceptual relationships become increasingly complex, even in the domain of any one sensory organization unit they are likely to be increasingly loaded by, i.e., to involve, some g_f or even some other sensory, or p organization. The question is whether this will show purely as a g_f loading—on the ground that any

---

[2] In discussing brain action and computer action in Chapter 9, it was pointed out that the barest logical symbolism, as in Boolean algebra, can be programmed very simply to generate decisions in deductive reasoning that would normally require, in humans, considerable intelligence and considerable brain mass. Much of the complexity of relations in such logic could be expressed in any one sensory form, e.g., visual diagrams, auditory patterns, or even tactile signals, without losing any of its challenge as an intelligence demand. However, we concluded (a) that the human mind usually does not handle its deductive reasoning in this way, and (b) that when it does, it has, in any case, first had to reach the level of insightful understanding of the propositions and their relationships. There is, in general, no one outside to "program" the individual of low intelligence to learn the propositions of Euclid by rote, but there is little hope that the rules will be followed as reliably as by the machine. There is also a possibility that the human mind has learned that it cannot proceed safely with the abstracted experience of a particular province of experience, so that it checks across domains and gives confidence to its most abstract rules only when there is redundancy across several provinces.

interaction between sensory areas is g_f—or whether one will find a more complex visual performance to show some loading also on, say, an auditory power. Certainly complex perceptions purely in the visual area get loadings on g_f as well as p_v, but there are suggestions of instances of their getting loadings also on p_m (motor ability).

Although "sensory" has been used at times for what we believe are better called provincial, p abilities, motor ability always has been tacitly but unquestionably included in the class (despite the usual "opposition" of sensory and motor in the stimulus-response habit of thought). For it stands in the same position factor-analytically, and its substrate can be pointed to in a cytologically recognizable area of the brain. Actually there is factor-analytic evidence for *two* motor ability factors—corresponding to the voluntary motor area and to the cerebellum. Their factorial delineation is admittedly not yet as clear as it should be. But neurologically the parallelism in terms of definiteness of localization is high, and the additional clear evidence phylogenetically of the independent development of the cerebellum points to such an expectation. Inasmuch as most voluntary motor dexterity involves not only the parietal motor area but also the "gyroscopic" functions of the cerebellum, one would expect a "cooperative factor" relation to appear, involving factors of goodness of voluntary motor skill and goodness of cerebellar coordination. (A test such as walking a chalk line would involve both.) And insofar as most motor judgment involves perceptual judgment (but not vice versa), a special factor-analytic relation (the motor factor being cooperative with all sensory factors) would be expected there too. A good perceptual understanding of anatomy may aid a wrestler, but some leading academic anatomists would almost certainly have made poor wrestlers!

This complexity may explain partly why many (admittedly rather superficially designed) motor ability factorial experiments have been inconclusive or contradictory. But by hypothesis one would expect that an individual with a highly developed voluntary motor area, compared with a person underdeveloped or damaged in that area, would show a generally higher level of performance in games of physical skill and motor judgment, quite apart from the level of excellence of the perceptual systems involved. And one would expect also a p factor corresponding to the level of cerebellar function (especially in cross-species factorizations).

Because of their differing roles in stimulus-response behavior, one would expect some differences of the sensory p factors on the one hand and the motor p factors on the other, justifying two subdivisions within the p's. But in relation to the general triadic structure, they should also have much in common, notably (a) a high genetic determination, inasmuch as neurological growth of particular brain areas may be considered constitutionally idiosyncratic to the individual or species; (b) nevertheless, some appreciable environmental susceptibility too, through the effects of early lack of exercise or later damage, e.g., by poor local circulation or differences in the working concepts acquired and stored in that area; (c) a position in the factor strata generally of second-stratum influences, the loadings showing effects of each across several agencies, and (d) a common susceptibility to direct influence by the general capacity parameters, e.g., speed, g_s, and g_f could spread their influences across performances in both kinds of provincial power.

Among the riddles awaiting solution in this p area is that concerning the position of "power to commit to memory." Is it a p, i.e., a cerebral regional influence, or a general, g, parameter? It is at first somewhat surprising that Thurstone found his M to be a primary, since one would expect that the capacity to commit figures to short distance memory by rote (in relatively meaningless material) would be a power that would influence the level of acquisition of many primary abilities (such as verbal, numerical, spatial, etc.), and thus stand at a higher factor stratum in regard to the primary stratum. That it appeared directly at the first-stratum level may be due to "committing to memory" in such experimental situations as he and many other experimenters have used being a relatively artificial performance in the test situation. It touches no main motivation and, in terms of the nature of everyday live performance (except in games and many social adjustments), it is atypical by reason of its deliberate nature and short term goal. For the bulk of our learning, e.g., in verbal, numerical, and mechanical primaries, proceeds in more casual, less deliberate, and less intense fashion, as R. L. Thorndike (1949), for one, has pointed out.

Indeed, the whole group of phenomena which, in one sense or another, we call memorizing has so far been attacked far too narrowly by the factor analysts. Its study, in fact, has "fallen between two schools." On the one hand stands the largely bivariate (but phenomenologically broad) attack of the learning theorists, and on the other the multivariate, but "test-oriented" approach of the last generation's factor analysts. Some questions that need to be asked are: "Are powers of recall, of retention, and of committing to memory dependent in part or whole on different factors?", "How much variance remains to be assigned to cognitive capacities, i.e., to 'abilities,' when differences in learning and forgetting due to motivation and interest variations have been partialled out?", "How far does g_f, presumably operating in the immediate reverberation and sorting phase of committing to memory, determine amount retained?" Consistent and appreciable correlations found between intelligence and most memorizing performances, suggest it acts rather powerfully.

Further one may ask: "If there are distinct retention and retrieval ability factors, are they general to all material or do they—alternatively or in addition—show 'area' factors corresponding to the provincial powers, e.g., good auditory memory, good motor memory?" Among the more sophisticated attacks on the problem are those of Kelley (1954) and others cited earlier which suggest a possible *general rote* memorizing capacity, as contrasted with power to commit meaningful, "intelligent" material to memory (but this does not preclude capacities with provincial boundaries in addition). Indeed, the small fraction of variance accounted for by the *general* rote and meaningful factors would not preclude quite substantial contributions from the p's and even the a's in addition. These factor studies also agree with the general learning experiment conclusions that distinct factors exist for short distance "immediate" and long distance "stored" memorizing. But the main questions above remain unanswered. One guesses that the memory parameters in general will come out as broad, common factors—g's like the g_r, we believe, can already be shown for retrieval—but it is also probable that fainter provincial factors will be found in the memory field, coming as a "bonus" from the amount of material already stored and structured in each. Research attention to date has concentrated so much on the cultural agency "primaries" or the "general factors," that we need more experimental data on the "provincial powers" before any more far-reaching generalizations on their nature become profitable.

4. THE RELATIONS OF GENERAL CAPACITIES (g'S), PROVINCIAL ORGANIZATIONS (p'S), AND AGENCIES (a'S)

Although the nature and growth of primary abilities and other structures which we have called agencies remains to be discussed below in more detail, it is evident from what has already emerged about their general character that the triadic theory commits us to a developmental relationship of g's, p's, and a's essentially as schematized in Figure 11–1.

The agencies must be regarded as developing in the areas in which they do develop through some convergence of experience and interest yet to be analyzed. For they so plainly represent—at least in several cases—special areas of culturally demarcated activity, such as numerical learning, mechanical learning, interest in words, etc. Any ability is, of course, partly a matter of such learning-motivation aggregates and partly of some innate potential, and in this case we may assume that most of the latter comes from the general relation-perceiving capacity of g_f.

In Table 11–1 the arrows indicate the direction of contribution *in growth*. The p's are given partly as independent constitutional powers, partly as stimulated by general capacity (arrow from above), and partly as ripened by general sensory experience (arrow from right). (The p's, among most persons enjoying normal experience, i.e., other than blind or deaf persons, would presumably, as discussed above, show lesser variations in their contributions than the g's and the motivational experiences.) The main direction of action of the g's and p's is upon the a's, which are also the products of unitary (molded) learning experiences—shown as d's (dynamic influences) on the right. All g's and all p's would normally operate upon any one a, though to avoid confusion not all arrows are drawn in Figure 11–1. Nevertheless they would differ in variance contribution. For example, verbal ability, a_v, is shaped more by g_f and g_m than

FIGURE 11–1
Developmental Implications of the Triadic Theory, Worked
Out Consistently with the Reticular Factor Model

The arrows indicate directions of influence and contribution to growth. Thus verbal ability, a_v, receives contributions from the capacities, g's, the powers, p's, a motivational factor, d_v, and a reinforcement in an experience area, t_v. To avoid complication of the diagram not all individual but only class connections are made.

The semi-circular arrows below the agencies indicate their self-development capacities as "aids."

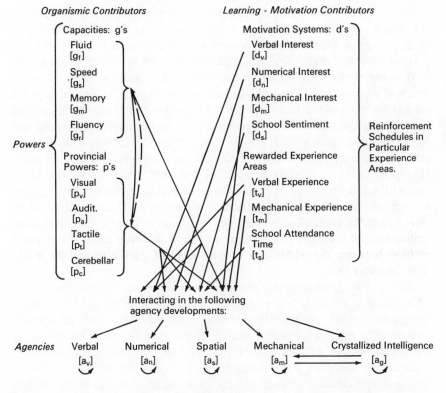

is, say, drawing ability, and it draws less upon p_m (motor ability) and more upon p_a (auditory) than does drawing ability.

The question of developmental interaction among the g's and the p's has been left partly unanswered in Figure 11–1, by putting only a broken "feedback arrow" from the p's to the g's. But earlier, above, we have speculated that some degree of contribution *would* occur in both directions, a higher g_f, for example, favoring higher relational developments in a sensory organization deposit, and high hierarchical relations in one sense domain contributing, possibly via g_f, to higher relational abstractions in another (see Figure 11–2, page 328). However, this remains speculative, because no factorial evidence of such interdependence is yet clear.[3]

Functionally, in performance at a given moment, in a wide range of variables like v_1 to v_n, we might expect as in Table 11–1 that all three classes of abilities might operate on any one performance. For example, handling a numerical classification test presented in Newland's (1962) tactile form (for the blind) might involve g_f for the more difficult relation eduction, p_t as a tactile organization development, and a_n as numerical ability. However, due to the developmental structuring shown in Figure 11–1, which would enter into the correlational observations in an experiment such as would yield the connections in Table 11–1, the relations in the latter would not be necessarily directly obtainable in that form.

Reverting to the possible developmental interactions of the g's and the p's, which we have toyed with speculatively in one or two places above, we must recognize that any more systematic unraveling thereof is going to involve some stiff methodological problems. Statistically and experimentally it is going to be hard to distinguish between a growth of g_f by some inherent process, on the one hand, and as a function of the interactions set up among the various p's, in virture of their level of dvelopment, on the other. Does the volume of telephone traffic and connections among five busy cities arise purely from the size and activity of each and all of those cities as separately developed? If the inter-city connections are naturally simply adjustive to existing demand, it will; but alternatively, the intercity wire traffic might be fixed and controlled quite independently by government decree or arise from stimulation *among* the cities, additional to any activity in each of the cities *per se*. That is to say, in correlations among several such five-city systems we might find that there is not much relation between the within-city activity level of each city and its traffic with the other four.

In the formal nature of this problem the reader familiar with the history of intelligence research will recognize a relatedness to the debate between Spearman and Sir Godfrey Thomson over the ways in which Spearman's undoubtedly existent statistical general factor could arise. The answer in the present instance is not to be reached by any one kind of multivariate experiment—we must have developmental experiment as well as cross-sectional, individual difference analysis. Nevertheless, as far as the present simple structure evidence is concerned, it would seem that the develop-

---

[3] In more detail, the first mode of action implies that the level of a sensory or motor p reflects not only its genetic endowment level, neurally, but also its development of stored "equipment." Insofar as the latter operates, the general capacities will have been instrumental in that development. For example, g_f presumably will help determine what complexities can be learned and stored even in a purely visual organization, and the general memorizing and retrieval powers also will have done something to define the limits of acquisition in the visual organization.

ment of the general factor is something distinct from the development of the provincial organizations—the p's. The size and activity level of the combining mass could be in part a function of the inherent developmental level of the p's, but we shall tentatively conclude that the g_f mass has a constitutionally set development of its own—a maturation course presumably set by an independent set of genes.

Although space here precludes pursuing the full implications of this aspect of the triadic theory in terms of research operations, the issue of this relation of g_f to the organizations is a very important one for the definition of intelligence—especially across species and across breeds and races. Species and races may differ appreciably in the balance of their largely genetically controlled p's—for example, the dog's olfactory world is far larger than man's, and one suspects that visualization plays a larger part in some human races than others. Certainly Figure 10-3 (page 292) shows that racio-cultural differences of pattern arise in the profile of primary abilities, which include both p's and a's. If g_f were simply a weighted sum of the total p developments, it would have a different meaning for different biological groups, and cross-cultural comparisons would have to face the complications on page 158 above.

Incidentally, the two-way action of g_f and the p's sketched above (Figure 11-1), supposing a definite action as shown by the dotted arrow, must be investigated seriously. At the factor-analytic level of investigation, this means that we go beyond the regular *stratum model* which, along with most current factor analytic writings, for the sake of simplicity we have usually followed. It accepts the possibility of what the present writer (1965c) has defined as the *reticular model,* which recognizes that the influences pursued in factor analysis may operate bi-directionally and circularly. Unravelling such connections from correlations presents a stiffer problem to the factor analyst's probe, but probably can be achieved (Cattell, 1965c).

To grasp more fully what is implied by such models as in Table 11-1 and Figure 11-1, it is necessary to graduate to a more explicit regard for the problems of using factor analysis, on the one hand, for unearthing historical, *developmental* connections, and, on the other, for describing immediately *functional* connections. Regard for this distinction has already been important to unravelling the higher-stratum factor relations of g_f and g_c (now a_g). There we accepted the appearance of a g_f pattern at two successive levels as meaning that the higher level represented the action of an earlier g_f, evident in present data as the result of an historically earlier formative process. The factor structure (Table 6-4, page 116) is interpreted to mean that g_f operates developmentally and historically in fixing the level and pattern of both g_c (a_g) and the present g_f. It was also brought out there that at any given moment the *present* g_f and g_c (a_g) operate *functionally* "on a par" in determining the level of some particular performance. This functional state of affairs is presented in Table 11-1.

The full complexity of the reticular model necessary for the developmental picture, in contrast to the functional model in Table 11–1, is perhaps not fully given in Figure 11–1 (page 309). Token connections have had to be substituted for a full set of arrows, and some possibilities have been omitted. It is shown, however, by the broken arrow line, that the neurological and functional level of p_1 (and other p's similarly) contributes to the building of a hierarchy of relation-educing powers into g_f. This would imply that, both in individual experience and in phylogenetic development, the level of growth of each sensory power exercises some limiting influence on the growth of the general relation-educing powers, despite the latter also having its inherent growth determiners. If so, a positive correlation between g_f and p levels should show up both in within-species and in interspecies comparisions. However, just what loading patterns, as just what strata of factor analysis (begun from various positions) should emerge if this reticular model is to be supported, is a complex matter needing discussions beyond the present volume.

The above, somewhat extensive discussion of the hypothesized g-p relations—even though left in the form of tentative alternative hypotheses—is necessary before proceeding to the next section's concern with the rise of the primary *agencies*. The theory growing out of the survey of evidence in the earlier chapters above has been that at least some of the primaries offer persuasive evidence of being acquired structures—the end result of a particular kind of learning process. This does not mean, however, that their nature-nurture ratios would not show appreciable "nature." For it has been suggested that environment provides their form but not all the "stuff"—the fluid intelligence capacity to acquire substance—out of which they arise. Indeed, in Chapter 10 this notion was taken to the level of a specific hypothesis; that (except for possible small genetic specifics in these primaries themselves) most of the *genetic* variance will come from the powers—the g's and p's—that are involved and woven into the learning processes and structures. For example, verbal ability will get some genetic component from the role of (genetic) fluid intelligence in determining progress in grasp of verbal complexities, but it will also receive some contribution from the visualization provincial, p_v, inasmuch as learning to read and spell is aided by visual ability, and from the auditory p_a, insofar as understanding the spoken word hinges on accurate perception of auditory patterns.

Our main concern in explaining the agencies, therefore, concentrates on the origins of the environmental, learning causes of their unitary form. To orient ourselves to later conclusions, let us state that the theory finally adopted is that this unity is *either* one of *cognitive consistency or of common learning experience* (common motivation and repeated common reinforcement). Each of the next two sections will handle the mechanisms in one of these and attempt to show how, together, they are sufficient to account for the phenomena observed.

5. AGENCIES: (1) TOOLS OR AIDS FROM COGNITIVE CONSISTENCIES: THE TRANSFER PROBLEM

What needs to be explained in the class of abilities—e.g., verbal, numerical, mechanical, reasoning—which we are calling *agencies* is the character of their form and nature of the development which leads to this form. Why, as factor-analytic structures, do they appear in the particular common trait forms now discovered, and how do they reach those forms? Incidentally, the same questions would arise with unique trait forms (as found from p-technique factoring of single individuals), as with *common* trait forms, but we shall carry the discussion along on the more usual basis of the latter.

The factorial phenomenon to be explained in the a's is that certain performances in individuals, motor, perceptual, or more commonly both together—x_1, x_2 . . . x_n—tend to rise together over time, and, as between individuals, to be correlated in level. The boy who is making more rapid progress in x_1, spelling ability, in general is also acquiring more rapid grasp of x_2, grammatical forms; and the man who can charm us with literary quotations, x_3, also tends to have the larger sheer vocabulary, x_4. Since several quite different p's are obviously at work in the development of any one a (e.g., verbal ability comes through visual, auditory, and motor avenues and expressions, and these latter thus get regrouped in each of such performances, as shown in Figure 11–1 and Table 11–1), we certainly cannot invoke *their* unities as an explanation. (Indeed, we tend to find in ordinary factor analysis that they are second-stratum to the a unities.)

Now, in general, psychometrists in the field of abilities have neglected those unities which could arise among abilities from single motivational sources—unities that would be perfectly obvious to the clinician and the personality researcher. If Mr. Brown had interests through which he repeatedly pursued a course of action only of desultory interest to Mr. Smith, it follows that a whole unitary pattern of acquired skills is likely to appear in Mr. Brown that is absent from corresponding cognitive measures on Mr. Smith. In fact, in a population composed of people stretching from Mr. Brown to Mr. Smith, a correlation cluster or factor for this "common ability" pattern must necessarily appear, though the unity is really laid down by dynamic sources. In this way a substantial proportion of agency unities—those we discuss in the next section—are a necessary consequence of interest unities and cultural unities. For example, a person who is interested in a church tends to acquire simultaneously a knowledge of his bible, a habit of social good works, an ethical judgment, and perhaps some ability to sing hymns. These go together (correlate) in people because they go together in the culture. The factor is, indeed, what is called an *environmental mold* (Cattell, 1946a) trait, and it presupposes a unitary interest in a social institution or activity as the basis of its formation. This source has been mentioned here, lest some reader be restive at our overlooking it. But, with this understanding that it will be considered in the next section, let us concentrate now on a first and different source—one of the two main sources of ability unity, which we shall call *cognitive consistency.*

Cognitive consistency embraces centrally not only the notion of *transfer of training,* but also some other concepts besides. Transfer of training once held an important position in educational psychology. (It was used, for example, to rationalize the preservation of as much as five years of Latin in high school, for the sake of its transferable "mental discipline!") However, such practices were struck down justifiably by the discovery of E. L. Thorndike and others that the transfer effect was altogether smaller than had been imagined. Further, it appeared that formal discipline carried over only to *very* closely similar performances. Nevertheless, it exists, and in the realm of problem-solving—as studied by Piaget (1960) in children, Guetzkow (1951), Laycock (1933) and many others—it can be shown definitely that a way of thinking learned in solving one problem does bring some improvement in solving certain others. For example, Laycock found that even such a general set as "try to approach the obstacle indirectly" managed to carry over to help solve new problems.

One must never overlook the fact that transfer can also be *negative,* as when a boy accustomed to a zip fastener accidentally tears the buttons off his pants! Indeed, it is perhaps a little surprising that Spearman, Guilford, and many others who have explored the domain of abilities rather widely have encountered so small a percentage of negative correlations. Of course, as Broverman et al. (1968) have pointed out, if one takes out the influence of general intelligence (which would leave zero correlations among specifics), one gets, in terms of "group factors" a number of significant negative loadings and correlations in the remaining abilities. And, as we turn specifically to the *dynamic* roots of certain agencies (abilities) in the next section, we shall see why such negative correlations would be expected theoretically to be *systematically* present.

Except for this cause squarely rooted in the nature of psychodynamic principles—and which we shall designate the *law of dynamic rivalry*—one can, however, find little systematic reason, in the ability performances as such, for persisting negative correlations (when general factors are removed) because negative cognitive transfer is largely a phenomenon of the learning stage. When you have learned that pencils can be held with any side up, but pens (with nibs) cannot, negative transfer ceases. Negative transfer is constantly naively begun and constantly corrected. One small source of systematic difference in the degree of positiveness of correlation matrices would therefore be expected between new performances, on the one hand, and old performances, on the other. In the latter the "mistakes" of making negative transfers have been gradually eliminated. The present writer has switched at about three-year intervals over forty years from driving on the right to the left side of the road, and back again. After some initial awkwardness at a roundabout or cloverleaf, the negative transfers disappear and the predominating positive transfers in general driving experience would almost certainly lead to good driving on the left being correlated (over say a few hundred people who learn both) with good driving on the right. But the "initial" stage—the problem-solving stage—is important, and one would expect systematically more negative correlations if the experimenter in question has chosen to investigate developing, adaptive, problem-solving habits than if his work refers to performances long adapted to circumstances. Even so, theoretically it would be necessary to partial out (or hold constant across the group) the most general of all problem-solving aids—the relation-perceiving capacities in g_f—if these negative correlations from more specific problem-solving habits are to be indubitably revealed. This amounts to performing nothing more than an ordinary multiple factor analysis and to looking for negative loadings as well as positive on the factors beyond g_f.

An enormous amount of discussion—and a very limited amount of psychometric experiment—has been given by Piaget and his followers to the area of acquisition of abilities by learning, with the theory of which we are here concerned. This discussion, beginning with valuable "naturalistic" observation of problem-solving in small children, has, in the main, failed to integrate with the main stream of quantitative experimental psychometric research, for lack of methodological sophistication. One cannot help observing that the preoccupation with finding "tools" of thought that transfer to new learning situations has conspicuously failed to keep in perspective the above aspect of negative transfer. It has also taken virtually no account of the role of g_f in making the perception of certain relations possible, which produces the well-documented correlation of acquisition of the more advanced tools with constitutional level on g_f. The most disabling lack of perspective, however, has occurred in implicitly considering the gains of the child in these experiences as an increase in his "general ability"—as some general power in the child himself without regard to their being tied up in a specific relation to a specific environment.

The first and second of these defaults will be evident from what has been covered above: the third needs more definition. The child's first discovery that a moderate wind needs appreciable allowance when he kicks a football at a goal, or that his penknife will cut a stick along the grain much more easily than across it; or that the result of multiplication is the same as serial adding, in each case becomes a "tool" capable of yielding positive transfer effects (and some negative) within a certain wider area. What that area will be has nothing to do with the child (except insofar as some children—those high on the U.I. 21, Exuberance, temperament trait discussed below (page 363)—pursue trial and error more irrepressibly than others). It is determined by the nature of the world itself—by the extent to which *cognitive consistencies* potentially pervade a given area of activity. An obvious area of high and sharply bounded cognitive consistency is the manipulation of numbers, where a few mastered rules will quickly enable one to deal with a variety of new problems. But these tools will not help the child to wheedle candy bars from Aunt Jane or wrestle more successfully with brother Jim.

In earlier writings I have used intentionally the abstract word "aids" for these positively transfering influences, but, despite its rather crude concreteness, the word "tools" is perhaps a better initial indicator of their nature. In the ability realm, a tool means some insightful device in thinking and acting which, once picked up, enables the user to handle a whole group of further performances. At a qualitative and almost anecdotal level, Piaget (1960) has instanced several in the child's growth of reasoning capacity. Ferguson (1956) has pursued the idea with a more controlled factorial and quantitative-experimental emphasis, sketching an interesting and clean-cut theory as to the expected overlap of ability factor structures.

The present theory of agencies, to account for the principal, discovered, primary abilities, considers them to be of two distinct types: (1) "tools" or "aids" developing within areas of cognitive consistency in the external world, and (2) dynamic "effector" systems, to be discussed in the next section. They justify being brought together in the single concept of "agencies" because, in the total dynamic action of the personality, they can be individually evoked and "turned on" as agencies in the service of any major dynamic goal-pursuing activity. Similarly, from the standpoint of a general ability factor, they are special agencies which come into operation (now unconsciously or consciously) as a special type of problem is approached.

The appreciable hereditary determination of verbal ability may be sufficiently accounted for by the role of g_f in its development, or it may depend on a specific ability and temperament contributions; but the form which the verbal ability primary finally takes obviously arises from the boundaries set by a cognitive consistency in the material. In infancy that form could be different, gradually changing into the factor pattern recognized in high school in a_v. It could begin with the discovery at about a year of age that sounds communicate his wants and result in rewards. Babblings are therefore emitted more freely when in want of food or company. At early school, when words come to be written, discovery of the phonetic principle opens a door to rapid increments in command of words, and their reinforcement through visual, auditory, and motor channels. Although the whole structure is thus not the result of generalization of any single tool, but rather of a hierarchy of tools, it is to be expected that it would have a unity in terms of an individual difference factor, because the child who starts ahead in the initial tools (as girls do, for example, relative to boys) is likely to hit on the later ones earlier too, and enjoy the bonus of early imprinting effects. No detailed studies yet exist mapping the transfer areas of verbal tools, the ages at which they appear, the role of g_f levels in permitting their appearance, and the changing form of a_v factor at different ages, so the agency theory strictly remains a theory, though surely a convincing one with present fragmentary evidence.

The important point to keep in mind in the "tool" theory of agencies is that the boundaries of ability pattern growth would be expected to be determined in each case by consistencies in the subject itself—not by anything in the human mind or brain such as accounts for the unity of, say, g_f. Consistencies similar to those just noted exist in the domain of mechanical things, where, for example, the notion of a regulator runs from steam engine to watch, in the care of plants (a green thumb factor has not yet been isolated, or even sought, but doubtless it exists), and, in the motor field, through most ball games.

Obviously, an important step toward understanding the growth and form of agencies consists in watching the way in which new concepts are formed and strategic and tactical habits acquired in the process of problem-solving or on day-to-day learning, in and out of school. Such developments have been discussed under the notion of "schemata" by Piaget and "phase sequences" by Hebb (1966). The organization of what can be found from such sources is considered mainly at two points in the present book—here and in the study of creative thinking in Chapter 13.

An enormous amount of work on learning, especially in the reflexological framework, has concerned itself with a succession of, at most, two or three acts. It might be described as the process of learning, but rarely as the learning of a process. The virtue of such "naturalistic" approaches as those of Bruner (Bruner, Olver and Greenfield, 1966) or Piaget (1958), as well as the series of attacks on problem solving by Laycock (1933), Maier (1945; Maier and Hoffman, 1961), Weaver and Madden (1949), Guetzkow (1951), Berlyne (1965), and others, has consisted in calling attention to the qualitative steps in the learning process. Unfortunately, most of the naturalistic study of process, from human thinking to the ethology of animal instincts, has not availed itself of the more formal, rigorous, and penetrating statistical treatment of processes as such that has now become available (Cattell, 1966; Fleishman, 1954; Tucker, 1966).

Piaget has driven home the essential (but casually overlooked) principle that, in the child's thinking process, if simple concepts are not understood, others cannot develop. This is especially evident in mathematics in the classroom where a child, who has been away a month and missed some integral step, limps ever afterward. Much has been said, in the problem-solving studies, about the gain on a wide front that occurs through a particular "breakthrough." Piaget has illustrated it in the child's grasp of the idea of causality. He has illustrated the opposite—the "hold up"—in his well-known instance of four-year-olds estimating a very tall cylinder to hold more water than an actually larger, short, fat one. Here advance waits upon more analytical thinking, which is probably largely tied to the development of specific concepts in specific fields.

Proper sequence, in the sense of ideas encountered in the right order in a learning process may thus be as important to early growth and high development in an "agency" as the occurrence of an early "breakthrough." In school, that order is generally arranged, and even in untutored learning, e.g., in learning in a swimming pool with only casual instruction, the need to control breathing, learned in the initial flounderings, becomes a prerequisite both for later swimming and diving.

From studying the process of problem-solving, one sees that it involves both the emergence of new concepts as such, and knowing how and when to "play" these cards. An old, yet anything-but-obsolete experimental study of the gradual emergence of concepts is that of Aveling (1930), who shows that if the relation-eduction (g_f) capacity of the subject is equal to the task, the natural result of repeated presentation of objects of a class is for a class concept spontaneously to emerge ("It's one of *those* things again."). The concept itself may be "held" in consciousness and reproduced (as the work of Bartlett, 1958, also shows) as a fragmentary sensory image, or, more commonly and if socially acquired, by a word.

In Chapter 9 it has been pointed out that even a computing machine can solve a lot of generalized "logical" problems if relations, e.g., syllogism forms, are programmed into it, and it has been suggested that crystallized (and perhaps even fluid) general ability may achieve much of its effectiveness through storage of relations (concepts) *per se*. It has been pointed out that C. W. Valentine at Birmingham reported (in conferences) improved performances in traditional intelligence tests through teaching subjects the elements of symbolic logic. Even in culture-fair tests, as some recent German research shows, some improvement of score occurs through the subjects being given words for the new concepts involved. It may be that fluid intelligence itself depends to an appreciable extent upon the growth and storage of suitable reference concepts, though not in any verbal or "cultural" framework. However, most handling of cultural concepts by humans probably operates with verbal reference symbols.

However, the fact that the growth of "universals" has been more intensively and lengthily studied (by Aveling, 1930; Bruner, Goodnow, and Austin, 1956; Bartlett, 1958; Maier, 1945; and numerous educational psychologists) must not allow us to underestimate the importance of those less-studied parts of the "agency" structure, which have been described above as strategies and tactical habits. When Gagné (1962) traces problem-solving from lower animals to humans, under such categories as trial-and-error reflex learning, concept formation, and the learning of principles, he brings into due proportion the role of the first, even in human learning. Games theory tells us that man or machine can learn that solving problems depends partly on blindly playing a certain "card" when past experience has taught that the probabilities of success are somewhat greater for that response than others, at that point in the game. Beyond these virtually unconscious tactical responses—such as a tennis player, for example, certainly makes without conscious decision as he hits a ball to the far side line—lie broader strategies, which are also part of the development of an agency. The hierarchy of TOTES, referred to in the work of Miller, Galanter, and Pribram (1960), is a generalized strategy for most mental activity. Resort to perceptual classification (e.g., recognition of types and attributes), attachment of explicit symbols, analysis into classes and concepts, seeking for (temporal) causal sequences, generalization about attributes or sequences, are also strategies common to virtually every kind of problem-solving. In more particular circumstances, one sees strategies in the form of particular mental sets, e.g., the *selection* and *reception* strategies discussed in Butcher's (1969) excellent account of problem-solving, or Sherlock Holmes's set also to observe what an interviewee did *not* say, i.e., to note the omissions from among the things he might be expected to say.

In connection with the growth of strategies, it has been a practically invariable finding of experiment that their development, in any particular agency area, is substantially correlated with the individual's intelligence. The notion that a good teacher and exceptionally favorable experience can raise a man's strategies above the level of his g_f is probably wrong. Napoleon was wont to remark that reading the wisest books on military strategy had not helped his opponents very much. *Without* the agency concepts and strategies the individual would not do so well, but *with* them he still has to perceive the relations that decide when they should be applied. This latter is probably the second-order g_f loading in the given a primary.

The literature of learning and problem-solving—even if one leaves out all that has been written on school education—is enormous. The above severe condensation has tried to summarize what is more relevant to understanding the origins, patterns, and operations of what the triadic theory recognizes as "agencies." Specifically, it has so far dealt with that half of the agency domain which we call "tools" or "aids." An aid is a primary factor explained by the triadic theory as a unity developed through an inherent similarity in the required activity in a particular domain of the environment. Proficiency tends to spread evenly through that domain (for any individual) because of this intrinsic cognitive consistency. The influences which tend to cause one individual to operate at a higher level than another across all manifestations of the primary "tool agency" are: (1) simply greater exposure to the area (when it is cultural "cut out" as a unity, e.g., numerical activity), (2) an earlier "breakthrough" in grasping a main conceptual or strategic tool, upon which all further advance depends, (3) a fortunate experience in developing concepts and strategies in the right developmental order. It is thus a coherent set of habit skills, knowledge, conceptual developments, and tactical and strategic "know-how" covering a domain in which there is positive transfer everywhere, i.e., a natural similarity which makes any skill advantageous over the whole area.

In any account of individual differences in learning it is appropriate to consider both repetition (length of exposure) and reinforcement (magnitude of motivation and reward). The triadic theory distinguishes among *agencies* a "tool agency," due to cognitive consistency, from a dynamic "effector agency," due to a motivational unity, though, of course, there is no reason why the two should not, by chance, operate together. This should be mentioned even before we study the "effectors," because a reader may well have been wondering what has happened to the dynamics which he also perceives in some tool agencies. For example, is the well-attested mechanical ability factor, a_m, due to the dynamic unity of an interest reinforcement, i.e., to the individual being recognized as good at "mechanical things" and rewarded for all such manifestations, or to some inner cognitive consistency, permitting and favoring transfer of mental habits, as occurs in mathematics? Anyone who takes either a vacuum cleaner or a car to pieces learns something about varieties of nuts and bolts and wheel bearings useful to him in meeting the next piece of machinery. Cognitive consistency is certain; but the rewards of a "sentiment" are also possible.

The argument for the second kind—the dynamic unity—is that interest in a given goal, and the enforced common learning due to the contiguity of problems, brings a new kind of agency unity (discussed in the next section), and that cognitive consistency unities may tend more frequently than by chance, to have this as a secondary contributor to unity. In consequence, in any given instance it may be difficult to decide what weight to give respectively to consistency and to interest. For example, in a group of high school boys, is the undoubted correlation we find between knowledge of how to handle nuts and bolts and how to deal with wheel bearings due to nuts telling us something about the nature of bearings, or to the fact that to get at bearings one has to undo nuts? In the broadest sense this latter is a means-end dynamic type of link.

The answer to "How much?" in these cases is still not known empirically, i.e., we do not know how much of the covariance in the observed primary ability structure is due respectively to one source or the other. A guess would be that the various primaries differ appreciably in their weighting on these, and that mechanical ability, social ability, and certain athletic dexterities, for instance, derive their unity more from a dynamic unity of experience (*effector* unity, as we have called it), whereas verbal, numerical, and spatial ability derive more from cognitive consistency (*aid* or *tool* unity). Incidentally, at the level of naturalistic observation, clinicians and others more impressed by the importance of dynamic influences may be inclined to doubt that the picking up of a "tool" can account for the substantial covariance of a typical primary ability. Grasping the phonetic principle in reading a year earlier than someone else, they may suggest, is surely not enough to account for one child tending to be higher simultaneously in vocabulary, grammar, style, and *every* other expression of the a_v factor. Here our answer has been, above, that cognitive consistency means more than a "breakthrough" in one or more major conceptual understandings, and consists of a branching tree of cognitive dependencies from initial concepts and strategies to continuing remunerative investments in ancillary aids which expand the use of the first. In short, this type of agency is not a tool, but a tool box. For example, such a tool box in numerical ability would encompass: a grasp of multiplication, a rule for handling the decimal point, laws for the manipulation of equations, and much else. Therefore, for precision let us keep the term "tool" for a single problem-solving discovery, and *use the word "aid" to apply to the whole tool box* of cognitively consistent habits. The rise of a primary ability, from inherent opportunities for cognitive consistency in the subject matter, is thus due always to an *aid,* within which individual *tool* discoveries are the building blocks.

Careful factor analyses, with strategically distributed choices of variables, presumably will eventually answer specific questions of this kind.

6. AGENCIES: (2) THE EFFECTOR PATTERNS CONNECTED WITH DYNAMIC STRUCTURES, NOTABLY SENTIMENTS: THE ISOMORPHISM PRINCIPLE

In many naturally occurring activities— farming, sailing, policing, accounting, skiing—what we shall now call the *environmental mold, or dynamic effector explanation* of unity—already touched upon above—must commonly be invoked as the main determiner of unity in an agency. For in these cases the problems to be solved in the area specified obviously require widely different skills. Cognitive consistency does not hold, as any farmer who likes farming but not marketing will agree. The farmer, indeed, has to handle matters as diverse as an internal combustion engine, signs of the weather, and the economics of the corn market. The more organized, sorted-out realms of special proficiency which we call academic or scholastic subjects, on the other hand, have typically a far higher cognitive consistency (indeed, it is the very basis of academic organization). But, in life, such areas of homogeneous activity are less common. The content of astronomy, of organic chemistry, of a language study hangs together in the sense that certain explicit and self-conscious skills and concepts in one part of the subject favor the development of proficiencies in other parts. The aid—i.e., the tool box of skills—in these cases develops by a nexus of cognitive interconnections. But, as we have seen above, even here a new influence for unity is sometimes seen at work. The tool agency begins as a (perhaps unconscious) product of cognitive consistency, but this is recognized consciously with pride as an esteemed expression of the self, and thus receives secondary, dynamic funding from the self-sentiment.

In this case one sees the interest as a secondary binding influence, but our preoccupation with abilities as such must not blind us to the instances on every hand wherein a unitary motivational system comes first and is father to a unified ability. It is a commonplace—at least among clinicians —that the skills are the servants of the interests. But, as indicated above, the educational psychometrists, among others, have not followed the implications of this generalization by hypothesizing an isomorphism between dynamic and ability structures. By what we may briefly call, in this section, "effectors" we mean unitary patterns of skill that are developed as agents, or means to ends, in what are primarily unitary motivation systems.

One suspects that the ignoring of effectors as an important origin of agencies is due partly to the lack of confidence of the precise psychometrist in the dynamic concepts handed down by psychoanalysis—or even by animal psychologists. Actually, there is no excuse for any continued isolation of dynamic from psychometric psychology today, since multivariate experimental research in the field of human motivation has progressed to precise and measurable concepts compatible with both clinical and psychometric concepts. This is most clearly expressed in what has been called the *dynamic calculus* (Delhees, 1968; Dielman and Krug, 1969).

In this connection it behoves us to remind the reader, if only in the space of one paragraph, on what foundations we may build in relating ability to motivation structure. The dynamic calculus researches have checked, over twenty years of experiment, the following concepts: (1) The existence of nine or ten distinct *ergs* or innate need patterns—sex, fear, hunger, self-assertion, etc. (2) Several patterns of *sentiments,* i.e., acquired aggregates of attitude-interests around some one life object, e.g., a sentiment to home, job, religion, and to the self concept. By the principles and procedures involved in the concept of the *dynamic lattice* (Cattell, 1957a), any desired course of action in any single attitude can be represented by a vector the *length* of which represents the total interest in making that response, while the *direction* defines the particular ergic composition of the reinforcements which sustain it. The reader should master elsewhere (Cattell, 1957a, 1958, 1959; Horn, 1966b; Dielman and Krug, 1969; Delhees, 1968) the integrating theory among these concepts, involving the notion of *integrated* and *unintegrated motivational components,* the *dynamic lattice* structure of attitudes, and the *dynamic calculus* of conflict resolution and learning.

The principles and concepts just mentioned will yield many rewards as we apply them increasingly in understanding, in the next chapter, the relations of abilities and dynamic traits. But let us first look at the situation with a commonsense, even if somewhat superficial, glance. The most obvious instance of abilities following a dynamic pattern is in the occupations and the hobbies. Men develop powerful unitary interest systems here, and it is obvious that unitary ability patterns in correlations of individual differences, must follow where unitary interest patterns arise. A "skilled surgeon" or a "great golfer" is sufficient to describe what undoubtedly would appear, in correlation over a suitable population, as a unitary surface trait or source trait—of surgical or golfing skill—simultaneously among interests and among ability measures. (Parenthetically, the distinction of "ability" and "aptitude" is sometimes an attempt to dissect out the surface trait (correlation cluster) of observed skills in such developments from the underlying "aptitudes," e.g., primary abilities, which are factors, and with which we have so far concerned ourselves. But as indicated in the first chapter, usage of these terms is now so utterly chaotic that one has no alternative but to abandon them for more technical terms.)

In the general context of the triadic theory—and specifically of agencies —we have agreed to call these acquired collections of skills "effector systems" (or, simply, effectors), meaning that they develop as motivation and skill systems effective in the pursuit of a dynamic emotional goal. The variables correlated are interest-attitudes, on the one hand, and skills, on the other, bound together isomorphically like the words and the melody of a song. To proceed now to a more rigorous terminology, let us call the unitary pattern as a cognitive-dynamic whole (and which reasonably could be assigned a single score for any individual) an *effector,* and when we show later just how the ability part can be separately measured we will call it a *proficiency.* There are, thus, effector trait levels for such as the surgeon, the electrician, the baseball player, and so on. Their proficiency parts are measured frequently by what, in education, would be thought of as an achievement test, and, as such, they are quite distinct from the underlying capacities and powers which occupy the other part of the triadic system. In some cases, their unitary structure may be a vast and changing or relatively ill-defined network. (Such might be the effector skills we would get from correlating the performances of "housewives.") But in other effector systems, e.g., the pattern of an air pilot or golf champion, the proficiencies would be a highly coherent correlation cluster. There will tend to be one other difference from the agencies and powers so far discussed, namely, that the latter have been practically universal patterns, whereas the coherence of the collection of skills seen in, say, a surgeon, will factor out clearly only in a group which is entirely, or maybe fifty-fifty, surgeons and non-surgeons. The extremely "skewed" distribution of many interest skills, in that only a small fraction of the population has them *at all,* is in keeping with the relatively idiosyncratic nature of interests, and explains why some ability patterns quite obvious to common observation are not found in the psychometrist's random samples of people, or recorded in his summaries of abilities.

Probably only the fact that dentists are scarcely more than about one in one thousand of the population has deprived factor analysts of the completeness of listing "dental ability" among the ability primaries, and similarly for most of these numerous but, population-wise, more restricted patterns.[4]

---

[4] In spite of these statistical obscurities created by extreme infrequencies, etc., the fact that ability patterns follow dynamic patterns is brought out in another way. It shows as a curious by-product, and from a new angle, in the last decade's investigations of the validity of objective motivation and interest measurement devices *per se* (Cattell, Radcliffe, and Sweney, 1963; Cattell and Horn, 1963). The high correlation which permits a measure of a level of skill, i.e., of an "ability" to be taken as the measure of an interest strength has brought out parallelism of factor structure. The validity holds, however, only for what has been designated the I or integrated motivational

Let us next pursue more formally the concept of *isomorphism* (or structural parallelism) between *interest structures* and corresponding *proficiency structures*. The notion of an *interest-ability isomorphism* is not new, but it needs today a statement and experimental demonstration in precise factorial form. The theory requires that the factorial loading form of *dynamic interest structures* measured by objective dynamic tests, on the one hand, and of the *proficiency part,* consisting of skills and abilities as ordinarily measured, on the other, should be the same. Now from multivariate experimental research we know that the major emerging dynamic interest structures are *ergs* (drives) and *sentiments*. In the latter, both at the level of social observation, and through correlational research, it is evident that we get dynamic patterns corresponding to occupations, hobby proficiencies, social institutions such as family and church, and language and subcultural loyalties. And it turns out that, among dynamic traits, it is in the sentiments, rather than the ergs, that we can look for the isomorphic ability-interest unities.

If there exists this marriage of corresponding proficiency and dynamic interest structures in the sentiment patterns, one may ask why we have accepted the improbability of a similar isomorphism of proficiencies in the dynamic structures of a more hereditary nature, namely, the ergic factors. Briefly, the reply is that in man, as distinct from the lower animals, the unlearned effector equipment is too vague and unspecified. However, if one turned to the insect world, or, in animals, considered the correlations one would get across species instead of individuals, the phylogenetic coherence of effectors and proficiencies would be very striking indeed. Ethologists have stressed constantly the closeness of innate impulse and innate ability structure (as well as, since Darwin, the innate somatic effector structure—in horns and fins). In the nest building, courtship, and pugnacious ergs the emergence in close association of interests, impulses, and skills is indubitable. Whether differential genetic endowments *within* a species would be strong enough to bring out in correlation matrices individual-difference factors binding ability and interest strength in the very same patterns remains doubtful, but is a challenge to sensitive research methods. At least we have terms like "gourmet," "Don Juan," "explorer," "boss," etc., for people whose skills center on expression of a particular corresponding erg (hunger, sex, curiosity, and domination respectively). But at least *among* species the counterpart of what we see as powerful individually-acquired sentiment structures among humans, appears also at the innate ergic endowment level, in appropriately interlocking dynamic-ability patterns (developed by mutational trial and error over the ages). Here, the parallelism of unitary ability and interest patterns is indeed

---

component (Cattell, 1957a), and the validity of a skill as an interest measurement is negligible for what has been recognized as the U or unintegrated component. Wishful, unadapted motivation, though it has its own demonstrable dynamic structure by other types of measures (as shown by the dynamic calculus methods) may generate ability structure later, but it has no immediate proficiency pattern counterparts.

understood in common speech, where an "instinct" for something means both an interest and an aptitude.

If the clustering of proficiencies around dynamic unities is supported by further dynamic structure research, it is of interest, at least to the historian of psychology, to return to the question of why the effector isomorphism principle has been largely ignored in conventional ability structure research. It would seem (as illustrated in Vernon, 1954; or Pawlik, 1966) that the explanation is partly that most ability researchers have been operating within the sectionalism of a traditional academic framework— "the psychology of sensation, perception, motor abilities," etc. For these archaic compartments from introspective psychology often continued to form the chapters of textbooks in the first half of this century. "Perception," for example, has been a specialty, largely tied to sensory-neurological work in the "brass instrument" type of laboratory rather than an aspect of the natural life environment seen by the ethologist. When encompassed in the broader experimental approach of the multivariate experimentalist, perception and other abilities are illuminated by motivational and general personality perspectives. To speak in the language of the sensory psychologist himself, traditional approaches have left in the "audible range of frequency," whole octaves of silence, unexplored and unmentioned.

The student will be helped in perspective—in understanding the distortions, gaps and paradoxes in our present knowledge—if he recognizes that the childhood of ability research suffered from the narrow tutelage of two mentors: the tradition of Wundtian brass instrument compartmentalism on the one hand, and the educational psychometrists, necessarily with strong classroom preoccupations, on the other. The very choice of variables which yielded our present patchwork quilt of primary abilities rested on these traditional origins. Until recently, in the work of Horn for example, no imaginative and comprehensive attack with a conception of variables akin to that based on the *personality sphere* concept in personality research had been made. Except for this recent attack, and work in the spirit of Spearman, Burt, Guilford, and Thurstone, the exploration of abilities has resembled an accidental drift across the ocean of the unknown, rather than an imaginative sequence of strategically planned voyages. In the new phase now beginning we can expect guidance from a "representative sampling" approach guided by an "ability sphere" concept; from such subjective but broad schemata as Guilford's; from animal ethology; from sociological surveys of occupational activities, and, especially, from considering abilities, as in this chapter, in their developmental setting in human dynamic structure.

In our present inherited poverty, it is true, we can claim nothing more than a patchy understanding of what is probably the real range of agencies of the cognitive consistency type, and almost no well-substantiated factor-analytic evidence on agencies of the proficiency, dynamic effector type. Nevertheless, leaning on the isomorphism principle, one can posit with some confidence a set of effector ability patterns corresponding to the chief known dynamic sentiments, i.e., those developing around such unitary social institutions as school involvement, home attachment, vocational ambition, athletics, religion, etc. There is a sense in which crystallized intelligence is such a proficiency, since it arises substantially from the attachment to and learning in the school situation. Regarding further research expectations, one may anticipate that the known broad dynamic factors will be found to generate corresponding proficiency patterns that will stand out as a relatively limited number of firm outlines among a boundless litter of smaller patterns peculiar only to particular social subgroups, special occupations, hobbies, and geographical localities. The last might be illustrated, for example, by the undoubted unitary proficiency of expertly finding one's way around on the New York or London subway. This is an agency in the satisfaction of dynamic needs, the pattern of which is necessarily fixed by the environment in which the individual happens to live out his needs. These less common, nonuniversal—but still "common factor"—patterns will merge, at the end of a continuum, into patterns absolutely unique to the single individual recognizable only by P-technique, e.g., the pattern of skills of Wells' invisible man, or the strategies of a university professor among the card indexes of his own specialty.

Although proficiencies can take on endless possible structural forms, as diverse as the environmental molds in which men live their lives, the mode of formation is uniform. To a reflexological learning theorist it suffices to say that the elements of the pattern come to cohere (as shown by correlations) because they experience the same *reinforcement schedule.* They have the same frequencies and occasions of reward. The skills at different parts of a golf course are very different in nature, but the man who plays one hundred times a year, compared to the man who plays a dozen times, has *all* of them subjected to greater reinforcement. To the personality theorist it suffices to say that we are speaking of an *environmental mold* factor (source trait), which implies that the unity is not one of internal powers of the organism, but of external impress; the impress being a matter of reward and frequency of experience in what may broadly be designated a unitary social institution. The personality theorist will normally dwell more on the attitudes, emotional interests, etc., measured in this acquired *sentiment.* But he can also observe the proficiency pattern associated with the dynamic effector system—the system which, within our culture, is the means of effecting satisfaction of ergic goals. A common form of the "social institution" pattern, incidentally, arises from the acceptance of a *role* in a social organization. The roles of a job, a leader in athletics, a wife and mother, each bring their characteristic interests, attitudes, and their characteristic isomorphic proficiency pattern.

It was pointed out in introducing the difference of "tool" agencies and "proficiency" agencies that there is no reason why they should not sometimes be superposed unities. It should be added that even without this juxtaposition it is sometimes difficult to distinguish them sharply. A student at an engineering school builds up a high level on a unitary mechanical ability factor, a_m, partly through the cognitive consistency of the intellectual "tools" used in handling all kinds of mechanical problems, and partly because of the sentiment—the environmental mold trait—he builds up through common frequency of experience and reward across the curriculum (based on the strength of his interest in becoming an engineer). But the two principles are nevertheless quite different. An art course in etching could produce transfer (cognition consistency) in regard to making counterfeit money, but the interest systems of art and crime would normally be totally different. Conversely, the unified interest in becoming an artist may require improved ability in matters with no mutual cognitive consistency, such as judging esthetic color combinations and in understanding the chemistry of pigments, between which no aid transfer exists.

7. AGENCIES: (3) SPLITTING EFFECTORS INTO PROFICIENCY AND DYNAMIC COMPONENTS BY CONDITIONAL FACTORING

So far we have defined a class of abilities called *agencies,* which fall into two subclasses: *aids* (or *tools*) and *effectors* (or *proficiencies*). In spite of the attempted comprehensiveness of our overview of the principles governing the growth of unitary organizations, the reader may justifiably still harbor doubts whether all types of possible determiners of agency ability structures have yet been handled. Notably, one wonders whether the coherence and high covariance in the elements of any aid, such as a verbal or numerical ability, are ever explained sufficiently by cognitive transfer within a cognitively consistent domain. Is it not a more likely hypothesis that the secondary dynamic binding through the dynamic subsidiation of a sentiment (or incorporation in the self-sentiment) mentioned above is in fact *always* present in these formations?

The basic objection to invoking dynamic coherence as the sole cause of coherence of skills in the agencies is that such an aid as numerical ability can subsidiate to (i.e., be the means-to-end servant of) a great variety of sentiments and ergic goals. Here is no longer something that is part of a single dynamic purpose, as in the effector of a sentiment or erg, but a type of agency or aid that is called in by the individual alike in the sentiment to his bank account, to his religious charities, and to his scoring in a game of tennis. True, it might be that it always subsidiates as a *whole,* so that all parts get equal exercise. But will there remain now any appreciable individual differences in the amount of learning of so universally used an agency? For, as the simplified dynamic lattice in Figure 11–2 suggests, individual differences in the dynamic development of sentiments will "even out" in terms of dynamic investments (since the instrument's use is a total of many diverse sentiment strengths) by the time we come to such an agency, so far down the line of subsidiation, i.e., so far to the left of the diagram.

Verbal proficiency, for example, has been built up on the motivation strengths of sentiments x, y, and z, which, in turn, subsidiate to the full

FIGURE 11–2

The Learning of Effector Proficiencies in the Framework of the Dynamic Lattice

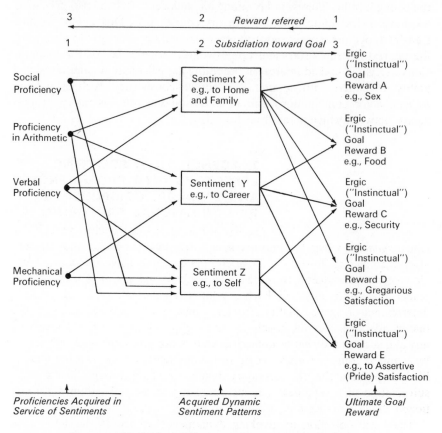

In terms of individual differences, the covariance of which
establishes unities, sentiments in column 2 are a function of
need strengths in column 1 and reward frequencies in 2. The
effectors in 3 are correspondingly derived from dynamic
strengths in 2 and experiences of learning reward frequency.
Individual differences in 3 are thus complexly determined,
but a unity is given to numerical, verbal, etc., agencies by their
being practiced in the same form for different sentiments,
and by their unitary reinforcement from incorporation in the
self-sentiment.

gamut of drives, A through E. Since people, in general, would be approximately equal in their total dynamic endowments, the verbal agency would receive about the same learning investment by everyone and (through lack of variance) would not appear as a factor on these grounds. More easily to grasp this and other important relations of ability structure and dynamic structure it is necessary to discuss a little further the concept of the dynamic lattice (Cattell, 1957a; Horn, 1966b; Dielman and Krug, 1969). It is, in effect, a precise reticular model to permit quantified "path analysis" of the naturally complex learning reinforcement schedules which apply in human life. It evokes methods, factor-analytic and other (Cattell, 1957a), for interpreting structural findings in personality dynamics in relation to learning principles. In the typical dynamic lattice, schematized in Figure 11–2, sentiments, if consciously entertained, appear as subgoals or common reinforcement patterns on the way to ultimate ergic goal satisfactions.

The dynamic lattice, besides showing the paths by which learning and reinforcement have occurred, offers (a) an algebraic summation relationship between any particular set of goal strengths and the courses which subsidiate to them, and (b) an explanation of why certain groups of attitudes get loaded (motivated) the way they do on various particular unitary dynamic factors (sentiments and ergs). Unfortunately, research has not yet clarified, with respect to (b), what the entire explanation is for the emphatic appearance in factor analysis of the unitary factors found for sentiments. It is, clear however, that much of it is due to each being always reinforced *as a whole*. Wherever arithmetic is used, one tends to use all arithmetic, and similarly with language or spatial sense. Thus, although the principles of the tool and the proficiency are distinct, one approaches the hypothesis that they will tend systematically to occur together. One invokes this secondary dynamic reinforcement of any aid unity because the transfer effect, which required high cognitive consistency and which, we have theorized, accounts for the unitary development of "aids," seems scarcely powerful enough to account for the factorial clearness with which such primaries as verbal, numerical, mechanical, etc., abilities stand out. One favors this conclusion also because there is psychological evidence that the initial unitary development of the "aid" type of agency normally tends to be succeeded by the reinforcement from the "effector" type of unity of a dynamic kind, as in a sentiment (a small and narrow sentiment, admittedly).

In any case, as we move distally (to the left) in the dynamic lattice (Figure 11–2), we come to what are quite narrow skills—mere splinter sentiments or specific attitude-skills. They are of the nature of quite specific means-end skills, such as driving a car, putting on one's clothes, writing letters, using a desk computer, etc. Obviously, these can be the servants of *any* erg or sentiment. Yet there is no reason why common dynamic reward for all parts of that small subsystem should not give it the status of a narrow unitary factor ("skill in car driving"), though factor-analytically it is likely to be at a lower-stratum level than what we now call the primary abilities, and such narrow factors, have been recognized rarely in factor-analytic research. However, already in some strategic experiments on abilities and dynamic traits in the simplified domain of *animal* research, where more specific, e.g., bar-pressing, behavior has been included, there are factorial observations in support of this position. In one such experiment (with thirst, shock, and gregariousness; Cattell, Dielman, and Schneewind, in press), three ergs stand out in rats clearly as factors across half a dozen diverse mazes (each *pair* of mazes sharing one common ergic motivation). But even there the operation of a particular instrumental agency, e.g., pressing two bars in succession in relation to a light signal, unmistakably appears as a factor. And bar-pressing, or paper hoop-handling, are quite close to the conceptual equivalents of verbal and numerical "agency" skills in man; for they enter similarly into a considerable variety of diverse dynamic goal services.

From such reasoning as the above we may hypothesize tentatively that— because verbal ability, numerical ability, etc., can (a) readily be conceived by their user as unities and consciously labelled as such, and because (b) they can be incorporated then in the individual's self-sentiment ("I am one of the best in my class at arithmetic;" "I am a man known to give competent after-dinner speeches."), and because (c) each is used still more in one person's total dynamic need system than in another's, they experience some unity of dynamic investment over and above their cognitive "aid" unity. This notion that some, but not all primary abilities may thus become "little sentiments," achieving the dynamic unity of an effector system calls for experimental checks in current research. Meanwhile, in moving tentatively toward such specific conclusions let us summarize and label some of the distinct concepts we have developed in this chapter.

The term 'agency' we shall retain to cover both *tool aids* and *effector proficiencies*. These subcategories of agencies refer respectively to origins primarily by the cognitive consistency transfer principle and to the dynamic sentiment development principle. By a *proficiency* we mean the cognitive skill part of a dynamic effector system—the last twig on the branch of a sentiment. Regarding this distinction of the cognitive proficiency part of a dynamic effector system from its isomorphic dynamic interest part, let us note that, from an early stage in factor-analytic work, a distinction has been drawn (Cattell, 1964a, p. 187) between a *wholistic* and a *conditional* factor. If, for example, we enter a research with measures of cognitive, temperamental, and dynamic variables, a sentiment of "athletics" will appear *wholistically* loading both interests *and* skills (and perhaps even some temperament). But by restricting the experimental measurements themselves[5] to certain variables, e.g., skills alone or interests alone, or taking conditions of administration in which, say, motivational differences cannot operate, we restrict our variables conditionally to either cognitive or dynamic modalities. When such variables are factored, one obtains what have been called conditional factors or trait descriptions. This slicing off of variance which is normally part of a "wholistic" trait has been done frequently and quite inadvertently by ability researchers when they equalize all motiva-

---

[5] This means altering and controlling the dynamic stimulus situation, as a rule. For example, one might so equalize the motivation situation for everyone e.g., by a powerful, ad hoc, monetary reward, unrelated to the usual motivation system, that differences in that modality, i.e., motivation, cannot contribute variance. Relative to the corresponding wholistic trait, the conditional trait thus factored out is one from which a whole region of expression has been sliced off.

tional stimuli as far as possible before testing. For example, there is some evidence, discussed in the next chapter, that the crystallized intelligence factor normally loads, in the total normal life behavior, not only the usual cognitive proficiencies, but also some personality behavior of conscientiousness, thoughtfulness, and general intellectual interest. But we try to give intelligence tests in classroom environment where all are constrained to concentrate, regardless of their natural thoughtfulness, and thus obtain a conditional factor, shorn of these features of the wholistic factor.

The conditional factor in the cognitive realm for *any* structure that is primarily an *effector* of a dynamic sentiment is what we are designating a proficiency. The dynamic effector factor and the cognitive proficiency factor have an isomorphism with regard to stimuli and response habits involved which should show up operationally in the "cooperative factor" phenomenon. Nevertheless (compared to what the "academic" ability taxonomist is accustomed to in tool agencies as neat, comprehensible primaries), proficiency patterns are likely to present quite strange and straggling shapes. For the sentiment to photography the proficiency pattern would include, on the one hand, skills in optics and, on the other, social skills in assembling portrait groups, and so on, to chemical know-how in development, etc. Similarly, if we factored 500 farmers and 500 random others, we should find (quite apart from the dynamic interest patterns in the wholistic factor) a conditional, proficiency factor, loading, perhaps, ability to milk cows, to run a straight furrow, and to know good from poor corn.

Although the effector-proficiency factor patterns may be "straggling" and awkward to design tests for, psychometrically, this is no reason for neglecting them either theoretically or practically, relative to the simple, restricted type of agency unity we are accustomed to in the aid primaries. The psychometrist whose world embraces only neat rows of primaries may not like it, but the fact remains that recognizing the experience of a man who has been a farmer or a locomotive engineer for twenty years is of importance in giving an account of, or making any prediction about, his abilities. Indeed, what we are finding out about the two kinds of agencies, and about dynamic effector systems has importance outside the measurement of narrow, primary proficiencies. It will soon become evident that a good understanding and use of the role and meaning of the *crystallized general* ability factor itself hinges on this appreciation. Except where the "sentiment-ability"—effector—patterns are too uncommon and idiosyncratic in the population, and too narrow and diverse for profitable recognition, classification, and measurement, there would be advantages in recognizing frankly, in all ability maps, that the common dynamic lattice structure of Figure 11–2, as worked out for our culture, is relevant to all ability structure concepts and measurements. It certainly implies that some of the variance in ordinary primaries, as now measured, belongs not only to the g and p higher-strata contributors we have recognized early in this book, but also to the action of relatively straggling higher-strata, dynamic-effector factor patterns. For example, among adults some of the variance in numerical performance is likely to be found due to the sentiments, in the occupational field, of "a housewife" or of belonging to a "number-using profession" such as accountancy. Again, the total measure of a_v (verbal ability) must receive some variance from a "teacher and allied professions" effector pattern, which will affect predictions from it.

One further reason why the main psychometric textbooks have given no real place to the complexity of the effector agencies is that the school psychologist is primarily concerned with children. The rich development of effector proficiencies is characteristic of adult life; in school the uniformity of curriculum divisions is likely to mold the compartively simple structure of the primary abilities, factor-analytically recognized at this period. (Twain's Hucklebery Finn, Wells's Joan and Peter, and Montagu's Bron, however, had a fair array of interesting effector skill patterns developed out of school hours.)

The importance of a taxonomy, as developed here and summarized in Table 11–2, lies not merely in clarity of description, but in the fact that the rise and decline, the physiological associations, the genetics, the learning requirements and—in short—the "fate," of these structures differs according to their kind. The *agencies* we have recognized as being systems of skills that can be brought to the assistance of any motivational system. They have a dual nature—*tools* and *aids*. The former, as brought out by Ferguson and by Piaget, are "discoveries" of problem solving concepts that will transfer positively to many areas, bringing a simultaneous advance in all. The latter —*aids*—are also transferable to assist *any* dynamic system in reaching its goals, but they owe their unitary character to an individual having to learn the whole if he learns one part (as in the N primary).

Each *proficiency*, on the other hand, has its unity established through being part of a unitary *dynamic system,* some contributory part of a sentiment which we have called an *effector,* e.g., learning a foreign language, initially as part of an interest in science; learning the route to X because one's girl friend lives at X. In regard to the relative importance and repe-

TABLE 11–2
Summary of Ability Component Concepts

1. *Capacities.* (g's) General *powers* operating through all brain action to affect all cognitive performances.

2. *Provincials.* (p's) *Powers*, limited to the functioning of particular, largely, constitutional, naturally delimited, neural zones of sensory, and motor input and output.

3. *Agencies.* (a's) 3a. *Aids. Acquired Cognitive Skills* in the pattern produced by transfer, resulting from cognitive consistency (with secondary reinforcement from 3b).

   3b. *Proficiencies.* (Cognitive parts of *effectors*)
   Acquired Cognitive Skills following the unitary pattern initially defined by the interest formation in a dynamic effector system.

tition and reward, as set out in Equation (11.3) below, it will be evident that repetition, working over the intrinsic linkages in the stuff of a domain, is the main producer of the unity of an aid, while a common reward, not necessarily tied to common repetition experience, is the main determiner of the unity of a proficiency (or the whole effector structure associated with a proficiency).

In the case of crystallized intelligency—which we have finally written as a_g rather than g_c, to bring out the fact that its nature is essentially that of an agency—one nevertheless encounters an extreme case of an agency, a supreme and general agency. It is a collection of agencies having a unitary factorial structure because all tend to be "taught" by the environment in mutual proportion. And since, in history, culture rarely completely turns a corner within the space of a couple of generations, this a_g measure will in general remain a tolerable measure of g_f. The I.Q. by a traditional test, of the omnibus variety, will work roughly.

Nevertheless, the discoveries to be made about *agencies* and proficiencies, will give us an understanding of important differences in a_g and g_f. It is true that at the present moment, barely past the conception of the two kinds of agencies, research has little to tell us about how the rate of acquisition, the permanence, and the predictive utilities of aids and proficiencies differ. But the theory indicates many respects in which they would be expected to differ, and which experiment can pursue. More of these differences may become apparent in examining, in the next section, more closely, the learning and motivational interactions of abilities.

8. THE FORMAL EQUATIONS CONCERNING MOTIVATION AND LEARNING EXPERIENCE IN RELATION TO ABILITY STRUCTURE

The present chapter has aimed to explain the development of ability in relation to learning theory, and in doing so has recognized that ability structure, at a given moment, is the child both of previous ability structure and of temperament and motivation. The latter is especially important in that the patterns of "effectors"—which are parts of dynamic sentiment systems—determine the pattern of "proficiencies." In the present section we aim to put this into precise equations, relating ability structure to motivation and learning in a formal way. The student not yet ready in background for this formulation might do well to skip it on a first reading.

In such formulation of the relations of ability to personality and motivation, it will clarify thinking if we notice that the relations can be studied in two ways:

(1) In terms of *immediate functional relationships of traits in being*. That is to say, we ask how a given piece of behavior can be accounted for by a combination of the individual's abilities, interests, and temperament

traits acting, as they stand at their given score levels, at the given moment. This is usually expressed in the standard specification equation already encountered in several instances in this book, and formally stated with full generality in Equation (11.7) below. It is our plan to present ample evidence on such relationships in the next Chapter—Chapter 12.

(2) In terms of *developmental relations and personal history.* This is the concern of the present chapter where we ask how interests, congenital abilities, and reward experience produce the structures that are seen by cross-sectional factor analyses.

Let us dismiss (1) to Chapter 12 with the brief reminder in the general form of (11.1), which is best designated the Present Action Specification Equation.

$$a_{ji} = b_{ja}A_i + b_{jp}\, P_i + b_{jd}\, D_i + \text{specifics \& error} \qquad (11.1)$$

Here what in a fully expanded equation would normally be a whole series of unitary ability traits, e.g., agencies—A_{1i}, A_{2i}, etc.—has been for brevity represented by a single A only. Similarly, a whole series of the individual's personality trait scores are represented by P_i only; and a whole series of his dynamic traits, e.g., ergic tension levels, by a D. (The subscript i simply says it is the A or P or D score of a given *individual.*) This linear equation states that the magnitude of any act is to be regarded as a function of the total personality represented by A's, P's and D's. The different weights, i.e., *behavioral indices* (loadings from factor analysis or tangents from a bivariate curve plot), b_{ja}, b_{jp}, b_{jd}—will be peculiar to each operating trait and the given focal stimulus j. Incidentally this equation could be carried—even as a present action equation—to greater precision by adding (1) a subscript k, for the general nonfocal, ambient stimulus situation, to the b's; (2) adding *states* or *state liability* terms, S's or L's, and (3) introducing modulator coefficients, s_k's, for the situations in (1) as they affect state liabilities and the D (motivation strength) terms.

To refresh the reader's memory on this present situation equation, it may be appropriate to add that the technical means by which the nature of the unitary traits is discovered, as well as the manner of getting the individual's score upon each, will be familiar from statistical texts on factor analysis. The behavioral indices, b's, also come from the factor analysis. The class of ability traits represented by A here could, in conformity with our whole analysis, be represented in actuality by subclasses, notably (1) a set of *agency* components (a's), (2) certain *provincial organizational* components (p's), and (3) *general capacity* components (g's), each with separate characteristic weights. But since among these will be a number of factors, e.g., agencies as primaries, capacities as secondaries, commonly found at different strata levels, this would take us to a "complex order" specification equation in which lower-order factors are bereft of that part of their variance which belongs in higher factors. The psychometry of such mixed strata equations, involving the Schmid-Leiman and Cattell-White formula, is complex and must be left to discussion elsewhere (Cattell, 1965b).

The way in which existent ability structure operates (in company with personality and motivation) in determining a person's level on some particular, new performance is one thing, and the way in which ability structures themselves grow out of existing structures is quite another. In moving to the latter we are basically concerned no longer with predicting a_{ij} but with predicting some increment in a_{ij} which can be written $a_{ij(t_2-t_1)}$ where t_1 is the first time of measurement and t_2 is the second, thus:

$$a_{ij\,(t_2-t_1)} = a_{ijt_2} - a_{ijt_1}$$

A person's ultimate level on any ability, will, of course, be the summation or integral of these increments from the time a_j may be said to have been zero. The typical learning theorist of the past, who has been bivariate rather than multivariate in his methods, has plotted learning curves of one variable, a_j, against time, repetitions or rewards. But if we are to succeed at all in the comprehensive purpose of linking structure with learning experience we must use the greater power of a multivariate learning theory. That is to say, since an ability factor A_x is recognized as a pattern in a_j, a_k, a_l, etc., and is scored as a sum of these, we need to show that the improvements in a_j, a_k, a_l, etc., are such as to create the pattern, and we need also to be able to write an equation like (11.1) above for A_x the trait itself, as well as a_j, a_k, etc., the separate components.

To attack this learning problem adequately it is necessary to resort to the recently developed multivariate learning theory incorporating what has been called the three-vector learning model. The latter states that whereas the learning theorist in the past has been content to describe the learning change as $(a_{ijt_2} - a_{ijt_1})$ it needs to be more analytically represented as a change in the *behavioral indices* (b's), the *trait levels* (T's), and the *modulating indices* (s's) for interests. If we take from (11.1) only one trait of each kind, for simplicity of representation, then we have:

$$a_{ijt_1} = b_{jat_1}A_{it_1} + b_{jpt_1}P_{it_1} + b_{jdt_1}s_{dt_1}D_{it_1} \qquad \textbf{(11.2a)}$$

$$a_{ijt_2} = b_{jat_2}A_{it_2} + b_{jpt_2}P_{it_2} + b_{jdt_2}s_{dt_2}D_{it_2} \qquad \textbf{(11.2b)}$$

It will be seen that three types of change can be represented on the right. First, the learning between t_1 and t_2 has changed the trait strengths, and this can be written as a vector of trait change, thus:

$$(A_{it_2} - A_{it_1}) + (P_{it_2} - P_{it_1}) + (D_{it_2} - D_{it_1})$$

Secondly, the behavioral indices, b's may have changed. That is to say the individual has learnt new ways of *combining* his traits to produce an improved result. The change vector (a vector is simply a series of numbers) here becomes:

$$(b_{jat_2} - b_{jat_1}) + (b_{jpt_2} - b_{jpt_1}) + (b_{jdt_2} - b_{jdt_1})$$

Thirdly, but in respect only to traits and states that can be modulated by a situation (which leaves out the A's and P's), the individual may learn to be more *interested* in a given performance. That is to say, his motivation

D, may itself be more stimulated when he comes again to that situation. Thus if there were three D's in (11.1) (instead of the one we took for simplicity) the modulation change vector would be:

$$(s_{d_1 t_2} - s_{d_1 t_1}) (s_{d_2 t_2} - s_{d_2 t_1}) (s_{d_3 t_2} - s_{d_3 t_1})$$

The researcher in the "learning of abilities" thus has a more intelligible, meaningful analysis of the learning change itself when he uses the *three-vector* model. But he still has to discover experimentally the laws which connect the changes in these three vectors with the experiences of reward and conditions of repetition in learning. The hypothesis used in the new and very recent experimental work on *structured learning theory* regarding gain, $a_{ij(t_2-t_1)}$, from session t_1 to t_2 (Cattell, 1971a) can be stated in equation form as follows:

$$a_{ij(t_2-t_1)} = b_{jat_1}A_{it_1} + b_{jpt_1}P_{it_1} + b_{jdt_1}D_{it_1} + b_{jest_1}(E_{ib} - E_{ia})_{t_1}S_{ait_1} \quad \textbf{(11.3)}$$

where E_a is the ergic tension at the end and E_b at the beginning of the particular learning experience. Thus the last term represents the magnitude of reward (reinforcement) at the end of each learning session, while S_{ait_1} shows the excitation level of the cognitive system a at the time. Both are multiplied by whatever constant b_{jest_1}, proves to be experimentally indicated. Note here that it is assumed that personality factors, P's, and dynamic factors, D's, will not themselves change with this kind of learning. But in other situations a formulation of change would be in order.

The level of a person in an element (variable) in an ability factor, A_x, after n learning experiences (t_0 to t_n) may be represented (assuming for simplicity that a_{ij} is at zero at t_1) by the definite integral:[3]

$$\int_{t=0}^{t=n} a_{ij}dt = \int_{t=0}^{t=n} b_{ja}A_i dt + \int_{t=0}^{t=n} b_{jp}P_i dt + \int_{t=0}^{t=n} b_{jd}D_i dt$$

$$+ \int_{t=0}^{t=n} b_{jes}(E_{i1} - E_{i2})S_{ai}dt \quad \textbf{(11.4)}$$

---

[3] Incidentally, equations (11.3) and (11.4) must be treated as an initial statement, needing further qualification, as to what makes the familiar learning curve, because we know that in fact, repetition tends to bring growth in a_{ij} eventually to a plateau, whereas (11.3) is linear. One suspects that a_{ij} reaches a plateau for each individual largely because the general capacities—g's—and provincial powers—p's—(being substantially dependent on physiological limits) do not lead to positive feedback as do the a's in the upswinging part of the learning curve but reach a genetic limit. Meanwhile the rewards in the form of ($E_1 - E_2$) decrease toward zero, because time and reward cannot be spread indefinitely over all the areas of possibly "desirable" learning. There are but 24 hours in a day, so the increments eventually fall to zero no matter how substantial the g's and p's. Moreover, as the work of Fleishman (1954) and of Tucker (1966) indicates, the b's change in magnitude according to the level reached in the skill (declining to zero at the plateau level). The pioneer experimental factorings of skills at different levels of learning by Tucker and Fleishman are an important beginning in our understanding of the roles of abilities in building abilities, as set out in general form in equation (11.3).

If the levels of several people on a_{ij} are compared, the differences among them can be due to (a) the original differences in their A, P, and D trait levels, (b) differences in the reward and arousal cumulatively experienced, and (c) differences in frequency of encountering the learning situation, i.e., in n. It follows that the factorial structure among a set of performances a_1 through a_n can reflect these three sources in varying degrees. In the case of the form of the crystallized intelligence source trait, a_g, it has been suggested that a major part of the determination of its "shape" is through a pre-existing A trait, fluid intelligence. In the case of *aids* (such as Thurstone's N (number facility)) it has been hypothesized that a common n across the elements accounts for their factor unity. By contrast, in the generation of proficiencies (such as the skills which make the repertoire of a good sales-man) it has been hypothesized that a common reward experience $(E_1 - E_2)$ has bound the a's into a unitary ability pattern. It is not so easy to point to a personality-temperament endowment shaping the form of acquisition of an ability, though one can surmise that a high surgency (F factor) favoring much social interaction when in groups might develop a pattern of social skills in a surgent individual, such as the "social intelligence" conceived by Thorndike.

With this brief "skeleton" of equations indicating the application of structured learning theory to research on the development of ability, it may assist understanding to turn to a concrete case—and a return to the relation of fluid to crystallized general intelligence provides such a case. However, in leaving the above formulations it should be pointed out that for the able student these precise statements of a theoretical model can be the beginning of major advances in the field through well-designed experiment.

The issue to which we are alerted by these equations (in contrast to traditional learning theory) is the role of existing A, P, and D source traits in generating new structures and the possible role of S—state of arousal level.

Some readers may have been taken aback by the final and explicit "demotion" in the last chapter of g_c from a power—a peer among the g's —to the status of an agency or acquired product. The change of conception, and the change of symbolism from g_c to a_g (the most general of agencies), will come hard after years of writing g_c, and the habit (never however, entirely justified) of thinking of g_c as the twin brother of g_f. The fact is that crystallized intelligence has all the properties of an agency. It mimics a general capacity by its great breadth, but this breadth exists only in one culture (and sometimes only in a school system) whereas fluid intelligence, speed, and retrieval, are as broad as biology, and run through mental performances in different cultures as ubiquitously as moisture through the world's atmosphere. Nevertheless, a_g is unique among the agencies in having, relative to any of them now known, a tremendous span over any sample of intellectual performances and also in being the special off-spring of a particular capacity, namely g_f (whereas all others appear as complex derivatives of various g's and p's). Thus, at the cost of a sharp break with history, we must no longer represent fluid and crystallized intelligence as the king and queen of the abilities, but rather as a father and his family of children—a well-knit and unified family, but still an aggregate of separate "agencies." It is strictly an a_g, not a g_c, and it would be best so to designate it henceforth.

On this basis, let us inspect its growth more closely. According to our initial sketch (Figure 6–2, page 123) the unitary character of a_g arises from what might appear an accidental (or, at any rate not *necessary*) circumstances of high overlap of two powerful factors in our lives—fluid intelligence and common school learning. But what exactly is "common school learning?" From the formula (11.3) above for the growth of an ability, it is evident that this is no passively received imprint from a curriculum. It involves the experience of a living individual, whose dynamics are represented by the P's and D's of that equation. What we have been connoting by common school experience is really the likelihood of certain repeated learning experiences having, simultaneously across all of them, large b and E terms applied to the shared g, p, a, P, and D factors. That is to say, we are recognizing that the "common experience" has so far, for convenient approximation, been sketched as more of a unity than it actually is. The impact of a number of personality factors, and, especially, an uneven distribution of interests will make the investment of g_f relatively uneven. And even within the ability part of the equation itself, we now realize through (11.3) that the learning is not through g_f alone, but depends on weights on several factors. Let us represent the relations we are to discuss concretely, though with guessed, approximate factual values, in the data of an experiment in Table 11–3.

The student will realize that the values in any *row* in a factor matrix—which is what Equation (11.2) or (11.3) is—are the b's in the specification equation which say by what weight each factor is to be brought in to predict the level of the variable named at the end of the row. The b describes the relevance or potency of the factor for that kind of learning. For discussion let us simplify loadings to rounded one-decimal-place figures, as shown in Table 11–3(b) A. (Let us repeat that these are not exact figures from a particular experiment, but representative central values from several experiments.)

Our concern is with the learning gain in several aspects of the school curriculum, but since we may suppose the children started from zero, the gain is also their present level. We are thus in the domain of equation (11.3), but since actual research has not yet progressed to that level and form of analysis, we shall suppose a formulation closer to the current factor-analytic model, as in (11.5).

$$A_{xi} = b_{xg}g_{fi} + b_{xm}M_i + b_{xd}D_i + b_{x1}L_i \text{ (plus specifics and errors)} \quad \textbf{(11.5)}$$

This states that an individual's level on a particular ability in school, A_x, results from his level of fluid intelligence, g_f; the goodness of his powers of memorizing, M; the level of the dynamic trait or traits, D, concerned with his motivation; and the totality of the learning conditions (repetition, reinforcement) which, to shorten the expression with ergic tension reduction, $(E_2 - E_1)$ and arousal, S, as in equation (11.4) we represent by L. The simplification in (11.5) consists in taking L out of its complex relations and letting it operate in a simpler model as just another factor—additively.

A factor analysis of the given correlation matrix, (11–3a) yields the factor matrix (11–3b), part A. Here we see that five tests—vocabulary, geometry, knowledge of literature, knowledge of history, and algebra performance—are unique in sharing loadings on all four factors as follows: (1) g_f, fluid ability demand, (2) L, learning (time taught and reinforcement in school), (3) D, the common interest (motivation) across school subjects (which could be called need for school achievement) and (4) M, goodness of memory. Other abilities, such as chess (not taught in school) and drawing skill are in some of these, but not all. Consequently (Note: the correlations in Table 11–3(a) can be obtained as the "inner products" of the rows concerned in the factor matrix, 11–3(b)A), although *all* these cognitive variables will tend to correlate positively, the *really high* correlations (such as could yield an unrotated general factor) occur, in Table 11–3 (a), among these five.

Now in Chapter 6 we have already noted that there tends—for historical pedagogic reasons—to be a coincidence between the activities chosen for the school curriculum and those which happen to demand high fluid intelligence. This means that the L factor values (column 2 in 11–3(b)A)—the time and reinforcement in school learning—will be substantial in this core, a little less in subjects like athletics and singing, and zero in gardening and motorcycling (also zero in *some* high g_f-loaded performances, like chess and culture-fair test use, which we have included here for another reason). The tendency for high values in column 1 to go with high values in column 2 (which would be more evident if we cut out 7 and 8 as artificial and had space to continue 15 and 16 into a host of other everyday and recreational activities like dishwashing!) is an instance of what is known in factor analysis as the action of *cooperative factors*.

Any phenomenon of cooperative factors, i.e., two independent factors manifestly settling on the same set of targets, merits inquiry, and this important case particularly does so. Actually, the essential explanation of this overlap has already been offered in Chapter 6 (page 117). The "coronet" of areas of fine judgmental skills, which clings like a circlet of intellectual gems around the brow of education in most advanced cultures, derives, as a curriculum in our western culture, from the trivium and quadrivium of the medieval schools, enriched by the Renaissance addition of scientific and humanistic interests. It has seemed reasonable to the schools of the last two centuries to continue to teach these intelligence-demanding subjects—even when they did not apply too obviously to the workaday proficiencies of the average man's job. (As we have seen, the illusion that they justify retention as intelligence-generating (by transfer) as *well* as intelligence-demanding exercises was dispelled by the researches of psychologists early in this century.) But the movement to shift to what is merely useful and applicable, in regard to job and everyday social life, lost its force because the crescendo of cultural complication threw up new and equally intelligence-demanding subjects of the level of complexity and intellectual challenge shown by chemistry, computer science, and physics —and which are also necessities for the new kinds of jobs! Latin may have fallen by the wayside, but the rest of the scholars' original intelligence-involving subjects, e.g., mathematics, have preserved their scholastic hegemony and new areas of the same quality have been added.

"General life experience" (no matter what the "progressive-casual" movement in education says) does not *necessarily* exercise g_f at all strongly. Everyday life may be better lived if g_f is strongly exercised, but there is no force to see that daily life *gets* that application. A statistically slender byproduct from a research by the present writer years ago gives a clue here. It was found in a group of diverse school performances whose "intelligence saturation" (factor loading: rate of increase of score with increased endowment and application of intelligence) was known, that a negative correlation of about -0.8 existed between the *g-demand* of a school subject and its popularity as voted by students. This rather vital observation has apparently not been checked by educators, but it suggests that people will

TABLE 11–3
Numerical Exemplification of the Correlational and Loading Relationships of Fluid and Crystallized Intelligence, Time in School, Interest in School, Memory, and Achievement

(a) Correlation Matrix of Variables, Consistent with Factor Matrix Below

	1	2	3	4	5	6	7	8	9	10	11	12	13	14	15	16
1	.58	.48	.45	.43	.46	.51	.36	.36	.36	.33	.40	.22	.30	.24	.15	.09
2	.48	.44	.37	.34	.41	.45	.30	.30	.27	.23	.30	.21	.29	.24	.08	.06
3	.45	.37	.43	.40	.34	.41	.18	.18	.23	.24	.41	.22	.28	.25	.15	.07
4	.43	.34	.40	.38	.32	.38	.18	.18	.23	.24	.39	.20	.25	.22	.15	.07
5	.46	.41	.34	.32	.39	.42	.30	.30	.27	.23	.28	.19	.26	.21	.08	.06
6	.51	.45	.41	.38	.42	.47	.30	.30	.29	.26	.35	.22	.30	.25	.11	.07
7	.36	.30	.18	.18	.30	.30	.36	.36	.30	.24	.12	.06	.12	.06	.06	.06
8	.36	.30	.18	.18	.30	.30	.36	.36	.30	.24	.12	.06	.12	.06	.06	.06
9	.36	.27	.23	.23	.27	.29	.30	.30	.29	.26	.20	.07	.12	.07	.11	.07
10	.33	.23	.24	.24	.23	.26	.24	.24	.26	.25	.23	.07	.11	.07	.13	.07
11	.40	.30	.41	.39	.28	.35	.12	.12	.20	.23	.42	.20	.24	.22	.17	.07
12	.22	.21	.22	.20	.19	.22	.06	.06	.07	.07	.20	.15	.18	.17	.04	.02
13	.30	.29	.28	.25	.26	.30	.12	.12	.12	.11	.24	.18	.23	.21	.05	.03
14	.24	.24	.25	.22	.21	.25	.06	.06	.07	.07	.22	.17	.21	.20	.04	.02
15	.15	.08	.15	.15	.08	.11	.06	.06	.11	.13	.17	.04	.05	.04	.10	.04
16	.09	.06	.07	.07	.06	.07	.06	.06	.07	.07	.07	.02	.03	.02	.04	.02

Variables bear same numbers as in (b) below.

(b) Factor Matrix, and Correlations Used as Basis for Weighting

	A. Factor Matrix (Ortho) (Loadings = Correlations with Factors[1])				B. Correlations of Tests with Estimated Scores on Achievement, Crystallized Intelligence and Present Fluid Intelligence[2]		
	g_f	L	D	M	Ach.	a_g	g_{f2}
1. Vocabulary	.6	.3	.2	.3	.73	.75	
2. Geometry	.5	.3	.3	.1	.63	.66	
3. Literature	.3	.3	.3	.4	.64		
4. History	.3	.3	.2	.4	.59		
5. Algebra	.5	.3	.2	.1	.59	.62	
6. Problem Arithmetic	.5	.3	.3	.2	.67	.68	
7. Culture-Fair Analogies	.6						.60
8. Culture-Fair Classification	.6						.60
9. Chess Success	.5			.2			
10. Life Problems	.4			.3			
11. Spelling	.2	.3	.2	.5	.57		
12. Drawing	.1	.3	.2	.1	.35		
13. Music and Linguistics	.2	.3	.3	.1	.45		
14. School Sports	.1	.3	.3	.1	.39		
15. Gardening	.1			.3			
16. Cycling	.1			.1			

g_f = Fluid intelligence at time of being in school.
L = Length of schooling time.
D = Dynamic interest in schooling learning at the time.
M = General goodness of memory
Ach. = School achievement (weights appropriately given to assessing it as a cluster)
a_g = Crystallized Intelligence
g_{f2} = Fluid intelligence at present time.

[1] Normally, with oblique factors, loadings do *not* equal correlations.

[2] g_{f2} in b is the centroid when g_f is estimated only from the tests indicated, and is thus not *identical* with g_f in a both because of error of estimate and because it is at a later time. Similarly Achievement (Ach.) and crystallized intelligence (a_g) are estimated only from the chosen variables agreed to represent each.

(c) Correlations Among Achievement, Fluid Intelligence and Crystallized Intelligence

	1	2	3
1. Fluid Intelligence	1.00	.50	.42
2. Crystallized Intell.	.50	1.00	.93
3. Achievement	.42	.93	1.00

learn willingly what they need to learn provided it does not demand much hard thinking! (A psychologist would be interested to see the experiment repeated with various branches and approaches, specifically in types of psychology courses, in relation to choice by the average psychology student!) In our culture the implication is generally accepted, as a reality of life, that children play games, learn hunting, do clay modeling, discuss emotionally-exciting literature, go on action parades, paint pictures, etc., almost on their own, but that involvement in more abstract and disciplinary thinking needs a (usually compulsory) school organization. That the school concentrates (relative to the nonschool world) on the higher g_f-saturated subjects is thus, historically and in terms of a viable culture, not an accident, but a necessity in the interests of human progress. In short, the parallelism that would exist in columns 1 and 2 in Figure 11–3, if continued over a wider range of activities, has, like most other instances of cooperative factor patterns, a systematic cause.

The role of the dynamic interest, D, and memory ability, M, column values will be discussed more in a moment. Meanwhile let us first note the "product variables" in Table 11–3(b)B. They are the products of the contributors—intelligence, interest, etc.—we have just been discussing, but assembled in commonly labelled major patterns—achievement and crystallized intelligence—instead of being left as single curriculum variables. The first column "Ach" shows correlations with variables representative of performances that normally would go with equal weight into a total measure of school achievement. That is to say, we have simply added up each individual's grades on all subjects in the curriculum and have given him a total school achievement score. Although the subjects go in with equal weight into the achievement total they do not finish up with equal correlation with the achievement vector, because they are variously correlated among themselves, and the eventual actual outcome in correlations is as shown in column 1. The second column consists of the kinds of performance (four of them) which are normally judged to demand high intelligence, and because of this and their high loading on a centroid through the cluster formed (see Table 11–3(a)), they are incorporated usually in traditional intelligence tests. (Geometry is not usually included as such, but its reasoning problems are.) The third column considers only the measures (7 and 8) which have neither school time in common, nor memory power, nor any effect from common interest—these are the culture-fair tests, taken as the best measures of g_f.

The loadings of all variables involved, upon the centroid of each of these three sets of variables can be computed, and they are the numbers set out in the B columns. Although the crystallized intelligence factor, a_g (column 2) uses achievement variables, it gives little weight to such things as drawing, athletics, etc., and the low values have been omitted altogether. Although the a_g has still less correlation with the "nonintellectual" school subjects, it is still much contaminated—relative to g_{f2}, the culture-fair test—with L, D, and M. Indeed, as seen starkly here, it is rather an odd and error-fraught way of going about the estimation of g_f—at least, when it is possible to estimate it directly by tests like 7 and 8 in Table 11–3. Certainly, to form our estimate of g_f through a_g is to see it through a glass darkly, as the correlation of 0.5 in Table 11–3(c) shows.

Some justification for using a_g as a measure for essential intelligence, i.e., for g_f, *in a culturally uniform group* comes from the fact that the L contribution—if not D and M—is a pretty constant contribution for all individuals over much of the school period. But for comparisons of persons in different subcultures, the method is poor, because the L values are now different. Even in one culture, as children grow up and go their different ways as adult citizens, the traditional test obviously becomes increasingly misleading, as we shall see factually in Chapter 14.

Table 11–3(c) shows the actual correlations among the three concepts —achievement, crystallized and fluid intelligence—worked out among the vectors constituted by the three centroids from Table 11–3(b)B. That is to say, assuming that achievement, a_g, and g_f were estimated with perfect validity on the basis of variables there used and others like them, how would the three intercorrelate? It will be seen that achievement and crystallized intelligence correlate better than the former does with fluid intelligence. As discussed in Chapter 15, this is taken frequently by teachers as an indication that they are more *valid* than culture-fair tests. But, in fact, it shows merely that they are more contaminated with the particular criterion which, in this case, they happen to be trying to predict. With other life criteria from other areas in which we believe the expression of intelligence to be important, their relative positions would be quite different.

9. THE DISTINCTION OF DEVELOPMENTAL AND ACTION STRUCTURES, AND THE CHANGING PATTERN OF CRYSTALLIZED INTELLIGENCE

Two further very fundamental questions will occur to the student looking at the analysis in Table 11–3, the essence of which is reproduced in geometric form in Figure 11–3. First, there is the theoretical question "How is it that we have been speaking of a_g as a *factor*

FIGURE 11–3
Crystallized Intelligence as a Surface and as a Source Trait

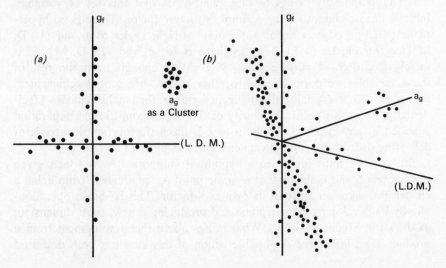

when the grouping of the six variables here (Figure 11–3) would indicate that they are behaving only as a correlation cluster or surface trait?" Secondly, there is the more practical question, "If a_g is the overlap and summation of fluid ability with amount of school experience (L), interest (D), memory (M), why do we not simply call this composite product "school achievement?" (This concerns the difference of column 1 and column 2 in Table 11–3(b)B.) Since we distinguish achievement and crystallized intelligence, what is the rationale for picking out the longest vectors in this common space—variables 1, 2, 5, and 6—as the basis of crystallized intelligence?" Since such questions may well have occurred earlier to the reader, one feels apologetic for neglecting them, but an adequate answer was not possible before sharpening the concepts treated in the last two sections.

For clarity and brevity of illustration, the data of Table 11–3 has been reproduced graphically in Figure 11–3 (which we have simplified by representing the factors L, D, and M which are only tangential to the argument as a single composite vector). In this drawing, the usual convention is followed of drawing any two tests as unit length vectors such that the cosine between them equals the experimentally given correlations. Factors are then coordinates, and initially, in 11–3(a), only two are shown. (This is a true two-dimensional diagram; but in 11–3(b) it has been necessary to draw three dimensions in perspective in two space.) The bunch of variables that shares both g_f and (L, D, M) loadings, and therefore consists of a definite correlation cluster, is shown by the variable numbers 1, 2, 3, 4, 5, and 6, as identified in Table 11–3. However, tests are represented by the *points* at the end of the vectors rather than by drawing in the vector lines too, in order to keep the drawing free of confusion. Normally the "coronet" of variables, 1, 2, 3, etc., which load high both on g_f and with emphasis in the school curriculum factor (L, D, M) would appear simply as a cluster of vectors, as shown in 11–3(a).

Regardless of details of representation, the important fact that Figure 11–3(a) graphically brings to our attention is that this set of variables initially has no claim to being a simple structure factor. There is no hyperplane (seen on edge as nebulae of points at right angles to g_f and (L, D, M) for this cluster in 11–3(a) as there is for g_f and (L, D, M). It is merely a cluster—a surface trait—segregating enough from the rest of those variables we normally add together to measure school achievement for us to call it crystallized intelligence rather than achievement. (Incidentally, up to this point, the clarity of this separation, like the separation supplied by any evidence about clusters, is unsatisfactory and incapable of delivering us from conceptual vagueness and disputes of opinion.)

But now we must introduce a hypothesis, supported by the facts given in Chapters 5 and 6 above, that at some point a_g "graduates" from being a cluster and takes on a life of its own as a factor. This is shown operationally by its developing a hyperplane and producing a new, third dimension, as shown in Figure 11–3(b). What brings about this development from a *product* to an *influence?* A possible action of this kind has been discussed under "aids." For there we have supposed that an agency as a tool tends to open up the possibility of grasping further tools, and that an agency as a proficiency tends to be consciously recognized and to receive reinforcement through the emotional satisfactions of the self-sentiment. In either case, what was a product becomes a more autonomous influence, catalyzing its own growth, appearing statistically as an interaction effect and operating as an influence, now partly independent of its origins, upon several specific intellectual performances. In the case of the agency, a_g, the integration of acquired verbal and reasoning skills escalates into a self-propagating unitary agency, invoked in a wide array of performances.

In terms of experimental evidence, the question of whether a hyperplane is visible for this new factor is even more important than whether a test of number of factors establishes the need for an extra factor. Actually, in the experimental data gathered in Chapter 5, such a hyperplane is found readily enough. The a_g hyperplane shows itself in several "culture-fair" performances, from the fluid ability factor which involves no school work; in rote learning performances, in skills in school and elsewhere that involve little or no "intelligence," and in personality factors (see Figure 6–1) which involve no ability of any kind. These are the things which the a_g factor shows that it does not affect, and which, as a hyperplane, have zero loading on it.

For the sake of establishing principles governing the kind of cluster-to-factor development occurring here (as well as in other instances in psychology) current research needs to concentrate on the ways—so far largely hypothetically stated here—in which a surface trait tends to become a source trait (factor or influence). The two main processes here suggested —*aid* (tool) transfer effects and dynamic unity as a sentiment *effector*— have been sketched above as hypothetically so acting in the case of crystallized ability. In more detail, one can see that the first principle works through the cognitive consistencies and overlaps inherent in the g_f saturated school subjects which enable each to help progress in the others. Geography makes history more intelligible; history adds to the meaning of literature; mathematics is a tool in every science, notably in economics, chemistry, and physics;[6] and vocabulary helps all. An increment of judgmental capacity in one is likely to bring about an increment—smaller but real—in all. Further, it is reasonable to suppose that the multiplied possibilities of associational links provide a basis for the rise—when sufficient g_f is present—of higher-order relation eductions. It is these relations higher

---

[6] If anything, some tendency to develop into three distinct, less broad "group" factors, one in the arts, one in literature, one in the sciences, might be expected from the natural structure of our school curriculum, in terms of the cognitive consistencies and transfers that should operate. Some intelligence test structures, such as the division into "verbal" and "quantitative" categories in the college entrance, seem to assume such patterns, but firm evidence for any such major separate *factor* nuclei within the main crystallized general ability factor is lacking still. Conceivably, the division may appear too late in school life to gain any separate variance as abilities—as distinct from achievements.

in the hierarchy that are presumably able to transfer more effectively to new fields—mathematical, statistical and logical relations would be instances—and thus make an individual's possession of a_g something which operates over a wide field of both old and new cognitive problem-solving.

On the dynamic side, unity is guaranteed by the demonstrated (Cattell, Sweney, and Radcliffe, 1960) existence of a "sentiment to school work and the school." Experimental, objective, dynamic studies also show that a conception of oneself as a good or an unenthusiastic scholar gets incorporated in the general self-regarding sentiment (Gorsuch, 1965; Horn, 1965). Thus reinforced and integrated by conscious realization and emotional investment, it is no wonder that the crystallized general ability pattern quickly takes on the character of an independent, productive, self-perpetuating, and expanding influence in any learning or problem-solving situation that the individual encounters.

If this explanation continues to fit new data, it will suffice also to give an answer to the *second* of our opening questions, namely: "Why are we not content to call a_g just "scholastic achievement?" A first answer has already been given in connection with equations (11.1) and (11.2) above, namely, that achievement as a whole is dependent on many factors, some of which—like rote memory, M, and bodily dexterity—have operated without any teaming-up with g_f. Such rote knowledge or athletic skill is not an essential part of that command of complex relations across many cognitive areas that we call a_g, and that is capable of operating across many areas. A second reason for conceptually separating them is that while there is comparatively little doubt about the areas of study in which g_f produces its harvest of a_g, there is considerable disagreement among citizens and teachers about what constitutes achievement! It is indeed an arbitrary domain, at the mercy of vagaries of values. If we could make no distinction between the sprawling achievement cluster and the crystallized intelligence factor, a debate would ensue in constructing every intelligence battery. Should it include grades for athletics? Should singing and music be counted as two sub-tests or one? And should the scoring weight for cooking and home economics be the same as that for chemistry? The definition of a_g has been, with many psychologists, it is true, nothing more precise than that of a preferred cluster—as witness countless traditional intelligence tests. It has amounted to designating a medley of "higher intelligence loaded" achievement variables as shown in column 1 in Table 11–3(b). Necessarily, as the values in column 1 show, some lower but appreciable weights still will have to be given in estimating this vector by this justification, to achievements that are acquired by the child through sheer rote memory, or length of attendance in school, requiring no midwifery from g_f.

On the other hand, when factor analysis separates out from these performances on a_g factor, it shows us a pattern which, though arbitrary in the sense of being local to the culture, is quite distinct from the sprawling achievement correlation cluster. Our argument is that it separates out as a functional unity because of the dropping out of the numerous nonintelligent, atomistically specific habits which have little or no transfer value in learning, and no common recognized part in a self-conscious sentiment. Because of their isolation from the hierarchy of relations, they do not continue to grow, and they constitute part of a new unitary influence in cognitive action and development. Such a character belongs, as far as present evidence goes, only to the spearhead collection of complex, transferable relations, concepts, and judgmental skills we call crystallized intelligence.

Any lingering doubts we have as to why the molten metal of fluid intelligence when poured into the definite school curriculum mold should create so unitary and influential a factor pattern as a_g, may be reasonably doubted in view of the fact that we have been content all along to accept just such transfer, cognitive consistency, and common learning experiences as sufficient to explain the more limited unitariness within each of the primary ability agencies themselves. The theoretical position on which we have finally converged is one in which a_g is definitely of the same qualitative nature and species as any single *agency*. It is not a capacity or power. A decent caution in reaching or emphasizing this conclusion is nevertheless appropriate because of its uniqueness among the a's in sheer size and in the great *range* of its effects. Indeed, if this pervasiveness of the predictive power of a_g has not so constantly manifested itself in school intelligence researches, psychologists would not have been so long hypnotized and misled by its full-moon face into taking it as *the* concept of intelligence, and as the model for all intelligence test design.

Some reluctance among psychologists to "demote" crystallized intelligence from a g to an a may persist from a less rational cause, namely, that one has long been accustomed to regard it, in its demonstrated role as a second-order factor, as having the *properties* as well as the rank of its "general power" peers. That factor-stratum level should not be considered at all closely related to properties has already been argued here. Nevertheless, the undoubted experimental fact of its higher-stratum level, showing that it shares some appreciable variance with each of *several* primary abilities, could confer some special properties upon it. In the sense that the height of a hierarchy depends on the breadth of its base, the cumulative contribution of the "committee" of primary agencies confers a level of abstractive capacity to a_g which is unrivalled by any a. The question arises whether it may also be unrivalled by g_f—at least after g_f declines. Is it possible that the only area in which g_f can exercise its most complex relation eductions is in a_g, and that no restricted area—as in some single a— suffices? In specific terms, can a high g_f find sufficient room to spread its wings only in a world philosophy, and not in numerical ability, or spatial or verbal skills? The fact that, so far, culture-fair intelligence tests, involving complex relations in the spatial domain, have proved complex enough to puzzle eminent philosophers, and to load as high as anything yet tried on the general relation-perceiving capacity running across all areas, argues against a broad base of knowledge or many sensory areas being necessary to permit higher relations. Crystallized intelligence is a *repository* for some of the highest among the abstractions mastered by g_f, but its cultural content is not essential for a severe exercise of g_f. The uniqueness of a_g among the a's resides in the high *generality* of useful application of the abstractions stored in it, not necessarily in their level of *complexity*. The best conclusion today would seem to be that a_g is the most general of agencies, but still an agency, and not a capacity or power.

In summarizing this summit view of our theory of ability structure as such, two emphases perhaps need to be made, even if at the cost of some repetition. First, in virtually all of the classes of concepts in Figure 11–1 —capacities, powers, or organizations, and agencies—we must recognize (a) that the triadic classification is according to *total properties* and definitely is not simply by factor-stratum position, i.e., breadth, which is only one source of evidence, and (b) that although each influence appears as a unitary factor, nevertheless, we have also the conceptual alternative, at any level below the top stratum, of considering and treating it developmentally as the result of a set of components. In the case of the agencies these are the components contributed by the capacities, by the provincials, and specifically by those aid or effector proficiencies which account for the rise of the agency as a primary structure. For example, in numerical ability we can literally estimate the numerical ability factor as a whole, as it stands as a primary. Alternatively, we can deal only with the component due to the specific primary when the second-order and higher-order factors have been partialled out. This is initially just a factor-analytic concept—the "stub" that remains in any primary when the secondary is taken out. But the stub probably also has a precise psychological meaning as the aid, or effector part contribution, apart from g_f. One can analyze out yet again the component which is from the visual and auditory organization—the provincial powers. And lastly, one can evaluate the third component in it, which is the contribution to its growth from fluid general intelligence.

The question of what the correct conceptual and experimental answer is in regard to these components arose earlier in the neurological discussions of Chapter 8, where we asked whether an individual's level of functioning on a provincial "neural organization," such as visualization power, p_v, is to be considered *apart* from the contribution which fluid general ability may make to that power or after fluid general ability has contributed to that provincial (standing as a presently functioning whole). As the factor analyst will recognize, both are operationally possible concepts, for they have their equivalents in two distinct ways of cutting up the factor-analytic variance contribution. They are, in fact, representable by two distinct formulae: the Cattell-White formula (Cattell, 1964) which pulls out at each stratum the factor as an organic whole (though overlapping with other wholes), and the Schmid-Leiman formula (Cattell, 1964) which refers each concept to that non-overlapping "specific" part—the "stub" remaining after all higher-stratum variance has been set aside. By political-economic analogy, one can say that in local and federal (central) government the local unit is a functional whole with respect to *all* the funds whose disposition it controls, regardless of source. (This is the equivalent of the Cattell-White formulation.) Alternatively one can define the "local" part as only that fraction of the local functioning and expenditure which is *not* sustained by central government contributions. (This is the equivalent of the Schmid-Leiman formula.) The alternative which one chooses to employ will determine both the concept (including its properties and natural history) and the actual numerical score an individual is assigned on that agency or power. This is a matter requiring some psychometric sophistication, but it is of too great general theoretical importance to be side-stepped.

Let us scrutinize a little more closely from this standpoint of analyzable components the general discussion above about the nature of crystallized ability. It will be noted that a two-way causal, developmental "feedback" has been hypothesized (in Figure 11–1) as the final theoretical statement of the relation of primary abilities and crystallized general ability. Either in development or in action, the possibilities to be considered here are (a) that the positive correlation which tends to exist among the agencies and which (with other evidence) is the basis of our inferring a second order a_g of crystallized general intelligence is solely due to the contribution *to* all of them *from* g_f, as we have posited in the first chapters here. However, if we hypothesize that a_g, so produced, tends to "graduate" from a surface trait to a source trait, by itself becoming a unitary influence, then it could aid and contribute to the agencies just as g_f did earlier. The psychological analysis above has favored this model, saying that the abstractions of high generality developed in a_g possess a wider transfer effect than any in the single aids. The dynamic part—through a self-conscious dynamic investment of all agencies as part of "what an intelligent man possesses"—would also show up statistically as part of this "feedback."

In regard to the first alternative—that conceiving the second order a_g as a static sum due to the individual growth of the agencies in the steady march of parallel curriculum demands—let us note that through the developmental years, as a result of cummulative experience alone, there would be a tendency for all primaries to increase with age as such. This alone would produce a common crystallized ability factor among them when populations of mixed age are factored. Some psychologists, with good reason, will consider this factor of simultaneous age maturation to be psychologically spurious, because it would vanish in equal age populations. But the a_g factor does not so vanish, so this cannot be the only cause, and, indeed, a final overview of the phenomenon must recognize causal actions of several kinds already indicated in the above formulae, namely: (a) the common growth of the a's through g_f aiding each; (b) their sharing the common effect of years of exposure to a curriculum and life experience; (c) their contributing to the rise of a relational hierarchy, which, in turn, becomes active in the growth of every agency; (d) some tendency of the inherent, self-catalyzing growth process in an a to generalize across a_g (thus requires the feedback arrow in Figure 11–1); and (e) the non-cognitive, motivational, common learning influences already discussed. Although only the arrow for (b) seems indicated definitely, it seems safer to posit both and leave research to show, if so proven, that the traffic in one direction is absent or at least far less than in the other.

Yet another aspect of these different possible emphases in subdividing these structures into components needing final perspective is that into the genetic and the environmentally acquired parts. Substantial evidence has been reviewed on g_f, showing that very little of its variance is environmental (except in the sense of brain injury or defective physiology). Regarding the primary abilities, appreciable evidence exists that they have much environmental determination, but regarding the provincials we remain uninformed. The most likely conclusion seems to be that constitutional neural structure first plays an important part in these, but one may hypothesize that, from the earliest years, the success of their storage by experience will also be important. In fact, in the only case analyzed (visualization in Table 6–1 and 6–2, pages 106 and 111, it is shown that, at the higher order, the p_v factor splits in two, almost equal parts, one part going with the presumed constitutional neural factor which affects also fluid intelligence and speed, and the other going with crystallized intelligence, suggesting an acquired part. The question of whether factor analysis alone may be capable of segregating out, as separate structures, the genetic and the threptic parts of a personality structure is a complex one discussed elsewhere (Cattell, 1946a; Thompson, 1957, 1966; Loehlin, 1962). But at present it admits no brief, simple answer. Some confidence can be given, however, to the answer that the genetic and threptic parts separate in still higher-order analyses, as we have seen for g_f and a_g in Table 6–3.

The second main emphasis needed in this final summary, if misunderstandings are to be avoided, is on the distinction maintained above, e.g., in equations (11.1) and (11.3), between the *developmental* equations and components, on the one hand, and the *present action* relations on the other. Consider either a provincial power or an agency. An agency stands at the level it holds today by virtue of a development in which several forces, e.g., one or two capacities, a dynamic sentiment, an aid, and a stated schedule of sociologically structured, reinforced experience have operated. On the other hand, the level of a given, specific *performance* stands where it does, in present action, by virtue of the capacities, dynamic sentiments, provincials, and agencies at their *present* levels, acting additively (the former no longer *through* the agency).

A less developed model for this analysis—but one closely tied to existing experimental evidence—was presented, in Tables 6–1 through 6–4, pages 106–116, in terms of higher and lower-strata concepts, and before reaching our present elaboration of the triadic theory. Our interpretation was that the third-stratum appearance of the fluid ability factor must represent, not the individual's fluid ability *today,* but his fluid ability years earlier when it was in process of building up his crystallized ability. Factor analysis was here undoubtedly revealing, as it can do, historical happenings, rather than present structure. Just so, an archeologist may find below some medieval castle whose structure he is exploring, not the expected foundations, but parts of the roof of a much earlier building. Developmental and present action equations are not easy to infer as separate contributions to the observed factor-analytic outcome; but sometimes we get powerful hints. When we simply do an R-technique factor analysis on variables measured upon, say, an adult group, we demonstrate that the ability to solve, say, an arithmetic problem today, hinges on the subject's level of functional numerical ability, crystallized general intelligence, and probably fluid intelligence. But the third-order factoring is likely to show, as just instanced, that the crystallized intelliegnce itself has been a product of substantial contribution from a fluid intelligence factor, which must be ascribed to earlier years. This is our hypothesis, but the R-technique factor analysis is not able to distinguish *directly* between present and past causal action. Only by dR-technique, and by the other indirect multivariate approaches and independent longitudinal experiments, which cannot be set out systematically here, can the developmental and the present action equations be separated fully.

Although in a treatment for general reading, such as this, it is not appropriate to pursue further the precise psychometric equations, one can perhaps succeed in glimpsing the intricacies of genetic and learned components which make up the structure of our abilities. Every individual contains in his present structure—with far greater sequential complication than the story in the growth rings of a tree—a record of the path of development. On page 335, a precise model has been presented in which learning can be expressed as changes in the (b's) behavioral indices (loadings) showing how abilities are combined in a performance, on the modulator indices (s's) showing how far interest and reactivity to the situation has been learned, and on the individual's levels of the various traits themselves. If psychometric subtleties could be pursued, it would be possible to show how the learning increments on the factors can be derived from the factoring of the same array of performances as yield the changing b and s patterns.

The full understanding of how abilities operate requires a grasp of this *tri-vectored learning theory,* as well as of the equation for performance at a given occasion, including the joint operation of abilities and personality-dynamic traits, to be pursued further in the next chapter. Without this more complete penetration of the mathematics of the model, we can nevertheless profitably take note of some important lemmas on those theorems, such as: (a) that the weights (b's) on abilities may alter continuously and appreciably for the same kind of performance with the level and the stage of learning (Fleishman and Ellison, 1969; Tucker, 1966);

(b) that the importance and role of an interest (a dynamic trait) may be very different in the learning *formation* of an ability agency from that which it plays in affecting *performance* at a given moment; (verbal ability, for example, might be much determined in shape and level over years by certain motivations, e.g., by interest in reading, but vocabulary performance *in a moment of school examination* might be very little affected by motivation level); (c) if the theory of autonomous growth of agencies is correct, we should expect to find on the loading patterns of traits with respect to learning on variables connected with one of them, high values for the trait itself, i.e., a self-perpetuating tendency; (d) some of the clearest evidence of transfer in shaping the structural form of new abilities is likely to be obtained by what has been described above as differential R-technique experiment.

These propositions can be readily illustrated by reference to one of the central concepts in the triadic theory—crystallized intelligence (a_g)—with which we have been much concerned. The developmental equation in early school makes it largely a function of g_f and the form of the curriculum. In later school, the self-conscious adoption of certain, proudly possessed, primary skills, realistically embodied in most students' self-sentiment, may lead to their growing more strongly than other curriculum aspects, i.e., the factor pattern begins to change. In the succeeding occupational years it continues to grow differently according to the subgroup in which the individual finds himself or even according to absolutely idiosyncratic interest molds. Indeed, already in childhood it will reflect to some extent such influences as the residential locale, the occupation of the father, the peer values, and so on. We do not, in fact, know how far the validity of a traditional crystallized intelligence test, even when explicitly aimed at g_c, is adequate, because we lack surveys of what the circumference of the child's knowledge and interests is, either for important subcultures or for the common overlap area of a good sample of subcultures. A beginning of a map of "what every child should know" (not in school terms, but in life terms) exists in various studies, e.g., that of Caldwell (1958) for young children. After that, there is greater uncertainty about the "map" than we commonly realize, though from what we know in educational sociology and administration about the constancy of the school curriculum, it is probably safe to conclude that the pattern of a_g is at least far more stable than it is later. As a factor pattern, we would expect a_g to become in later adult life relatively attenuated in variance and vague in outline, except for the common deposit which all adults retain from school, and apart from the most common—largely social and verbal—experiences of everyday life. The notion of a single general crystallized ability consequently begins to lose usefulness and validity among adults, though if we adopt tests highly adapted to an occupational or social subgroup pattern, perhaps a_g validity can still be obtained. Nevertheless, the structure is, by now, the integral of several different successive development equations.

The practical consequences and predicaments, in the use of ability measures in applied psychology, to be expected on the basis of this analysis will be met in Chapters 12 and 13.

CHAPTER TWELVE

PERSONALITY-ABILITY INTERACTIONS AND THE PREDICTION OF ACHIEVEMENT

1. BASIC PRINCIPLES IN DISSECTING ABILITY FROM PERSONALITY AND MOTIVATION TRAITS

The last chapter should have left no doubt that a fundamental treatment of abilities is impossible without a thorough understanding also of psychological principles in personality and motivation. The latter enter into understanding of both (1) the development of abilities, and (2) the action of abilities, and soon we shall encounter a third interaction in which (3) abilities shape personality and motivation. So far we have edged our way into this realm of interaction in connection with the two topics above, but the time is ripe to study systematically the whole issue of interaction of ability, personality and motivation.

In the substance of folk wisdom as developed from the observations of everyday life, few topics are more movingly discussed than that of the fate of individuals having great disparities between the level of their abilities and the maturity of the rest of their personalities. Outstanding character and personality with very limited abilities is a not uncommon picture which leaves us with a sense of respect, but also a sad awareness of waste, while brilliance with a defective character or warped personality presents us with a sinister Dr. Moriarty or a disastrous Cellini or Cagliostro!

Ability, temperament, and dynamic traits are commonly referred to in psychology as three trait *modalities*. But they are far more frequently used than defined. At the very outset of any study of the interplay of these three modalities, we should make clear how we recognize and define the nature of each. One might think, from the confidence with which psychologists speak of ability, temperament, and motivation traits, that infallible methods exist for distinguishing them. On the contrary, only "commonsense" agreement, aided by a long, uneasy truce in analytical criticism, prevails. Far-fetched positions—such as McDougall's attempt (1932) to explain Spearman's "g" as a motivational phenomenon (note the somewhat similar recent position of Hayes [1962])—can be asserted still with nothing but embarrassment to refute them. Even in everyday psychometric practice it is brought home to us with painful frequency that common sense is not good enough to effect a decisive separation. For example, among the personality traits covered in the 16 Personality Factor Questionnaire there are factors such as E, dominance, or G, superego strength, which are viewed by some psychologists as dynamic traits, and by others as virtually temperamental. And in the domain of objective, nonquestionnaire, miniature-situational personality tests, as in the O-A (Objective-Analytic) Battery, there are dimensions such as U.I. 19, Independence, or U.I. 21, Exuberance which powerfully affect certain performances (Gottschalk figures and Witkin's field independence in the former; word fluency and fast judgment in paired comparisons in the latter) frequently treated as sheer ability measures.

Before a more explicit rationale can be given for modality distinction, and, indeed, before the whole theme of ability-personality interaction can be knowledgeably discussed in this chapter, it would be desirable to remind the reader, by the briefest thumb-nail sketch, of the present status of structural measurement in the personality field.

The recognition, description, and measurement of structures in the personality and motivation fields naturally reduces to the same basic principles of research as the reader has seen in operation in the ability field. After the first rough clinical perceptions of functional unities described as drives (with much disagreement), ego strength, anxiety, schizothyme temperament, and superego structure, there followed the same psychometric, quantitative, correlational tightening of observation and analysis. Fundamentally there is no proof of a unity, either as a trait structure or as a state (such as anxiety), except by showing "what goes together," and this reaches its greatest methodological penetration and precision in factor analysis—cross-sectional and longitudinal. Across ability, personality-temperament, and dynamic-motivational realms, the same principles of investigation apply, but with local tactical adjustments, e.g., to the fact that dynamic patterns are more complex and fluctuant than those of abilities, and that there is, in general, no single "positive" or desirable direction of scoring in temperament measures, as there is in abilities.

Again, whereas ability research usually has not trusted to ratings by observers, and certainly not questionnaires ("Just how intelligent are you?"), personality and motivation researchers have worked frequently with these two media of data gathering, at least until the objective test "miniature situation" approach developed (Cattell and Warburton, 1967) and added the precision of laboratory measures. Problems still exist in equating across the three media, though it is evident that the dozen or more independent patterns—surgency, F, ego strength, C, affectothymia, A, superego strength, G, dominance, E, etc.—found in questionnaire items are matched by corresponding factors of outward behavior that emerge from factoring *skilled and objective* ratings. On the other hand, for reasons as yet only half understood, the first-order factors found in objective personality measurement devices (and which are indexed by universal index numbers, e.g., U.I. 24 for anxiety) correspond to *second*-stratum patterns in the life observation and questionnaire media.

In the following discussion of relation of ability to personality we shall deal with the questionnaire-rating factors by the A, B, C, D, E, etc., symbols as above, and as measured by such questionnaires as the 16 P.F. (and in some cases the Guilford-Zimmerman) for adults, the High School Personality Questionnaire (HSPQ), the CPQ, etc., for children. We shall also deal with the second-stratum factors measured by the adult or the child O-A battery, or in questionnaires by Eysenck's tests for the same second-order derivatives as are scored from the 16 P.F., the HSPQ, etc. The objective personality test factors (such as U.I. 16, Ego Strength, U.I. 17, General Inhibition, U.I. 22, Arousal or Cortertia, U.I. 23($-$), Regression (Eysenck's "neuroticism"), U.I. 24, Anxiety, U.I. 29, Superego strength, U.I. 32, Extraversion), being new as measurements, are as yet not so widely known, and the researches showing their relation to ability and achievement have appeared only in the last two or three years.

Back of these concepts and measurements there is now a very extensive analysis of their genetic development in nature-nurture terms, their normal age growth curves, their constancy of pattern and difference of level across cultures, their patterns in occupational profiles; their physiological, e.g., drug and EEG associations; their clinical diagnostic utility, and so on. This conceptual and factual background must, in a book on abilities, be assumed understood by professional students, though it would be helpful, e.g., in relation to any uncertainty when ability is related to a particular personality dimension, see Bischof (1964), Cattell (1957a), Dreger (1962), Hundleby, Pawlik, and Cattell (1965), Hall and Lindzey (1957), Pawlik (1968), Sells (1962a), Pervin (1970), and others.

Our glance over advances in determining motivation structure by objective analysis and objective test devices, must also be very compressed. Whereas the Strong, the Kuder, and virtually all interests tests until the mid-1960s were based on *asking* the subject what he preferred, and the TAT used only one objective device—projection—(and that with subjective scoring which confounded the testers and the subject's projections), the developments in what has become known as the *dynamic calculus* rejected this clinical subjectivity. Over one hundred extremely varied devices (Cattell and Warburton, 1967) representing a dozen different theories about the manifestation of motivation strength, were compared over many hundreds of adult and child subjects, and those of the highest validity were selected and improved. They included the GSR response, immediate memory, spontaneous eye movements, distortion of belief (autism) and perception, projection, muscle tension, and so on. A central finding here is that every attitude-interest has two components which can be measured as distinct factors—an *unintegrated* and often unconscious component, appearing in autism, the GSR, etc., and an *integrated* component, manifesting itself in word association, information, etc.

Possessing the objective instruments of motivation-interest intensity measurement, of experimentally checkable validity, the researchers in this area set out to explore factor-analytically the whole domain of dynamic structure. Hundreds of diverse attitude-interests, over a broad "human motivation sphere" of home, career, hobbies, religious and political interests, etc., were correlated over thousands of adults in our culture (and later in others) and carefully factor analyzed. The results were a striking vindication of the clinical and ethological view that the interests of human beings are organized about "drives," "instincts," or "propensities" continuing the pattern perceived in the primates. These, as precise factor patterns discernible in objective tests have now been called *ergs;* and it turns out that this first objective demonstration of the number and nature of ergs in man confirms such Freudian hunches as that sex is separable into two patterns—an object-directed mating erg and a narcissistic erg, though on the whole this list of ergs best supports those observed by ethologists in the higher mammals.

Additional to the approximately ten ergs, a further set of factors has been found among dynamic structures called *sentiments* because they represent acquired emotional reactivity centered on such things as home, religion, school, etc. These are obviously formed by simultaneously rewarded attitudes integrated by some social institution. They have already been discussed in connection with the learning of effectors with their associated proficiencies, as studied in the last chapter.

With an instrument such as the Motivation Analysis Test (Cattell, Horn, Radcliffe, and Sweney, 1964) or the School Motivation Analysis Test (Cattell and Krug, 1970), it is possible to measure (in both integrated and unintegrated terms) an individual's level of development on a particular sentiment structure, or of ergic tension on a particular drive. Unlike abilities, the ergic tension levels, along with arousal and anxiety, vary appreciably from day to day (with stimulation and gratification), though a characteristic central level seems to exist for each person. The basic model in the dynamic calculus uses the same linear additive relation (for initial simplicity) as we use in the abilities. Thus the strength of interest in any course of action j in a stimulus situation k—a measure called an attitude-interest and represented by I—can be written:

$$I_{ijk} = b_{je_1}s_{ke_1}E_{1i} + \cdots + b_{jep}s_{kep}E_{pi} + b_{jm_1}s_{km_1}M_{1i} + \cdots$$

$$+ \; b_{jmq}s_{kmq}M_{qi} \; \text{(plus specifics)} \tag{12.1}$$

where the E's represent the individual's scores on p ergic tensions and the M's his developmental levels on q sentiments. The b's are loadings—behavioral indices psychologically—and the s's are situational modulators. These can be omitted if we are speaking of a person's interests in a relatively fixed life situation. The ergic and sentiment patterns have been found to maintain their patterns over both cross-sectional and longitudinal analysis (the latter by P- and dR techniques, Cattell, 1957a).

The fuller developments of the dynamic calculus in such concepts as vector resolution of conflict, and the dynamic lattice must be taken up as we proceed. The above sketch of the actual taxonomic findings was given initially to provide substance for a meaningful distinction of ability from personality and dynamic modalities. Although that separation in current psychometry is casual and confused, a separation by basic principles is possible. It involves making measurements of factors under different conditions and observing the changes of mean and sigma. Dynamic traits are those which change most with changes in incentive, an incentive being whatever signals a consummatory goal. Abilities change score most with changes in complexity, changes in complexity being situational changes that are not changes in incentive. Temperament traits are scores—frequently ratio scores, that change minimally with changes in incentive (reward) or complexity. The more operational illustration of these objective criteria for modality may be followed elsewhere (Cattell, 1946a; Cattell and Warburton, 1967).

Since abilities can, in principle, always be measured by speed, or the fewness of errors, in attaining an agreed result despite complexities, there is always a known positive direction, and, as Spearman and Thurstone independently observed, when a large variety of performances is so measured and factored, the result, in factor plots, is a "positive manifold." That is to say, most performances load positively on most ability factors extracted. And since motivation performances analogously possess a goal of incentives, and can be positively measured as strength of interest in that goal, they also, when so measured from the beginning, end by yielding a positive manifold in the.plots of dynamic traits.[1] But temperament traits have neither the criteria of complexity nor incentive, and can be given no direction from the beginning. It is highly characteristic therefore of personality-temperament factor plots that the points are equally distributed over all quadrants. There are as many positive as negatively loaded performances on a personality dimension.

Another aspect of this difference is that though one can speak of a "good" pole on an ability, or a "strong" pole on a dynamic factor, there is no "good" or "strong" pole to a personality factor. Any value judgment is

---

[1] The dichotomy of "approach" and "avoidance" labels often used for animal drives is a superfluous and even misleading piece of pedantry. Fear is not avoidance, but a positive and powerful search for the goal of safety. In that course of action, as in any other, objects can appear as impediments. But the measures of the safety-seeking drive can be positively scored uniformly with those of all other drives.

arbitrary. On the sizothyme-vs-affectothyme factor A on the 16 P.F. one finds that some occupations are performed better by A+ and some by A− individuals. On the objective test factor U.I. 17 of general inhibition-vs-general expressiveness, again some performances are better done by a U.I. 17+ and others a U.I. 17− score. Another way of looking at this is to realize that natural selection in our environment cuts off too much impulsiveness, in some situations, and too much inhibition in others. Evolution shepherds the species along a delicate balance.

However, within the narrower segment of concern we have with the interaction of abilities, it means that the prediction of any performance by a specification equation is likely to be almost invariably positively loaded on the ability factor, to be often positively loaded on dynamic, but to have positive and negative loadings with about equal frequency on various personality factors. It is systematic differences in properties of this kind, and the fact that dynamic traits can be manipulated whereas abilities and temperament cannot, as well as other regular differences of properties, which make the recognition of the three different trait modalities worthwhile. Their separation in measurement and natural history is not a mere academic exercise in taxonomy; it pays off in understanding and prediction.

Regardless of whether the tyro in psychology is prepared to pursue the above operational definition of modalities in theoretical depth or not, he usually recognizes the practical worth of the distinction and is alert to the evidence of their intrinsic separability, together with normal joint action. For instance, he recognizes that two people of similar personality, through different educational and environmental influences, may finish up even on opposite sides of some political or religious issue. Dynamic sentiment traits and personality temperament traits are combinable in almost any way. Conversely, he sees that people with the same interests and motivations may differ widely in temperament. One often notices, for example, in some extreme radical groups, e.g., the 1918 Bolshevic leaders, that temperaments cover much the same range as in some extreme right wing group. Regarding modality combinations, the psychologist nevertheless realizes that the flavor of an interest or belief will be affected by the personality traits, and that the qualities of an ability seem different in persons of different temperament. His expectation is that these intuited "qualitative" differences can be supported by formulae following from scientific methods for dissecting out the separate influences.

2. PERSONALITY TRAITS THAT SIMULATE ABILITIES

Although the three modalities of traits can be separated, with scientific profit, this does not mean that the separation may not sometimes be difficult. It behooves us to start out in our study of interaction of abilities and personality traits by recognizing that certain personality traits act almost like abilities, and have often been mistaken for abilities.

That this confusion has not been observed earlier and handled incisively is due to so much personality research having been content with inventories or ratings. But once personality measurement moved to objective personality factor tests, as in the O-A batteries, it became clear that the loading of personality factors on "miniature situation tests" sometimes makes a large contribution to what would be called ordinarily "general competence" in much the same areas as those affected by abilities. The recognition that a broad factor so found in an area of ability-like measures—such as personality factors U.I. 19, 21, or 23—is nevertheless *not* general intelligence in a new guise is given by the fact that the general intelligence factors g_f and a_g *also* turn up in the very same factor analysis. An instance of a personality-temperament factor which affects many ability-like performances and has sometimes (without g_f to contrast it with) been mistaken for intelligence is U.I. 23, mobilization-vs-regression. Eysenck (1947), Cattell (1947) and others (Scheier, Cattell, and Horn, 1960) repeatedly have isolated this factor independently, Eysenck (in the regression direction) labeled it "neuroticism," but our work favors the interpretation *regression-vs-capacity to mobilize*. Here several performances sometimes included in intelligence tests, e.g., coding, short distance memory, judging spatial positions, handling mirror images, are found to be "cooperatively" loaded simultaneously on U.I. 23. By the theory in the label "Capacity to Mobilize" (for U.I. 23) we imply that it is one thing to be able to *perceive* relationships (g_f) and quite another (U.I. 23) to be able to *mobilize* and use them, marshaling decisions and actions effectively around them. Such personality factors conveniently can be called "ability factor simulators."

From the early days of objective measurement of personality (Cattell, 1933b) and motivation (Murray, 1938; Cattell, 1937b; Eysenck, 1947), it became evident that *perceptual* performances, particularly, could be loaded appreciably by such factors. Soon the bivariate experimental investigation of perception as a purely cognitive ability performance took on the "new look" of the late 1940s and 1950s, and began seeking systematically for personality expressions in perception. This took two forms: (1) the search for motivation and dynamic structures by *misperception* measures (of which projection is one), pursued widely by clinicians and by systematic multivariate methods in the motivation measurement researches described above (Cattell *et al.,* In press, 1971), and (2) the search for temperament in perception, as involved in the work of Thurstone (1950) and later of Witkin et al. (1954), Gardner (1958), and others. The association of perception differences with dynamics is a vast study in itself, and the reader must be referred to the domain of *defense mechanisms and motivation components* (Anderson and Anderson, 1950; Cattell, Heist, Heist, and Stewart, 1950; Cattell and Wenig, 1952; Cattell, Radcliffe, and Sweney, 1963) covering analysis of "misperception," "autism," etc., in relation to a great range of performances, in order to understand such interactions. Dynamic needs sharpen and distort cognitive perceptual ability in particular directions and in particular areas. But the more general heightening of perceptual competence, under the second of the headings above, arises from temperament factors, and it is these that need to be studied in the present glance at personality factors simulating general abilities.

After his pioneer work in factoring primary abilities, Thurstone in 1945 turned to factoring perception (provoked in part, he said, by the excessive faith of clinicians in the Rorschach test) and found some six to twelve factors stable in such performances as gestalt completion, accuracy of complex reaction time response, flicker fusion, the number of objects seen in unstructured drawings, speed of alternating perspective, peripheral span of perception, etc. About this same time the Personality Analysis Laboratory at the University of Illinois espoused the alternative theory that such broad factors in perceptual performances are not cognitive aptitudes but expressions of temperament. The "marker variables" for Thurstone's concepts were included accordingly among personality measures in researches over 1945 to 1952 by coworkers of the present writer. The result was a confirmation for both laboratories, each in a different sense, for we found that perceptual performances essentially did group themselves just as Thurstone's results were showing, but that these groupings embedded themselves in still larger behavioral manifestations of temperament, most of the other manifestations of which had nothing to do with perception or cognition. Later, when Witkin and his associates (1954) began very systematically exploring the correlations of "field independence" in perception, the Illinois group again put forward strong arguments that this undoubted perceptual general tendency is really part of the already demonstrated unitary temperament factor of *Independence,* U.I. 19.

To illustrate the general nature of the relations, we may take a "cognitive" factor which Thurstone had called perceptual slowness or delay, marked by slow speed of gestalt closure, narrower peripheral span of perception, and slowness to name objects in the dark after exposing the eyes to a bright light (styled "dark adaptation"). This same group of performances was found in personality research to be embraced in a wider, but clearly unitary factor which had been called *General Inhibition* and indexed as U.I. 17. The U.I. 17 loading pattern includes also measures of unduly large magnitude of GSR response to threat; tendency to avoid "disturbing" reading preferences; low ratio of inaccuracy to speed in motor performance; much cautious slowing of response decision as a problem becomes more complex; much reduction of finger maze exploration by threat of shock; and various other measures of proneness to inhibition. They agree in showing U.I. 17 to be a highly general temperament dimension of timid inhibition, extending far beyond perception. The theory in fact is that this unitary factor gives substance and support to Pavlov's speculation (never verified) of a *general inhibition* factor in the nervous system of animals. The factor-analytic experiments of Royce (1950, 1966) directly with animals uses variables which now enable us to say with more confidence that we have the same temperament factor of inhibition-timidity, U.I. 17, in both man and higher mammals. And we now realize that the extensive tendency in the field of cognitive perception to "go slowly" to "underperceive"—which operates in many performances to change scores in the same direction as occurs from a low perceptual *ability*—is actually a personality trait.

Similarly, the perceptual ability factor which Thurstone temporarily labeled C, proved to be embedded in the personality factor U.I. 22, *Cortertia* (for "cortical alertness," and which many neurological experimenters are calling arousal or activation). The chief expressions of this source trait pattern comprise fast speed of alternating perspective; rapidly seeing many objects in unstructured drawings; fusion of light flicker only at high speeds; rapid reaction time; good eidetic imagery; and high fidgetometer frequency. This general cortical alertness factor obviously aids all kinds of cognitive performance of a routine speediness nature, e.g., cancellation in clerical material, but its main domain is equally clearly a temperament expression, as shown, for example, by its strongly significant negative association with neuroticism (Cattell, Scheier, and Lorr, 1962).

As mentioned above, a second area in which perceptual ability and temperament are suspected to be one and the same is with respect to the ability to abstract shapes from their background ("field independence"). The latter was a popular theme among students of perception with the "process" approach to learning and perception in the fifties. In Thurstone's novel, multivariate, factor-analytic approach to perception in the 1940s, he had already shown the existence of an individual difference perceptual factor (E, "suppressive manipulation of configurations," in his series) covering abilities of this kind. Witkin (1954, 1962) and his co-workers, similarly showed a coherence of such performances in a correlation cluster ("surface trait") of field independence. Meanwhile, as mentioned above, in the broad investigation of the personality sphere, an independent *source trait* (not a surface trait) indexed as U.I. 19 and called Temperamental Independence, had been discovered and confirmed (Cattell, 1948, 1951; Cattell, Dubin, and Saunders, 1954).

General temperamental independence, U.I. 19, of which "field independence" is an outcropping in the perceptual performance realm, has been matched as a factor pattern across a dozen adult and eight child experiments. It covers, with significant loadings, the test performances (see Cattell and Warburton, 1967, for operational descriptions): high accuracy in gestalt completion; absence of slips in maintaining complex mental sets; ability to keep several instructions operative at once; performance in Gottschalk figures; carefulness in following directions; ratio of accuracy to speed in numerical problem-solving; ability to draw mirror images of drawings; high ratio of color to form emphasis in sorting cards; high critical hostility of judgment; low motor-perceptual rigidity; accuracy in placing cut-out patterns on templates; ability to invent adjectival attributes in describing familiar things; and freedom from error on an easy series "intelligence test."

It is easy to understand a psychologist mistaking this for some kind of "perceptual intelligence" test if he did not enter an experiment with enough variables to yield g_f too, and the factor analytic finish to separate out g_f by its markers. Nevertheless, what marks its true nature as a temperament factor is the breadth of expression in areas outside perception, such as general criticalness, low rigidity, self-assured independence, a certain masculinity of interests, and marked self-control. It is not surprising that this factor has predictive importance in the purely personality domain. It appears to correspond, for example, with the second-stratum factor, QIV, Independence (Cattell, Eber, and Tatsuoka, 1970) in the personality questionnaire domain. It also has considerable clinical predictive value, in that it distinguishes neurotics from normals (in its negative direction, as Subduedness, U.I. 19−) with a significance of P < .001. Nevertheless, in the way it contributes to subtests normally considered abilities—even the series test used in intelligence tests—it could be (and has repeatedly been) mistaken for a pure ability.

Another marked—and extremely interesting—instance of doubt about modality, arising from the "projection" of a temperament factor into the ability field is that of U.I. 21, Exuberance. In this case perception is not the main area, but instead we see a trait operating in the area of memory retrieval and the general fluency ability factor, g_r, or, in Guilford's concepts, in "divergent thinking." The pattern called Exuberance has been found repeatedly in objective personality tests, and covers such behavior as high fluency, e.g., in completing a story; more hand tremor (eagerness?); more unreflective acceptance of unqualified statements (but resistance to control by authority, as shown by suggestibility shift on attitudes when authorities are quoted) a much reduced likelihood of neuroticism (Cattell, Scheier, and Lorr, 1962); fast speed of social judgment; larger myokinetic (muscular) movements; fast reading tempo; and other signs of an expansive temperament. The present theory (Hundleby, Pawlik, and Cattell, 1965) is that U.I. 21 (which also correlates with basal metabolic rate and strong reaction of pulse under stress) is a physiologically determined temperament factor, perhaps expressing the level of a chemical pacemaker in the midbrain or cortex. It declines steadily with age.

As just indicated, this temperament trait loads quite strongly on a number of what were previously considered ability manifestations, notably the fluency of association factor and one of Thurstone's perceptual closure factors. Since Spearman first recognized a general fluency factor across both verbal and nonverbal (drawing completion) tests there has been constant reproduction in experiment of some kind of fluency or "divergent thinking" factor, and the triadic ability analysis above defines this as the general retrieval capacity, g_r. The moot question now is "Are U.I. 21, Exuberance, and g_r, fluency-retrieval, two distinct factors, and if so, what is their relation?" The theory that the present writer would consider most promising—but with crucial experiments still to be done—is that they *are* distinct factors, affecting fluency for different reasons. General retrieval, g_r, is considered an *ability* concerned entirely with the fluency-retrieval performances, and having to do with storage and accessibility facility.

Exuberance, U.I. 21, is a temperament trait of impulsiveness and emotional vitality (it has been called the "Churchill" factor) extending over wider realms of behavior than ability. If this is correct, when g_r and U.I. 21 variables are factored together they should (a) split into two factors, and (b) divide the variance of the fluency measures (and those only) between them.

Two other general personality factors have shown striking overlap with abilities, and in this case they are entirely out of the perceptual field. The first is U.I. 16, Competitive Ego Strength. It loads all kinds of speed and determination, particularly in situations of rivalry. It is a substantial factor in speed of decision, speed of carrying out most tasks, and is probably considered in common language just "Competitiveness." However, it can add as much as half the variance to individual differences in success in, for example, social decisions, running mazes, checking simple sums at speed, etc. It is the prime instance of the contribution of temperamental assertiveness in ability test performance.

More subtle and intriguing is the contribution of the important personality source trait U.I. 23, *Mobilization-vs-Regression,* already briefly introduced above as an illustration. This pattern was discovered simultaneously by the London University and the University of Illinois personality research laboratories and since then has been pursued intensively by both independently. It is certainly a major associate of neuroticism (in the negative, U.I. 23− direction) and by Eysenck's theory is *"the* neuroticism factor." But, since three or four other personality factors are associated even more strongly with neuroticism, our theory is that it is *one* contributing condition describable as *regression* (Cattell and Scheier, 1961). In the regression (U.I. 23−) direction it is responsible for poor performance in several behaviors that would be considered cognitive, notably for high motor perceptual rigidity; poor two-hand coordination; high ataxia; susceptibility to suggestion (Hull's sway test, 1933); rapid increase of inaccuracy with speed; poor immediate memory; and low dynamic momentum in disentangling cues.

Regression (low U.I. 23) also seems to produce poor performance in an examination or intelligence-test-taking situation. Indeed, the general parallelism of the "poor grasp" pattern to g_f would make one suspect that at times it has been accepted in some researches as the (low) intelligence factor. Actually, it can be seen readily from its total nature that it is quite distinct from either g_f or g_c (a_g). What produces the poor performance here is not inability to perceive relations or lack of good equipment in judgmental skills, but clumsy "tiredness" in the coordination of ideas and an inability to mobilize the skills one has—a general regression of interest and control from sharp reality contacts. Although temperamental it is certainly a "generalized incompetence"—as general and pervasive in extending across simpler cognitive performances as is the effect of a low score on the general intelligence factor. Yet when closely scrutinized, the performance decrement has the character that would be expected from a withdrawal of interest, or from the presence of a general, chronic, mental fatigue. Since this fatigue does not diminish overnight it is more like a neurasthenic fatigue. It has seemed best to designate the trait at a non-committal, operational level as Inability to Mobilize (U.I. 23−), to be contrasted with lack of insight and relation perception as such (g_f-).

The five examples just considered of general personality traits contributing to ability performances—U.I. 16, Ego Strength, U.I. 19, Independence, U.I. 21, Exuberance, U.I. 22, Cortertia, and U.I. 23, Capacity to Mobilize—exhaust only the major instances, and they do not touch motivation apart from temperament. Obviously there is a semantic looseness in which *all* personality and motivation could be considered ability, since it contributes to "capability," "achievement" or the sheer capacity to survive. But the above statements, in precise factorial terms, have to do with performances that, in a quite narrow sense, have been called "abilities," and they show that definite fractions of the variance on such tests are overflow effects of temperament into the ability area.

3. WHAT DOES INTELLIGENCE DO FOR PERSONALITY DEVELOPMENT?

As indicated in the opening comments, the interaction of abilities, on the one hand, and temperament and motivation traits on the other, needs to be studied systematically and comprehensively with respect to some four main possibilities, two concerning developmental process and two having to do with interactions in the living present. They are: (1) in development—ability affecting personality growth; (2) in development—personality affecting ability growth; (3) in immediate performance—ability modifying personality expression, and (4) in immediate performance—personality affecting ability performance (not by simulation, as above, but by aiding ability).

This section will concentrate principally on the first. A glance has already been taken at the second, which might be represented by the hypotheses that a personality high in factor A, affectothymia, i.e., warm, sociable, and emotionally expressive, will develop more social ability agency (a_s) skills than would a more sizothyme (A−) person, by reason of encountering greater interpersonal, trial-and-error learning opportunities. Instances of type (1) connections are common, as when the school frustrations of a borderline mental defective create the morose personality of a delinquent. Instances of (3) are seen when a high verbal capacity favors the expression of aggression in, say, satire, and of (4) when a high temperamental patience and restraint enables a player at chess to beat an impulsive opponent of equal intelligence. These varieties of causal action will be looked at in due course, but the first is perhaps of greatest interest.

An appreciable folklore suggests that giftedness in abilities brings risks to character equal to those from inheriting a fortune. Forgetting the statistics for all children it is easy to be overly impressed by the neighbor's unpleasantly precocious child, by the Neros and Cellinis of history, or by our more recent anti-establishment cases, such as Oscar Wilde, Baudelaire, Frank Harris, or Maupassant. But the data gathered by psychologists early in this century, by the Chassells (1935), by Terman (1925), by Burt (1925), by Healy and Bronner (1936) and many others, working at both ends of the intelligence distribution, did not support a negative correlation of intelligence and fine character as the *general* rule. As far as this general giftedness is concerned, the law seems to be that a moderate *positive* correlation holds through the population as a whole between intelligence and such characteristics as conscientiousness, consideration, foresight, and self-control.

At the lower end of the range, the careful quantitative studies of Healy and Bronner (1936) and the classic of Burt on child delinquency (1925) consistently showed an increased likelihood of delinquency and crime with lower intelligence. The monumental study of the Chassells on *Morality and Intellect* (1935) showed a general tendency at *all* levels for higher ideals and moral self-discipline to go with higher intelligence, and many correlations were even at the level of +0.6. Terman's extensive survey of the characteristics of the top one or two percent by intelligence tests showed them also to be, on an average, less often in moral trouble, more dependable, persistent, and contributory (in mature years)to their societies.

However, when psychology and history get together, so that historians utilize precise psychological measurements to plot changes in attitude, personality, abilities, etc., some very interesting trends may come to light. Certain recent investigations, in the turbid back streams of a morally confused society, have shown absences and even occasional inversions of the positive ability-character relation. Recent data on the 16 P.F. test shows that on factor G—basic superego strength—the highest level is reached by the middle class and especially the lower middle class. (Actually history has shown frequently, as in the times of Cromwell and Charles I, a lower morality among the spoiled aristocrats and the slum dweller, with the fiber of society in between.) In an opulent society, the leisured and unearning student may momentarily play the part of the spoiled aristocrat, free of the restrictions of a workable morality. The striking results of Graffam (1967) show by the 16 P.F. that four years of college (as contrasted with noncollege) produce, on an average, an increase in radicalism and in dominance, and a decrease in guilt proneness (O factor) and superego strength (G factor). This may be characteristic of a purely intellectual education, and judged by biography, does not seem to be true of Napoleon, Wellington, Eisenhower, or MacArthur in a military and action-oriented education, or of Loyola, Wesley, and others in theological schools, or of the statesmen, such as Churchill, raised in the character-oriented English public schools.

The correlation of character with intelligence is thus, to an appreciable extent, what society makes it. And in periods of change, when one set of moral values gives way to another, those who are against morals all the time are momentarily allied with those against a particular conservative set of values (not that, in fundamentals, morality changes). In such periods of chaotic inversions, where the more intelligent reformers spurn the moral restraint still preserved in their society by the less intelligent, an inversion of the correlation may arise. It is also likely to arise, as in the days of ancient Rome when the leadership was corrupt but the legions were faithful (for a time) in a moribund society. But apart from such periods of history it seems the rule for higher intelligence to be moderately associated with less antisocial and more morally elevated behavior.

Combining with rough allowances the various rating and measurement results, one might estimate that the correlation across the full range of society is slight—perhaps about 0.2. This figure is no simple relation, but the complex end result of many causes operating in various directions. Some of the relation to delinquency is undoubtedly roundabout; children of low intelligence will tend to have had parents of low intelligence, and parents of low intelligence will tend to provide poorer socioeconomic conditions and less wise discipline (often impeded by oversize families). Another connection is more directly in the realm of psychodynamics as implied in Freud's *Civilization and its Discontents.* The thesis there is that a more developed culture demands greater instinctual restraints, which it rewards by greater security, longevity, and opportunity for *sublimated* emotional satisfactions in art, music, and science. But an individual with an I.Q. of 70 to 80 will find Bach and Boolean algebra a poor thrill compared with boxing, bullfighting or street rioting. Probably the most fundamental and persistent dynamic relation over all periods of society, however, is that between low intelligence and the personality difficulties occasioned by an excess of agression due to frustration. Studies with the School Motivation Analysis Test (Cattell and Butcher, 1968) show higher ergic tension levels in pugnacity in those failing in school. Incidentally, the majority of discussions of campus discontent in this decade have busied themselves with superficial ideational causes and said no word about the basic frustration inevitable when intellectual standards and styles that have grown up for centuries in adaptation to the top 10% of I.Q.'s are applied to a third of the population (age group). The fundamental frustration in the demands of a complex society pressing hardest on those of lower intelligence is the perennial cause of the association of lower intelligence with higher delinquency. The association may fluctuate with social conditions, but it remains.

However, let us not slip into thinking of a single relation with something called "character stability," but remember the whole specification equation and the whole array of personality dimensions. Higher intelligence, for example, is also an aid to rationalization and evasion, and no low intelligent simple delinquent is quite as revolting, or even as dangerous to society, as the highly intelligent but irresponsible antimoralist, e.g., the publisher of pornography, or the intellectually dishonest professor who grinds his own ideological axe in the guise of instruction in the social sciences.

As to the variety of personality facets systematically correlated with intelligence, preliminary evidence has accumulated across sufficient subcultures to give reliable empirical figures on the relation to perhaps twenty measured personality dimensions. The central tendency in the closing year of high school, according to the 16 P.F. test, is for intelligence to be correlated, positively but slightly (+.18), with superego strength, G; +.23 with self-sentiment (self-concept organization) development, Q_3; and +.12 with premsia, I (protected emotional sensitivity). In university students it tends to become correlated also with dominance, E (.20), with radicalism, Q_1 (.28), and with autia, M (.20) (intensity of inner mental life). The relations to superego strength and self-sentiment strength in high school are apt, as instanced in Graffam's results, to become inverted in the college "emancipation" period.

Similar evidence, but less analytical, has long been obtained outside the test area in correlations (or test intelligence) with observers' ratings. Thus, among adults, correlations of intelligence were found (Cattell, 1945b) with "analytical mindedness" (.40); intellectual interests (.31); conscientiousness (.30); persistent, alert, vigorous character (.29); wisdom and maturity (.26); polished manners (.26); and with "cleverness," "smartness," or "assertiveness" (.24). Other significant correlations are with cooperative, reliable, industrious in school work, and higher moral ideals and habits.

To set out the reasonably promising theories about many of these connections obviously needs more space than we can give. Some associations are directly generated through the experience of the individual, but others come in roundabout ways through parental inheritance, social status associations, etc. The associations with dominance, smartness, and assertiveness, etc., are probably generated in the experience of the individual himself through the status and success which intelligence brings. Other associations may be due to the statistical probability discussed above that the less intelligent person will experience more ergic frustration and therefore more provocation to impulsive, antisocial activity. As regards the self-sentiment (Q_3) and the delinquency associations, the more intelligent person, seeing further into consequences of his behavior, builds up more inhibitions and acquires more socially desirable habits. Incidentally, the correlation of a_g with self-sentiment, Q_3, in well-knit groups is so considerable that the psychologist may see acceptance of the school culture, of the realities of the physical world, and values of culture, the social culture as part of a single learning process all parts of which are aided by a high g_f. Factor analysis might then expect to reveal a tie-up of a_g and Q_3 as common products of a single investment process, and this indeed is seen in the second-order 16 P.F. factors from some analyses (Cattell, Eber, and Tatsuoka, 1970; Cattell and Gorsuch, 1971; Horn, 1965).

An interesting personality correlation with intelligence—at least with intelligence when exposed to the academic learning situation, is that with personality factor M, autia. The student life, as mentioned in connection with Graffam's and others' results, produces not only an increase in independence and dominance (E) and in readiness to depart experimentally from the culture (Q_1), but also (as common observation suggests and despite the young poet's bemoaning of "the weary weight of thought"), a strong increase in intellectual interests and the "analytical mindedness" of the ratings. It also produces a rise in M (autia, inner mental activity), which means a greater interest in abstractions as well as in the subjective products of imagination as contrasted with the facts of the external world. In fact, the possibility must be considered that the higher interest in the symbol world, which higher intelligence makes possible, detracts to some extent from interest in and respect for the concrete realities. The fact is that, in the general population range of M (autia) scores, higher levels are associated with poorer social adjustment and higher accident proneness vis-à-vis the physical world. Persons of high philosophical or abstract mathematical attainment, like Russell or Oppenheimer in our own time, or Diogenes and Socrates of old—as well as all the "absent-minded professors" in between—have not been conspicuously good at managing their concrete personal affairs. "Dynamic competition" brings about some defects from high g_f, visible in the M correlations.

Another aspect of this association of high intellectual gifts and activity with the E+, Q_1+, Q_2+ and M personality factors, i.e., with dominance, radicalism, and subjectivity of judgment, is the suggestion that high E, Q_1, and Q_2 are the results of the constantly greater experience of success that goes with higher intelligence. This increase of self-assurance and even arrogance reminds anyone with moral perspective of "that sin of pride by which Lucifer fell." It will evoke reflections that there is some sense in which character develops more by adjustment to failure than by success, and that, consequently, there must be a backward eddy in the correlation structure of intelligence and character over and above the main trend in which intelligence relates positively to G and Q_3 above. The beginnings of this eddy are seen in the negative r's of intelligence with Q_3 in college student populations. In short there is one sense in which the more intelligent person is more advanced in character development (organization, persistence, foresight, and an appreciation of social conscientiousness) and another in which he is backward, for example, in a religious type of resigned but emotionally realistic adjustment to the ultimate frustrations.

When dealing with the results of frontal lobe injury on planfulness of behavior (page 197) we adopted the interpretation that discovery of frontal neural projection areas from the hypothalamus indicates that this zone is not a purely "general intelligence" associational area. Instead, it has a particular concern with associational, relation-perceiving powers *applied to the emotional control and impulse deferment (inhibition) processes.* This activity corresponds in the analysis of behavioral structure to the C, G, and Q_3 personality factors (ego strength, superego strength, and self-sentiment development) which have been shown to become correlated in a second-order factor, QVIII. In fact, this second-order behavioral factor could well be identified with frontal lobe neurological action. Positive relations (Gorsuch and Cattell, 1967; Horn, 1965) are also beginning to become apparent between intelligence and this Q_3, G, and C plexus, though it is still not entirely clear just how they will resolve factorially. However, one can see that the nicety of judgment breadth and balance on this governing dynamic system ultimately must have a limit set by the individual's capacity to perceive relationships—in this case as applied in the satisfaction-balancing, dynamic world. In this factorial domain lies one of the most important of all intelligence-personality relationships now needing research investigation. The most likely theory is that the second-stratum "behavioral control" factor, loading C, G, and Q_3, is partly determined in its development by the third stratum g_f, just as is a_g.

Nevertheless, this projection of intelligence into a dynamic control system, probably neurologically located in the frontal lobes, and expressed in personality factors, Q_3, G, and C, does not complete the story of how intelligence helps shape personality. There is a curious finding with young children, as yet, on somewhat slender samples and certainly still needing confirmation (or rejection) of higher anxiety with higher fluid intelligence (Cattell, 1963a, 1967b). Since the general relation in the school years—via achievement, as discussed below—is one showing *lower* anxiety with higher achievement, and probably higher a_g, an intriguing paradox may exist here. In general, the more machinery that an organization possesses, either in the biological or the mechanical world, the more there is to go wrong! Conceivably the young child of high fluid intelligence, with massive associational area development, has more possibilities of imaginative trauma, or even of cumulative physiological, e.g., acetylcholine, imbalances than one of smaller intelligence. One may begin to speculate that perhaps the anxious depressions of such men as J. S. Mill, Pascal, William James, and others of great gifts might hark back to such childhood emotional vulnerability due to the large "combining mass." The possibility that high intelligence in a very unstructured phase of environmental relations might create an "imaginative" magnification of fears and depressions such as a less intelligent child would not experience is at least worthy of investigation —biographically in the infancy of highly intelligent individuals and psychometrically with testing of young children today.

Yet another, more special problem has to do with the possibility of sharp nonlinear relations, existing within the broad, apparently linear relations, of intelligence to certain personality qualities discussed above. There is evidence that in any trait whatsoever, good or bad, an *extreme* endowment—toward the upper or lower tip of the population range—creates adjustment problems. It does so by virtue of what the present writer has called "the law of coercion to the bio-social mean" (Cattell, 1950a). Eysenck, among others, has brought evidence that maladjustment connected with intelligence is higher at both ends of the I.Q. range. Despite Terman's initially surprising, but later confirmed, findings that high I.Q. children are better adjusted than the average, some unpublished results of our own show more neurotic scores on the 16 P.F. in certain high intelligence groups. Probably two distinct principles are in conflict: that for higher intelligence to produce higher C, G, and Q_3 development as discussed above, and that for extremity to produce frustrations, notably of gregariousness (*vide* the rise of the Mensa Society, see page 507) and shared emotional life. This deprivation of group life, and the pressures of coercion to the bio-social mean which operate at extremes, add to still greater frustrations at the lower limit. In all, they would lead us to expect curvilinear personality-intelligence correlations to modify the primary linear ones.

4. PERSONALITY AND THE SPECIAL ABILITY AREAS

The fourfold scheme in which we set out to study personality-ability interactions (Section 3, page 365), has been covered as far as intelligence effects on personality and personality factor simulating abilities. In the present section we propose to consider some interactions not so well understood as to causal direction, and more concerned with special than general abilities. The notion that such specific connections exist is deep in our folklore, wherein the artist, for example, is expected to be temperamental, the poet melancholy, and the mathematician absent-minded and impractical. But what is the evidence?

The man in the street sometimes rejects the idea of measuring intelligence saying it has a different "quality" in different people. It would seem that there is nothing but a verbal misunderstanding here, for what he calls different *qualities* the psychologist represents as differing *vector quantities*. A vector in factor space can represent, in one case, so much g_f with, say, little projection on the verbal proficiency axis, and, in another case, the same amount of g_f with less projection on verbal proficiency, a_v, but more on reasoning proficiency, a_r, and so on. This recognition that what is felt in personal interaction as a difference of quality appears, instead, as a precisely representable vector measurement in the dimensions of the full triadic ability space is only the beginning of a still more comprehensive understanding of representation. In this latter, instead of drawing the vector only in the ability space we place the specific kind of performance also in the broader domain of personality factors. Perhaps, for example, we should represent some artistic talent performance as three parts ability and one part some personality factor, and mathematical ability (of a certain kind) as having much more to it than a score on the N agency.

Spearman and his coworkers, despite their preoccupations with mathematical models, found time to consider, as sensitively as any clinician, this "quality" question, and in regard to general intelligence they particularly investigated the difference of "cleverness" and "wisdom." They traced it to concepts outside the ability field—to dimensions which became the precursors of what we know now as the surgency (F factor) and ego strength (C) source trait measures. The surgent individual is able to express his intelligence with rapidity, which favors the growth of a habit of repartee, and his wit and liveliness make him the "life and soul of the party." Surgent intelligences offer us a delightful spectacle. Frank Harris, himself far more conspicuous for cleverness than wisdom, said he would give years of his life to have been present at a dinner party consisting of Lord Birkenhead, Oscar Wilde, and himself. Such meetings have left quotable treasures which, by accident of meaning more than inherent profundity, can be wise as well as witty.

In spite of our enjoyment of sparkling wit, some shrewd observers of human nature always have suspected that certain questionable personality traits may go with glibness—as witness at least two of the above three characters, and numerous TV characters admired by the young. Certainly, the known criterion associations of the temperament factor F—surgency— bear out the inverse correlations of "cleverness" with dependability. The desurgent (F−) person's prudence and depth are correspondingly witnessed by such findings as the low F of leading scientists (Cattell and Drevdahl, 1955). These systematic findings nevertheless have not sufficed to prevent some recent writers on creativity confusing surgency (F) and exuberance (U.I. 21) with creativity! It is inhibition—keeping the lid on— that generates enough pressure to drive the mind to more fundamental originality.

It is the restraint of second-thoughtedness that also contributes to wisdom. That term in its full depth of meaning, is something that a wise man would hesitate to define, but perhaps Coleridge's "common sense in uncommon degree" is a good start. For it is a painful fact of history and everyday observation that admittedly highly intelligent men can be extremely foolish from the standpoint of a person of "common sense." This has been illustrated by the dicta of some academic men in the last decade, during expeditions into politics, and by the dicta of brilliant young writers on morals and social values. When careful observer ratings on the general run of humanity are correlated and factored, as in various summarized studies (Cattell, 1957a; Hammond, 1957; Norman, 1963; Tupes, 1957) one finds associated with the current cultural definition of wisdom, over and above intelligence, such traits as foresight, reality-contact, patience, emotional control, and self-insight as opposed to subjective prejudice.

In short they show a belief in Euripides' injunction that "among mortals second thoughts are vital," or in terms of underlying personality factors known to the personality theorist, a high probability that the C factor of ego strength, i.e., realism, balance, self-control, is here linked to intelligence. That the C factor of ego strength or "character" enters was the main upshot of Hargreaves' early investigation with Spearman, and it fits recent criterion correlations. For example, there are few places where wisdom is needed more than in handling difficult individuals as a psychiatric technician has to do, and the specification equation for success there is positively loaded (Cattell, Eber, and Tatsuoka, 1968) with ego strength (and, incidentally, desurgency and superego (G factor) over and above intelligence). It would be valuable to have similar 16 P.F. or other ability and personality factor measures simultaneously on successful and unsuccessful magistrates and judges, stockbrokers, and others whose survival depends on wisdom and shrewd judgment. The occupation profiles for occupations in which the demand for mature judgment is exacting—physicians, accountants, school superintendents, university administrators, and business executives —all show the pattern of below-average surgency (F−, desurgency) and above-average shrewdness, N, while most show above-average ego strength, C (Cattell, Eber, and Tatsuoka, 1970).

These considerations of the "quality" of intelligence generally account for specific disappointments in intelligence test predictions which users may report. They have not separated sufficiently the real characters of a_g or g_f from some persisting, personal, subjective concept of intelligence of their own preference. If the latter were brought out as a definable vector, it would be found to include much more than true intelligence. If the "intelligence" in the required criterion includes much wisdom, wit, prophecy, or creativity, then additional measures, several of which are important personality measures, are definitely needed in the test battery and the specification equation.

That intelligence is often given particular flavor or timbre by the predominance of some primary ability has already been discussed. One thinks of the wealth of a_v in Shakespeare's thinking; of a_s in Einstein's grasp of space; or the abundant a_{mk} in the inventiveness of Edison. These are particular angles given to the vector of ability by projections on agencies in the ability space itself. Less obvious, and of greater interest to our present direction of analysis, are the special qualities given to agencies (usually "primary abilities") by association with personality factors. These associations are sometimes more marked than those with general intelligence itself. For clarity, research results in this domain are best examined after general ability (g_f) has been statistically partialled out of the correlations with a primary ability scale as such.

In an early research on personality-ability relations by personality *ratings* (Cattell, 1945a) in over two hundred young men in an Army Specialist Training Program (the observer ratings on personality reaching the unusual reliability of .88) several significant personality correlations were found with verbal and mathematical ability, after partialling out intelligence as advocated above. Verbal ability was associated with affectothymia (A factor), −.25; with surgency (F), −.35; and with premsia (I) as much as 0.5. The association with premsic upbringing is not surprising, for the closer contact with a parent in a protective and sustaining home could be one of the main determiners of more advanced verbal performance. But the negative relation of a_v with the level of outgoing, exviant personality activity, as measured in A and F, will come as a surprise to many. What the first popular stereotype perhaps overlooks is that, though the "extravert" will talk more, he will read less. And except for a few professors' children (who may have serious doubts about their privilege) most children can get a much larger and sophisticated vocabulary from books than from their immediate associates.

Certainly a glance over the lives of poets and others should convince us that the great wielders of language were mainly inviant and solitary individuals. Of the seclusive habits of many writers, Gray's lines would be descriptive:

> Hard by yon wood, now smiling as in scorn,
> Muttering his wayward fancies he would roam.

Indeed, where the fostering of a love of verbal music and a sedate precision of word choice is concerned, the inward direction of attention is surely most favorable. At any rate it is in the verbal field that we see one of the best examples of Goethe's comment quoted earlier: "Es entwickelt sich ein Talent in den Stille." And who should know better than the lonely Werther, image of Goethe's own adolescence, that talent "blooms in silence and stillness?"

Discoverable personality correlations with mathematics are slighter (when intelligence is partialled out). This is perhaps not surprising—for there is perhaps little left in the way of special proficiency in so abstract a subject as mathematics when the gains from the pure insight of abstract intelligence are taken out. Nevertheless, one can conceive that a certain fortitude and an absence of need for emotional sustenance, also favors sustained interest in this abstract world, and this is, in fact, what is found. The correlations (significant but now down to 0.1 to 0.2) are with ego strength, C (positive with mature; negative with changeable, frivolous, emotional), with higher superego, G (positive with conscientious) and, negatively, with neurotic, psychopathic, paranoid, and infantile-demanding behavior. There are also very slight positive relations to surgency and affectothymia, and negative to dominance. Altogether the personality picture of the mathematically gifted is one of benign, mature adjustment, with such unusual frustration tolerance as the great figures of mathematics—Newton, Gauss, Euler, Lagrange, and others—typically have shown. (Galois is an exception, and his "maladjustment" arose in an exceptionally difficult environment.) Incidentally, there is no trace of the obsessive-compulsive traits which psychoanalysts glibly have theorized *should* be attached to mathematics. Indeed, the correlations are negative with "rigid" and "tyrannical" and other obsessive and paranoid traits.

Other primary abilities in relation to which we have already some research hints of significant personality associations are mechanical aptitude, drawing ability, and the still ill-defined factor of "social intelligence." Repeated hints crop up (see the occupational profiles of engineers, electricians, and mechanics on the 16 P.F. and various special studies) of association of mechanical aptitude with sizothymia $A(-)$, ego strength, C, parmia, H, strong self-sentiment, Q_3, and sometimes dominance, E, and harria, $I(-)$. Personality-wise, the engineers and electricians show a "tough," somewhat introverted, realistic, independent profile. It is, at first sight, strange that, in comparisons of delinquent and nondelinquent children, investigators have often noted higher mechanical aptitude as a characteristic of the former. However, in the first place, some of these comparisons have defined "high" as relative to verbal, and the educationally poor home background of many delinquents means low verbal ability. Nevertheless, some connection seemingly remains here, and it may be that, in unfortunate environments where the high ego strength and dominance normally associated with mechanical ability cannot lead to a good self-sentiment development, they lead to aggression. The interesting, more basic connection is that mechanical and engineering talent evidently depend on an essentially realistic, balanced, and independent type of personality, with other positive qualities. (Even in delinquency, the types of delinquency in the mechanically gifted tend to be primarily connected with a nonhostile and nonemotional, but self-determined "taking of the law into one's own hands.")

Correlations with drawing ability in the writer's 208 sample stand up across eight subgroups in the direction of artist talent being associated with A+ (responsive, warmhearted, easygoing), F(+) (talkative, high-spirited, quick), I(+) (intuitive, careless, lethargic), H(+) (self-confident, socially interested), and less significantly, E(+) (dominance) and J(+) (self-directing). This set of factors, practically constituting the second-order exvia factor, entirely fits the popular stereotype—which is perhaps based on centuries of experience—of the extravert (A, F, H, L−, Q₂−), bohemian, self-directing artist. Furthermore, the contrast with the mechanical interest profile just seen excellently fits (at the level of contrasting whole cultures) McDougall's data (1902) revealing statistically an antithesis of the extravert, Mediterranean, artistic culture and the introvert, Northern European, mechanically inventive, scientific culture. As one looks at individual artists, however, one may get the impression that this temperament description fits the general classical period better than the experimental era of the last eighty years, with the tortured, introverted Van Gogh and his modern almost schizophrenic successors. Nevertheless, so long as we deal, not with artistic creativity as a whole, but concretely with drawing ability as rated by art teachers, and with normal ranges of ability, the "extrovert" and high premsic (I+) individual evidently is given more to seeing the world around him, and to cherishing the motor skills necessary to depict it.

Turning next to "social intelligence," we encounter a primary which is conceptually important but still lacks a good factorial foundation. Indeed, it is a concept which, in various actual experimental analyses, apparently has vanished when general intelligence has been partialled out. Nevertheless, one suspects that if the skills involved were measured more effectively, as by going beyond pencil-and-paper perceptions and skills, into actual social reactions and emotional communication, a major primary ability *would* stand revealed. From the 16 Personality Factor Questionnaire profiles of those in such occupations as salesmen, executives, priests, administrators, psychiatric technicians, teachers, and others who have to show skill in dealing with people (see Cattell, Eber, and Tatsuoka, 1970), a common profile emerges positive in affectothymia, A; ego strength, C; parmia, H;

premsia, I; low guilt proneness, O−; and high self-sentiment, Q_3. The pattern is definite and significant enough, but whether it means that these traits are "auxiliaries" (in the "action" specification equation) to intelligence in producing effective social interaction, or whether, as in other instances in this section, we are supposing a "developmental equation" in which "social intelligence" factors are built up as a real proficiency, necessarily correlated therefore with these traits, remains to be seen.

Apart from the intrinsic psychological value, for counseling, education, and guidance, of the above psychological findings, they are put forward here as illustrations and arguments for certain general principles. First, they illustrate the principle that although the ability modality is conceptually, definably distinct from the temperament modality of traits, we must expect quite significant correlations to appear between them. Thus verbal, mathematical, and artistic performance systematically tend to be associated with certain personality traits, over and above abilities. Secondly, they bring out the principle that what are often thought of as different qualities of ability are actually combinations of ability and temperament traits which incidentally, can now be precisely represented as vectors in personality-ability space. This is, of course, quite different from the phenomenon of "ability-simulating personality traits" in Section 2 above. In the present phenomenon it is as if the personality trait is necessary to the criterion performance by aiding the ability to express itself with certain controls and directions of temperamental sensitivity. At present it is not certain how much of the interaction is immediate and how much developmental, but such significant connections call for systematic further investigation with well-defined personality source traits.

5. PERSONALITY AND ABILITY MEASURES IN THE PREDICTION OF ACHIEVEMENT

So far the analysis of results has been largely concerned with what are probably developmental effects, using variables expressing definite test performances, scored in some easily defined fashion. But achievement in some broader sense, even in the still not so wide sense of getting through college or apprenticeship to a vocation, surely would be expected to involve the admixture of personality qualities with abilities to a still greater extent. Our opening chapter indeed has quoted some famous observers to the effect that personality and character are *more* important to life success than are abilities.

In trying to get objective and quantitative answers to these questions about the broader drama of life, however, the psychometrist quickly realizes that defining life achievement and measuring success on occupational and family life criteria demand more psychometric skill than he is accustomed to bring to the simpler task of scoring a test ability performance. What is achievement in life? What, indeed, is success in an occupation? Jesting Pilate might well have followed up his query "What is truth?" with "What is success?" and stared just as blindly. In evaluating the great and unusual achievements in our own time (as witness even the task facing a compiler of *"Who's Who"*), we undoubtedly bungle. Contemporary fashions and disputes and the shouts of the crowd confuse our judgment, and we seek solace for our confessed incompetence in the thought that "the verdict of history" will tell. But even history cannot allow for differences of opportunity. Would Napoleon have been a great figure if not born on the surge of the French revolution? If Darwin had wandered off with the Patagonian boy, York Minster, and missed the Beagle when it sailed home, how much of a recognized genius would he have been among those bleak mountains? Which psychologists are making the vital contributions to our science in this decade? One has to suspect also a systematic error, appreciated by the poet who called success "the bitch goddess," since fairly obviously she may be won by those ready to sacrifice honor and standards to her whims.

When asked to predict relative success on some criterion of occupational or social achievement, many psychologists prefer simply not to ask where the criterion came from. Give them a criterion measure of achievement and they will usually do a pretty good job of weighting test measurements to predict it. They may, further, (if they understand functional measurement, i.e., testing for known source trait structures) employ psychological insight to see why weights are what they are. But all too frequently, like a capable servant at the beck and call of a peremptory master, the psychologist is asked by the public and sometimes by administrators to work with criteria he definitely distrusts or knows are wrong. For example, selection for scholarships for higher education commonly is made against a criterion of subsequent performance *in college* (or even academic achievement in the same year) whereas, the purpose of college being to prepare for life, the criterion really should be the goodness of *adult life* performance for which college education is a preparation. Existing selection procedures undoubtedly choose the facile college-examination-passer—and *sometimes* he turns out later to be a contributor to culture.

The first major advance from this worship of pedantry was the shift of emphasis in the early part of this century to selection by intelligence tests, and later by culture-fair intelligence tests. But this shift from what a student *has* done—in a school atmosphere—to what he may do in the future—in any broad, intelligence-demanding life situation—is not enough. It currently satisfies some aspirations in scholarship selection to select by the individual's promise as an individual rather than by his parents' financial good fortune; but public opinion should learn that this is still not good enough by the psychologist's standards. Unless it is balanced by adding personality and motivation tests (weighted against a post-school criterion) this "promotion by talents" *could* be poorer than what we had before. Intelligence tests may select merely bright, facile individuals lacking the character qualities to be anything but genteel parasites in some sheltered position for the rest of their lives. A true criterion of life achievement would undoubtedly put far more emphasis on personality test selection in the prediction battery. But, alas, for the present, we must admit that evaluation of the criterion, e.g., one of magnitude of social contribution, is in its infancy, and that we must make do with the best achievement criteria we have and ask how personality and ability measures can predict them. The fact is, however, that even in academic prediction, personality factors over and above intelligence contribute to accuracy.

Achievement is a many-faceted thing, and except for a few, relatively carefully studied occupational and examination performances, which we shall illustrate, the greater number of achievements—from driving fifty years without an accident to raising a family of effective citizens—as yet remain undocumented and experimentally unanalyzed. School achievement has been the big theme in achievement prediction research, and, except for certain provisos above, it is at least measured with high reliability. However, until the advent of factored personality and motivational source trait measures, and the more refined concept of fluid intelligence, many educational psychologists seemed content with very short perspectives in achievement analysis and estimation. For example, they would take any weighted sum, from any old shopper's basket of psychological tests, that would give the highest multiple correlation (in the sample) with the criterion, regardless of any basic structural psychological meaning in the published tests. More frequently the educational psychologist has taken nothing but an intelligence test, obtained the usual 0.4 to 0.6 prediction (regression) on next year's examination performance, and washed his hands of any responsibility for predicting the remaining 64% to 84% of variance in the criterion. Along with this goes the habit of partialling out the attainment due to intelligence and expressing the rest (or the rest divided by age) as an "achievement quotient," i.e., a statement of how well the individual is achieving "relative to his intelligence." We will not pause to evaluate the varieties of achievement of attainment quotient designs, because conceptually, they remain a crude half-step to the formulation that is really needed, namely, a full specification equation across all ability and personality factors, as set out below. For by this we can evaluate for the given case what the main roots of his achievement or nonachievement are. In fact, by the older notion, an "achievement quotient" could be written for every one of his capacities, e.g., "How well is he achieving relative to his powers of memory, or his emotional stability (C factor), or his anxiety level (second order, QII), and so on?"

So long as we examine prediction purely from an intelligence test, the fact will come up repeatedly in further discussion that educational psychologists have been inclined to evaluate (and even validate) an intelligence test by how well it *alone* predicts achievement. In that case crystallized ability, or any achievement-contaminated intelligence test will obviously become evaluated as better than a test which, though measuring intelligence well, measures *only* intelligence. True, a poor achievement prediction can arise from a test being intrinsically a poor intelligence test, not able even to account for all the variance in achievement due to intelligence. But the moment an alleged intelligence test passes the fraction that intelligence *should* predict, it must be convicted of having a contaminant in it, as surely as one detects alcohol in the excessive friendliness of a neighbor at the bar. It is no virtue in an intelligence test to predict more school achievement than it should. In general, correlations of intelligence test with school performance that exceed 0.6 (or even 0.5, depending on the population) show that the intelligence test is itself contaminated with school achievement and is anything but a pure culture-fair measure.

We are beginning to acquire tolerably stable figures on the relative role of fluid and crystallized intelligence, the primary abilities, and the chief personality and motivation source traits in performance in high school, and it may not be long before we have the same for colleges. The work of Cattell and Butcher (1968), Butcher, Ainsworth, and Nesbitt (1963), Graffam (1967), Radcliffe and Cattell (1961), Cattell, Sealy, and Sweney (1966), Warburton (1952), and other experienced psychometrists and factor analysts, e.g., at the Educational Testing Service in the United States and the National Foundation for Educational Research in Britain, has supplied us with a reasonably complete and stable estimation of the normal weights for the abilities and personality factors in a fairly complete spectrum of contributors. In particular, the studies (Cattell and Butcher, 1968) with relatively factor-pure measures of personality and motivation source traits (as in the 16 P.F., HSPQ, MAT, and SMAT) have at last clarified the total picture regarding the contributions from different trait modalities. One sees now just how the prediction builds up (from about 0.55 from abilities to 0.75 with personality traits, and so on) as each new modality adds its contribution.

The contribution from intelligence and the primary abilities has long been known. Table 12–1 shows actual correlations, first, for predictions from the abilities, namely Thurstone Primaries (including by implication, crystallized intelligence as a weighted sum) and secondly, from general intelligence as specifically represented by fluid general intelligence.

As would be expected, the weights for verbal *ability* are highest on verbal achievement, and so on for other agents. "Space" does practically nothing for these academic achievements, but number, reasoning, and fluency have significant contributions at suitable places. The fluid intelligence level helps *all,* but assists least in such a specialized rote performance as spelling. The multiple correlation from all these ability sources can rise to about 0.7, though the most common, central tendency for pure fluid intelligence is about 0.5 (sometimes dropping to 0.4 or rising to 0.55 or 0.60). Whenever the value for the intelligence regression weight falls below 0.5 we may suspect unsatisfactory reliability in test or criterion—or an unusually selected sample, e.g., of university students. On the other hand, although a crystallized intelligence test measure—estimated as a weighted sum of the primary abilities or by a traditional intelligence test— may reach a predictive value of even 0.7, we should not expect fluid intelligence (a culture-fair test), in the normal ranges of ability, to correlate

TABLE 12–1
Typical Levels of Predictions of School Achievement from Fluid Intelligence and Primary Abilities

Correlations and Weights of Tests in Estimating School Performance

Tests of Primary Mental Abilities and Intelligence	Paragraph Meaning		Word Meaning		Spelling		Language		Arithmetic Reasoning		Arithmetic Comprehension	
	r	β	r	β	r	β	r	β	r	β	r	β
Verbal	.60	.44	.60	.50	.57	.38	.54	.30	.52	.25	.46	.14
Space	.36	.12	.25	.03	.20	−.03	.26	.03	.36	.11	.33	.08
Reasoning	.37	.06	.36	.09	.38	.05	.40	.09	.43	.11	.45	.13
Number	.28	.01	.27	.00	.44	.20	.35	.08	.40	.15	.50	.30
Fluency	.33	−.01	.34	.01	.45	.15	.46	.19	.35	.00	.38	.05
Fluid Intelligence (culture-fair)	.45	.19	.35	.07	.31	.04	.37	.11	.51	.26	.45	.19
Multiple correlation	.64		.61		.63		.60		.64		.64	

This table is formed by combining two groups, N = 153, N = 125, urban and rural samples respectively.

From *The Prediction of Achievement and Creativity* by Raymond B. Cattell and H. John Butcher, copyright © 1968, by The Bobbs-Merrill Company, Inc., reprinted by kind permission of the publishers.

Primary Mental Abilities	Spelling	Social Studies	Typing	Shorthand
Verbal	.54	.50	.19	.44
Space	.36	.26	.16	.16
Reasoning	.44	.35	.27	.24
Number	.51	.48	.32	.27

From *Tests and Measurements: Assessment and Prediction* by J. C. Nunnally. Copyright 1959, McGraw-Hill Book Company. Used with permission of McGraw-Hill Book Company.

TABLE 12–2
Correlations of Primary Ability Agencies and Fluid Intelligence with Broader Achievements Outside the Classroom

Teachers' Ratings On

Primary Mental Abilities	Total Score on Stanford Achievement Test		Personal Adjustment		Interest in School Subjects		Behavior Record		Leadership		Social Adjustment		Achievement in Sports		Interest in Sports	
	r	β	r	β	r	β	r	β	r	β	r	β	r	β	r	β
Correlations and Weights in Multiple Correlation of Tests on Performances																
Verbal	.64	.44	.31	.09	.54	.30	.25	.15	.46	.23	.37	.19	.28	.08	.28	.10
Space	.34	.08	.24	.12	.30	.06	.10	.01	.28	.08	.22	.06	.12	–.02	.12	–.03
Reasoning	.43	.08	.35	.22	.49	.20	.29	.22	.45	.25	.35	.19	.30	.16	.27	.10
Number	.39	.10	.21	–.02	.42	.14	.18	.04	.26	–.05	.25	.05	.19	–.01	.21	.02
Fluency	.41	.06	.30	.13	.42	.10	.14	–.02	.38	.15	.27	.04	.27	.14	.30	.17
Fluid Intelligence (culture-fair)	.44	.14	.24	.03	.38	.07	.14	–.01	.38	.11	.26	.06	.25	.12	.26	.13
Multiple Correlation	.68		.42		.64		.32		.57		.43		.37		.37	

From *The Prediction of Achievement and Creativity* by Raymond B. Cattell and H. John Butcher, copyright © 1968, by the Bobbs-Merrill Company, Inc., reprinted by permission of the publishers.

more than about 0.45 to 0.55 with school achievement. Whatever the crystallized (traditional) test adds beyond that, is a conglomerate of personality and motivation traits—and a dash of the criterion itself! By contrast, any truly scientific analysis of the causes of achievement (and therefore of a given individual's problems in achieving) would prefer to have—clearly set out as such—the distinct contributions of personality, intelligence, and motivation components. Least of all does one want any chasing of one's own tail by "predicting" school attainment *from* school attainment, using an empirical correlation which yields no increase of insight whatever and no lawful extrapolation to new circumstances.

To obtain a more complete and balanced perspective on personality-ability interactions in the school environment, it is interesting to compare the prediction of nonscholastic achievements from the same kind of predictors. As Table 12–2 shows, the correlations of less centrally "scholastic" performances are negligible with the fluid intelligence factor, but both adjustment and interest in school subjects have some slight, significant, positive correlations with primary abilities. These are best with verbal ability and reasoning, and least with spatial ability. Incidentally, the lack of correlation with the last shows that, as an agency, it cannot be explained as a *proficiency* (page 323), i.e., as a dynamic, school sentiment "effector" product, as the other primary agencies may in part be. It is more likely, therefore, to be explicable as a "tool" or "aid" unity. (For we must not forget that correlation can be two-way causation, and school experience and achievement may themselves account for levels on what some statistical psychometrists (e.g., Horst, 1962, 1966) too blithely call "the predictors." On the other hand, when the multiple correlation of all these agencies, plus intelligence, is worked out with respect to teachers' ratings of interest in school work, the value (0.64 in Table 12–2) is virtually the same as with school attainment. Allowing for some misperception on the part of the teacher, it is still convincing that agency development is appreciably connected with the dynamic "effector" action of interests. Incidentally, if we calculate from Table 12–2 an estimate of the most general of agencies—a_g, crystallized intelligence—by adding the agencies, we again get a correlation (here and elsewhere) of about 0.4 to 0.6 between school interest and crystallized intelligence (higher than the 0.38 with fluid intelligence). This argues again for crystallized intelligence being a joint product of g_f and cultural exposure and interest.

Table 12–3 shifts the analysis to a straight evaluation of the role of personality factors in the classroom subjects of Table 12–1 and the school ratings of Table 12–2. It is virtually the first evidence available on the educational importance of a broad spectrum of verified personality factors. The results derive from the High School Personality Questionnaire in which the intelligence measure—Factor B—is actually quite a short intelligence test, though operating effectively for its length. The "achievements" in Table 12–3 are of special interest in that they cover a broader assessment than scholastic achievement alone. In passing, one notes the sub-

TABLE 12–3

The Balance of Intelligence and Personality in Predicting a Variety of Life Criterion Performances in Children

Achievement Measures and Teacher Ratings	Personality Factors														Multiple Correlations
	A	B	C	D	E	F	G	H	I	J	O	Q₂	Q₃	Q₄	R
Interest in Sports	.11	.25	.08	−.02	−.08	.12	.08	−.05	−.05	−.01	.00	.13	.03	.01	.42
Achievement in Sports	.19	.25	.10	−.09	−.10	.07	.13	.03	.00	−.06	−.03	.13	.09	−.05	.41
Social Adjustment	.15	.27	.06	−.08	−.12	.13	.15	.09	−.02	−.08	−.12	.09	.16	−.05	.38
Leadership	.18	.40	.03	−.10	−.16	.08	.23	.05	.00	−.06	−.11	.18	.19	−.04	.53
Behavior	.12	.22	−.07	−.17	−.21	−.02	.17	.06	.17	−.04	−.09	.07	.27	.02	.47
Interest in School Subjects	.22	.46	.03	−.12	−.21	.01	.33	.04	.03	.04	−.14	.20	.20	−.07	.58
Personal Adjustment	.19	.35	.06	−.14	−.21	−.03	.25	.01	.07	.02	−.10	.14	.22	−.10	.49
Total Score on Stanford Battery	.14	.56	.01	−.05	−.12	−.03	.25	.00	−.06	.04	−.07	.25	.14	−.02	.65
Paragraph Meaning	.17	.42	.03	−.06	−.07	−.02	.24	.03	−.09	−.02	−.10	.27	.13	−.04	.54
Word Meaning	.08	.52	.05	−.05	−.01	−.05	.25	.00	−.09	.01	−.07	.25	.11	−.04	.62
Spelling	.17	.48	−.04	−.06	−.19	.00	.27	.02	.06	.03	−.01	.14	.07	−.01	.60
Language	.16	.48	−.05	−.07	−.17	−.01	.24	−.04	.00	.08	−.06	.10	.07	.02	.58
Arithmetic Reasoning	.15	.48	.03	−.09	−.04	−.01	.21	.06	−.13	.03	−.10	.24	.11	−.07	.57
Arithmetic Computation	.17	.39	−.03	−.03	−.11	−.01	.29	.02	−.05	.05	−.11	.19	.07	−.07	.52

stantive role of personality source traits in such achievements as leadership, sports, etc. Nevertheless, the multiple correlation is even higher for scholastic attainment, partly because intelligence (B in the HSPQ series) begins to contribute substantially and probably partly because the criterion is more objective and reliable.

This is as far as we can go at present toward that prediction of youthful performance in a wider context, which was the ideal we stated at the beginning of this section. At this age, for lack of wider criterion data, we shall pursue in the next section our intended, more intensive, theoretical analysis of the balance and interaction of ability and personality traits specifically in the domain of school achievement.

6. ANALYSIS OF INTERACTION OF ABILITIES, PERSONALITY, AND MOTIVATION IN SCHOLASTIC ACHIEVEMENT

That personality plays a substantial part in achievement of various kinds has been documented sufficiently in the last section. However, we wish now to go beyond bare documentation to some theoretical understanding, introducing at the same time new findings on motivation. In so doing, it is necessary to concentrate on that area of achievement we call scholastic attainment, for there alone do we find reasonably complete data.

Incidentally, the absence of investigation of the relation of intelligence to all sorts of "life achievements" is at first surprising. We become less surprised when we find that there are only four studies in existence (Fryer, 1922; Cattell, 1934; Harrell and Harrell, 1945; Himmelweit and Whitfield, 1949) directly determining intelligence levels for many occupations (see Chapter 14). Educators have been the active users of intelligence tests, and the social and biological sciences come out a very poor second. For example, there exists no data with culture-fair tests and on an adequate sample relating intelligence to income (for any given age level), though half the world is ready to take this as a firm criterion of success ("If you're smart why aren't you rich?"). Since success is an elusive concept, we could at least tie correlations to reliably measurable supposed "criteria" of adaptation. Sociology and economies might well have been expected to find the relations of intelligence to such variables as income, freedom from accidents, longevity, contributions to charity, dependence on welfare, delinquency record, marital stability (inverse of divorces), number of children, etc. (The last is, for married people, even *negatively* related to intelligence.) So far we know only that a correlation of about 0.3 exists between intelligence and social status (Chapter 14) by status of parents.

In school achievement the assertion that scholarship selection should depend on more than intelligence will probably be greeted by experienced teachers with a hearty "Amen." Before the arguments can be evaluated properly, however, we must turn to some finer methodological issues. It is necessary, in fact to bring out the difference between the psychometric, actuarial examination made above, and the scientifically causal formulation. In the former the word "prediction" is used statistically in the sense of "providing an estimated figure for" not in the sense of "causally producing according to scientific laws" or even of "foretelling" (in the sense of future reference). Research necessarily *starts* with psychometric analysis of data (including multivariate, experimental, manipulative evidence). But its aim is to reach scientific, causal explanations. And, as instanced in the last section, in reference to alleged prediction from traditional intelligence tests, what the pure psychometrists (Horst, 1962, 1966; Guilford, 1959; Vernon, 1960; Cureton, 1955; Kendall, 1957) call the "predictors" may actually include a substantial part of the "predicted." In that sense we can as readily predict the individual's score on a traditional intelligence test from his school achievement as the converse, though we believe that causally a *fluid* (culture-fair) test acts to produce the school attainment.

In discussion we may necessarily use much the same jargon as the statistician, but our aim at this point is to reach conclusions about causation. Naturally the operational conditions, e.g., the sequences we impose, whereby one can recognize that the factor is an influence, are important for such conclusions. But the main requirement is that all experiment be based on pure factor measurements, wherever possible (i.e., unitary ability and personality source traits) rather than upon any ad hoc tests that happen to predict. By taking out a straight g_f measurement, for example, from the jumble of components in the typical intelligence test, as used in the last generation, we can re-combine that score in varying causative weights with personality, achievement, and motivation influences as each new situation requires. Applied psychology, correspondingly, would gain from having such measurements at hand, instead of working with the gross conglomerates of the traditional intelligence test score.

As a first step, let us add only personality-temperament information to intelligence predictions and compare, in Table 12–4, the magnitude of prediction from abilities alone and from abilities plus personality. This table re-analyzes the evidence from the tables (12–2 and 12–3) above in terms of the *total* contribution to predicting the criterion from intelligence alone, all abilities and all abilities plus all personality, and so on. All differences but one are highly significant between columns 2 and 3 in Sample A. However, as pointed out above, column 8 in Sample B—the "all abilities prediction"—of the variance has a disguise which needs penetration. It hides much personality and interest variance which has gone into the development of primary abilities. In fact, as we saw in Chapters 5 and 6, personality factors significantly remain correlated with crystallized intelligence and the specific abilities in the primary agencies. Consequently, for the total school achievement as objectively represented by the Stanford, the percentage variance (Table 12–2) accounted for by purely fluid intelligence is no more than $(.44)^2 \times 100 = 19.4\%$ (other samples give about 25%). By contrast, that accounted for by all assorted abilities is $(.68)^2 \times 100 = 46\%$ and that by fluid intelligence and personality source traits together is 59% to 62% (Table 12–4). *The goodness of scholastic attain-*

TABLE 12–4
Combined Prediction of Performance from Abilities and Personality Source Traits

(Sample A)	R			Percentage Variance		
	Culture-Fair Alone	All Abilities Alone	Abilities and Personality	Culture-Fair Alone	All Abilities Alone	Abilities and Personality
Total Achievement (Stanford)	.44	.70	.77	19.3	49.0	59.3
Paragraph Meaning	.64	.67	.73	41.0	44.9	53.3
Word Meaning	.61	.63	.73	37.2	39.7	53.3
Language	.60	.63	.70	36.0	39.7	49.0
Arithmetic Reasoning	.64	.64	.71	41.0	41.0	50.4
Arithmetic Computation	.64	.66	.70	41.0	43.6	49.0
Leadership	.57	.58	.66	32.5	33.6	43.6
Behavior Record	.32	.35	.54	10.2	12.2	29.2
Interest in School Subjects	.64	.64	.70	41.0	41.0	49.0

(Sample B)	Six Personality Factors		Thirteen Personality Factors		Entire HSPQ plus Abilities		All Ability Factors	
	R	var'ce	R	var'ce	R	var'ce	R	var'ce
Interest in Sports	.22	4.8	.40	16.0	.52	27.0	.33	11.0
Achievement in Sports	.34	11.6	.40	16.0	.54	29.2	.36	13.2
Social Adjustment	.32	10.2	.38	14.4	.53	28.1	.37	13.7
Leadership	.32	10.2	.42	17.6	.69	47.6	.55	30.0
Behavior Record	.35	12.3	.46	21.2	.50	25.0	.19	3.8
Interest in School Subjects	.46	21.2	.50	25.0	.70	49.0	.49	24.0
Personal Adjustment	.40	16.0	.43	18.5	.56	31.4	.36	12.9
Total Achievement (Stanford)	.36	13.0	.47	22.1	.79	62.4	.63	40.3

The prediction is shown separately for all thirteen personality dimensions in the HSPQ and for the six largest contributions, namely, A, affectothymia; D(−), low excitability; E(−), submissiveness; G, superego strength; Q_2, self-sufficiency; and Q_3, self-sentiment strength. The contraction of abilities (The IPAT Culture-Fair, g_f, and the B factor in the HSPQ, an a_g measure) is 40.1% of the variance, corresponding to a correlation of .63 (unusually high for a sheer ability prediction) compared to .47 for personality alone. However, that is for scholastic achievement, and this table shows how small (though always positive) the increment from abilities is in *other* fields, e.g., achievement in sports, behavior record.

ment prediction achieved from intelligence alone (in round values) may therefore be said to be *doubled by adding personality source traits from a sufficiently wide personality sphere,* as in the 16 P.F., HSPQ, etc., personality scales and the prediction from traditional intelligence tests is then surpassed.

Evaluating the situation more broadly than in the above specific results, from accumulation of many studies, we may write down a best rounded estimate of the high school weights in a specification equation as follows:

$$\text{Ach.} = .15A + .50B + .10C - .10D - .15E + .10F + .25G \\ + .10H - .10I + .15J - .10O + .20Q_2 + .20Q_3 - .10Q_4$$

(12.2)

For further explanations and more detailed discussions of probable modes of action of personality traits, the reader may peruse Cattell and Butcher (1968). The multiple correlation from this (the B, intelligence value, being taken as that for a culture-fair test) is about 0.7, i.e., this specification accounts for about half the variance.

As every psychologist will understand, these values will alter with change of educational situation, e.g., teaching methods and accidental selection affecting the samples. Thus among undergraduate university students, where the range of intelligence has been trimmed, the intelligence correlation and the associated I.Q. weight in the specification will fall, while personality factors also shift, as follows:

$$\text{Ach.} = - .10A + .35B + .15C + .05E - .20F + .10G - .10H \\ + 20I - .15L + .10M - .05N - .10O - .20Q_1 \\ + .20Q_2 + .20Q_3 - .10Q_4$$

(12.3)

The symbols are, of course, for the same personality factors in both the adult and child range though the (adult) 16 P.F. contains one or two later-evolved dimensions than in the roster representing the slightly simpler structure in the high school pupil (HSPQ) age range. Among the changes in emphasis with age, one notices principally (a) that introversion (the second-order factor loading A, F, H, etc.) becomes more favorable to performance in the older student group. This is probably associated with the shift of instruction from an interactive classroom situation to individual reading. It can also be related to the higher need for writing skills, since we have noted before that V factor is correlated with personality factor $A(-)$, etc. One also notes (b) that docility—$E(-)$—favors learning in the younger child, whereas some independence and critical attitude $(E+)$ is more demanded in university studies.

For the student of personality the mode of action of the other personality source traits will not be hard to see. "Emotional stability" (C+, Ego strength) aids almost any long term enterprise. Superego strength $(G+)$ perhaps operates through homework being conscientiously done. Self-sufficiency (Q_2+) means that the individual will tend to solve problems on his own, instead of being dependent on aid from teachers and fellow students at every step. The negative correlation of achievement with guilt proneness (O) and ergic tension (Frustration, Q_4) on the other hand, calls for a sequential experiment to see whether these may not be products of relative school failure, rather than causes.

Finally, in seeking a comprehensive understanding of the roots and associations of achievement—in any area—one must turn to the third great modality of trait measures—motivation and dynamic structure measures. In a general way most western peoples subscribe to the dictum of Schiller that "Man is made great or little by his own will." Certainly the majority of people are able to point to arresting and desolating examples in their own circle of persons of outstanding intelligence and talent who have failed miserably despite their talents. The range in subsequent magnitude of contribution to their science among men who share the high ability necessary to get a Ph.D. degree, for example, is very wide. The contributions, for example, to subsequent research in their own subjects, between the most and the least active is nearer 100 to 1 than 10 to 1. When the abilities are held constant, the full effect of differences of motivation and personality organization is vividly exposed, but, in the specification equation weights for the general population range, we see ability and motivation playing more equal parts.

To obtain a meaningful figure for the relative variance contribution of abilities, personality traits, and dynamic traits, the psychologist must first assure the critic that he is including the major traits in each modality in his battery. Certain refined psychometric methods, e.g., canonical correlations, offering results to the third decimal place, are pointless if the whole question of proper sampling from the domain of personality, motivation, and ability, in a *psychological* perspective, has been neglected. What we have taken in the above school achievement predictions from the ability field is a reasonable array of the chief confirmed agency patterns, and the same is explicitly guaranteed by the way the fourteen to sixteen personality traits of the HSPQ and 16 P.F. are taken from a spanning of the personality sphere.

A little more discussion is needed regarding a sampling of the motivation modality. It has been pointed out in the brief survey of motivation structure research (page 357) that factor analyses of a stratified sample of the world of interests in our culture, akin to the sampling of the personality sphere population of behaviors which gave us the primary personality source traits, has yielded some eight or nine drives or ergic structures and several sentiment structures. Only ten of these, five of the more important ergs and five of the major sentiments, have been embodied so far in the objective test devices of the Motivation Analysis Test (MAT) and the School Motivation Analysis Test (SMAT). Those in the Edwards' inventory are similar, but not based on varied objective devices, while Guilford's (1959) factoring of interests yields similar structures (Cattell, 1957a) to those in MAT and SMAT. Although our measurable variety of common dynamic structures in standardized objective scales thus lacks completeness, notably in regard to the numerous, relatively narrow sentiments which contribute like small streams to the rivers of interest in everyday life, yet at least those major sources of energy we call hunger, sex, need for security, gregariousness, self-assertion, etc., are now represented in the main ergs factor-analytically isolated in humans.

The first researches adding objective batteries of these drive strengths to ability and personality measures in investigating school achievement were launched over the last ten years by Butcher, Sealy, Warburton, and their students in England; Barton, Dielman, Sweney, and Cattell in the United States, and Radcliffe in Australia. Their results agree in assigning an importance to individual differences in motivation of the same general magnitude as that of ability and temperament differences. The results of the research carried out by Butcher on 144 children are given in Table 12–5.

At so early a stage of research, and for one sample, the precise values in Table 12–5 should not be taken too seriously. (In two cases, second samples and determinations have appreciably changed the given correlations). Also, we know that in the case of ergic tension levels, the scores do not remain constant for the individual from occasion to occasion as with temperament and ability trait scores. They *do* maintain a stability coefficient of about 0.6 over a four-month interval in groups in which there is

TABLE 12–5
Dynamic Source Trait (Erg and Sentiment) Strengths
Related (by Objective Measures or SMAT) to School
Achievement

Dynamic Structure (Motivation) Factor	*Correlation with School Achievement*
Constructiveness	+.36
Curiosity	−.20
Fear	−.24
Pugnacity	−.21
Gregariousness	+.17
Assertion ("Need Achievement")	−.23
Religion	−.34
Submissiveness	+.50
Self-Sentiment ("Need Achievement")	+.40[1]
Superego ("Need Achievement")	+.44
Narcissism	−.33
Sex	−.15
Acquisition	−.39
Protectiveness	+.21

Note that the above values must be regarded as completely corrected for attenuation of criterion and dynamic factor, since they are obtained as correlations among the pure factors (see Cattell and Butcher, 1968).

[1] The original table published in Cattell and Butcher (1968) has a clerical error reversing the sign of this loading.

little change in environment and opportunities of self-expression. Consequently, when the criterion performance is one that would depend on *average* motivation level over a year, e.g., grades, rather than instant motivation, as in a momentary performance situation, we should not expect criterion correlations to reach the levels for personality and ability traits.

Although it has so far been impracticable to retest children repeatedly over the year to get a good estimate of average level, significant relations are reached even with single measures. In particular several studies have consistently shown that school achievement is related positively to self-sentiment and superego strengths and negatively to tension level on the sex and pugnacity ergs. The negative relations to narcism are also reasonably consistent. These make sense, and agree very well—as far as self-sentiment and superego are concerned—with measures made independently in the questionnaire medium. (These two factors in the 16 P.F.—G, superego, and Q_3, self-sentiment—are conceptually the same as two in MAT and SMAT and correlate well with them.) But other relations, such as the negative correlations with curiosity and acquisitiveness, which might be expected to favor a well-stocked mind, are at present puzzling. If, as experts in the objective motivation measurement fields may do, one goes further into the complexities of integrated and unintegrated ergic components, more definite but complex statements are possible. Thus the negative relation to achievement is larger and more consistent with *unin-*tegrated sex and pugnacity tensions. Probable reasons for this will be discussed below (page 402), but let us first proceed a little further with the quantitative evidence.

For before specific hypotheses are entertained one should perhaps answer the general question: "Just how effectively *does* motivation add to the total prediction of school achievement?" Table 12–6 shows that approximately one-fifth of the total achievement variance is contributed by each of the three modalities (assuming we represent ability by intelligence rather than the "agencies," which are, after all, the *products* of interest and ability). Actually, the quantum from dynamic traits is, in presently available results, a little less than one-fifth. But we know that the validities of these rough pioneer tests were those of relatively crude instruments. Psychometrists familiar with the typical history of test progress in regard to reliability and validity might make a shrewd guess that correction for attenuation could raise these validities by 20% (see below).

Meanwhile, the central indication in these researches is that a combined modality prediction can account at present for 60% of the variance (corresponding to a correlation of about 0.78), which is definitely at an augmented level compared with what psychologists have been accustomed to when using ability measures alone. For the sake of guiding theory and research planning, it is interesting to ask what our estimate is of how much *would* be predicted if the tests in each of these modalities reached the same realized validity and reliability. If we were able to correct for (a) attenuation from present test *and* criterion unreliability, and (b) incompleteness

TABLE 12–6
Relative Contributions of Three Modalities of Traits to
School Achievement (Standardized Achievement and
Average School Grade Measures)

	Correlation with Criterion	*% Variance of Criterion Predicted*
1. Abilities:		
Fluid Intelligence	.45	20.3
2. Personality:		
13 HSPQ Personality Factors		
(Intelligence Factor B Abstracted from the		
14 total)	.43	18.5
3. Motivation		
15 SMAT Dynamic Factors	.40	16.0
4. Ability and Personality (1 and 2)*	.79[1]	62.4[1]
5. Personality and Motivation (2 and 3)	.53	28.1
6. Ability, Personality, and Motivation		
(1, 2, and 3)	.78	60.1

[1] This value is on a different sample (153 boys and girls in 7th grade) from the rest (144 7th and 8th graders) and is uncorrected for shrinkage. Hence, it exceeds (6).

Note: (1) The figures here are estimates, derived by Cattell and Butcher (1968) by averaging values from two (and in some instance three) studies and are smaller than those actually obtained because allowance has been made for the expected shrinkage in going to a new sample.

(2) The variances from the three sources as put together in 4, 5, and 6 will not add exactly to the combined values because there are some small correlations across the three different modalities.

(3) These values are not yet corrected for attentuation by test or criterion unreliability.

From *The Prediction of Achievement and Creativity* by Raymond B. Cattell and H. John Butcher, copyright © 1968, by The Bobbs-Merrill Company, Inc., reprinted by permission of the publishers.

of sampling of the modality domains, it is a reasonable conclusion that the increase in the personality quantum would be a little greater than that for intelligence, while the increase for the dynamic realm would be a little greater than for personality. Thus, we are suggesting that the actual magnitudes of the predicted variance in fact should finish close to 25% of the criterion ascribable to each. This would point to 75% of the criterion being predicted from characters of the examinee and 25% from accidents of environmental conditions. (For well-designed measures from the three modalities are correlated only trivially.)

The manner of causal action accounting for the observed personality and motivation contributions has been briefly psychologically sketched above and can be pursued further from the data in the tables by any dynamic psychologist. What remains relatively obscure, with our dearth of home background data, is the origin of that 25% (assuming fully reliable tests) of the criterion variance not accounted for by characteristics in the individual. Such variance as family attitude to the child's school work already has expressed itself appreciably, but not entirely, in the measures of the child's personality and motivation. But intermittent illnesses, slips in the examination, differences in the conception of the criterion among teachers, variations in book and study facilities at home, could enter to reduce the correlation between the child's essential achievement capacity and the criterion measure. The remarkable feature of these findings indeed, is, as Cattell and Butcher (1968) comment, that the estimate of how much of the individual's achievement is resident in the student himself approaches this high asymptote of 75%. Even allowing for the fact that his characteristics at the given year express what environment has done for him already, it is somewhat surprising that so little remains for current environment. When Henley wrote "I am the master of my fate; I am the captain of my soul" many who would grant the second would be more likely to agree with Ecclesiastes (9:11) on the first, that "time and chance happeneth to them all." But at least in this precious artificial realm—the school—in which justice, equality of opportunity, and objectivity of valuation are fostered more than they will be later, it does indeed seem that the individual may be the master of 75% of his fate!

Throughout this chapter's discussion of achievement and ability we have employed a distinction between *action equations* and *developmental equations*. The former tell us in what degrees success in a present action are due to various personality and ability traits; the latter tell us how the level of present development of traits is a function of the interaction of past traits with experience. When we find what weights are to be given to traits in predicting a child's achievement test performance we are actually dealing with values that are, in a sense, a combination of these two. On the one hand, we can conceive a "trait" of school achievement which has been built up over the year by the P's, A's, D's, and experience. On the other hand, there remains a question of how well he will show this achievement on the morning of the examination. For the latter—the examination-taking performance—there is surely a distinct specification equation, and it is one which many students believe treats them badly.

Future psychometric practice may well embrace the sophistication of separating these, thus:

$$S_t = b_p P + b_a A + b_d D + \text{Experience terms} \qquad \text{(12.4a)}$$

$$S_p = b_s S_t + b_p' P + b_a' A + b_d' D \qquad \text{(12.4b)}$$

where S_t is the trait of achievement as built up at the end of the school year and S_p is the actual examination performance. Most, but not all the variance of S_p comes from S_t, and the weights b_p', b_a', b_d', certainly are going to be very different from b_p, b_a, and b_d. What we get when, as usual, we express S_p *directly* as a function of P, A, and D (personality, ability, and dynamic traits) is a derivative of these two. But for many purposes we would like to have (12.4a) itself—the cumulative effect of intelligence and personality qualities upon real achievement—not just the way it is able to express itself in a given examination on a given bilious morning. Even then, we would have to analyze further the purely statistical equation (12.4a), for, as pointed out above, it is always possible that the correlational relationships are due to two-way effects—the effect of achievement upon personality and vice versa. Beyond this analysis is the further analysis needed into (a) the equation for relating present (accumulated) learning levels to personality (which, in ninety-nine cases out of a hundred, is what the educational investigator gives us), and (b) the equation for increments in achievement related to traits. A tentative answer to the latter is provided by Cattell and Sealy's (1965) correlations of personality and dynamic traits with *increase* of school performance over a year. As might be expected, the weights are of the same general pattern as in the integrated resultant commonly seen (page 389).

7. MEMORY, MOTIVATION, AND ABILITY

The influence of motivation has been approached in an introductory manner in the above section in relation to scholastic achievement, for its action is comparatively simple there and good empirical findings exist. In this and the next section we plan to probe more subtle kinds of interweaving of motivation and ability—in this section we will examine that which takes place through the interaction of motivation and memory. In so doing we propose to knit together, by drawing threads from a new angle, what has been said about memory in brain physiology (Chapter 8) and about the place of memory in the triadic theory of abilities (Chapter 11).

The triadic theory of abilities describes the rise of a class of unitary abilities recognized by factor analysis as "primaries," by designating many of them *agencies,* created by common experience in the case of *aids* and common interest and reward in the case of *proficiencies.* It links structured learning theory with ability theory, by claiming that the structures actually found in the latter can be predicted from the structured learning theory specification equation. Thus if a pre-existing ability, e.g., g_f, is predominant in the learning (Equations 11.3 and 11.4), the acquired ability, a_g, will turn out to be largely a projection of the patterns of that pre-existing ability. On the other hand, if a need system with its particular reward schedule, such as build up a dynamic sentiment structure, have most of the weight in equation (11.3 and 11.4), then we shall expect a proficiency structure to be shaped as a common trait with outlines matching the interest system.

The study of ability growth in relation to interest and motivation now needs to be explored further in two directions: (1) concerning the two-way interaction of ability and interest and the limits which this imposes on the equation, and (2) concerning the interaction of motivation and memory, in relation to the specific properties of memory.

Regarding the first, whereas in the laboratory learning is commonly studied with a fixed (and, one may add, relatively trivial) motivation, in life the motivation alters with the performance. It may alter by the interest failing long before the characteristic plateau of the repetition learning curve is reached, or, in the opposite direction, by the individual becoming so proud of the new ability, or receiving such a crescendo of unexpected rewards for it, that it shoots to new heights. In life the casual interaction of ability and interest works both ways. This is recognized in the structured learning theory formulation, which, by the changes in the vector of *modulators* (s's) measures learning change as an increase in interest (page 395). This increase in interest depends on reward from success, which may not be comparative social success, or self-sentiment reward, or straight ergic reward (though all these play their part) but simply greater ease (less energy expenditure) in the new way of performing.

The absence of recognition of this two way interaction of Equation (11.5) is partly a consequence of excessive dependence in learning theory on bivariate animal experimentation, where interest is always a manipulated independent variable. Here one must point out that the main reason why rats are not interested in electronic engineering, despite their modern maze environment being full of it, is that they cannot understand it!

Nevertheless, at least as far as the primary drives—the ergs—are concerned, the dynamic structure is obviously primary, and the abilities develop as agents to the ends of these ergs, as we have seen in "tool agency formation." This occurs notably in the effector patterns of the sentiments, which in turn are shaped by the institutions studied by the cultural anthropologist and the social psychologist. All this we have surveyed above, in regard to the reasons why abilities shape themselves in the unitary agency patterns discovered.

It may be desirable to remind the reader again at this point of the three vector proposition in *structured learning theory*. These vectors are (1) a vector of the change scores for each individual on the k ability factors (or personality and motivation source traits—the T's); (b) a vector of changes in the behavioral indices—the b's; (c) a vector of changes in the modulator indices—the s's. The important contribution of the last is to tell us how people's *interest involvements* change as they are repeatedly exposed to a learning situation—for the s's modify mainly the sentiment and ergic source traits. It is vital to note that the use of modulators implies that every situation has two aspects (for one aspect is tied to the b's and the other to the s's). This is the concept that the total *global situation* has two parts: (1) a focal stimulus, which triggers the particular response to which it is bound. This is the j subscript to the b's and to the act (response) a, as in the above equations, a_{ij} (i being the individual, j the focal stimulus) and (2) an ambient (surrounding) stimulus situation, k. This calls for the complete designation a_{ijk} for a given act, and for b_j and s_k in the equation. For example, a child might be responding to an intelligence test item j either in a group testing situation, k_1, or an individual testing situation, k_2, or in yet a third, k_3, in which the presence of a parent is added.

Now the central concept in *modulation,* is that the ambient situation, k, changes the factor level itself, by a modulating index, s_k, when the factor is of the kind that *can* be modified, e.g., a general state of anxiety, elation or fatigue, or a drive level. That is to say, it changes the involvement of interest itself by raising the effect of any one of several ergic tension or E levels. The result is that the familiar specification equation now has to be rewritten with s's (modulators) as well as b's (behavioral indices) thus:

$$a_{ijk} = \sum_{x=1}^{x=l} b_{jx}T_{xi} + \sum_{y=1}^{y=m} b_{jy}s_{ky}L_{yi} + \sum_{z=1}^{z=n} b_{jz}s_{kz}E_{zi} \qquad (12.4)$$

The Σ's simply remind us that there are a whole series of traits (T's)— 1 of them—to take into account, covering abilities and personality—as well as m different state liability scores, L's e.g., to anxiety, arousal, etc., and n different ergic tensions, e.g., sex, fear, self-assertion, pugnacity. The b's are factor loadings and the s's show how much the ambient situation k raises the anxiety, etc., state levels or stimulates the ergic tensions.

The fact that structural learning theory analyses a learning change into a change of level on the T's, e.g., ability traits, and a change on the b's, describing the extent to which the trait changes its involvement in the performance is merely in keeping with general knowledge from learning experiments. The additional notion now incorporated is that learning experience changes also the modulator indices (s's), i.e., the extent to which the increasingly familiar situation stimulates interests it did not much invoke before. As has been stated in the previous chapter, this theoretical framework has been called the *three vector model* in structured learning theory. Formally it is the statement that a learning change needs three vectors to describe it, namely, a change vector of T's, of b's and s's. The task of learning theory now becomes that of predicting these vector changes from learning experiences and the pre-existing personality. As pointed out above (pages 335 and 387) the initial predictions of change are made in structured theory, as in traditional learning theory, in terms of change in performance, on the a_{ij}'s. But these changes are translated into changes in the traits (T's, including A's, abilities), on the behavioral indices, b's, and on the interest modulation coefficients, the s's. This translation is necessarily complex (see Cattell, 1971a); but we can at least set down in Equation (12.6) the general truth that the change in any one modulation term s, (any modulator from occasion t_1 to t_2) must be a function of the ability traits (A_t's), the behavioral indices (b_t's) and modulators (s_t's), and the reward experience, ($E_1 - E_2$) at the t_1^{th} occasion thus:

$$s_{jlc(t_2-t_1)} = \sum b_{jat_1}A_{at_1i} + \sum b_{jbt_1}P_{bt_1i} + \sum b_{jct_1}s_{lct_1}D_{ct_1i} \qquad (12.5)$$

$$+ \; b_{j(e_1-e_2)}(E_1 - E_2)_{t_1}$$

where j is a specific response, l an ambient situation, A_a, P_b and D_c are any ability, personality and dynamic traits, ($E_1 - E_2$) is the reward (fall in ergic tension) from the beginning, E_1, to the end E_2, of the learning experience, the b's are functions yet to be found and so on.

If b_{jat_1} should turn out by experiment at time t_1 to be as large as $b_{j(e_1-e_2)}$ it would mean that a high ability on the trait A_a is as important as a high reward $(E_1 - E_2)$ in determining this aspect of learning (or the specific learning performance itself if we substitute $a_{ijl(t_2-t_1)}$ for $s_{jlc(t_2-t_1)}$).

Since we know that any learning curve eventually reaches a plateau, and since the abilities—A's—do not themselves decline (and are, moreover, unlikely to decline to zero b_a values) it must be supposed that the limit is imposed by changes in the b_d's on the dynamic traits and the approach of the b_e's to zero (presumably as a result of the behavior impairing other ergic satisfactions when it goes beyond a certain level).

The second issue that we promised to discuss here is a more intensive analysis of the role of powers of memory in the rise of ability. So far, in the above, capacity to remember has been "taken for granted" as an adjunct to or condition of learning. Actually it is considered hidden in Equation (12.5) as one of the A's determining the rate of learning. However, it obviously occupies a very special position among the series of abilities that determine the acquisition of a new ability—special in being different from the other abilities as such, and special in its unique relation to motivation.

As pointed out in discussing the physiology of memory in Chapter 8, and computer simulations in Chapter 9, the essential structure of memory is still an enigma—due to absence of report on certain essential correlations. For example, there is reasonably sound evidence (Thurstone, 1938; Kelley, 1954) that capacity to commit "meaningless" material to memory ("rote memory") is an independent factor of capacity to commit meaningful material to memory, but the exact factorial separation of the latter from intelligence is uncertain. Similarly, there is evidence that the capacity to remember for a few seconds is different in kind (and in endowment from person to person), from the capacity to remember over long time intervals. However, the correlations of these latter two with the former two have not been reliably established, nor has the effect of a probably independent capacity to retrieve been separated from the capacity to store.

In consequence of these and other gaps the position adopted here is a theoretical construction, with which other "schools" of psychology may disagree, and which the present writer may want to modify as new data appears in the next few years. In terms of process it is tolerably well established (Haber, 1970) that an immediate sensory impression, e.g., a picture, is assimilated to memory in about ¼ of a second. If some second impression intrudes on the first during those 250 milliseconds, the reproduction is in some degree upset. If the person wishes to retain the impression longer, for immediate memory, he can introduce some repetitive device, as a person repeats in auditory-motor imagery a telephone number. This short distance memory, the present writer would hypothesize, has no distinction of rote and meaningful factors, as has long distance memory. It is limited by the "span of attention" limit to about five or six things at a time. This power is quite strongly correlated, according to Jensen's (1968) and Horn's results with the fluid intelligence factor, presumably because the initial impact of a new perception momentarily involves not just one provincial sensory zone but the whole cortical association mass (see Horn, 1968; Ertl, 1966).

It has been claimed by clinical psychologists on the one hand (Freud) and by experimentalists (such as Haber, 1970) on the other that these immediate sensory impressions are at times 100% reproducible, and the personal experience of exact reproduction of "long forgotten" scenes as well as their production by electrical stimulation of the brain suggests that—but for failures of retrieval—we should be more commonly aware of their persistence. However, we have supposed in this theory (page 205) that a "processing" takes place over seconds, minutes and even hours, of the direct sensory impression, so that it becomes linked with other sensory experiences at a "perception of relations" level, i.e., by the building up of abstract symbolic reference. For example, the visual perception of a Blank's beer can link with the auditory and motor storage of the word beer, with the symbol C_2H_5OH for an important part of its content, with thoughts of a famous party; and an anti-pollutionist's sad image of the can thrown in a public park. Haber suggests that this commitment to the permanent symbol and associative storage is less efficient than the direct image storage, but in fact we are comparing two different things: the likelihood of finding a man in when you call at his house and the likelihood of reaching him from files and phonebooks at remote parts of the country.

Our theory of memory as far as it was developed in Chapter 8 stated that the effectiveness of this symbolic, abstract, or "distributed" memory would be correlated with intelligence, and in fact would be identical with and measured by Kelley's "meaningful memory" factor. The latter is not all intelligence, and is presumably far from perfectly correlated with it, because it depends, as measured in his and similar experiments, also on (a) the number of referent experiences that the person has already accumulated, by which a concept could be reached, (b) a power of retrieval which, we have seen, is appreciably dependent on neurological efficiencies in certain brain areas and on motivation strength, and (c) the intactness of the brain areas connected with the original sensory impressions. As Luria (1970) and many others have pointed out, the use of words is an excellent illustration of this last, in that damage to the motor memory area permits one to remember words visually but not to write them, and damage to the auditory area, to write words but not to avoid confusion with words of roughly similar sound, and so on through various combinations.

Our concern here, however, is with the "broad" capacities not the sensory or motor "provincials," and here there seems to be at present factor analytic evidence for three powers: a long distance rote memory, g_{mr}, a long distance meaningful memory, g_{mm}, and a "fluency" or capacity to retrieve,

g_r—in addition to the immediate, short-term, reverberatory memory, which correlates with g_f. The theory has been put forward here that these are systematically inter-related and therefore oblique factors. For example, it is theorized that g_r is not power of retrieval alone, but power of retrieval plus the total volume of storage. However, just as the water flow from a reservoir is normally far more dependent on the size of the pipe than the amount in storage, so g_r—until the limits of the person's reservoir of stored content is reached—is a single factor across the various performances. In as much as the total meaningful storage is a cumulative function (an integral) of the g_f and g_{mm}, these two factors should be correlated positively with it; so that g_r when measured on performance which comes near to "draining the reservoir" should correlate positively with g_f and g_{mm} measures. Similarly a_g should be a cumulative function of *interaction* of g_f and g_{mm}. If substantial correlation with the first has been well demonstrated, its correlation with the second is open to experiment.

Since the majority of provincial powers, as usually measured, and, especially, all *agencies* however measured, depend not only on the investment of g_f, as already closely followed, but also on the cumulative effect of memorizing, and on the presently existing capacity to retrieve, we should expect the appearance of g_{mm} and g_r to be almost as broad at the higher order factor analyses as g_f. In particular, a_g should show g_{mm} running as a secondary across its primaries as broadly as does g_f. The tables shown earlier are not inconsistent with this, and, in particular, at the pre-school level, factor No. 6 in Table 7–4 suggests a broad memory power influence.

The reason that such broad memory powers as g_{mm} and the power of retrieval would not be expected to appear with such powerful variance as g_f (at the second stratum or higher) is to be found, in our theory, in the influence of specialized motivation, as studied in this chapter. Unfortunately there is still little agreement in the scanty experimental findings, as to the relative power with which the restricting effect of specialized motives acts on (a) the committing to memory, (b) the maintenance of storage (if "maintenance" by some motivational force is necessary) and (c) the power of retrieval. Clinicians following Freud, put most emphases on (c). Physiologists may look to (b). Experimental psychologists, such as Underwood (1957), have demonstrated that strength of interest affects (a). Although quantitative answers on relative importance are desirable, they do not affect the conclusion we can draw here that the action of the different aspects of memorizing in terms of the cumulative build up of abilities-in-being is strongly affected by the dynamic (motivation-interest) history in that domain. The general principle that *proficiencies* will take the *form* of the dynamic structure, and, in any given individual, reach a *level* determined by his dynamics, is clear. However, if we were to know more about the points and manners of application of motivation in memory, its role in the action and growth of abilities at different stages and ages could be more specifically formulated.

8. THE RELATION OF MOTIVATION AND ABILITY TO PERFORMANCE IN AN IMMEDIATE SITUATION

The last section has been concerned with the role of motivation and memory in the long-term, cumulative build up of abilities. In the preceding section we took a brief look at evidence on the immediate interaction of motivation and ability in the specialized, school achievement area. It is proposed here that—having fully distinguished the cumulative from the immediate action situation—we return to the latter for broader analysis than that provided by school achievement evidence alone.

A central principle which stands out at first glance over this area is that where performances are of low complexity most of the variance therein is associated with dynamic differences, while with high complexity it is determined more by ability differences. (Indeed, this has been proposed as the basic operation for separating ability from dynamic trait modalities (Cattell and Warburton, 1967).) For example, where the number of pegs being correctly placed in holes is the performance, motivation predicts much of it; but where the number of items correct in an intelligence test is involved, motivation has a negligible role over any ordinary range. Similarly, the speed of a rat in a straight maze run is a better indication of his motivation than of his learning level in running the maze.

This is evident in a qualitative sense also in temperament, as well as in motivation *per se*. What a person will learn, in a free living situation, is much more determined by temperamental inclinations than by ability. For example, whether a person will remember more faces or more inanimate objects from exposed pictures is related significantly to the personality factor, exvia-invia, U.I. 32, over and above the goodness of his memory, while his tendency to do much in the first as compared to the second minute in the cursive miniature situation test performance depends on his endowment in the hypomanic source trait, U.I. 18, and his tendency to get a higher number correct relative to number done, in gestalt completion, will depend on his level in the independence trait, U.I. 19.

Probably more experiments have been done in motivation in relation to school achievement, as discussed above, than to any other area of performance. Unfortunately, not many of these educationist's researches can be brought into the psychologists' more motivationally developed conceptual systems, because they have not been identified as to their dynamic structures involved and they have been measured by self-evaluative (opinionnaire check list) rather than objective motivation component measuring devices. McClelland's and Atkinson's (1953) researches on the achievement motive have, it is true, used one or two objective devices, principally projection on the TAT. But, as has been overwhelmingly proved (Cattell, Radcliffe and Sweney, 1963), projective measures alone achieve very poor validity as a motivation factor measurement. Research on motivation component factors shows that at least six diverse types of positively loaded subtests, as in the MAT and SMAT, are needed to achieve acceptable validities. The MAT researches described above actually show that sheer competitiveness (self-assertive erg) makes only a minor contribution to school performance. The largest contribution are from the superego and from the self-sentiment, the structure of which is well understood and which would be poorly described by stretching the term "need for achievement" to cover them. In short, "need for achievement" needs to be understood as a complex, composite entity, better reduced to clear-cut MAT and 16 P.F. factors in any insightful analysis of relation to academic or other performance.

A general overview of the importance of motivation in immediate performances tends to agree with the precise work reported in Table 12–3, that about as much prediction of school achievement is likely to be made from motivation as by all ability or by all personality dimensions. However, if one may make a shrewd guess at what future research will show, it could be that a fair part of this is really not in the "immediate performance" equation but has appeared through the developmental equation, in the building up of knowledge and skill. For the motivation levels at the time of examination probably also represent those which have prevailed over much of the year of study. The measurement of momentary levels in ergic tension factors has not yet reached the point where dependable experimental evidence can be presented regarding the effect, in humans, of increased effort only in the immediate action situation. Yet the question of what motivation level does to the final expression of ability in the immediate action situation is of importance in many contexts, and particularly in intelligence measurement. For example, recent debates (see Chapter 14) on practical social uses of intelligence tests have concerned the argument that certain cultural groups do not do well on intelligence tests because they are not interested in taking them.

The early work of Spearman's associates showed surprisingly little increment on average test performance from adding monetary and other motivations to the standard classroom situation, and still less effect upon the rank order of the students. The present writer found the same when motivating small children to do intelligence tests by including candy as an immediate goal (as Köhler had used bananas with chimpanzees) in the puzzle boxes. From the structural learning theory arguments above, one would conclude that the fact that duller children apparently show less motivation for intelligence testing is as much a consequence as a cause of their poor performance. They do not "light up" at the intellectual challenge of a puzzle, as do brighter children who have had frequent experience of being reinforced by success. Incidentally, this is an argument for chopping off the difficult upper part of an intelligence test when using it with duller groups and also for interspersing very easy examples instead of having a steadily increasing difficulty level, in order to maintain the level of motivation, the standardization being appropriately adjusted.

In a recent survey Burt and Williams (1962) repeated the type of comparison of high and low motivation in testing made by Spearman, but in more natural settings. Again, the increments with substantial motivation change were small, but they were statistically significant. Obviously, if we consider the general principle above that increase of motivation does little for complex judgments, some differences between experimental results could be explained by the relative difficulty of the tests used. From the standpoint of practical conclusions from tests, it is worthwhile to note that Burt and Williams, in readministering the same tests under different motivation, were not always able to separate the two- or three-point increment of I.Q. due to doing the test again (test sophistication) from that due to motivation change. But, making allowances for what is known about test sophistication, it seems that students who take an intelligence test for scholarship competition or an immediate attractive monetary reward show, respectively, a three- and a four-point (I.Q.) increment over the situation where the test is simply done as an impersonal classroom exercise. The increment in the mean is accompanied by heightened test reliabilitv ana by an increase in standard deviation, i.e., separation, in the group. However, the rank order is little affected. More attention undoubtedly should be given in routine testing to maximizing and equalizing motivation in all students before considering the test result to represent largely intelligence. (Alternatively, one can give motivation tests and partial out the motivation differences.)

Other issues of importance in motivational theory in which speculation has run ahead of good experimental analyses is Eysenck's invocation, as a general principle, of the very narrowly applicable Yerkes-Doddson law. Yet another has been the equating, by Spence and other learning theorists, of motivation with anxiety. The former "law" argues that the effect of abilities is augmented by the increase of dynamic strength up to a certain maximum on the curve, and that, thereafter, further effort produces a decrease. The studies above, e.g., by Cattell and Butcher (1968) show no such curvilinear relation of the motivation strength measurements to school achievement. Subjective reports of curvilinear relation of effort to performance must be regarded with suspicion because in most real life situations, "in situ," the highest degrees of effort are applied only when the performance begins to be perceived as unsuccessful. The person straining to hear certain whispers, or finding himself losing in a game of tennis, is apt to associate his sense of strain with not doing so well.

Most laboratory experimental curves relating motivation to performance, it is true, are not exactly linear, but approach a plateau. However, a true downward trend with increased effort is extremely uncommon, and when it occurs it is generally (a) in complex performances, and (b) associated with new psychological byproducts of failure at high effort, such as anxiety, giddiness, or overexcitement.

The last comment brings us to the second of the misunderstandings mentioned above, in which anxiety is unquestioningly equated with motivation.

Then it is said that a little anxiety is good, but too much interferes with the best application of abilities. Fortunately for the happiness of mankind, the bulk of motivation stems primarily from ergic tension levels—sex, gregariousness, self-assertion—which, as in the MAT, we are beginning now to measure—and from which anxiety appears only as a byproduct. Equations have been put forward elsewhere (Spielberger, 1966) which fit much existing experiment, and suggest that anxiety is no more to be considered as motivation than the steam escaping from a safety valve is to be counted as power. Most situations in which anxiety is objectively measured as the standard anxiety factor (Cattell and Scheier, 1961; Spielberger, 1966; Di Mascio and Barrett, 1965), show it operating as a form of motivational disorganization and waste. This interpretation is supported by the great majority of correlations between anxiety and achievement being found to be negative[2] (Cattell and Butcher, 1968).

When we get to objective measures of known ergic tension factors, as in the SMAT, we find that only two drive factors have consistently shown negative correlation with school performance, namely unintegrated sex drive tension and pugnacity tension levels (see Figure 12–1 and Table 12–5) though narcissism, fear, acquisitiveness and gregariousness do so also in certain samples (as in Figure 12–1 or Table 12–5). (Incidentally, some negative correlations in Table 12–5 are due to the ipsative mode of scoring, and disappear when no negative correlation is thus forced among the ergs.) The most likely explanation of the negative correlation with gregariousness and narcissism is that they are motivations in the wrong direction with regard to the performance under consideration, leading to "wasting" time in sociability and personal adornment. The negative correlation with unintegrated, undischarged, sex drive and with pugnacity could arise from a two-way causal action: the resort to sexual interests and to aggression through the frustration of achievement and the distraction which such interests offer to school work. That the causal action is, in part, in an analogous direction in anxiety has been shown by Tsushima, who "failed" members of a class at random, and found significant increases on anxiety in those who failed (as scored on the IPAT Anxiety Scale which measures the uniquely defined second-order anxiety scale in the 16 P.F.).

---

[2] As Scheier and others have shown, *rate of conditioning,* in the autonomic field, correlates significantly positively with anxiety level. This relation seems peculiar to classical conditioning, "excitation learning," as it has been analyzed elsewhere (Cattell, 1971a) rather than instrumental (means-end) learning, and it may even be mainly effective only in autonomic learning. But even if it were not, the learning theorist who reduces all learning to classical conditioning would be forced to draw a wrong conclusion about the relation of anxiety to school learning. For this overlooks that much or even most school learning is insightful. The current conclusions also overlook that the poor *state* measures of anxiety commonly used have failed, in much experimental work reported in the learning journals, to separate anxiety (P.U.I.9, in the factor series) from excitement or arousal (P.U.I.1 in the factor series). Since rate of conditioning is bound also to the latter it is easy to see that erroneous conclusions could easily be reached about the role of anxiety in cognitive performance.

FIGURE 12–1
**Comparison of High and Low Achievers on Motivation
Factor (Ergic Tension) Levels Measured by Objective
Test Devices**

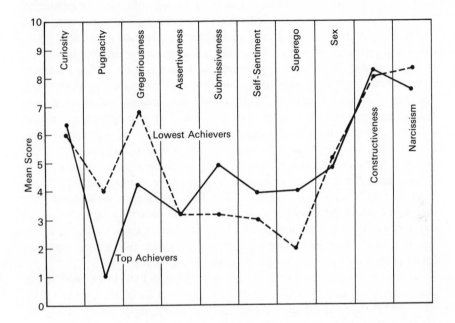

Most existing research would point, however, to some causal action in both directions: poor performance evokes anxiety, and rising anxiety brings poorer performance.

Except for anxiety, sex emotion, and pugnacity (and some "distracting" interests, as above), a positive relation exists, as far as has been explored, between increasing motivation and increasing performance. Furthermore, the higher and more consistent correlations make psychological sense, as in, for example, the fact that both the self-sentiment and the superego strength correlate positively with school achievement. In the case of the self-sentiment, one can see the possibility, however, also of two-way inter-action, in that school success might assist the growth of self-regard and encourage the acquisition of self-standards generally. But in the case of the superego, and probably of most of the self-sentiment action, one sees increased performance through an increased motivation to achieve.[3]

---

[3] As pointed out above, it does not fit any known psychological evidence to consider a "need to achieve" as a useful unitary concept. Repeated experimentation (Cattell, 1965a; Cattell, Radcliffe, and Sweney, 1963) shows the various main attitudes concerned with achievement to have three distinct factorial dynamic roots, each with its own quality and goals. They are the superego, with its drive toward service to justify

It is worthy of note that the personality factors found to load school achievement are consistent with these results obtained from objective motivation tests. In the first place, the superego and self-sentiment measured by questionnaire correlate in just the same way as when measured in the new medium (objective motivation devices). The self-sufficient temperament, Q_2 (see equation, page 387) also assists school performance, but dominance, E, guilt proneness, O, and excitability, D, reduce it. Premsia (I +, overprotected sensitivity), aids English achievement—perhaps due to the overprotected child's closer dependence on adults and their larger vocabulary—but is negatively related to mathematics and science, presumably because of their cold impersonality. There are, indeed, several instances akin to the premsia case, where one can see that a temperament endowment itself would tend to channel motivation broadly along certain lines. For this reason, and in the interests of perspective it is imperative to study personality-temperament differences along with motivation differences in motivation-achievement experiments. The negative correlation of achievement in school with dominance, E, has been checked several times, and seems to contain the principle that docility favors learning by reducing the frequency of critical and unreceptive behavior. Arrogance is a bar to learning. However, later, in driving independent research and artistic creativity forward (see next chapter) high E becomes desirable.

As one penetrates further into the motivation achievement field, it becomes evident—though data is scanty as yet—that there are important differences between the integrated and unintegrated components in any given erg or sentiment. In school achievement one sees fairly often a positive relation to the *integrated* component of some sentiment or erg together with a negative correlation with the strength of the *unintegrated* component. This is very evident in the sex, self-assertive, and pugnacious ergs. The full meaning of the integrated and unintegrated component factors is still under investigation, but we may be on the threshold of a more satisfactory explanation of apparent curvilinear relations than by the Yerkes-Doddson law. The law one begins to see emerging agrees with the Y-D in saying that learning performance is not a function simply of the total strength of motivation. If we accept the conclusion that in many drives a high unintegrated motivation actually may militate against success, but that learning is proportional through the whole range to the strength of integrated motivation, a gross measure confusing the two could give curvilinear effects.

About the personality-motivation interactions in achievements beyond the school we know very little, for none has been the object of such concentrated research. We have accepted above that the term ability or achievement is used by the man in the street in a way which gets far from the spe-

one's existence; the self-sentiment, which is primarily a motivation toward social performance fitting to one's self-concept; and the self-assertive erg, which is a purely innate primitive ergic impulse to mastery. The loading of the last on school achievement is negative (or negligible) compared with the first two, possibly because school work at this age is not seen in a "mastery" context.

cial use of abilities as made here, but which recognizes the interweaving of personality and dynamic structures in many combinations with true ability. One talks of "ability to drive a car," and many ability and skill tests have been set up to select safe drivers, on the strength of that "ability" notion. Such skills as reaction time, judgment of distance, and other true abilities often measured in driver selection may be useful, but, as shown below (Equation 12.7), most of the distinction between good and bad driving is to be found in personality. The man in the street also speaks of "ability as a politician," ability to attract the opposite sex, and even ability to bear the toothache. Examined by the same broad conceptions of interacting ability, personality, and dynamic structure factors as in the above section, one gets, typically, as in the three following equations, at least as much personality as ability entering into the decision, i.e., into the specification equations.

Freedom from accidents

$$= 0.2B + 0.3C - 0.2E - 0.2F + 0.5G - 0.5M - 0.3O$$
$$+ 0.3Q_3 - 0.3Q_4 \tag{12.7}$$

Success as a Psychiatric Technician

$$= 0.2A + 0.1B + 0.5C - 0.2E + 0.3G + 0.3H - 0.3M$$
$$- 0.2O - 0.3Q_1 + 0.3Q_3 - 0.2Q_4 \tag{12.8}$$

Success (Measured as Income) in Salesmanship

$$= 0.2A + 0.1B + 0.1C + 0.1E + 0.2F + 0.1G - 0.1L$$
$$- 0.3M + 0.2N - 0.3Q_2 + 0.2Q_3 - 0.2Q_4 \tag{12.9}$$

With the help of *The Scientific Analysis of Personality* (or the 16 P.F. Handbook) the reader not familiar with the settled notation for personality factors will ascertain readily from the above that the driver more given to accidents has been found to be more dominant, of lower ego strength, more autistic, and of lower self-sentiment. He can read the above quantitative research outcome, also, to the effect that a good psychiatric technician needs great ego strength; and that successful salesmanship correlates principally with the constituent primaries in the extraversion secondary. However, he will notice that in these three important achievements the role of intelligence (Indexed as B in the 16 P.F. HSPQ, etc., test series) is relatively small. Looking at the success of his classmates as reached in middle life, and remembering their intellectual level at school, the top boy on the classroom list sometimes is considerably surprised. Chance enters everywhere and probably into later life more than school, but often it is the systematically differing weights given by school life to intelligence and personality-motivation qualities that account primarily for the disparities he sees. However, the increasing complexity of our culture probably means more weight in the future for intelligence in the specification equation for success even beyond the school years.

CHAPTER THIRTEEN

GENIUS AND THE PROCESSES OF CREATIVE THOUGHT

1. SOME MYTHS AND FACT ABOUT GENIUS

Creativity has come into the full glare of fashionable limelight in this decade. In the right places it has always held a revered status, but today it is coaxed like a hothouse plant. The definitions currently given for creativity range from originality of thought, through problem-solving and inventiveness, to the merest nonconformity or pointless fluency. Let us look at its "natural history."

The creativity that is important for culture, and which has been identified with the definition of genius, shows itself in scientific discovery, literary, musical, and artistic creation, technological invention, political and social innovation, and religious leadership. Rather than set up artificial definitions of creativity (since laboratory operationism is scarcely applicable here) it seems better to begin by studying the living process, recognized in its natural cultural context. After that we can relate it, as a criterion, to laboratory measures of ability and personality.

Before examining data, some cobwebs of folklore should be scrutinized and perhaps swept out. Because what is newly created is strange, folklore has connected genius with oddity. Any new, successful biological variant —such as a hairless ape—is also strange, but it may be perfectly normal, if by normal we mean healthy and effective. On the other hand it is probably true of cultural variations as of biological mutations, that only about one in a thousand is an improvement on the status quo, and the rest are unhealthy misfits, quickly to be eliminated in the course of nature. If by a genius we mean someone who produces a *better* remedy against disease, or a *better* play, then a genius may seem unconventional, but bo-hemianism is a poor indication of genius; nevertheless, love of the occult continues to favor a belief in the transcendental strangeness of genius. Socrates may have begun it, when he convinced the young that he possessed a "demon" and went into trances therewith. Aristotle claimed that "men illustrious in poetry, politics, and the arts have often been melancholic and mad." Such views descending through Roman times (Seneca), and epito-mized in Dryden's oft-quoted couplet:

> Great wits are sure to madness near allied
> And thin partitions do their bounds divide.

linger also, as a speculation, in more recent writings on genius by Havelock Ellis, Galton, Lombroso, Hirsch, Kretschmer, and many others. One is forced to repeat that much of this identification springs from the ever-blooming logical fallacy that if genius is odd, oddity is genius. Careful bio-graphical research does not support this contention; the genius *may* be neurotic, partly because of the stress of his loneliness or rejection;[1] but the incidence of mental ill health and psychosis is actually below normal in the ranks of the creators.

The variety of ideas about the causes of creativity in genius are endless, ranging from Moorman's (1940) theory of germ stimulation by tubercu-losis (Voltaire, R. L. Stevenson, Bashkirtseff, Keats, Shelley, Sidney Lanier, Hood, Bessemer, Schiller, and others), to Lombroso's "equivalent to crime," to Kretschmer's "warring heredities," to Adler's overcompensation for inferiority, and even to Freud's "evasion of reality."[2]

The modern and quantitative study of genius can be said to begin with Galton (1870), who stressed the centrality of sheer g, and demonstrated the substantial hereditary connections of that g. Havelock Ellis may be said to have added the importance of temperament, in his finding from statistical analyses in the National Portrait Gallery (unfortunately not since followed up) that in Britain the Nordic strain (Newton, Kelvin, Edison, Rutherford) expressed itself in mathematics and science, and the Celtic strain (dark-eyed and haired) in religion, history, and verbal-social skills. Kretschmer

---

[1] Hirsch (1931) penetratingly observes "Genius is constantly forced to solitude . . . (It is) its *refuge* not its *goal*." (Italics ours) However, our demonstration below of high introversion in creativity does suggest that solitude can be embraced neither as a refuge, nor as a goal, nor yet as a result of social rejection, but as a means sys-tematically to develop unusual and fragile ideas without interruption. As for social rejection (to give the average man in the street his just due) some cold shouldering of genius, such as Havelock Ellis documented (*A Study of British Genius*, 1926), can be sympathetically understood. For, as Sir John Seely summed it up, the genius is apt to be "alarming, perplexing, and fatiguing."

[2] "If the individual who is displeased with reality is in possession of that artistic talent which is still a psychological riddle, he can transform his phantasies into artistic creations. So he escapes the fate of a neurosis." Freud, quoted by Hirsch (1931).

(1931) followed Nietzsche ("Where is the madness with which you should be inoculated?") and the Greeks in believing that there must be some element of the fanatic in genius. He stressed hybridization of talented races, and, (as followed up later by Sheldon) the importance of temperament, rooted in body build, in deciding the direction of expression, here reaching views essentially consistent with those of Havelock Ellis.

More careful documentation followed, in this tradition, in the work of Cox and Terman (1926), who studied 301 men of genius from the past, and then in Terman (1925) who began that monumental follow-up of children actually selected by intelligence tests to lie within the top 1% of the ability range. The former study fully confirmed the general emphasis by Galton on high absolute magnitude of general intelligence in geniuses. When rated by independent judges operating on childhood biographical data, 84% of the 301 geniuses received, by modern I.Q. standards (sigma = 15 to 16), I.Q.'s of 120 or more, and 21% of 150 or more. Additionally, Catherine Cox (1926, Vol. 2, p. 218) called attention to the pervasive frequency of "persistence of motive and effort, confidence in their abilities and great strength or force of character," which Galton has also commented on as "great energy and zeal."

From there, the chief developments have been studies on living subjects: (a) of abilities *other* than general intelligence, by Guilford, Merrifield, and a group of able associates (1961); (b) of the criterion of creative performance in life, by Calvin Taylor and his associates (1963), Barron (1963) and others; and (c) of personality and motivation, in terms of modern, measurable dimensions by Cattell and Drevdahl (1955), Cox (1926), Drevdahl and Cattell (1958), Jones (1959), Sprecher (1959) and others. The second of these lines of research is vitally necessary, for until we know how the actual criteria correlate we do not know whether we are trying to predict one thing or several. Taylor's work shows definitely that among scientists in industry the publication of research articles, the number of patents obtained, etc., are different from and little correlated with the evaluation by peers and supervisors. The personality analyses (in this field and by Lowell Kelly in medical research) give a clue to this discrepancy between criteria, because they show that creative persons are apt to be unpopular. Incidentally, finding firm criteria is the toughest part of this area of research. It is not an intellectually defensible escape from this problem of an objective criterion of creativity to say it cannot be documented and *must* rest on ratings. For "ratings" are merely personal opinions, changing with the cultural affiliations, intelligence, etc., of the rater.

This issue also affects the approach to creativity by measures other than intelligence. Guilford and his co-workers who have gone to abilities beyond intelligence, nevertheless have defined creativity in *the test performance itself,* instead of by some life criterion through which the designation of a test as a "creativity" measure could be validated. The result is that the verdict that a test measures creativity is only a projection of the test constructor's personal view about what creativity is. Thus in the intellectual tests designed by Guilford's students, and many others who have worked on creativity in this decade, creativity has finished up by being evaluated simply as oddity or bizarreness of response relative to the population mean or as output of words per minute, etc. This indeed comes close to mistaking the shadow for the substance. Mere unusualness, without adaptive value, is, as Eysenck shows (1957) actually a good measure of psychopathy or neuroticism, not creativity. Again one must repeat that many creative products are odd; but oddity is not creativity. For some, additional, vital condition must be met by the latter.

Of course, in the last resort, a similar charge of circularity could be brought also with regard to intelligence, if Galton, Terman, and others had not located their geniuses first and *afterward* evaluated their intelligence. Terman found, as we have seen, that geniuses of the past, vindicated by history, were generally of exceptionally high intelligence. But this makes intelligence only a necessary, not a sufficient condition. It was only when Terman came to his study of *living* children of high intelligence and allowed it to be called a study of genius that a doubtful logical assumption crept in. A writer can be the victim of his readers, and in this case perhaps the mistake is in assuming that Terman intended that the label "genius" apply to these bright individuals before later life performances had confirmed their status. Another instance of this dictatorship of the follower may have occurred in the followers of Guilford, whose emphasis on abilities other than intelligence has become for the moment the popular view that intelligence is unnecessary! It remains true, as Burt (1967), Butcher (1969), Thorndike (1943), and Vernon (1960) have reminded neophytes in the field, that general intelligence is *still* the main essential *ability* (apart from personality traits) and that the one, sure, common feature of many and varied tests of creativity is their high "g" saturation. As Burt has pointed out: "the new tests for creativity would form very satisfactory additions to any ordinary battery for testing the general factor of intelligence."

2. SOME ABILITY AND PERSONALITY ASSOCIATES OF HIGH CREATIVITY

If, as suggested above, we stand by *actual life performance* (rather than performance in a two-hour test of artificial "creativity measures") as the necessary criterion, then—after intelligence—the most important determiners are unquestionably personality factors. Biographical studies by Roe (1953), Barron (1963), the present writer (1963b) and especially Drevdahl and Cattell (1958) agree with the view inherent in Havelock Ellis, Kretchmer, Terman, Galton, and other shrewd observers that the creative person does possess, over and above intelligence, some very characteristic personality qualities. These may or may not be considered healthy, normal qualities—this is often a matter of values—but the psychologist today can at least analyze them as meaningful source traits which point to clear theories of causal action.

Without space to present separately the profiles from the various personality factor surveys of highly creative people in physical science, biology, psychology, art, and literature (see Cattell and Drevdahl, 1955; Drevdahl and Cattell, 1958)—which, incidentally, agree amazingly well, considering the diversity of interest of the groups—we present in Figure 13–1 the composite, central profile found. Its greatest deviations from the average are (apart from intelligence) on high self-sufficiency, introversion, dominance, and desurgency.

The selection of outstandingly creative individuals was made in these cases by committees of peers, and is thus, in essence, the same as, say, a Nobel prize selection procedure. It differs from direct personality rating in that it is made with documents and productions. In the case of the common (three area) scientist's profile the raters also were asked to contrast their choices with choices of equally academically distinguished men (administrators and teachers) *not* creatively gifted. Since abbreviated discussion most easily proceeds with the broader second-stratum level of personality factors (though the more accurate prediction and understanding rest on the primaries), we may point out that at a rough glance these people would be described as introverts (second-order Factor I). They also show high self-sufficiency and dominance in the primaries. Both the intensive *biographical* researches of Anne Roe (1953) and the more discursive biographical survey by the present writer (1963b) strongly support the main conclusions of these systematic *test* results. Cavendish hiding from society in a remote wing of his mansion, Newton forever wandering on "strange seas of thought, alone," Einstein remote in the patent office library, Darwin taking his solitary walks in the woods at Down—these are the epitome of the way of life of the creative person. If this introversion and intensity is the essence, it is easy to see why a committedly extravert, impulsive and casual society has had to begin frantically chasing—and vulgarizing—creativity over the last decade.

In this latter connection let us note that acceptance of the idea that measures of fluency are measures of a creative ability has led to generalizations to the effect that the temperamental and personality associations of fluency are conditions of creativity. Thus, inferences drawn from the empirical research of Getzels and Jackson (1962), for example, (who used certain tests from the Objective-Analytic Personality Factor Battery, but not enough to measure any one factor) and the theorizing of Maslow (1954), have led to the picture of the creative person as an incontinent, unrestrained, over-self-expressive individual. In the latter's descriptions of the self-actualizing personality, one scarcely can escape the impression that, without some daily assault upon convention, such a personality feels futile. That some kind of true *flexibility* of temperament and thinking habits are necessary to genius no one can doubt. But according to personality research, this is a very different trait from the uninhibited (U.I. 17) dimension or the "exuberance" or U.I. 21 dimension. In 1948 Tiner and the

FIGURE 13–1
Personality Profile Common to Those Creative in Science,
Art, and Literature

Source Trait	Direction		Scientists	Artists	Literary	Artistic and Literary Creators same or different from scientists
			(114)	(64)	(89)	
A	(−)	Sizothyme	3.4*	3.0*	3.9*	S
B	(+)	Intelligent	9.1*	8.3*	8.8*	S
†C	(+, −)	Ego strong and Ego weak	6.9*	5.1*	4.2*	D
E	(+)	Dominant	7.2*	5.6	6.0*	S
F	(−)	Desurgent	3.5*	3.3*	4.0*	S
G	(−)	Casual	3.4*	5.1*	4.7*	S
†H	(+, −)	Parmic and Threctic	6.5*	5.2*	4.9*	D
I	(+)	Premsic	7.1*	8.9*	7.8*	S
L	(−)	Alaxic	4.1*	5.2	5.4	S
M	(+)	Autious	5.5	8.8*	6.8*	
N	(+)	Unaffected	5.5	4.7*	5.2	
O	(+, −)	Poised and Guilt Prone	3.8*	6.1	6.1	D
Q_1	(+)	Radical	6.2*	6.9*	7.3*	S
Q_2	(+)	Self-Sufficient	6.5*	8.9*	9.2*	S
Q_3	(+)	Strong in Self-Sentiment	6.8*	6.0*	5.9*	S
Q_4	(−)	Low in Ergic tension	5.1*	5.2*	5.3	S

* = Significantly different from general population at $P < .05$ or beyond.
† A plus *and* a minus means above average in one area of creativity and below in another.

The data are from Cattell and Drevdahl, 1955, and Drevdahl and Cattell, 1958, in nationally eminent U.S. figures. Drevdahl's general writers and science fiction writers have been pooled in the literary group. The intelligence results are on a revised standardization of Factor B, the earlier translations of the 1956 values being too low. The artists and writers always deviate the same way, but the scientists differ, in agreement with Terman's observations, in being more emotionally stable and less anxious (C+, H+, O−).

As is found in occupational selection, so here, what distinguishes the group from the general population is now always what distinguishes the better from the poorer number. Thus in later work by Drevdahl (unpublished at his death), it was found in a comparison of creative and uncreative psychologists that the former showed significantly higher super-ego strength, G, and lower autia, M, though in other respects, e.g., B, E, F, etc., they deviated as the group does from the general population. Similarly Cattell and Drevdahl found that researchers relative to equally gifted administrators, were more A−, F−, and Q_2+, just as they are in regard to the general population. Drevdahl also found on the MAT test (Cattell, Horn, and Sweney, 1964) a significantly greater attachment of the creative to their home interests. (See also, on the artist profile, Cross, Cattell, and Butcher (1967), who found artists introverted (in contrast to the popular stereotype) but still more anxious and emotional, and lower in superego, than here.

TABLE 13–1
Behavior in the Dimension of Ideational Flexibility versus Firmness

Performance and Direction of Measurement	Loading in the Factor
High ability to reconstruct hidden words	.51
High success in finding solutions to riddles	.41
Rapid speed of flicker fusion	.41
Plasticity (changes in exactitudes of repetition of Werner tone rhythm test)	.34
Good ability to restructure habitual visual perception	.29

present writer (Cattell and Tiner, 1949) completing a decade of study of rigidity (Cattell, 1933a)—defined as a motor-perceptual personality trait —by exploring its intellectual expressions, found that after putting aside the *classical* motor-perceptual rigidity factor (see Luchins and Luchins, 1959), and the general fluency factor (U.I. 21 or g_r), a new behavioral factor remained. This had the pattern reproduced in Table 13–1, and was called Ideational Flexibility-vs-Ideational Inertia or Rigidity, g_x. It suggests some kind of energy, and the question immediately arises whether we are unearthing a new kind of general ability capacity—a "g"—or whether this is some temperamental tendency which expresses itself partly in the cognitive domain. Against the former view is the fact that it has not appeared clearly as a second or third-stratum general power in cognitive measures only. Against the latter is the fact that Table 13–1 shows only one variable that could be definitely temperamental (flicker fusion) and that Guilford and his associates picked up this pattern later in pure ability traits. (It appeared, however, in their data, with that lopping off of part of the pattern which is due to the restriction of their researches to orthogonal rotations, thus making final interpretation somewhat difficult (page 18).

Until factorial searches are made over a wider spectrum of variables, such dilemmas as to ability or temperamental origin will remain. Indeed, we need constantly to be reminded that when tentatively we conceptualize the behavior of rigidity, fluency, and flexibility as expressions of cognitive performances, we are actually in a complex and insufficiently analyzed field in which much of the variance probably will turn out to be due to personality and temperament factors, notably those now indexed as U.I. 16 through U.I. 33. Thus the relation of Guilford's assumed ability factors, such as the above flexibility factor, to temperament, in any adequate sense still has to be investigated. Certainly much of the variance in classical motor-perceptual rigidity is due specifically to personality factors U.I. 21, 23, 26, etc., which could readily account for 90% of its variance.

Elsewhere in this volume we have made a more detailed analysis of the concept of flexibility-vs-rigidity. Rigidity is the most overused and underanalyzed term in the whole of personality psychology. It is used by the psychiatrist as a synonym for compulsiveness—or even strength of character. It was used by the early investigators, such as Gross, Heymans, and

Wiersma (see Spearman, 1927) and has more recently been used by Biesheuvel as a concept of secondary neural function, i.e., a kind of reverberation after a primary process. For some experimentalists it has meant a persistent mental set to solve a problem in a given way, and for some social scientists (Rokeach and Fruchter, 1956) the root of prejudice. As Spearman's *Psychology Down the Ages* (1937) and Luchins and Luchins's comprehensive *Rigidity of Behavior* (1959) show, it has indeed been all things to all men.

The scientific way out from this mesmerized preoccupation with a word is to take the actual operations by which the various writers would consent to their subjective visions being represented by behavior, and to do an extensive factor analysis covering all manifestations. This has been accomplished up to a point by the work of Coan, the present writer, (1933a and b, 1935a and b, 1943, 1946 (a and b), 1949, 1955a and b, 1965a and c, and 1967a) Damarin, Eysenck, Howarth, Hundleby, Knapp, Pawlik, Peterson, Rethlingshafer, Ryans, Saunders, Scheier and many others with less systematic attacks. The performances have ranged from perceptual (seeing new shapes or objects embedded in old objects) to motor (writing familiar letters in unusual combinations, calling the names of a string of colors by prescribed wrong names), and from physiological (hangover of a visual contrast effect, pulse rate persistence) to social and characterological (instability of attitudes, change of opinion under fact and authority). The verdict is perfectly clear that there is no such factor as general rigidity.

The view which emerges is that the concept has been under-analyzed, both experimentally and in conceptual definition. For example, an appreciable fraction of what the casual psychologist calls rigidity is due in the final place to low g_f, either innate or through brain injury. The mental defective goes on doing the same thing inappropriately because he does not have the relation-perceiving capacity to see that a more effective alternative presents itself. Secondly, the widespread derogation of rigidity (notably by psychiatrists and alleged progressive social issues psychologists) overlooks the fact that much "rigidity" is operationally simple character stability, C factor (such as is notoriously absent in neurotics) in the face of persuasion ("obstinacy" to the tempter). Human learning is based on a certain probability of constancy in the external world. The internal stability of a habit should match the external stability of the world, as Humphreys (1962) and others have shown in more technical detail experimentally. There is an optimum "plasticity" of habits. Probably our habits, if anything, err on the side of being insufficiently rigid, for memory is fallible, and the cue from the fact that would be correct (assuming some constancy in the external world) is lost. Low rigidity is here poor memory.

Strictly in the domain of cognitive process it is questionable whether flexibility-rigidity, in its myriad manifestations, is affected by more than g_f, g_r, and g_m—intelligence, fluency, and memory trace persistence. What emerges very clearly from the broader analyses is that, on the other hand, several distinct personality-temperament factors are involved, and that they determine more of the variance on flexibility-rigidity than do any cognitive factors. For example, the variance on the most widely used perceptual-motor rigidity battery (that investigated by Pinard, Spearman, Stephenson, Eysenck, and the present writer, and consisting of performing old motor-perceptual tasks in new "interfering" ways) is significantly contributed to by no fewer than five personality factors: U.I. 23, Mobilization-vs-Regression; U.I. 24, Anxiety; U.I. 26, Narcissistic Self-Determination; U.I. 29, Superego; and U.I. 33, Depressive Tendency. These act to determine the total rigidity on this common measure in psychologically understandable ways. For example, the self-exactingness in superego strength, self-determination and depressive guilt work to overcome the tendency of the organism to accept the rigidity of its own natural process ("laziness," pleasure principle). In the case of the large effect of Regression (U.I. 23)—and probably the small effect of anxiety (U.I. 24)—however, we see an effect on the very energy resources themselves needed to combat rigidity.

The role of these same personality factors in creativity in the broader sense (as distinct from this operational flexibility-rigidity) remains to be investigated. But if the questionnaire measurement of personality may be temporarily accepted as a guide, we should expect superego (U.I. 29), and what is virtually the self-sentiment (U.I. 26) to act as they do here, contributing to flexibility. In the questionnaire domain, it must not be overlooked that there is also a powerful contribution to creativity (see Section 2 below) from the dimension of radicalism-conservatism first demonstrated by Thurstone and, as Q_1, in the 16 PF, since shown to be broader than the religio-political items in his analysis. It seems to be some kind of temperamental tendency to restless critical adoption of the new, as opposed to a phlegmatic, tolerant conservatism.

The personality factors—other than intelligence—which favor creativity are not, by any means, highly advantageous or even adaptive in other realms of behavior. For example, higher rated mental hospital attendants (psychiatric technicians, see Shotwell, Hurley, and Cattell 1961) are lower on Q_1, the more radical being presumably unable to tolerate the unreason of lunatics. The higher superego and self-sentiment, on the other hand, would be helpful in most situations. The plasticity contribution which comes from poor memory and high inherent lability, as in the dreamer who forgets his own telephone number, puts on socks of two different colors, and goes tortuously back to basic principles on the simplest decisions, operates in most situations undoubtedly as a defect rather than as a virtue of "flexibility." (Note, for example, in Table 13–1, the failure of the highly flexible to reproduce familiar sounds accurately.) This matter of fields of effectiveness is scrutinized more closely in the next section.

Flexibility is thus of considerable importance, but it is a complex entity traceable to several distinct events. Fluency, on the other hand, seems to be largely a general cognitive trait of ease of retrieval (plus local storage levels, according to the hypothesis in Chapter 6), together with whatever impulsiveness or energy is ascribed to the highly inherited temperament trait of Exuberance (U.I. 21). These are certainly important in determining the productivity or "divergence of thinking" in a test situation in a fixed short interval of time, as the work of Guilford and his collaborators abundantly proves; but it is still an open question whether g_r and U.I. 21 correlate positively, negatively, or insignificantly with *creativity in life,* over long periods, such as we examined in our leading physicists, biologists, artists, and writers. One suspects the correlation would be positive, but not as high as for the personality traits in Figure 13–1. In real performance, it was doubtless important that Kekulé had the flexibility of thought and the retrieval capacity to conjure up many images from which he culled at last the benzine ring structure, that Newton hearing the apple fall had the notion of universal gravitation, and that Archimedes' principle finally occurred to him daydreaming in his comfortable bath. But in what fraction of a second, after the thud of the falling apple in the still autumn evening, the idea came to Newton, or at what stage of the bath it came to Archimedes matters little. Output per minute is unimportant, compared to quality and aptness. The speed and productivity measures taken on artificial test situations are on a very different and possibly irrelevant level in relation to the productivity we encounter in real life originality.

Evidence on high creativity in life careers points to the necessity first of high intelligence, and second of a very characteristic, "concentrating," personality profile. In respect to life-long and fundamental originality, as shown in problem-solving and cultural contribution, these together are more important than any restricted special abilities or fluencies, and when we look at the personality associations more closely, the psychologist will recognize that our rough introductory interpretation of the creative personality as "introverted" stops far short of all the information contained in the profile of primary personality factors in Figure 13–1. Indeed, first he will notice that there is a curious paradox within the second-stratum introversion pattern itself. For among these researchers, sizothymia (A−), desurgency (F−), and self-sufficiency (Q_2+) appear strongly in what is normally the right direction for the second-stratum introversion factor, whereas threctia (H−) is in the wrong direction, i.e., creative researchers are parmic (H+). Another, and at present admittedly more speculative, way of saying this is that creative people are those who would constitutionally be extraverts (H+) but who have somehow been made introvert (A−, F−, Q_2+) by heavy cultural pressures, and an environmental training in the depth-increasing value of inhibition. It is of much psychological interest to ask how—granted their association—the introvert qualities of A−, F−, and Q_2 operate to augment the creativity of the individual.

Let us look at personality dimension A–affectothymia-vs-sizothymia. Compared to the emotionally expressive and responsive affectothyme, the sizothyme according to ratings and questionnaire items, is dry, realistic, sceptical, and even "cranky." He does not see life in terms of easily given promises and of widely humanly acceptable, casual compromises with reality. Occupational data shows that A− makes a person a poor teacher of young children and a hopeless salesman (both high on A+), but a more effective house electrician or physicist (both A−). Considering next the F factor, we encounter, at the F−, desurgent end, the general inhibition component in introversion. Unlike the surgent wit—the happy-go-lucky "life and soul of the party"—the desurgent individual is cautious in statement, aware of many possibilities of failure and possessed of a deep feeling for responsibility. It is the inhibition we call desurgency (F−) that is responsible for his having second, third, and fourth thoughts where the surgent person expresses a superficial originality in the first. The self-sufficiency of the next factor, Q_2, is a very pervasive influence in the creative personality. Here we see the vital set of values necessary for living the kind of life which receives little social reinforcement and requires dogged pursuit of lonely trails. (The "lonely seas of thought" in which Newton confessed he had desired some company.)

To distinguish the precise and measurable pattern of the second-stratum (A, F, H, Q_2−) pattern from the battered popular expression extraversion-introversion, it has been called in personality theory *exvia-vs-invia*. This dimension of exvia-invia has been checked as a second-stratum factor at all post-infancy age levels, and, as the work of Eysenck and the present writer shows, it is very stable in form and characteristically measurable. One can readily see in psychological terms how the inviant adjustment favors intensive concentration on original production. It is interesting also, however, to consider the exvia-invia balance in energy-economic terms by the computer model considered a couple of chapters back. The computer model of abilities has elements of input, storage, processing, and output. If one needs much internal working over of material, the fewer working elements given over to input and output transactions, the better. The individual who is constantly immersed in "journalism" (derived from the French for "the day"), in current fashions in clothes, art, and what else, and in living the lives of all around him (as the A+, F+, H+, and Q_2− individual is) cannot obtain either the quiet or the sustained reserve of "working elements" for the actual processing. As the title of Balchin's novel of the life of scientists characterizes the situation, there is a necessity for living in *The Small Back Room*.

Other personality characteristics which differentiate the creative researcher, writer, and artist from the equally intelligent teacher, administrator, or journalistic writer are higher E (dominance), higher L (protension), and higher M (autia). The higher L—with its egotism and paranoidlike features—is responsible for some of those unpopular features of the scientist which a penetrating and realistic observer like Roe has not hesitated to draw for us (1953), and which incidentally, account for some of the asperity of scientific debates. Rightly or wrongly, most scientists are predisposed to the conviction that theirs is *the* conception needed, and high L helps them to exhaust its possibilities. The higher M, or autia factor, bespeaks a greater intensity and spontaneity of inner mental life (the relation of such inner imaginal activity is obvious). The higher dominance (E factor; see Figure 13–1) combined also with some tendency to higher radicalism, permits the scientist to sustain more comfortably the socially egregious positions into which his original thoughts get him. (Newton perhaps had insufficient of this, for he nearly gave up publishing after all the unpleasant disputes with Linus and Pardies into which his treatise on "Opticks" pitchforked him.)

Obviously the personality qualities that are most functional in enabling high intelligence to produce new ideas and father them to ultimate survival will vary with the social setting of the occupation of the scientist, the writer, and the artist. The setting and incentive system have changed in the last generation appreciably for the scientist; but the required core of personality qualities discussed above seems to remain the same. Without them high ability is only high ability.

3. THE CREATIVE PERSONALITY AND THE CULTURE PATTERN

It is an impoverishing abstraction to keep personality and cultural concepts separated. The factor analyst extracts and recognizes the dimensions of personality and the dimensions of culture only that he may proceed to the laws by which they interact. The historian and the sociologist deal with the status and the flow of group life in general descriptive terms, but it is the task of the social psychologist to get at underlying summary dimensions and explanatory mechanisms. In the field of abilities generally the next chapter deals with this most systematically, but a section here must now be devoted to the social interaction with creativity and genius.

To do this it is necessary to digress briefly into the description of epochs and cultures. Even the scantiest acquaintance with history and cultural anthropology is enough to bring home the enormous variations in the production of genius between different cultures, races, and epochs. The distinctive flowerings of Greek, Jewish, Sumerian, Chinese, and Egyptian cultures occurred in an otherwise mediocre world. In the artistic world, it is true, anyone is free to assert his taste that the ebony statuettes of the Congo are superior to the frieze of the Parthenon, or that Aztec pyramids show greater esthetic feeling than early Chinese paintings. But when objective standards enter, as in mathematics, science, engineering, and exploration, the egalitarian must admit that there are peoples and periods —such as classical Greece, the Confucian period of civil organization in China, and Western Europe at the Renaissance—richer in creativity.

The historian and the anthropologist give colorful detail and, in such writers as Toynbee (1947), intriguing explanations for these appearances. The social psychologist sets out to reach the basic explanations by the slower, more difficult, but eventually more positive and law-producing path of measurement and correlation. It was around 1950 that the first attempts were made to discover the stable dimensions of groups, as organisms, by the same correlational techniques as had proved successful for human personalities. Groups—especially national and religious groups—show a consistency and persistence of character at least as impressive as that for individuals, and they exhibit common traits, i.e., traits in the behavior of all groups that are possessed at different levels.

When a wide array of group characteristics, e.g., democracy of government, amount of crime, percent of national income spent on education, number of revolutions, frequency of declaring war, number of Nobel prizes per million, etc., is correlated over some eighty nations, a dozen or more independent factorial dimensions are found to account for much of the variance. A profile of scores can be set up on these for each nation, just as for the ability and personality dimensions (the A, B, C's, etc., and the U.I. dimensions) for individual personalities. The term *syntality* has been used, analogously to personality in individuals, for this, and it has been shown that (a) various aspects of international and internal cultural behavior can be predicted from these traits, and that (b) when the resemblances of nations are objectively worked out by applying the pattern similarity coefficient, r_p, to these profiles, they group themselves in ways which fit the historical criteria, of, for example, Toynbee's "civilizations" and other criteria of essential cultural type (Cattell, 1950c; Cattell, Breul, and Hartmann, 1952; Rummel, 1970).

Similar research has been done on measured behavior of small groups, revealing dimensions of morale, "intelligence," efficient role organization, etc., to describe syntalities in group dynamics. Further, just as the individual's behavioral structure can be examined both by R-technique (correlation across individual differences) and P-technique (correlation measures on one person as they co-vary from day to day over a long period), so they can both be applied to cultures. Thus P-technique analyses over a hundred years have been made on Britain (Cattell, 1953), the U.S.A. (Cattell and Adelson, 1951) and Australia (Gibb, 1956). Through the latter approach, the historian's conceptions of cultural trends can be given precise expression in unitary dynamic concepts and plotted curves.

To pursue this analysis of group and cultural dynamics into study of the various dimensions is not the scope of the present book, but we *are* concerned about what has been revealed regarding the "creativity" variables— number of mechanical inventions, musical compositions, Nobel prizes, etc. —in these analyses. The answer is comparatively straightforward: they almost all fall on a dimension of "cultural pressure," as shown in Table 13–2, which includes also variables bunching about the expressions of (a) high urbanization, (b) riots and indications of internal irritability, (c) involvement in wars and political interactions with many countries, and (d) indications of internalized aggression, as in suicide and neurotic conflict. This factor, incidentally, is virtually unrelated to the factors of educational expenditure, affluence, morality level, and sheer size.

Table 13–2
The Nature of the Cultural Pressure Dimension

	Factor Loading
High creativity in science and philosophy	.91
High frequency of cities over 20,000 (per 1,000,000 of population)	.78
Large number of clashes (short of war) with other countries	.70
High musical creativity	.70
Many Nobel prizes (per 1,000,000) in science, literature and peace	.67
Large number of riots	.66
High ratio of tertiary (complex) to primary occupations in population	.64
Large number of foreign treaties contracted	.60
More frequent involvement in war	.58
Climatic stimulation (Huntington's Index)	.37

In countries for which reliable records exist, the factor loads also more patients in mental hospitals (per 1,000,000), higher control of typhoid and epidemic diseases, higher suicide rate, lower birth rate, higher divorce rate, lower illegitimate birth rate, and fewer deaths from syphilis, but the values are all much lower than the above.

Combined data, over some 69 countries from Cattell, 1949, and Cattell, Breul, and Hartmann, 1952, and Cattell and Gorsuch, 1965.

The theory of cultural pressure (Cattell, 1950a) is that an inevitable increase in the complication of life (through previous inventions, urban aggregations, etc.) produces a frustration of direct ergic expression to which the natural reaction is pugnacity. This expresses itself partly in aggression, as in the correlations with war and riots, and partly in what follows when aggression is itself blunted, namely, anxiety and sublimation. It is the sublimation not just of aggression but of all ergs, which is responsible for the creativity.

This brings us back to the above findings on the correlation of creativity with introversion and with self-sentiment and superego standards. For what characterizes a society which is *adjusting* to complexity is probably an increase in introversion, and certainly an increase in superego control (possibly, as Freudians assert, at some cost in terms of neurosis). Unfortunately, prior to the location of extraversion as a unique second-order factor, psychologists were as loose as the general public in confusing extraversion with other things. One suspects that the educational psychologists of the "progressive" movement of the 1920s in England and the corresponding popular view in North and South America (exclusive of Canada) confused "healthy adjustment" with "extraversion." Regardless of whether this impulsive exvia appears in New York or the western frontier, there is every indication that it is antipathetic to true creativity, and the fact that it has been held up as a norm and an ideal in school is not unconnected with the present belated search for a lost creativity.

Creativeness must come from the individual, but it is the task of society to produce the climate in which introversion and restraint are viable styles of life. The ordinary noise level of conversation should not be such that a wise or subtle remark needs to be shouted to be audible. It is at first surprising to find that high creativity actually has not been a feature of plastic and turbulent frontier societies, but of refined societies with highly internalized controls. The cultural flowering in America came in New England homes like those of Emerson, Emily Dickinson, and Willard Gibb, not on the frontiers. And in Europe a totally disproportionate contribution came from the bourgeoisie of which Lavoisier would be a typical instance, especially, the Victorian bourgeoisie, of which countless instances from Darwin to Pasteur could be given in nineteenth century France, Britain, Germany, and Italy, and from the lesser or higher aristocracy, of which Galileo, Boyle, Humboldt, and Cavendish would be examples. In this matter of social origins, the "genius in a garret" stereotype has created a popular myth. As Terman's genetic studies of genius, and various checks since have shown, creative intelligence comes four or five times as often (relative to the number of homes) from the middle than the lower class. As typified in Bernard Shaw, who lived at his mother's expense till age thirty-five, the genius is more often of a middle class background, but one who has substituted more subtle for more obvious ambitions.

There are various other discovered facts (and countless theories) about the relation of creativity to the social matrix. An interesting viewpoint expressed by Drever (XIII International Congress of Psychology, Edinburgh) in support of which he instanced the periods of highest scientific, philosophical, and artistic productivity in Scotland and Holland, is that wars, instead of interrupting cultural progress, actually stimulate it. Possibly the intensifying of effort communicates itself to other fields, or the loosening of habits permits new integrations. On the other hand, peace and leisure might be expected to produce more experimentation, as some economists argue. The facts are complex, in that funds for cultural activity are obviously important, yet they may merely favor sybaritic pursuits, and some stress and earnestness in life may be vital to sincere and fundamental creativity.

An objective approach to finding out what wars do to creativity may be sought partly from a time plot of the cultural pressure factor (not itself *all* of creativity, however) from the above two P-technique studies of one hundred years of British and American history.

The score is a composite (weighted by factor weights) of such variables as those listed below the plots (from Cattell, 1953, and Cattell and Adelson, 1951). If wars do give a stimulus to the curve, they are certainly followed, at least in the figures for Britain after 1918, by a relapse. However, the striking and important message of the results in Figure 13–2 lies not in the slight bends in the curve, but in its soaring character, for both countries, through the whole period of observations. We are in a period of cultural crescendo such as few epochs have known, and may expect, along with the creativity, the ergic frustrations, the tensions and aggressions, that the culture pressure theory indicates.

FIGURE 13–2
The Course of Cultural Pressure Factor in Three Western Cultures

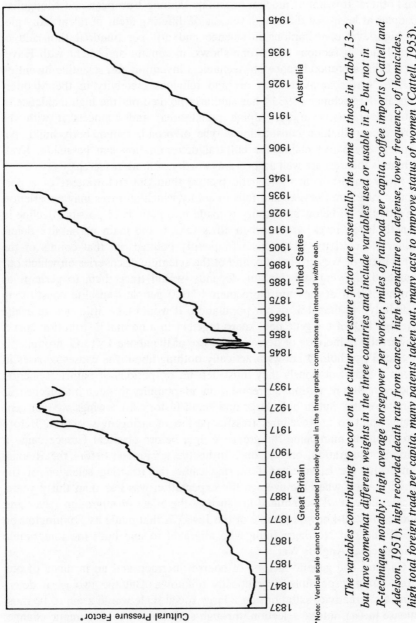

Note: Vertical scale cannot be considered precisely equal in the three graphs; comparisons are intended within each.

The variables contributing to score on the cultural pressure factor are essentially the same as those in Table 13–2 but have somewhat different weights in the three countries and include variables used or usable in P- but not in R-technique, notably: high average horsepower per worker, miles of railroad per capita, coffee imports (Cattell and Adelson, 1951), high recorded death rate from cancer, high expenditure on defense, lower frequency of homicides, high total foreign trade per capita, many patents taken out, many acts to improve status of women (Cattell, 1953).

Even climate has its role, and as the fine work of the geographer-sociologist, Huntington (1945) shows, temperate and cool regions have in fact perennially contributed most. Huntington has also documented relations to racial origins, as objectively as did Havelock Ellis, McDougall, Kretschmer, and others. It is not as much a question—among European and Mongolian peoples at least—of differing levels, as of differing areas of talent. Any plot of high-level contributions in science and art, per hundred thousand of population in sections of Europe shows, in general agreement with Havelock Ellis, a preponderance of mechanical invention and scientific invention in the Nordic areas, and of art and religious creativity in the Mediterranean. Kretschmer (1931) has similarly pointed out the high incidence of musical creativity in the Alpine racial area, and connects it with the Kretschmer-Sheldon constitutional type of broad, round, body build. Although alternative claims for cultural determination can be made, Kretschmer's theories are well argued and worthy of more research.

More important in the genetic picture than the endowments of a particular race, are the rises and falls in ability which all races may experience. In Chapter 14 below an enquiry is made into periods of possible decline in genetic levels in g_f, which, when all is said, is the main permissive determiner of creativity. It has been frequently pointed out that counts of the great ideas of Western culture, and of the scientific discoveries on which our standard of living and thinking depends, would trace them to perhaps as few as 500 or at most no more than 10,000 people—an elite constituting definitely less than 1% of our population. It would take little change in the average I.Q., if the gene pool keeps together in a normal distribution curve, powerfully to increase or decrease the size of the above 150 I.Q. group.

Social psychology knows practically nothing about the causes or rises in mean I.Q. but obviously they must depend on periods of natural selection under conditions putting a premium on adaptability through intelligence. It is noteworthy that in both large and small historical upswings we can generally point to a preceding stressful period of stringent selection. Before Cro-Magnon man came the great ice age; before classical Greece came a period of migration, on and on into hostile territories; before the Renaissance and the Elizabethan flowering came the exacting selection of the Middle Ages, when the average life expectation was less than thirty years. Incidentally, a well-examined instance of the effect of migration (over and above the well-known example of the Jews) is that made by Huntington on the Khmers of Northern India who migrated to and built the remarkable cities such as Angkor Wat.

Cultural and genetic factors, of course, interact, and an instance of one alone being responsible is practically unknown. But the two great determiners of creativity saltations on a large social scale would seem to be most intense in (a) natural selection, through such influences as climatic change, war, and migration under difficulties, and (b) the environmental effect which we have called cultural pressure.

Religious affiliations also yield significant relations to scientific creativity, in the U.S. academic population. The statistical analyses of Knapp (1963), McKeen Cattell (1906), Visher (1947), and others have shown that within America the Protestant and Jewish traditions have contributed, to a statistically significant degree, more than others to scientific creativity. Their analysis, and those of Wispé (1965) also show that in the last resort, even certain types of university educational organizations consistently produce a higher percentage of creative alumnae.

No glance at factors in creativity outside the ability and personality traits of the individual would be complete without considering influences from the stage of the individual in the life cycle of youth and age. The careful studies of Lehmann (1943) indicate that an individual's greatest contribution is likely to be made quite early. The salient contributions are earlier (e.g., at the beginning of the twenties) in some areas, such as physics or mathematics, than in others, such as biology, history, or politics. Wayne Dennis (1958) has criticized this interpretation of such data as Lehmann and others found, saying that (a) since scientific discoveries are now made with greater frequency every year, the "magnitude" of the earlier discoveries becomes overestimated, like the prominence of the first small mountain appearing among foothills, relative to the large mountains which come later, and (b) that a man's energies become partly tied up in defending his first discovery, leading us to underestimate what he would do later if unencumbered. Actually, though real, this latter burden is probably small compared to that involvement in administration, in fostering the work of younger, oncoming men, and in the increase in correspondence around the world which robs the older man of his creative hours.

The biologically-minded psychologist is likely to be so impressed by the resemblance of creative output curves (if accepted without the Dennis correction, which is difficult to quantify) to the life curve (Table 7–3, page 161) for g_f that he feels little need to go further into the above sociological explanations. The g_f curve might, indeed, partly explain creativity trends, especially in the abstract subjects, e.g., mathematics, where sheer relation-perceiving capacity is the first demand. But where experience and content are necessary, e.g., in biology, history, or depth of emotional experience in art, music, and literature, creativity should depend more on a_g, crystallized intelligence, which does not diminish and probably increases. This brings us, in the next section, to the more intensive examination of these powers.

4. THE SYNTHESIS OF CAPACITIES, PERSONALITY, AND DYNAMICS IN CREATIVITY

Some discussion of the environment in which creativity can fulfill itself, and from which it derives its stimulus, as given above, is essential to understanding creativity, but it cannot be our main theme here. The reader may pursue it in relation to home conditions, laboratory organization, demography, college environment, and intellectual tradition in the penetrating articles respectively by Roe, Kaplan, Knapp, Thistlethwaite, and Kuhn in Calvin Taylor's excellent collection of contributions on creativity (Taylor and Barron, 1963). He may also wish to ponder on the Marxist theoretical position of Hogben, in *Science for the Citizen,* that "necessity is the mother of invention," in contrast to the view that creativity is play, an adventure of the human spirit, best pursued freely, without reference to economic pressures.

Throughout the moderate ranges of environmental condition and incentive seen nowadays, however, the abilities and personality traits necessary to invention and discovery remain much the same. Our plan at this point is to return to the discussion of these contributors begun in Sections 1 and 2 above, and attempt a more formal integration of the way in which capacities and traits synthesize a creative outcome. It has been the scientific intention of this book to proceed wherever possible from general discussion to precise models—models necessary for the student who pursues psychology as a science. In previous chapters, starting with the linear, factor-analytic, "influence model," we have proceeded to a formula combining abilities, temperament traits, and dynamic traits—still in a linear form—in a way which empirically has been shown successfully to predict general scholastic achievement. Secondly, we have made the distinction between the equation for accounting for *actual performance at a given moment,* known as the *present action* equation ((11.1), page 334 above), and the *structural acquisition* or *learning product* equation ((11.3), page 336 above). We have now to consider a third expression, for the accumulated creativity of a person over time. For it is this which distinguishes the genius from the brilliant individual, and which, as we have seen, is a complex product of conscious and unconscious motivations, of abilities, and of the guiding personality traits, as shown in equation (11.3). (Parenthetically, the reader will have understood from the outline of the dynamic calculus findings above, that the D terms—for unitary dynamic traits—include unconscious as well as conscious structures.)

Before attempting a further step in the model for integration of ingredients, let us in fact take a brief inventory of the abilities, personality traits, and dynamic traits involved. In the ability area, though it remains to discuss (Sections 5 through 7 below) the special character of fluid and crystallized intelligence in more detail in regard to creativity, we have already taken the position above that g_f is the prime source of new relation perceptions, but that ffuency-retrieval and flexibility are more important here than in scholastic achievement and routine intellectual performances.

However, our conclusion has been that in current literature "divergent thinking" has been both misconceived and overrated as to its role in creativity. It is misconceived because the orthogonal rotational procedures, throughout the work of Guilford and his colleagues, have divided up the variance of what we center here on the concepts of fluency and flexibility in a different and falsely simplified way. Until the current researches by Horn (1967, 1970) and others in effect re-rotate this area of correlational analysis of extensive areas of ability, the conclusions cannot be entirely clear. But our tentative conclusion has been, if one may sketch in some smaller gaps in the data underlying the triadic theory, that the main variations in creative performance emerge, in the ability field, from the general capacities, g's, rather than the provincial powers, p's, or the agencies, a's.

Over and above fluid and crystallized intelligence, g_f and a_g, we see among the capacities a general fluency ("divergent thinking contributor"), which, in the cognitive field, is a retrieval capacity, g_r, and a general ideational flexibility factor, g_x, as in the Cattell-Tiner (1949) experiments and (rotationally somewhat different) in Guilford's experiments. Our present hypothesis contains the assumption that, with wider exploration of cognitive manifestations, the latter (a) will be established as a "g" rather than as an "a," and (b) will show the qualities of a bi-polar dimension—*flexibility-vs-tenacity* (Table 4–1 above)—rather than the appearance of a uni-directional ability. That is to say, the "low score" pole is a retention of concepts in their original form, which is a kind of cognitive tenacity with utility and survival value. For its opposite is a plasticity and instability of cognitive habits that can be disabling and even dangerous—though permissive for creativity. (Among the world's cultures, Oriental cultures perhaps have shown a relatively high degree of this cognitive tenacity, as have members of those cultures.) Experimentally, what we see as yet is that the highly flexible person is relatively poor at reproducing exactly some given data, such as a heard rhythm, and, by inference, at preserving concepts and habits efficiently, without some intrusion of instability and error. He is by hypothesis liable to sporadic, spontaneous, and unrecognized departures in long-accustomed ideas, which contrast with the precision and dependability of application by the "tenacious" individual. On the other hand, loadings on such performances as solving riddles and restructuring visual patterns show that he can see things in new groupings, can perceive possibilities of constructing new words by dissolving the rigid forms and obstinate debris of the old, and has ability to escape from habitual approaches to problems. The hypothesized new general capacity, still awaiting checks on its breadth, will index g_x (the subscript f being already used in g_f).

The classical "rigidity" dimension, in any sense of a broad capacity, we have abolished from the psychometric scene. The numerous rigidities become either the above ideational flexibility-tenacity capacity, g_x, or what are, operationally, perceptual-motor rigidities expressing an inability to execute a known pattern in a new way. The latter reduce to the effect of a whole set of factors—largely personality factors—namely, low g_f, and, in the U.I. series:—low U.I. 23, 26, and 29, and high U.I. 33. The effect of this last on creativity is unknown, though there are indications that U.I. 23 and 26 do contribute somewhat to creativity as they contribute to reduce motor-perceptual rigidity. Just as in flexibility, so in fluency, we have to recognize an appreciable contribution from the personality domain, in this case about half the variance on a fluency ("divergent thinking") performance being due to g_r and half to the U.I. 21, Exuberance temperament factor. Thus g_f, g_r, g_x, and U.I. 21 might well account for most of the variance in creativity in an "immediate action" situation.

As argued above, it is the personality factors that become important in the cumulative effect situation, and still more the dynamic factors. When we ask how many propositions Euclid wrote, or how many kinds of bacteria Pasteur isolated, or by what steps Kepler eventually concluded that the planets move in ellipses rather than the long-accepted circles—in short, when we are talking about a life's creativity—we are speaking of the cumulative process equation summed over time. Incidentally, it may be objected that it is easy to do this for a brick wall or a factory product, but difficult for the creation of ideas. Granted the difficulty, still the proposition holds in principle.

What we have been saying about the inadequacy of certain currently popular test approaches to predicting creativity in life is brought out more clearly by the above proposition, for we are saying that: (a) The output through the year has a process specification equation which depends much more on personality factors than does the railroad track performance in a three-hour test session with "creative ability" measures. The contention is that personality and interest measures rather than specified abilities determine how *frequently* the person will return to the task and with what degree of *intensity and inspiration*. For every Faraday or Pasteur or Darwin there must have been thousands of individuals of equal level in "creative abilities" on a pencil and paper examination. These people taught well, or directed businesses, or made shrewd bets on horse races—or perhaps just lived a life of leisure. (b) Since, in fact, the most important creative steps in science and elsewhere have been long-continued *unconscious* processes (Beveridge, 1950), which depend powerfully on a properly organized motivation system, the probable importance of personality and motivation over special abilities is raised to yet a new level.

In connection with this last interaction, let us recognize that the summarizing specification equation does not include all of the mathematical model necessary to describe the interaction of ability and motivation. The dynamic calculus recognizes a dynamic lattice structure (Cattell, 1957a, 1965a) showing how various behavioral and thought activites are subsidiated, by conscious and unconscious paths, to ultimate ergic goals. Within the dynamic lattice there are hierarchies toward "instinctual" ergic goals and toward sentiment goals. Ability structure may also be considered in part a hierarchy. At least within crystallized intelligence more generalized, abstract, problem-solving habits and more specific sets of skills, numerical, mechanical, verbal, are invoked at particular points. There is a sense in which the interaction of abilities and interests (dynamic traits) can be understood as the interplay of two distinct hierarchies, though at the moment this lacks expression in a due extension of our model and its equations.

In that interplay we see now this sentiment and now that making use of some given skill in the ability hierarchy. Any interest at any level in the dynamic hierarchies of the dynamic lattice is, in general, free to avail itself of any skill. Nevertheless, as seen in the concept of tools (effectors) in Chapter 11 above, there are tendencies for particular skills to get tied to particular dynamic traits, i.e., there are "adhesions" which deny complete randomness of interaction between the two hierarchies. In the lives of most geniuses these areas of especial intensity of application of the dynamic system to an ability system are far more prominent than in the average man. When Edison said that "inspiration is 99% perspiration" or Kretschmer (1931), that "genius is concentration at a point" they had this truth in mind. Like an acrobat who astonishes us by some motor performance, possible through the remarkable development of some muscle system, the creative person generally has focused conscious and unconscious attention, day in and day out, on some problem until sensitivity of perception is such that a breakthrough occurs. As a process, we shall return to this below, in the observations of Poincaré and others, but as a systematic relation of ability and dynamic hierarchies, let us formulate it in what we have indicated above as a third type of performance specification equation—the cumulative performance equation.

Wherever we deal with a product within a life setting, whether it be an essay, a painting, a mathematical treatise or the solution of a scientific technical problem in the laboratory, *time* must enter the equation. Consequently, our first "present action" equation ((11.1) above, page 334), commonly worked out for a one-hour examination, or some instant of time, must be written in integral form:

$$C_{ijn} = \sum_{t=1}^{t=n} a_{ijt} = \sum_{t=1}^{t=n} b_{jat}A_i + \sum_{t=1}^{t=n} b_{jpt}P_i + \sum_{t=1}^{t=n} b_{jdt}D_{it} \qquad (13.1)$$

where C_{ijn} is the creative output of individual i in area j over time n, and the other symbols have their usual meaning. As usual, for simplicity, only one representative trait is taken from each modality. The summation over time must be for the same period over all three modalities, because the output concerns their joint action, in which D and the b's are likely to oscillate, whereas A and P are fixed ability and personality traits.

Although immediate additional uses for this equation will not be pursued, it has the useful function of reminding us that performance on "divergent thinking" tests from 3 to 4 on Friday afternoon is not creativity. Actually, since learning would occur, in "concentration at a point" the prediction would also require attention to the *structure acquisition* equation ((11.3) above), and therefore to the incentive system as well as the dynamic traits. Furthermore, the time given to the creativity would, in a free environment, itself be a function of the level of the D's and the magnitude of the incentive. However, (13.1) takes one more step toward adapting more academic performance and learning equations to the life situation.

5. THE ROLES OF g$_f$ AND a$_g$ IN PROBLEM SOLVING AND CREATIVE PROCESS

Although real-life creativity involves conscious and unconscious work over time, and equation (13.1) is thus to (11.1) as the physicists concept of work is to force, it behooves us to study (11.1) again more closely in terms of focusing the processes of thought in problem-solving at a given moment. "Problem-solving" here does not mean solving familiar problems by familiar recipes, in routine work, but entirely new problems, and can then be considered cognate with creativity. At this juncture, moreover, let us consider the dynamic forces as given, and also take for granted the lesser more specialized ability factors in the triadic theory—the p's and a's—since their action is no different, except for area, from the general capacities. Our focus is thus on the understanding of the problem-solving process in terms of g_f, a_g, and g_x.

The vital role of g in problem-solving, very adequately described by Spearman and his coworkers fifty years ago, covers much of the action of what now we should call g_f. He described this role as the capacity in problem-solving to perceive relationships and to educe correlates. The process can be seen in high degree as pointed out earlier, in such tests as series, classifications, matrices, etc., that are particularly valid in g-saturation. However, as Burt pointed out when inventing the analogies subtest in intelligence tests, relation and correlate eduction reach their clearest expression in analogies and metaphors, and this form will therefore be taken here for illustration, in Figure 13–3.

Whether an *inherently present* relationship actually will be *perceived* depends on the person's level of intelligence. If the individual concerned

FIGURE 13–3
Eduction of Relations and Correlates Variously Illustrated

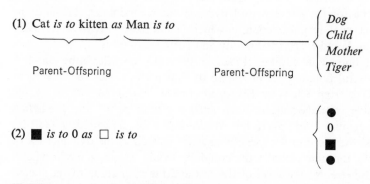

(1) Cat *is to* kitten *as* Man *is to* _____ { Dog / Child / Mother / Tiger

⎵ Parent-Offspring ⎵ Parent-Offspring

(2) ■ *is to* 0 *as* □ *is to* _____ { ● / 0 / ■ / ●

(3) Distance *is to* automobile *as* Time *is to*

(4) 16 is to 4 *as* 9 is to 3 *as* 4 is to 2 *as* −1 is to

has sufficient associational mass for a relationship of that level of complexity to rise into consciousness, when presented with the fundaments "cat" and "kitten," he will educe the relation "parent-offspring" (which he may or may not verbalize). Then he can apply it to the given third fundament "man" and educe the new correlate "child." The retrieval from memory of the word "child" is a process distinct from the location of the *meaning* of that which should stand as the fourth fundament.

That the retrieval is a separate process can be shown by the fact that in suitable experimental conditions the thinker can be permitted to solve the eduction problem *without* being able to find and fit the concrete example into the intellectual "slot" which he has located. For example, he can carry the meaning, for which he knows no word or picture, as a nonsense syllable, or an "x," showing that his concept is clear by the use he makes of it. The first man to think of the square root of -1 must have done something like this, and Moseley's conception of what we now call the proton, when he thought of atomic numbers, had the same imageless but meaningful quality. Once the thinker passes from grasping the meaning to the step of completing the solution by finding an object that actually fits that meaning ("child" in the above example), the limits to his problem-solving are set by other parameters of ability, such as fluency (to supply the concrete instance) or flexibility (to pull the new form out of an older, "binding" context).

Because of the high loading commonly found in school for verbal ability on traditional intelligence tests—measures of a_g—there has been a widespread tendency to use it as *the* medium for intelligence measurement. However, in fact, very complex relations can be put to the subject without any use of words. A simple instance is shown in the second example in Figure 13–3. Incidentally, in the first two examples in Figure 13–3, we have used *selective* rather than *inventive* examples to eliminate the role of retrieval. Selective and inventive forms of a test usually correlate so highly that nothing but the convenience of being able to machine score the former by a key causes it to be preferred. However, in the last resort, the inventive form *does* introduce some g_r over and above g_f, and is best avoided.

The third example shows the essence of creativity, wherein no such object as the required fundament exists in human knowledge, and a real invention had to occur. In this case H. G. Wells's stimulating fantasy of the *Time Machine* is the product of the given relation eduction. In this instance more than retrieval would be involved for the inventive answer. "Filling the slot" by construction of an effective machine—a time machine—so far has baffled us, except as a fantasy, but the flying machine, the moving picture, the general anesthetic, and the electronic computer, beginning necessarily as newly educed fundaments, ultimately were realized in practice. Whether the correlate necessary for fourth example, $i = \sqrt{-1}$, is "realized," is a matter for mathematicians to answer, but it certainly is a creation!

As Spearman (1930) himself illustrated in an excursion into the arts, much of the pleasure of art and music comes from suitable insights—the sudden sense of the beauty of order where no order at first was evident. Artist and composer have built into their products hierarchies of intricate relations on which we may continue to feast. The insight may give only the simple and sedate pleasure of the rhythmically repeating relations among pillars in a Greek temple. Or it may deliver a secret of delicately balanced proportions in a "cubist" picture. Or it may permit us the more complex experience of recognizing a musical fugue. Or again in literature it enlightens with the magnificent metaphors of Shakespeare or such modern gamin expressions as "overworked as a dog with four children to follow" or "TV is a kind of chewing gum for the eyes." Or in poetry, it may offer the double delight of getting an order in *sound* (rhyme, alliteration, assonance) with the penetration of *meaning* by metaphor and simile. Consider Tennyson's "Yet all experience is an arch wherethrough, gleams that untravelled world," or Browning's "Ay, note that Potter's wheel, That Metaphor! and feel, Why time spins fast, why passive lies our clay," or Brooke's "Love sells the proud heart's citadel to Fate," and note how each introduces essentially a set of revealing, possible, relation eductions. By a conspiracy of such artfully hidden relations, a veritable conflagration of cognitive processes can be started, which illuminates a whole landscape of ideas.

The same relation-perceiving insights are the vital ingredient also in practical problem-solving. The artist, the engineer, the scientist, the musician, the poet, and the architect live on totally different technical foods, but they digest them with the same intellectual wine. Regarding such solutions to technical problems, there have been many ingenious researches, such as those of Laycock (1933), Strasheim (1926), Guetzkow (1951) and others too numerous to list. Except for occasional "serendipity" solutions, in which a lavish use of retrieval or laboratory time has produced a solution by sheer fecundity of trial-and-error responses, practical problems also get solved by eduction of relations. Such a relational insight must have come to Trevithick when he suddenly realized that the valves of the steam engine need not be opened by hand, as they had been in mine pumps, but could be tagged to the connecting rod movement which naturally occurred at the same time.

A book could be filled with the history of glorious human insights, creating the fabric of the culture on which we now live and depend as a matter of course. But a handful of examples is enough, for, as psychologists we need to be off on a further trail. The power of g_f—the working of the neurological associative mass—is essential to relation eduction, but it is also not sufficient alone. The dynamic states and directions of the human mind decide when and to what purpose the relation eduction shall take place. What solution the individual prefers will obviously depend also on repressive blockings and facilitations, retrievals of relevant examples from storage, and much else. The natural and the test setting are different. The several naturalistic studies of, for example, scientific discovery, in its ordinary daily setting, by Beveridge (1950), Poincaré (1914), as well as many frank scientific autobiographies such as those of Edison, Cannon, Huxley, Osler, and Watson, tend to show certain dynamic rhythms, in which the crest of a tide of high insight is driven still farther by some gale of demoniacal enthusiasm and application. One detects a rhythm, in which there are phases, lasting days or months, such as (a) clarifying the elements in the problem, (b) deciding what the central question really is, (c) experiencing a heightened tension as effort at solution mounts, (d) marking time (apparently) in what is often a fairly long incubation period. Therein much work is done unconsciously, while consciously the individual feels in the doldrums, aware of no progress, (e) a sudden thrusting up from the subconscious of a solution, often rough, and sometimes as symbolic and poorly communicable as a dream, but generally true, and (f) a working out of detail and explicitness and a tidying of the means of communication.

Now in this process one can see clearly, in any actual example, the working of the main general powers—g_f, g_r and g_x—that we have described. Often the chief obstacles in the early phase are certain wrong assumptions and configurations maintained by the tenacity of cognitive structures, and awaiting the dissolving action of such swings toward high flexibility as the individual's g_x can produce for him. The physician Harvey perceived an intriguing relation—the resemblance of structures in veins to valves in the common pump—and decided that the blood circulated; but the authority of Aristotle's concepts kept other physicians from seeing and accepting this for another twenty years. Similarly, the theory of phlogiston kept chemists from accepting the necessary complete reversal of thinking required to accept oxygen, when weighing showed that burned metals were heavier, not lighter, than the unburned. (A factor analyst may perhaps be allowed to add that in psychology today the high school training in drawing coordinates orthogonally blocks many from recognizing that oblique factors better fit all the facts!)

The whole problem of tenacities of accustomed concepts versus new flexibilities has never been handled better than by Francis Bacon nearly four hundred years ago, and he pointed rightly to words as the chief villains of reactionary thought. (This is one reason why rhetorical and journalistic "freedom of speech" can be dangerous unless accompanied by the education that gives freedom of mathematical and scientific formulation an equal chance.) Psychology, for example, has been plagued badly by the implicit, tenacious assumption that if there is one word—e.g., "intelligence," "rigidity," the "authoritarian personality," "need achievement," "cognitive dissonance" or "field independence"—there must be one thing. Writers are often far into their second volume on such a theme before the multivariate analyst can awaken them and their readers to the fact that, say, two or three quite distinct phenomena have to be explained mathematically.

6. THE ROLES OF EDUCTIVE, ASSOCIATIVE, AND DISSOLVENT THINKING

By eductive, associative, and dissolvent thinking we mean, respectively, the action of g_f (and its derivative a_g), of g_r as retrieval (deliberate or automatic) of an association, and of g_x as flexibility shown in the capacity or tendency to undo past cognitive structures.

Of these, we know least about dissolvent thinking. This is partly due to insufficient factor-analytic researches following up the first rough delineations of the flexibility factor (Table 13–1). But probably it is due also to dissolvent thinking acting less prominently in controlled, artificial test situations than in odd moments and unwatched intervals of everyday life. In any single test item performance, e.g., in a hidden picture test as in Figure 13–4, the perception of the necessary visual relations themselves and the flexible separation of new forms from older, predominating forms—respectively the work of g_f and g_x—may be virtually instantaneous. But in the life history of creativity—as when Kekulé at last thought of the benzene ring as a solution to the valency problem, or Oken saw the skull as the last enlarged vertebra; or when Bohr concluded that the arrangement of electrons in orbit must relate to the position of the element in the periodic table —much of the dissolution of obstructive older formulations must go on intermittently and subconciously. Nevertheless, the amount of such activity in a given individual presumably still depends on the general level of the tested g_x power of flexibility that he possesses.

FIGURE 13–4
Eduction and Dissolvent Thinking in Hidden Pictures

By kind permission of the Institute of Personality and Ability Testing, 1602 Coronado Drive, Champaign, Illinois.

A problem to be faced in the conception of flexibility as dissolvent thinking, i.e., as a general reduction of the strength of existing cognitive habit structures, relative to newly presented combinations, concerns its relation to dynamic principles. Since Freud, psychologists have developed considerable evidence, clinical and experimental, that the obstinacy of particular beliefs and conceptions, the distortions imposed on new perceptions, and the particular groupings brought about in one's ideas, depend to a high degree upon the nature of the dynamic systems, the occurrence of conflict, and the operation, e.g., in producing "complexes" of various defense mechanisms, such as repression, projection, and reaction formation. Consequently, one may well ask such questions as "Is there need for any additional concept, such as that of the general factor g_x in accounting for the ideational flexibility and ideational firmness attributed clinically to dynamic causes?" and "If there is evidence for some general flexibility over and above that induced at specific junctures of conflict and repression, should it not be itself considered a dynamic trait rather than of ability modality?"

As pointed out above, we believe there is evidence in the work of Cattell and Tiner, extended by Guilford and his associates, of the existence of a new factor beyond any previously recognized capacity, and which, in the triadic theory, is placed as a general capacity, g_x. When two people of equal intelligence are faced with a riddle, one fails and the other solves it, apparently because his thinking is not so firmly held in the conventional thinking system encouraged by the façade of the riddle. His thoughts easily do a somersault, and, presto, he has bounded through the blinding paper hoop to the intended solution. Since this happens with all kinds of items, i.e., is relatively independent of the particular interests and dynamic systems involved, we seem safe in saying it is a general factor, not explicable in terms of dynamic structures alone. However, to repeat the caution above, we possess still only fragmentary researches on the boundaries of this factor, and especially on its role in dissolvent operations on ideas in everyday life and over time long periods.

If this generality and consistent extra variance contribution of g_x should continue to be confirmed, the second question still would remain, i.e., we might yet have to conclude that it is more of a personality factor than an ability factor. Actually, in systematic personality factor researches some twelve forms of behavior have been measured that either overlap precisely or in general intuition with ideational flexibility, and are listed under Master Index numbers in the compendium of over 1,000 behaviors (Cattell and Warburton, 1967). With their M.I. (Master Index; Hundleby, Pawlik, and Cattell, 1965) numbers preceding them for exact identification they are: 26, Riddles; 7, Gestalt completion; 38, Ratio of consonant to dissonant opinion recall; 170, Hidden pictures; 198, Perceiving anagrams; 327d, Logical consistency in emotional syllogisms (later developed as cognitive dissonance by Festinger); 680, Tendency to use neologisms; 711, More logical sequences in story telling; 808, Solutions to novel situations; 1443, Lability versus constancy in paths on successive days (Howard and

Diesenhaus, 1965, already showed 16 P.F. associations to this), and 1865, Preference for more unconventional proper names. Although the experimental evidence is clear that they do not fall entirely on a single factor (Hundleby, Pawlik, and Cattell, 1965), they are, nevertheless, largely contained by four of the twenty known personality source trait patterns, namely, U.I. 19, 25, 27. and 28. U.I. 19, Independence, is a positive tendency to impose one's own conscious set in interpretation (as in field independence, Witkin, 1962) and is definitely *not* the ideational flexibility here discussed. U.I. 27 is an Emotional condition of apathetic discouragement, in which past cognitive sets are weak for dynamic reasons. The concept we have so far built up in ideational flexibility would therefore be competed for chiefly by the two remaining patterns, U.I. 25, Realism and U.I. 28, Asthenia. The former has been called by Eysenck (1956) "psychoticism" (when measured negative to our "realism"). The latter has been called *asthenia,* because its personality associates are those of debilitated neurasthenia-like behaviors.

It would seem a logical concomitant of increasing ideational flexibility, as conceived above, that it could end in the loss of such reality contact as is general to the various behaviors we call psychosis. Actually, our more recent work (Cattell and Tatro, 1966) shows U.I. 25 to distinguish simple schizophrenics better than psychotics in general. Interesting though this theory is that binds flexibility to the psychosis pole of U.I. 25, we must not ourselves lose contact with the reality that an appreciable though not equal contribution to number of hidden pictures seen, speed of gestalt completion, and tendency to recall what one agrees with is made by U.I. 28. A monistic theory for this kind of behavior just will not do, and the g_x which appears as an ability factor could, if not truly cognitive, be viewed as an unrecognized, combined outcrop of three or four personality factors. However, the kind of flexibility defined here in riddles, letting visual structures restructure themselves (not imposing structure, as in U.I. 19), lower logical consistency of attitudes, and greater eccentricity fits the "subjectivity" (psychosis) end of U.I. 25 and the asthenia of U.I. 28. This agreement checks also with the concept of greater cognitive firmness as the opposite of flexibility. For at the "realism" pole of U.I. 25, we have more reliable simple arithmetic, more correct speeded color naming, and greater speed and accuracy in matching (Hundleby, Pawlik, and Cattell, 1965).

It may well be that the attempts of various writers (Section 1 above) to describe some kind of mental "asthenia" in the genius are in fact a perception of this U.I. 28 dimension, or of g_x (however these two may prove to be related). Geniuses, contrary to popular folklore, do *not* have an excess of mental derangements. Though instances of manic depressive geniuses can be quoted, *perhaps* almost up to the incidence rate in the general population, instances of schizophrenia (the largest class of psychotics) in genius have been estimated at well *below* the general population frequency.

On the other hand, an asthenic and depressive form of neurosis, like that which some think plagued Darwin most of his life (others ascribe it to Chagas' disease), can be seen in the "nervous breakdowns" of many very creative persons, e.g., John Stuart Mill, Pascal, Pasteur, Newton, and Faraday. The plasticity and flexibility of thinking necessary for restructuring when new ideas are formed is bought apparently at the cost of efficiency, economy of effort, and avoidance of fatigue in handling everyday matters by cut-and-dried methods. It helps explain why our profiles for the researcher and the administrator are so different. Doubtless the heavy inhibition and prolonged concentration necessary for the long-circuited thinking of profoundly creative work could account for the type of "neurasthenia" which seems the only type of nervous breakdown truly likely to be more frequent in genius. Whether the asthenia we measure in personality factor U.I. 28 always is determined environmentally or whether, as seems more likely, it is also due to a constitutional tendency to this kind of flexibility, research is equipped now to decide. Meanwhile, it is evident that the creative process is aided through g_x (which may be contributed to by the joint action of U.I. 25 and 28). It is aided precisely as the creation of a new building is aided when the task of demolition of existing structures does not encounter excessive resistance.

So much for dissolvent thinking. By contrast, the positive work of construction arises from eductive and associative processes. The creation of new mental content by eduction of relations and correlates has been discussed sufficiently above in connection with g_f. However, before grappling with the problem of associative thinking, we should pause to deal with the question that will occur to many readers regarding eduction: "Does not crystallized intelligence, a_g, also play a role in eduction?"

Examination of the loadings of performances by a_g (called g_c at that stage of exposition) in, say, Table 5–1, shows that performances we would regard as creative, e.g., verbal analogies, *do* have some contribution from crystallized intelligence. However, by its very definition and nature, a_g deals with things that are already known, and judgmental skills that have already been applied before. One would expect that its contribution, as shown by such correlations, must reside in the knowing of the fundaments, and the practiced habit of deciding on a certain direction. On the opposite side of the ledger, we have to recognize that g_f cannot educe relations between fundaments the nature of which is unknown. (Those used in culture-fair tests are in fact chosen to be overlearned.) Most relation eduction is actually carried out at the upper levels of a hierarchy, for fundaments are often themselves relations, or relation among relations. (If I divide a box of twelve oranges equally among three boys, and one of ten equally between two girls, and then ask whether a girl or a boy has more, I ask for such a relation among relations.) To the extent that educing a new "creative" relation depends on relational fundaments already practiced in a_g, the existing quicker and surer perception of the latter will facilitate a quicker and surer response on the new possibility higher in the hierarchy. One cannot perceive that the area of a circle can be estimated from a series of isosceles triangles, unless he knows that he can calculate the area of a single triangle. Faraday could not have perceived the relation of a magnetic field to plane polarized light, if he had not had clear conceptions of these two; and a tactic in tennis to play twice to the opponent's backhand, followed by a quick drive to the forehand, is too slow to succeed, if the player has no automatic command of forehand and backhand placement.

But the role of crystallized intelligence would seem to be that of supplying a foundation, or at least supplying it more quickly than if all had to be worked out from scratch. Any truly new eduction of relations or correlates is, by all we have analyzed, an act of g_f. Crystallized intelligence may load a creative act because it permits and facilitates. Obviously, of two persons in a creative, mathematical problem-solving, the person with long investments of his fluid intelligence in that field will produce answers more quickly and be less liable to errors. But if the two are equally familiar, the new creative steps are likely to be made by the more highly endowed in fluid intelligence, in proportion to his endowment.

In most creations that have to be communicated or made, the mental operation must draw not only on flexibility, which makes new structurations feasible, and fluid intelligence which brings the new relation to birth, but also on memory and associative powers. As in the example in Figure 13–3, fluid intelligence shows where the "slot" is, in the field of meaning, but to finish the creative task, memory has to supply the suitable spare part for the slot. In the area of association, we have recognized (Chapter 4) three processes: committing to memory ("gramming"), retention, and retrieval. (Recognition may be considered an abbreviated retrieval procedure.)

The debatable view needing to be examined here is that these associative processes are not just *adjuncts* to the creative process constituted by educing relations and fundaments, but a means of creativity in themselves. It is frequently claimed that associative processes, i.e., without prior eduction, can be creative, and that creativity is "nothing but a marriage of ideas that were previously strangers." Koestler (1964) for example, tells us that cogito comes from coagitare "to shake together," and on this linguistic derivation would have us consider oddity of juxtaposition as creativity. Here again we meet the notion, not that what is created is unusual and strange—which of course, it is—but that what is strange and odd is "creative." If nightmares and bedlam are creative, this would be true. But our definition of creative has been functional from the beginning, namely, that the invention must work, the short story must grip our attention, and the discovery must bear scientific checking by other techniques. By this functional definition, any merely odd "shaking together" does not constitute creativity—else the glacier that leaves an erratic boulder in the plain would have to be commended for its creativity.

Nevertheless what sometimes rightly earns the name of cultural creativity for accidental juxtaposition is one that (a) happens to be functional too, and (b) is intelligently perceived to be functional. When Charles Lamb's Chinaman accidentally burned his house down, thus roasting his domestic pet, the pig, he made the delicious discovery of crackling as he licked his fingers. The perception that here was a way to a new culinary triumph constituted the discovery. When scientists and artists are in a humble mood, they will confess that a decidedly higher percentage of scientific and artistic advances are due to accident than theorists usually like to admit. (Indeed experienced researchers will recognize that the perception of the value of an "irrelevant" byproduct (in terms of the main theory) is often more important than the main theory.) If we now look at such undoubted discovery and creativity in terms of the qualities in individuals necessary to bring it about, it is obvious that we must turn to gifts (over and above curious and alert observation) in the realm of fluency and fantasy, which generate "ideational" experiments. Enough real experiments will in time generate some fruitful juxtapositions, but fantasy is the carrying out of experiments in imagination, and therefore includes much trial and error at the mental level—which is quicker. Even creative thought processes of an eductive kind depend a good deal upon fantasy—as do some less clinically healthy activities—and they benefit from the free play which is possible in fantasy. Thus, not all fantasy is sheer trial-and-error play at a purely associative level, since it can be play also with relation eduction. Nevertheless, for most people, most fantasy is casually reproductive, waywardly directed by dynamic needs, and, at the dream level, likely to bring together elements in an almost random way, as far as realism and logic are concerned. As Freud argued, and others have since found by experimental dream recordings ("REMS"), dreams may function to explore emotional solutions for the individual, but it is rare for the dream *per se* to solve, say, an engineering problem.

This last instance demands that for clarity we recognize two meanings to "functionality" in creativity, namely, functional in that an invention or discovery "works" by standards of the real world, and functional in the sense of playing aptly upon human emotions. The creations of Lewis Carroll in *Alice in Wonderland* were an intriguing mixture of mathematical logic and emotional entertainment, but mostly art and literature aim to create certain emotions in human beings, while science and mathematics create what has to "work" and meet the test of interlocking with reality and logic. Our emotions are captured by the notion of an "angel" with the purity of a saint and the freedom of a bird to soar. But anatomists tell us that, in order to use the wings, the angel would have to have a breastbone standing out about three feet! In science, mathematics, engineering, and medicine, creation has to be judged by hard standards. A vaccine against children's polio is a beautiful idea, but it must also work. The great majority of purely conglomerative creations, formed by random association in fantasy or otherwise, do not work. If they work, it is a remote accident, not guaranteed by any eductive insight regarding necessary properties. And they do not work even in the emotionally functional sense of artistic communication except where a personal fantasy aptly and powerfully captures the emotions of a fantasy belonging to all mankind.

It is a mistake, therefore, to consider high fluency (or speed of retrieval, g_r, as we have called it) directly creative. Most of the time, it does not even produce what is new; it only reproduces. But if, by a random shake of the dice, it produces something new, say a beanstalk that climbs to the clouds, it is only a wishful-thinking, entertaining notion, not a jet that actually carries you over the clouds. Thus some pointless debates would be dissolved if, as suggested above, we recognize *two* creativities: primary creativity that creates something new in terms of effectively solving external world and emotional problems, and secondary creativity that may produce the new and the bizarre which accidentally has usefulness. Associative, reproductive processes thus have only a limited role in creativity in the primary sense, through (a) supplying the material to complete the correlate eduction carried out by g_f, (b) possessing the probability of hitting upon a few, lucky, blind, trial-and-error solutions, if the sheer fertility of supply is very high, and (c) as in crystallized intelligence supplying the necessary judgments lower in the hierarchy as a basis for new relation eduction.

The role of sheer memory storage and fluency can be illustrated by Edison's success in producing the incandescent filament lamp, which depended partly on having a rich store of ideas about where to turn for the hundreds of different substances to which he gave a trial for the filament. In the theoretical field, one can instance how the Bondi-Gold-Hoyle "steady state" theory versus the "big-bang" theory of Lemaitre and Gamow was unilluminated for a time by anyone having thought of the fact that the latter would require radiation reverberations. When Dicke eventually thought of it, it was found that Gamow had had the idea implicitly in an overlooked paper ten years earlier. Just how far wide reading and good memory and retrieval powers are vital in an era of computer encyclopedias and retrieval systems is debatable. But within individual minds themselves, we would argue—in conflict with some divergent thinking theory—that g_f is of prime importance for creativity, followed by a_g, g_r, and that combination of retention capacity and wide experience which determines the magnitude of storage.

This perspective on factors in creativity would not be complete without a word on group creativity, which a decade ago was fashionable in, for example, the notion of "brainstorming." In spite of a number of impressive instances, from the King James version of the Bible to the atom bomb, most who have seriously studied the processes of discovery and invention conclude that the real steps come from individuals as individuals, and that "discovery by committee" is a poor plan. (One recalls the gentleman who became an atheist because, he said, the world was in such a mess that it could only have been constructed by a committee!) Studies of problem-solving in some hundred groups of ten men each (Cattell and Stice, 1960) provided much evidence as to why this inferiority in creative (as contrasted with a superiority in routine judgmental) activities exists.

Briefly, one may enumerate: (1) Such activities as brainstorming—pooling ideas—undoubtedly give a ten-man group a greater memory and fluency than any single man, but no similar cumulative effect takes place in g_f. (2) In g_f, the intelligence of a group is not even that of the single brightest individual. With one man at I.Q. 150, another at 100, and eight at 75, the group decision could be that of I.Q. 75. (3) By the nature of truly creative, new ideas, they are the hardest to communicate. Often no words exist for them. Their fragility renders them vulnerable; they break up and are superseded by readily understood and communicated notions. (4) The unconscious gestation of ideas, described in the phase of consolidation mentioned above, or in the persistent inner development characteristic of introvert activity, has no chance to take place in the extravert life of the group. (5) Actions and decisions in individual creativity are part of an unconscious process—a hunch—not capable of explicit defense, as in the compass course set by Columbus, or the brushstroke of a Michelangelo. Committees do not paint pictures. Some further aspects of group inter-actions of abilities will be noted in the next chapter. But as far as specific creations by a "group spirit" is concerned, the result shows some sort of summation of abilities only in highly role-structured groups. There is cer-tainly no evidence for summation—in group performances of a specific, measured nature—of the g_f level of the members, and the group decision, at best, reflects the g_f level of the brightest member.

7. A CLOSER LOOK AT CRYSTALLIZED INTELLIGENCE IN CREATIVE THOUGHT

The somewhat brief dismissal above of crys-tallized intelligence from any major role in creativity may strike many readers as inviting more debate. It was argued that the correlation that undoubtedly exists between a traditional intelligence test score, a_g, and some criteria of creativity is due to the a_g skills providing the foundation of knowledge, but that the final relation perception, which is new, comes from the g_f action, and is decided by its level. This says the correlation is due to a_g contributing to the creativity variance, though a purely statistical alterna-tive is that the correlation exists because a_g correlates 0.5 to 0.6 with g_f, and thus is likely to correlate with whatever g_f causally affects.

A somewhat more intensive inspection of the action of a_g in creativity is justified because it pushes still further our hypothetical definition of a_g itself. Immediately above we have supposed that the facilitation of creative work in a new field depends on the fact that nothing is entirely new, and that a high level of development of a_g brings with it (a) knowledge neces-sary to understand the nature of the lower fundaments (between which relations are made) and (b) habit skills in quickly perceiving and applying relational perceptions used before (these we have briefly called "judgmen-tal skills"). But "knowledge" has usually been considered by us a function of good retention and good retrieval, g_r. How then is it a function of a_g? The answer is that knowledge is also a function of the history of experience, and that what we call a_g is, by all our earlier analyses, a function of experi-ence. However, we *have* argued that mere rote absorption of experience is not a_g, but that the latter is experience accepted through the action of g_f. That is to say, it is organized, relationally interpreted experience, built into effective analytical thinking habits. In the analogy: "thermometer" is to "temperature" as "clock" is to "——" it is supposed that we are acquainted with the fundaments "thermometer" and "clock," though failures of retrieval, as in aphasia, would upset this. Logically, one must therefore admit that the "knowledge of fundaments" depends on effective functioning of various aspects of memory.

This opens the door to the recognition that all *agencies,* including a_g, are abilities which depend for their functioning on memory being intact. We are now going to argue that this applies to their use of remembered relations as well as remembered fundaments. If this admission that *some* determination of a_g functioning depends on the level of present storage and facility, over and above past g_f and breadth of experience, is correct, then appreciable loadings should be found on most a_g (but not most g_f) loaded performances for g_r itself and for whatever factor or factors power of retention is yet to be resolved into. As far as present data on sufficient ranges of variables and with competent factor analyses goes, as in the work of Horn and Cattell (1966a), it *does* seem that this relation holds.

The assertion that the habits of relational perception in a_g, though fathered by g_f and mothered by experience, are in the keeping of memory powers may be better evaluated if we consider examples. What are some actual illustrations of such judgmental, discriminatory skills? They should appear in correct verbal usage of similar-appearing words, such as complacent and complaisant; in nice application of near synonyms such as consummate and superlative; in distinguishing between survival of the fitter as used by Darwin and by Nietzsche; in not setting out to solve for six unknowns from five simultaneous equations; in deciding that a bottle of cider spoiled by being left open to the air may be used safely in a salad dressing; in refusing to be drawn into an apparently purely philosophical argument between a man and his mother-in-law; and in deciding whether to replace the spark plug or the distributor points in a misfiring automobile. In all of these, a suitable level of g_f was necessary, initially, in order that the individual might insightfully acquire the rather complex judgment necessary to respond to the right elements in the situation in the way indicated. Further, we concluded that whatever the amount of teaching, the individual could not acquire real *judgment* response to the right abstraction of situational elements, beyond that attainable from his particular level of g_f. A typist of lower intelligence may be taught that principal is more often used in its sense as an adjective, and occurs rather often in referring to people, while principle is a noun and will appear more often in the realm of rules or ideas, but in taking such dictation as "Men of principle know that the principal rules are . . ." the acquired judgment may fail. There is no substitute for insight. When there is age decline of g_f, a person who has *had* insight will continue to handle the complex situation well by the acquired judgmental skill, reacting to the right elements. But the above assertion, that this a_g skill is a g_f deposit, may be shown by lack of true insight ("I simply remember that this process gives you a square root. I cannot prove it.") and by error, if entirely new elements demanding a different response, appear in the situation.

The essence of a_g, therefore, is a set of learned response habits to complex cues—responses which are highly adaptive in a persisting, stable environment. As an engineer, for example, the individual knows that the calculation to decide a certain construction requires computing a partial differential. But he may no longer have—indeed, he may never have had, since he accepted his teacher's authority—complete insight as to why this is done. As a writer, he may use what are felt by new readers to be sparkling phrases, but which are nevertheless clichés from old writers, and not of his own invention. As a chess player, he may use a potent opening gambit unknown to his neophyte opponent, but not understand in the least why it succeeds. He may be able to state formally, by the rule, why the conclusion from a given syllogism is wrong, yet draw the wrong conclusion himself, if the problem is not arranged and presented in syllogistic form. In all these cases, in order to bring out the difference, we have used as illustrations instances where the individual's g_f has fallen below his a_g level (or where he has accepted a decision process beyond his g_f level, on a teacher's authority, and where a change in the present situation calls for an insightful new and different response.

Although g_f and a_g have differences of loading pattern—indeed our initial separation of them depended (Chapter 5) on finding such crucial instances —they are nevertheless on the main *cooperative* factors, i.e., they tend to load the same variables. This fits the observation that, although many complex situations in which much learning has occurred can be largely handled by the learned judgmental responses stored in a_g, they can rarely be entirely so handled. They are apt to incur slight changes in situation or setting that involve complex new relation perceptions and therefore invoke g_f. No two engineering problems or chess games are just the same. It is apparently easier to set up a problem that requires *pure* fluid ability performance than *pure* crystallized ability (though it is easier to find tests that are *largely* a_g). Presumably this "contamination" of a_g arises also through individuals in the usual sample range lacking acquaintance with the particular a_g requirements and turning to find a solution by invoking g_f. (This use of a general relation is brought out clearly by the young man who was asked if he could play the violin, and answered that he could not say for sure, as he had never tried.)

This last illustration is not entirely frivolous; for it reminds us that g_f and a_g may sometimes work in opposition—"pure reasoning" upsetting what experience might better suggest, and experience interfering with a correct answer from reasoning. Indeed, having admitted that a_g may help in truly creative acts, by supplying a better springboard for the final acts of g_f, we must next give attention to the well-known fact of "negative transfer" of decision habits in a_g, and the sad generalization from the history of research that "specialists" and "authorities" in a field have often been the last to recognize, accept, and support a creative movement in that field. Thus, classical learning theorists in psychology promise to be the last to utilize structured learning theory, and so on.

The fundamental causes for the limitation of contribution to creativity, or even negative contribution, from an individual's high endowment in a_g, crystallized general ability, would seem to be (a) that a relationship he uses is not as easily maneuverable or applicable to a new situation as would be a g_f-perceived, insightful relation—he uses it, but does not "understand" it; and (b) that if he deliberately set out to apply it elsewhere it might be applied to an inapt situation. In that case, it would have no higher chance of success than has the chance association which very occasionally produces originality in some fantasy trial-and-error. Thus, a person with reduced g_f relative to a_g might continue to use two near-synonyms, like those cited above, in apt distinction in their verbal contexts, but not be able accurately to abstract a relation between them that could be carried over, in an analogy, to produce a new pair of words similarly related. It would be interesting, in this connection, to analyze age distribution of production of new similes and metaphors in the lives of poets.

In contrast to this negative effect of a_g, due to its strong, inveterate habits of perception drowning out the new ideas that the "still small voice" of g_f might offer, it can also make a positive contribution. For g_f may often proceed to its new relation eductions on an insufficient knowledge of the real nature of the fundaments involved. In these two effects, incidentally, we encompass the origins of most of the differences in reasoning that occur between youth—higher on g_f—and age, higher on a_g. There is a constantly active function of a_g in ruling out, in the experienced person, certain avenues of approach that are false. An expert has been well defined as a person who has made every possible error in a given field. Some of the continuously improving a_g score throughout life is due to this wisdom of knowing what not to do. Every researcher of experience has seen—especially in psychology— his able research assistants re-entering old blind alleys with the enthusiastic belief that they are making new discoveries.

Play and trial-and-error being more frequent in childhood, one probably encounters there more numerous instances of insightless, chance application of learned relations to new fundaments. The boy who sees that boiling improves eggs may proceed to boil his father's watch. Some of the most egregious examples of applying complex relations, once perhaps learned with insight but later, as a part of crystallized intelligence, applied more mechanically, probably occur in mathematical abilities. It has been cited above how, for example, by programming certain rules of inference, in Boolean algebra, the computer, with far fewer relation-perceiving elements than the human brain, can accurately solve logical problems of a kind often presented in intelligence tests, and indeed develop propositions which leading logicians have failed to recognize before. This behavior nevertheless corresponds to a_g rather than g_f. It is a cut-and-dried application of rules that could produce absurdities but for the human director's insight in seeing that rules and material appropriately go together. It suggests, incidentally, that inductive reasoning ability should be a more saturated and reliable measure of g_f than is deductive reasoning, especially in a population where many subjects have been exposed to training in deductive reasoning. If this experimental evidence on the origins and the factor loadings of the inductive and deductive modes of reasoning is sustained, it will lead to a somewhat surprising reversal of the esteem in which scholastically they have been held, but it will add to our grasp of the implications of the g_f and a_g distinction.

A developmental issue that must be related to the present examination of the creative or noncreative role of a_g resides in the theory stated earlier, that a_g "graduates" from a correlation cluster to an independent factor through achieving, at any early stage, self-perpetuating powers. The suggestion therein was that a set of habits employing higher-level relations will generate additional habits, by the mechanism we have described in the growth of "aid" agencies generally, namely, through the inherent consistency of a domain calling for the creation of new associated habits to fill a gap. This formation of new, perceptual, judgmental habits is correctly to be described as a form of creativity. The student who has learned some geometry and some algebra will more easily take the requisite steps in trigonometry: the a_g habits are the requisite foundation and contribution to the creative steps taken by virtue of g_f.

In summary, it would seem that the level of creativity that an individual can reach is determined, among abilities, largely by one major and three minor contributions from his general capacities. The major power is still g_f, fluid intelligence (including in the last resort the local organization, p's, too). The lesser contributions come from a_g, crystallized ability (with added contributions from all primary agencies); g_r, ability to retrieve or reproduce (fluency, when timed); and g_x, flexibility, a general cognitive or personality characteristic still insufficiently mapped in research. However, in life, as distinct from brief, artificial, problem-solving test exercises, the role of g_r and all ability factors except g_f is probably quite small, compared to the variance contributions from personality dimensions, A−, F−, E, M, Q_1, Q_2, Q_3, U.I. 19, U.I. 21, etc., which determine habits of concentration and restriction of impulse in favor of inner activity.

CHAPTER
FOURTEEN

INTELLIGENCE AND SOCIETY

1. WHEN WILL SOCIETIES TAKE A CENSUS OF THEIR ABILITY RESOURCES?

Modern prophets are increasingly insisting that unless the social sciences receive as much development and application as the physical sciences we are doomed. However, the necessary steps are not so simple because (a) we know less in the behavioral than the physical sciences, (b) more complex social and ethical problems arise in the application of the behavioral sciences, and (c) the man in the street is not really very cooperative. The first will be all too obvious to the reader who has seen how thin our data become here as we approach social research. The difficulties in the second will become more obvious as we investigate in this chapter attempts to apply social psychology. The major difficulty is, perhaps, that men try to combine explicit scientific reasoning with inexplicit, inspirationally revealed, dogmatic, ethical principles, repeating the error of putting new wine in old bottles.[1] The third is illustrated by the recent attacks on psychological testing in schools and elsewhere, and also by the ancient retort "my behavior is entirely my own business"—though, obviously, for anyone who lives in society, it is not.

---

[1] I propose to do no more here than to state the principle that every social application calls for a marriage of science and ethics. Ethics cannot be discussed here. However, inasmuch as I have suggested that this marriage will never be happy until the ethical principles are themselves derived as objectively and scientifically as scientific laws, I must refer the reader to possibilities discussed at greater length elsewhere (see Cattell on *Beyondism,* in 1938a, 1950b, 1971b).

In any case, to apply behavioral science in a society requires, first, some knowledge of its human resources, its distribution of abilities, attitudes, educational levels, etc. A society is a living organism, and one index of the developmental level of an organism is the extent to which it has internal receptors keeping a brain informed of its hungers, its working resources, its moods, and the present disposition of its parts. Before appropriate social action can be planned, the means of obtaining, storing, and analyzing information on the human lives concerned must be set up. Since our concern here is with intelligence and other abilities, we naturally turn to information about intelligence. How much do we know (especially how much does our government know) about the real magnitude of our resources of high, medium, and average intelligence? What are birth rates and educational forces doing to change intelligence levels in the oncoming generation? And what are the needs of various occupations, in terms of the national gains that might result from possible redistributions of ability?

From costly national censuses, governments and private research organizations increasingly bombard us with information regarding numbers of persons born, income distributions, magnitude of economic product, buying habits, religious affiliation, and much else. An elected government surely has the right and duty to know the mental income as well as the monetary income of its citizens. And, in historical fact, in spite of the perennial reactionary sloth of mankind (sometimes sincerely believed to be liberalism, as in Orwell's *1984* or Young's skit on "meritocracy"), societies have continually demanded better records of their citizens, as to numbers, income, incidence of disease, educational level, family size, and so on. Advances in psychological and medical diagnostic and measurement techniques make the well-organized recording of individual scores in health and ability levels increasingly practical. Such knowledge would be highly advantageous in avoiding disease and maximally adjusting educational opportunities to the individual. Yet only a few advanced countries have actually initiated psychological surveys of educational levels, mental health, etc., during the last few years. We have only the beginnings of knowledge of intelligence distributions in occupations, economic class, etc., through the Royal Commission Reports to which Burt, Thomson, and others have contributed in Britain, and through enquiries on national resources of intelligence made by Dael Wolfle, Lentz, and others in the United States.

Manpower resources, in terms of numbers of trained doctors, scientists, engineers, etc., are, on the other hand, now known with comparative precision in several developed countries. For example, the total of qualified scientists and engineers in the United States climbed over the years 1954 1958, 1961, and 1965 by the steps of 237,000, 356,000, 429,600, and 503,600. In the last year 69,000 were employed by government, 66,000, by colleges, and 351,200 by industry (plus 17,400 in nonprofit research institutions). Information on trends of this kind is important in itself for calculating resources for medical research, national defense, etc., but to the psychologist studying abilities, calculations in these terms alone pose a different, rather disturbing issue. If there is a largely biologically determined g_f normal distribution curve, and a biologically plus scholastically determined derivative a_g curve, can our population meet the demand for an increasing percentage of Ph.D.'s without lowering the standards implied in that qualification? Indeed, this same issue has to be faced in yet broader terms in the question "Has this generation's increase in the percentage of the population admitted to universities lowered educational standards represented by various grades or the character of the curricula?" Many experienced faculty members, especially in the older universities, acknowledge that it has insidiously introduced a spoon-fed education, in which methods of the high school (some even say the nursery school) have invaded the universities. The hope that this impression may not be true rests on the anticipation that selection for ability is actually more effective now. Burt rightly points out that if the 1.5% of eighteen-years-olds who entered British universities before World War II were truly the top 1.5% by ability, it would correspond to an admission cutting point at an I.Q. of 135. He points out now that even though the examination selection and the provision of scholarships are reasonably good, the cutting point goes below 115. Obviously, if university doors are opened indefinitely wide, the average level of complexity of the curriculum must fall. But, could such a fall be avoided by a more efficient search for untapped ability resources?

The issue is by no means the only one to which our call for better psychological survey information is relevant and important. But it is worth pursuing further because it offers excellent illustration of the difficulties and the utilities encountered. To illustrate the difficulties in clear conclusions with present data, those who assert that standards are not lowered when an increasing fraction of the population enters higher education—in the case publicly discussed, scientific education—can argue as follows: (1) Improved efficiency of education can more than offset the need to dip lower into the fluid intelligence distribution. We have seen that regarding *average* intelligence on traditional tests, increased educational efficiency has actually raised the crystallized general intelligence level over the last two generations. (2) The higher demands and rewards in science during the past century have almost certainly diverted talent from the arts; while this incentive condition endures, the standards in science can be maintained. (3) All the natural resources have never been utilized fully, for with every man of I.Q. 135 and over who took a Ph.D., the distribution curve shows there were three or four others at the same intelligence level who apparently lacked opportunity to work toward a Ph.D.

Let us set aside until Section 3 the first of these effects, and deal with the last (and, by implication, the second), namely, the question of sheer available community resources of intelligence. Obviously, with two kinds of intelligence to be considered, the question must be asked twice, and it will be appropriate to begin with the largely innate (Chapter 10) form—

fluid intelligence. Since the 100 I.Q. average is set by standardization within each community (except when culture-fair tests span several countries), it is not easy to compare resources across countries, as one might with agricultural production or the resources of a mineral such as gold. The picture within a single country has meaning, however, in terms of the magnitude of *standard deviation* of I.Q. (for that relates to age units) and whether the distribution is that of the usual, bell-shaped normal curve, or is, alternatively, skewed in some way, showing shortages at certain levels. However, the wider use of culture-fair intelligence tests will obviate present dependency on an artificial 100 I.Q. set separately for each nation or culture. By this means it will be possible to bring all tests into a common world standardization, so that nations and subcultures *can* be compared in mean I.Q. Lastly (and again we need culture-fair tests), some additional meaning to expressions of "levels of resources" develops through culture-fair tests inasmuch as we become able to make comparisons across successive *generations* despite changes in breadth or style of education. For example, one might begin to answer the question "Is there more really high intelligence available today than there was a generation ago?" Once such comparisons are possible, the performance of a particular generation in a particular country could serve as an "absolute" standard (in the sense of the standard platinum bar or caesium wave length in the physical sciences) against which change could be recorded.

Naturally any complete ability census would cover not just fluid intelligence, but the actual school achievements, the general capacities such as a_g, g_r, g_s, etc., the p's or provincial powers (since visual and auditory powers, for example, might easily differ), and the primary abilities or agencies, especially the most general—a_g. In America, Britain, France, Australia, and some other countries where objective achievement tests have been employed for a generation or more, a precise basis exists for many kinds of analyses through such enterprises as ETS at Princeton, the surveys of cities by Thorndike, Flanagan's Talent Survey, the National Foundation for Educational Research in Britain, the Scottish and London surveys of Sir Cyril Burt and Sir Godfrey Thomson, and the Leicester survey by the present writer.

Incidentally, the one trend that emerges clearly from all these diverse areas is a fairly steady rise in standards of school achievement over the past fifty years. Beyond that, and on the more vital subject of fluid and crystallized intelligence, there exist only the sporadic individual researches to be discussed in the next section. The present nervous system of society—its arrangements for systematic information about its own resources and needs—is, by a metaphor from animal phylogeny, at about the jellyfish level! Vague awarenesses of levels and trends on just one or two dimensions filter down to us. The development of a sophisticated and reliable awareness of the psychological characteristics of our social organism is still something to be hoped for in the future.

2. THE INTELLIGENCE DISTRIBUTION AND ITS EFFECTS ON SOCIETY

It is practically impossible to write on what *is* without one's adjectives implying what *should be*. Yet it can properly be asked "Does society *need* more intelligence?" or "Should this occupation rather than that receive our reserves?" And beyond traits such as intelligence—for example, when we talk of exvia-vs-invia or high or low anxiety—value judgments are still more equivocal.[2] Perhaps one can take the position, temporarily, that although much dispute prevails about the desirability of other traits, such as sociability, kindness, emotional stability, etc., greater resources of intelligence are almost universally valued. Granted a sound personality and value attitudes, a better intelligence enriches life for its possessor and vastly increases the help he can give to others.

A realm in which there is an almost complete failure to recognize the effect of individual differences in intelligence is that of real wealth and the standard of living. Economists talk of production, distribution, and resources without seeming to recognize that people lie at the root of the causal sequence that leads to the numbers with which they deal. That which to an I.Q. of 80 may be a rocky hillside, fit for a few sheep, to an I.Q. of 180 may be, as a uranium deposit, a tremendous energy resource, or, as the home of a genetic mutation in wheat, a potential huge food reserve. In their egalitarian preoccupations, few sociologists have taught the truth that the tremendous gains in average real wealth and health since the Renaissance are essentially the result of the application of intelligence to nature and natural resources by a few people. They are not the result of improved social organization, of a sudden access to new resources, or of a rise in individual education or of average civic virtue. Politicians can distribute wealth, but they cannot make it. This latter has been the gift of scientific geniuses. Unintelligent people will starve with natural resources all around them no matter what their political organization. Man's ultimate natural resource is therefore his intelligence—especially if shaped and trained with awareness of scientific advances. Furthermore, history demonstrates that the discoveries, inventions, and enterprises which gave Western man his start are the product of but a few thousand men of genius (see Chapter 13). Without the contributions of this minute fraction of a percent of the total population, the millions today would be living much as their ancestors lived and as people still live in countries backward for lack of cultural leadership.

---

[2] As indicated in the first footnote above, I shall not attempt in this chapter the impossible task of excluding value judgments, but shall refer the reader to my writings on *Beyondism* (1938a, 1944, 1950a, 1971b) for what I feel to be the truly defensible values in the application of social sciences to human affairs. At present the bulk of applied science—social or physical—is suspect of having implicit values that are adopted ready-made and unexamined from sources totally inconsistent with the logical basis of science.

Although the larger gifts—nuclear energy, anesthetics, the chemistry of agriculture and improved education systems—come from high intelligences, the level of *average* intelligence of a community probably also affects significantly the average community prosperity. In the first place, it does so also in terms of the effect, just discussed, of the bright few, for since distributions tend to be symmetrical about the average, an increase in the average tends to be accompanied by an increase in the number of persons above, say, a 130 I.Q. (by the original norms). This tendency of the extremes to move with the average is primarilly a genetic effect. In a freely intermarrying group, a gene pool is defined and constant, and the frequencies of the gene combinations which make the extremes tend to become constant as stability is reached. (Other special effects, such as assortive mating, which spreads out the range of the normal curve, can be considered later.) If, as seems probable, appreciable differences in the real wealth of communities are associated with small differences in average intelligence, it may turn out to be largely because small differences in the mean I.Q. between groups have this relatively large effect on the numbers in the highest I.Q. range. As more data accumulates, statistical tests can be invoked to decide how much the increased group performance stems from a change in mean *per se* and how much from this augmentation of high "managerial" ability at the uppermost levels.

The question of relation between real wealth and average community intelligence will be discussed below, but it is interesting to note in passing that the constructive reaction to perceiving that at any rate the *highest* I.Q.'s are vital has encountered conservative opposition, particularly from Marxists. Constructive measures at the genetic level, for eugenic increase of high I.Q.'s by Darwin, Huxley, and the present writer (1937b) for example, have been attacked with doctrinaire arguments, by, for example, Hogben, and Penrose (not to mention various sociologist-environmentalists), and at the educational level on the ground that giving most education to the most gifted will create an elite. (For some reason, Young, in his book on "meritocracy" (1958), considered this reprehensible.) Nevertheless, the fact remains that the standard of living of a nation in peace, and its security in war, depends strongly on possessing such an elite (by whatever term it is called). Incidentally, several penetrating analyses of the last decade of economic malaise in Britain trace it to the failure of the educational system to funnel high native ability into industrial and managerial channels.

There is really no conflict between humanitarian goals and the aim of fostering high intelligence. The suggestion that the low intelligence individuals will be neglected has been simply a rationalization for doing nothing in the field of eugenic exploration. The reformer is as sensitive as any to the worth and dignity of every individual, regardless of gifts. But the greatest happiness of the greatest number, even in the lower ranges of intelligence, demands a birth rate adjusted to competence. Nor does the reformer's position deny the need for citizens at every level of intelligence. For example, a gap in the distribution curve between the topmost level of genius and the I.Q. 100 level would grievously deprive the community of interpreters and adaptors to understand and apply the discoveries of genius. If mechanization and computerization eliminate the need for large numbers of I.Q. 80 individuals (those typically socially contributory only in "drawing water and hewing wood"), society is obliged to avoid the maladjustments that would be created by an oversupply at that level.

While there is as yet no exact, quantitative proof, indirect evidence and sound logical reasoning support the position that a community's wealth and health is a function of its average level of fluid intelligence. Studies of cities by E. L. Thorndike (1931) (and others by R. L. Thorndike, his son (1941)), show consistently positive correlations over any series of two hundred or more cities among such variables as mean income, length of school, number of books read per 100,000 people, and mean performance on nationally standardized school achievement tests. These differences among cities in a "general goodness of living" index have some correlation with the proportions of professional, skilled, semiskilled, and (negatively) unemployed families.

The arguments for correlation of mean g_f level of a community—be it city or nation—with real standard of living are several. Of these we may glance at (1) the argument from distribution of occupations, (2) the argument that achievement in school tends to be proportional to g_f, and (3) the nature of the discovered cross-national cultural dimension of "affluence-intelligence." In the surveys mentioned above, the proportions of people in higher level to lower level occupations is higher in the communities with better "goodness of living" indices, *not* merely higher mean salaries, as would naturally be expected. If, by reason of examinations, etc., the g_f mean for more complex occupations is higher—as in fact we know empirically it is from such data as in Table 14–1—then a higher fraction of the population in more complex occupations means a higher average community level in intelligence.

As to educational achievement in the schools, the analysis of Chapter 12 above shows that it depends on many things besides intelligence, e.g., personality qualities and home attitudes to learning, among others. But unless it can be proved that these are for *independent* reasons, i.e., not as a by-product of low intelligence itself, poorer in the lower achievement communities, the statistician must accept as the *most probable* conclusion that lower achievement in communities is partly due to lower intelligence.

Perhaps the best evidence available at the present time for systematic relations between performance levels in the schools and economic performance of the community is presented in the nature of the "socioeconomic level factor" in the Hadden and Borgatta (1965) studies of American cities, and in the educational achievement level studies of R. L. Thorndike (1941). With small towns, Hadden and Borgatta found a correlation of .60 between percentage of college graduates and the socioeconomic level of the town as a whole. But our contention here, perhaps in some contrast to

TABLE 14–1
Distribution of Intelligence in Occupations

Occupation	Mean
Professors and Researchers	134 (C1)
Professors and Researchers	131 (C2)
Physicians and Surgeons	128 (C1)
Lawyers	128 (H&H)
Engineers (Civil and Mechanical)	125 (C1)
School Teachers	123 (C)
School Teachers	123 (H&H)
School Teachers	121 (H&W)
General Managers in Business	122 (C)
Educational Administrators	122 (C)
Pharmacists	120 (H&H)
Accountants	119 (C)
Accountants	128 (H&H)
Nurses	119 (C1)
Stenographers	118 (C)
Stenographers	121 (H&H)
Efficiency (Time Engineer) Specialists	118 (C)
Senior Clerks	118 (C)
Managers, Production	118 (H&H)
Managers, Miscellaneous	116 (H&H)
Cashiers	116 (H&H)
Airmen (USAF)	115 (H&H)
Foremen (Industry)	114 (C)
Foremen	109 (H&H)
Telephone Operators	112 (C)
Clerks	112 (C)
Clerks, General	118 (H&H)
Salesmen (Traveling)	112 (C)
Salesmen (Door to Door)	108 (C)
Salesmen	114 (H&H)
Psychiatric Aides	111 (C&S)
Electricians	109 (H&H)
Policemen	108 (C)
Fitters (Precision)	108 (C1)
Fitters	98 (H&W)
Mechanics	106 (H&H)
Machine Operators	105 (H&H)
Store Managers	103 (C)
Shopkeepers	103 (H&W)
Upholsterers	103 (H&H)
Butchers	103 (H&H)
Welders	102 (H&H)
Sheet Metal Workers	100 (C)
Sheet Metal Workers	108 (H&H)
Sheet Metal Workers	76 (F)
Warehouse Men	98 (H&W)
Carpenters and Cabinet Makers	97 (C)
Carpenters, Construction	102 (H&H)
Machine Operators	97 (C)
Cooks and Bakers	97 (H&H)
Small Farmers	96 (C)

TABLE 14-1 (Continued)

Farmers	93 (H&H)
Drivers, Truck and Van	97 (H&W)
Truck Drivers	96 (H&H)
Laborers	96 (H&H)
Unskilled Laborers	90 (H&W)
Gardeners	95 (H&W)
Upholsterers	92 (C)
Farmhands	91 (H&H)
Miners	91 (H&H)
Factory Packers and Sorters	85 (C)

The figures in this table are from samples varying in size from some thousands to a couple of dozen, but centering on about 100. They are taken largely from the studies by Fryer (1922), Cattell (1934), Harrell and Harrell (1945), Himmelweit and Whitfield (1949), and some occupational analyses by the present writer, using 16 P. F. Factor B scores, from the Institute for Personality and Ability Testing. The initials C_1, C_2, F, H&H, H&W, indicate these origins. An attempt has been made to bring the various sources to the same standard score I.Q., namely, a sigma of 16 points, and in so doing, a number of approximations have had to be made which makes it pointless to calculate to more than a whole number mean I.Q. These are, thus, results intended to give perspective rather than to be the basis of a definitive occupational list, which, hopefully, will be undertaken soon by institutions with sufficient resources and in terms of culture-fair tests.

The sigmas may be calculated from some of the original sources, but for illustration it is about 12 for accountants, 16 for salesmen, 15 for electricians, 16 for mechanics, 19 for carpenters, 20 for truck drivers, 12 for teachers, 13 and 14 for stenographers, 9 for physicians, 14 for nurses, and practically reaching the general population value (16) for carpenters, factory workers, and laborers. The general tendency is for selection to a lesser value than that of the population (perhaps actually about $\frac{2}{3}$), and this is particularly potent in the professions, but scarcely exists in the less skilled occupations.

the conventional assumption, is that both the educational and goodness-of-living indices are consequences of a single cause—the mean level of community intelligence. To social and political activists unaccustomed to viewing mankind as one more biological species with the usual ecological variation, the idea that innate endowment of communities may differ appreciably in the means and distributions of their fluid intelligence levels may appear alarming and unacceptable. But to the scientist, the explanation that requires least elaboration ("natura est simplex") is the best. And in this case the theory here offered makes the lower standard of real earning (or community production) and the lower performance of school children of low production communities partly due to a single cause—lower g_f.

Let it not be overlooked that the mean differences here discussed are quite small—perhaps one point of mean I.Q. between say, an industrial town, a county agricultural center, and some university and research centers (such as, say, Palo Alto, Boulder, and some university towns in the Northeast). Differences of this size could readily be produced by differential migration. Another obvious influence on community intelligence levels is the differential birth rate. A community with extensive birth control clinic service might be expected to avoid proliferation of large families of low intelligence. As to migration, there is well-documented sociological research showing that migration can be differential for intelligence. However, it also shows that migration in one geographical direction is not always in the same *psychological* direction! For example, in normal or prosperous times, those who migrate to urban areas average more on intelligence than those left behind in the country. But in certain agricultural depression periods, the less able farmers migrate, presumably because they fail before the more able. Ellsworth Huntington cites the historical instance (which we have cited above) of the Khmer migration from India to Cambodia where the Khmers built the remarkable civilization which left the magnificent ruins of Angkor Wat. He argues that not only the original decision to move from a crowded situation in India, but also natural selection in face of obstacles along the way, raised the average constitutional intelligence level of the survivors. The same explanation fits the good cultural record of the early settlers of America or of the Jews, with their long migrations through hostile environments. Huntington also documents the striking difference in cultural productivity between the inhabitants of Newfoundland and Iceland, where the geographically and climatic conditions are very similar, but the source of migrants was very different.

Let us now consider the third source of evidence—the cross-national cultural dimensions found by factor analysis. The procedures by which these "source traits" to measure the syntalities of nations are reached has already been explained in discussing the *cultural pressure* dimension in Section 3 of Chapter 13 above. One of the next largest factors after cultural pressure in the series of some 12 required to cover the culture pattern differences of nations was one variously called "Enlightened Affluence," "Affluence-Intelligence" and "Education-Affluence" in certain factorizations. The loading pattern as found by Cattell, Breul, and Hartmann (1952) is shown in Table 14–2. It has since been confirmed by Cattell and Gorsuch (1965), Rummel (1963), Jonasson and Peres (1960) and others. Some awareness of social causality and the meaning of loadings is required for adequate interpretation. Tuberculosis may mean infection in the individual, but in the mass it means poverty, unwise living (alcoholism, for example) and poor living conditions. Above a third of the variables, starting with this, are standard of living; others are education, liberal culture, and communication (telephones, trains); others are discretion, foresight, and wiser living (low syphilis, delayed marriage, more expenditure on housing).

In other contexts, e.g., comparisons of cities, counties, and states, this nexus of educational achievement and affluence variables has been interpreted by one sociologist as a tendency of wealth to be spent on education just as on any other luxury, and by another (looking also at nations) as a tendency of higher education to mean better use of resources, etc., and thus better production. The theory propounded here is that both are a function of higher intelligence, g_f, and, in defense of that, one can point to variables which suggest enlightened common sense itself. The argument that at least wealth is not primary, but educated intelligence is, receives some support from slightly higher correlations with technical than luxury education, suggesting that the wealth derives from better technology. Another weakness of the "wealth first" argument is the difficulty in explaining the origin of

TABLE 14–2

**The Factor of Enlightened Affluence as a Dimension of
National Cultures**

Factor Loading	*Variable*
−0.73	Low death rate from tuberculosis
0.67	High expenditure of tourists abroad
−0.60	Lower marriage rate[1]
−0.58	Low death rate from syphilis[1]
0.55	High real standard of living
0.51	High real income per head
0.50	More miles of railroad per person[1]
−0.42	High expenditure (all sources) on education
0.40	High musical creativity
−0.40	Low density of population and of persons per house[2]
−0.39	Low percentage of men eminent in art
0.37	High sugar consumption per head
−0.36	Low degree of government censorship of the press
0.31	More telephones per person[1]
−0.27	Low suicide rate
−0.25	Low death rate
0.23	High ratio of exports to imports

[1] These items from Cattell and Gorsuch (1965); main items from Cattell, Breul and Hartmann (1952).
[2] This item is composite of values from these and other studies; some taking density generally, some density in home. Both are inversely related to the factor.

the wealth in some other way than by earning it. "Accidental differences of natural resources in the areas where these populations happen to live" is only a partial answer. For a people driven to the last resorts of ingenuity, almost anything is a natural resource. Germany has poor resources of agricultural land for its population; but it had the genius of a Haber who made nitrogenous fertilizers out of air. Similar ingenuity has transformed the deserts of Israel. We are approaching a period when the relative wealth of nations has to be explained more by their differences in technological level and intelligence of organization.

The historian and the sociologist are likely to object to this last step in our argument: that differences of wealth, arising from differences in educational levels, trace to differences in crystallized intelligence, a_g, levels, and partly, ultimately to differences in g_f levels. (Note that we do not conclude wholly innate g_f levels, since a disease like malaria or hookworm might reduce g_f, and a humid tropical climate might reduce the periods of time in which intelligence is actively used.)

It certainly is true that historical traditions, as in the "underdeveloped countries," and various environmental conditions account for large fractions of the variance, but they are decreasing fractions. The spread of education, the rapidity of communication are likely to even up cultural stimulation. Even in this process, we notice difference rates of learning; Japan, for instance, was far quicker than some other previously nonindustrialized countries. When borrowing has reached its maximum, there will still be according to the present theory, relatively "developed" and "less developed" communities, corresponding to the g_f distributions in the peoples and fraction of peoples in various areas.

The argument is that the *enlightened affluence* dimension, though partly determined by history is also partly determined by biology—in this case the biology of intelligence—and that cultural differences will continue, to some extent, to be associated with biological differences. For if the rate of learning in an individual is partly a function of g_f, there is no reason to expect this relation suddenly to disappear when we consider the rate of learning of groups of individuals. So far this theory is an inference, admittedly on scanty data, from the three sources here discussed—the relation of school achievement level to standard of living across cities, the difference proportions of persons in complex occupations where economic demands are similar, and the enlightened affluence dimension that factors out across the nations of the world. *Direct* evidence, such as would arise from using culture-fair intelligence tests on large and carefully stratified samples from many cities and many countries, has so far lacked researchers and resources. It will come as nations begin to value their human resources enough; but meanwhile it is but a promising theory, that the level and distribution of native intelligence is one determiner of the wealth of nations.

An examination of intelligence and the life of society would not be complete unless we added to a study of the steady performances of culture a glance at what is likely to happen in the great emergencies—war, epidemics, natural catastrophes. In regard to war, that remarkable man Lord Fisher, father of the dreadnought battleship, summarized tactics with the dictum "In war you want surprise. To beget surprise, imagination must go to bed with audacity." In national defense the imagination of even one man—an Archimedes, a Napoleon, a Maxim, or the inventor of an atom bomb—can save countless lives and preserve the culture of the country possessing such resources of imagination. That high intelligence has value in national survival can be inferred also from countless historical instances at a less personalized level. Of World War I and the near success of the German submarine blockade, Admiral S. S. Hall (Cattell, 1937a, p. 79) emphasized "the overwhelming importance in submarine matters of the character and abilities of those who command them. Germany had some four hundred submarine captains during the war, but over sixty percent of the damage they did was accomplished by but twenty-two of these four hundred officers [who were able to] rise superior to the intricacies of these complicated vessels." And in the following war, when Churchill said that never in the history of war had so many owed so much to so few, he was speaking of a group of airmen who, in selection for a fitness level on intelligence, decidedly exceeded the national average.

Even today more draftees are rejected for defective psychological than inadequate physical standards. Eighteenth century governments had the illusion that armies could be made out of unemployed and criminals.

France changed that with the introduction of conscription at the Revolution, and Napoleon's steady succession of victories was not due to his imagination alone, but to the superior adaptability of the individual French conscript soldier (the father of Pasteur and many another very able man being among them).

But greater emergencies than war exist. When three billion people are in a space ship hurtling into an unknown space in which dark stars may be on collision courses, with another ice age as the least of their impending domestic troubles, it behooves them to achieve some understanding and control of their environment as early as possible. The question is no longer the sybaritic one: "What balance of distribution of intelligence makes for a comfortable society?" but rather, "How can we increase our resources of top-level intelligence to ensure man's eventual survival?" It follows that steps must be taken to "bring up the rearguard," since the functioning of democratic institutions and a true feeling for the brotherhood of man demand a capacity for common interests which is unattainable with an extreme range of ability.

Burt has convincingly demonstrated in some startling illustrations that the present range of ability in our population is enormous compared to the range in other human characteristics. Ruling out any pathological, physiologically odd forms of imbecility, and starting with healthy microcephalics, the range of mental age still goes all the way from three or four years to the equivalent of an abstract mental age (see Chapter 7) of twenty-five years. We do not have to adjust to such a range of physical stature, weight, or most other natural individual differences. The span is such that, in level of brain evolution, the population ranges from the greatest genius of modern man back to types prevalent 100,000 or even 500,000 years ago. By a kind of domestication, we carry forward in our midst various strains with brain capacities less than the average of races which, on their own, barely survived the primitive conditions of prehistoric times. This retention is not planned humanitarianism, but sheer neglect of the need for raising the intelligence resources of society. It is anything but humane to develop a complicated society and then imprison in it individuals who suffer from an oppressive sense of inadequacy, who have difficulty in finding respected employment, and who may express their frustration in a chronic conflict and delinquency.

The ease of cultural borrowing between classes and nations is increasing at a tremendous rate, as is the efficiency with which any set of habits—except top judgmental habits—can be taught. As educational opportunities become more equitable, the differences among societies will be based increasingly upon their genetic levels, especially the level of genetic resources in intelligence. The latter partly determine what kind of culture and forms of creativity and recreation the society will show; what educational achievement levels it will reach; how well it will survive war and disaster, how far it can maintain full genuine employment and a high standard of living, and perhaps even what social reforms and spiritual values it can truly assimilate. Though each individual determines most of his own morality and character, society, in the previous generation, is responsible for his intelligence.

3. WHAT IS PRESENTLY HAPPENING TO OUR INTELLIGENCE RESOURCES?

A certain type of environmentalist with his head in the clouds does not acknowledge the problem of raising the resources of ability in a society to the demands that progress will make upon them. His belief, like that of the prebiological rationalists of the French Revolution, remains that education can do everything. This contains, of course, all the danger of a half-truth. Education can succeed in ensuring the acquisition of simple conditionable responses, and the learning of symbols for concepts, though the meaning of the latter reaches only the level set by the individual's intelligence. After all, we recognize that even in areas not controlled primarily by intelligence, some innate component in special abilities can set limits. Training in dexterities, even if it were continued ten hours a day, would not fashion top-notch trapeze artists out of certain individuals. In acquiring dependability in complex judgments, the limits set by g_f are even more definite. Nevertheless, if one type of crystallized intelligence is desirable—say that expressed in the academic, scholastic abilities of modern man rather than in the hunting and tracking abilities of the Australian aborigine—an educational system can raise the population's level of performance considerably. But what we have called, in Chapters 11 and 12, the law of temporal rivalry still holds. Investments of g_f cannot be made simultaneously on all environmental fronts. Even if education could absorb for its purposes all the money that society earns, another limit to acquisition even more inexorable than g_f, appears in the restriction to twenty-four hours a day.

Education can raise the community level on some forms of achievement and in what our culture chooses to define as crystallized intelligence. But it cannot raise the level indefinitely on all motor, perceptual, and judgmental skills. Einstein confessed that he was no good at throwing a boomerang, and, but for self-teaching, he would not have been so expert at sailing a boat. No experiments yet exist to show it, but it seems highly probable that the rise in crystallized intelligence in our society over the last fifty years (as shown by traditional intelligence tests) has actually been accompanied by a loss of intellectual skills in many other directions, e.g., in telling by its smell whether the hay crop is good, in recognizing good taste in manners, in ethical discrimination in everyday social problems, in judging horses, in parsing Greek, or in insight into character.

For a moment, let us grant the environmentalist that society is unanimous as to what skills are important, and that the goal is to raise everyone to the highest possible level on the traditional crystallized intelligence test beloved by the educational psychologist. From the analyses of variance made in Chapter 10, we could calculate, by a certain rate of exchange, that individuals of I.Q. 90, given twenty years of schooling, would reach the same final level as individuals of I.Q. 110 given twelve years of schooling. That is to say, we are granting that a wide variety of performances exists on which just the same level can be reached by either of the two avenues. The important difference appears, however, when we compare the cost of starting with half the population at 90 and half at 110, with that incurred when we start with all at 110! To lift the 90's to the finishing level of the 110's demands, according to careful estimates, at least twice the educational cost. At the lower levels—of borderline defect in the I.Q. 70–75 region—the cost of special classes more than trebles the cost per child. Moreover, the end result in these cases is still not an averagely wise citizen. When enough of such citizens are caught by Madison Avenue adverts or by the slogans of the less conscientious politician, society staggers in its decisions as unstably as a waterlogged ship.

Teachers of special classes of the "backward," i.e., I.Q.'s in the 65–75 range, are a devoted and even enthusiastic group, for which society may be thankful. Their triumphs with these individuals measured in small increments of adjusted citizenship are not to be underestimated. Specialists in such teaching justifiably reassure the citizen that some progress can be made, and they may add that such really low intelligences and those still closer to the imbecile level constitute only about one to two percent of the population. Farther in the imbecile group, perhaps half of the deviations below 60 I.Q. are not normally inheritable.[3] This two percent of the population is not however, the real problem that we are discussing. That problem concerns the forty-eight percent of the population from I.Q. 70 to I.Q. 100 which is statistically correctly designated as subaverage. In this range we are usually dealing with intelligence inheritance that follows the usual laws of polygenic determination, and since the numbers here are far greater, the effect on the population average of an excessive birth rate is marked (see Burt, 1948; Cattell, 1950c).

Unless society musters the courage to think afresh on these problems, we are committed to drift, for decades and perhaps for centuries, repeating the inefficient educational process of the last century. The I.Q. 90's will remain as numerous as or become more numerous than the 110's, and, as every institutional medical officer knows, we shall even be keeping in expensive, care institutions the children and grandchildren of those kept

---

[3] A typical and recent research—that of B. G. Scully, reported at the International Association for the Scientific Study of Mental Deficiency at Montpelier, in 1966—showed that, from the 342 defectives studied, about a thirty percent incidence of mental defect could be expected in children when parents are defective. Higher figures have appeared elsewhere; but due to "regression to the mean" the Scully figures are fairly typical. In this group incidentally, the illegitimate birth rate was twenty times that of the average citizen.

before. Charity for the unlucky is justifiable; a stupidly incurred welfare burden for a systematically recurring and even expanding drain on all efforts at cultural progress is quite another matter. It is a burden which, in a dire emergency, could hazard the very survival of a nation in a competitive world where nothing is as important as the quality of people. The laissez-faire defense of doing nothing about genetics is that "it takes all kinds to make a world." This "wait and see" attitude is entirely correct when we are ignorant of the genetic origin and social value of a trait. But we know much about the origins and the social and educational effects of intelligence. We know too that in our technologically changing world, where demand for unskilled work is vanishing, and where the constant, pressing need is for individuals of the highest educable capacity, the below 90 (say) I.Q. is faced with increasing maladaptation. Psychology and genetics are advancing to the point where a positive social program could confidently be undertaken to raise the mean g_f I.Q. of the population by suitable encouragements in family planning.

To plan such an upward shift in I.Q. requires recognition, as every biology student knows, that a shift in any inherited group character occurs partly through mutation, partly from differences of death rates, and partly from differences of birth rates. The human species under civilization is heavily dependent for its "progress" on differences of birth rates, since differences of survival in a welfare state are reduced by all economic and medical means possible. Forty years ago it was well documented from censuses, e.g., in the work of Heron, Leonard Darwin, Galton, and others, that size of family was inversely related to level of social status (the latter essentially defined as complexity and educational demand of the occupation). Since, as Table 14-1 shows, intelligence and occupational complexity are related (actually to a correlation of about 0.2 on culture-fair and 0.3 on traditional tests) there is a substantial probability—but not certainty—that such an inverted birth rate implies a declining community ability level. (However, our results below did show that even within one occupation, e.g., postmen, a relation (negative) persisted between size of family and intelligence.) This inverse relation was apparently characteristic of most Western cultures at the turn of the nineteenth century, and historians argue that it had been characteristic of Rome, and perhaps of other civilizations prior to their collapse (McDougall, 1930).

These ominous historical precedents and the current signs in our own culture induced many social psychologists to research on the question of whether, in fact, the socially inverted birth rate implied a real negative correlation of intelligence and family size. The curiosity of the present writer, and his conviction that this is one of the most important applied problems in sociology and social psychology, led him with the help of Leonard Darwin and Sir R. A. Fisher, to make in 1935 a complete cross-sectional testing of a British city of about 250,000 (Leicester) at the ten-year-old level, and similarly of a rural area (Devonshire) sample. The results showed quite consistently that larger families were then being produced[4] at the lower intelligence levels, as shown in Figure 14–1. Incidentally, this research was unique among prior studies and subsequent studies over the next twenty years in (a) the early use of culture-fair intelligence tests, so that effects of class education were minimized, and in (b) completing the research by actually returning to check the prediction by a retesting of the next generation of ten-year-olds in the same city.

FIGURE 14–1

Intelligence Related to Number of Children per Family: Urban and Rural Samples

URBAN SAMPLE (CATTELL, 1937a)

I.Q.	SIZE OF FAMILY		NO. OF CASES
160–180	2.33		61 Families
140–160	2.92		112 Families
120–140	2.76		291 Families
100–120	3.00		848 Families
80–100	3.60		1160 Families
60– 80	4.13		368 Families

RURAL SAMPLE (CATTELL, 1937a)

I.Q.	SIZE OF FAMILY		NO. OF CASES
160–180	1.80		5 Families
140–160	2.31		26 Families
120–140	2.62		47 Families
100–120	3.27		115 Families
80–100	3.72		451 Families
60– 80	4.21		159 Families

BURT (1946)

I.Q.	SIZE OF FAMILY	
130–up	2.3	
115–130	2.7	
100–115	3.3	
85–100	3.6	
70– 85	4.2	
up to 70	4.7	

Largely London Data, 1920
Not a culture-fair intelligence test

Note the standard deviation of I.Q. in these urban and rural samples is respectively approximately 21.9 and 36.9 points of I.Q. This is larger than on traditional intelligence tests because, as described in the experiment (Cattell, 1937a; 1951) a culture-fair test was used with the usual larger sigma.

---

[4] The alternative explanation, which must logically be entertained, that larger families environmentally lower the intelligence of the children, does not hold water. Only on crystallized intelligence tests, and especially on vocabulary size, has a slight decline been demonstrated between earlier and later-born children—hypothetically due to later children having a less direct influence from adult vocabulary.

The calculation of population I.Q. change from data gathered in this way is quite complex. The differential birth rate is only one of several determiners of what change shall occur; other principal influences are (Cattell, 1950a):

(1) A differential death rate (before age of reproduction);

(2) A differential celibacy rate (about 70% of girls born were married by age forty in this period);

(3) A differential *completely* barren marriage rate (about one couple in seven were completely childless at this time, and would not have been included in our survey by *children*);

(4) A differential length of generation (later marriage in upper classes effects the calculation if made by time periods);

(5) Differences in completeness of the families we sampled (this causes underestimation of the size of larger families);

(6) Genetic mechanisms notably any dominance effects, which would modify the outcome of the simpler calculation we made at the time. This simpler calculation assumed that the mean of the children of a marriage would resemble the mid-parent value, but regress toward the mean in accordance with the correlation in Table 10–1. Thus, from a frequency distribution for one generation, it is possible to move to a frequency distribution for the next, and so to the new average. The mechanisms that would produce some slight change in the estimation are called by the geneticist epistacy, dominance, linkage, and gene frequencies.

The calculation—a statistical estimate with several unknowns—suffered principally from having no data on death rates in relation to intelligence; the projection from birth rates was therefore given as "tentative," with the shrewd guess that the unknown influences would operate toward restoring the loss in I.Q. (For example, there is indirect evidence that (a) the less intelligent are less frequent among the married, and that (b) death rate tends to be higher in the less intelligent.) The tentative, uncorrected calculation predicted a drop of approximately one point of I.Q. per decade, and, like most unpleasant conclusions, it was attacked in journals and in the popular press. World War II postponed a retest to check on the prediction until 1949 when, with the dedicated help of Diana Millis, a complete retesting of the ten-year-old population of the city was accomplished. The 1949 retesting, done in the same sixty-eight public and private schools as in 1936 (about 5000 children), revealed three interesting facts: (a) The intelligence level had remained unchanged. (I.Q. = 100.487 in 1936; 101.764 or 100.023—according to method of calculation—in 1949. The difference in either case is not significant.) (b) The differential birth rate was, over most of the I.Q. range, still in the negative direction, but *much* smaller. (c) In the upper part of the intelligence range, the dangerous trend had actually reversed itself. Among parents above about I.Q. 115 the more intelligent were having larger families, the less intelligent (but still more than averagely intelligent) were keeping family size proportional to income. This trend had been predicted to occur through planned parenthood when the 1936 test results and full discussions were published (Cattell, *The Fight for Our National Intelligence*, 1937) (see Figure 14–2). The 1949 results actually showed the turn of the tide—at least among citizens of more than average intelligence.

FIGURE 14–2
Evidence of Reversal of Dysgenic Birth Rate in
Upper Intelligence Range of Population

URBAN SAMPLE

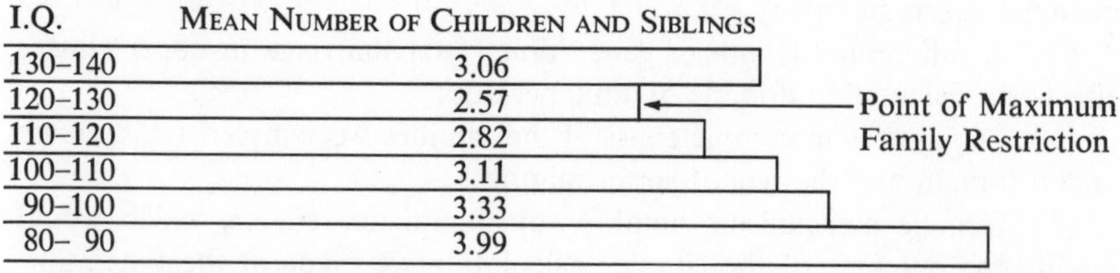

I.Q.	MEAN NUMBER OF CHILDREN AND SIBLINGS	
130–140	3.06	
120–130	2.57	◄———— Point of Maximum
110–120	2.82	Family Restriction
100–110	3.11	
90–100	3.33	
80– 90	3.99	

Sample of 10 year olds (1936b); analysis is on the whole group, approximately 2837 families.

RURAL SAMPLE

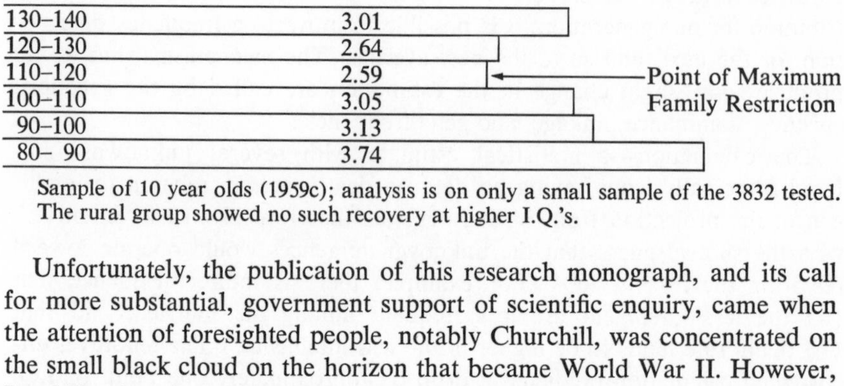

I.Q.	MEAN NUMBER OF CHILDREN AND SIBLINGS	
130–140	3.01	
120–130	2.64	
110–120	2.59	◄———— Point of Maximum
100–110	3.05	Family Restriction
90–100	3.13	
80– 90	3.74	

Sample of 10 year olds (1959c); analysis is on only a small sample of the 3832 tested. The rural group showed no such recovery at higher I.Q.'s.

Unfortunately, the publication of this research monograph, and its call for more substantial, government support of scientific enquiry, came when the attention of foresighted people, notably Churchill, was concentrated on the small black cloud on the horizon that became World War II. However, Lord Horder, the king's physician (see Cattell, 1937a, p. vi) wrote, "The evidence seems overwhelming, from this intensive study of two typical areas, that in this country the birth rate is inversely related to the intelligence level. . . . If we really want to build an A-1 nation, we must take this matter to its logical conclusion and employ the whole machinery of our medical services, not merely for "preventive medicine" in the narrow sense, nor even for 'anti-natal hygiene' but for large scale efforts along eugenic lines." In anticipation of the action research philosophy of thirty years later, a note was added by Charles Darwin's son, "We cannot afford to wait for further, detailed knowledge before beginning to take action, and we must boldly face the risks which will inevitably accompany our proposed reforms." The only heated criticism came from segments of the political press which objected to the view—a mere side-issue from the main argument—that a substantial fraction of the chronically unemployed were unemployable by reason of inadequate ability and/or disabling personality problems. As Serebriakoff sums up, in his incisive book (1966) on social aspects of intelligence: "Not everyone accepted Cattell's view that the decline was so rapid or that there was a decline, but in Professor Burt's memorandum of evidence to the Royal Commission on Population he confirmed that there must be such a trend. Britain's leading medical geneticist, Frazer Roberts, estimated the decline at about one and a half points per generation and both Professor Sir Ronald Fisher and Professor Haldane have agreed with this estimate. There would seem to be few fields where there is greater need for research and for remedial action."

With today's better resources the requisite data could be gathered also to allow for the six modifying factors above and to promote better public understanding of the issues. It is strange, therefore, that at the moment only one new research since then has added to our knowledge, that of Higgins, Reed, and Reed (1962) on the intelligence test records from a small-town, Minnesota high school. The findings concur with those given above in showing a tendency for the positive relation of intelligence and family size to assert itself among the more intelligent, and for a lower marriage and possibly lower survival rate to compensate over the rest of the distribution. However, this study, and a smaller one by Bajema, as well as the present writer's second Leicester experiment, are made in communities which, relative to the countries as a whole, are of good civic morale, with a reputation for prudence and order. (The fact that they went to much trouble to aid and facilitate these researches marks them from the majority of the world's communities.) One can no more draw inferences from these as to what is happening in the world generally than can a student of water pollution draw a *generally* optimistic view from samples of water from the Tweed and the Penobscot Rivers. The Higgins and Reed study, though much quoted for its optimism, is on a particularly small and shaky basis.

The best estimate on this problem as of 1970 is that, during this decade, especially in countries and classes where family planning is not powerfully brought to bear, a drift toward general *diminution* of world resources of better intelligence has not been stopped, and will be sporadically and miserably corrected only by selection through famine and epidemics. In advanced Western cultures, on the other hand, there seems a good prospect that the family-planning values of the middle class will spread effectively into the ranks of the unskilled—at least down to the limiting levels of intelligence and responsibility at which even swallowing a pill is too much. At that point, to maintain a healthy increase of total population, in a country such as the United States, which can afford such an increase, it may even be necessary to encourage four- and five-child families as a norm for parents in the professions and with managerial capacities.

Meanwhile—questions of morale aside—the social scientist must consider several contingencies in regard to the future of the curve of intelligence distribution. In particular he needs—for countries in the world with uncontrolled birth rates—to consider the alternatives of a fall in the *general* average with and without a drop at the upper end of society's intelligence range. If the "bell curve" does *not* shift downward as a whole, problems of inner tension and discontent would be expected (Cattell, 1938c) from the extension of the I.Q. range and the maladaptations of one segment to the cultural complications created by another. If it *does,* then, as Burt has pointed out, a decline of one and one-half points in the average I.Q. per generation would in fifty years, almost halve[5] the number of gifted children at one end and double the number of retarded at the other. This presupposes a freely intermarrying population, such that the gene pool behaves in a typical way and the distribution curve, when certain genes are reduced in frequency, moves as a whole.

A view of intelligence resources would not be complete without noting the implications of the age and sex distributions with respect to intelligence considered in Chapter 7. With better health measures, most countries are experiencing an increase in average age of their population, i.e., the central age is greater and the percentage over, say, 60, is considerably increased. Since the g_f curve declines steeply and the g_c curve stays practically level, this age shift should produce no change in crystallized intelligence but some drop in the former. The probability is that the age decline in g_f is physiologically determined, and due partly to avoidable conditions such as atherosclerosis and anemias. As a practical issue, any medical research that could postpone such deterioration could make a quite substantial contribution to the national average of intelligence. In magnitude it should easily exceed the mean effect of the present extensive expenditure in school attempts to raise the a_g performance level of genetically low g_f individuals, and it certainly deserves a comparable research endowment.

A more delicate issue, perhaps, concerns the community's action on its resources of intelligence in women. On g_f there are no sex differences, and on a_g they are slight and changing with age and situation. In school, girls are apt to be a bit ahead of boys, especially in traditional tests with a heavy a_v (verbal primary) representation; but after 40 there are indications that a_g falls lower in housewives than in their husbands out in the world. In some social classes, and in premechanized homes, there is no doubt that women were too fully occupied to make any contribution outside the home, and that nothing is more important than the intelligent upbringing of children in the home (as important as in the school). Nevertheless classes and epochs have seen lapdog nursing, and bridge-playing, unemployed wives reaching proportions which Dean Inge described as "the largest and least responsible leisure class that history has ever seen." Really high ability in women of 40–70 has often created its own valuable social function; but no survey of community resources of intelligence in times of shortage can overlook that the sexes are equally endowed, but that one pool of ability has been systematically neglected.

---

[5] On an I.Q. sigma of 16, a drop of 3 points in the average would reduce I.Q.'s above the former value of 130 from 3.5% to 1.9% of the population.

4. INTELLIGENCE AND SOME MAJOR SOCIO-POLITICAL PROCESSES

So far, the relation of intelligence to society has been considered largely in terms of the gross totality of intelligence resources. These resources affect the cultural level of society and, in turn, are determined in part by the habits and values of society. Except for the level and direction of crystallized intelligence, determined by the nature of schooling, the culture can affect its resources—the resources of g_f—mainly through birth rate effects, and the control of physical disease. There are other two-way affects, however, than that on the totality of intelligence, namely, effects from distributions of intelligence on various social processes, and from various processes upon the distribution of intelligence. They offer us no single theme, but each requires brief comment if the relations of intelligence to society are to be systematically covered. The topics we shall treat are social status and promotion; drafting the population for emergencies, such as war; political organization processes; unemployment and occupational competence; "hurdle" and assortive mating effects on elites; cultural morale and decline; and relations to economics and education.

That a significant correlation of intelligence and social status exists has long been known. It stands at about 0.3 with traditional, a_g, tests (Vernon, 1965) and about 0.2 with culture-fair, g_f, tests (McArthur and Elley, 1963). Depending on the country, the method of estimating social status, and the age at which it is measured, it seems to vary from about 0.1 to 0.5. Social promotion of ability occurs partly in the stream of the school (about ¾ of Oxford and Cambridge students are scholarship winners from lower middle class homes) and partly on the occupational ladder of adult life. Obviously, any social system which makes these ladders efficient will benefit by using its high ability to good advantage, and one that blocks them will be both inefficient and exposed to disruptive revolutionary pressures. But cautions are necessary even in regard to what the French Revolution demanded as "careers open to talents." So long as school scholarship selection continues to be only on intelligence tests and exams, and ignores the personality measuers important in school work (Cattell and Butcher, 1968) and in later life, its selection is askew. It is likely, for example, to repeat the error of the old Chinese civil service mentality, intelligent but lacking in enterprise and character. Secondly, the end result of fair and efficient promotion (even if it includes the personality traits) is to comb the lower status free of ability.

The latter can be done, as far as living persons are concerned, in one generation, but as far as the genetic distribution across social status is concerned, it may take a long time. Nevertheless, in older societies such as France and Britain, and with at least three generations of increasingly effective school scholarship selection, there are already clear signs that the correlation of child intelligence with parental occupational status is mounting.

The scholarship children, even if picked out by culture-fair intelligence tests, are increasingly from higher-class homes. We even see a paradoxical outcry against meritocracy, and complaints from the political left wing that the "working" class is being drained of its leadership talent. (Men with university degrees, often from the older universities and largely from the middle class, are the predominant leaders in the British Labor Party.) Discontent and injustice are two very different things, and the former is unavoidable in human life. The real weakness of the efficient intelligence selection is that, if society needed to head in a radically different direction, e.g., through new scientific discoveries, the previous placement of all high ability in the establishment makes such a readjustment extremely difficult to bring about. Either the establishment must be educated to a saintlike unselfishness and to a firm creed of readiness to change, or a reserve of high ability should be deliberately kept outside the main axis of promotion.

A successful instance of the latter, though in only a special aspect of society, is encountered in the next process to study—adjustment to an emergency. Through "catastrophes" large and small—from wars to epidemics and economic upsets—the necessity is suddenly created to draft men—more men of high ability—from accustomed paths into new ones. The clearest instance is war, and, as has been pointed out above, battle is a contrived situation in which each side tries to put the highest (and hopefully excessive) demands for adaptability upon the other, so that high g_f becomes extremely important for survival. The part which the intellectual Archimedes played in the defense of Syracuse is legendary, and, to the dismay of those who seek peace in too simple-minded a fashion, support of science by the defenders has increased in the interval.

The psychological problem faced by the military in the emergency of a war is that the small, professional, military group cannot possibly contain as much ability, defined as g_f, as resides in the larger civilian pool. Naturally, at most times and places, the professional has rationalized a tendency to keep this new ability subordinate by claiming that special knowledge is necessary too, and that the military art is not learned in a day. However, in Western cultures beginning in World War I, and increasingly in World War II, a more efficient outlook prevailed in which intelligence tests were used, and rapid promotions made accordingly. (It is interesting to speculate how history might have been changed if the unquestionably talented Hitler had come through World War I as a fulfilled and disenchanted general, instead of a discontented and revolutionary corporal.)

Britain's World War I losses of great poets like Owen and Brooke and great scientists like Moseley need not be deplored simply in terms of their death in comparatively useless roles, since they themselves believed it equally the duty of intelligent and unintelligent men to die for their country, if necessary. But in the rush of recruitment, the positions to which they and thousands like them were almost randomly assigned meant that their extremely high abilities could make no comparable contribution to national survival. Imagine the prolongation of World War II that might have occurred if Fermi, Bethe, Teller, Oppenheimer, Gamow, and others had been drafted to the cookhouse or the regimental band.

The technical story of the—on the whole—remarkably efficient work of psychologists in the various branches of the U.S. armed forces in World War II is too well known to require sketching here. Just as in scholarship selection—only more so—it could, however, have been improved by adding to ability instruments the more developed personality and motivation measures available today, and by more use of culture-fair intelligence tests. The latter is particularly important when the judgmental skills of a_g are less appropriate than usual to this strange new domain, and where a wider range of ages renders the prediction from a_g measures to g_f more erroneous.

A third important area of vital relations of intelligence to social processes is that of politics—as it concerns both the politicians and the voters. Doubt is perennially cast by the latter upon the intelligence of the former, and vice versa. Among the highly skilled professions, that of politics is surely unique in having no professional standard set by a qualifying examination. Bernard Shaw, H. G. Wells, Bertrand Russell—to name but a few earnest writers on the situation—have suggested that at least an intelligence test, and hopefully also an examination in social science should be required as a preliminary to asking for votes. Admittedly, the rough and tumble of politics is itself a powerful selector—but of what? Who knows but that the game of politics would be played much better if the players were selected by other criteria, as they could be in an orderly society.

Compared with the reasonable sample of evidence available on intelligence scores of other professions, little indeed is available on politicians and statesmen. Judging by those included in Terman and Cox's survey of leaders, and sporadic data in studies by the present writer with his Scale III "superior adults" intelligence tests (the traditional, 1933; the culture-fair, 1960) there is little to complain of regarding the intelligence of politicians at the national level. The I.Q.'s center on the same values as for doctors, lawyers, and higher-level teachers. Since an intelligence test can be made more difficult without losing its high correlation with either a_g or g_f by speeding it up a little, there has never been any technical problem with tests for "superior adult levels" in providing a high enough ceiling to outreach any adult yet tested. This seems to be true, at least, for such tests as Roback's measure for superior adults, the Miller Analogies, the two Scale III tests (for a_g; Cattell, 1933) and g_f (The IPAT Culture-Fair) by the present writer. The latter have been tried with Nobel Prize Winners and are used by the Mensa Society in selecting the top 2% of the population for admission to that society.

At any rate, even as research, it would be valuable to know the I.Q.'s of politicians who have affected history. (One surmises, for example, that those of Woodrow Wilson and Churchill would be exceptionally high.) And in practice—though Shaw's idea of a "selected panel" of qualified available politicians may be chimerical—it would still be useful if such testing were treated only as evidence to put before the voters. For it would permit the intelligent citizen to focus his choice far better than he can by looking at the façades fabricated by the publicity agency and the press.

However, the more serious problem in a democracy is almost certainly not so much the ability of the candidate as the intelligence of the voters! It has well been said that "a people gets the government it deserves," and Plato argued that the poor perception of most citizens made any democracy merely a preliminary to the development of a tyranny. Somewhere in the 70 to 100 I.Q. range, depending on the character qualities too, is a group which is almost certainly unable to perceive the subtleties of remote compared to immediate ends, and which can be swayed by any unscrupulous manufacturer of emotional slogans. Here, in the rushes of "activist" mob rule, is a danger as serious as loosely shifting ballast in a storm-tossed vessel. Political education, like any other, can proceed only as far as the intelligence of the "students" will allow. Except in a few gifted societies, intelligent, long-term aims, such as eugenic aims which better only the next generation, or financial aims to maintain a firm currency, have been unable to prevail against unrealistic promises of obvious, immediate gratifications.

Intellectual leaders, like Plato, Shaw, Graham Wallace, Bentham, Mill, and many other wise observers, have proposed restricting the vote to those who pass certain intelligence and educational levels—which, in a refined form, means "weighting" votes by qualification levels. Actually, in this generation, movement has gone in the opposite direction, toward giving votes to less mature age, ability, and responsibility levels. It is the period in which Britain revoked the arrangement whereby a person with a university degree had two votes, one for his local candidate and one for his university M.P., and that in which America and some other countries dropped the voting age to include those still only half-way through secondary education. On the question of using intelligence tests and adjusting the voting age, there is much to be said both ways. Some would cheapen democracy by using a vote frankly as a therapy for discontent, rather than as an aid to wise government. But, insofar as a vote continues to have directive power, a random, unweighted pooling of the judgment of fools and wise men is not the best mechanism for group health and survival. In the more hard-headed areas of scientific, industrial, military, and medical matters where mistakes are costly, group judgments are systematically made to take account of the intelligence and experiential qualifications of the participants. Democracy still has to work out an improvement whereby every stomach counts for a "want," but every head does not count equally in giving technical direction on the best instrumentality for satisfying wants.

A fourth vital issue in any brief survey is that of unemployment and vocational competence. It has already been pointed out and illustrated (for example, in Table 14–1) that wherever intelligence tests have been applied in surveys on sufficient samples—either in specialities of different rank in military organizations and large industries or in society generally

—significant occupational differences have appeared. There exists a regular tendency for the higher occupations (in earnings, status, and complexity), to be occupied by people of higher average intelligence. They also indicate that the unemployed—specifically the chronically unemployed—are lower than the average for all steady occupational groups. (This finding extends, e.g., in the Leicester evidence (Cattell, 1937b) to the children of unemployed, presumably partly by inheritance.) Table 14–1 also reveals that there is a broad spread of intelligence within each occupation, such that the brightest nurses are more intelligent than the less intelligent doctors, and the dullest teachers are less intelligent than the brighter shop assistants.

Do such anomalies argue that there is real misplacement—or some systematic failure of our selection and promotional methods? To some extent yes, for it remains true today that much placement is close to random, and that, as Pascal complained in the seventeenth century, "Le hasard en dispose." Nevertheless, even good vocational guidance and selection with modern psychological aids would not lead to a complete reduction of overlaps of occupation in intelligence. For, as has been stressed constantly in these pages, e.g., in regard to achievement and creativity, the specification equation tells us that other characteristics, especially personality source traits, may be as important as intelligence for successful job performance. If, according to the specification equation for success in a job (see page 405), the *summed* values of ability and personality scores were plotted for all persons in a given occupation, we should almost certainly find a much *narrower* spread of the final competence figure than Table 14–1 presents for intelligence alone.

In this connection, the psychologist needs to take notice of what has been called "the hurdle effect." If we look as psychological test results in a group of people who have passed a given hurdle, e.g., a difficult examination or the qualification for a competitive profession, we may actually expect a *negative* relation among the required "virtues." For example, persistence and intelligence may be *inversely* related in the group of students who have succeeded in hurdling a difficult examination, since the bright can "make it" without needing to be persevering, and those with great powers of work can make it without being brilliant. Positive qualities of ability and personality may be slightly positively correlated in the general population, but negatively correlated *within* subgroups, due to the hurdle effect. These changing correlations have sometimes been a puzzle to the psychology student, but are clarified by "hurdle selection."

Another failure of perception—or "illusion" if one will—to which psychologists, like everyone else, are subject, might be called "unicausal thinking." The multivariate experimental psychologist, in contrast to the classical experimental psychologist (which latter some departments still persist in calling *the* experimental psychologist), operates with several causal variables at once, not just manipulating one at a time. Consequently, he succeeds in keeping in his mind's eye several interacting causes for any phenomenon in nature. Unless he is so trained, the student of any one cause, be it learning, creative fluency, or intelligence, is apt to forget the other contributors. In particular, as emphasized in the opening paragraph of this book, the guidance psychologist in schools has been apt to think of intelligence tests only, and omit personality and motivation. He and others have even been inclined to think of it, not only as the sole contributor, but as the only excellence. Perhaps there is always a tendency, when thinking of one excellence, to consider it the *only* excellence. A society is formed (Mensa, for example) to contain only the top two percent of the population by intelligence. "The top," in this specific sense, quickly becomes considered to be the top in some more general sense, and discussion soon succumbs to talking of them as "the best people in our society." If any abbreviation of statement in these pages has lent itself to such a possible inference, let it be forthwith corrected. In one group of recognized "intelligentsia" (which must be nameless) tested by the present writer, the 16 P.F. revealed a rather high representation of neurotic and misfit personalities. Some other aspects of an intelligentsia are discussed below under education; but this group beloved of newspaper leading-article writers is cited here to illustrate (a) the danger of making one excellence *the* excellence, and (b) that occupational selection is not only for positive powers, but for deficiencies which have caused the person to fail in other occupations. Members of the Bloomsbury and Greenwich Village "intelligentsia," and the hangers-on around a few creative writers and artists on the Parisian left bank, often merit on intelligence tests the label "intelligentsia," but conspicuously lack the realistic personality qualities that make other very intelligent persons effective scientific researchers, statesmen, surgeons, teachers, and creators of big businesses and public services.

Nevertheless, in society as a whole (as contrasted with subgroups subject to the "hurdle effect," producing negative correlations *within* special groups) the correlation of intelligence and most other "virtues" does tend to be somewhat positive. One can see this partly as environmentally produced, through the more intelligent tending to start in and to seek a better environment in value terms, but it also could have systematic genetic causes. A genetic component in this association (covariance) needs to have, for its full action, the conditions provided by a socially effective social status hierarchy. Let us suppose that higher intelligence and higher ego strength (emotional stability) are each, separately, conducive to social promotion. Then, in some higher-status group, there will be some individuals who have "arrived" largely by intelligence, while others will have succeeded more through their above-average ego strength. Marriage, even in such democracies as America and Britain, tends to be mostly within the individual's socially interacting occupational and social stratum. It is, in any case, *assortive* in terms of individual tastes, i.e., the more intelligent prefer the more intelligent, and so on. Thus, the offspring of a higher-status marriage may tend to bring together (insofar as intelligence and ego strength have genetic components) above-average values on both, and conversely at the bottom of the social scale. There will also be some tendency

for acquired good qualities to go together through purely family and class *environmental* reasons. What evidence yet exists definitely supports this theory of a slight positive correlation of "desirables," and some of the positive association discussed above (page 366) between intelligence, conscientiousness, etc., could have this social and genetic, as well as the individual environmental origin.

Fisher, who has offered us the most penetrating discussion of this issue available, in his *Genetical Theory of Natural Selection* (1930) pointed, however, to at least one sinister connection. He showed that, since low fertility is an aid to social climbing (in six generations of only children, the wealth of $2^6 = 64$ families converges on one person), whatever genetic causes operate for infertility get tied to intelligence and emotional stability. (The association would arise also, less reliably, on the environmental side, if we consider that family attitudes and values are systematically handed down.) Let us add to Fisher's generalization the observation that social climbing does not occur *only* through good qualities. Greed, dishonesty, neglect of social and altruistic duties, and, in authoritarian regimes, a cruel and ruthless disposal of rivals, are the "cheating" ways to success in the game of social competition. The character of an "aristocracy," therefore, in its sense of the quintessence of the upper strata, is only as good as the ethical and selective conditions of the society in which it has arisen. A meritocracy, i.e., promotion as far as possible by sheer merit in achievement and creativity, is, in this respect, a definite advance on an aristocracy. For there is obviously a sense in which, in an unbridled poltical struggle such as prevails in the Mafia, the "cream of the crop" is also the "scum" of the melting pot. And since, in even the best communities we can devise, the conditions for promotion are never perfect (at best they still favor the person abnormally preoccupied with eminence at the expense of service), a governing class is never simply a best possible selection of the community's resources of desirable traits.

In hereditarily rigid societies like that of prerevolutionary France and doctrinally rigid societies like postrevolutionary Russia, the power group will accumulate in its ranks some peculiar psychological selections, such that progress occurs only through sloughing it off, as a growing insect or reptile does with its skin casing. In flexible societies, the pattern of the selected group is continuously being replaced by that of a new breed. Indeed, history shows that in more tolerant, flexible societies (on the "vertebrate" model), such as in Britain and Scandinavia (which have continuously opened their "aristocracies" to any talent) or in the continuously mobile and reconstituted classes of America, intelligence and other desirable qualities constantly flow into the upper and governing groups.

Apart from the effect of this "law of contamination" in regard to the qualities of an aristocracy, the main scientific objection to hereditary aristocracy is a genetically simpler one. It resides in Galton's law of filial regression to the mean—the fact that a correlation of only about 0.5 in intelligence exists between father and son. The offspring of a brilliant father, of

I.Q. 150 is likely, as seen in Chapter 10, to reach an I.Q. of only 125. Or, stated in other terms, the *within*-family variation in heredity is typically about the same magnitude as that *between* families (page 258 above), so that a system for rigid transmission of power by primogeniture does not make much sense. (Incidentally, many who, on the other hand, resist accepting the role of heredity, now so clearly demonstrated for many mental traits, are confusing the idea of between-family heredity variation, the role of which they wish to minimize, with *within*-family heredity variation, which they recognize readily enough in their own children.) However, the heredity of a whole inbreeding *group* nevertheless breeds more true than that of a single family. Consequently, the objection to preassigning opportunity and status to a whole class cannot be so well sustained by obvious genetic principles. If an objection exists, it is more subtle than this simple rule that variations within offspring of a family are as important as those between families. The only visible, genetically based objection stems from that "law of contamination"—the tendency to biased and deleterious associations of promotion—in the original selection of the group.

Some sociopolitical processes, on which distributions and levels of intelligence have a bearing, are vaster and vaguer than those encapsuled above. One that is nevertheless of vital importance is the relation of intelligence to morale. The notion that lower and untutored intelligences are better fed and more health-protected in a higher intelligence group, but are nevertheless more frustrated, has been introduced in connection with discussing the relationship between delinquency and lower intelligence. Delinquency is only one symptom and itself has other causes too, but there can be little doubt that, when the range of intelligence deviation gets very wide, sympathy fails between the two extremes and there is a tendency for the intelligent to create cultural complexities and standards that are bewildering and frustrating to the subnormal. More specific theories on this issue have been set out by the present writer elsewhere (1937b, 1938c) and are discussed on a more philosophical basis in Freud's *Civilization and Its Discontents*. The emphasis in the former is on the effect of large standard deviation, as by cultural standards being set by the creativity of a certain intelligence distribution, followed by a high breeding rate at the lower level which produces a group out of tune with the culture. But the alternative process is also recognized in the theories, namely, that in which assortive mating lengthens the deviation at the upper end of the I.Q. range (where it is likely to occur most strongly) and leads to new cultural growth and complication. In either case, if we believe in social progress, the tensions and frustrations of simpler ergs, and the dissonance of values, require a reduction of the "tail" by birth control and education.

A different, but historically equally frequent process is that in which there is a loss of morale at the upper end of the intelligence distribution— as expressed in the mixture of lack of faith in the culture, despair, and sybaritic self-indulgence which is evident in the writings of cultured, intelligent persons in the declining years of the Roman Empire. This abdication

of leadership has characteristically been accompanied also by a failure to breed (as in the decay of preliterate cultures encountering Western cultures, and in animals kept in captivity or under crowding and stress conditions). In man this failure to breed may not appear primarily as biological, but may be expressed or rationalized as reaction to economic complexities or changes in social mores. How much high intelliegnce, of the kind needed for good organization on a national scale, was lost from the Roman Empire in the recorded dying-out of the leading classes can in part be realized from the succeeding Dark Ages. Although the other aspects of this repeating story of cultural decline go deeper, on the one hand into emotional adjustments, on the other into organizational aspects of the social system per se, yet one root of this change can certainly be understood in terms of our concept of crystallized intelligence.

A culture in a state of high morale goes far in developing a particular crystallized pattern, appropriate to its needs. It does not leave the available, native, fluid intelligence uninvested, but develops it to the utmost possible level of resultant a_g. Conversely, when morale is low, the a_g level declines, and finally even the g_f level falls from the birth rate effects noted above. The biology of human beings is tied even to the most abstract values.

Much progress and cultural trial-and-error is less dramatic than these examples, known through Gibbon's *Decline and Fall of the Roman Empire* or Prescott's *Conquest of Mexico,* but involves the minor deaths of cultural and biological subpatterns as studied by Darlington (1969). Crystallized intelligence, in the leading schools of Britain and some other European countries in the 18th and 19th centuries, meant primarily Latin and Greek grammar, literature, and history. The governing class of Victorian times had its intellectual flowering in rhetoric and its finest judgmental skills in classical history, but knew virtually nothing of the physical and biological sciences. Even Churchill, a generation later, needed his Professor Lindemann to lead him slowly to the implications where, had his youthful intelligence crystallized in that field, he would have taken profound insights in his swift stride. It is possible—even probable from the data of Heron—that to some degree a class died also biologically with the passing of the Victorian pattern. But, in any case, our understanding of sociopolitical processes needs to recognize that the crystallized a_g pattern is probably shifting constantly in level and direction with the morale and vitality of communities, and that there is a constant causal feedback interaction of crystallized intelligence, fluid intelligence, and the morale of a culture.

5. INTELLIGENCE AND LIVING STANDARDS: THE PSYCHO-ECONOMIC THEORIES OF ABILITY DISLOCATION AND SHIFT

Of the social interactions with intelligence set out for study at the start of the last section, economics and education remain to be examined. Since economics—or at least occupational life—goes far to delineate the adult activities for which education prepares us, it needs prior treatment. At the time when the present writer was a university student, it was fashionable for the intellectual world to look with irritated disdain on the industrialist, the entrepreneur, and the commercial executive, and with deeper but more benevolent disdain on blue-shirted men with hammers and sickles. The arrogance of intelligence and immaturity in the bright student was fostered by the stereotypes in universities where a medieval curriculum, begotten at the time when the line between students and vagabonds was thin, held no place for the social and behavioral sciences, business management, engineering, and the sciences of administration. According to a writer surveying European universities in a 1970 issue of a leading scientific journal, the situation has not altered much, and the behavior of the more violent students on our campuses in the same year suggest the same separation from the realities of creation. Nevertheless, an appreciation of the unrivalled intellectual challenges in technology is dawning. From scientific farming, to education, medicine, and big business, the applied studies have developed an increasing intellectual content, theoretical fascination, and practical challenge. The pedant's disdain of technology, industry, and commerce has become vestigial and obsolete. It is fine for the 10,000[th] man to build himself defenses from immediate pressures, that basic research and theory may receive his whole attention, but there is no point in having ten times as many shrines as geniuses.[6]

The issue of values among the highest group in I.Q. is important, because the sense of many findings in "group dynamics" is that the productive capacity of the group (and therefore its real standard of living) depends far less on the ability level of the average worker than on the levels of the upper ranges of ability recruited to leadership (morale being constant). It is not surprising to find that the *enlightened affluence* level[7] (page 453) is low in those countries (of which some South American and Indian communities are examples) where society consists of peasants and of intelligentsia interested only in nontechnological professions (see Myrdal, 1968).

---

[6] This would still mean 20,000 pure scientists in the United States, roughly one-fifteenth of all registered scientists. Cross-cultural comparisons (to which Russia *may* be an exception (but see the "affluence" factor on page 454 above) show that the actual prosperity and vigor of universities, and the available support for research, particularly in new and promising fields, is greatest in societies where no apology is made for technological interest or for private enterprise in industry and commerce, and where the prestige of demonstrated excellence in the managerial arts is high. In Britain, and even more so in some Mediterranean cultures of strong classical affiliations, it is almost *de rigeur* for the academic man to look down upon his brother in applied science. Yet as indicated by the number of Nobel Prizes in the United States and the flight of scientists from Britain and Continental countries to the United States, these attitudes are out of touch with the organic realities of healthy cultural development.

[7] Countries with high output, with universities which do not expect professors to live wholly on outside consultation, with more fellowship-supported students, with stronger support to scientific research, continue to be those in which the prestige of the managerial, business-inventive, and technological man is at least as high as that of the

As areas of creativity constantly shift with changing values, a wise society will periodically question how realistic the current interests are. Unless the values foster the recruitment, by selection and education, of enterprising "entrepreneurial" types, any cultural productivity which depends on massive cooperation of many disciplines—space exploration, medicine, and geophysics—must lose vitality. Furthermore, in "applied" as distinct from "pure" research, success depends on the existence of a very able, but not "top I.Q." group of *supportive* individuals, themselves highly trained, e.g., computer operators, technicians, etc. The threat of failure appears again unless *this* group receives recruits of adequate g_f from an appropriate birth supply, and of adequate a_g and training levels from good channels of selection and education. Some countries seem to be in a chronic state of deprivation at this level. However, the main thesis above is that economic productivity is determined most of all by the particular levels reached in the upper executive and planning levels. Except for results in miniature with group dynamics experiments, this thesis is not easy to demonstrate with scientific conclusiveness, because it depends upon ongoing social processes that cannot be manipulated for the sake of experiment. However, the history of invention in technical fields, as by the introduction of the steam engine and the power loom, in organizational fields, as in Henry Ford's subsequently much-imitated innovations, and in distribution facilities, as by the eighteenth century use of canals and the twentieth century use of the airplane, suggests that real wealth is most dependent on the activities of a few at the near-genius level.

The specters which have haunted community well-being since the early days of the industrial revolution (and in less obvious ways, much earlier) are those of chronic unemployment and of uncontrollable cycles of expansion and depression. The economic remedies proposed for these, from Adam Smith, through Marx and Keynes, to the latest economic theories, can be applied only at the cost of unforeseen or unwanted changes in political freedom, cultural vitality, and much else. A social psychologist is entitled to the conviction that this springs from treating symptoms only, an approach which might be expected from a science—economics—which sets out to study "exchange behavior" in isolation from principles of total behavior. For example, one can see that psychological upsets result from attempts to solve unemployment by creating special, unnecessary work—the awareness of which damages the individual's sense of personal worth.

Increasing application of automation and cybernetics is accompanied usually by relative unemployment in lower skill ranges. Some econo-

"intelligentsia" and the handworker. Incidentally, T. S. Ashton, in *The Industrial Revolution* (1948), describes how strongly in the expansive Victorian era of the British culture, the values here described prevented the artificial academic-nonacademic split into which universities tended later to degenerate. "Inventors, contrivers, industrialists, and entrepreneurs—it is not easy to distinguish one from the other at a period of rapid change—came from every social class and from all parts of the country." "[Leading] physicists, chemists . . . were in intimate contact with the leading figures in British industry."

mists and "social reformers" suggest that this unemployment should be artificially spread over the community under the more palatable title of leisure. The economist who views "work" as an undesired burden, accepted to earn subsistence and leisure, is likely to be surprised at the indignant objections that the psychologist can foresee arising against enforced leisure. The craftsman, the scientist, the bus driver, or airpilot who enjoys his vehicle, the artist, the competitive and creative manager—all these will want to go on with their real business rather than play games. Even for those who welcome it, leisure beyond a moderate dosage creates many problems. A flexible system of a half-week of serious work, with an option on diversions for the rest, decided according to psychological needs, is very different from fixing leisure by the "accidental" needs for economic adjustments. Wholehearted activity in the great adventure of exploring space, for example, is more meaningful than hours spent daily before a TV. Unfortunately, what may decide the matter for the economist is the need to adjust the whole system, regardless of the interests of the active half of the community, by catering to the abilities and qualification levels of the other half. If more people should have abilities that permit them more easily to dig ditches than to build airplanes (after training), the politically oriented economist may back legislation for more ditches, though the need at the consumer end may be for airplanes.

These thoughts lead to complex philosophical issues beyond the present book. But those elements in the problem which hinge on the study of abilities lead us to scrutinize employment in present world conditions in terms of an admittedly simplified, but still real, model. In this model we can refer either to the g_f or a_g distribution. It would be more correct, since the discussion concern adults educated in the culture, to deal with the latter. The argument will be simpler, and will remove certain objections, however, if we suppose an ideal system of education in which every individual is raised to the fullest a_g expression relative to his g_f. Thus, our equation in which g_f and e, educational experience, are additive, would consider $e = cg_f$ where c is some constant. With this relation we start with a normal g_f distribution and end with a normal a_g distribution, in which the rank of the individuals is unchanged. However, the subsequent argument is not changed in essentials if we go to a random relation of g_f to education, though the determination of rank order of "fitness" by g_f will not be so precise. Actually, in terms of the model settled upon in Chapters 6 and 11, i.e., independence of g_f and e, the relation will be a little more complex, for we must now suppose that a person's job role complexity level, which we will call r, is a function of his crystallized intelligence level and his training time, t, and that his crystallized intelligence level, as in Table 6–4, is an additive function of his g_f and the effectiveness of his education, e. Thus:

$$r = t(a_g + g_f) = t[(g_f + e) + g_f] \tag{14.1}$$

to which we may add an x for the accidents of life.

$$r = t(2g_f + e) + x. \tag{14.2}$$

But in an educational system where free scholarships and selection to class streams purely according to merit place every individual in a learning situation appropriate to his ability, e would be made proportion to g_f, and t in any case quickly reaches a limit of occupational training time at which all must stop, so that r will finish, in these circumstances, close to a linear function of g_f.

So much for the distribution of the *supply* of intelligence: but what about the cultural *demand?* Although there is no guarantee, even in a long-settled culture, that the jobs and roles it regards as necessary will be nicely adjusted to fit everyone's biological capacities, as in the upper part of Figure 14–3, there is a high probability of such an adjustment. For the initial occupations are in fact those invented by the members of the culture (and their ancestors) by direct self-expression, i.e., of what they actually find it feasible to do. This gives the relationship of supply and demand distribution shown in the upper part of Figure 14–3. Dislocation of curves S

FIGURE 14–3
Supply and Demand Curves of Intelligence

(1) Stable State

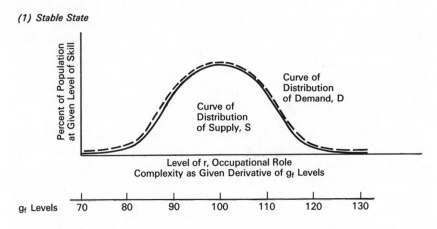

(2) Present Two-Way Dislocation

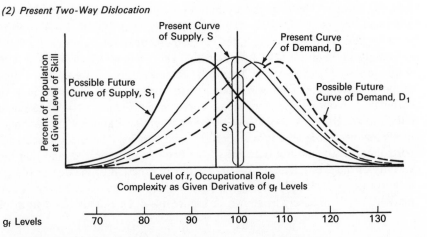

and D—supply and demand for capacity—may begin with the growing implementation and accumulation of inventive products. In the industrial and automation revolutions, the complications become such that the dislocation has at certain periods—especially present times—become very great.

In previous discussion it has been illustrated how the dislocation of S and D could arise from either of two distinct causes. There could be a change in the biologically given distribution curve, through new birth or survival rates operating on different parts of the S curve, or there could be a change in the demand curve through invention and culturally complicating changes. Whatever the detailed causes, we have to deal with a possible misfit of two distinct curves, arising from two largely independent determiners of distribution as shown in the lower part of Figure 14–3. By economic incentives and other ways of influencing family planning, a wise society *can* hope to bring about a coordination of the biological (S) to the cultural demand (D) curve at least within the space of one or two generations. But unless S is adjusted to D or the cultural demand is controlled by a "moratorium" on invention (another name for "machine wrecking"), there is nothing to stop the development of all kinds of dislocation between the two curves, as shown in the lower part of Figure 14–3. It is not easy to quantify, with present crude approaches, exactly what is happening to the D curve, but in regard to S, the general evidence suggests, as seen in Section 3 above, that in some parts of the world a discrepancy is systematically being produced by birth rates skewing the supply curve to a lower average. If, at the same time, rapid invention changes the D curve upward, then, indeed, circumstances have "ganged up" on society to increase the S-D gap dangerously.

Since the laws of supply and demand which fix the price of goods tend also to fix the wages for services, the amount that has to be paid to get services at various levels of skill will be a function of the discrepancy of the S and D curves at that level. Thus since there might, for example, be twice as many people available for unskilled factory work as there is demand for factory goods, and only half as many qualified doctors as people need, people would be willing to pay much more per hour to the latter than the former. The discrepancy may be expressed as a ratio by drawing a vertical line as at I.Q. 100, where the D/S ratio in Figure 14–4 is given as .86. This D/S ratio is plotted against occupational complexity level separately in Figure 14–4. Just how this ratio would translate itself into wages in a free market can be left to the economist, but if we take a simple proportionality, and then work out a distribution curve for frequency of earnings, we obtain the nonnormal curve as in Figure 14–4(2). Such a curve, in which many people live at a low wage level and few at very high levels has been frequent across countries and epochs. The theory here suggests that it is the natural outcome of the two causes indicated, and that the severity of the skewedness in 14–4(2) will be a function of the degree of dislocation in 14–2(3). The literal economic outcome may not be the "open market" result precisely as shown in Figure 14–4(2). For the final form of the economic return for people and services, as distinct from goods is, of course, determined by humanitarian and political considerations, in which economists, trade unions, and sundry government departments play a role. (Nevertheless, the Soviet Union, in order to make hard study and stressful managerial positions more attractive, raised the real wage maximum differential from the original 10 to 1 to 50 to 1 within one generation after the workers' revolution.) However, these interferences do not negate the fundamental law; they merely pass the maladjustment on into more devious expressions, e.g., inflation and shortages.

The ingenuity of the economists may be said to have postponed recognition of the fact that the most important factor is people—the distribution of intelligence in the people. For the rest of what economics deals with, the rule is allowed to hold that what is valuable and useful will be produced in

FIGURE 14–4
Effect of Supply and Demand on Distribution of Earning Rates

*(1) Ratio of Demand to Supply : Price.***

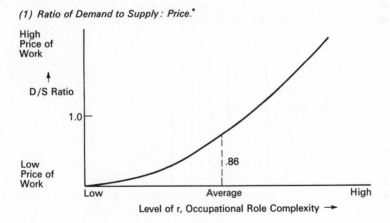

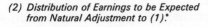

*(2) Distribution of Earnings to be Expected
from Natural Adjustment to (1).***

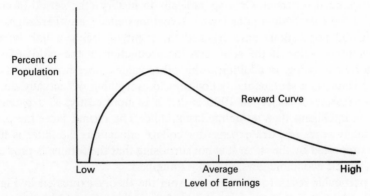

*These curves are illustrative, not based on any exact data.

(3) Ratio of Demand to Supply, i.e., Price of Earning Rate.

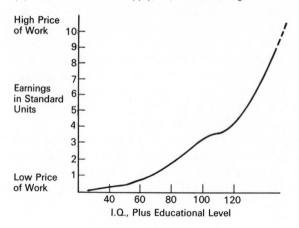

*(4) Distribution of Earnings to be Expected
   from Natural Economic Adjustment of (3) to (1).*

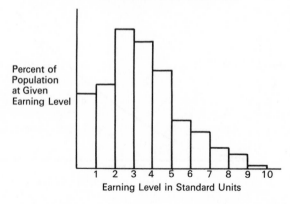

proportion to the demand for it. No arrangements whatever have been considered by government for connecting the supply of various ability levels to the demand for them. Only sporadically in history (the period of enactment of the Elizabethan poor laws is sometimes cited) are there signs that foresighted populations have reached the point of seeing a link between the economic value of the adult and the production of the child. (To say that a human being, in addition to his other values, does not have an economic value, is a sentimentality contrary to everything we actually do.) A sinister feature of society in 1970 is that it is more costly, as a parent, to have an intelligent than an unintelligent child. The former faces the parent with many years of extra expense for college education; the latter is likely to be supported by the state. It is not surprising that the former is produced, by inevitable economic laws, in smaller numbers.

A particular result to be expected from the theory expressed in Figures 14–3 and 14–4 is that the appearance of dislocation from either cause will produce a pool of permanently unemployed—or, at least, what would normally appear as such. It may not appear immediately and directly at the lower intelligence level where the supply·most grievously exceeds demand, but so long as an employer takes the better qualified employee, there persists an occupational game of "musical chairs" in which unemployment is passed down the line to appear most persistently at the lowest intelligence level. (Assuming, of course, that employees are willing to migrate and employers are ready to employ without prejudice.)

Without getting at the root of the problem, our society has drifted into the position that since humanitarian considerations do not allow people to be unpaid, those who do not meet the demand curve are paid to do nothing. This creates the anomalous situation in which the greatest leisure is given to the least intelligent and least educated. A pleasant phrase like "Work is for machines; thinking is for people" is dangerously wrong in both terms. First, even with all the automation in the world, much work will always remain. We quoted above Edison's "Invention is 1 percent inspiration and 99 percent perspiration," and it is likely that creative people will always be fully extended to the point of stress. And in any case, for the services of such as dentists, power plant engineers, garbage collectors, nurses, university administrators, and mothers, there is always more work than can be done. There are two reasons for rejecting a system which inevitably culminates in giving the greatest leisure to people with no fondness or capacity for thinking. First it is a waste so to place leisure, and secondly, the boredom of those who have nothing to do could boil bloody.

An interesting second lemma on the intelligence supply theorem deals with business cycles. The volume of writing by economists on this issue fills whole libraries, but again, little of it does justice to the fact that economics is a branch of psychology. At a purely empirical level, such investigation has at least indicated that a variety of wave lengths exist from depression to depression. The oscillations named spread from the 40 to 50-year cycle of Kondratieff through the old Juglar 7 to 9-year cycle, to the brief 3⅓-year cycle of Kitchin, as well as to some cycles peculiar to particular markets. Without any detailed argument for a particular cycle, we may yet see in the ability dislocation theory, a delayed feedback mechanism. (For it is delayed feedback systems that are often responsible for cycle phenomena *per se.*)

When business prospers, more people will be employed from the lower range. At the same time, due to prosperity, more managerial leaders at the upper boundary of the ability range will be able to retire and devote themselves to cultural good works, art, or just nothing at all. In the shift to Phase 2 (see Figure 14–5) the productive capacity characteristic respectively of the people newly included at the lower level and the people newly excluded at the upper will tend to reduce the efficiency of production, for the first would be expected to be below average and the second above. Consequently the real price of goods tends to rise, and less frequent purchases and declining business bring a return to Phase 1. Similar theories have been proposed, notably with respect to plant efficiency, money, and market conditions, but the *ability shift theory* as propounded thirty years ago in *psychological* journals (Cattell, 1937b) does not appear to have made its way into economists' writings—so fabulously high are the walls among academic specialties.

FIGURE 14–5
Illustrating the Ability-Shift Theory of Business Cycles

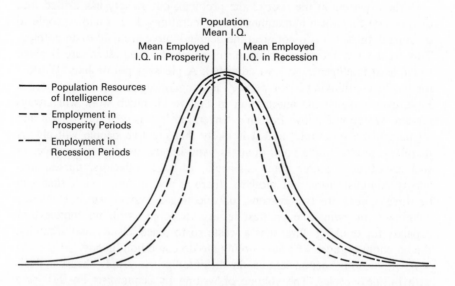

The "dislocation" concept is so vital to all three of the above psychosocial inferences (wages, unemployment, business cycles) that, ideally, more exact determinations should be presented for alleged changes in the D and S curves. What is known about the S curve changes has been given in Sections 2 and 3 above, and, although in Britain one might infer hopefully that it is on the way up, the probability in many countries lacking such widespread birth control centers is that a bulge is developing at the lower levels. In regard to the upward trend on the S curve, the argument has depended so far simply on the general observation that technology gets more complex, e.g., that diagnosing trouble in a car is more complex than finding what went wrong with a cart. However, much detailed evidence exists from which one might quote virtually at random, that between 1911 and 1951, Britain's census showed professional and administrative workers increasing from 5.3% to 11.2%; the foreman and clerical from 6.1% to 12.9%; and skilled handworkers falling from 68.6% to 55.9%.

Various features of what has been rather coarsely stated in Equations (14.1) and (14.2) above also deserve more attention and research. Our assumption has been stated that both e and t level off at some limit—at least at a limit set by resources of time and money for education and occupational training. Nevertheless, how *big* is e, relative to $2g_f$ in (14.2)? A figure of 15% to 20% of the variance, relative to that of g_f, has been reached in terms of individual difference determination, but what of determination of the average of the population, in successive generations?

The data of Tuddenham, Thomson, and Finch, discussed in Chapter 10, leaves no doubt that a significant upward shift of a_g occurred in the early part of this century, perhaps of three or four points of I.Q. in Britain and eight to twelve in America. However, as has been pointed out, this is in the main adaptation to a particular culture (in which, nevertheless, the universal culture of mathematics, among others, is embedded). At least one can say that it is no more remote from the present needs of the culture than targets fixed by the preceding generation are bound to be. In the main, the store of judgmental skills made available through the individual's g_f working on the school curriculum helps the S curve considerably. Nevertheless, despite devoted teachers and unstinting taxpayers, there is a limit to the augmentation of level possible for the general population on these judgmental skills. Most of the possible rise may, indeed, already have been accomplished in the last two generations. First, there is a limit to learning time and teaching efficiency, and secondly, there is a limit to the level of judgmental skills that can be taught to any given fluid intelligence level. Like Pavlov's unhappy puppies, who were conditioned to expect food when an ellipse and not a circle was presented, and were reduced to howling madly when the distinction of these shapes became too fine, tomorrow's students of the teaching machine must come to a limit of judgment fixed by their fluid ability.

With this overview, in Sections 4 and 5, we must conclude pursuit of the broader socio-economic and political give and take of intelligence and social processes and begin to ask more technical questions, notably, in Section 7; what available psychological tools and treatments—in the realm of intelligence—can effect the school system itself?

6. TECHNICAL CONDITIONS AND PRACTICAL EFFECTS OF TESTING PROGRAMS IN SCHOOLS AND OCCUPATIONS

Most of what psychologists know about intelligence in relation to education has been incorporated into everyday parent-teacher discourse already familiar to most readers. Some popularly accepted concepts, however, based on uncritical research, need revision; other parts of modern educational lore have been overdiscussed to the point where the distinction between essentials and nonessentials has been lost. Wherever we deal with an essential and well-established finding about intelligence in schools, it can stand up to expression in quantitative equations. (See the specification equations such as 12.1, 12.2, and Table 6–2, Figures 7–3 and 7–5.) Such equations have stated that school achievement is a complex outcome of particular ability, personality, and motivation source traits in the individual, and of certain types of environmental experiences. With the suggestion that these summary equations may in fact contain more than is at first seen, we will leave them to tell their tale.

Any question concerning the effective use of ability measures *per se* in schools must address itself first to good technical standards in the testing, and secondly to the proper use of the reliable information from a good test in various aspects of education. In the testing field, in the light of the research findings presented in chapters above, the practical issues become: (1) should school psychologists now set out to measure two intelligences, g_f and a_g, instead of one as formerly, and (2) whether personality and motivation should not be as carefully appraised as ability. In the use of test results we encounter such controversial issues as the grouping of students according to intelligence level, and weighing the motivation and moral effects connected with a student's being informed (or not informed) of his own psychological performances. These issues are not unrelated. Thus, any adaptive streaming must be conducted on a scientifically rational basis, not on the muddled concept of the traditional intelligence test I.Q., so that the requirement of two I.Q. measures is already endorsed in that case.

Virtually everyone would agree that, if intelligence testing is to be used —whether it be for scholarship selection, direction to appropriate schools, vocational counselling, analysis of causes of backwardness, clinical examination of brain damage, or anything else—it must (1) be such as to yield the most accurate possible quantitative value, with a definable known degree of inaccuracy, and (2) be properly understood conceptually by the psychologist and the client. In regard to both of these, we must now enter on some technical discussion of test properties, such as occupy much of the attention of that psychological specialist we call a psychometrist.

An intelligence test, like any other psychological test, can have a *validity evaluation* and a *consistency evaluation*. Validity can be *concrete* or *conceptual*, according to whether the correlation which evaluates it is made with some particular single measure (job or school achievement, income, an older intelligence test) or with a uniquely determined factor defining a construct or concept. (A concept can be quantified by various other formulae, but in the psychological field these are generally pointless unless the concept is first demonstrated to be a unitary entity.) In the case of an intelligence test, agreement with any concrete criterion is scarcely a validity but rather a *relevance,* since there is no single *concrete* (particular) performance with which intelligence *should* correlate perfectly. The conceptual (construct) validity of intelligence tests is the only rock on which they can stand. No one has yet found any logically and mathematically satisfactory avenue to evaluate concept validity except by correlating the given test with a uniquely defined and indicated general cognitive ability factor. When properly executed, this gives us exactly what we want to know. However, let us remember that, in the case of a culture-fair test, the referent is properly the *fluid* ability factor, g_f, while with most traditional tests, the conceptual target has clearly been the crystallized ability factor, a_g.

The correlations (validity coefficients) of tests and subtests with the appropriate, distinct, general factors are shown for (a) a culture-fair (fluid intelligence) and (b) a traditional (crystallized intelligence) test—both well-known tests—in Table 14–3. With allowance for a slightly shorter times in the WAIS subtests, they reach about the same figures.

TABLE 14–3
The Conceptual (Construct) Validities of Culture-Fair and Traditional Intelligence Tests [1]

LOADINGS (SATURATIONS) OF TESTS ON THE GENERAL INTELLIGENCE FACTORS: g_f AND a_g

(i) Culture Fair (The IPAT Scale 3: Adult)

American Sample (200 Undergraduates) on IPAT Scale 3	Factor Loading on g_f	German Sample (300 Business Schl. Studs.) on Same Test [2]	Factor Loading on g_f
Form A	.84	Form A	.86
Form B	.83	Form B	.91
Full Test (A + B)	.96	Full Test (A + B)	.97

Validities of Eight Culture Fair Subtests ($2\frac{1}{2}$ to 3 minutes each) on g_f.

Series A	Class A	Matr. A	Topol. A	Series B	Class B	Matr. B	Topol. B
58	56	67	51	70	53	63	56

[1] See Tables 12–1, 12–2, and Figure 14–1 for Concrete Validities.
[2] Data from Rudolf Weiss, Die Branchbarkeit des Culture Free Intelligence Tests Skala 3 (CFT 3) bei Begabungspsychologischen Untersuchungen. Unpublished doctoral dissertation, University of Würzburg, 1968.

(ii) More Traditional Test (The WAIS) [3]

Subtest	Loading on a_g	Subtest	Loading on a_g
Information	83	Digit Symbol	65
Comprehension	72	P. Completion	75
Arithmetic	71	Block Design	70
Similarities	77	P. Arrangement	70
Digit Span	62	O. Assembly	64
Vocabulary	83		

[3] J. Cohen, "The Factorial Structure of the WAIS between Early Childhood and Old Age," *Journal of Consulting Psychology*, 121, 1957, 283–290. Copyright 1957 by the American Psychological Association, and reproduced by permission.

(iii) Cross-cultural Concrete Validation

(a) Equality of Score across Racio-cultural Groups

Test		*Chinese*	*Taiwanese*	*American*
Culture) Mean		27.33	26.69	27.00
Fair B) Standard Deviation		4.53	4.47	4.50

Nowhere among these raw scores do differences approach statistical significance.

(b) Similarity of Predictive Power across Groups [4]

Language	Chinese	.30	*Math*	Chinese School	.47
	English	.40		American School	.64

[4] Prediction from same Culture Fair Scale of Student Achievement in U.S. and China.

It might perhaps be expected that a_g subtests would correlate mutually more highly, in the sense that they share common educational variance as well as common g_f variance, but the g_f variance which they share is that of an earlier age, and somewhat shot with error through the passage of time. Thus if we look at, say the 13- to 14-year-old data in Table 6–4 (page 116) we find the loading of g_f on historical g_f, i.e., $g_{f(h)}$, is better than that for g_c (a_g); but the latter also loads the educational experience factor .32. Thus the communality (on $g_{f(h)}$) of the g_f test is .69, while that of g_c (a_g) is $\sqrt{.63^2 + .32^2} = .71$. But, there seems no intrinsic reason why tests for g_f should not eventually be constructed that have relatively little specific factor variance (J. L. Horn and H. H. Anderson, and the present writer are at present experimenting with some promising forms) whereas it seems unlikely that the specificity in such tests as vocabulary size, deductive reasoning, and the N primary will ever be severely reduced.

The culture-fair and crystallized ability intelligence tests first must be validated against different factors (conceptual criteria) consistent with their different meanings and purposes. Secondly, the extra properties demanded of the culture-fair test must not be expected of the traditional test. It must show no difference of level among groups in widely different cultures when they are otherwise equal, as evidenced on page 485 above, and, in the present validity context, it must show the same factor structure across cultures.[8] The upper part of Table 14–3 compares the loading of the identical C. F. test—the IPAT Scale 3, Adult form—given in America and in Germany, with excellent agreement. Thirdly, one must recognize that *the correlation agreement of culture-fair and traditional tests should not be indefinitely high* "in support of" a spurious conception of validity. They should, in a typical group of, say, eighteen-year-olds, correlate only about 0.5. For the *pure* g_f and a_g factors would normally correlate about 0.6 and, with imperfect test validity, an r of about 0.5 might be expected between two good tests.

This last point deserves stressing, because of the frequency with which it is overlooked, and also because of the habit of taking a pool or first principal axis factor out of a battery of several intelligence tests simultaneously administered, and estimating the validity of each by its correlation with that pool. The probability is that the newer, culture-fair tests will be outnumbered by the others, and that the centroid of the group—while

---

[8] The question of establishing the identity of a particular concept—such as intelligence or anxiety—as it expresses itself across different cultures or at different ages, is a complex but vital one for any acceptance of generality of psychological laws. It has inevitably been encountered and touched on briefly at several points in this book, though the reader concerned seriously to answer it must be referred to more technical reading elsewhere (Cattell, 1969b, 1970a; Meredith, 1966). An answer acceptable to statistical opinion is to use, in comparisons of scores across cultures (on a culture-fair test) the weights for estimating a factor taken from which has been called a *transcultural factor* (Cattell, 1957a). This is the factor obtained by taking the means of N cultures on each of n variables and factoring them. It deals only with intergroup covariance, but is directly applicable to the differences of groups and uses the same intelligence concept for all. The more subtle alternatives for comparing across cultures are the isopodic and equipotent methods given elsewhere (Cattell, 1969b, 1970a).

obviously representing neither a clean-cut g_f or a_g—will be much nearer to crystallized intelligence. This confused assumption was not made by McArthur and Elley in the experiment reported in Table 14–4, but the correlations are actually correlations with such a centroid or principal axis of many tests, a second factor, which they called "education" being set aside. Some further rotation to a more complete simple structure could be done, and, in our view, the first column is not pure g_f, but has some admixture with a_g. Nevertheless, perhaps because of their relative freedom from specifics, it is noteworthy that the Culture-Fair and the Raven Matrices rank highest in validity against this general factor in a representative array of such intelligence tests.[9]

TABLE 14–4
Loadings (Saturations) When General Factor is Defined
by Varied Collection of Intellectual Ability Measures

Test	Presumed[1] g_f	Presumed Cryst. Intell. or Educ. Factor
IPAT Culture-Fair (Scale 2A)	.75	
Rav. Progressive Matrices	.71	
Lorge-Thorndike Fig. Class.	.58	
Lorge-Thorndike No. Series	.55	
Lorge-Thorndike Fig. Anal.	.74	
Holz-Crowder Fig. Ch.	.50	
Holz-Crowder Series	.46	.21
Holz-Crowder Spatial	.40	
Occupat. Status Parent	.25	
Home Index	.25	.21
Reading Vocabulary	.34	.74
Reading Comprehension	.50	.62
Arith. Reasoning	.46	.34
Arith. Fundamentals	.45	.44
Language	.42	.59
Spelling	.20	.62
Laycock	.68	.51
Cal. Test Ment. Matur. Spatial	.61	
Cal. Test Ment. Matur. Logical	.66	
Cal. Test Ment. Matur. Number	.64	.20
Cal. Test Ment. Matur. Verbal	.46	.66

[1] On 271 Canadian Grade 7 boys and girls. Rotation, not fully for simple structure, by R. S. McArthur and W. B. Elley, The reduction of socioeconomic bias in intelligence testing. *British Journal of Educational Psychology*, 1963, 33, 107–119. Correlations below .20 omitted.

[9] The IPAT Culture-Fair tests have matrices as one of four subtests, whereas in Raven's test they are the entire measure. Since it is certain, by the reliability of these tests exceeding the validity, that *some* specific is present in any such single test, the design of the Culture-Fair recommends itself, in reducing the effect of any one specific by including four (or more in the lower age C. F. Scale 1) subtests.

TABLE 14–4 (continued)

LOADINGS IN DIFFERENT ANALYSIS, TOGETHER WITH CORRELATIONS WITH
ACHIEVEMENT AND SOCIAL STATUS OF PARENTS[2]

Test	g loading	Soc. Status	Achiev. Tests
IPAT Culture-Fair	.79	.24	.35
Raven Matrices	.78	.23	.41
Lorge-Thorndike Fig. Class.	.58	.15	.31
Lorge-Thorndike No. Series	.55	.19	.41
Lorge-Thorndike Fig. Anal.	.74	.26	.39
Lorge-Thorndike Total	.75	.27	.47
Holz-Crowder Series	.46	.31	.49
Holz-Crowder Fig. Ch.	.52	.22	.39
Cal. Test Ment. Matur. Non-Lang.	.62	.18	.38
Cal. Test Ment. Matur. Lang.	.58	.41	.66
Cal. Test Ment. Matur. Total		.38	.65
Laycock Intelligence Test	.68	.35	.64

[2] McArthur and Elley conclude: (1) Culture-reduced tests sample the general intellectual ability factor as well as or better than conventional tests. (2) Most culture-reduced tests show negligible loadings on verbal and numerical factors. (3) Culture-reduced tests show significantly less relationship with socio-economic status than do conventional tests. (4) A conventional verbal test (Cal. Test Ment. Matur.) showed significant increase in relationship with socio-economic status over four years, whereas the culture-reduced show no change.

The extensive work of McArthur and Elley has also asked and answered (as far as one research center can) a number of other necessary questions. They conclude, for example, that culture-reduced tests in general (samples covered in the lower part of Table 14–4): (1) measure the Spearman general ability factor as well as or better than conventional tests and (2) show reduced or even negligible correlations with the specific primaries in, for example, verbal and numerical ability. Farther, their results (McArthur and Elley, 1963) agree with the experience of the present writer in sampling different cultures, in that they demonstrated (3) that the CF tests show significantly less relationship with socioeconomic status than do conventional tests (compare the first three with the last three loadings of column 2 on the lower half of Table 14–4), and (4) that conventional tests (California Test of Mental Maturity) showed significant increase of correlation with social status as the child grows older, whereas the culture-reduced show no such change.

Continuing the psychometric examination of test properties, as they concern the choice of tests in ability measurement and applied psychology, we encounter, after *validity,* the important concept of *consistency*—the agreement of a type of measurement with itself. The consistency of a test has three distinct facets of possible evaluation: (1) its *dependability,* calculated by correlating *one administration with another* with only a trifling time interval between; (2) its *homogeneity,* the degree to which *its part cor-*

relate mutually. This need not be high for a good test; it depends on the object of the test. And (3) its *transferability,* the extent to which *it continues to measure the same psychological trait* when used on different populations (to which it claims to apply).[10] Regarding consistency, Polonius's dictum "but to thyself be true, and it follows as the night the day, thou canst not then be false to any man" applies as well to tests as to men, since a test of low consistency cannot maintain the validity it has. The dependability coefficient is usually not only an evaluation of the consistency of the test itself, but of the precision of the administrative conditions and the people who administer it. Dependability coefficients are usually around 0.85 to 0.95 for intelligence tests, the higher values for tests of an hour or more, the lower for fifteen-minute lengths.

Homogeneity can be calculated either by correlating random split halves or as a "herringbone" homogeneity, in which parts are symmetrical. If a school attainment test, covering English, math, geography, etc., had its homogeneity calculated in the first way, there would be something wrong with the test if it were not low. It would be much higher, in such a "patterned" test, if geography items were split in two and so on, by the herringbone coefficient. A high homogeneity—in the sense of the alpha coefficient as calculated by Cronbach—is by no means always desirable. An intelligence test is strictly a patterned rather than an homogenized test, because subtests do and should spread over different specifics. Consequently only a herringbone index is appropriate.

The concept of *transferability* is a new and important one in test evaluation. For example, it is obvious that one of the important differences of culture-fair and traditional tests is the far higher transferability of the former. To measure transferability one must obtain the factor structure of the test in the two populations to be compared, thus:

$$t_1 = b_{11}T_1 + \cdots + b_{k1}T_k \qquad \text{(14.3a)}$$

$$t_2 = b_{12}T_1 + \cdots + b_{k2}T_k \qquad \text{(14.3b)}$$

where t_1 and t_2, b_{11} and b_{12}, etc., are the test scores (for any individual) on populations 1 and 2, and the loadings on populations 1 and 2. A pattern similarity coefficient, r_p, worked out between the two series of b's (k in each) has been called the *fidelity coefficient* (Cattell and Warburton, 1968), though the simpler expression of transferability, T_x, is

$$T_x = \frac{1}{\sigma_{r_v}}, \qquad \text{(14.4)}$$

where σ_{r_v} is the standard deviation of the concept validity coefficient (as Fisher's Z) over the standard set of populations to which the test should apply.

---

[10] Corresponding to each of these *coefficients,* there is also an *index,* expressing the shift of *mean score* when changing from one situation to another. A full discussion of these validity and consistency concepts and their operational use is given in Cattell and Warburton, 1967.

If a certain species of test type has some degree of validity, both its reliability and validity will increase with its length. In any talk of relative validity, therefore, one must beware of generalizing without knowing the length of each test and without correcting for this. Obviously the first and biggest mistake any practitioner can make is to use a test of less validity *per half hour* than other available tests. A concept of *standard validity,* and the rather more complex concept of an *index of efficiency* (amount of effective decision-making per unit of time) have been proposed by Cattell and Warburton (1967) for final evaluation of intelligence tests in general practice. By these standards the new CF—culture-reduced—type of intelligence test is equal to or better than most conventional tests now so prevalent in the applied fields.

The first, most widespread fallacy in discussing intelligence test validity arises from a failure to distinguish *concept* ("construct") and *concrete* validities, and clearly to abandon the myth that some single, universal concrete validity is possible for intelligence tests. The latter is implicit in the notion that a good intelligence test should correlate higher with school performance, or some old intelligence test, than a former one. But intelligence is a *concept,* fixed by a particular, defined factor, and the true evaluation of any test is by a validity coefficient against that factor. The mere observation that Test X correlates with some older intelligence test may mean little. Two older tests may correlate +0.7 with each other, but a new test can still correlate 0.7 with one of these associated criteria and zero with the other! Apart from such statistical embarrassments, the whole principle of assigning validity to a new test by correlating it with an old one is as ludicrous as validating a recent estimate of the sun's distance against one made by Copernicus, or the boiling point of pure hydrogen against the value accepted fifty years ago. Truth in science is not handed down by apostolic succession, and the validity of, say, a culture-fair intelligence test has little to do with its correlation with the Binet, but only with a precise, experimentally determined correlation with g_f (or in the case of a traditional test with a_g)—the concept it aims to measure. Actually, few conventional tests in popular use have provided good evidence of their simple structure factor saturation, and fewer still have checks across several factor-analytic experiments on different samples. Results, as in Table 14–3 for the IPAT Culture-Fair and the WAIS, are not easy to obtain.

A second common weakness in testing is to use too short a test to get adequate reliability. The Stanford-Binet typically takes thirty to forty minutes for children, the WAIS forty to ninety minutes, and the Otis thirty minutes. The IPAT Culture-Fair[11] Scales are made in four equivalent

---

[11] Regarding the use, in intelligence test titles, of the terms culture-fair, culture-free, culture-reduced, etc., there has been much unnecessary hedging. No one—even when using the term culture-free—means this in the *absolute* sense, i.e., in any sense other than that in which a city says its water is "pure." The standard tribal reaction of sociologists has been to deny the possibility of a culture-free test. Thus Goslin (1966, p. 138) asserts, "Unless someone can succeed in creating a test to be given as the

forms, on the "telescopic" principle, so that the psychologist in dire straits for time can take, with *one* form only twenty minutes (just twelve and one-half minutes of actual testing time), but can extend to forty minutes or even an hour and a half (using Scales 2 and 3, A and B).

Since, as Horn has shown (1967), a person's ability as such, not merely his performance on a test, suffers some *function fluctuation* from day to day, no ascertainment of intelligence for any important decision should rest on a single test session, regardless of its length. Fatigue, sickness, etc., take their toll of examination performance. A testing on perhaps four occasions, spread over as many months, would be a reasonable practical standard for scholarship selection. No accurate data yet exists on the actual magnitude of function fluctuation. It is usually a hidden part of the total unreliability of a measure (the rest being test undependability), as indicated by the following:

$$\sigma^2_s = 1 - r^2_s = \sigma^2_f + \sigma^2_d \tag{14.5}$$

Here s refers to the obtainable *stability coefficient*, r_s, simply from retesting after a lengthy interval. But the variance σ^2_s is composed of both administrative test error, σ^2_d, estimatable from the obtainable dependability coefficient, r_d, and the unknown function fluctuation, σ^2_f, in the trait itself. Since $\sigma^2_d = 1 - r^2_d$ we can obtain σ^2_f, and a corresponding function fluctuation coefficient, r_f, thus:

$$r_f = \sqrt{1 - \sigma^2_f} = \sqrt{1 - r^2_d + r^2_s}$$

whence

$$\sigma^2_f = r^2_d - r^2_s \tag{14.6}$$

The work of Horn, as well as certain dR analysis of the 16 P.F. by the present writer, show that r_f for intelligence, fluid or crystallized, is not unity. That is to say, intelligence is not to be treated as an absolutely fixed trait, variable only because the test varies, but as intrinsically given to its own unitary but slight diurnal fluctuation. In fact, if σ_s is accepted as about five points of I.Q., a present guess might be that σ_f is about three points of I.Q.

In connection with estimating error in intelligence measurement in various applied situations, it has sometimes been suggested that (a) the score will fluctuate primarily with *motivation* change (not the *intrinsic* intelligence change above) for the same person, and (b) that the individual

---

physician removes the infant from the mother's womb, it is unlikely that anything approximating a culture-free test will be developed." This statement both confuses *culture free* and *innate* (physiology does its bit to alter the innate) and overlooks the fact that science proceeds by abstraction. Such remarks are on a par with great-grandma's assertion, "How can those astronomers know how hot a star is? When they get up there with the oven thermometer I'll believe it." The evidence for a high degree of culture-fairness has been given above, pages 294, 488, and justifies, as MacArthur (1968, p. 121) has recently said, the firm conclusion that such tests "as the IPAT [Culture-Fair] and the Lorge-Thorndike Non-Verbal should be included in testing programs" where good intelligence assessments are vital.

differences in actual test score are, to an appreciable extent, actually differences in *motivation*. Equation (12.5) above recognizes that ergic tension and sentiment development levels play their part, but technical analyses suggest that the strength of motivation in test-taking does not play nearly so large a role as the layman is inclined to suppose.[12] Lay critics have wished to account for significant differences found between whole groups and classes as due to differences in interest in school work and perception of community role (and interest in social service and personal ambition being called "middle class" morality, forsooth!). In commenting on this, let us be clear that lesser interest may powerfully effect the *generation* of crystallized from fluid intelligence. (This is an instance of an effect in the *developmental* as opposed to the action equation [page 334.]) Interpretation of such motivation-intelligence relations is then misleading only if we confuse crystallized and fluid intelligence. Naturally, in any large group there will always be a few individuals who "sabotage" a test by sheer noncooperation, and the frequency of these will vary with the morale of the group. In the past, such gross effects have been included in *impressions* of the general unreliability of testing, but psychometrists now have techniques for detecting such cases and analyzing the distinct sources of unreliability.

This raises the intriguing question of whether one can estimate a person's intelligence without his being willing for one to do so—instances of which arise in management, with business executives too dignified to be tested, and in criminal cases where mental defect is pleaded. As to "rights" of being tested, it is everyone's right to estimate anyone's intelligence and to hide his own if for some peculiar reason he wishes to do so. When Julius Caesar, as an unknown, was captured by pirates, he gave them such an impression of a "good-natured-stupid" person that he was able, as he jocularly promised them, to come back and hang the lot. Had they recruited a psychologist, as some modern pirates in Madison Avenue do, they might have escaped their deserts, since a number of means are now available for indirectly estimating intelligence.

Insofar as interests relate to intelligence, in the ways discussed in Chapters 11 and 12, relative galvanic skin reflex, blood pressure or breathing

---

[12] To recapitulate what was discussed above, it is found generally that increased motivation will strongly affect scores on simple activities, like rate of tapping or cancellation, but not correctness in more complex judgments. Average changes of the order of two or three points may be expected from motivation differences (probably less if the test is unspeeded). Outside the laboratory motivation manipulative experiments, part of the slight correlation found between lower performance and lower motivation is almost certainly due to causal action in the opposite direction, i.e., to experience of relative failure reducing motivation. A modicum of intrinsic motivation suffices in the test situation. For even with preliterate primitive tribes, who certainly had no motivation system into which they could incorporate intelligence testing, Porteus (1937) found that the spirit of play was sufficient to get all attention necessary for dependable judgmental performance. Some part of the effectiveness of testing must naturally be left to the training of the psychologist, whose skills should encompass approaches which generate an adequate "rapport" and motivation level in any group he is testing.

change to a range of stimuli, some of which would convey emotional meaning only to an intelligent person, could provide an avenue to noncooperative intelligence testing. A second approach, with reasonably good correlations is indicated by the work of Ertl (1966) and of Horn (1969) measuring the brain wave response to virtually any kind of stimuli. A third form of indirect and hidden intelligence tests exists in the humor test of intelligence, beginning with the work of Luborsky and developed by Tollefson (1959) and the Institute for Personality and Ability Testing. The humor test depends in principle on having two levels of sophistication in each joke, such that if the subtle point is seen, joke A is intrinsically, emotionally, more humorous than B, but if only perceived at a gross level, B is funnier than A. Disguised as a "taste in humor" test, it is useful with groups whose role status or personal insecurity might make them unwilling to take a labelled intelligence test.

Of all conditions, short of actual test sabotage, that contribute to invalidity of intelligence testing, none is so serious as inequalities in what is technically defined as *test sophistication*. As pointed out in the work of Adkins (1937), Thouless (see Cattell, 1936c, Vernon, 1954), Burt and Williams (1962), Heim (1949–1950), Vernon (1954), and others, when children first meet intelligence tests and are given repeated exposure to them, a steady improvement of score occurs. It may be four I.Q. points on the first occasion, three on the second and so on, in slight, but statistically significant increments for the first two or three repetitions. This gain, through getting familiar with "the rules of the game," the layout, the timing conditions, etc., is greatest from the first to the second occasion, but may be detectable as late as between the fourth, fifth, and sometimes sixth administrations. Test sophistication is just as operative in culture-fair as in traditional tests. As far as testing in school is concerned, both this effect and function fluctuation could readily be reduced to trivial proportions by planning a wise "test installation" scheme. Thereby children would be routinely tested once a year, as in an annual medical examination, from nursery school years onward, without any connection with stressful competitions hanging on the result. Then, at an age when some important advice has to be given, e.g., in vocational counselling, or at scholarship selection, evidence would be available free of individual differences from test sophistication, and averaged across different situations of testing. In testing a new individual—possibly unsophisticated in tests—for something of importance, and especially in carrying out research comparisons of means between disparate social groups, it should be routine to test, with intervals between, on A, B, C, etc., forms of the intelligence scale, and to "throw away" the first two.

In decisions on whether, when, and how to test, one must never forget that the obtaining by examination of a psychological measurement has several diverse functions and effects. It may act as a guide for decision-making on classifications and curricula in educational and occupational institutions. It may, alternatively help the individual to evaluate his past and plan his future. As he comes to know his capacities (and to integrate them in his plans) it may even affect his personality. Testing is also likely to affect the organization and fate of society as a whole, in ways glimpsed in the last section. If the diverse purposes of selection, guidance, group organization, self-appraisal, etc., are kept in perspective, and the psychometric properties of tests are not properly understood, tests can be misused and complaints against testing can accumulate. Testing programs, like any other procedures affecting admissions to this and that important opportunity, job and school promotions, and various human contacts and contracts (seen most fatefully in psychometric marriage counselling!), are bound to become the focus of emotional disputes, and such disputes need to be intelligently avoided or settled.

Two rules are vital here: (1) that the nature of the test results, including their degree of reliability, should be understood by all concerned, and (2) that misguided philosophies that would effect selection and attitudes to selection when these are effected by *any* technical means should not be allowed to mistake the means for the end and attack testing *per se*. These can be illustrated, first, by the vexed question of whether a student, or other client, should be allowed to know his own test results. There are an alarming number of teachers and psychologists who, in one and the same hour, will preach in class the philosophers' ideal "Know thyself," and shake their heads in a professional stand against giving the individual knowledge of his test results.

Obviously, the results can only be given to the student if enough is explained for him to understand their true nature, if he is not so immature and unstable that he cannot absorb them, and if he is given enough understanding of their unreliability not to treat them more seriously than they deserve. Although documentable experimental evidence for this is scarce, it seems certain that knowledge of test results affects not only a person's plans, but also his personality. Indeed, as we have seen in Chapter 12, knowledge of one's abilities and their limitations, even if obtained roughly, through life experience, rather than more exactly through tests, affects personality, as evidenced by ensuing correlations of personality development with abilities. It is sometimes said that such self-knowledge is not always for the best: that awareness of a low intelligence test result discourages and blights an individual's motivation, while a high score may cause superciliousness. Experiment shows, however, that people usually have a far more exact (but not publicly confessed) self-image in a great number of areas, than the onlooker would suspect. They have several evaluations of how good-looking they are, how intelligent, how physically fit, etc.—even without an "intrusion" of testing. The argument that an intelligence test, or a labelled classification into streams in school, or rejection from a university does damage to personality ignores the main evidence. Discoveries may be painful, but that does not mean they are not salutary for adjustment, and decidedly less painful than if made too late!

Important though it is, the issue of whether a person should get a somewhat more accurate view of his talents by ability testing or continue with the costly, delayed, and less accurate one which life experience may offer, is not the most vital. The vital issue concerns by what philosophical or religious values he is encouraged to meet these facts. In a recent, widely read book, John Gardner (1958) points out that a child can adjust to being good or bad at games, whereas a statement about his intelligence is a "total judgment" which is "central to his self-esteem." As a commonsense observation, no one would want to disagree with this, but there is something wrong with the human value system if it cannot give consolation to all individuals in accepting the facts of individual differences in gifts. It is one thing to say that society, for its own good, must reduce the number of low intelligence births; it is quite another to say that an individual at those levels, being born, should not be fully esteemed as a human being in the community. The value system or religion to which humanity has striven is one which seeks to preserve the individual's serenity in face of success or failure, superiority or inferiority to others, life or death—though as individuals, in misfortune even the best formula may come hard.

It is instructive to the social psychologist in this area to gain perspective from cultural anthropology by contrasting the philosophies of Russia and the liberal West. Russia uses educational examination systems but not psychological tests, and rejects the notion that any ability difference can be innate. The West seeks a philosophy, mainly in Christianity and Judaism, that individual differences are to be accepted without envy and malice. The former seeks to handle the problem of adjustment and self-respect in the citizen who eventually perceives his lowly status in an occupational meritocracy by the *ad hoc* device of inverting class snobbery. The lowly handworker deserves his full dignity; it is questionable whether the inversion of telling the proletarian worker that he is the supreme dictator is the best solution. Western culture seeks to handle these differences of social role by recognizing the equality in worth and in communion of every human soul. The ultimate excellence is moral goodness, not worldly success or intelligence (which latter St. Paul and other saints have repeatedly "put in its place"). Freedom, equality of human value, and equality of opportunity might be called Democracy I, but there is also abroad in politics and in newspapers a Democracy II, which asserts that all could be actually equal in talents, and resents adjustment of opportunity to talents, e.g., in the schools. Since education, even if applied inversely, cannot, according to our evidence, obliterate differences in intelligence, this bastard form of democracy would be reduced to manipulating the birth rate to reduce the standard deviation of I.Q. Whether this were done by leveling up, leveling down, or squeezing to the middle, it would probably give the desired result of greater social solidarity and conformity. Social engineers of the future may decide that some movement of that kind, by leveling up, is humanly desirable (since there is a sense in which even Democracy I is born, not made; for it has proven unworkable with too great a range). But since, in any yet conceivable society, a wide diversity of tasks must exist, there probably exists for each society an optimum standard deviation of I.Q., which needs to be maintained.

The object of the last few paragraphs of digression into values is to make clear that much dispute about psychological testing is by no means new, and certainly not inherent in testing, but belongs to any method, however ancient, of estimating differences in capacity and promise, and its settlement belongs to morality and values. The increased precision and analytical and predictive power of testing have simply brought the issue to a sharper focus. Testing has been demonstrated (Eysenck, 1960) to be decidedly more accurate than interviewing, and, passed through the computer anonymously, its judgments are obviously more free of prejudice than those made socially. What could be more ironical, therefore, than the recent regressions in some British and a few American schools from *testing* for scholarship or promotion with its alleged "invidious selections" to disposal according to the headmasters' opinions of many only vaguely known pupils!

Nevertheless, the sheer increase of scientific precision through testing, and the guidance of lives which increasingly opens up through knowledge of genetics, learning theory, and the natural history of abilities, may have profound effects on social organization. For example, if it were true (as, in sophisticated analysis it is not) that the decline of fluid intelligence from ages twenty-five to sixty-five invalidated promotion by seniority, rational organization would turn upside down much that we now take for granted. For example, if this fluid intelligence curve held for all men, and if social science were a real science and absorbable in six years at the university, the limiting age for election to the Presidency of the U.S.—30 years—might need to be retained as now—but as an upper rather than a lower boundary!

Regardless of these more speculative excursions, testing is accepted as a valuable aid, and it should be technically well done. If the triadic theory of capacities, powers, and agencies survives further research, the practice of ability testing must, in due course, begin to follow the theory. Prediction of an individual's performance and due counseling on his best areas of future accomplishment will then require a broader spectrum battery in the regular installation testing which covers not only g_f, but also g_s and g_r. Such a design of the battery would provide also a firm view of the distribution of his provincial powers—the p's for visualization, auditory ability, and so on—and record the stage of development of his agencies—a_v, a_n, a_s, and, of course, their summation in crystallized intelligence, a_g. With improved delineation of these abilities, and more efficient testing in a given time (as in Horn's primary abilities test), it should surely become possible to make a comprehensive triadic survey of an individual's abilities in about three hours. Though we have a relatively spotty coverage in existing tests, we can at least test the main primaries and obtain separate measures of crystallized and fluid general intelligence by traditional and culture-fair tests.[13]

---

[13] The IPAT Culture-Fair Scales 1, 2, and 3 (for children, high school students, and superior adults) representing the outcome of the present writer's basic research over the years since 1940 on fluid intelligence, use four different subtests in the search for a compromise between time and variety (contrast the Raven matrices test). A not infrequent first reaction of teachers and laymen, on casual inspection of such tests, is

7. ON THE EFFECTIVE EDUCATIONAL AND COMMUNITY USE OF ABILITY RESOURCES

It is endemic in educational circles—especially in parents' associations—to believe that schools are not doing as well as they might. These misgivings lead to some solid research, but they also open the door to cycles of fads and fashions. These latter make the house of education, for a reasonably skeptical but constructive scientist, as uncomfortable and unsuitable for steady life work as a house where the wife is forever changing the furniture around. Most "action researchers" are at the end of their scientific tether and in a state of frantic guesswork. Our concern in this book, however, can fortunately be sharply focused on that aspect of education that has specifically to do with the effective use of resources of ability.

The psychologist contributes to this field, hopefully, a clearer recognition of the structure of abilities, of their nature-nurture ratios, their growth, and their contribution. His research has affected ideas about the age at which certain topics can be profitably taught; it has pointed to "streaming," i.e., classification by mental age similarity, to ensure a less scattered class interest and to permit faster progress of the above-average; and it has enabled clearer ideas to be formed on issues concerning the fraction of the population that can attend universities without their ceasing to be institutions of advanced learning.

Among the valuable soul-searchings of educators is the concern that not all the resources of ability in the country may be properly utilized. At one time, many European children, fit for advanced, selective education, e.g., in the English Grammar school or the German Gymnasium, missed this education through lack of parental means. To remedy this situation, psychologists came forward to support scholarship systems with intelligence tests, in one of the most socially effective uses of psychological testing yet recorded. However, public dissatisfaction has been registered even at the most just and technically efficient selection of bright children into the desired classes where they can move together faster. Teachers of other classes object that the cream has been taken off their student group, and parents are unconvinced that their children are not as bright as the Jones's. In the 1940s and 1950s, Britain handled the issue not on scientific merits but on social and political terms; the defunct and unreliable interview and teacher rating on intelligence were substituted for the objective test. The real

---

that (a) they must involve much spatial ability, and (b) they cannot possibly predict verbal learning ability because they have no verbal content. Experiment shows these hasty conclusions to be incorrect. Some overemphasis on visualization power may exist and must be corrected in the future by additional approaches through auditory and tactile powers. But the prediction of verbal learning, as shown by both English and Chinese languages, is essentially as good from the CF tests as from a crystallized intelligence measure in either of those languages.

remedy lay in a change of values which would dissolve academic snobbery and recognize the equal worthiness of the man with the hammer and sickle.

If we assume that a reasonably satisfactory testing installation has directed, e.g., via scholarships, the best ability to the available educational services, another problem still arises in the modern world. If an institution —the university—which in Europe shaped itself to take 1 in 50 of the school-leaving group, now takes in 1 in 5, can it remain the same in methods and aims, or must it be completely recast? Some hope for the former is offered by what we have seen in the plot of the cultural pressure factor (page 419) namely a four- or five-fold increase in the need for persons in professional and more complex occupations. Except for the question of whether we have resources in the distribution curve of g_f to meet these needs, it seems functional for the university to take in more students and still aim at the same curricula. On the other hand, some writers justly point out that we are in danger of converting children of fine craftsmen, skilful carpenters, and master electricians, into mediocre novelists and second-rate musicians.

The question of internal changes of curricula being beyond our present assignment, let us assume that the problem is one of finding talent for the universities as we now know them, catering expressly for the professions such as law, engineering, teaching, and medicine. Let us assume—the figure is not exactly known—that (on a sigma of 16 points) the student who expects to be successful in obtaining the Ph.D. has to stand at I.Q. 130 or above. Then, since a country like America has, according to the I.Q. distribution curve, between one and two million above I.Q. 130, but only 50,000 to 100,000 Ph.D.'s, one might conclude that at least nine-tenths of those capable of such education never get to this level of qualification. There is a systematic fallacy in such simple calculations that our study of human resources above exposes. It arises again from "single factor thinking." The psychologist fully recognizes (Equation 12.3 above) that achieving a Ph.D. with an I.Q. of 130 requires also an emotional stability (C factor) not less than average (possessed by only half the population), and similarly for superego strength (G factor), and desurgency (F factor). Since these three factors are virtually uncorrelated, it is evident with even three factors only, that but one person in 2^3, i.e., one in eight will have the necessary qualities despite an I.Q. over 130 to sustain the necessary doctoral study. Consideration of one or two other necessary qualities involving additional reduction, leave an estimate not far from the present actual figure. This dwindling from what the intelligence curve alone might suggest occurs in many other intelligence-demanding occupations. In medicine and teaching, for example, the practical demands of internship and classroom teaching commonly eliminate many who had at least the fortitude required to apply their intelligence quite successfully in written examinations, but whose personality was inadequate to the demands of the personal and social situations in medicine and teaching.

Although we have presented some evidence, e.g., from Terman's study of the gifted and from factor-analytic findings, that intelligence is positively related to character qualities and freedom from neurosis, a sense of perspective requires one to remember that the correlation is very slight. The precise calculation would not be very different from the rough one above, simplified by assumption of independence. Further, in student pools selected mainly for intellectual performance, the hurdle effect (page 470) may induce even a *negative* correlation of intelligence and character qualities. Some such negative relation is believed by many to be evident in the academic profession, for example, which has a rather egregious reputation for impracticality, unrealism, and the espousing of what this generation calls beatnik fads. The unpleasant and seldom publicly stated probability is that—like some other groups selected for sheer intelligence—it contains many with a neurotic or a frivolous incapacity to bring any undertaking to completion, who would fail and be unemployed in an unprotected, competitive world of individual enterprise. On the other hand, it contains some of the community's most effective and creative individuals. In short, any selection for an occupation that is carried out on one factor only—in this case crystallized intelligence, a_g—is likely, by any other criteria of effectiveness[14] to show a very wide range, since the other factors in effectiveness, e.g., the personality source traits, may vary across the whole range.

Similar illustration of the phenomenon of a great range of effectiveness, as well as diversity of area of successful expression, despite intensive selection to a narrow high band in intelligence, is given in Serebriakoff's fascinating story of the Mensa Society (1966). This group also offers some illustration of the personality hazards of high intelligence in growing up in the regular school system. As mentioned above, admission to this society requires proof that the individual belongs to the top two percent of the distribution curve.[15] Since members have been willing to submit to many kinds of psychological experiments, some very interesting statistics are known about its properties, as described in Serebriakoff's book. The latter

---

[14] Even if we take the still rather abstract performance expressed by contribution of acceptable publications to scholarly journals, not because it is necessarily the best criterion, but because reliable data can readily be obtained on it, we find the median publication rate for faculties of typical universities is less than one article per year; yet the range is from 0 to 9 or 10.

[15] The development of the present "two general factor" theory, g_f and a_g, has a special bearing on Mensa and on several "scholarship" selection schemes which were worked out originally accepting the theory of a single Spearman "g" intelligence. The split into fluid and crystallized intelligence concepts presents the disturbing question "On which of the two factors, a_g or g_f, is the selection ultimately to be made?" For although they may correlate between $+0.5$ and $+0.7$ (the r would be higher in an educational system which adjusts opportunity to talent and lower in an older and more age-scattered group), a correlation as high as 0.6 will still lead to much discrepancy in the membership of the top two percent on each. In fact, it can be shown that with a correlation of 0.6, the top 2% by the a_g intelligence test will share only 30% of its 2% with the top 2% by the g_f test. When Mensa examiners have used both the Cattell Test (Harrap, London)—a crystallized ability test—and the IPAT

shows that, like a group of academic prima donnas, the community of Mensa has not been an easy one to run. Though its members have the redeeming quality (in a world where serious reading habits are sadly reduced), that "most of them seldom or never watch television" (Serebriakoff, 1966, p. 143), it is also true according to a senior member, that "Their beliefs are provisional, their intellectual loyalties temporary, they are undisciplined, errant, unorthodox, and they disagree both with authority and with each other" (*op. cit.*, p. 121).[16]

Culture-Fair Scale 3—a fluid ability test—on the same group of candidates, they have in fact been disconcerted as the above indicated magnitude of discrepancy became concretely evident.

There is a point in all such social selection procedures at which the problem ceases to be one for psychological technicians and must be solved by makers of policy and values. It has long been recognized that the top 2% by an a_g test is likely to consist substantially of university-educated persons. Serebriakoff (1966, p. 114) says "The largest single group [in the 1963–1964 Mensa Register] is that of teachers. There are eighty-one university lecturers . . . fourteen barristers . . . twenty-four journalists . . . forty-six company directors . . . forty-seven lecturers in mathematics [but only] one steel smelter . . . one wireman . . . one toolmaker . . . one fitter . . . and two machinists." While this predominance of the highly educated among those selected for high crystallized intelligence witnesses to the excellence of the design of the 11 + scholarship machinery operating a generation earlier (and set up by Sir Cyril Burt and others), it also permits the interpretation that present Mensa selection by conventional a_g measures is missing many individuals of high g_f and low a_g. For in spot sampling with the highest (Scale 3) IPAT Culture-Fair, the present writer has encountered several instances of very high intelligence indeed in farmers, sailors, garage mechanics, and others whose formal education happened to be slight. Although the policy of a group like Mensa is not our concern, a strong argument could be made for more selection by culture-fair tests. It would enrich the group with ideas and experiences outside the academic, such as many historical figures like Jack London, Darwin, Dostoevski, and Ramanujan might have brought in when picked by fluid intelligence selection (assuming they would have failed the crystallized intelligence performances of their day). The need for at least an equal representation in the qualifications by g_f and a_g is particularly evident in an adult group, where a_g and g_f pull rather far apart, and represent very different kinds of competence.

In most scholarship selection for an education which still lies in the future, among candidates of very different social background, an instrument such as the IPAT Culture-Fair is certainly logically indicated.

[16] To explain what appears to be a certain frivolity in the personality type selected here, one may point out that this group volunteers for membership in a purely social and conversationalistic society; and that volunteering generally brings significant personality selection (Cattell and Scheier, 1961) toward low anxiety and extravert qualities. In a world where unoccupied leisure is generally more common in the less intelligent, and any person of high intelligence and serious obligations is likely to be hard-worked, any highly intelligent person who deliberately seeks new commitments is obviously atypical! A proposal which the present writer made to Terman years ago for studying the intelligence and personality of *living* geniuses fell through, incidentally, because tentative enquiries found them quite unable to give the time for testing. One should be extremely cautious, therefore, in considering information on a group selected under these conditions as reliable evidence about the typical highly intelligent person.

Nevertheless, the consensus of data from this and other "high test" groups shows, first, that their members are largely in the professional occupational status range as expected (Serebriakoff, 1966, p. 114) and—more importantly for our present educational enquires—that they had been successfully located and aided by the scholarship system. In spite of this during their school experience, they did not escape scars arising from their unusual intelligence. Their autobiographical reports suggest that the chief hazards of the highly intelligent child are: (1) boredom and resentment when having to "mark time" in class with the average; (2) becoming the target of jealousy from others aroused by their high classroom performance and their being "teacher's pet;" (3) having to simulate popular interests and to avoid true self-expression in order to be well accepted by the peer group.

At the opposite end of the "exceptional child" range are the hazards of the borderline mental defective intelligence, which again include: (1) boredom and resentment at having to try the (to him) difficult and meaningless tasks done by the ordinary class; (2) a sense of failure in the whole school situation; and (3) a difficulty in sharing interests with peers in the social world. Most school systems have solved this problem as far as possible by special classes for one or both of these types of exceptional child. But every child is in a sense exceptional, and some systems have accordingly gone the whole way and made in large schools as many as three or four streams of progress by segregating according to ability.

These indications of maladjustment from deviation toward either end of the intelligence scale provoke us to turn next to the controversies which have sprung up about "streaming" in connection with the British "eleven plus selection," and in America in connection with varying emphases on advanced classes in high school. First, the allocation of children of widely different intelligence to different types of school (in this case, or streams in general) undoubtedly aids class teaching, enables the bright to move much faster, and the less bright to have a more kindly adapted curriculum. Secondly, the objection that the average class performance is "lifted" by having more bright children in it is beside the point. The coercions are, in the end, equal and opposite—the bright is equally bent to the world of the less bright—and the question is rather, how much tension and frustration from mixing different levels can be tolerated.[17] Thirdly, labeling as

---

[17] Coercion to the biosocial mean is a very real experience. A recent editorial in *Mensa* comments, "To force a child who is *not* average to conform to an educational system which is concerned solely with the mass production of 'average' robotic exam-passers, can amount (and often does amount) to no less than cruelty." Even National Health schemes do not require doctors, in the name of justice, to give the same prescription to all patients. The hostility is also real. There was applause around the guillotine when Lavoisier was condemned as a middle class intellectual with the judge's comment "The revolution has no need of scientists." (Reminiscent of Hitler and his failure—shortsighted even from the standpoint of his own ambitions—to support "basic" scientists.) Individual differences and superior variants are the necessary conditions for evolutionary advance; any society which cannot tolerate excellence

more or less advanced is criticized as bad for the self-respect of the duller child. The alternative is for the less able child to be aware of lesser ability by contrasts forced upon his own consciousness *within* the class. *Either* way he does not escape dangers of knowing he is less able, nor the bright child the reciprocal dangers of arrogance from feeling he is so precocious. (If anything, the better cure for the latter is competition with other equally bright children.) As suggested above, the real remedy here is one of deeper ethical values in regard to the acceptance of individual differences and retention of respect for all people as striving human beings.

A fourth and last criticism of classification by intelligence, and specifically of doing so at an early age, is a purely technical one. It is asserted that decision on a "stream" at eleven years of age, as in Britain, or similar ages elsewhere—is too tender an age for reliable determination of one's educational fate. Just how validly can general ability be measured at, say, ten to twelve years of age? Is enough known about the laws of ability development to make decisions affecting the next five or six years? Answers can be given only in statistical expressions. To go first to a more extreme case, let us admit that intelligence testing at age four, and our knowledge of structure there will not permit us to predict about the next five years with greater confidence than the weatherman predicts tomorrow's weather.

But concerning a child eleven years of age, if we are asked what a stipulated environment is likely to lead to from a present stipulated set of structural test results, our estimate has considerable reliability, provided the questions are asked in clear analytical form, e.g., what will be the level of fluid intelligence provided (a) there is no intercurrent illness, (b) assuming the person suffers brain injury? Or, what will be the level of crystallized intelligence (a) if he continues in his present environment, and (b) if he is chronically short of vitamin B? Or, what will be his attainment three years hence in English provided (a) he stays in a nonselective class, and (b) if he moves to a selective secondary school. Test accuracies and knowledge of learning laws, especially after more aspects of the triadic theory of ability have been checked, should enable answers of appreciable accuracy to be given to questions such as these. Meanwhile we must make up by more extensive sampling of measurements for what we lack in predictive power from single measures. It would, in short, be desirable practice to measure more frequently—say once a year—to base action on averages, and to arrange promotion and selection schemes to permit reclassifications among the educational streams at shorter intervals.[18]

---

pays ultimately a heavy price. Left wing reformers of the nineteenth century were inclined to see the managerial and entrepreneurial classes as parasites upon the manual laborer; our generation perceives that the creative scientist and the far-sighted industrial organizer are sources of wealth for the whole community. Parasitism seems a questionable concept in either direction, for each level of ability has its distinct needs and its distinct services.

[18] Actually, even under the eleven-plus selection system, such readjustments occurred. The present writer, in teaching Workers' Educational Association classes in Devon-

The improvement in allocation of individuals to appropriate education that the personality psychologist would like to see, but which has so far not been much thought of either by popular reformers or by more conventional educational psychologists, is the addition of personality and motivation measurements to the ability batteries. For the evidence of Chapter 12 is to the effect that they add substantially to the prediction of school achievement and would eliminate many of the errors in scholarship selection, for example, made by using ability measures alone. Incidentally, the doubts about giving weight to personality measures because of the assumed greater plasticity of personality traits are not entirely well founded. The relative stability depends on the particular abilities and personality traits compared. General intelligence—as g_f—is (barring brain injury) admittedly a more fixed characteristic than, say, area of intellectual interest, or conscientious work habits; but it is just as true that temperament traits such as exuberance (U.I. 21), or independence (U.I. 19) are more steadily characteristic over years than are abilities such as typing speed or facility in a foreign language. Personality and even motivation measures have enough stability to justify their use in academic achievement or job performance predictions over several years. However, the argument for their inclusion in educational psychological work is supplemented and sustained by quite independent reasons, namely, that inasmuch as a clinical psychologist can manipulate personality, the removal of obstacles in personality and motivation can bring movement to abilities that have been marking time and can unlock creative capacities.

In our searches for possible sources of society's needs for ability, and better uses of existing sources, we have considered the birth rate, fuller use of neglected age and sex groups, better recruitment to schools and universities, segregating for more effective development, and more skillful education of personality and motivation in relation to abilities. It remains to consider the directions in which ability might be better trained, and then, in Section 8 which follows, attempts at more basic augmentation of the very springs of ability. Parenthetically, it will be evident to any social scientist

---

shire villages, found a few instances of able young men missed at eleven years of age who nevertheless entered universities later by the W.E.A. scholarships. The irony is that they entered, i.e., were accepted, by this "back door further down the corridor" more easily, i.e., at a *lower* I.Q. level than was required for those who took the main path to the university at eleven-plus. Sir Cyril Burt, whose sixty years of professional experience with intelligence testing in all kinds of educational situations is unrivaled, concludes: "In my opinion, eleven-plus is not too early to start the screening; but it should be the beginning of a continual scrutiny." The American system of avoiding separate types of high school, but developing all kinds of aptly adjusted streaming within one type, is probably a better device than the distinct schools which have been criticized in Britain. The latter bring *social* segregation; and it is surely a vital part of education to know all kinds of people (in Kipling's phrase "to walk with kings, nor lose the common touch"). The general high school permits social interaction without losing the advantages of efficiency of teaching and learning from a common natural pace among those in one class and from an appropriate degree of competition by real peers.

that most of the problem of resources with which the social psychologist is here concerned simply does not exist for most sociologists and economists. An eminent writer in those fields has written quite recently (Myrdal, 1963, p. 29) that, because modern society "needs less and less manual labor" to produce goods, "more and more of our labor force can then be engaged in educating our youth . . . preventing and curing illnesses, advancing sciences, and intensifying and spreading culture." This daydream might be taken seriously if human beings were the "universal robots" that they often become in sociological and economic theory, i.e., indefinitely interchangeable units in economic calculations. The reality seems very different to the psychologist. He recognizes that the resources of intelligence for "curing illnesses" are strictly limited. They are defined by the present, approximately normal, distribution curve of g_f, which, at least for a generation and probably much longer, is fixed at a mean value that education is unlikely to shift more than trivially.

Although the resources of fluid ability (but not all the general capacities), and the provincial powers (in the triadic model) are largely *given,* the *agencies* are as free to develop as the basic fluid ability generator and time will permit. However, as the reader has been cautioned once or twice above, the educator must not unrealistically set the sky as his limit in these aids and proficiencies; for the law of rivalry of expenditures still controls him. Human energy and the twenty-four-hour day still dictate that what he teaches in one area is at the cost of possible increments of ability in another. He is therefore still faced with two questions: (1) in which direction shall the teaching of agencies on an *average* be aimed, e.g., to more numerical, more verbal, or more mechanical ability development; and (b) how much *diversity* of direction is desirable? The first question is, of course, the same as the question encountered earlier in the context of cultural emphasis. Crystallized intelligence, a_g, is the center of gravity of the a factor developments, and therefore we are asking here: "What kind of fluid intelligence is best for our culture?" The educational philosopher's answer to the former question has been given above. The answer often given to the latter is: "as much as possible," though the practical administrator, who wants as much education as possible for limited funds, often finds it more effective to aim at the opposite, for mass production of a standard product is more economical.

The ideal of diversity is commonly based on the belief that the community benefits from producing a manifoldness of talents, inasmuch as they can be expected to summate in some way. Everyone knows how well a picnic goes when one man can cut wood skilfully, another is an expert at cooking, and so on. One of the clearest expressions of the ideal of educating for an array of experts is offered in Dael Wolfle's (1960) comment: "In the selection and education of persons of ability, it is advantageous for a society to seek the greatest achievable diversity of talent: diversity within an individual; among the members of an occupational group, and among the individuals who constitute a society." Nevertheless, this is a somewhat unguarded and "popular" statement for so good a statistician to make. Is there not some *optimum* degree of diversity, beyond which disintegration is risked? The evidence from small group experiment (Hare, Borgatta, and Bales, 1955; Cattell and Stice, 1960) is that, for many types of group performance, there is an ideal degree of diversity that can easily be overshot. Does "diversity within an individual" mean a "jack-of-all-trades and master of none?" Does it mean that among airline pilots it is good to have some who fly well only in fine weather and others who excel in storms?

Economy and the conditions of class teaching and school administration almost certainly lead to a less than optimum variability, but to aim at "the greatest achievable diversity," even if we had infinite resources and educational machinery for achieving it, should surely not be our goal. Society actually needs a superbly judged balance of specialists and integrators. Like an advancing army, it needs scouts in all directions, but also a uniform core of coordinated performers. On the one hand, the too unique individual is not likely to be happy and may not even be socially effective, if he gets too "far out" to be heard. Nevertheless, Wolfle is right that, as a society, we suffer from a mass-produced man. (This is particularly true of the society of which he was once president, the APA.) Abilities are valuable social resources to the extent that they are not redundant, but fill gaps in the social network of available abilities. Maximal utilization of resources, in the area of abilities highly subject to training—the agencies—therefore means arranging education with due regard to the principal of rivalry and the particular diversity of talents that society needs. And the word "needs" applies not just to today, but implies a vigilant scanning of the horizon ahead.

8. AUGMENTING THE SPRINGS OF ABILITY

If a trifling meteorite fifty miles in diameter hit the Pacific, it could cause such survival problems that, without a sufficiency of men of genius, we should all perish. Crawling on a planet's precariously stabilized skin, under which exist incredible pressures and temperatures, and gazing at the vast explosions in an as yet superficially understood outer universe, how can we doubt that understanding through intelligence is our only hope? Whatever other psychological qualities are desirable in man, our concern must be to augment, with all possible means, the level of human intelligence.

The directions we have explored above, for increasing and utilizing resources of intelligence, boil down to working (1) genetically, by fostering the birth of more individuals at higher intelligence levels, (2) environmentally, by maximal educational developments, (3) in terms of survival within a generation, by increasing the survival rate of the gifted, (4) physiologically, by preventing loss of intelligence through disease and the aging process, (5) by redistribution, placing available intelligence more skilfully where it is needed, (6) by calling on little used groups, e.g., the older, especially among women, and, as far as one society is concerned by encouraging immigration of more bright and fewer dull from other societies, and

(7) by constructing mechanical servants, such as computers that will not only do routine tasks but perform feats of reasoning. These seven seem exhaustive of all possibilities. The third—helping the death rate to favor the more intelligent—was objectively discussed by Plato, but can be set aside as relatively unimportant and ethically complex in a medically advanced community. The last has been discussed sufficiently in Chapter 9. Of the remaining five, let us briefly discuss and dismiss immigration, because, on a world stage, it only "robs Peter to pay Paul."

Migration can sometimes be considered as more than a mere shifting without effect on the world average, inasmuch as it comes under the heading of more effective redistribution. Certainly "brain drain" has been going on for some years, consisting of high talent moving from Britain (and other European countries) to the U.S.A., and being partly replaced by doctors and others moving from Commonwealth countries such as India and Malaya to Britain. In 1966, the last year for which data is given, some 5,300 highly qualified scientists migrated to the U.S.A. Except where advanced education is paid for by its recipient, through loans later repaid, the "exporting" country loses both talent and the costs of the individual's education. H. G. Johnson (1968) advises such countries, if they wish to retain talent, to alter the tax structure and the artificially low (relative to open market value) salaries of skilled and professional workers. Economic incentives, at any rate, have been effective means of moving higher ability about the world. It is a pity that economics has not been invoked more in the basic *production* of ability—by making the birth of a bright child less expensive to parents than a less able one, instead of the converse, as pointed out above.

Of the remaining four possibilities, redistribution by selection and placement in educational and occupation areas has been fully discussed, and thus we are left with what have always been the three major constructive possibilities: (1) educational augmentation of basic potentials, i.e., the production of a high level of crystallized intelligence, (2) eugenic augmentation of fluid intelligence and other capacities and powers, and (3) elimination of loss of intelligence and other powers (including sensory powers) over the life span from the erosion by physiological loss and accident.

The augmenting of crystallized intelligence requires the best possible application of learning theory. However, modern learning theory itself still has much to learn about the type of learning which we described as "acquiring tools" (aids) and "learning proficiencies," i.e., raising the level of the "a's." This is learning in which broad, problem-solving skills, appropriately oriented to a particular area (to avoid negative transfer), are built up systematically. Teaching with this kind of apt orientation of agency development to the later cultural demands requires, first, the establishment of a taxonomy describing and classifying the skills within our culture. This would lead to what may be briefly designated "the optimum investment," but over and above this regard for a wisely chosen and adequately pursued investment of fluid intelligence in crystallized intelligence for *everyone,* the adjustment of education to the differing g_f levels of individuals has to be managed. The basic fact remains that the best environmental use of potential requires adjustment of different intensities of education according to g_f levels, as discussed above. Together, these aims require all that the psychologist can do for talent search, and an educational philosophy which does not condemn us to the equal and identical treatment of unequals and the individually different.

The environmental building up of crystallized intelligence has its dangers of gross mistakes as well as its opportunities. First, we can cause frustration and maladjustment by demanding a greater complexity than can be reasonably reached with the biological, fluid ability levels of the given populations. Secondly, education can go wrong in direction, setting up a bad choice of acquired skills. (And if a mistake is made, relative to the developing direction of the culture, a generation has to pass before any new direction of judgmental skills can be easily set up. For, although it is never too late to learn, negative transfer can arise between one set of skills in the individual's educational history and another, and the fluid ability level is reduced by age so that late acquisition of high-level skills at least proceeds with more difficulty.) In the English Public Schools and the two older provincial universities, Oxford and Cambridge, the classics lasted long as the touchstone and centerpiece of crystallized intelligence. In China, the education of the literati and the civil service grew even more out of touch with the new cultural skills actually required for the survival of that country. Crystallized intelligence is a great aid to problem-solving in an agreed area, but in a rapidly changing world its augmentation can be no substitute for high "mother wit," i.e., g_f.

Actually, the socially most neglected, and potentially most vast improvement of community ability resources awaits us in the eugenic improvement of the large genetic component in fluid intelligence. Modern genetics is making rapid strides as a science and the possibilities of dependable positive action are not far away. Basically such action could include: (a) instituting a positive differential birth rate throughout the intelligence range, (b) encouraging mutations toward still higher intelligence, and (c) trying promising hybridizations. Improvement by (a) is the main resource and can operate through the length and breath of society. However, in technical fact, there must come an end to redistributions by multiplication within the existing gene pool. Hopes have arisen since the Crick-Watson understanding of the DNA molecule that "gene surgery" or "euphenics" (by X-rays or chemical means) might directly produce advantageous new mutations, but they would still have to be tried against the verdict of behavior and social life, just as in the prosaic method of waiting for nature to produce mutations.

However, increasing the resources of mental capacity by action within the existing gene pool has two other possible aids besides the inauguration of a positive differential birth rate and watching for advantageous mutations, namely, (a) increasing assortiveness of mating and (b) eutelegenesis.

Increased assortiveness, i.e., improving the means by which the more intelligent find and marry the more intelligent, leads to increased standard deviation of the I.Q. of the nation's offspring. Such a change would result in both a higher proportion of very low and very high I.Q.'s than before. To increase the proportion of very high I.Q.'s within a generation might be the saving of society in emergency situations.

Eutelegenesis, proposed by the Nobel Prize geneticist, Herman Muller and others, is a plan (now being implemented by Robert Graham and others) for artificial insemination of women whose husbands are sterile, from a sperm bank of fathers highly selected for intelligence and other qualities. Since the differential birth rate for mothers is limited, say over a range from 0 to 30 births (or, more practically, 0–10), whereas fathers could range from 0 to many thousands of offspring, this is inherently a more powerful technique than the setting up of a differential family birth rate alone. Enough artificial insemination births have already been medically directed and psychologically observed—many thousands—to show that with, say, the degree of selection of fathers presented merely by taking young doctors as the donors, the intelligence level of offspring is good—significantly above average. So far, this method involves no interference with family structure, but ethical decisions could arise if other possible developments, beyond aiding the infertile, were adopted.

There is enough genetic and statistical understanding and enough community experience to know that both the environmental improvement of a_g and the genetic improvement of g_f will work. About the last of the methods now to be discussed—postponement of ability erosion during life by introducing physiological aids—however, we are as yet in a largely speculative stage. It has already been pointed out that any adequate discussion of community distribution of intelligence resources must consider not only the typical and familiar normal curve distribution *at any one stage,* but also what happens to intelligence over the whole life period. We know that fluid general ability, g_f, typically falls steadily from the early twenties, while crystallized ability, a_g, stays at about the same level, but follows a devious transformation according to the sequence of the individual's life interests, laying down fresh deposits of judgmental skill to compensate for some decay of the old.

Socially and economically, the losses and transformations of these two general intelligences—a_g and g_f—during the prime of life and late middle age, constitute one of the most important determiners of our pool of ability resources. And since government is more in the hands of this age group than any other, the maintenance of high ability here becomes crucially important. It has often been said that the ideal combination for intellectual performance would be that of the mental energy of youth with the wisdom of age, and that youth is wasted on the young. How far are the losses inevitable and how far remediable? As far as a_g is concerned, a wider community acceptance of the fact—well-substantiated experimentally—that "it is never too late to learn" might, with continuing adult education, do much. But on this sustaining of a_g levels there is essentially nothing new to say. With g_f, on the other hand, since we are dealing with a physiological efficiency, one naturally turns to the new hopes of physiological and pharmacological discoveries that might be used to restore to action this immense reservoir of community ability. Our enquires in Chapter 8 leave little expectation that anything in the pharmacopoeia, today or tomorrow, can carry a healthily functioning young brain *beyond* the maximum level for the given brain mass and structure. But where some loss of function from a previous high level has occurred, there are indications that physiological aids could, at least for some periods of time, restore action to its original maximum. At present we simply do not know how much of the g_f decline is due to a normal biological process and how much to various assaults on the brain, e.g., from violent accidents, anesthetics, carbon monoxide, smoking, transient inflammations and fevers, and avoidable atheroschlerotic conditions.[19] Even when the decline is due to normally expected physiological changes, such as the decline in DNA production in brain cells found by Hydén (1959), there is no intrinsic reason why remedial measures should not be possible. From the standpoint of society, there is an enormously greater potential increment from any discovery which would offset this *universal* loss of g_f than from all the educational efforts now devoted to remedying largely hereditarily irremediable structural defects in the one or two percent of mental defectives and retardates in the population.

In advanced countries—but, alas, not in three-quarters of the world's population—the prospects of successfully marshaling these aids to augment community resources of ability are good—if morale survives the population explosion. And granted success in directing social attention to the real foundations of cultural advance—human ability—we could find ourselves in the midst of an unprecedented flowering of civilization. Nevertheless, despite all this attention to the importance of intelligence, let us end this book, as we began, with the perspective-giving recognition that, for the individual himself, intelligence is but an instrument. Sir Cyril Burt, whose long lifework has been the study of intelligence in all its forms, recently concluded a review in *Mensa* (Burt, 1967) of intelligence and achievement with the words: "But the most important factor of all is the individual's character and temperament." Certainly intelligence is valueless, or even positively dangerous, unless it is the servant of character and clear moral values.

---

[19] Dr. D. Harman, University of Nebraska, has shown that rat "intelligence" can be reduced by atherosclerotic changes from feeding excess saturated fat, and partially avoided by unsaturated fat. Extension of such researches would be one approach to answering the question raised here.

Wherever (as in phenylketonuria) individual mental defect, like the decline in g_f in the general population, is not primarily a matter of *structure,* but of physiological function, remedies may hopefully be envisaged. Remedies for structural inadequacy—sheer absence of development of brain tissue—are, on the other hand, at present doubtful and wholly speculative.

GLOSSARY

Abative Scores. Scores for one individual on one test, repeated many times, in which each occasion is given a standard score with respect to the population of occasions. (Distinguish ipsative scoring, in which standardization is for one person across tests.)

Ability Dimension Analysis Chart (The ADAC). A theoretical schema proposing a specific, substantially exhaustive, set of parameters, according to which any ability should be classifiable. It has three domains, action phase, content, and process, each divisible, e.g., action phase into input, storage, and output.

Ability Distribution Dislocation. A theory of wage change and unemployment through a dislocation of the intelligence distribution curves of supply (birth rates) and demand (technological advance).

Ability Shift Theory of Business Cycles. The theory that some conditions cause unemployment at lower and full employment at higher intelligence levels; and that at other times, the two distribution curves (supply and demand) involved shift into the opposite phase. These shifts produce price changes and business cycles.

Ability Sphere. A sub-set of the personality sphere, q.v., of largely ability-modality performances. Therefore, a population of all variables, from which samples can be taken.

Action Equation (or Present Action Equation). An equation estimating an individual's ability (or other) performance at a given time in terms of ability, temperament, dynamic traits, and conditions existing at the time. (Contrast with Developmental Equation, q.v.)

Adjustment Process Analysis. A means of investigating and expressing personality learning by the frequency of following certain adjustment paths and by their effect upon personality factors in a matrix multiplication design.

Affluence-Intelligence. A factor found in factoring syntalities of modern nations which links real standard of living with years of education and behaviors that could reflect level of intelligence. Hence, a component in relative national affluence that seems independent of fortune in natural resources.

Agencies. Unitary abilities that develop as primary abilities through investment of general abilities and dynamic traits in problem solving developments.

Aids. The development of systems of cognitive ability to cope, through the discovery of some particular response formula which is successful and generates many associated performances.

Ambient Stimulus. That part of a total environmental situation which is *not* the focal stimulus, q.v. Roughly, all kinds of background and circumstantial conditions other than the stimulus to which the organism is primarily reaching.

Assortive Mating. The tendency of like to marry like, expressed in most traits by a positive correlation of husband and wife of about 0.1 to 0.6.

Behavior Specification Equation. An estimation of the magnitude of an individual's response (performance) in terms of loadings (descriptive of the situation) and trait scores (descriptive of the individual), each loading multiplying one factor trait score.

Behavioral Situation Indices. The values, which are factor loadings, usually written b or s in the behavioral specification equation, which show how much a given source trait is involved in that specific situation and response.

Bipolar Factor. A factor having roughly as many negative as positive loadings. Not to be confused with Holzinger's "bifactor."

Bloated Specific. A factor which, in true perspective (see Personality Sphere), would be a specific or very narrow, but which, through the experimenter multiplying highly similar tests, is "blown up" into a seemingly broad common factor.

Coercion to Cultural-Genetic Mean, Law of. The tendency of social pressure to force behavior to the existing central norm.

Combining or Associational Mass. That part of the neurological brain mass which is not assigned to particular sensory, motor, or behavioral control areas, and is concerned purely with associating and combining (in the cortex) elements from more specialized areas.

Common or Broad Factor. A factor (trait or state) that affects many variables (of *all* in a matrix, it is common or general), contrasted with specific, q.v.

Communalities. The correlation values put in the diagonal of a correlation matrix before factoring (initially as estimates, finally as exact values), expressing the extent to which each variable shares common variance with all other variables.

Conditional Factors and Factoring. Factors obtained from variables administered under restrictions, particularly as to modality, e.g., by holding motivation or complexity constant. (Contrasted with Wholistic Factors, q.v.)

Confactor Rotation. A means of reaching unique rotational resolution, giving trait meaning to factors, in which the factors from two researches are rotated to congruence, and shown by proportionality of loading pattern on corresponding factors.

Conspect Reliability Coefficient. The degree of agreement of two psychologists scoring the same recorded or observed responses.

Cooperative Factor. A factor having the loading pattern on salient variables very similar to that of another independent factor with which its correlation may be negligible.

Correlation Matrix. A triangular or square arrangement of cells which gives the correlation between all possible pairing among the variables (e.g., test scores, etc.) studied.

Cortertia, U.I. 22. The factor of cortical alertness and arousal, in objective tests, such as reaction time, flicker fusion speed, etc.

Criterion and Predictor Variables. Criterion variables are usually real life performances, and predictors are tests. But, this is not necessary (any grouping is possible), nor are predictors "causes" and criterion "consequence." A multiple correlation of predictors on the criterion is usually calculated.

Criterion Rotation. A form of factor rotation in which the difference existing between a control and an experimental or criterion group is made to be the expression of a single factor.

Cultural Pressure. A dimension of syntality found among modern nations which appears to express the extent to which ergic long-circuiting of satisfactions ("restraint") is required in the culture. It affects cultural productivity, aggression, and mental disorder.

Culture-Bound Factors. Personality factors which are recognizable only in one culture and are presumably peculiar to the effect of its institution.

Culture-Fair Test. (Also, culture reduced, culture free, etc.) A test which, by operating only with material and habits common to all cultures, seeks to minimize the effect of special cultural skills in educing complex relations. It need not eliminate differences of races and classes, since such differences could be real.

Culture-Free Factors. Personality factors which appear with much the same loading patterns in varied cultures. (Distinguish Transcultural Factor, q.v.)

Delayed Discriminatory Response Test. A test in which the motor response must be delayed (if reward is to be gained) some time after the sensory presentation determining the choice has been made.

Dependability Coefficient. That coefficient, in the class of *test consistency coefficients,* calculated by correlation scores of a testing and an immediate re-testing. (Distinguish from Stability Coefficient, q.v.)

Developmental Equation. A specification equation which analyzes the present level of an ability (or other trait) in terms of traits and learning processes operating over previous years. (Contrast with Present Action Equation, q.v., involving most of the same terms.)

Disposition Rigidity. The resistance which a habit offers to change, independently of its particular dynamic strength, as shown by difficulty in re-structuring particular elements in motor and perceptual tasks. Sometimes called perseverative tendency.

Dissolvent Thinking. That contribution to the creation of a new idea in certain area which is made by the dissolution of incompatible existing ideas. It may be greater in some persons through greater endowment in a flexibility vs. rigidity factor, g_x.

Dual File System. A system in industrial personnel work of summarizing all information in two files: (a) individual endowment profiles, and (b) job profiles.

Dynamic Calculus. The model, objective measurements, and principles concerned with inter-relating attitude strengths, interests, conflict, and learning using vectors, ergs, engrams, etc.

Dynamic Lattice. A representation of the habit systems, attitudes, subgoals, and ergic goals to bring out their full subsidiation pattern, as chains intersecting in a lattice.

Dynamic Structure Factors. Source traits found among attitude-strength measures of very varied content and representing both ergs and engrams. (Distinguish from Motivation Component Factors, q.v.)

Ecogenic Component Curve. That part of the obtained age curve for any trait which is due to the characteristic nature of the typical environment across different epochs. (Contrast Epogenic, q.v.)

Eduction of Relations. The tendency of the possible logical relations between two objects to rise into consciousness on focusing attention on those objects.

Ego Strength. A source trait found in behavior ratings and questionnaire responses, labeled C, or U.I.(L) or (Q) 3, and corresponding to the clinical concept of ego strength.

Endogenous Curve Component. The component in an age curve that is due to the typical internal maturational and involutional qualities of people.

Engram. Possibly a single element, but more commonly a unitary factor pattern, M, found in the analysis of dynamic trait manifestations. The M's cover sentiments and complexes, and represent the contribution to interest strength through past experience of reward and conditioning of the reaction tendencies in the pattern. Engramming is a general term for that part of memorizing which consists in setting up permanent storage.

Epogenic Curve Component. A component of an age trend curve on intelligence or other trait that is due to the historical peculiarity of the time epoch concerned.

Equipotentiality, Law of. (See Mass Action.)

Erg. A pattern, discovered by factor analysis of dynamic trait measures, which corresponds by its goal quality to an instinctual pattern in the higher mammals. Consequently, it is hypothesized to be an innate reactivity toward a goal, though stimuli and means are learned. The terms "drive" and "instinct" have been used, but they lack the operational precision and statistical support of ergic patterns.

Ergic Tension (Q_4+). The objectively measurable (see Motivation Components) level of drive strength in an erg. Also, in personality testing, the source trait interpreted as the total aroused unexpressed drive tension (from ergic sources). It covers tense, driven, over-active behavior.

Excitation Learning Principle. The principle that if two cognitive or action systems experience excitation at the same time, excitation, henceforth, of one evokes the other. This covers association and classical conditioning, but not operant conditioning (reward learning).

Exogenous Curve Component. The component in a trait age change curve (including epogenic and ecogenic components) that is due to exposure to the typical environment which people encounter.

Exuberance. The name given to a trait, in objective tests, indexed as U.I. 21, and showing itself in high fluency, rapid decision, spontaneity, etc.

Factor (or Factor Analytic) Homogeneity (of a Test). The quality of a test by which all items or subtests tend to have the same factor composition, that of some single factor.

Factor Analysis. A method of accounting for the observed correlations among many variables in terms of a much more limited set of underlying determiners, called factors. It decides the number of influences required, and gives information on their nature, instead of leaving trait definition to the subjective choice of the psychologist.

Factor Loading. A loading of a variable by a factor (represented by b, for behavior index, in many psychological predictions) is the fraction of a unit change in a variable produced by unit change in a factor. (In orthogonal factors, it is a correlation.)

Factor Matrix. A matrix of n rows (corresponding to variables) and k columns (corresponding to factors) in which each number describes how much the given factor contributes to the variance of a given variable.

Factor Pattern. The pattern (vector) of loadings of a factor on a series of variables.

Factor Strata. Factor orders—primary, second order, tertiary—refer to factoring operations. Factor strata are conceived levels of factors, as influences believed influences, only partly determined by factor order findings.

Fidelity Coefficient. The extent to which a test, e.g., an intelligence test, continues to measure the same factor or factors as the sample moves toward the extremes of the range of intended use.

Focal Stimulus. That element in the total environment to which the organism is primarily reacting, e.g., by instruction, by consciously singling it out, etc.

Function Fluctuation. The real variation on a source trait from time to time with internal and external conditions (not in the focal stimulus), differentiating the stability coefficient from the consistency coefficient.

General Capacity, written "g". A cognitive ability which, as a unitary factor, seems to run across virtually all cognitive performance, as with intelligence, speed, capacity to retrieve memory material, etc. (Contrast p's and a's.)

Genetic Maturation Rate of Intelligence. The rate of inner motivation of intelligence, presumably different for different genetic constitutions, and producing instability in the I.Q. as commonly calculated.

Genetic Pattern Method of Cross-Cultural Trait Comparison. The identification of a trait for comparison of measures across cultures by sorting factor patterns for the same variables in several cultures into "types" by the pattern similarity coefficient, r_p, and taxonome.

Genetic Regression to the Mean. The tendency of a relative of a person, measured on some genetically composite trait, to be nearer the average than the person himself. Pearson's law of filial regression to the mean, showing sons nearer to the mean than fathers on intelligence, is the classical case.

Genothreptics. The science concerned with studying the interaction of heredity and environment. Genothreptic ratio is the same as nature-nurture ratio, q.v.

Guilt-Proneness (O+). A source trait distinct from super-ego strength but predisposing to guilt-prone, depressive, apprehensive behavior.

Heritability Coefficient. The ratio of the genetic to the total observed variance ratio, written h. (See Nature-Nurture Ratio n, q.v.)

Hierarchy of Correlations. A correlation matrix in which it is possible to arrange values so that they decline uniformly from top to bottom and left to right—indicative of a single general factor being sufficient.

Hierarchy of Relations. The fact that relations can arise among relations leads to the field of cognitive understanding being a hierarchy, starting with sensory elements, leading to hierarchies within provinces (p's), and so to the highest general abstract concepts.

Higher Order Factors. With oblique factors, one can take second order factors from their correlation matrix, and third orders from the correlations of second orders, and, possibly, further. They stand to factors as primary factors to variables.

Homogeneity Coefficient. That test consistency coefficient, differing from reliability-dependability and from transferability, which evaluates the agreement between parts of the test. It includes the case of agreement of two parts, as in the equivalence coefficient.

Homostat Type. A type defined by a set of people who are placed close together by their scores on factor coordinates.

Hurdle Effect. The unusual correlation produced between two variables in a group selected by having to pass a "hurdle" in which the variables are mutually substitutable, i.e., loaded in the same sense on the criterion. A negative correlation, e.g., of intelligence and persistence, could thus be produced among those passing a difficult examination.

Hyperplane. A plane in the hyperspace representation of test vectors and factors, formed by a concentration of tests unaffected by the factor perpendicular to the hyperplane.

Hyperplane Stuff. Variables introduced into a factor analysis that are unlikely to have any correlation with the main ability studied to create a hyperplane to help exact rotation. A ground for a figure.

Ideational Flexibility (vs. Firmness). A unitary cognitive tendency, distinct from fluency, intelligence, and low rigidity, which favors easy restructuring of the cognitive field, as in seeing riddles, puns, etc.

Imprinting. The tendency of a learning experience at one stage in an inner, genetic maturational phase to have greater consequence than at another.

Inventive-Response Test. An "open-ended" test in which the subject is restricted in response only by the instructions, as opposed to a selective-response test in which given response alternatives restrict the possible responses.

Investment Theory of Crystallized Intelligence. The theory that both the general unifactor form and individuals' levels on a_g arise from variations in the degree of investment of fluid intelligence, g_f, by different people, in the total area of learning activities. Primary abilities are also explained by investment theory, but with agencies predominating.

Ipsative Scores. Scores expressed with respect to a standardization within one person. Different tests must be measurable in a common metric in order to do this, and his score on one is a standard score with respect to the distribution of all his scores. (Distinguish from the somewhat similar Abative Score.)

Isomorphism of Interest and Ability. A principle that ability structure as "proficiencies," q.v., tends to follow and parallel dynamic interest structures, as "sentiments," q.v.

Itemetrics. That part of psychometrics which has to do only with tests resolvable into items and is concerned with relating properties of items to properties of scales.

L Data. Life-record data, covering behavior *in situ* instead of in a test and, therefore, including the specifically important behaviors of criteria. Often evaluated by behavior rating.

Loading. The extent to which variance on a factor contributes to variance on the behavior concerned. A value obtained by factor analysis.

Mass Action, Law of. The tendency of all parts of the cortex to be equal in potential for determining learning that involves intelligence. Hence, the neurological theory that the whole cortex participates in intelligent actions.

Medium. A medium of personality behavior observation, of which there are three: life record, questionnaire self-evaluation, and objective test.

M.M.P.I. The Minnesota Multiphasic Personality Inventory by Hathaway and McKinley, which is a questionnaire for recognizing surface traits or syndromes of an abnormal nature.

Modality. The class of a trait in respect to ability, temperament, and dynamic traits.

Modulation Theory. A model which supposes that ambient situations change the levels and group variance on states according to a certain law. Modular indices, multiplying state liability trait scores in the specification equation, express this modulator action of a stimulus.

Morale. The dynamic state of a group, measurable largely in factors of reward morale, immediate synergy, and leadership synergy.

Motivational Components. The components, principally integrated and unintegrated, found when manifestations of motivation strength are factored.

Multiple Abstract Variance Analysis (M.A.V.A.) Design. A research design for discovering relative proportions of environmental vs. hereditary determination for personality traits (Nature-Nurture Ratio).

Nature-Nurture Ratio. The ratio expressing the percentages contributed in a given social and racial group, respectively by *hereditary* and by *environmental* differences, to the observed interpersonal variability in a trait. As a variance notion written n.

Negative Transfer of Training. The situation in which learning more on performance A reduces one's performance in B, usually due to some interference of skills.

O-A Battery. The Objective-Analytic Personality Factor Test Battery, an experimental battery from recent research covering eighteen factors.

Objective Test. A test in which the subject's behavior is measured, for making inferences about his personality, without his being aware in what ways his behavior is likely to affect the interpretation. A test of this kind is to be distinguished from a questionnaire in which there is semiobjectivity (Conspection, q.v.), in which he himself estimates his acts.

Oblique Factors. Correlated factors, as distinct from orthogonal factors, as they initially appear from a factor analysis.

P Technique. The factor analysis of a set of variables, each measured over the same series of occasions for the same organism (or group mean). P means single *person* factoring.

Pattern Similarity Coefficient. A coefficient summarized as r_p which indicates the degree of similarity between the personality profiles of two people or of one person and the ideal pattern for an occupation, etc., and which varies from $+1$ to -1 like a correlation coefficient.

Penetrance. The percentage of the persons known to possess a certain gene who actually show one possible phenotype expression for it, in a given social environment.

Permissive Relation. The relation of one factor to another such that a certain level must be reached on the former before the latter can function on the criterion at all.

Personality Sphere. A population of variables, measures of behavior, which covers the totality of the interactions of people with other people and the physical world, in a given culture. A representative set of personality expressions.

Positive Manifold. A factor solution in which variables have only positive loadings on the factors.

Primary Abilities. The dozen or more primary factors found from correlations of ability performances, including verbal, numerical, spatial, etc.

Process Parameters. The dimensions in terms of which an ongoing process can be plotted.

Proficiencies. Common measurable patterns of ability which grow around dynamic structures. The whole being called effector agencies but the cognitive part a "proficiency." A *Proficiency* and an *aid* due two kinds of *agency*.

Provincial Organizations or "Powers," p's. Factorially unitary ability traits which apparently correspond to neurological sensory and motor areas. To be distinguished from *capacities* g's, that one completely general *agencies,* a's, that represent culturally learnt unities.

Purposive vs. Purposeful. The former term indicates behavior that is dynamic in the sense of having a purpose and a goal. The latter behavior in which, additionally, the person himself fully realizes the goal.

Q Data. Evidence on personality from self-evaluative, introspective report, as in the consulting room or filling out a questionnaire.

Q Technique. A factor analysis from correlating persons (scored over a series of tests) instead of tests. The transpose of R technique.

Rate Retentivity, g_m. A factor determining good retention which is independent of intelligence, and shows itself basically in retention for "meaningless" material.

Reference Vectors. The coordinates in factor analysis that are drawn orthogonal to hyperplanes. They are not, technically, factors; but they fix the position of factors.

Reflexology. A system of laws in the field of learning experiment in which a simple reflex connection, such as might be due to a neurological reflex arc, is supposed to exist between the stimulus and the response.

Reticular Model. A model to guide the interpretation of structure by factor analysis which is the principal alternative to the strata model. It supposes a network of influences, with positive and negative feedback.

Retrieval Capacity, g_r. A general ability factor showing itself in rate of recall of material in memory storage. It is close to general fluency, but the latter represents also size of store.

Saturation in Intelligence. The degree to which a test performance is loaded by the g factor. (See Loading, q.v.)

Second-Order or Higher-Order Factors. Factors of wider influence obtained by correlating factors themselves and factor analyzing them. Thus, factors among factors.

Segregate Type. A set of people between whom and another set there are no persons intermediate in factor score profile.

Self-Sentiment. The factor and system of attitudes centered on the conceived, contemplated self, and directed to maintaining its physical, social, and moral integrity as a basis for other sentiment and ergic satisfactions.

Sentiment. A factor among attitudes corresponding to an acquired pattern from a social institution. Such factors may be either object intersection or subgoal centered.

Simple Structure. A unique rotational resolution of a factor analysis which allows each factor to affect a minimum number of variables. Since a real influence is unlikely to affect all variables, this suggests alignment with real influences has been attained.

Simplex Scaling Theory. The assignment of equal intervals on a scale on the theory that correlations among scales for diverse variables will be maximized when all scales stand at the equal interval condition.

Source Trait. A trait defined as a uniquely rotated (simple structure or confactor) factor. Thus, a pattern of behavior due to a single source.

Specific Factors or Trait. An influence found only in one performance, measured by what remains when broad factor contributions are removed.

Stability Coefficient. The correlation of a test with itself after appreciable time lapse. It thus measures the sum of the test undependability (See Dependability Coefficient, q.v.) and the function fluctuation characteristic of the trait itself (not the test).

Standard Score I.Q. The I.Q. calculated from a distribution of scores at one age, assuming a normal distribution from an agreed sigma of I.Q., usually 16 points.

Standard Validity. The validity of a test corrected for the range and other parameters of the population sample to make a reliable choice among alternative tests feasible.

State Liability Trait Score. A score assigned to a trait-like liability of an individual to experience a certain state when provoked. His actual level on a state is thus estimated by his liability, L, multiplied by the situational provocation level, expressed in the modulator index, s.

Stens. Units in a standard ten scale in which ten score points are used to cover the population range in fixed and equal standard deviation intervals, extending from 2½ standard deviations above the means (sten 10). The mean is fixed at 5·5 stens. In this book, questionnaire raw scores are usually converted to stens, when intending to use them normatively (to compare obtained values with population values).

Structured Learning Theory. A development beyond classical, bivariate reflexological learning theory, arising from multivariate experiment. It employs as "intermediate variables" the concepts of traits, behavioral indices (factor loadings), modulator indices, ergic tension states, ergic reward patterns, co-excitation, and dynamic sets. (See Cattell, 1971 in bibliography.)

Subsidiation. A stable sequence in the learning, and the temporal functioning, of attitudes and habit systems, arising because the completion of one course of action provides, by its subgoal, the necessary condition for the starting of another course.

Super-Ego Strength $(G+)$. A source trait governing conscientious, persevering, unselfish behavior and impelling the individual to duty as conceived by his culture.

Surface Trait. The pattern of a correlation cluster, fixed by its centroid. It is "surface" rather than "source" because it may be the composite resultant of several factors.

Surgency. A source trait of happy-go-lucky, heedless, gay, uninhibited, and enthusiastic, behavior.

Synergy. The energy, representable by an ergic vector, by means of which a group operates. It sums the attitude vectors representing the interest strengths of members in the group life.

Syntality. That which determines a group's performance when its situation is given. Analogous to personality in the individual, and measured on trait dimensions.

T Technique. Factor analysis of a correlation matrix from correlating, on a sample of people, the various occasions on which the same test is repeated.

Taxonome Program. A computer program which illuminates the taxonomy of a domain, employing the pattern similarity coefficient, r_p, segregate search methods, etc.

"Telescopic" Principle in Test Construction. Constructing a test in many parallel A, B, C, etc., forms so that the user may find always a suitable compromise length for the validity desired and time available.

Test Sophistication. The component in the score of a test due purely to the subject having taken the test (or one like it) before.

Test Vector. A series of numbers expressing the projections of a test on factor coordinates, hence describing how various factors enter into success in that test.

Three Vector Learning Analysis. This rests on the notion in *structured learning theory,* q.v., that learning on a set of variables can be fully described by (a) a vector of *trait* gains, (b) a vector of changes on *behavioral indices,* and (c) a vector of changes on *modular indices,* q.v.

Tractability. Defined as a trait of passive plasticity or openness to acquire new responses. No adequate factor analytic definition as yet. (See Dissolvent Thinking.)

Transcultural Factor. A basis for measuring numbers of different cultures on an identical, unique factor trait, from correlating the mean performance of many variables on many cultures.

Transferability Coefficient. A correlation showing how much a test measures with one group of subjects the same thing that it measures with other kinds of subjects.

Transposed Factor Analysis. Factoring people over tests is the transpose of factoring tests over a series of people. One score matrix is the transpose of the other. R and Q; P and O; T and S-techniques are transposes.

Unicausal Thinking. The habit of looking for one cause for one effect or phenomena. Most psychological phenomena are multiply determined and require multivariate experimental analysis to understand them.

Universal Index (U.I.) Number. Number on a proposed indexing system for thrice-confirmed factors, to avoid premature interpretive names.

Utility Coefficient of a Test. The mean contribution of a test to the prediction of a standard, stratified sample of practical criteria in a given area, e.g., education. This represents both its *validity* and the *relevance* of the factor which it measures.

Validity. The capacity of a test to predict one or more performances outside itself, measured by the correlation of the test with these responses to other situations. The coefficients may be divided according to basis into *concrete* (test or cultural performance referent), *concept* (or construct), direct, indirect, and standard validity; as well as certain spurious forms such as face, intrinsic, and content validities. Breadth of validity and utility are further derived concepts from these.

Variance. The magnitude of variability of a score. Technically, $\frac{\sum_{o}^{N} d^2}{N}$ where d is the deviation of each person from the mean and there are N persons.

Wholistic Factors. Factors from "naturalistic" variables in uncontrolled conditions, and therefore wider than conditional factors, q.v. Thus, a motivational "school interest" factor would wholistically run across intelligence subtests too, except where children's motivations are essentially equalized by powerful conditional motivation.

REFERENCES

Adkins, Dorothy C. The effects of practice on intelligence test scores. *Journal of Educational Psychology*, 1937, 28, 222–231.

Adkins, Dorothy C., & Lyerly, S. B. *Factor analysis of reasoning tests.* Chapel Hill: University of North Carolina Press, 1952.

Adrian, E. D. *The physical basis of perception.* Oxford: Clarendon Press, 1947.

Alexander, W. P. Intelligence: Concrete and abstract. *British Journal of Psychology Monograph*, 19, 1935.

Allport, G. W. *Pattern and growth in personality.* New York: Holt, Rinehart and Winston, 1961.

Altus, W. D. Birth order, intelligence, and adjustment. *Psychological Reports*, 1959, 5, 502.

Alvi, S. A. Traditional and "culture fair" aptitude test performance of college students from different academic and cultural background. Unpublished doctoral dissertation. Indiana University, 1963.

Ampère, A. M. *Essai sur la philosophie des sciences.* 1834.

Anastasi, A. A. A group factor in immediate memory. *Archives of Psychology*, 1930, 18 (No. 120), 5–61.

Anastasi, A. *Differential psychology.* New York: Macmillan, 1958. (a)

Anastasi, A. Heredity and environment, and the question How. *Psychological Review*, 1958, 65, 197–208. (b)

Anastasi, A. A., Fuller, J. L., Scott, J. P., & Schmitt, J. R. A factor analysis of the performance of dogs on certain learning tests. *Zoologica*, 1955, 40.

Anderson, H. H., & Anderson, M. *Projective Techniques.* New York: Prentice Hall, 1950.

Andrews, F. M. Factors affecting the manifestation of creative ability by scientists. *Journal of Personality*, 1965, 33, 140–152.

Ardrey, R. A. *African Genesis.* New York: Dell, 1961.

Asch, S. A study of change in mental organization. *Psychological Archives*, 1936, #195.

Ashby, W. R. Design for an intelligence amplifier. In C. E. Shannon and J. McCarthy (Eds.), Automata studies, *Annals of Mathematics Studies,* Vol. 34. Princeton, New Jersey: Princeton, 1946. Pp. 215–234.

Ashby, W. R. *Design for a brain: The origin of adaptive behavior.* (2nd ed.) New York: Wiley, 1960.

Ashton, T. S. *The industrial revolution,* 1948.

Aveling, F. A. P. *The consciousness of the universal.* London: University of London Press, 1930.

Babbage, H. P. *Babbage's Calculating Engines.* London: Macmillan, 1888.

Baggaley, A. R. *Intermediate correlational methods.* New York: Wiley, 1964.

Bagshaw, M. H., & Pribram, K. H. Effect of amygdalectomy on transfer of training in monkeys. *Journal of Comparative and Physiological Psychology,* 1965, 59 (1), 118–121.

Bakwin, H. Glutamic acid and mental functioning. *Journal of Pediatrics,* 1947, 31, 702–703.

Balinsky, B. An analysis of the mental factors of various age groups from 9–60. *Genetic Psychology Monographs,* 1941, 23, 191–234.

Ballard, C. S. *Group tests of intelligence.* London: Harrap, 1927.

Baltes, P. B. Longitudinal and cross sectional sequences in the study of age and generation effects. *Human Development,* 1968, 11, 145–171.

Barron, F. *Creativity and psychological health.* Princeton, N.J.: Van Nostrand, 1963.

Bartlett, F. C. *Thinking. An experimental and social study.* London: Allen and Unwin, 1958.

Barzun, J. *The house of intellect.* New York: Harper, 1959.

Bass, R. I. An analysis of the components of tests of static and dynamic balance. *Research Quarterly of the American Association of Health and Physical Education,* 1939, 10, 33–52.

Bayley, Nancy. Mental growth during the first three years: a developmental study of sixty-one children by repeated tests. *Genetic Psychology Monographs,* 1933, 14, 1–92.

Bayley, Nancy. Consistency and variability in the growth of intelligence from birth to 18 years. *Journal of Genetic Psychology,* 1949, 75, 165–196.

Bayley, Nancy. Some increasing parent-child similarities during the growth of children. *Journal of Educational Psychology,* 1954, 45, 1–21.

Bayley, Nancy. Research in child development, a longitudinal perspective. Merrill-Palmer *Quarterly of Behavior Development,* 1965, 11, 183–208.

Bayley, Nancy. Learning in adulthood: the role of intelligence. In H. J. Klausmeier & C. W. Harris (Eds.), *Analysis of concept learning.* New York: Academic Press, 1966. Pp. 177–238.

Bayley, Nancy, & Oden, M. H. The maintenance of intellectual ability in gifted adults. *Journal of Gerontology,* 1955, 10, 91–107.

Beach, F. A. *Sex and behavior.* New York: J. Wiley & Sons, Inc., 1965.

Beach, F. A., & Jaynes, J. Effects of early experience upon the behavior of animals. *Psychological Bulletin,* 1954, 51, 239–262.

Beach, F. H. *Hormones and behavior, a survey of interrelationship between en-*

docrine secretions and patterns of overt response. New York: P. B. Hoeber, 1948.

Bechtoldt, H. P. Factorial investigation of the perceptual speed factor. *American Psychologist,* 1947, 2, 304–305.

Bechtoldt, H., & More, R. Correlational analysis of test-retest data with a thirty-year intertrial interval. *Proceedings of the Iowa Academy of Science,* 1957, 64, 514–519.

Bell, H. M. Retention of pursuit rotor learning after one year. *Journal of Experimental Psychology,* 1950, 40, 648–649.

Benjamin, B. Social and economic differences in ability. In J. E. Meade and A. S. Parkes (Eds.), *Genetic and environmental factors in human ability.* Edinburgh: Oliver and Boyd, 1966.

Bennett, G. K., Seashore, H. G., & Weisman, A. G. *Differential aptitude tests manual.* New York: Psychological Corp., 1952.

Benton, A. L. Influence of incentives upon intelligence test scores of school children. *Journal of Genetic Psychology,* 1936, 49, 494–497.

Berger, F. M. Classification of psychoactive drugs according to their chemical structures and sites of action. In L. Uhr & J. G. Miller (Eds.), *Drugs and behavior.* New York: Wiley, 1960. Pp. 86–106.

Berlyne, D. E. *Conflict, arousal and curiosity.* New York: McGraw-Hill, 1960.

Berlyne, D. E. *Structure and direction in thinking.* New York: Wiley, 1965.

Bernstein, A., Klein, E., Berger, L., & Cohen, J. The influence of institutionalization and several pre-morbid and demographic variables on the structure of intelligence in chronic schizophrenics. *Newsletter in Research Psychology,* 1963, 5, 34–35.

Bernstein, E. Quickness and intelligence. *British Journal of Psychological Monograph Supplements,* 1924, 7.

Beveridge, W. T. B. *The art of scientific investigation.* New York: Vintage Books, 1950.

Bianki, V. L. O roli mozolistogo tela (corpus callosum) v osuschestvlenii parnoi deyatel'nosti zritel'nogo i kozhonogo analizatorov krolika. *Zh. vyssh. nervn. Deyatel.,* 1959, 9, 116–125.

Bianki, V. L. Kmekhanizmu vzaimodestviia simmetrichnykh korkovykh tsentrov zritel'nogo analizatora. *Zh. vyssh nervn. Deyatel.,* 1959, 9, 872–879.

Bianki, V. L. CR to light and sound in fish deprived of cerebellum. *Zh vyssh. nervn. Deyatel.,* 1962, 12, 5, 962–968.

Binet, A., & Simon, T. Méthodes nouvelles pour le diagnostic du niveau intellectuel des anormaux. *L'Année Psychologique,* 1905, 11, 191–244. (a)

Binet, A., & Simon, T. Le developpement de l'intelligence chez les enfants. *L'Année Psychologique,* 1905, 14, 1–94. (b)

Birren, J. E. Age changes in speed of behavior: its central nature and physiological correlates. In A. T. Welford and J. E. Birren (Eds.), *Behaviour, ageing and the nervous system.* Springfield: C. C. Thomas, 1965. Pp. 191–216.

Bischof, L. J. *Interpreting personality theories.* New York: Harper & Rowe, 1964.

Bitterman, M. E. The evolution of intelligence. *Scientific American,* 1965, 212, 92–100.

Blackwell, A. M. A comparative investigation in the factors involved in mathematical ability of boys and girls. *British Journal of Education,* 1940, 10, 143–153, 212–222.

Bloom, B. S. *Stability and change in human characteristics.* New York: Wiley, 1964.

Borg, W. R. Ability grouping in the public schools. *Journal of Experimental Education,* 1965, 34, 2–97.

Botzum, W. A. A factorial study of the reasoning and closure factors. *Psychometrika,* 1951, 16, 361–386.

Bowlby, J. Some pathological processes set in train by early mother-child separation. *Journal of Mental Science,* 1953, 99, 265–272.

Bowlby, J., Ainsworth, Mary, Boston, M., & Rosenbluth, D. The effects of mother-child separation: a follow-up study. *British Journal of Medical Psychology,* 1956, 29, 211–247.

Boyd, W. C. Genetics and the races of man. In S. M. Garn (Ed.), *Readings on race.* Springfield, Illinois: Thomas, 1960. Pp. 17–27.

Boyne, A. W., & Clark, J. R. Secular change in the intelligence of 11-year-old Aberdeen school children. *Human Biology,* 1959, 31, 325–333.

Bradway, Katherine P. Paternal occupational intelligence and mental deficiency. *Journal of Applied Psychology,* 1935, 19, 527–542.

Bradway, Katherine P., & Robinson, N. M. Significant IQ changes in twenty-five years: a follow-up. *Journal of Educational Psychology,* 1961, 52(2), 74–79.

Brazier, Mary A. The analysis of brain waves. *Scientific American,* 1962, 206(6), 142–153.

Broadbent, D. E. *Perception and communications.* New York: Pergamon Press, 1958.

Broadbent, D. Short term memory. *The New Scientist,* 1965, 16, 20–21.

Broverman, D. M., Klaiber, E. L., Kobayashi, G., & Vogel, W. The roles of activation and inhibition in sex differences in cognitive abilities. *Psychological Review,* 1968.

Brown, A. W., Jenkins, R. L., & Cisler, L. E. Influence of lethargic encephalitis on intelligence of children as determined by objective tests. *American Journal of Diseased Children,* 1938, 55, 304–321.

Brown, M. H., & Bryan, G. E. Sex as a variable in intelligence test performance. *Journal of Educational Psychology,* 1957, 48, 273–278.

Brown, W. Lynn, Overall, J. E., & Blodgett, H. C. Novelty learning sets in rhesus monkeys. *Journal of Comparative and Physiological Psychology,* 1959, 52, 330–332.

Brown, W., & Stephenson, W. A test of the theory of two factors. *British Journal of Psychology,* 1933, 23, 352–370.

Brozek, J., Guetzkow, H., Keys, A., Cattell, R. B., et al. A study of personality of normal young men maintained on restricted intakes of Vitamin B. *Psychosomatic Medicine,* 1946, 8, 98–109.

Brubaker, M. L., & Pierson, W. R. The effect of dexadrine on primary mental abilities scores. *Journal of Clinical Psychology,* 1962, 18 (4), 518–519.

Bruner, J. S. On perceptual readiness. *Psychological Review,* 1957, 64, 123–152.

Bruner, J. S., Goodnow, J. J., & Austin, G. A. *A study of thinking.* New York: Wiley, 1956.

Bruner, J. S., Olver, R. R., & Greenfield, Patricia. *Studies in cognitive growth.* New York: Wiley, 1966.

Bryan, A. I. Organization of memory in young children. *Archives of Psychology,* 1934, 162.

Budd, W. C. Educators and culture fair intelligence tests. *Journal of Educational Sociology,* 1954, 17, 333–334.

Burke, W. E., Tuttle, W. W., Thompson, C. W., Janney, C. D., & Weber, R. J. The relation of grip strength and grip strength endurance to age. *Journal of Applied Physiology,* 1953, 5, 628–630.

Burks, Barbara S. A study of identical twins reared apart under differing types of family relationships. In Q. McNemar & Maud A. Merrill (Eds.), *Studies in personality.* New York: McGraw-Hill, 1942.

Burks, Barbara S., & Roe, Anne. Studies of identical twins reared apart. *Psychological Monographs,* 1949, 63, No. 300.

Burnett, A., Beach, H. D., & Sullivan, A. M. Intelligence in a restricted environment. *Canadian Psychology,* 1963, 4, 126–136.

Burns, R. B. Age and mental ability: re-testing with thirty-three years' interval. *British Journal of Educational Psychology,* 1966, 36, 116.

Burt, C. Experimental tests of general intelligence. *British Journal of Psychology,* 1909, 3, 94–177.

Burt, C. L. *Distribution and relations of educational abilities.* London: P. S. King, 1917.

Burt, C. *The young delinquent.* London: University of London Press, 1925.

Burt, C. *Factors of the mind.* London: University of London Press, 1940.

Burt, C. Ability and income. *British Journal of Educational Psychology,* 1943, 13, 83–98.

Burt, C. *Intelligence and fertility.* London: Hamilton, 1946.

Burt, C. The distribution of intelligence. *British Journal of Psychology,* 1948, 48, 161–164.

Burt, C. The structure of the mind. *British Journal of Educational Psychology,* 1949, 19, 190.

Burt, C. Intelligence and social mobility. *British Journal of Statistical Psychology,* 1961, 14, 3–24.

Burt, C. Francis Galton and his contributions to psychology. *British Journal of Mathematical and Statistical Psychology,* 1962, 15, 1–15.

Burt, C. Is intelligence distributed normally? *British Journal of Statistical Psychology,* 1963, 26, 178.

Burt, C. Intelligence and achievement. *Mensa,* December, 1967, 1–2.

Burt, C., & Howard, M. The multifactorial theory of inheritance and its application to intelligence. *British Journal of Statistical Psychology,* 1956, 9, 95–131.

Burt, C., & Williams, E. L. The influence of motivation on the results of intelligence tests. *British Journal of Statistical Psychology,* 1962, 15, 129–136.

Bush, R. R., Galanter, E., & Luce, R. D. Characterization and classification of choice experiments. In R. D. Luce, R. R. Bush, and E. Galanter (Eds.), *Handbook of Mathematical Psychology.* New York: Wiley, 1963. Pp. 77–102.

Butcher, J. *Human intelligence: its nature and assessment.* London: Methuen, 1968.

Butcher, J. Creativity in multivariate personality research. In R. M. Dreger (Ed.), *Contribution to the understanding of personality in honor of R. B. Cattell.* Urbana: University of Illinois Press, In press.

Butcher, J., Ainsworth, M. D., & Nesbitt, J. E. Personality factors and school achievement. A comparison of British and American children. *British Journal of Educational Psychology,* 1963, 33, 276–285.

Caldwell, Bettye M. An evaluation of psychological effects of sex hormone administration in aged women: II. Results of therapy after eighteen months. *Journal of Gerontology,* 1954, 9, 168–174.

Caldwell, Bettye M. The cognitive development scale. Chicago: S.R.A., 1958.

Campbell, D. T. Blind variation and selective retention in creative thought as in other knowledge processes. *Psychological Review,* 1960, 67, 380–400.

Cancro, J. (Ed.) *Intelligence: Its nature, genetics and development.* Urbana: University of Illinois Press, 1971.

Cannon, W. B. *The wisdom of the body.* New York: W. Norton, 1932.

Carlson, H. B. Factor analysis of memory ability. *Journal of Experimental Psychology,* 1937, 21, 477–492.

Carmichael, L. The physiological correlates of intelligence. In G. M. Whipple (Ed.), *Yearbook of the National Soc. Stud. Educ.,* 1940, 39, 93–155.

Carpenter, C. R. Field study of the behavior and social relations of howling monkeys. *Comparative Psychological Monographs,* 1934, 10, 48.

Carroll, J. B. A factor analysis of verbal abilities. *Psychometrika,* 1941, 6, 279–307.

Cattell, J. McK. A statistical study of eminent men. *Pop. Sci. Mon.,* 1903, 62, 359–377.

Cattell, J. McKeen. A statistical study of American men of science: The selection of a group of one thousand scientific men. *Science,* 1906, New Series, 24, 658–665.

Cattell, P. *The measurement of intelligence of infants and young children.* New York: The Psychological Corporation, 1940.

Cattell, Psyche & Gaudet, F. J. The inconstancy of the I.Q. as measured by repeated group tests. *Journal of Educational Research,* 1930, 21, 21–28.

Cattell, R. B. The effects of alcohol and caffeine on intelligent and associative performance. *British Journal of Medical Psychology,* 1930, 13, 20–33.

Cattell, R. B. Temperament tests: I. Temperament. *British Journal of Psychology,* 1933, 23, 308–329. (a)

Cattell, R. B. Temperament tests: II. Tests. *British Journal of Psychology,* 1933, 24, 20–49. (b)

Cattell, R. B. The Cattell Intelligence Tests, Scales I, II and III. London: C. Harrap & Co., 1933. (c)

Cattell, R. B. Occupational norms of intelligence, and the standardization of an adult intelligence test. *British Journal of Psychology,* 1934, 25, 1–28.

Cattell, R. B. On the measurement of "perseveration." *British Journal of Educational Psychology,* 1935, 5, 76–92. (a)

Cattell, R. B. Perseveration and personality: some experiments and a hypothesis. *Journal of Mental Science,* 1935, 61, 151–167. (b)

Cattell, R. B. Temperament tests in clinical practice. *British Journal of Medical Psychology,* 1936, 16, 43–61. (a)

Cattell, R. B. Is national intelligence declining? *Eugenics Review,* 1936, 27, 181–203. (b)

Cattell, R. B. *A guide to mental testing.* London: London University Press, 1936. (c)

Cattell, R. B. *The fight for our national intelligence.* London: King, 1937. (a)

Cattell, R. ⁻ Some further relations between intelligence, fertility and socioeconomic factors. *Eugenics Review,* 1937, 29, 171–179. (b)

Cattell, R. B. *Psychology and the religious quest.* New York: Nelson, 1938. (a)

Cattell, R. B. A study of the national reserves of intelligence. *Human Factor,* 1938, 12, 127–136. (b)

Cattell, R. B. Some changes in social life in a community with a falling intelligence quotient. *British Journal of Psychology,* 1938, 28, 430–450. (c)

Cattell, R. B. A culture-free intelligence test. I. *Journal of Educational Psychology,* 1940, 31, 161–179.

Cattell, R. B. Some theoretical issues in adult intelligence testing. *Psychological Bulletin,* 1941, 38, 592.

Cattell, R. B. The measurement of adult intelligence. *Psychological Bulletin,* 1943, 40, 153–193.

Cattell, R. B. The place of religion and ethics in a civilization based on science. In R. Wulsin (Ed.), *A revaluation of our civilization.* Albany: Argus Press, 1944. Chapter 2.

Cattell, R. B. The description of personality. Principles and findings in a factor analysis. *American Journal of Psychology,* 1945, 58, 69–90. (a)

Cattell, R. B. Personality traits associated with abilities. I. With intelligence and drawing ability. *Educational and Psychological Measurement,* 1945, 5, 131–146. (b)

Cattell, R. B. *The description and measurement of personality.* New York: World Book, 1946. (a)

Cattell, R. B. The riddle of perseveration: I. "Creative effort" and disposition rigidity. *Journal of Personality,* 1946, 14, 229–238. (b)

Cattell, R. B. Personality structure and measurement. I. The operational determination of trait unities. *British Journal of Psychology,* 1946, 36, 88–103. (c)

Cattell, R. B. Confirmation and clarification of primary personality factors. *Psychometrika,* 1947, 12, 197–220.

Cattell, R. B. Primary personality factors in the realm of objective tests. *Journal of Personality,* 1948, 16, 459–487.

Cattell, R. B. The dimensions of culture patterns by factorization of national characters. *Journal of Abnormal and Social Psychology,* 1949, 44, 443–469.

Cattell, R. B. *Personality, a systematic theoretical and factual study.* New York: McGraw-Hill, 1950. (a)

Cattell, R. B. The scientific ethics of "Beyond." *Journal of Social Issues,* 1950, 6, 21–27. (b)

Cattell, R. B. The fate of national intelligence: test of a thirteen-year prediction. *Eugenics Review,* 1950, 42, 136–148. (c)

Cattell, R. B. The principal culture patterns discoverable in the syntal dimensions of existing nations. *Journal of Social Psychology,* 1950, 32, 215–253. (d)

Cattell, R. B. A factorization of tests of personality source traits. *British Journal of Psychology,* 1951, 4, 165–178. (a)

Cattell, R. B. Classical and standard score I.Q. standardization of the IPAT Culture-Free Intelligence Scale 2. *Journal of Consulting Psychology,* 1951, 15, 154–159. (b)

Cattell, R. B. *Factor analysis.* New York: Harpers, 1952.

Cattell, R. B. A quantitative analysis of the changes in the cultural pattern of Great Britain 1837–1937, by P-technique. *Acta Psychologica,* 1953, 9, 99–121.

Cattell, R. B. The personality and motivation of the research scientist. Wenner-Gren Prize Essay. New York: Academy of Sciences, 1954.

Cattell, R. B. Psychiatric screening of flying personnel. Personality structure in objective tests—a study of 1000 Air Force students in basic pilot training. *USAF School of Aviation Medicine* (Project No. 21–0202–0007), Report No. 9, 1955, 1–50. (a)

Cattell, R. B. The Objective-Analytic (O-A) Personality Test. Champaign, Illinois: Institute for Personality and Ability Testing, 1955. (b)

Cattell, R. B. *Personality and motivation structure and measurement.* New York: World, 1957. (a)

Cattell, R. B. A universal index for psychological factors. *Psychologia,* 1957, 1, 74–85. (b)

Cattell, R. B. The dynamic calculus: a system of concepts derived from objective motivation measurement. In G. Lindzey's *Assessment of human motives.* New York: Rinehart, 1958. Chapter 8.

Cattell, R. B. The dynamic calculus: concepts and crucial experiments. In M. R. Jones (Ed.) *The Nebraska symposium on motivation.* Lincoln, Nebraska: University of Nebraska Press, 1959. Pp. 84–134.

Cattell, R. B. The dimensional (unitary-component) measurement of anxiety, excitement, effort stress and other mood reaction patterns. In L. Uhr & J. G. Miller (Ed.) *Drugs and behavior.* New York: John Wiley & Sons, Inc., 1960. Pp. 438–462.

Cattell, R. B. The relational simplex theory of equal interval and absolute scaling. *Acta Psychologica,* 1962, 20, 139–158.

Cattell, R. B. Theory of fluid and crystallized intelligence: a critical experiment. *Journal of Educational Psychology,* 1963, 54, 1–22. (a)

Cattell, R. B. The personality and motivation of the researcher from measurements of contemporaries and from biography. In C. W. Taylor and F. Barron (Eds.) *Scientific creativity: its recognition and development.* New York: John Wiley & Sons, 1963. Chapter 9. (b)

Cattell, R. B. The nature and measurement of anxiety. *Scientific American,* 1963, 208, 96–104. (c)

Cattell, R. B. *The scientific analysis of personality.* London: Penguin Books, 1965. (a)

Cattell, R. B. Factor analysis: an introduction to essentials. I. The purpose and underlying models. *Biometrics,* 1965, 21, 190–215. (b)

Cattell, R. B. Higher order factor structures and reticular-vs-hierarchical formulae for their interpretation. In Charlotte Banks & P. L. Broadhurst (Eds.), *Studies in psychology.* London: University of London Press, 1965. (c)

Cattell, R. B. The IPAT Culture Fair Intelligence Scales 1, 2 and 3. (3rd ed.) Champaign, Illinois: Institute for Personality and Ability Testing, 1965. (d)

Cattell, R. B. *Handbook of multivariate experimental psychology.* Chicago: Rand McNally, 1966.

Cattell, R. B. The theory of fluid and crystallized general intelligence checked at the 5–6 year-old level. *British Journal of Educational Psychology,* 1967, 37, 2, 209–224. (a)

Cattell, R. B. La théorie de l'intelligence fluide et cristallisée, sa relation avec les tests—culture fair—et sa vérification chez les enfants de 9 a 12 ans. *Revue de Psychologie Appliquée,* 1967, 17, 3, 135–154. (b)

Cattell, R. B. Handbook for the Jr.-Sr. High School Personality Questionnaire. Champaign, Illinois: Institute for Personality and Ability Testing, 1968.

Cattell, R. B. The profile similarity coefficient, r_p, in vocational guidance and diagnostic classification. *British Journal of Educational Psychology,* 1969, 39, 131–142. (a)

Cattell, R. B. Comparing factor trait and state scores across ages and cultures. *Journal of Gerontology,* 1969, 24, No. 3, 348–360. (b)

Cattell, R. B. The isopodic and equipotent principles for comparing factor scores across different populations. *British Journal of Mathematical and Statistical Psychology,* 1970, 23, 23–41. (a)

Cattell, R. B. Separating endogenous, exogenous, ecogenic and epogenic component curves in developmental data. *Journal of Developmental Psychology,* 1970, 3, 151–162. (b)

Cattell, R. B. Structured learning theory, applied to personality change. In R. B. Cattell (Ed.), *Handbook of Modern Personality Theory.* Urbana, Illinois: University of Illinois Press, 1971. Chapter 15. (a)

Cattell, R. B. *Beyondism: Values for applying science to human affairs.* New York: Pergamon Press, 1971. (b)

Cattell, R. B., & Adelson, M. The dimensions of social change in the U.S.A. as determined by P-technique. *Social Forces,* 1951, 30, 190–201.

Cattell, R. B., & Baggaley, A. R. The salient variable similarity index for factor matching. *British Journal of Statistical Psychology,* 1960, 13, 33–46.

Cattell, R. B., Blewett, D. B., & Beloff, J. R. The inheritance of personality. A multiple variance analysis determination of approximate nature-nurture ratios for primary personality factors in Q-data. *American Journal of Human Genetics,* 1955, 7, 122–146.

Cattell, R. B., Breul, H., & Hartmann, H. P. An attempt at more refined definition of the cultural dimensions of syntality in modern nations. *American Sociological Review,* 1952, 17, 408–421.

Cattell, R. B., & Bristol, H. Intelligence tests for mental ages of four to eight years. *British Journal of Educational Psychology,* 1933, 3, 142–169.

Cattell, R. B., & Butcher, J. *The prediction of achievement and creativity.* Indianapolis: Bobbs-Merrill, 1968.

Cattell, R. B. & Cattell, A. K. S. *Handbook for the Culture-Fair Intelligence Test. Scale 3.* Champaign, Ill.: IPAT, 1959.

Cattell, R. B., & Coulter, M. A. Principles of behavioral taxonomy and the mathematical basis of the taxonome computer program. *British Journal of Mathematical and Statistical Psychology,* 1966, 19, 237–269.

Cattell, R. B., & Damarin, F. L. Personality factors in early childhood and their relation to intelligence. *Monograph of Society for Research in Child Development,* 1968, 33.

Cattell, R. B., & Dickman, K. A dynamic model of physical influences demonstrating the necessity of oblique simple structure. *Psychological Bulletin,* 1962, 59, 389–400.

Cattell, R. B., Dielman, T., Schneewind, K. Dynamic structure and learning in the rat. Monograph, In press.

Cattell, R. B., & Drevdahl, J. E. A comparison of the personality profile of eminent researchers with that of eminent teachers and administrators. *British Journal of Psychology,* 1955, 44, 248–261.

Cattell, R. B., Dubin, S. S., & Saunders, D. R. Verification of hypothesized factors in one hundred and fifteen objective personality test designs. *Psychometrica,* 1954, 19, 209–230.

Cattell, R. B., Eber, H. W., & Tatsuoka, M. The 16 P. F. Handbook. Champaign: Institute for Personality and Ability Testing, 1970.

Cattell, R. B., Feingold, S., & Sarason, S. A culture free intelligence test. II. Evaluation of cultural influence on test performance. *Journal of Educational Psychology,* 1941, 32, 81–100.

Cattell, R. B., & Gorsuch, R. L. The definition and measurement of national morale and morality. *Journal of Social Psychology,* 1965, 67, 77–96.

Cattell, R. B., & Gorsuch, R. L. Personality and socio-ethical values: The structure of self and superego. In R. B. Cattell (Ed.), *Handbook of Modern Personality Theory.* Chicago: Aldine Press, 1971. Chapter 30.

Cattell, R. B., Heist, A. B., Heist, P. A., & Stewart, R. G. The objective measurement of dynamic traits. *Educational and Psychological Measurement,* 1950, 10, 224–248.

Cattell, R. B., & Horn, J. An integrating study of the factor structure of adult attitude-interests. *Genetic Psychology Monographs,* 1963, 67, 89–149.

Cattell, R. B., Horn, J. R., Radcliffe, J., & Sweney, A. B. The Motivation Analysis Test. Champaign: Institute of Personality and Ability Testing, 1964.

Cattell, R. B., & Jaspars, J. A general plasmode (No. 30–10–5–2) for factor analytic exercises and researches. *Multivariate Behavior Research Monograph,* 1967, 67, 3.

Cattell, R. B., Korth, B., & Brace, C. L. The isolation of temperament dimensions in dogs. *Journal of Comparative Psychology,* 1970.

Cattell, R. B., & Krug, S. The School Motivation Analysis Test. Champaign: Institute for Personality and Ability Testing, 1970.

Cattell, R. B., & Kulhavy, R. Ability structure at ages 3 through 6 years. *Child Development Monograph* (In press).

Cattell, R. B., Maxwell, E. F., Light, B. H., & Unger, M. P. The objective measurement of attitudes. *British Journal of Psychology,* 1949, 40, 81–90.

Cattell, R. B., & Miller, A. A confirmation of the ergic and self-sentiment patterns among dynamic traits (attitude variables) by R-technique. *British Journal of Psychology,* 1952, 43, 280–294.

Cattell, R. B., & Muerle, J. L. The "maxplane" program for factor rotation to oblique simple structure. *Educational and Psychological Measurement,* 1960, 20, 569–590.

Cattell, R. B., & Nesselroade, J. R. Likeness and completeness theories examined by 16 P.F. measures on stably and unstably married couples. *Journal of Personality and Social Psychology,* 1967, 7, 4, 351–361.

Cattell, R. B., & Nesselroade, J. Interaction of heredity and environment in behavior: an introduction to genothenic methodology, 1971.

Cattell, R. B., Radcliffe, J. A., & Sweney, A. B. The nature and measurement of components of motivation. *Genetic Psychology Monographs,* 1963, 68, 49–211.

Cattell, R. B., & Saunders, D. R. Inter-relation and matching of personality factors from behavior rating questionnaire and objective test data. *Journal of Social Psychology,* 1950, 31, 243–260.

Cattell, R. B., & Scheier, I. H. The objective test measurement of neuroticism U.I. 23(–). *Indian Journal of Psychology,* 1958, 33, 217–236.

Cattell, R. B., & Scheier, I. H. *The meaning and measurement of neuroticism and anxiety.* New York: Ronald Press, 1961.

Cattell, R. B., & Scheier, I. H. Personality measurement in applied psychology as illustrated by the 16 personality factor test. *Revista de Psicologia Normal e Patalogica,* 1965, 9, 42–58.

Cattell, R. B., Scheier, I. H., & Lorr, M. Recent advances in the measurement of anxiety, neuroticism, and the psychotic syndromes. *Annals of New York Academy of Science,* 1962, 93, 815–856.

Cattell, R. B., & Schuerger, J. The Objective Analytic (O-A) Battery for Personality Measurement at High School Age. Champaign, Illinois: Institute for Personality and Ability Testing, 1969.

Cattell, R. B., & Sealy, A. P. The general relations of changes in personality and interest to changes in school performance: An exploratory study. Cooperative Research Project Number 1411, U.S. Department of Health, Education and Welfare. Urbana, Illinois: Laboratory of Personality Assessment and Group Behavior, 1965.

Cattell, R. B., Sealy, A. P., & Sweney, A. B. What can personality and motivation source trait measurements add to the prediction of school achievement? *British Journal of Educational Psychology,* 1966, 36, 3, 280–295.

Cattell, R. B., & Stice, G. F. The dimensions of groups and their relations to the behavior of members. Champaign, Illinois: Institute for Personality and Ability Testing, 1960.

Cattell, R. B., Stice, G. F., & Kristy, N. F. A first approximation to nature-nurture ratios for eleven primary personality factors in objective tests. *Journal of Abnormal and Social Psychology,* 1957, 54, 143–159.

Cattell, R. B., & Sullivan, W. The scientific nature of factors: a demonstration by cups of coffee. *Behavior Science,* 1962, 7, 184–193.

Cattell, R. B., Sweney, A. B., & Krug, S. The School Motivation Analysis Test. Champaign, Illinois: Institute for Personality and Ability Testing, 1966.

Cattell, R. B., Sweney, A. B., & Radcliffe, J. A. The objective measurement of motivation structure in children. *Journal of Clinical Psychology*, 1960, 16, 227–232.

Cattell, R. B., & Tatro, D. F. The personality factors, objectively measured, which distinguish psychotics from normals. *Behavior Research Therapy*, 1966, 4, 39–51.

Cattell, R. B., & Tiner, L. G. The varieties of structural rigidity. *Journal of Personality*, 1949, 17, 321–341.

Cattell, R. B., & Tsujioka, B. The importance of factor-trueness and validity, versus homogeneity and orthogonality, in test scales. *Educational and Psychological Measurement*, 1964, 24, 3–30.

Cattell, R. B., Tsujioka, B., & Ishikawa, A. Nature-nurture ratios for the primary personality factors in a Japanese sample. Monograph in press.

Cattell, R. B., & Warburton, F. W. *Objective personality and motivation tests: a theoretical introduction and practical compendium.* Urbana, Illinois: University of Illinois Press, 1967.

Cattell, R. B., & Warburton, F. W. *Objective tests of personality and motivation.* Cincinnati, Ohio: Bobbs-Merrill, 1968.

Cattell, R. B., & Wenig, P. Dynamic and cognitive factors controlling misperception. *Journal of Abnormal and Social Psychology*, 1952, 47, 797–809.

Cattell, R. B., & Williams, H. F. P-technique, a new statistical device for analyzing functional unities in the intact organism. *British Journal of Preventive and Social Medicine*, 1953, 7, 141–153.

Cattell, R. B., & Willson, J. L. Contributions concerning mental inheritance. I. Of intelligence. *British Journal of Educational Psychology*, 1938, 8, 129–149.

Cattell, R. B., & Winder, A. E. Structural rigidity in relation to learning theory and clinical psychology. *Psychological Review*, 1952, 59, 23–39.

Cattell, R. B., Young, H. B., & Hundleby, J. D. Blood groups and personality traits. *American Journal of Human Genetics*, 1964, 16, 4, 397–402.

Cattell, R. B., *et al.* Systematic motivation study. (In press, 1971)

Charles, D. C., & James, S. T. Stability of average intelligence. *Journal of Genetic Psychology*, 1964, 105, 105–111.

Chassell, C. F. *The relation between morality and intellect.* New York: Columbia University Press, 1935.

Churchill, J. A. The relationship between intelligence and birth weight in twins. *Neurology*, 1965, 15, 341–347.

Clark, Mamie P. Changes in primary mental abilities with age. *Archives of Psychology*, 1944, #291.

Coan, R. W. Child personality and developmental psychology. In R. B. Cattell (Ed.), *Handbook of multivariate experimental psychology.* Chicago: Rand McNally, 1966. Pp. 732–752.

Cobb, S. Brain size. *Archives of Neurology*, 1965, 12, 555–561.

Cohen, J. A factor-analytically based rationale for the Wechsler-Bellevue. *Journal of Consulting Psychology*, 1952, 16, 272–277.

Cohen, J. The factorial structure of the WAIS between early childhood and old age. *Journal of Consulting Psychology*, 1957, 21, 283–290.

Cohen, J. The factorial structure of the WISC at ages 7–6, 10–6 and 13–6. *Journal of Consulting Psychology,* 1959, 23, 285–299.

Comrey, A. L. A factorial study of achievement in West Point courses. *Educational and Psychological Measurement,* 1949, 9, 193–209.

Connor, D. V. The effect of temperament traits upon intelligence test responses. Unpublished doctoral dissertation, University of London, 1952.

Conway, J. Class differences in general intelligence. *British Journal of Statistical Psychology,* 1959, 12, 5–14.

Coon, C. S. *The story of man.* New York: Knopf, 1962. (a)

Coon, C. S. *The origin of races.* New York: Knopf, 1962. (b)

Corning, W. C., & John, E. R. Effects of ribonuclease on retention of conditional response in regenerated planarians. *Science,* 1961, 134, 1363–1365.

Corter, H. M. Factor analysis of some reasoning tests. *Psychological Monographs,* 1952, 66, 340.

Cox, Catherine, Terman, L. M., & others. The early mental traits of three hundred geniuses. *Genetic studies of genius.* Vol. II. Stanford: University Press, 1926.

Cox, J. W. *Mechanical aptitude.* London: Methuen, 1928.

Cox, J. W. *Manual skill: Its organization and development.* Cambridge: Cambridge University Press, 1934.

Crandall, V. J., Katkavsky, W., & Preston, Anne. Motivational and ability determinants of young children's intellectual achievement behaviors. *Child Development,* 1962, 33, 643–661.

Cranston, R. E., Zubin, J., & Landis, C. The effect of small doses of thonzylamine, dexedrine, and phenobarbital on test performance and self-ratings of subjective states. *Journal of Psychology,* 1952, 33, 209–215.

Cravioto, J. Malnutrition and behavioral development in the pre-school child. *Courrier,* 1966, 16 (2), 117–127.

Cronbach, L. J., & Gleser, Goldine C. *Psychological tests and personnel decisions.* Urbana: University of Illinois Press, 1965.

Cross, P. G., Cattell, R. B., & Butcher, H. J. The personality pattern of creative artists. *British Journal of Educational Psychology,* 1967, 37, 292–299.

Cureton, E. E. A note on the use of Burt's formula for estimating factor significance. *British Journal of Statistical Psychology,* 1955, 8, 28.

Cutler, M., Little, J. W., & Strauss, A. A. The effect of benzedrine on mentally deficient children. *American Journal of Mental Deficiency,* 1940, 45, 59–65.

Dabrowska, J. Multiple reversal learning in frontal rats. *Acta Biologiae Experimentalis,* 1964, 24 (2), 99–102.

Dailey, J. T. A survey of the use of tests in public high schools. From Project Talent Data, A. I. R., Pittsburgh, 1962.

Das, G., & Broadhurst, P. L. A note on the Hebb-Williams test of intelligence in the rat. *Canadian Journal of Psychology,* 1959, 13, 72–75.

Delhees, K. Conflict measurement by the dynamic calculus model, and its applicability in clinical practice. *Multivariate Behavioral Research,* 1968, 3, 73–96.

Denenberg, V. H., & Bell, R. W. Critical periods for the effects of infantile experience on adult learning. *Science,* 1960, 131, 227–228.

Dennis, W. Age and productivity among scientists. *Science,* 1956, 123, 724–725.

Dennis, W. The age decrement in outstanding scientific contributions: Fact or artifact. *American Psychologist,* 1958, 13, 457–460.

Dentler, R. A., & Mackler, B. Originality: some social and personal determinants. *Behavioral Science,* 1964, 9, 1–7.

DeRenzi, E., & Faglione, P. The comparative efficiency of intelligence and vigilance tests in detecting hemispheric cerebral damage. *Cortex,* 1965, 1 (4), 410–433.

Dielman, T. E., & Krug, S. Trait description and measurement in motivation and dynamic structure. In R. B. Cattell (Ed.), *Handbook of modern personality theory.* Urbana, Illinois: University of Illinois Press, 1971. Chapter 5.

Dielman, T. E., Schuerger, J. M., & Cattell, R. B. Prediction of junior high school achievement from I. Q. and the Objective-Analytic personality factors U.I. 21, U.I. 23, U.I. 24, and U.I. 25. *Personality: An International Journal,* 1970.

DiMascio, A., & Barrett, J. Comparative effects of oxazepam in "high" and "low" anxious student volunteers. *Psychosomatics,* 1965, 6, 298–302.

Donaldson, M. C. *A study of children's thinking.* London: Tavistock, 1963.

Dreger, R. M. *Fundamentals of personality.* Philadelphia: Lippincott, 1962.

Dreger, R. M., & Miller, K. S. Comparative psychological studies of Negroes and whites in the United States. *Psychological Bulletin,* 1960, 57, 361–402.

Drevdahl, J. E. An exploratory study of creativity. Unpublished doctoral dissertation, University of Nebraska, 1954.

Drevdahl, J. E. Factors of importance for creativity. *Journal of Clinical Psychology,* 1956, 12, 21–26.

Drevdahl, J. E., & Cattell, R. B. Personality and creativity in artists and writers. *Journal of Clinical Psychology,* 1958, 14, 107–111.

Drever, J. Presidential Address: Psychology and history. XIII International Congress of Psychology, Edinburgh, 1951.

Drever, J. The teaching of psychology. In C. A. Mace and P. E. Vernon (Eds.), *Current trends in British Psychology.* London: Methuen, 1953. Pp. 248–254.

Drever, J., & Stephenson, W. Contemporary American and British psychological scenes. *American Psychologist,* 1948, 3, 547–550.

Dudek, F. J. The dependence of factorial composition upon population differences among pilot trainees. I. The isolation of factors. *Educational and Psychological Measurement,* 1948, 8, 613–633.

Duff, J. F., & Thomson, G. H. The social and geographical distribution of intelligence in Northumberland. *British Journal of Psychology,* 1923, 14, 192–198.

Duncan, D. R., & Barrett, A. M. A longitudinal comparison of intelligence involving the Wechsler-Bellevue I and the WAIS. *Journal of Clinical Psychology,* 1961, 17, 318–319.

Duncanson, J. P. Intelligence and the ability to learn. Research Bulletin (RE–64–29). Princeton, New Jersey: Educational Testing Service, 1964.

Eccles, J. C. *The neurophysiological basis of mind.* Oxford: Clarendon Press, 1959.

Eccles, J. C. Brain and conscious experience. Study week, September 28 to October 24, 1965, of the Pontificia Academia Scientiarium. New York: Springer, 1966.

Eells, K., Davis, A., Havighurst, R. J., et al. *Intelligence and cultural differences.* Chicago: University of Chicago Press, 1951.

Eibl-Ebesfeldt, I. *Grundriss der vergleichenden Verhaltensforschung. Ethologie.* München: Piper, 1967.

Einstein, A. *Time,* September 29, 1967.

El Koussy, A. A. H. The visual perception of space. *British Journal of Psychology Monograph Supplement,* 1935, #20.

Ellis, H. *Man and woman.* 1894.

Ellis, H. *A study of British genius.* New York: Houghton Mifflin, 1926.

English, H. B., & Killian, C. D. The constance of the I.Q. at difference age levels. *Journal of Consulting Psychology,* 1939, 3, 30–32.

Enslein, K. An approach to pattern recognition. In K. Enslein (Ed.), *Proceedings of 1961 at Rochester Conference Data Processing in Biology and Medicine.* New York: Pergamon Press, 1962.

Enslein, K. A general purpose perception simulator. *Computers and Biomedical Research,* 1967, 1, 187–214.

Ericksen, C. W. Discrimination of learning without awareness: a methodological survey and evaluation. *Psychological Review,* 1960, 67, 279–300.

Ericksen, M. R. H. Brain lesions and mental functions. *Yearbook of the National Soc. Stud. Educ.,* 1940, 39, Part I.

Erlenmeyer-Kimling, L., & Jarvik, L. F. Genetics and intelligence; a review. *Science,* 1963, 142, 1477–1479.

Ertl, J. P. Evoked potentials and intelligence. *Revue de l'Université d'Ottawa,* 1966, 36 (4), 599–607.

Ertl, J. P., & Schafer, E. W. P. Brain response correlates of psychometric intelligence. *Nature,* 1969, 223, 421–422.

Essman, W. B. Awareness of reinforcement in "learning without awareness." *Psychological Review,* 1957, 3, 399–400.

Eysenck, H. J. *Dimensions of personality.* London: Kegan Paul, 1947.

Eysenck, H. J. *The dynamics of anxiety and hysteria.* London: Kegan Paul, 1957.

Eysenck, H. J. *The structure of human personality.* 2nd ed. London: Methuen, 1960.

Eysenck, H. J. *Handbook of abnormal psychology.* New York: Basic Books, 1961.

Eysenck, H. J. Intelligence assessment: a theoretical and experimental approach. *British Journal of Educational Psychology,* 1967, 37, 81–98.

Eysenck, H. J., & White, P. O. Personality and the measurement of intelligence. *British Journal of Educational Psychology,* 1964, 34, 197–201.

Eysenck, S. B. G. Neurosis and psychosis: an experimental analysis. *Journal of Mental Science,* 1956, 102, 517–529.

Ferguson, G. A. On learning and human ability. *Canadian Journal of Psychology,* 1954, 8, 95–112.

Ferguson, G. A. On transfer and the abilities of man. *Journal of Canadian Psychology,* 1956, 10, 121–131.

Ferguson, G. A. *Statistical analysis in psychology and education.* New York: McGraw-Hill, 1959.

Ferguson, G. A. Human abilities. *Annals Rev. Psychol.,* 1965, 16, 39–62.

Finch, F. H. Enrollment increases and changes in the mental level of the high school population. *Applied Psychology Monograph,* 1946, 10, 75.

Findlay, D. C., & McGuire, C. Social status and abstract behavior. *Journal of Abnormal and Social Psychology,* 1957, 54, 135–137.

Fisher, R. A. The correlation between relatives on the supposition of Mendelian inheritance. *Transactions of the Royal Society of Edinburgh,* 1918, 52, 399–433.

Fisher, R. A. *The genetical theory of natural selection.* Oxford: Clarendon Press, 1930.

Fiske, D. The analysis of tests and test taking situations. In R. B. Cattell (Ed.), *Handbook of modern personality theory.* Urbana, Illinois: University of Illinois Press, 1971.

Fleishman, E. A. Dimensional analysis of psychomotor abilities. *Journal of Experimental Psychology,* 1954, 48, 437–454.

Fleishman, E. A. A comparative study of aptitude patterns in unskilled and skilled psychomotor performances. *Journal of Applied Psychology,* 1957, 41, 263–272.

Fleishman, E. A., & Ellison, G. D. Prediction of transfer and other learning phenomena from ability and personality measures. *Journal of Educational Psychology,* 1969, 60, 300–314.

Fogel, L. J., Owens, A. J., & Walsh, M. J. *Artificial intelligence through simulated evolution.* New York: Wiley, 1966.

Forgus, R. H. Advantage of early over late perceptual experience in improving form discrimination. *Canadian Journal of Psychology,* 1956, 10, 147–155.

Fortes, M. A new application of the theory of noegenesis of the problems of mental testing. Unpublished doctoral dissertation, University of London, 1930.

Fortes, M. A study of cognitive error. *British Journal of Educational Psychology,* 1932, 2, 297–318.

Frankenhaeuser, M., & Myrsten, A. Performance decrement after intake of meprobamate as a function of task difficulty and learning level. Reports of the University of Stockholm Psychology Laboratory, 1968, No. 246.

Franks, C. Personality factors and the rate of conditioning. *British Journal of Psychology,* 1957, 48, 119–126.

Franz, S. I. On the functions of the cerebrum: the frontal lobes in relation to the production and retention of simple sensory-motor habits. *Amer. J. Physiol.,* 1902, 8, 1–22.

Fredericksen, N., Jensen, O., Beaton, A. C., & Bloxom, B. Organizational climates and administration performance. Research Bulletin 6841. Princeton, New Jersey: Educational Testing Service, 1966.

Freeman, F. N., Holzinger, K. J., & Mitchell, B. C. The influence of environment on the intelligence, school achievement, and conduct of foster children. *Yearbook of the National Society of Student Education*, 1928, 27, Chapter 9.

French, J. W. *The description of aptitude and achievement tests in terms of rotated factors.* Chicago: University of Chicago Press, 1951.

French, J. W. Social class and motivation among Meties of Alberta. University of Alberta, unpublished paper, 1962.

French, J. W. *Kit of Reference Tests for cognitive factors.* Princeton, New Jersey: Educational Testing Service, 1963 (Revised).

Freud, S. *Civilization and its discontents.* Garden City, New York: Doubleday, 1958.

Fruchter, B. The nature of verbal fluency. *Educational and Psychological Measurement*, 1948, 8, 33–47.

Fryer, D. Occupational intelligence levels. *School and Society*, 1922, 16, 273–277.

Fuller, J. L., & Scott, J. P. Heredity and learning ability in infrahuman mammals. *Eugenics Quarterly*, 1954, 1, 28–43.

Fuller, J. L., & Thompson, W. R. *Behavior genetics.* New York: Wiley, 1960.

Furneaux, W. D. The Nufferno manual of speed and level tests. London: National Foundation of Education Research, 1956.

Furneaux, W. D. Intellectual abilities and problem-solving behavior. In H. J. Eysenck (Ed.), *Handbook of abnormal psychology.* London: Petman Medical Publishing Co., 1960. Chapter 5.

Gabriel, R. F. The influence of order information and stimulus display time on short term retention. Unpublished doctoral dissertation, University of Southern California, 1963.

Gagné, R. M. The acquisition of knowledge. *Psychological Review*, 1962, 69 (4), 355–365.

Gagné, R. M. (Ed.) *Learning and individual differences.* Columbus, Ohio: Merrill, 1967.

Gagné, R. M., & Paradise, N. E. Abilities and learning sets in knowledge acquisition. *Psychological Monographs*, 1961, 75, No. 14.

Gainer, W. L. The ability of the WISC subtests to discriminate between boys and girls of average intelligence. *California Journal of Educational Research*, 1962, 13, 9–16.

Galton, F. *Hereditary genius.* New York: Appleton, 1870.

Galton, F. *Inquiries into human faculty, and its development.* London: Macmillan, 1883.

Gardner, I. C., & Newman, H. H. Mental and physical tests of identical twins reared apart. *Journal of Heredity*, 1940, 31, 119–126.

Gardner, J. *The pursuit of excellence.* New York: Doubleday, 1958.

Gardner, R. A multiple choice decision behavior. *American Journal of Psychology*, 1958, 71, 710–717.

Garrett, H. E. A developmental theory of intelligence. *American Psychologist*, 1946, 1, 372–378.

Garrett, H. E. The SPSSI and racial differences. *American Psychologist*, 1962, 17, 260–263.

Garrett, H. E., Bryan, Alice J., & Perl, Ruth E. The age factor in mental organization. *Archives of Psychology,* 1935, #176.

Garwood, Dorothy S. Personality factors related to creativity in young scientists. *Journal of Abnormal and Social Psychology,* 1964, 68, 413–419.

George, F. H. *The brain as a computer.* Oxford: Pergamon Press, 1961.

Gesell, A., & Amatruda, C. S. *Developmental diagnosis.* New York: Hoeber, 1947.

Gesell, A., Halverson, H. M., Thompson, Helen, Ilg, F. L., Coslner, B. M., Ames, L. B., & Amatruda, C. S. *The first five years of life: a guide to the study of the preschool child.* New York: Harper, 1940.

Gesell, A., & Ilg, F. L. *Infant and child in the culture of today.* New York: Harper, 1943.

Getzels, J. W., & Jackson, P. W. *Creativity and intelligence: explorations with gifted students.* New York: Wiley, 1962.

Ghiselli, E. E. Intelligence and managerial success. *Psychological Reports,* 1963, 12, 898.

Gibb, C. A. Changes in the culture pattern of Australia, 1906–1946, as determined by P-techniques. *Journal of Social Psychology,* 1956, 43, 225–238.

Giessel, Gerda. Vergleichsuntersuchung zur Intelligenzstruktur verwahrloster und nicht verwahrloster jugendlicher Hilfsschüler. (Comparative study of the structure of intelligence in neglected and not neglected retarded adolescents). *Praxis der Kinderpsychologie und Kinderpsychiatrie,* 1967, 16, 143–146.

Gilgash, C. A. Effects of thorazine on Wechsler scores of adult catatonic schizophrenics. *Psychological Reports,* 1957, 3, 561–564.

Ginsberg, B. E. Coaction of genetic and non-genetical factors influencing sexual behavior. In F. A. Beach (Ed.), *Sex and behavior.* New York: Wiley, 1965. Pp. 53–75.

Glass, Jean. Educational Piltdown man. *Phi Delta Kappan,* November 1968, 148–151.

Goldstein, K. The mental changes due to frontal lobe damage. *Journal of Psychology,* 1944, 17, 187–208.

Goodman, A. *The attainment and ability of Hong Kong primary iv pupils.* Hong Kong: University of Hong Kong Press, 1964, 86.

Goodman, C. H. A factorial analysis of Thurstone's sixteen primary mental abilities. *Psychometrika,* 1943, 8, 141–151.

Gopalaswami, M. "Intelligence" in motor learning. *British Journal of Psychology,* 1924, 14, 274–290.

Gorsuch, R. L. The clarification of some superego factors. Unpublished doctoral dissertation, University of Illinois, Dissertation Abstracts, 1965, 26 (1), 477–478.

Gorsuch, R. L., & Cattell, R. B. Second stratum personality factors defined in the questionnaire realm by the 16 P.F. *Multivariate Behavioral Research,* 1967, 2, 211–224.

Goslin, D. A. *The search for ability, standardized testing in social perspective.* New York: Russell Sage Foundation, 1966.

Graffam, D. T. Dickinson College changes personality. *The Dickinson Alumnus,* 1967, 44(1), 2–7.

Grams, A., Hafner, A. J., & Quast, W. Child anxiety: self estimates, parent reports, and teacher ratings. *Merrill-Palmer Quarterly,* 1965, 11(3), 261–266.

Gray, S. W., & Klaus, R. A. An experimental preschool program for culturally deprived children. *Child Development,* 1965, 36(4), 887–898.

Gross, O. *Die cerebrale sekundär Funktion.* 1924.

Guetzkow, H. An analysis of the operation of set in problem-solving behavior. *Journal of General Psychology,* 1951, 45, 219–244.

Guilford, J. P. *Psychometric methods.* New York: McGraw-Hill, 1954.

Guilford, J. P. *Fundamental statistics in psychology and education.* New York: McGraw-Hill, 1956. 3rd ed.

Guilford, J. P. *Personality.* New York: McGraw-Hill, 1959.

Guilford, J. P. *The nature of human intelligence.* New York: McGraw-Hill, 1967.

Guilford, J. P., Christensen, P. R., Kettner, N. W., Green, R. F., & Hertzka, A. F. A factor analytic study of Navy reasoning tests with the Air Force AC Battery. *Educational and Psychological Measurement,* 1954, 14, 301–325.

Guilford, J. P., Christenson, P. R., Frick, J. W., & Merrifield, P. R. Factors of interest in thinking. *Journal of Genetic Psychology,* 1961, 65, 39–56.

Guilford, J. P., Kettner, N. W., & Christensen, P. R. The nature of the general reasoning factor. *Psychological Review,* 1956, 63, 169–172.

Guilford, J. P., & Lacey, J. I. Printed classification tests: Army Air forces aviation psychological research program report #5. Washington, D.C.: Government Printing Office, 1947.

Guilford, J. P., Merrifield, P. R., Christenson, P. F., & Frick, J. W. Some new symbolic factors of cognition and convergent production. *Educational and Psychological Measurement,* 1961, 21, 515–541.

Guilford, J. P., & Zimmerman, W. S. The Guilford-Zimmerman Aptitude Survey. Beverly Hills, California: Sheridan, 1948.

Guttman, L. A generalized simplex for factor analysis and a facetted definition of intelligence. *Psychometrika,* 1955, 20, 173–192.

Guttman, L. The structure of interrelations among intelligence tests. In C. W. Harris (Ed.), *Invitational conference on testing problems.* Princeton, New Jersey: Educational Testing Service, 1965. Pp. 25–36.

Haber, R. N. How we remember what we see. *Scientific American,* 1970, 222, 104–115.

Hadden, J. K., & Borgatta, E. F. *American cities.* Chicago: Rand McNally, 1965.

Haggard, E. Social status and intelligence: An experimental study of certain cultural determinants of measured intelligence. *Genetic Psychology Monographs,* 1954, 49, 141–186.

Hall, C. S., & Lindzey, G. *Theories of personality.* New York: Wiley, 1957.

Halstead, W. C. A power factor (P) in general intelligence; the effect of Brain injuries. *Journal of Psychology,* 1945, 20, 57–64.

Halstead, W. C. *Brain and intelligence.* Chicago: University of Chicago Press, 1947.

Hamilton, J. A. Intelligence and the human brain. *Psychological Review,* 1936, 43, 308–321.

Hammond, W. H. The constancy of physical types as determined by factor analysis. *Human Biology,* 1957, 2, 40–61.

Hare, A. P., Borgatta, E. F., & Bales, R. F. *Small group.* New York: Alfred A. Knopf, 1955.

Hargreaves, H. L. The "faculty" of imagination. *British Journal of Psychology Monograph Supplements,* 1927, 10, 74.

Harlow, H. F. The formation of learning sets. *Psychological Review,* 1949, 56, 51–65.

Harlow, H. F., & Warren, J. M. Formation and transfer of discrimination learning sets. *Journal of Comparative and Physiological Psychology,* 1952, 45, 482–489.

Harrell, R. F., Woodyard, E. K., & Gates, A. I. The influence of vitamin supplementation of the diets of pregnant and lactating women on the intelligence of their offspring. *Metabolism,* 1956, 5, 555–561.

Harrell, T. W., & Harrell, M. S. Army General Classification Test Scores for civilian occupations. *Educational and Psychological Measurement,* 1945, 5, 229–240.

Harrell, W. A factor analysis of mechanical ability tests. *Psychometrica,* 1940, 5, 17–33.

Harris, C. W. On factors and factor scores. *Psychometrika,* 1967, 32, 363–379.

Hartson, L. D. Influence of level of motivation on the validity of intelligence tests. *Educational and Psychological Measurement,* 1945, 5, 273–283.

Havighurst, R. J., & Janke, Leota L. Relations between ability and social status in a midwestern community. I. Ten-year-old children. *Journal of Educational Psychology,* 1944, 35, 357–368.

Hayes, C. *The ape in our house.* New York: Harper, 1951.

Hayes, K. J. Genes, drives and intellect. *Psychological Reports,* 1962, 10, 299–342.

Healy, W., & Bronner, A. F. *New light on delinquency and its treatment.* New Haven: Yale University press, 1936.

Hebb, D. O. Intelligence in man after large removals of cerebral tissue: report of four left frontal lobe cases. *Journal of General Psychology,* 1939, 21, 73–87.

Hebb, D. O. Human intelligence after removal of cerebral tissue from the right frontal lobe. *Journal of General Psychology,* 1941, 25, 257–265.

Hebb, D. O. The effects of early and late brain injury upon test scores and the nature of normal adult intelligence. *Proceedings of the American Philosophical Society,* 1942, 89, 275–292.

Hebb, D. O. *The organization of behavior.* New York: Wiley, 1949.

Hebb, D. O. Intelligence, brain function and the theory of mind. *Brain,* 1959, 82, 260–275. (a)

Hebb, D. O. A neuropsychological theory. In S. Koch (Ed.), *Psychology: A study of a science.* Vol. 1. *Sensory, Perceptual and Physiological Foundations.* New York: McGraw-Hill, 1959. Pp. 622–643. (b)

Hebb, D. O. The semi-autonomous process: Its nature and nurture. *American Psychologist,* 1963, 18 (1), 16–27.

Hebb, D. O. *A textbook of psychology.* Philadelphia, London: W. B. Saunders Co., 1966.

Heber, R. F. The relation of intelligence and physical maturity to social status of children. *Journal of Educational Psychology,* 1956, 47, 158–162.

Heber, R., Dever, R., & Conry, S. The influence of environmental and genetic variables on intellectual development.

Heim, A. W. et al. The effects of repeatedly retesting the same group on the same intelligence test. *Quarterly Journal of Experimental Psychology,* 1949–50, 1, 151–159; 2, 19–32, 182–195.

Hempel, W. E., Jr., & Fleishman, E. A. A factor analysis of physical proficiency and manipulative skill. *Journal of Applied Psychology,* 1955, 39, 12–16.

Herzberg, F., & Lepkin, M. A study of sex differences in the Primary Mental Abilities Test. *Educational and Psychological Measurement,* 1954, 14, 687.

Herzka, A. F., Guilford, J. P., Christensen, P. R., & Berger, R. M. A factor-analytic study of evaluative abilities. *Educational and Psychological Measurement,* 1954, 14, 581–597.

Hess, E. H. The relationship between imprinting and motivation. In M. R. Jones, Ed.), *Nebraska Symposium on Motivation.* Lincoln, Nebraska: University of Nebraska Press, 1959. Pp. 47–77. (a)

Hess, E. H. Two conditions limiting critical age for imprinting. *Journal of Comparative and Physiological Psychology,* 1959, 52, 515–518. (b)

Heymans, G., & Wiersma, E. Beiträge zur speziellen Psychologie auf Grund einer Massenuntersuchung. I–VII. *Zeitschrift für Psychologie und Physiologie der Sinnesorgane,* 1906–1912.

Higgins, J. V., Reed, E. W., & Reed, S. C. Intelligence and family size: a paradox resolved. *Eugenics Quarterly,* 1962, 9, 84–90.

Hilgard, E. R., & Atkinson, R. C. *Introduction to psychology.* New York: Harcourt, Brace & World, 1967.

Himmelweit, H. T., & Whitfield, J. W. Mean intelligence scores on a random sample of occupations. *British Journal of Industrial Psychology,* 1949, 1, 224–226.

Himwich, H. E. Boichemical and neuropsychological action of psychoactive drugs. In L. Uhr and J. G. Miller (Eds.), *Drugs and behavior.* New York: Wiley, 1960. Pp. 41–82.

Hindley, C. B. Stability and change in abilities up to five years: group trends. *Journal of Child. Psychol. Psychiat.,* 1965, 6, 85–100.

Hirsch, N. D. M. A study of natio-racial mental differences. *Genetic Psychology Monographs,* 1926, 1, 231–406.

Hirsch, N. D. M. *Genius and creative intelligence.* Cambridge: Science-Art Publishers, 1931.

Hoagland, H. Adventures in biological engineering. *Science,* 1944, 100, 63–67.

Hoagland, H., & Burloe, R. W. *Evolution and man's progress.* New York: Columbia University Press, 1962.

Hobson, J. R. Sex differences in primary mental abilities. *Journal of Educational Research,* 1947, 41, 126–132.

Hoepfner, R., Guilford, J. P., & Merrifield, P. R. A factor analysis of the symbolic evaluation abilities. Report #33 of Psychology Laboratory of the University of Southern California, 1964.

Hofstaetter, P. R. The changing composition of intelligence. *Journal of Genetic Psychology,* 1954, 85, 159–164.

Holmes, J. A., & Singer, H. *Speed and power of reading in high school.* Washington, D. C.: Government Printing Office, 1966.

Holmes, P. A., & Bitterman, M. E. Spatial and visual habit reversal in the turtle. *Journal of Comparative and Physiological Psychology,* 1966, 62, 328–331.

Holzinger, K. J. Preliminary report on Spearman-Holzinger unitary trait study. Chicago: Statistical Laboratory Department, University of Chicago, No. 2 and 4, 1934–1935.

Honzik, M. P. A sex difference in the age of onset of the parent-child resemblance in intelligence. *Journal of Educational Psychology,* 1963, 54(5), 231–237.

Horn, J. L. Fluid and crystallized intelligence: a factor analytic study of the structure among primary mental abilities. Unpublished doctoral dissertation, University of Illinois, 1965.

Horn, J. L. Integration of structural and developmental concepts in the theory of fluid and crystallized intelligence. In R. B. Cattell (Ed.), *Handbook of multivariate experimental psychology.* Chicago: Rand McNally, 1966. Chapter 18, Section 7. (a)

Horn, J. L. Motivation and dynamic calculus concepts from multivariate experiment. In R. B. Cattell (Ed.), *Handbook of multivariate experimental psychology.* Chicago: Rand NcNally, 1966. Chapter 20. (b)

Horn, J. L. *Short period fluctuations in intelligence.* Denver, Colorado: Denver Research Institute, 1966. (c)

Horn, J. L. Intelligence—Why it grows, why it declines. *Trans-Action,* 1967, 5, 23–31.

Horn, J. L. Organization of abilities and the development of intelligence. *Psychological Review,* 1968, 75, 242–259.

Horn, J. L. The relationship between evoked potential recordings and intelligence test measurements. *International Conference of Society of Multivariate Psychology,* Oxford, 1969.

Horn, J. L., & Bramble, W. J. Second-order ability structure revealed in rights and wrongs scores. *Journal of Educational Psychology,* 1967, 58, 115–122.

Horn, J. L., & Cattell, R. B. Vehicles, ipsatization and the multiple method measurement of motivation. *Canadian Journal of Psychology,* 1965, 19, 4, 265–279.

Horn, J. L., & Cattell, R. B. Refinement and test of the theory of fluid and crystallized intelligence. *Journal of Educational Psychology,* 1966, 57, 253–270. (a)

Horn, J. L., & Cattell, R. B. Age differences in primary mental ability factors. *Journal of Gerontology,* 1966, 21, 210–220. (b)

Horn, J. L., & Cattell, R. B. Age differences in fluid and crystallized intelligence. *Acta Psychologica,* 1967, 26, 107–129.

Horn, J. L., & Little, K. B. Isolating change and invariance in patterns of behavior. *Multivariate Behavioral Research,* 1966, 1, 219–229.

Horn, W. O. Primary Ability Tests. Göttingen, Germany: Hogrefe, 1960.

Horst, P. Generalized canonical correlations. *Journal of Clinical Psychology Monograph Supplement* #14, 1962.

Horst, P. An overview of the essentials of multivariate analysis methods. In R. B. Cattell (Ed.), *Handbook of multivariate experimental psychology.* Chicago: Rand McNally, 1966.

Howard, K. I., & Diesenhaus, H. I. Personality correlates of change-seeking behavior. *Perceptual and Motor Skills,* 1965, 21, 655–664.

Howarth, E., Instincts and their vicissitudes: a discussion of ethological models. *Journal of Psychological Researches,* 1966, 10 (3), 110–115.

Hull, C. L. *Aptitude testing.* New York: World Book Co., 1928.

Hull, C. L. *Hypnosis and suggestibility.* New York: Appleton Century, 1933.

Humphreys, L. G. The organization of human abilities. *American Psychologist,* 1962, 17, 475–483.

Humphreys, L. G. Critique of Cattell's "Theory of fluid and crystallized intelligence: a critical experiment." *Journal of Educational Psychology,* 1967, 58, 120–136.

Humphreys, L. G. Footnote to the Scottish survey of intelligence. *British Journal of Educational Psychology,* 1970, 40, 72–74.

Hundleby, J. D., Pawlik, K., & Cattell, R. B. *Personality factors in objective test devices.* San Diego: R. R. Knapp & Co., 1965.

Hunt, E. B. *Concept learning: an information processing problem.* New York: Wiley, 1962.

Hunt, E. B. Simulation and analytic models of memory. *Journal of Verbal Learning and Verbal Behavior,* 1963, 2, 49–59.

Hunt, J. McV. *Intelligence and Experience.* New York: Ronald Press, 1961.

Huntington, E. *Mainsprings of civilization.* New York: Mentor, 1945.

Hurley, J. R. Parental acceptance-rejection and children's intelligence. *Merrill-Palmer Quarterly,* 1965, 11, 19–31.

Hurst, C. C. *Heredity and the ascent of man.* London: Cambridge University Press, 1935.

Hurst, J. G. A factor analysis of the Merrill-Palmer with reference to theory and test construction. *Educational and Psychological Measurement,* 1960, 20, 519–532.

Hurst, J. G. Factor analyses of the Merrill-Palmer at two age levels: structure and comparison. *Journal of Genetic Psychology,* 1963, 102, 231–234.

Husen, T. The influence of schooling upon I.Q. *Theoria,* 1951, 17, 61–88.

Hydén, H. Biochemical changes in glial cells and nerve cells at varying activity. In *Proceedings of IVth International Congress of Biochemistry.* London: Pergamon, 1959.

Jenkins, J. J., & Paterson, D. G. (Eds.) *Studies in individual differences.* London: Methuen, 1961.

Jensen, A. R. Rote learning in retarded adults and normal children. *American Journal of Mental Deficiency,* 1965, 69(6), 828–834.

Jensen, A. R. Social class, race, and genetics: implications for education. *American Educational Research Journal,* 1968, 5, 1–47.

Jensen, A. R. How much can we boost I.Q. and scholastic achievement? *Harvard Educational Review,* 1969, Winter Issue.

Jerison, H. J. Brain to body ratios and the evolution of intelligence. *Science,* 1955, 121, 447–449.

Johnson, D. M. Application of the standard score I.Q. to social statistics. *Journal of Social Psychology,* 1948, 27, 217–227.

Johnson, D. M., Johnson, R. C., & Mark, A. L. A mathematical analysis of verbal fluency. *Journal of Genetic Psychology,* 1951, 44, 121–128.

Johnson, H. G. The economic approach to social questions. *The Public Interest,* 1968, 12, 68–80.

Jonassen, C. T., & Peres, S. H. *Interrelationships of dimensions of community systems.* Columbus: Ohio State Press, 1960.

Jones, H. E. Seasonal variations in I.Q. *Journal of Experimental Education,* 1941, 10, 91–99.

Jones, H. E. The environment and mental development. In L. Carmichael (Ed.), *Manual of child psychology.* New York: Wiley, 1954. Pp. 631–696.

Jones, H. E. Intelligence and problem solving. In J. E. Birren (Ed.), *Handbook of aging and the individual.* Chicago: University of Chicago Press, 1959.

Jones, H. E., & Conrad, H. S. The growth and decline of intelligence. *Genetic Psychology Monographs,* 1933, 13, 223–298.

Jones, R., Terrell, D. L., & De Shields, J. I. Intellectual and psychomotor performance of preschool children from low-income families. *Psychology in the schools,* 1967, 4, 257–259.

Kagan, J., & Moss, H. A. *Birth to maturity: a study in psychological development.* New York: Wiley, 1962.

Kaplan, O. J. *Mental disorders in later life.* Stanford: Stanford University Press, 1945.

Karlin, J. E. Musical ability. *Psychometrika,* 1941, 6, 61–65.

Karlin, J. E. A factorial study of auditory functon. *Psychometrika,* 1942, 7, 251–279.

Keehn, J. D., & Prothero, E. G. Non-verbal (culture fair) tests as predictors of academic success in Lebanon. *Journal of Educational and Psychological Measurement,* 1955, 5, 497.

Kelley, F. L. *Crossroads in the mind of man.* Stanford: Stanford University Press, 1928.

Kelley, H. P. *A factor analysis of memory ability.* Technical Report. Princeton, New Jersey: Educational Testing Service, 1954.

Kelley, T. L. *The influence of nurture upon native differences.* New York: Macmillan, 1926.

Kellogg, W. N., & Kellogg, L. A. *The ape and the child. A study of environmental influcence upon early behavior.* New York: Whittlesey House, 1933.

Kendall, M. G. *A course in multivariate analysis.* London: Griffin, 1957.

Kettner, N. W., Guilford, J. P., & Christensen, P. R. A factor analytic study across the domains of reasoning, creativity and evaluation. *Psychological Monographs,* 1959, 73, 479.

Kiev, A., Chapman, L. F., Guthrie, T. C., & Wolf, H. G. The highest integrative functions and diffuse cerebral atrophy. *Neurology,* 1962, 12(6), 385–393.

Kimura, Doreen. Some effects of temporal-lobe damage on auditory perception. *Canadian Journal of Psychology,* 1961, 15, 156–165.

Kintsch, W. All-or-none learning and the role of repetition in paired associate learning. *Science,* 1963, 140, 310–312.

Kipnis, D. Intelligence as a modifier of the behavior of character disorders. *Journal of Applied Psychology,* 1965, 49, 237–242.

Kirk, S. A. *Early education of the mentally retarded.* Urbana: University of Illinois Press, 1958.

Klausmeier, H. J., & Wiersma, W. Relationship of sex, grade level, and locale to performance of high I.Q. students on divergent thinking tests. *Journal of Educational Psychology,* 1964, 55, 114–119.

Kleinmuntz, B. *Problem solving research, method and theory.* New York: Wiley, 1966.

Kleinmuntz, B. *Formal representation of human judgment.* New York: Wiley, 1968.

Knapp, R. H. *The origins of American humanistic scholars.* Englewood Cliffs, New Jersey: Prentice-Hall, 1964.

Knapp, R. R. Demographic cultural and personality attributes of scientists. In Taylor, C. W., & Barron, F. (Ed.), *Scientific creativity: Its recognition and development.* New York: Wiley, 1963.

Koestler, A. *The act of creation.* New York: Macmillan, 1964.

Köhler, W. *The mentality of apes.* New York: Harcourt Brace, 1925.

Konorski, J. *Conditioned reflexes and neuron organization.* London: Cambridge University Press, 1948.

Konorski, J. Faits nouveaux et hypothèses concernant le mécanisme des réflexes conditionnels du deuxième type. *Psychologie Franc.,* 1960, 5, 123–134. (a)

Konorskii, I. U. [Konorski, J.] I Avliaiutsia li otsrochenne reaktsii sledovymi uslovnymi refleksami? *Fizrol. Zh. SSSR,* 1960, 46, 244–246. (b)

Krech, D. Nasledstvennost', sreda, mozg i reshenie zadach. [Heredity, environment, brain, and problem solving]. *Voprosy Psikhologii,* 1966, 3, 39–43.

Krech, D., Rosenzweig, M. R., & Bennett, E. L. Effects of environmental complexity and training on brain chemistry. *Journal of Comparative and Physiological Psychology,* 1960, 53, 509–519.

Kretschmer, E. *The psychology of men of genius.* London: Kegan Paul, 1931.

Krug, S. E. Personality and motivation components in measured ability. In preparation.

Lamson, Edna E. To what extent are intelligence quotients increased by children who participate in a rich, vital school curriculum? *Journal of Educational Psychology,* 1938, 29, 67–70.

Lansdell, H. Evidence for a symmetrical hemispheric contribution to an intellectual function. *Proceedings,* 76th Annual Convention of the American Psychiatric Association, 1968, 337–338.

Lashley, K. S. *Brain mechanisms and intelligence.* New York: Dover, 1963.

Lashley, K. S., Chow, K. L., & Seemes, Josephine. An examination of the electrical field theory of cerebral integration. *Psychological Review,* 1951, 58, 123–136.

Laycock, S. R. *Adaptability to new situations.* London: University of London Press, 1933.

Leaky, A. M. Nature-nurture and intelligence. *Genetic Psychological Monographs,* 1935, 17, 236–308.

Lehman, H. C. Man's most creative years: then and now. *Science,* 1943,

Lehman, H. C. *Age and achievement.* Princeton, New Jersey: Princeton University Press, 1953.

Lesser, G. S., Fifer, G., & Clark, D. H. Mental abilities of children from different social class and cultural groups. *Monograph of Society for Research in Child Development,* 1965, 30, No. 4.

Levine, S., & Mullins, R. F., Jr. Hormonal influences on brain organization in infant rats. *Science,* 1966, 152(3729), 1585–1592.

Lewis, M. M. *Language, thought and personality.* London: Harrap, 1963.

Lilly, J. C. *Man and dolphin.* New York: Doubleday, 1961.

Lindholm, B. W. Changes in conventional and deviation IQ's. *Journal of Educational Psychology,* 1964, 55, 110–113.

Lindsley, D. B. The reticular motivating system and perceptual integration, in D. E. Sheer (Ed.), *Electrical stimulation of the brain.* Austin: University of Texas Press, 1961.

Line, W. The growth of visual perception in children. *British Journal of Psychology Monograph Supplement* #15, 1931.

Line, W., & Kaplan, E. Variation in I.Q. at the preschool level. *Journal of Experimental Education,* 1933, 2, 95–100.

Lingoes, J. C. *New computer developments in pattern analysis and nonmetric techniques.* Computing Center Report No. 4. Ann Arbor: University of Michigan, 1965.

Livesay, P. J. The rat, rabbit and cat in the Hebb-Williams Closed Field Test of animal intelligence. *Australian Journal of Psychology,* 1966, 18(1), 71–79.

Loehlin, J. C. Heredity, environment and personality inventory items. Paper read at American Psychological Association, St. Louis, 1962.

Loevinger, Jane. A systematic approach to the construction and evaluation of tests of ability. *Psychological Monographs,* 1947, 61, No. 4.

Lombroso, C. *The man of genius.* London: Walter Scott, 1891.

Lorenz, K. *King Solomon's ring.* London: Macmillan, 1958.

Lorge, J. Influence of regularly interpolated time intervals on subsequent learning. *Teachers College Contribution to Education,* 1930, No. 438.

Lorge, J. The influence of the test upon the nature of mental decline as a function of age. *Journal of Educational Psychology,* 1936, 27, 100–110.

Louittit, R. T. Chemical facilitation of intelligence among the mentally retarded. *American Journal of Mental Deficiency,* 1965, 69, 495–501.

Lowes, G., & Bitterman, M. E. Reward and learning in the goldfish. *Science,* 1967, 157, 455–457.

Luchins, A. S., & Forgus, R. H. The effect of differential post-weaning environment on the rigidity of an animal's behavior. *Journal of Genetic Psychology,* 1955, 86, 51–58.

Luchins, A. S., & Luchins, E. H. *Rigidity of behavior.* Eugene, Oregon: University of Oregon Books, 1959.

Luria, A. R. L. S. Vygotsky and the problem of localization of functions. *Neuropsychologia,* 1965, 3, 387–392.

Luria, A. R. The functional organization of the brain. *Scientific American,* February 1970, 66–78.

MacArthur, R. S. Assessing intellectual potential of native pupils: a summary. *Alberta Journal of Educational Research,* 1968, 14, 115–122.

Maier, N. F. R. The behavior mechanisms concerned with problem solving. *Psychological Review,* 1940, 47, 43–58.

Maier, N. R. F. Reasoning in humans: III. The mechanisms of equivalent stimuli and reasoning. *Journal of Experimental Psychology,* 1945, 35, 349–360.

Maier, N. R. F., & Hoffman, L. R. Organization and creative problem solving. *Journal of Applied Psychology,* 1961, 45, 277–280.

Maier, N. R. F., & Schneirla, T. C. *Principles of animal psychology.* New York: Dover, 1964.

Maller, J. B., & Zubin, J. The effect of motivation upon intelligence test scores. *Journal of Genetic Psychology,* 1932, 41, 136–151.

Malmo, R. B. Reduction in general intelligence following frontal gyrectomy and frontal lobotomy in mental patients. *American Psychologist,* 1948, 3, 277.

Marquart, D., & Bailey, L. L. An evaluation of the culture fair (IPAT) test of intelligence. *Journal of Genetic Psychology,* 1955, 86, 353–358.

Marron, J. E. A search for basic reasoning abilities: A review of factor analysis. *USAF, Human Resources Research Center Research Bulletin,* No. 53–28, 1953.

Maslow, A. H. *Motivation and personality.* New York: Harper, 1954.

Matarazzo, J. D., Ulett, G. A., Guez, S. B., & Seslow, G. The relationship between anxiety level and several measures of intelligence. *Journal of Consulting Psychology,* 1954, 18, 201–205.

Maxwell, A. E. Trends in cognitive ability in the older age ranges. *Journal of Abnormal and Social Psychology,* 1961, 63, 449–452.

Maxwell, J. *Social implications of the 1947 Scottish mental survey.* London: University of London Press, 1953.

McArthur, R. T., & Elley, W. B. The reduction of socio-economic bias in intelligence testing. *British Journal of Educational Psychology,* 1963, 33, 107–119.

McClelland, D. C., Atkinson, J. W., Clark, R. A., & Lowell, E. L. *The achievement motive.* New York: Appleton-Century-Crofts, 1953.

McClelland, W. *Selection for secondary education.* London: University of London Press, 1942.

McDade, D. F. Language, intelligence and social class. *Scottish Educational Studies,* 1967, 1, 34–39.

McDougall, W. The physiological factors of the attention process. *Mind,* N.S.I.X., 1902, 109–132, 216–229, 324–340.

McDougall, W. *National welfare and national decay.* London: Methuen, 1930.

McDougall, W. *Energies of men.* London: Methuen, 1932.

McFie, J. Psychological testing in clinical neurology. *Journal of Nervous and Mental Disorders,* 1960, 131, 383–393.

McGaughran, L. S., & Moran, L. J. Differences between schizophrenic and brain-damaged groups in conceptual aspects of object sorting. *Journal of Abnormal Psychology,* 1957, 54, 44–49.

McGraw, Myrtle B. Later development of children specially trained during infancy. Johnny and Jimmy at school age. *Child Development,* 1939, 10, 1–19.

McGuire, C., Hindsman, E., King, F. J., & Jennings, E. Dimensions of talented behavior. *Educational and Psychological Measurement,* 1961, 21, 3–38.

McGurk, F. C. J. On white and Negro test performance and socio-economic factors. *Journal of Abnormal and Social Psychology,* 1961, 48, 450–455.

McNemar, Q. A critical examination of the University of Iowa studies of environmental influences on the I.Q. *Psychological Bulletin,* 1940, 37, 63–92.

McNemar, Q. *Revision of the Stanford-Binet Scale.* Boston: Houghton Mifflin, 1942.

McNemar, Q. On growth measurement. *Educational and Psychological Measurement,* 1958, 18, 47–55.

McNemar, Q. Lost: Our Intelligence? Why? *American Psychologist,* 1964, 19, 871–882.

Meehl, P. E. *Clinical versus statistical prediction.* Minnesota: University of Minnesota Press, 1954.

Meili, R. Sur la nature des facteurs d'intelligence. *Acta Psychologica,* 1949, 6, 40–58.

Mellone, Margaret A. A factorial study of picture tests for young children. *British Journal of Psychology,* 1944, 35, 9–16.

Melton, A. W. Implications of short-term memory for a general theory of memory. *Journal of Verbal Learning and Verbal Behavior,* 1963, 2, 1–21.

Meredith, G. M. Contending hypotheses of ontogenesis for the exuberance-restraint personality factor, U.I. 21. *Journal of Genetic Psychology,* 1966, 108 (1), 89–104.

Meredith, G. M. Observations of the origins and current status of the ego-assertive personality factor, U.I. 16. *Journal of Genetic Psychology,* 1967, 110(2), 269–286.

Merrifield, P. R. An analysis of concepts from the point of view of the structure of intellect. In H. J. Klausmeier and C. W. Harris (Eds.), *Analyses of concept learning.* New York: Academic Press, 1966. Chapter 2.

Meyer, W. J., & Bendig, A. W. A longitudinal study of the Primary Mental Abilities Test. *Journal of Educational Psychology,* 1961, 52, 50–60.

Meyers, C. E., Dingman, H. F., and others. Primary abilities at mental age six. Child Development Publications, Society for Research in Child Development, 1962.

Michael, W. B., Guilford, J. P., Fruchter, B., & Zimmerman, W. S. The description of spacial-visualization abilities. *Educational and Psychological Measurement,* 1957, 17, 185–199.

Miles, Catherine C., The influence of speed and age on intelligence scores of adults. *Journal of General Psychology,* 1934, 10, 208–210.

Miles, W. R. Changes in movement time and reaction time with age. In E. V. Cowdry (Ed.), *Problems of aging*. Baltimore: Williams and Wilkins, 1942.

Miller, G. A., Galanter, E., & Pribram, K. H. *Plans and structure of behavior*. New York: Holt, 1960.

Miller, J. G. Drugs and human information processing: perception, cognition and response. In L. Uhr & J. G. Miller (Eds.), *Drugs and behavior*. New York: Wiley, 1960. Pp. 335–351.

Minsky, M. Artificial intelligence. *Scientific American*, 1966, 215(3), 246–260.

Moorman, L. J. *Tuberculosis and genius*. Chicago: University of Chicago Press, 1940.

Moreton, C. A., & Butcher, J. H. Are rural children handicapped by the use of speeded tests in selection procedures? *British Journal of Educational Psychology*, 1963, 33, 22–30.

Morrison, J. R. Effects of time limits on the efficiency and factorial composition of reasoning measures. Doctoral dissertation, University of Illinois, 1960.

Moss, H. A., & Kagan, J. Maternal influences on early I.Q. scores. *Psychological Reports*, 1958, 4, 655–661.

Mukherjee, B. N. The factorial structure of aptitude tests at successive grade levels. *British Journal of Mathematical and Statistical Psychology*, 1902, 15, 59–70.

Murray, H. A. *Explorations in personality*. New York: Oxford University Press, 1938.

Myrdal, G. *Challenge to affluence*. New York: Vintage Books, 1965.

Myrdal, G. *Asian drama; an inquiry into the poverty of nations*. New York: Pantheon Press, 1968.

Nash, H. Psychological effects of amphetamines and barbiturates. *Journal of Nervous and Mental Disorders*, 1962, 134, 203–217.

Nesselroade, J., & Cattell, R. B. Personality structure in objective tests at the child level. In press, 1971.

Netchine, G., & Netchine, S. Organisation psychologique et organisation bio-électrique cérébrale dans une population d'arrièrés mentaux. *Psychol. Franc.*, 1962, 7(4), 241–258.

Newland, T. E. The assessment of exceptional children. In W. M. Cruikshank (Ed.), *Psychology of exceptional children and youth*. New York: Prentice-Hall, 1962.

Newman, H. H., Freeman, F. N., & Holzinger, K. J. *Twins: a study of heredity and environment*. Chicago: University of Chicago Press, 1937.

Nilsson, N. J. *Learning machines*. New York: McGraw-Hill, 1965.

Nisbet, J. D. Intelligence and age: retesting with twenty-four years' interval. *British Journal of Educational Psychology*, 1957, 27, 190–198.

Nisbet, J. D., & Entwistle, N. J. Intelligence and family size, 1949–1965. *British Journal of Educational Psychology*, 1967, 37, 188–193.

Nissen, H. W., Chow, K. L., & Semmes, J. Effects of restricted opportunity for tactual, kinesthetic, and manipulative experience on the behavior of a chimpanzee. *American Journal of Psychology*, 1951, 64, 485–507.

Norman, W. T. Toward an adequate taxonomy of personality attributes: replicated factor structure in peer nomination personality ratings. *Journal of Abnormal and Social Psychology,* 1963, 66, 574–583.

Nunnally, J. C. *Tests and measurements: assessment and prediction.* New York: McGraw-Hill, 1959.

Nunnally, J. C. *Educational measurement and evaluation.* New York: McGraw-Hill, 1964.

Ochs, S. *Elements of neuro-physiology.* New York: Wiley, 1965.

Osler, Sonia F., & Fival, M. W. Concept attainment: I. The role of age and intelligence in concept attainment by induction. *Journal of Experimental Psychology,* 1961, 62, 1–8.

Ostow, M. Psychodynamic disturbances in patients with temporal lobe disorder. *Journal of Mount Sinai Hospital,* 1954, 20(5), 293–308.

Owens, W. A. Is age kinder to the initially more able? *Journal of Gerontology,* 1959, 14, 334–337.

Owens, W. A. Age and mental abilities: a second adult follow-up. *Journal of Educational Psychology,* 1966, 57, 311–325.

Page, J. D. The effect of nursery school attendance upon subsequent I.Q. *Journal of Psychology,* 1940, 10, 221–230.

Paolino, A., & Friedman, I. Intellectual changes following frontal lobe procainization. *Journal of Clinical Psychology,* 1959, 15, 437–439.

Parsley, K. M., Jr. Further investigation of sex differences in achievement of under-, average-, and over-achieving students within five I.Q. groups in grades four through eight. *Journal of Educational Research,* 1964, 57 (5), 268–270.

Paterson, D. G. *Physique and intellect.* New York: Appleton Century, 1930.

Patterson, R. F. A longitudinal analysis of the relationship between growth rate and mental development in children between the ages of four and ten years. *Dissertation Abstracts,* 1958, 18, 1869.

Pavlos, A. J. Sex differences among rural Negro kids on the WISC. *Proceedings of the West Virginia Academy of Science,* 1961, 33, 109–114.

Pavlov, I. P. *Conditioned reflexes.* London: Oxford University Press, 1927.

Pawlik, K. Concepts and calculations in human cognitive abilities. In R. B. Cattell (Ed.), *Handbook of multivariate experimental psychology.* Chicago: Rand McNally, 1966. Chapter 18.

Pawlik, K. *Dimension des Verhaltens.* Stuttgart: Verlag Hans Huber, Bern, 1968.

Pawlik, K., & Cattell, R. B. Third-order factors in objective personality tests. *British Journal of Psychology,* 1964, 55, 1–18.

Pawlik, K., & Cattell, R. B. The relationship between certain personality factors and measures of cortical arousal. *Neuropsychology,* 1965, 3, 129–151.

Pearson, K. On the relationship of intelligence to size and shape of head. *Biometrika,* 1906–1907, 5, 105–146.

Pemberton, C. The closure factors related to other cognitive processes. *Psychometrika,* 1952, 17, 267–288.

Peterson, H., Guilford, J. P., Hoefner, R., & Merrifield, P. R. Determination of "structure-of-intellect" abilities involved in ninth grade algebra and general mathematics. Report of the Psychology Laboratory, University of Southern California, 1963, No. 31.

Piaget, J. *The origins of intelligence in children.* Translation by Margaret Cook. New York: International University Press, 1952.

Piaget, J. *The growth of logical thinking.* London: Routledge, 1958.

Piaget, J. *Psychology of intelligence.* Paterson, New Jersey: Littlefield Adams, 1960.

Piaget, J. The stages of the intellectual development of the child. *Bulletin of the Menninger Clinic,* 1962, 26, 120–128.

Pickford, R. W. Two artists with protan colour vision defects. *British Journal of Psychology,* 1965, 56(4), 421–430.

Pierce-Jones, J., & Tyler, F. T. A comparison of the A.C.E. Psychological Examination and the Culture Fair Test. *Canadian Journal of Psychology,* 1950, 4, 109–114.

Pierson, G. R., Barton, V., & Hay, G. SMAT motivation factors as predictors of academic achievement in delinquent boys. *Journal of Psychology,* 1964, 57, 243–249.

Pilkington, G. W., & Harrison, G. T. The relative value of two high-level intelligence tests, advanced level, and first-year university examination marks for predicting degree classification. *British Journal of Educational Psychology,* 1967, 37, 382–388.

Pinard, J. W. Tests of perseveration. I. Their relation to character. *British Journal of Psychology,* 1932, 23, 5–19.

Pinneau, S. R. *Changes in intelligence quotient: infancy to maturity.* Boston: Houghton Mifflin, 1961.

Pintner, R. Pintner general ability tests. Non-language series. New York: World Book Co., 1945.

Pintner, R., & Forlano, G. Season of birth and mental differences. *Psychological Bulletin,* 1943, 40, 25–35.

Poincaré, H. *Science and method.* London: Nelson, 1914.

Pont, H. B. A review of the use of information theory in psychology and a study of the effect of age on channel capacity. Ed.B. thesis, University of Aberdeen Library, 1963.

Porteus, S. D. *Primitive intelligence and environment.* New York: Macmillan, 1937.

Porteus, S. D. Mental changes in psychopharmacology. In L. Uhr, & J. G. Miller (Eds.), *Drugs and behavior.* New York: Wiley, 1960.

Pressey, S. L., & Ralston, R. The relation of the general intelligence of school children to the occupation of their fathers. *Journal of Applied Psychology,* 1919, 3, 366–373.

Pribram, K. On the neurology of thinking. *Behavioral Science,* 1959, 4, 265–287.

Pribram, K. K teorii fiziologecheskoi psikhologii. *Vop. Psikhol.,* 1961, No. 2, 133–156.

Prosser, C. L., & Buehl, C. C. Oxidative control of spontaneous activity in the nervous system of the crayfish. *Journal of Cellular and Comparative Physiology,* 1939, 14, 287–297.

Quereshi, M. Y. Patterns of psycholinguistic development during early and middle childhood. *Educational and Psychological Measurement,* 1967, 27, 353–365.

Radcliffe, J. & Cattell, R. B. Factors in objective motivation measurement in children, a preliminary study. *Australian Journal of Psychology*, 1961, 13, 65–76.

Radinsky, L. Relative brain size: a new measure. *Science*, 1967, 155, 836–837.

Raven, J. C. *Progressive matrices*. London: H. K. Lewis, 1947.

Reed, S., Reed, E., & Palm, J. Fertility and intelligence among families of the mentally deficient. *Eugenics Quarterly*, 1954, 1, 44–52.

Reitan, R. M. Investigation of the validity of Halstead's measures of biological intelligence. A.M.A. *Archives of Neurology and Psychiatry*, 1955, 73, 28–35.

Reitan, R. M. Impairment of abstraction ability in brain damage: quantitative versus qualitative changes. *Journal of Psychology*, 1959, 48, 97–102.

Rheingold, H. L. Mental and social development of infants in relation to the number of other infants in the boarding home. *Psychological Bulletin*, 1942, 39, 594.

Richard, Suzanne. Mental organization and age level. *Archives of Psychology*, 1944, #295.

Richards, J. W., & Nelson, Virginia L. Abilities of infants during the first eighteen months. *Journal of Genetic Psychology*, 1939, 55, 299–318.

Riesen, A. H. Arrested vision. *Scientific American*, 1950, 183, 16–19.

Riesen, A. H., Chow, K. L., Semmes, J., & Nissen, H. W. Chimpanzee vision after four conditions of light deprivation. *American Psychologist*, 1951, 6, 282.

Rimoldi, H. J. A. Personal tempo. *Journal of Abnormal and Social Psychology*, 1951, 46, 283–303. (a)

Rimoldi, H. J. A. The central intellective factor. *Psychometrika*, 1951, 16, 75–102. (b)

Roberts, J. A. F. Intelligence and family size. *Eugenics Review*, 1939, 30, 237–247.

Robinson, S. Experimental studies of physical fitness in relation to age. *Arbeitsphysiologie*, 1938, 10, 279.

Rodd, W. G. A cross-cultural study of Taiwan's schools. Unpublished doctoral dissertation, Western Reserve University, 1958.

Roe, A. *The making of a scientist*. New York: Dodd, 1953.

Roe, A., & Shakow, D. Intelligence in mental disorder. *Annals of New York Academy of Science*, 1942, 42, 361–490.

Roff, M. Personnel selection and classification: perceptual tests. A factorial analysis. Randolph Field, Texas: USAF School of Aviation Medicine (Project No. 21–02–009) (cf. also: *Psychometric Monographs*, 1952, No. 8), 1950.

Roff, M. A factorial study of tests in the perceptual area. *Psychometric Monographs*, 1953, No. 8.

Rokeach, M., & Fruchter, B. A factorial study of dogmatism and related concepts. *Journal of Abnormal and Social Psychology*, 1956, 53, 356–360.

Rosenblatt, F. *Principles of neurodynamics*. Washington, D. C.: Spartan Books, 1962.

Rosenthal, R. Covert communication in the psychological experiment. *Psychological Bulletin*, 1967, 67, 356–367.

Rosenthal, R., & Jacobson, L. Teachers' expectancies: determinants of pupils' I.Q. gains. *Psychological Reports,* 1966, 19, 115–118.

Rosenzweig, M. R., Krech, D., & Bennett, E. L. Heredity, environment, brain biochemistry and learning. In *Current trends in psychological theory.* Pittsburgh: University of Pittsburgh Press, 1961. Pp. 87–110.

Ross, A. O. Brain injury and intellectual performance. *Journal of Consulting Psychology,* 1958, 22, 151–152.

Royce, J. R. The factorial analysis of animal behavior. *Psychological Bulletin,* 1950, 47, 235–259.

Royce, J. R. Concepts generated in comparative and physiological psychological observations. In R. B. Cattell (Ed.), *Handbook of multivariate experimental psychology.* Chicago: Rand McNally, 1966. Chapterf 21.

Rummel, R. J. Dimensions of conflict behavior within and between nations. *General systems: Yearbook of the Sociology for General Systems Research.,* 1963, 8, 1–50.

Ryans, D. G. A study of the observed relationship between persistence test results, intelligence indices, and academic success. *Journal of Educational Psychology,* 1938, 29, 573–580.

Sanford, G. A. Selective migration in a rural Alabama community. *American Sociological Review,* 1940, 5, 759–766.

Sarkisov, S. A. *The structure and function of the brain.* Bloomington: Indiana University Press, 1966.

Saunders, D. R. Further implication of Mundy-Castle's correlation between EEG and Wechsler Bellevue variables. *Journal of National Institutes of Personnel Research* (Johannesburg), 1960, 8, 91–101.

Schade, Alice F., & Bitterman, M. E. The relative difficulty of reversal and dimensional shifting as a function of overlearning. *Psychonomic Science,* 1965, 3(7), 283–284.

Schaedeli, R. Untersuchungen zur Verifikation von Meilis Intelligenzfaktoren. *Z. exp. angew. Psychol.,* 1961, 8, 211–265.

Schaefer, E. S., & Bayley, Nancy. Maternal behavior, child behavior, and their intercorrelations from infancy through adolescence. *Monograph of the Society for Research in Child Development,* 1963, 28, No. 3 (Serial No. 87), 127.

Schaie, K. W. Occupational level and the Primary Mental Abilities. *Journal of Educational Psychology,* 1958, 49, 299–303. (a)

Schaie, K. W. Rigidity-flexibility and intelligence: a cross-sectional study of the adult life span from 20 to 70 years. *Psychological Monographs,* 1958, 72(9), 26. (b)

Schaie, K. W. Cross sectional methods in the study of psychological aspects of aging. *Journal of Gerontology,* 1959, 14, 208–215.

Schaie, K. W., Rosenthal, F., & Perlman, R. M. Differential mental deterioration of factorially "pure" functions in later maturity. *Journal of Gerontology,* 1953, 8, 191–196.

Schaie, K. W., & Strother, C. R. A cross-sequential study of age changes in cognitive behavior. *Psychological Bulletin,* 1968, 68.

Scheier, I. H., Cattell, R. B., & Horn, J. Objective test factor U.I. 23: Its measurement and its relation to clinically-judged neuroticism. *Journal of Clinical Psychology,* 1960, 16, 135–145.

Schiller, B. Verbal, numerical and spatial abilities of young children. *Archives of Psychology,* 1933–1934, 24, #161.

Schneewind, K. *Methodisches Denken in der Psychologie.* Berne, Stuttgart, Wien: Hans Huber, 1969.

Schuerger, J. M., Dielman, T. E., & Cattell, R. B. Objective-analytic personality factors (U.I. 16, 17, 19 and 20) as correlates of school achievement. *Personality: An International Journal,* In press.

Schwartz, F., & Lippman, F. Cognitive and associative structures in recall. *Psychological Reports,* 1962, 11, 91–101.

Scott, Eileen M., & Nisbert, J. D. Intelligence and family size in an adult sample. *Eugenics Review,* 1955, 46, 233–235.

Scott, J. P., Fuller, J. L., & King, J. A. The inheritance of animal breeding cycles in hybrid basenji-cocker spaniel dogs. *Journal of Heredity,* 1959, 50, 254–261.

Scott, Peter. An Isonoetic Map of Tasmania. *Geographical Review,* 1957, *3,* 47, 311–329.

Scottish Council for Research in Education. *The trend of Scottish intelligence.* London: University of London Press, 1949, Pub. No. 30.

Scottish Council for Research in Education. *Gaelic-speaking children in Highland school.* London: University of London Press, 1961.

Seashore, C. E. *In search of beauty in music: a scientific approach to musical esthetics.* New York: Ronald Press, 1947.

Selfridge, O. G., & Neisser, U. Pattern recognition by machine. *Scientific American,* 1960 (August), 203, 60–68.

Sells, S. B. *Essentials of psychology.* New York: Ronald Press, 1962. (a)

Sells, S. B. (Ed.) *Stimulus determinants of behavior.* New York: Ronald Press, 1962. (b)

Semler, I. J., & Iscoe, I. Structure of intelligence in negro and white children. *Journal of Educational Psychology,* 1966, 57, 326–336.

Serebriakoff, V. *I. Q.: A Mensa analysis and history.* London: Hutchinson, 1966.

Sholl, D. A. *The organisation of the cerebral cortex.* London: Methuen, 1956.

Shotwell, Anna M., Hurley, J. R., & Cattell, R. B. Motivational structure of an hospitalized mental defective. *Journal of Abnormal and Social Psychology,* 1961, 62, 422–426.

Shotwell, Anna, & Shipe, Dorothy. Effect of out-of-home care on the intellectual and social development of mongoloid children. *American Journal of Mental Deficiency,* 1964, 68, 693–699.

Shub, D. *Lenin.* New York: New American Library, 1948.

Shuey, A. M. *The testing of Negro intelligence.* New York: Holborn Publishing Co., 1958.

Skeels, H. M. Some Iowa studies of the mental growth of children in relation to differentials of the environment: a summary. In *Yearbook of the National Society of Student Education,* 1940, 39, Part II. Pp. 281–308.

Skeels, H. M., & Skodak, Marie. Adult status of individuals who experienced early intervention. Paper presented at 90th annual meeting of the American Association on Mental Deficiency, Chicago, May 12, 1966.

Skinner, B. F. *Science and human behavior.* New York: Macmillan, 1953.

Skodak, Marie. Mental growth of adopted children in the same family. *Journal of Genetic Psychology,* 1950, 77, 3–9.

Slater, P., & Sargant, W. Influence of sodium amytal in intelligence test scores. *Lancet,* 1942, 676–677.

Smith, I. M. *Spatial ability.* London: University of London Press, 1964.

Sokal, R. R., & Sneath, P. H. *Principles of numerical taxonomy.* San Francisco: Freeman, 1964.

Spearman, C. The proof and measurement of association between two things. *American Journal of Psychology,* 1904, 15, 72–101. (a)

Spearman, C. General intelligence, objectively determined and measured. *American Journal of Psychology,* 1904, 15, 201–293. (b)

Spearman, C. *The nature of "intelligence" and the principles of cognition.* London: Macmillan, 1923.

Spearman, C. *The abilities of man.* London: Macmillan, 1927.

Spearman, C. *A measure of intelligence.* London: Methuen, 1929.

Spearman, C. *Creative mind.* London: Misbet, 1930.

Spearman, C. *Psychology down the ages.* London: Macmillan, 1937.

Spencer, H. *The principles of psychology.* London: Williams and Norgate, 1855.

Sperry, R. W. The great cerebral commissure. *Scientific American,* January 1964, 240–250.

Spielberger, C. D. *Anxiety and behavior.* New York: Academic Press, 1966.

Spitz, R. A. Hospitalism: a follow-up report. In *The Psychoanalytic Study of the Child,* Vol. II. New York: International University Press, 1946.

Sprecher, T. B. A study of engineers' criteria for creativity. *Journal of Applied Psychology,* 1959, 43, 141–148.

Spuhler, J. N., & Lindzey, G. Racial differences in behavior. In J. Hirsh, *Behavior-genetic analysis.* New York: McGraw-Hill Co., 1967. Chapter 19.

Stake, R. E. Learning parameters, aptitudes, achievement & *Psychometrics Monog.* 31, 9, 1966.

Stephenson, W. *The study of behavior: Q-technique and its methodology.* Chicago: University of Chicago Press, 1953.

Stern, C. *Time,* September 29, 1967.

Stettner, L. J., & Matzniak, K. A. The brain of birds. *Scientific American,* 1968, June, 218, 64–76.

Stevens, S. S. The psychophysics of sensory function. *American Scientist,* 1960, 48, 226–253.

Stoddard, G. D. *The meaning of intelligence.* New York: Macmillan, 1943.

Stone, G. C. Attainment of color, form, and size concepts by rhesus monkeys. *Journal of Comparative Physiology and Psychology,* 1961, 54, 38–42.

Stott, L. H., & Ball, R. S. Infant and preschool mental tests: review and evaluation. *Monographs of the Society for Research in Child Development,* 1965, 30, 2–151.

Stott, L. H., & Ball, Rachael S. The identification and assessment of thinking ability in young children. Final Report Project No. 6–1106 U.S. Department of Health, Education and Welfare, Office of Education, Bureau of Research. October, 1968.

Strasheim, G. *A new method of mental testing.* Baltimore: Warwick and York, 1926.

Studman, L. G. Studies in experimental psychiatry. V. "W" and "f" factors in relation to traits of personality. *Journal of Mental Science,* 1935, 81, 107–137.

Stutsman, Rachel. *Mental measurement of preschool children.* New York: World Book, 1931.

Sweney, A. B., & Cattell, R. B. Relationships between integrated and uninte-grated motivation structure examined by objective tests. *Journal of Social Psychology,* 1962, 57, 217–226.

Swineford, F. General, verbal, and spatial bi-factors after 3 years. *Journal of Educational Psychology,* 1949, 40, 353–360.

Tapp, J. T., & Markowitz, H. Infant handling: effects of avoidance learning, brain weight, cholinesterase activity. *Science,* 1963, 140, 486–487.

Taylor, C. W. A factorial study of fluency in writing. *Psychometrika,* 1947, 12, 239–262.

Taylor, C. W., & Barron, F. *Scientific creativity: its recognition and develop-ment.* New York: Wiley, 1963.

Terman, L. M. *Mental and physical traits of a thousand gifted children.* Lon-don: Harrap and Co., 1925.

Terman, L. M., & Oden, H. M. *The gifted child grows up.* Vol. 4 of the Genetic Studies of Genius. Stanford: Stanford University Press, 1947.

Terman, L. M., & Oden, M. H. *The gifted group at mid-life.* Vol. 5 of the Genetic Studies of Genius. Stanford: Stanford University Press, 1959.

Thistlethwaite, D. L. The recognition of excellence. *College and University,* 1961, 36.

Thompson, W. R. The inheritance and development of intelligence. *Proceedings of the Association for Research on Nervous and Mental Disorders,* 1954, 33, 209–231.

Thompson, W. R. Traits, factors and genes. *Eugenics Quarterly,* 1957, 4, 8–16.

Thompson, W. R. Multivariate experiment in behavior genetics. In R. B. Cattell (Ed.), *Handbook of multivariate experimental psychology.* Chicago: Rand McNally, 1966. Chapter 23.

Thomson, G. The Northumberland Intelligence Tests. London: Harrap, 1935.

Thomson, G. H. *The factorial analysis of human ability.* London: University of London Press, 1939.

Thomson, G. H. Intelligence and fertility. *Eugenics Review,* 1949, No. 4.

Thorndike, E. L. *The original nature of man.* New York: Columbia University Press, 1913.

Thorndike, E. L. *Human learning.* New York: Appleton-Century-Crofts, 1931.

Thorndike, E. L. *Intelligence of animals and man.* Chicago: University of Chi-cago Press, 1932.

Thorndike, E. L., & Woodyard, E. Differences within and between communities in the intelligence of children. *Journal of Educational Psychology,* 1942, 33, 641–656.

Thorndike, R. L. *Analysis of a further 300 American cities.* New York: Harcourt, Brace, 1941.

Thorndike, R. L. The origin of superior men. *Scientific Monographs,* 1943, 56, 424–433.

Thorndike, R. L. The psychology of invention in a very simple case. *Psychological Review,* 1949, 56, 192–199.

Thorndike, R. L. Community variables as predictors of intelligence and academic achievement. *Journal of Educational Psychology,* 1951, 42, 321–338.

Thorndike, R. L. Intellectual status and intellectual growth. *Journal of Educational Psychology,* 1966, 57, 121–127.

Thurstone, L. L. Multiple factor analysis. *Psychological Review,* 1931, 38, 406–427.

Thurstone, L. L. *Primary mental abilities.* Chicago: Chicago University Press, 1938.

Thurstone, L. L. *A factorial study of perception.* Chicago: University of Chicago Press, 1944.

Thurstone, L. L. Some primary abilities in visual thinking. Psychometric Laboratory Report No. 59, University of Chicago, 1950.

Thurstone, L. L., & Thurstone, T. G. Primary mental abilities test. Chicago: Scientific Research Associates, 1948.

Thurstone, T. G. SRA PMA Examiner's Manual, 1963.

Tinbergen, N. *The study of instinct.* Oxford: Clarendon Press, 1951.

Tollefson, D. Differential responses to humor and their relation to personality and motivation measures. Unpublished doctoral dissertation, University of Illinois, 1959.

Townsend, A. M., & Mirsky, A. F. A comparison of the effects of meprobamate, phenobarbital, and d-amphetamine on two psychological tests. *Journal of Nervous and Mental Disorders,* 1960, 130. 212–216.

Toynbee, A. J. *A study of history.* New York: Oxford University Press, 1947.

Tryon, R. C. Genetic differences in maze-learning ability in rats. *39th Yearbook of the National Society of Student Education.* (Part I) Bloomington, Illinois: Public School Publishing Co., 1940. Pp. 111–119.

Tucker, L. R. Learning theory and multivariate experiment: illustration by determination of generalized learning curves. In R. B. Cattell (Ed.), *Handbook of Multivariate Experimental Psychology.* Chicago: Rand McNally, 1966. Chapter 16.

Tuddenham, R. D. Soldier intelligence in world wars I and II. *American Psychologist,* 1948, 3, 54–56.

Tupes, E. C. Relatonships between behavior trait ratings by peers and later officer performance of USAF Officer Candidate School graduates. Lackland AFB, Texas: USAF Personnel and Training Research Center, Report No. AFPTRC–TN–57–125 (ASTIA Doc. No. 134257), 1957.

Turing, A. M. Computing machinery and intelligence. *Mind,* 1950, 59, 433–460.

Tyler, L. E. *The psychology of human differences.* New York: Appleton-Century-Crofts, 1956.

Uhr, L. Objectively measured behavioral effects of psychoactive drugs. In Uhr, L., & J. G. Miller (Eds.), *Drugs and behavior.* New York: Wiley, 1960. Pp. 610–634.

Underwood, B. J. Interference and forgetting. *Psychological Review,* 1957, 64, 49–60.

Unger, S. M. Relation between intelligence and socially-approved behavior: a methodological cautionary note. *Child Development,* 1964, 35, 299–301.

Vandenberg, S. G. The primary mental abilities of Chinese students: a comparative study of stability of a factor structure. *Annals of the New York Academy of Science,* 1959, 79, 257–304.

Vandenberg, S. G. The hereditary abilities study: hereditary components in a psychological test battery. *American Journal of Human Genetics,* 1962, 14, 220–237.

Vandenberg, S. G. *Methods and goals in human behavior genetics.* New York: Academic Press, 1965.

Vaughn, C. L. Factors in the rat. *Comparative Psychological Monograph,* 1937, 14, 3.

Vernon, P. E. Changes in abilities from 14 to 20 years. *Advanced Science,* 1948, 5, 138.

Vernon, P. E. Practice and coaching effects in intelligence tests. *Educational Forum,* 1954, 18, 269–280.

Vernon, P. E. *Intelligence and attainment tests.* London: University of London Press, 1960.

Vernon, P. E. *The structure of human abilities.* London: Methuen, 1961.

Vernon, P. E. *Personality assessment: a critical survey.* New York: Wiley, 1964.

Vernon, P. E. Environmental handicaps and intellectual development. Parts I and II. *British Journal of Educational Psychology,* 1965, 35, 1–22.

Vernon, P. E. *Intelligence and cultural environment.* London: Methuen, 1969.

Vernon, P. E., & Parry, J. B. *Personnel selection in the British forces.* London: University of London Press, 1949.

Very, P. S. Differential factor structures in math ability. *General Psychology Monographs,* 1967, 75, 169–207.

Visher, S. S. *Scientists starred, 1903–1943.* Baltimore: Johns Hopkins, 1947.

Vogel, W., & Broverman, D. M. A reply to "relationship between EEG and test intelligence: a commentary." *Psychological Bulletin,* 1966, 65, 99–109.

von Neumann, J. *The computer and the brain.* New Haven: Yale University Press, 1958.

Vygotsky, L. S. Psychology and the localization of functions. *Neuropsychologia,* 1965, 3, 381–392.

Wackwitz, J. H. Abilities as a function of age: an alternative to levels of performances. *Psychological Bulletin,* 1971.

Walter, W. G. Where vital things happen. *American Journal of Psychiatry,* 1960, 116, 673–694.

Wand, B. Flexibility in intellectual performance. Princeton, New Jersey: Educational Testing Service, 1958, Project NR 151–113.

Warburton, F. W. *The selection of university students.* Manchester: University of Manchester Press, 1952.

Watson, J. B. *Behavior: An introducton to comparative psychology.* New York: Holt, Rinehart & Winston, Inc., 1914.

Weaver, H. E., & Madden, E. H. Direction in problem solving. *Journal of Psychology*, 1949, 27, 331–345.

Wechsler, D. *The measurement and appraisal of adult intelligence.* London: Bailliere, Tindall and Cox, 1958.

Wechsler, D. Intelligence et fonction cérébrale. *Revue Psychologie Appliquée*, 1958, 8, 143–147.

Weiner, M. Organization of mental abilities from ages 14 to 54. *Educational and Psychological Measurement*, 1964, 24, 573–587.

Weiskrantz, L., Gross, C. G., & Baltzer, V. The beneficial effects of meprobamate on delayed response performance in the frontal monkey. *Quarterly Journal of Experimental Psychology*, 1965, 17(2), 118–124.

Weiss, R. Die Brauchbarkeit des Culture Free Intelligence Tests Skala 3. (CFT 3) bei begabungspsychologischen Untersuchungen. Unpublished doctoral dissertation, University of Würzburg, 1968.

Welford, A. T. *Aging and human skill.* Oxford: Oxford University Press, 1958.

Wellman, B. L. Iowa studies of the effects of schooling. In *Yearbook of National Society of Student Education*, 1940, 39, Part II. Pp. 377–399.

Wellman, Beth L., & Pegram, E. L. Binet IQ changes of orphange preschool children: a re-analysis. *Journal of Genetic Psychology*, 1944, 65, 239–263.

Wells, H. G. *The way the world is going.* New York: Benn.

Werdelin, I. *Geometrical ability and the space factors.* Lund, Sweden: University of Lund, 1959.

Wherry, R. J. Determination of the specific components of maze ability for Tryon's bright and dull rats by factorial analysis. *Journal of Comparative Psychology*, 1941, 32, 237–252.

Widrow, B. Generalization and information storage in networks of adaline "neurons." In *Self organizing systems.* Washington, D. C.: Spartan Press, 1962. Pp. 435–461.

Windle, W. G. Brain damage by asphyxia at birth. *Scientific American*, 1969, 221, 76–87.

Wiseman, S. (Ed.) *Intelligence and ability.* Harmandsworth: Penguin, 1967.

Wiseman, S., & Wrigley, J. The comparative effects of coaching and practice on the results of verbal intelligence tests. *British Journal of Psychology*, 1953, 44, 83–94.

Wispé, L. G. Traits of eminent American psychologists. *Science*, 1963, 141, 1256–1261.

Wispé, L. G. Some social and psychological correlates of eminence in psychology. *Journal of the History of the Behavioral Sciences*, 1965, 1(1), 88–98.

Wispé, L. G., & Ritter, J. H. Where America's recognized psychologists received their doctorates. *American Psychologist*, 1964, 19(8), 634–644.

Witkin, H. A. *Personality through perception, an experimental and clinical study.* New York: Harper, 1954.

Witkin, H. A. *Psychological differentiation; studies of development.* New York: Wiley, 1962.

Witkin, H. A., Lewis, H. B., Hertzman, M., Machover, K., Meissner, P. B., & Wapner, S. *Personality through perception.* New York: Harper and Row, 1954.

Wolfle, D. L. Diversity of talent. *American Psychologist,* 1960, 15, 539.

Woodrow, H. The relation between abilities and improvement with practice. *Journal of Educational Psychology,* 1938, 29, 215–230.

Woodrow, H. Intelligence and improvement in school subjects. *Journal of Educational Psychology,* 1945, 36, 155–166.

Woodworth, R. S. *Experimental psychology.* New York: Holt, 1938.

Wrigley, J. The relative efficiency of intelligence and attainment tests as predictors of success in grammar schools. *British Journal of Educational Psychology,* 1955, 25, 107–116.

Young, M. *The rise of the meritocracy.* London: Thames and Hudson, 1958.

Zangwill, O. L. The cerebral localisation of cortical function. *Advancement of Science,* 1963, 20, 335–344.

AUTHOR INDEX

SUBJECT INDEX